Baile Átha Cliath
Dublin City

Date D

Dublin City Council
and the
1916 Rising

Dublin City Council
and the
1916 Rising

John Gibney, *editor*

Dublin
Dublin City Council
2016

First published 2016 by
Dublin City Council
c/o Dublin City Library and Archive
138-144 Pearse Street
Dublin 2

Comhairle Cathrach
Bhaile Átha Cliath
Dublin City Council

Decade of Commemorations

www.dublincommemorates.ie

Series editors: Mary Clark and Máire Kennedy
Designed by Yellowstone Communications Design
Indexed by Julitta Clancy
Printed by Johnswood Press

ISBN hardback   978-1-907002-33-5
ISBN paperback   978-1-907002-34-2

Distributed by
Four Courts Press
Malpas Street
Dublin 7
www.fourcourtspress.ie

POBLACHT NA H EIREANN.

THE PROVISIONAL GOVERNMENT
OF THE
IRISH REPUBLIC
TO THE PEOPLE OF IRELAND.

IRISHMEN AND IRISHWOMEN: In the name of God and of the dead generations from which she receives her old tradition of nationhood, Ireland, through us, summons her children to her flag and strikes for her freedom.

Having organised and trained her manhood through her secret revolutionary organisation, the Irish Republican Brotherhood, and through her open military organisations, the Irish Volunteers and the Irish Citizen Army, having patiently perfected her discipline, having resolutely waited for the right moment to reveal itself, she now seizes that moment, and, supported by her exiled children in America and by gallant allies in Europe, but relying in the first on her own strength, she strikes in full confidence of victory.

We declare the right of the people of Ireland to the ownership of Ireland, and to the unfettered control of Irish destinies, to be sovereign and indefeasible. The long usurpation of that right by a foreign people and government has not extinguished the right, nor can it ever be extinguished except by the destruction of the Irish people. In every generation the Irish people have asserted their right to national freedom and sovereignty; six times during the past three hundred years they have asserted it in arms. Standing on that fundamental right and again asserting it in arms in the face of the world, we hereby proclaim the Irish Republic as a Sovereign Independent State, and we pledge our lives and the lives of our comrades-in-arms to the cause of its freedom, of its welfare, and of its exaltation among the nations.

The Irish Republic is entitled to, and hereby claims, the allegiance of every Irishman and Irishwoman. The Republic guarantees religious and civil liberty, equal rights and equal opportunities to all its citizens, and declares its resolve to pursue the happiness and prosperity of the whole nation and of all its parts, cherishing all the children of the nation equally, and oblivious of the differences carefully fostered by an alien government, which have divided a minority from the majority in the past.

Until our arms have brought the opportune moment for the establishment of a permanent National Government, representative of the whole people of Ireland and elected by the suffrages of all her men and women, the Provisional Government, hereby constituted, will administer the civil and military affairs of the Republic in trust for the people.

We place the cause of the Irish Republic under the protection of the Most High God, Whose blessing we invoke upon our arms, and we pray that no one who serves that cause will dishonour it by cowardice, inhumanity, or rapine. In this supreme hour the Irish nation must, by its valour and discipline and by the readiness of its children to sacrifice themselves for the common good, prove itself worthy of the august destiny to which it is called.

Signed on Behalf of the Provisional Government,

THOMAS J. CLARKE.

SEAN Mac DIARMADA.   THOMAS MacDONAGH.
P. H. PEARSE.   EAMONN CEANNT,
JAMES CONNOLLY.   JOSEPH PLUNKETT.

Contents

Brollach

Ardmhéara Bhaile Átha Cliath
Críona Ní Dhálaigh

Cuireann sé an-áthas orm fáilte a chur roimh an leabhar tábhachtach seo ina dtugtar eolas nua ar ghné d'Éirí Amach 1916. Chuir Comhairle Cathrach Bhaile Átha Cliath go mór leis an ngluaiseacht bharrthábhachtach seo i stair na hÉireann ach tugadh neamhaird air sin go dtí anois. Rinneadh foirgneamh garastúin de phríomhfhoirgneamh na Comhairle Cathrach, Halla na Cathrach, nuair a ghabh Arm Cathartha na hÉireann é Luan Cásca le fórsa ina raibh a lán ban. De réir mar a lean Seachtain na Cásca ar aghaidh, bhí Briogáid Dóiteáin Bhaile Átha Cliath chun cinn ó thaobh cosaint a thabhairt do shibhialtaigh a gortaíodh sa troid nó a raibh a mbeatha i mbaol ag an ionsaí sliogán agus ag an tine. D'éirigh leo bean thorrach a shábháil fiú – thug siad leo í ó Fhionnradharc trí cheantar cogaidh na cathrach go dtí Ospidéal Shráid Holles. Is iomaí comhalta tofa de Chomhairle Cathrach Bhaile Átha Cliath a throid in 1916 nó a cuireadh i bpríosún ina dhiaidh sin. Duine acu sin ná an Comhairleoir Richard O'Carroll ar mharaigh an Captaen míchlúiteach Bowen Colthurst é. Bhí a lán d'fhostaithe Bhardas Bhaile Átha Cliath amuigh in 1916 freisin. Áirítear orthu sin Éamonn Ceannt a shínigh an Forógra agus a bhí ina oifigeach a raibh ardmheas air i Roinn na Rátaí; an Maor Seán Mac Giolla Bhríde, báille uisce na cathrach; Harry Nicolls, innealtóir le Bardas Bhaile Átha Cliath; agus a lán ball de sheirbhís leabharlainne na cathrach.

Is é eagarthóir an leabhair, John Gibney, a chuir na haistí seo a dtoll a chéile le scil mhór. Tréaslaím leis as ucht eolas úrnua a chur i láthair sa leabhar seo agus tá mé muiníneach gur iomaí duine a léifidh é agus a chuirfidh suim ann.

Foreword

Ardmhéara Bhaile Átha Cliath
Críona Ní Dhálaigh

I am very pleased to welcome this important book, which sheds new light on an aspect of the 1916 Rising. The contribution of Dublin City Council to this seminal movement in Irish history has been immense but to date has been neglected or at best overlooked. The City Council's premier building, City Hall, became a garrison building annexed by the Irish Citizen Army on Easter Monday, by a force which included a large cohort of women. As Easter Week progressed, Dublin Fire Brigade was to the fore in protecting civilians who were injured in the fighting or had their lives threatened by shelling and fire – they even rescued a pregnant woman from Fairview and brought her safely through the city war-zone to Holles Street Hospital. The roll-call of elected members of Dublin City Council who fought in 1916 or were imprisoned afterwards is impressive and it includes Councillor Richard O'Carroll who was effectively executed by the notorious Captain Bowen Colthurst. A large number of Dublin Corporation employees were also out in 1916. These include Éamonn Ceannt, signatory to the proclamation, who was also a valued official in the Rates Department; Major John MacBride, the city's Water-Bailiff; Harry Nicolls, an engineer with Dublin Corporation; and many members of the city's library service.

This set of essays has been drawn together with much skill by the book's editor John Gibney. I commend him for breaking new ground with this book and am confident that it will reach a wide and interested readership.

Acknowledgements

The editors would like to thank the many organisations and individuals whose kind assistance was called upon in different aspects of this publication. We would like to thank Dublin Fire Brigade Museum; Seán McDermott at Dublin City Council Survey and Mapping section; Dr Brian Kirby, Provincial Archivist, Capuchin Provincial Archives; Hugh Beckett, archivist, at the Military Archives; Mark Duncan from Century Ireland; Alastair Smeaton for photographing images; Lewis Foreman and the estate of the late Arnold Bax for permission to use the poem 'A Dublin ballad'; the family of Seamus Kearns; Francis Devine and the trade unions IMPACT and SIPTU. In particular we would like to thank the families of those councillors and Council employees who fought in 1916, who generously gave of their time, family papers and photographs, especially the families of Laurence O'Neill, Tom Kelly, Michael McGinn and Patrick Stephenson.

We are very grateful for the support of Dublin City Council Decade of Commemorations who funded the project, and to the Dublin City Librarian, Margaret Hayes, and Deputy City Librarian, Brendan Teeling, for unfailing support and encouragement. Special thanks are due to the staff of Dublin City Library and Archive for their constant support and help. Finally and especially we would like to thank the contributors, who provided original and well researched essays and who made this book possible.

John Gibney
Mary Clark
Máire Kennedy

List of abbreviations

AOH	Ancient Order of Hibernians
ASU	Active Service Unit
BMH	Bureau of Military History (Military Archives)
BOR	Birth of the Republic Collection (DCLA)
CQMS	Company Quartermaster Sergeant
CSORP	Chief Secretary's Office Registered Papers
DBC	Dublin Bread Company
DCC	Dublin City Council
DCC *Minutes*	*Minutes of the Municipal Council of the City of Dublin*
DC *Reports*	*Reports and printed documents of the Corporation of Dublin*
DCLA	Dublin City Library and Archive
DDA	Dublin Diocesan Archives
DFB	Dublin Fire Brigade
DIB	*Dictionary of Irish biography*
DLP	Dublin Labour Party
DMOA	Dublin Municipal Officers Association
DMP	Dublin Metropolitan Police
DTC	Dublin Trades Council
FJ	*Freeman's Journal*
GAA	Gaelic Athletic Association
GPO	General Post Office
GRO	General Register Office
GSWR	Great Southern and Western Railway
ICA	Irish Citizen Army
II	*Irish Independent*
ILGOU	Irish Local Government Officers' Trade Union
INA	Irish National Alliance
INV	Irish National Volunteers
IPP	Irish Parliamentary Party
IRA	Irish Republican Army
IRB	Irish Republican Brotherhood
IT	*Irish Times*
ITGWU	Irish Transport and General Workers Union
ITUC	Irish Trade Union Congress
IV	*Irish Volunteer* (newspaper)
IV	Irish Volunteers

IWW	Industrial Workers of the World
LRC	Labour Representation Committee
MGWR	Midland and Great Western Railway
MRA	Municipal Reform Association
MSPC	Military Service Pension Collection
NAI	National Archives of Ireland
NDU	North Dublin Union
NLI	National Library of Ireland
OBU	One Big Union
ONFP	O'Neill Family Papers
RDF	Royal Dublin Fusiliers
RIC	Royal Irish Constabulary
SDU	South Dublin Union
SF	Sinn Féin
SFRH	*Sinn Féin rebellion handbook*
SPI	Socialist Party of Ireland
TCD	Trinity College Dublin
TUC	Trade Union Congress
UCDA	University College Dublin Archives
UIL	United Irish League
WoI	War of Independence
WS	Witness Statement
YIS	Young Ireland Society

Introduction:
Dublin's Rising, 1916

John Gibney

Seán T. O'Kelly (DCLA, BOR Collection)

Seán T. O'Kelly was the son of a cobbler from Dublin's north inner city and, like many on the radical fringe of Irish political life, he was a member of a wide range of cultural and political organisations: the Gaelic League (of which he became national secretary), the Irish Republican Brotherhood (IRB), and, of course, Arthur Griffith's Sinn Féin. By his own account, on Easter Monday 1916 Seán T. O'Kelly left 19 Ranelagh Road, the family home of his future wife Mary Kate Ryan, which had become something of a hub for many 'advanced nationalists', and went into Dublin city centre. Later that day he made his way down Sackville (O'Connell) Street, where just after noon he witnessed the seizure of the General Post Office (GPO); the smashing of its windows left a 'strange impression' on him and at 3 p.m. that afternoon James Connolly despatched him to Liberty Hall to collect flags, and later again to tell those still in Liberty Hall to bring all their available equipment to the GPO. At some point O'Kelly was also given the task of pasting up copies of the republican proclamation in the city. Later still Connolly sent him to Fairview with 20-30 men to engage troops coming from Dollymount (though by his own admission he had no military training). O'Kelly was imprisoned at Frongoch and Reading after the Rising, and later became Sinn Féin representative to the Paris peace conference before becoming a key member of Éamon de Valera's Fianna Fáil, minister for public health and local government and, in 1945, president of Ireland.[1] One could look at his career and assume that O'Kelly, like many, had his

---

1   BMH WS 1765; *Dictionary of Irish biography.*

career launched by the shift in Irish public opinion towards the separatist politics of the revitalised Sinn Féin after the Easter Rising. But this is to overlook the fact that O'Kelly had been part of Sinn Féin from the start; and, alongside his many other appointments over the course of his career, from 1906 O'Kelly had been a reforming Sinn Féin member of Dublin City Council, a position he held until his elevation to government in 1932. Dublin City Council was the elected body that governed the city, and had been established in 1841 when Dublin Corporation had been remodelled in a manner that made it unrecognisable from its medieval origins (though the name Dublin Corporation was still employed for the body that oversaw the Council's property and employed its staff). Over subsequent decades the remit of both Council and Corporation expanded dramatically to encompass a wide range of administrative responsibilities, but in April 1916 they were faced with the unprecedented reality of an armed rebellion in Dublin in the midst of a global war.

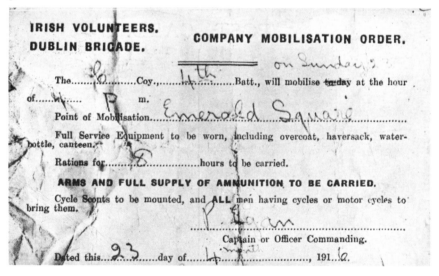

Mobilisation Order Irish Volunteer Brigade - Emerald Sqaure, off Thomas Street (DCLA, Seamus Kearns Postcards)

The Easter Rising of 1916 was primarily a Dublin affair. Ireland's capital went to war for a week in April 1916 in the course of a rebellion planned and orchestrated by a cabal within the secretive IRB spearheaded by Thomas J. Clarke and Seán Mac Diarmada; as early as September 1914, they had identified the outbreak of the war as an opportunity, and resolved to carry out a rebellion against British rule before the war came to an end. The footsoldiers were to be members of the Irish Volunteers (the paramilitary organisation founded in 1913 to oppose unionist opposition to Home Rule), though some smaller groupings such as Cumann na mBan and the Irish Citizen Army (ICA) also became involved. The Rising was originally meant to begin on Easter Sunday, 23 April 1916. On that day the

Irish Volunteers were to assemble for regular weekend manoeuvres, where they would then be informed of the rebellion that they were expected to participate in. Clarke's obsession with secrecy meant that the rank and file were kept in the dark until the last minute, though many suspected that something was being planned. But the failure of an abortive attempt to obtain weapons from Imperial Germany precipitated attempts to call off the Rising, and so the putative leaders of the rebellion - Clarke, MacDiarmada, James Connolly, Éamonn Ceannt, Thomas MacDonagh, Joseph Mary Plunkett and Patrick Pearse - were deprived of both weapons and the numbers they had hoped to mobilise. They were also faced with the prospect that the attempt to import weapons might trigger a British crackdown that would deprive them of even a limited oportunity for insurrection. From their point of view, it was better to act rather than lose that opportunity. In that sense the Easter Rising was a desperate gesture, and was not necessarily the Rising that the leaders may have intended to bring about.[2]

The Easter Rising that actually broke out, as opposed to whatever had been planned, was largely confined to Dublin. There seems to have been a plan for a bigger uprising outside Dublin, contingent on the arrival of weapons from Germany. The Rising that broke out, however, did so without the numbers that its leaders had hoped to muster or the weapons that they had hoped to equip them with. On 24 April 1916, having initially assembled at the Irish Transport and General Worker Union (ITGWU) headquarters at Liberty Hall on Beresford Place, members of the Irish Volunteers and the Irish Citizen Army occupied a number of districts in the city, along with key buildings within them. The GPO became the headquarters and, by extension, the most famous location associated with the Easter Rising. Originally opened in 1818, the GPO was seized by members of the Irish Volunteers and Irish Citizen Army under Pearse and Connolly early on the afternoon of 24 April 1916. The rationale for seizing it remains unclear, but the GPO was a key communications hub in Dublin. It was also a very visible symbol of official authority north of the River Liffey, and its location on the wide expanse of Sackville Street ensured that its seizure, and thus the outbreak of the rebellion itself, would be widely seen and reported. It had both a practical and propaganda value. In the early days of the Rising many observers noted an almost surreal atmosphere in its vicinity, complete with looters and sightseers, but as the week wore on Sackville Street and the GPO came under heavy bombardment and fires broke out in the commercial district around the building. Moving west along the north inner city, the area directly behind the Four Courts, extending up Church Street towards Phibsborough, was, after the GPO, the other main area of insurgent

---

2   For general accounts of the Rising see Charles Townshend, *Easter 1916: the Irish rebellion* (London, 2005); Fearghal McGarry, *The Rising: Easter 1916* (Oxford, 2010).

activity north of the River Liffey during the Rising. This area took in North King Street, the Linenhall Barracks (which was burned down), and the North Dublin Union. Its location gave it a strategic importance. It was adjacent to the north quays, which ensured that Volunteers in this area were in a position to hinder troop movements to and from both the Royal Barracks and Kingsbridge (now Heuston) Station, which was the terminus of the Great Southern and Western Railway. North of the area seized by the Volunteers was Broadstone Station, the terminus of the Midland Great Western railway, which was another venue that could facilitate the arrival of British reinforcements; a consideration that seems to have influenced the choice of a number of insurgent locations throughout the city. In line with the manner in which fighting intensified as the week went on, the area around Church Street, North Brunswick Street and North King Street saw some of the heaviest and most intense fighting in the city during the Rising. North King Street was also the location of one of the most notorious incidents of the Rising, when members of the South Staffordshire Regiment killed a number of unarmed civilians in house to house searches.

The Four Courts from Wood Quay (DCLA, Postcard Collection)

The remaining centres of insurgent activity were south of the River Liffey. Between the Four Courts and the Guinness Brewery was the Mendicity Institution, a charitable body whose premises on Usher's Island housed a small garrison under Seán Heuston. A more substantial position that was also occupied was the South Dublin Union, located on the site of what is now St James' Hospital, south-west of Dublin city centre. This was Ireland's largest workhouse, housing 3,200 inmates on a sprawling complex that covered 50 acres. Given that the majority of military installations in Dublin were located to the west of the city, the seizure of such a large complex would have enabled the Volunteers to impede the movement of troops from Richmond Barracks, or even the Royal Hospital in Kilmainham. It was seized by the 4th Battalion of the Dublin Volunteers under Éamonn Ceannt, who assembled in the Liberties before moving along Cork Street to seize the complex. A number of outlying buildings were also seized in this area: Watkins Brewery in Ardee Street, the Jameson Distillery in Marrowbone Lane, and Roe's Distillery in Mount Brown (though the insurgents declined to sample any of their wares). There was no attempt made to seize Kingsbridge Station, which was a major oversight. The South Dublin Union was the site of intense fighting on Monday 24 April, Tuesday 25 April, and Thursday 27 April. Part of the complex was occupied by troops, but their attention shifted elsewhere as the week went on.

Staying south of the Liffey but moving eastward, back into the city centre, one of the first buildings seized during the week was Dublin City Hall, located at the intersection of Parliament Street and Dame Street in the south inner city, which was originally opened as the Royal Exchange in the 1770s and was reopened as the City Hall in 1852. On the afternoon of 24 April members of the Irish Citizen Army led by Seán Connolly seized City Hall and a number of other buildings in the immediate vicinity. City Hall is located just outside the entrance to the upper yard of Dublin Castle. City Hall's location ensured that it was a natural vantage point from which to ambush troops who might emerge from the castle (the castle itself was not seized, presumably due to the small number of insurgents involved). The occupation of City Hall saw the killing of Dublin Metropolitan Police (DMP) Constable James O'Brien, who is often classed as the first victim of the Rising: he was shot by Connolly, who later became the first insurgent victim of the Rising after he was shot on the roof of City Hall. The British garrison in Dublin Castle was immediately reinforced when the Rising broke out, and heavy fighting took place in the vicinity of City Hall until troops broke into the building later that day and overwhelmed the small rebel garrison; the building itself suffered only minor damage.

Continuing east but moving away from the Liffey, Volunteers under Thomas MacDonagh seized the enormous Jacob's biscuit factory located on the 'block' enclosed by Bishop Street, Bride Street, Peter's Street and Peter's Row, between St Patrick's Cathedral and St Stephen's Green. The factory had two large towers that could act as observation points, while its location was very close to both Camden Street and Patrick Street: natural routes for troops entering the city centre from Portobello Barracks in Rathmines and Wellington Barracks (now Griffith College) on the South Circular Road. As it happens, little fighting took place here, though the roughly 100 volunteers who seized the factory were abused by local residents, many of whom were Jacob's workers themselves or were the families of soldiers serving in the British Army (MacDonagh surrendered in nearby St Patrick's Park on Sunday 30 April). The other major location seized by insurgents in the south inner city was St Stephen's Green itself, at the southern end of Grafton Street, which was originally laid out in the 1660s but had been redeveloped in the 1870s. It was a natural junction that commanded the approaches to a large tract of the south-east inner city. On 24 April members of the Irish Citizen Army led by Michael Mallin seized the Green and were met with considerable hostility as they ejected civilians from the park, which was magnified into outrage after a civilian was shot while trying to retrieve his handcart from a barricade the insurgents had erected near the Shelbourne Hotel. Within the park itself, trenches were dug as members of the Citizen Army sought to fortify their positions. In the early hours of Tuesday morning troops who had been sent to the district began to attack the Citizen Army positions in the park; the Shelbourne Hotel provided a natural vantage point overlooking the park, and troops were able to fire down into the trenches that had been dug. Within a matter of hours Mallin and those under his command were forced to abandon St Stephen's Green and retreated to the Royal College of Surgeons on the west side of the green. The fighting eased off as British attention shifted elsewhere, and Mallin and the garrison surrendered the following Sunday.

Boland's Bakery (DCLA)

Finally, the easternmost Volunteer outpost was in and around Boland's Bakery, overlooking the Grand Canal (the current Treasury Building is built on the site). This complex of buildings was seized by members of the Volunteers led by Éamon De Valera: perhaps as few as 100-130 poorly armed Volunteers were involved. Boland's Mill was to serve as the headquarters of the Volunteers in a large region of Dublin's south inner city that was quite diverse in socio-economic terms: it incorporated commercial and industrial regions in Dublin's docklands, while the residential districts within the area seized by the Volunteers ranged from slum tenements near the docks to the middle-class residential districts in and around Merrion Square, and between the canal and Ballsbridge. The location of the area was significant, as it contained important transport links that connected Dublin to the southern ferry port of Kingstown: the rail terminus at Westland Row, and the roads leading into the city that crossed the Grand Canal at Mount Street. There were apparently plans to seize a number of buildings within the district, but these were curtailed. The Volunteers established outposts outside Beggar's Bush Barracks, near Mount Street Bridge, and near Westland Row, where rail tracks were torn up in order to disrupt rail transport. This region also saw some of the heaviest fighting of the Rising, as British reinforcements who had disembarked at Kingstown were ambushed as they attempted to cross the canal at the junction of Northumberland Road and Mount Street.

There was, it seems, logic to the seizure some of these areas and buildings, but the stark reality was that the Easter Rising was doomed to failure. In the midst of a global war the British authorities would not - could not - tolerate an uprising of this nature in what was then still a substantial city in the United Kingdom that had, since August 1914, already been profoundly affected by a war being fought elsewhere. The outbreak of the Rising, less than two years after the outbreak of the First World War, took Dublin's citizens by surprise. It took the British authorities by surprise. In truth, it even took some of those who participated in it by surprise. On 24 April 1916, the day on which the Rising broke out, the news as reported by the major Dublin dailies was dominated by the 'Great War'. In the letters pages of *The Irish Times*, 'an Irish nationalist' who had spent 'many months at the front in Flanders' suggested that conscription should be extended to Ireland if it applied to England and Scotland: 'Why should Irishmen suffer the indignity of allowing other countries to sacrifice everything for our sakes, while our foolish young men play at soldiers in the streets of our cities and the roads and lanes of our country districts?' This was presumably a swipe at groups like the Volunteers; events over the next few days may have changed this correspondent's opinion.[3]

---

3   *Irish Times* 24 Apr. 1916.

Slum Buildings in Dublin (DCLA, Dublin City Council Collection)

The population of Dublin city in the second decade of the twentieth century was perhaps 304,000 people, of whom 87,000 lived in slums: a higher proportion of the population than any other UK city. The poverty of tenement Dublin had been starkly highlighted in the massive industrial dispute and lockout of 1913-14, prompted by the attempt of ITGWU leader James Larkin to organise a union to represent the vast ranks of Dublin's unskilled labouring poor; itself an indication that Dublin's socio-economic profile was different to that of its peers. The Irish capital was not a city that was defined by the presence of heavy industry, though a 'war economy' of sorts had developed in the city, as after August 1914 Dublin port morphed into a manufacturing centre for the British war effort while also carrying out its perennial function as a transit point for agricultural goods making their way across the Irish Sea. Demand intensified during the war and supplies became scarce; for ordinary Dubliners, the problems they faced in 1915 and 1916 were quite literally of the bread and butter kind. The war affected virtually every walk of life. Its outbreak had derailed the prospect of slum clearance, and its requirements placed an enormous material burden on many in the city. On the other hand, it had opened doors into employment for many, including many women, in institutions such as the new shell factory on Parkgate Street.

First World War Irish Recruitment Poster (DCLA)

But the war took a human toll as over 25,000 Dubliners enlisted in the British Army between 1914 and 1918. Many were drawn from the ranks of the labouring poor, and others from the nationalist and unionist professional classes. Soldiers were a visible presence on the streets of Dublin prior to the Rising (in early 1916 most of the crimes faced by the DMP apparently related to deserters). The British war effort had been vociferously supported by the Home Rule leader John Redmond, but as the human cost mounted (especially during the abortive Gallipoli campaign of 1915), the war had become increasingly unpopular even before war came to the streets of Dublin in April 1916.[4] Of those 25,000 men from Dublin who enlisted in the British Army during the First World War, approximately one in five were killed, even aside from the wounded and maimed.

---

4   Padraig Yeates, *A city in wartime: Dublin 1914-1918* (Dublin, 2011), pp 26-89.

Yet the circumstances of the First World War acted as both an opportunity and a rallying point for 'advanced' nationalists who opposed it; an undercurrent of dissent had remained visible in the city throughout 1914, 1915 and 1916, though, as the authorities noted, 'Up to the fourth week of April nothing unusual occurred to cause anxiety in reference to the general peace of Ireland except the continued disloyal and dangerous activity of the Sinn Féin movement'.[5] But by the beginning of May much of Dublin's central commercial districts lay in ruins; over £2,600,000 worth of damage was caused by both fires and fighting, while nearly 500 civilians and combatants were killed due to the combat that had taken place in and around the various insurgent positions throughout the city.[6] All of this death and destruction had been visited on the jurisdiction of what was then Dublin Corporation.

How did Dublin City Council fit into the upheaval of 1916? The overall purpose of this book is to provide answers of a sort, by exploring how Dublin Corporation dealt with, was affected by and was essentially intertwined with the Easter Rising. It is divided into two sections; one dealing with the Council itself, and the other dealing with the institutions and employees of the Corporation. It begins with a wide-angle perspective, in the form of Padraig Yeates' overview of how the Council as a whole responded to the war in general, and the crisis of 1916 in particular. From there it moves to examine the diverse careers of a number of those who sat on the Council: Richard O'Carroll was the only councillor to be killed during the Rising (and Laurence White's examination of O'Carroll and William Partridge is a salutary indication of the importance of the politics of labour in Dublin). Other councillors such as Tom Kelly and Laurence O'Neill, studied here by Sheila Carden and Thomas J. Morrissey respectively, were affected by the events of Easter Week while aldermen such as W. T. Cosgrave, examined here by Anthony J. Jordan, saw the trajectory of their careers ultimately transformed by their role in the Rising.

These are, however, and with the exception of Yeates' essay, studies of individual responses to the events of Easter 1916; there were also corporate responses, on the part of the Corporation's various departments. The most immediately pressing issue that fell upon such civilian institutions was that of dealing with the destruction of the city; a task that fell to Dublin Fire Brigade, whose role in tackling the impact of the Rising in the city is explored here by Las Fallon. Yet employees of the Corporation proved to be active participants in the Rising: Seán T. O'Kelly was a distinctive example of a councillor who fought in the Rising, but, as Evelyn

---

5   Breandán MacGiolla Choille (ed.), *Intelligence notes 1913–16* (Dublin, 1966), p. 228.
6   Fearghal McGarry, 'Violence and the Easter Rising' in David Fitzpatrick (ed.), *Terror in Ireland, 1916-23* (Dublin, 2012), pp 39-57; Daithí Ó Corráin, '"They blew up the best portion of our city and … it is their duty to replace it": compensation and reconstruction in the aftermath of the 1916 Rising', *Irish Historical Studies*, 39, no. 154 (Nov. 2014), pp 272-95.

Conway explores, a number of the city's library staff also fought in the Rising. Martin Maguire explores the career of a radical, in the form of the engineer Harry Nicholls. And David Flood's meticulous register of employees who fought in 1916 reveals the full extent of the manner in which Corporation staff participated in the Rising and indeed, the Irish revolution as a whole.

Alongside those employees who were active participants in the Rising were two who were executed for their involvement in it. Donal Fallon examines the early career of Major John MacBride in both Ireland and South Africa. MacBride also brings us to one of the venues for the fighting: the occupation of Jacob's Biscuit Factory, where MacBride spent his Easter Rising, is examined in detail by Séamas Ó Maitiú. The second of the executed leaders examined here is Éamonn Ceannt, and Shay Cody examines Ceannt's multifaceted life as both republican and trade unionist. Ceannt is commemorated with a plaque on the Rates Office (formerly the Newcomen Bank), directly across from City Hall; and Conor McNamara examines how the Rising was fought in the official headquarters premises, so to speak, of the Council and Corporation.

The Easter Rising is naturally the subject of intense debate and scrutiny in its centenary year. This book will hopefully offer a set of fresh and unfamiliar perspectives on this most prominent of events. It is concerned not so much with the meaning of the Rising but with its reality, in terms of how it affected and shaped the city in which it mainly took place, and many of the individuals who took part in it or were affected by it. What connects them all is their link to the municipal authorities of Dublin. In that sense, while many will claim the legacy of 1916, the chapters in this volume deal with what was, unequivocally, Dublin's Rising.

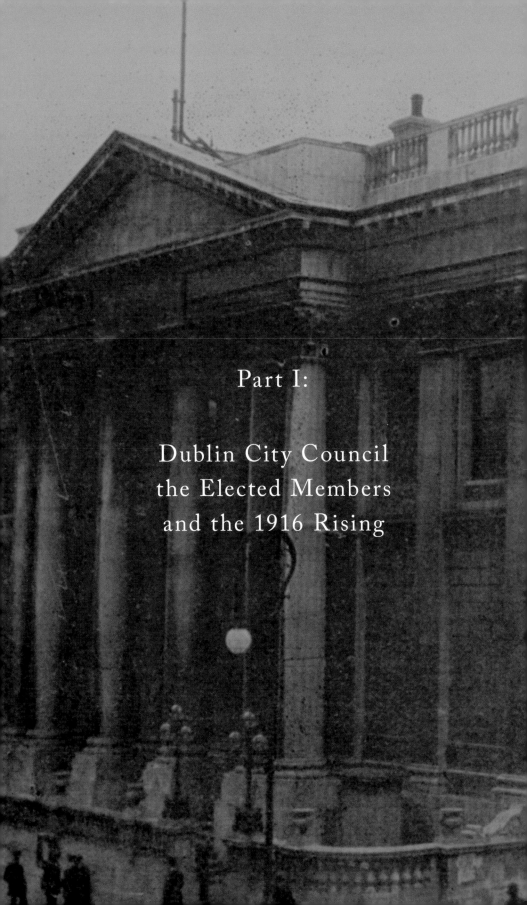

Part I:

Dublin City Council
the Elected Members
and the 1916 Rising

The politics of
Dublin City Council
and the 1916 Rising

Pádraig Yeates

In the years before 1916 Dublin City Council took itself quite seriously as Ireland's leading representative assembly, and a model for the eagerly awaited Home Rule parliament on College Green. Yet its predominantly Redmondite members were largely detached from the burgeoning revolution on the streets of the capital. Only two councillors, Richard O'Carroll and William T. Cosgrave, were members of the Irish Volunteers while only one, William Partridge, was a member of the Irish Citizen Army (ICA) and Councillor Sean T. Ó Ceallaigh was a member of the Irish Republican Brotherhood. O'Carroll and Cosgrave held the rank of lieutenant and Partridge was a captain in the ICA. A fourth councillor, Dr James McWalter, was the only member of the 80 strong City Council to join the British army. He served as a member of the Royal Army Medical Corps from late 1916 until the war's end.

O'Carroll would die after being taken prisoner and shot out of hand by the notorious Captain John Bowen Colthurst on Wednesday 26 April 1916, in Camden Street.[1] Partridge was part of the ICA garrison on Stephen's Green a short distance away. He survived the Rising only to die of nephritis in 1917, contracted while a prisoner in Lewes Jail.[2] Cosgrave survived to become Minister for Local Government in Dáil Éireann, and, later still, was President of the Executive Council of the Irish Free State. McWalter also survived the war and returned to lead the Municipal Reform Association (MRA), an alliance of former Home Rule colleagues and unionists on the City Council. Ironically, given his war service, he died suddenly in early 1921 when he collapsed after rushing home from an MRA meeting to beat a military curfew.[3]

All four men were representative of minorities in the Council Chamber of 1916. O'Carroll was leader of the Labour group, of which Partridge was a fellow member. Both were trade union officials, as were all the Labour councillors, who comprised

---

1   Richard O'Carroll (MSPCW1D237). John Bowen Colthurst was from Cork. His other victims included 19 year old James Coade and three journalists, Thomas Dickson, P. J. McIntyre and Francis Sheehy Skeffington. He was only charged with the murders of the three journalists and was found guilty but insane.
2   Lawrence William White , 'Partridge, William Patrick 'Bill'' in *Dictionary of Irish biography*, (Cambridge, 19 June, 2014).
3   *Freeman's Journal*, 8 Feb. 1921; *Irish Times*, 6 Feb. 1921; Pádraig Yeates, *A city in turmoil: Dublin 1919-1921* (Dublin, 2012), pp 231-2.

the largest opposition group to the nationalist majority. O'Carroll was secretary of the Ancient Guild of Stonemasons and Bricklayers, while Partridge was a member of the Amalgamated Society of Engineers and a fulltime official in the Irish Transport and General Workers Union (ITGWU). Both had played leading roles in the 1913 Lockout and were advocates of the 'new unionism' that was realigning the revolutionary syndicalism of class war with militant nationalism; a not uncommon phenomenon in contemporary Europe, where national freedom from London, Moscow or Vienna were often seen as a necessary precondition to the economic emancipation of the working classes. It was probably the greater momentum of the Irish Volunteers that drew trade union militants such as O'Carroll into that organisation, as the Irish Citizen Army was almost moribund for several crucial weeks after the Lockout ended and was also seen as being too small and too closely associated with the ITGWU to attract craft workers such as O'Carroll. Although an engineer, or fitter, by trade, Partridge tied his fortunes to those of the ITGWU's founder Jim Larkin and his successor James Connolly.

Cosgrave was the antithesis of his revolutionary colleagues and had much more in common with the Redmondite majority on the Council. His family were publicans and shopkeepers (he managed their main premises on James's Street in 1916). He had been attracted to the writings of Arthur Griffith from an early age, and by 1909, was a Sinn Féin Councillor for Ushers' Quay in the south west of the city. He had the support of local trade unionists, despite sharp policy differences which had emerged between Griffith and some of his former trade union supporters in 1907. Before this Sinn Féin had seemed set to become the main opposition to the traditional Redmondite majority on the Council. Yet Griffith's insistence that the needs of Irish business should take precedence over trade union demands for better pay and conditions that would endanger competitiveness, followed by his ferocious attacks on Larkin and the ITGWU prompted figures such as Richard O'Carroll and P. T. Daly, Secretary of the Irish Trades Union Congress to defect to Labour. Daly would also become a City Councillor. Despite their differences, the larger Labour group often voted with Sinn Féin on issues when their interests coincided, such as slum clearance and public health initiatives. Labour and Sinn Féin could also find common cause with regard to the promotion of Irish culture, asserting aspirations to greater independence beyond what Home Rule seemed to offer, and supporting the use of Irish made goods by the Corporation. Although leading Labour figures, such as Jim Larkin and James Connolly, espoused revolutionary socialism, the Labour Party's policy on Dublin City Council was essentially one of municipal socialism, which focused on improving public amenities, such as housing and public health, as well as the working conditions of Corporation employees (This approach might have changed after Larkin's election to the City

Council in 1912 but he was unseated because he was an undischarged bankrupt). Nor was the Labour Party anti-clerical, unlike many of its fraternal movements in Europe and the United States. O'Carroll, Partridge and their colleagues were as conscientious in the practice of their religion as their nationalist fellow-councillors; and Partridge, judging by his correspondence with Dr William Walsh, Archbishop of Dublin, was probably more devout than most. During the Lockout he was at pains to explain to the archbishop how close Labour policies were to his own pronouncements, and in 1916 Partridge led decades of the rosary for the ICA garrison in the Royal College of Surgeons.

Any shift towards the espousal of more radical policies by the Labour councillors was checked by the outcome of the 1914 local elections, when only one of ten 'Larkinite' candidates running on the Dublin Labour ticket was elected, and even then only in the traditional Labour stronghold of New Kilmainham. Walter Carpenter, who ran on a Socialist Party of Ireland ticket, did even worse than his 'Larkinite' colleagues. It is possible that more seats could have been won if Labour had run fewer candidates and had not relied on mass rallies and the *Irish Worker* to mobilise support, while spurning the traditional door to door canvassing and blatant clientelism of its opponents. It still managed to poll a respectable 12,026 votes to the nationalists' 16,627.[4]

Even more importantly, the outbreak of the First World War in 1914 brought about a shift in attitudes towards the idea of armed revolution. By 1915 Larkin, Dublin's leading advocate of syndicalism, was in America and its other ablest advocate, James Connolly, was looking to an armed insurrection as a more effective means of establishing a Workers Republic than municipal elections. Indeed Connolly's new newspaper, launched on 29 May 1915 to replace the *Irish Worker* (which had been banned) was called the *Workers Republic*. Its message was unequivocal: 'The time for Ireland's battle is now, the place for Ireland's battle is here'.[5]

'a false step might ruin the work of 35 years'

When the *Irish Worker* carried out its post-mortem into the 1914 municipal elections, it identified Dr McWalter as one of two 'Nationalists in Sympathy with Labour' on the Council. The other was Laurence O'Neill, who became Lord Mayor after 1916.[6] The nationalist majority on the council was far from homogeneous. Only 16 of more than 60 aldermen and councillors who declared themselves nationalists ran formally as members of the United Irish League (UIL), the

---

4   *Irish Times*, 16 Jan. 1914.
5   *Workers Republic*, 19 Feb. 1916.
6   *Irish Worker*, 24 Jan. 1914.

official constituency organisation of the Irish Parliamentary Party. The league was essentially a rural-based body that had emerged from the land war, which may help to explain its relative weakness in the capital. One nationalist, Councillor John Dillon Nugent, ran as an Ancient Order of Hibernians (AOH) candidate, of which organisation he was national secretary. Five councillors described themselves as independent nationalists in 1916. Apart from O'Neill and Lorcan O'Toole the rest, including Dr McWalter, invariably rallied to support Redmond and the Irish Party on important issues. There were only two genuine independents, both of whom were former unionists no longer able to secure election as such. An unaligned 'independent nationalist', Sarah Harrison, had lost her seat in 1915 during the last municipal election held before the British government banned all elections for the duration of the war.[7]

Unionists had once dominated Dublin City Council but the gradual widening of the franchise had reduced their numbers to one alderman and three councillors by 1916. However, they remained a force in the southern townships of Pembroke, Rathmines, Blackrock and Kingstown (Dún Laoghaire). Sinn Féin had briefly eclipsed the unionists as the largest opposition party only to be overtaken in 1912 by Labour, but neither posed any threat to the nationalists. The restrictive property and residency qualifications of the franchise were a particular handicap for Labour: only 38,000 of the 300,000 inhabitants of the city had a vote.[8] What held the Nationalists together was that their majority on the City Council enabled them to share the spoils of office, culminating in the salary of £3,688 a year for the Lord Mayor. This made it an attractive position for even the most successful businessmen, let alone the clutter of publicans, tobacconists and shopkeepers who made up the bulk of councillors (almost a quarter of whom were also slum landlords). Anyone advocating even modest reforms in areas such as housing and public health faced a sisyphean task as the city fathers were also among the ratepayers liable to foot the bill. Patronage was the lifeblood of municipal life. If the great issues of the day were rarely discussed, the granting of a painting contract, the appointment of a rate collector, or even a slot meter reader could spark bitter debates and often led to named votes in which those granted or denied largesse could see which of their elected representatives they should thank or blame.

---

7   An exception was by-elections to fill parliamentary vacancies caused by death or resignations. Harrison was one of only two women elected to Dublin City Council before 1920. Women were eligible to vote and stand in local elections if they satisfied a property qualification..

8   P. Murray, 'Electoral politics and the Dublin working class before the First World War', *Saothar 6*, (1980).

Politics were therefore irremediably local and the Council Chamber was not a place where the great issues of the day were debated. For instance, the outbreak of the First World War barely registered. When the first full Council meeting took place on 10 August it was to discuss housing and finance issues and to unanimously condemn the 'savage crime' of Sunday 26 July, when members of the King's Own Scottish Borderers opened fire on a crowd that had taunted them on Bachelor's Walk after their unsuccessful attempt to seize the rifles landed at Howth earlier that day for the Irish Volunteers. Even unionist councillors supported the motion, which was hardly surprising as three Dubliners had been shot dead and dozens more injured, many seriously. There was no vote for King and Country, but rather concerns over rising food prices and resentment that the British government had not included Irish local authorities in new legislation to finance slum clearance. By the time the 1914 Housing Act was amended to include Ireland the funds had already been spent by British local authorities, while the city fathers never managed to rein in food prices, a doomed cause in a chamber full of shopkeepers.

John Redmond (DCLA, BOR Collection)

If, therefore, Redmond's passionate declaration of support for the British war effort aroused no response in City Hall, there was no outright opposition either. Rather, it was the slow attrition of the war effort on the quality of life in the city that gradually generated a reaction. It was not until 14 July 1915, that what might be termed the first anti-war motion was moved by Councillor John Ryan, a builder from Clontarf and leading UIL member. He proposed a motion that 'We demand as the right of the Irish Nation that the Home Rule Act agreed and accepted by the English Government and signed by His Majesty King George V be put into operation for all Ireland on September 17ᵗʰ next.' If passed the motion would have been deeply embarrassing to Redmond, and other nationalist councillors rallied to defend their leader, with an amendment welcoming the passing of the Home Rule Act as 'a solemn Treaty between the British and Irish Nations'. It congratulated Redmond and the Irish Party 'on their success in securing this settlement in the face of terrible and unlooked for difficulties and we look with confidence to Mr Redmond and the Irish Party, to select the best and speediest means and the proper moment for bringing the Home Rule settlement into operation by the summoning of the Irish Parliament'. The amendment was only adopted by 30 votes to 22, with several nationalist councillors voting for the original motion alongside Labour and Sinn Féin members.[9] Even the watered down version of the motion was too much for Redmond, who on 20 July 1915 wrote back testily from Aughavanagh, expressing concern at the damage it could do when times were 'extremely critical' and 'a single false step might ruin the work of 35 years'. Unabashed, at the following meeting a declaration that the Council 'will not have Conscription' was passed by 31 votes to seven. Only three nationalists voted with the unionist councillors against the motion.[10] Attitudes were hardening, and some nationalist councillors such as Laurence O'Neill were already realigning with Sinn Féin and Labour colleagues.

Half-pay for Corporation employees who had joined the British army was another contentious issue. In October 1914 any employee who joined the colours was granted half-pay but by August 1915 this was being withdrawn from men who were considered 'well provided for'. When a renegade Labour councillor, John Saturninus Kelly, who was employed as a 'civil recruiting officer' by the War Office, objected to the withdrawal of half pay from one Francis Fitzpatrick in the paving department, he was ruled out of order. Kelly protested that such men were being penalised for joining 'the Army in response to the call to arms … by Mr John E. Redmond M.P. to save Ireland and the Empire from the Pre-Mediated (sic) German and Prussian Murderers', only to be told that the grant of half pay to families of employees 'who join the British Army or Navy was a voluntary act of grace on the part of the Council and they are not bound by any law or regulation to continue it in any case in which they see fit to suspend it'.[11] When a choice had to be made between political principles and saving money on the rates, it was usually the ratepayers' interest that prevailed.

---

9   *DCC Minutes* (1914), p. 248.
10 *DCC Minutes* (1914), pp 416-7.
11 *DC Reports* (1915), vol. i, p. 279.

'to resist by every means in their power any proposed increase in tax'

In many ways the Council appeared cocooned from the outside world. There were no debates over the disaster at Gallipoli, or the battles on the western front, not to mention events nearer home such as the funeral of the veteran Fenian Jeremiah O'Donovan Rossa in August 1915 or even the two by-elections that year caused by the deaths of Irish Party veterans Joseph Nannetti and William Abraham. Nannetti was replaced by the secretary of the AOH and City Councillor John Dillon Nugent, who saw off a strong challenge from Labour candidate Thomas Farren. Publican Alfie Byrne won Abraham's seat in a three-way contest with fellow nationalists, Councillor J. J. Farrell and 'The O'Mahony'. Ominously, Labour chose not to contest with several of its leaders now preoccupied with paramilitary politics rather than those of a constitutional variety.

O'Donovan Rossa, lying in state in City Hall, August 1915 (DCLA)

In January 1916 it was very much business as usual with the High Sheriff Patrick Shortall being congratulated by colleagues on his recent knighthood for services to the war effort. The subsequent debate turned on the usual issues, such as rising Corporation wage bills, fuel prices and housing funds. For once there was good news on the latter front, with 113 Corporation houses nearing completion on a site donated by the Oblate order in Inchicore. These would be allocated to men working in the area 'in order that they may enjoy the ... mid day meal in their own homes, that will prove so efficacious to employers and employees'. However an anti-conscription motion, from Labour councillors P. T. Daly and Michael Brohoon, both fulltime ITGWU officials, was passed overwhelmingly. It warned the government that conscription would be met with 'vigorous resistance'. Only the four unionists and four moderate nationalists sought unsuccessfully to move next business.[12]

Prices, including those of coal and potatoes, which had doubled since 1914, was a war induced issue that dogged the Council's agenda. It had lost most of its powers to tackle such problems under the 1914 Defence of the Realm Act, but this at least had the virtue of enabling councillors to blame the British government.[13] In February 1916 the onset of price-driven wage inflation raised hackles. A war bonus for Corporation employees threatened to push up the rates and the cost of services such as electricity to citizens.[14] But the issue that caused most anger was taxation, which stood at £17 million in 1916, compared with £8 million a decade earlier. A motion proposed by Alfie Byrne and seconded by W. T. Cosgrave called for 'the Irish representatives in Parliament to resist by every means in their power any proposed increase in tax'. A UIL amendment calling on the Irish Party to follow suit was only accepted by 23 votes to 18. The fact that it was proposed by Dublin's newest nationalist M.P. was an indication of growing anti-war sentiment, for Alfie Byrne was arguably Dublin's most accurate political weather vane. Byrne had opposed conscription, and now distanced himself from the rest of the Irish Party by telling fellow councillors that he was the only Irish M.P. to vote against increased taxation in the Budget. Cosgrave, for his part, said Britain had no more right to levy taxes on Ireland than Germany had on Belgium.[15]

In March 1916 Councillor Andrew Beattie proposed that representations be made to the government and the Minister for Munitions, Lloyd George, to bring 'orders to Dublin for Munitions of War in fair and reasonable amounts in proportion to our increased taxation and per capita of the population as compared with the population of England, Scotland and Wales'. This was another straw in the wind for Beattie, although an independent, came from a family with strong unionist and military connections.[16]

The vast majority of Council members approached Easter 1916 blissfully unaware of what was impending. However, in the week prior to the outbreak of the Rising they found themselves playing an unsuspecting role in seeking to justify armed insurrection. The occasion was a special meeting to set the city rates on 19 April,

---

12   *DCC Minutes*, 10 January 1916, pp 26-31; *Irish Times*, 11 Jan. 1916.
13   *DCC Minutes*, 17 January 1916; *Irish Times*, 18 Jan. 1916.
14   *DCC Minutes*, 7 February 1916; *Irish Times*, 8 Feb. 1916.
15   *DCC Minutes*, 7 February 1916; *Irish Times*, 8 Feb. 1916. For a breakdown of voting see p. 146 of Minutes.
16   *DCC Minutes*, 14 March 1916.

including that for the Dublin Metropolitan Police (DMP). This particular levy was deeply resented because although ratepayers had to meet around 20 per cent of the cost of the DMP, the city had no role in overseeing or managing the force. It was answerable only to Dublin Castle. The rate should have been struck a week earlier, but the meeting had adjourned in protest at remarks by Justice William Kenny to the Grand Jury on the state of the city. Kenny, a former unionist M.P. for the Stephen's Green division who was now a High Court judge, had expressed concern 'at the existence of a spirit amongst a small section of the population of a disquieting nature. There was propaganda of an openly seditious character. There were anti-recruiting meetings and the seizure of seditious literature ... Firearms were freely used in street disturbances'. Kenny went on to denounce the 'large and attractive posters' displayed outside shops with slogans such as 'England's last ditch' and 'Pretence of the Realm Act'.[17]

Cosgrave, who was chairing the reconvened meeting, proposed a motion condemning Kenny's 'tainted' elevation to the bench, adding that the Judge's remarks had more in common with his old role as 'a Crown Prosecutor rather than a person administering justice to all'. It was seconded by Sir Joseph Downes, a pillar of the Home Rule establishment, and it provided an ideal opportunity for the leader of the Sinn Féin group, Alderman Tom Kelly, to make an intervention. He told his fellow councillors that he had received a letter from P. J. Little, editor of *New Ireland* and similar seditious tracts of the type which Justice Kenny had been complaining about, which contained 'an enclosure' of Dublin Castle files showing that the government intended 'to cause bloodshed in Ireland by an attack on the Irish Volunteers'. Kelly quoted extensively from the document, citing plans sanctioned by Dublin Castle on the recommendation of the military authorities to arrest 'All members of the Sinn Féin National Council, the Central Executive of the Irish Sinn Féin Volunteers, the County Board Irish Sinn Féin Volunteers, Coiste Gnotha Committee Gaelic League' and other bodies. The DMP and RIC were to be confined to barracks during this operation, which included plans for the seizure of the ITGWU headquarters in Liberty Hall, the Sinn Féin head offices in Harcourt Street, the Irish Volunteers headquarters in Dawson Street, the National Foresters Hall in Rutland (now Parnell) Square, 'all National Volunteers premises in the city', the Dublin Trades Council premises in Capel Street, the offices of Arthur Griffith's *Nationality* newspaper in D'Olier Street; along with the 'isolation' of the Catholic Archbishop's house, the Mansion House, the Plunkett family's Larkfield estate in Kimmage where many expatriate Irish Volunteers who had returned from England were now based, and Patrick Pearse's school St Enda's in Rathfarnham. The original documents had probably been given to the IRB's

---

17   *Irish Times*, 12 Apr. 1916

Military Council by Eugene Smith of the 'G' Division of the DMP. He can lay claim to being the rebels' first 'spy in the Castle', but his originals had certainly been doctored afterwards by the Military Council of the IRB to influence not just public opinion but, crucially, Eoin MacNeill, the Chief of Staff of the Irish 'Sinn Féin' Volunteers as they had been mistakenly dubbed by the authorities. The inclusion of MacNeill's home address in Herbert Park, mistakenly given as 40 rather than 19, as the only private residence on the list of suspect locations was clearly intended to secure his acquiescence with the conspirators' plans.[18]

'I believe if I had a beads I would be safe'

Tom Kelly said that if the document was false the responsibility for any consequences lay with him, but if it was true he had done a public service 'to prevent these military operations being considered in a city which was the most peaceable in Europe'. There is no reason to think that Kelly had not been duped, as his poor health precluded membership of the Volunteers and he was not part of the revolutionaries' inner circle. The document, however, was greeted with some scepticism at the meeting, with the recently knighted High Sheriff, Sir Patrick Shortall complaining that the chairman had given Kelly 'a good deal of latitude'. He objected to the Council 'being turned to the purpose of political propaganda'.

> We have some rights and privileges and we don't want them to be filched, whether by Judge Kenny on the one side, or by our extreme political opponents on the other. They were governed constitutionally and the Government of Ireland was in a position to see that every man's life and property was protected, and there was no such thing as Alderman Kelly wanted to put before them of an outbreak of rebellion. Alderman Kelly's words would do nothing but stir up the worst passions of Irishmen.

However Alderman Lorcan O'Toole, an independent nationalist sympathetic to Sinn Féin, reminded Shortall that when he was sitting on the Bench at the opening of the Assizes a week earlier as High Sheriff, beside Justice Kenny, 'you did not object to his remarks'.[19]

In any case Kelly's 'Sensational Document' was generously covered by the *Irish Independent* while being ignored by the Liberal Unionist *Irish Times*. Kelly's amendment to reduce the police rate to 4*d*. in the £ was ultimately defeated.[20] Far

---

18   The doctored document is generally thought to have been the work of Joseph Plunkett.
19   *DCC Minutes*, 19 April 1916; *Irish Independent*, 20 Apr. 1916.
20   It was reduced marginally to 7*d*. in £.

from helping to avert bloodshed in the city, the doctored document was intended to justify it and Shortall's critique of it was accurate, if self-serving.

The Council as a body played no role in the Rising, though individual councillors were involved. The incumbent Lord Mayor, James Gallagher, distinguished himself in helping to protect Grafton Street from looters, with the assistance of the Trinity College defence force, for which he was subsequently knighted. He also acted as a character witness at the court martial of Cosgrave, testifying that he was 'a very good citizen and of exceptional ability'. A former Lord Mayor, Councillor Lorcan Sherlock, also testified on Cosgrave's behalf.[21] Other councillors arrested included Labour's P. T. Daly and the independent nationalist Laurence O'Neill, who had an unusual conversation with a soldier on night duty at Richmond Barracks, who asked O'Neill for 'beads'. When asked why, the soldier said,

> I have been with two firing squads in Kilmainham Jail. Your fellows came out with beads in their hands, a smile on their faces, and they died like men. As I am under orders for the Front, I believe if I had a beads I would be safe.[22]

O'Neill was subsequently released but his temporary incarceration helped to transform his political standing over the coming months as one of the few city councillors to be associated in the public mind with the rebels. Sinn Féin's Tom Kelly, Sean T. O Ceallaigh and W. T. Cosgrave, as well as Labour's P. T. Daly and William Partridge, also benefited from a newfound celebrity as temporary rebel prisoners.

Dublin was placed under martial law once the Rising erupted and those members of the Council who sat on the Dublin Port and Docks Board voted unanimously with their colleagues to endorse the curfew imposed by the military authorities. It is unlikely the vote would have been unanimous were it not for the enforced absence of Labour Councillor and ICA Captain William Partridge, now in military custody. Despite the disturbed state of the city, a meeting of the Council was convened on 10 May, 1916, while the executions of the rebel leaders were continuing. The reason was a letter from A. R. Barlas, secretary of the Local Government Board, calling on the Corporation to invoke Section 13 of the 1898 Local Government (Ireland) Act. This was required so that the North and South Dublin Unions (NDU and SDU) (municipal workhouses) could obtain bank overdrafts to deal with 'the destitution caused by the Sinn Féin Rebellion'. It was supplemented by letters from

---

21   M. Laffan, *Judging W. T. Cosgrave: the foundation of the Irish state* (Dublin, 2014), p. 55.
22   T. J. Morrissey, *Laurence O'Neill (1864-1943): patriot and man of peace* (Dublin, 2014), p. 53.

J. P. Condon, the clerk of the SDU and his counterpart at the NDU, John O'Neill, confirming the 'exceptional distress' in the city.

Children receiving bread (DCLA, *The Graphic*, 13 May 1916)

At this stage various convents in Dublin were baking emergency bread supplies, the commercial bakeries were limiting customers to two loaves of bread a day and the British army had established an emergency soup kitchen in the city centre. The weekly rates of relief — 8*s.* for a man and wife, 1*s.* 6*d.* for the first child falling to 1*s.* for the second and 6*d.* for each child thereafter — were hardly generous, but there were still councillors who questioned the need for emergency relief. Clontarf builder and independent nationalist John Ryan warned colleagues that if they invoked the legislation 'it would only mean stampeding ourselves into very large expenditure of which they did not know the end'. It was unfair to impose further charges on the 'already heavily burdened' ratepayers who were 'in no way accountable for the misfortune'. Andrew Beattie questioned if there was 'any real distress', and had heard that 'very poor children had been coming' into his area 'for relief from other wards in the city' unaffected by the fighting. Despite the absence of so many of the radical Sinn Féin and Labour councillors who were in custody or gone into hiding, there were enough concerned nationalist representatives on the council who were prepared to accept their responsibilities. Dr McWalter, whose dispensary in North Earl Street had been in the eye of the storm, warned that existing agencies could not cope with the 80,000 to 100,000 civilian Dubliners affected by the Rising. James Gately, who also represented the North City ward and served on the SDU Board of Guardians, said there were people seeking help who had never done so before. The only female councillor, Martha Williams, who had been elected as a nationalist in 1915, said that her local dispensary was dealing with 700 people a day: the Council 'could not allow people to starve'. The necessary funding was approved.[23]

It was 5 June before normal business resumed in the Council Chamber, with a series of carefully choreographed votes of sympathy acknowledging recent deaths. The first was proposed by the unionist alderman for Glasnevin, William Dinnage, to the family of his recently deceased constituency colleague John Thornton. This was seconded by a nationalist councillor for Glasnevin, James Cummins. Nationalist councillor James Higgins proposed a vote of sympathy for the family of Richard O'Carroll, the only councillor killed in the Rising. This was seconded by another nationalist, the High Sheriff, Sir Patrick Shortall, who had taken such exception to Tom Kelly's dramatic revelation of 'secret' military documents on the eve of the Rising. A nationalist alderman, William O'Connor, proposed and a party colleague, councillor Patrick Lennon, seconded a vote of sympathy to Sir Thomas Esmonde on the death of his 'youthful son … through the destruction of His Majesty's ship *Invincible*'. Esmonde was a former chairman of the Irish Party who had flirted with Sinn Féin a few years earlier. The decision of his youngest son, John, to enlist as a midshipman in the Royal Navy at the outbreak of war saw him firmly re-ensconced in the Redmondite ranks. Like so many other major engagements of the First World War, the Battle of Jutland, where the *Invincible* failed to live up to its name, was never discussed in the council chamber. The focus remained determinedly parochial. Finally nationalist councillors Murty O'Beirne and Patrick Lennon proposed a vote of sympathy 'to the relatives of the citizens who lost their lives during the recent rebellion'.

---

23   *DCC Minutes*, 10 May 1916; *Irish Times*, 11 May 1916.

Eden Quay from O'Connell Bridge after the Rising (DCLA, BOR Collection)

The delicate and potentially divisive issue of condolences being dealt with, the Lord Mayor, James Michael Gallagher and Council tackled the even more perilous issue of the Rising. Gallagher said, 'the awful calamity of rebellion fell upon the City like a thunderbolt' and placed the blame for what had happened on the 'incredible inaction' of the Irish Executive. The city now 'displayed the same scene of heart breaking destruction' as much of Europe. 'The Government had blown down the centre and most beautiful part of their City', yet it expected the ratepayers of Dublin to foot the bill for its reconstruction according to the best principles of town planning and architectural science. Gallagher put the loss of annual revenue to the city from rates on destroyed premises at £30,000 a year. He pointed out that the Public Health and Housing Acts were totally inadequate to meet the needs of the situation. After consulting with the Town Clerk and Law Agent he had presented a draft bill to the Under Secretary for Ireland on behalf of the Corporation to be given powers to rebuild the city centre and he predicted, accurately as it turned out, that this could be done within five years. Meanwhile, he opened a fund to relieve distress with a target of £5,000. Some £1,650 had already been raised by a concert in New York, thanks to Count John McCormack and Cardinal Farley.

Another expense confronting the Council was the demand for pay rises from clerical staff, who had seen the wages of manual workers outstripping theirs in the price-wage spiral accelerated by war inflation. W. T. Cosgrave had proposed a motion prior to his arrest that the pay structures of the clerical and administrative staff should be adjusted to ensure 'no one is paid less than a labourer'. While Cosgrave remained in prison, the motion remained on the order paper and Alfie Byrne, sensing an opportunity, proposed its adoption. An amendment from nationalist and unionist councillors to refer the matter to the Estates and Finance Committee for a report was defeated by 25 votes to 9. The latter included Dr McWalter, who always sought to maintain a balance between the mutually conflicting aims of social reform and municipal economy, as well as by the Lord Mayor himself, who declared 'it was shameful for the Corporation to pass such a motion without knowing the cost at such a time'. He was mindful that increases to one set of employees would inevitably lead to demands from others.

Undeterred, Byrne now proposed 'That having regard to the undisputed fact that food and fuel prices have increased 50 per cent since the outbreak of the War, this Council are of the opinion that the Old Age Pension should be increased to 7s. 6d. so as to enable its recipients to purchase the same quantity of food and fuel they were using previous to the War, and that we are of the opinion that the new age qualification should be reduced to 65'.[24] This was, of course, passed with alacrity, as the bill would fall on the British exchequer if ever implemented. That these might be expensive chickens coming home to roost under a Home Rule parliament or a Republic does not seem to have occurred to the city fathers.

BODIES OF VICTIMS OF SUNDAY'S TRAGEDY BORNE THROUGH THE SCENE OF SLAUGHTER

Press coverage of the funerals of the victims of Bachelor's Walk (DCLA, *Irish Independent*, 30 July 1914)

If it appeared that council business was returning to normal, the consequences of the Rising continued to make themselves felt. The trial of Captain Bowen Colthurst for the murder of Francis Sheehy Skeffington, and fellow journalists Thomas Dickson and P. J. McIntyre, dominated the news in early June. That he was tried at all was largely due to the persistence of Sheehy Skeffington's widow Hanna and to Major Francis Vane, a fellow officer appalled at what had happened. Bowen-Colthurst, who was not charged with the murder of any of his other

---

24   The age to qualify as a pensioner was 70. *DCC Minutes*, 5 June 1916; *Irish Times*, 6 June 1916; *Irish Independent*, 6 June 1916.

victims, including Richard O'Carroll, was found guilty but insane. There was even more outrage at the discovery of the bodies of 15 civilians killed by members of the Staffordshire Regiment in North King Street, and at the defence put in by the military authorities at the inquest. Not alone did the officer in charge fail to identify the culprits, but he added that 'the troops under my command showed great restraint under exceptionally difficult and trying circumstances'. A specially convened meeting of the City Council condemned the deaths, and those of 'other offending citizens'. The only dissenting voice was that of Alderman David Quaid, a former unionist and now an independent representing Drumcondra, a middle class suburb with a large residual unionist electorate.[25]

'it would be extremely serious if ... any large proportion of their stud were put out of action'

There was a significant break with tradition at the next council meeting on 19 June when the question of co-opting new members to replace the unionist Councillor John Thornton and Labour's Richard O'Carroll arose. Traditionally a nominee from the party of the former member was accepted, but the sympathy expressed over Thornton's death was in scarce supply a fortnight later. The nationalist bloc, supported by Labour and Sinn Féin members, proposed Michael Maher, a dairyman and cow-keeper, who comfortably won by 31 votes to 10. Alderman William Dinnage protested that Maher did not even live in the constituency, only to have his own candidate, James Hubbard Clark, falsely denounced as the director of a British owned company (he was a painting contractor). The outcome was worrying for unionists because the suspension of elections for the duration of the war meant they had no means to replenish their ranks in the event of further deaths or resignations. When the Labour candidate to replace Richard O'Carroll, John Long, was proposed, the former unionist and now formal independent Andrew Beattie proposed stationery manufacturer John Shuley in protest, and then withdrew the nomination. But Alderman James J. Kelly, a nationalist but also a tobacco manufacturer insisted on a vote. Long was elected with Kelly casting the only vote for Shuley. It was a case of one businessman crossing the confessional divide to vote for another. None of the unionists voted for Shuley but two of them, Alderman William McCarthy and Councillor William Coulter voted for Long.[26] It was perhaps significant that Quaid and Beattie, former unionists now sitting as independents, displayed the most dogged resistance to the increasingly militant nationalist consensus over the North King Street massacre and the Council co-options respectively.

---

25 *Irish Independent*, 15 May 1916; *DCC Minutes*, 2 August 1916; P. Yeates, *A city in wartime: Dublin 1914-1918* (Dublin, 2011), pp 114, 131.
26 *DCC Minutes*, 19 June 1916; *Irish Times*, 20 June 1916.

On 3 July the war intruded directly into the Council chamber when the Lord Mayor informed his colleagues that he had received a letter from Dr McWalter informing him that 'I have received orders from the War Office to take up duty at "some place in the Mediterranean" and therefore I cannot attend the Council for some time'. McWalter was the only member to respond to John Redmond's call for volunteers to serve wherever the British firing line extended, and had been placed on reserve, possibly because of his age. Now he was called to the colours. Under Corporation rules any member who failed to turn up for meetings over a six month period was deemed no longer to be a member and was replaced by a co-option; however an exception was made for Dr McWalter. By contrast, when the cases of Sinn Féin's W. T. Cosgrave and Sean T. O Ceallaigh and Labour's P. T. Daly and William Partridge came up in September a different policy prevailed. Alderman Tom Kelly, who had himself been imprisoned briefly, read out a letter from O'Kelly explaining why he could not attend meetings: he was in Reading Prison. A nationalist councillor, William Reigh proposed that the four imprisoned 'corporators' be re-elected by the chamber but the Town Clerk said the law required that vacancies be declared in each case.[27]

Property around Sackville Street destroyed in the Rising (DCLA, 'Dublin areas destroyed by fire during Rebellion' 1917)

Of more immediate interest to many councillors and property owners was the question of compensation for property destroyed in the Rising, 70 per cent of which was located in Lower Sackville (O'Connell) Street, where Dublin's premier

27   DCC Minutes, 4 September 1916.

businessman, William Martin Murphy suffered the greatest losses. He had set up a committee to lobby for emergency legislation and the Council approved a special delegation led by the Lord Mayor to demand this from the Prime Minister, H. H. Asquith. Thanks to the good offices of John Redmond, Asquith met the delegation on 6 July, but as councillors had to pay their own travel expenses it was dominated by unionists and wealthier members of a nationalist persuasion. The Dublin Reconstruction (Emergency Provisions) Bill was introduced in August and became law in December. It made no provision for civilians injured in the fighting and would not have done so but for the intervention of one of Dublin's two unionist M.P.s, Sir Edward Carson. A pittance was provided for personal injury claims and nothing to the families of the men killed in North King Street; to do so would have been an admission by the British government that they died at the hands of its soldiers. By contrast Hanna Sheehy Skeffington, who stood to receive substantial compensation after Captain Bowen Colthurst had been found guilty of the murder of her husband, refused to apply on principle.

If the Corporation displayed a predictable attitude in prioritising the rights of property owners and ratepayers over those of families who had lost members in the cross fire, there was growing anger over the extent and duration of martial law in the city. The Lord Mayor, who was very much a Redmondite, expressed concern at the 'hundreds of citizens, men, women and boys who had been arrested on suspicion of involvement with the insurrection'. He warned that 'only the promptest action on the part of the Government in restoring to their homes people against whom there was no serious evidence, could allay the public resentment which had thus been occasioned'. Motions put forward a fortnight later by Alfie Byrne and seconded by Labour councillor Michael Brohoon calling for 'the immediate withdrawal of Martial Law' and payment of compensation to all Corporation employees released by the authorities for loss of earnings were passed with large majorities. However, most councillors drew the line at the next motion from Byrne and Brohoon, which proposed that they condemn 'in the strongest possible manner the action of the Dublin employers who have victimised their employees by dismissing them because of their relationship with those who participated in the recent rising'.[28]

The Council also took the military authorities to task over the shortage of fodder for farmers and cow-keepers in Dublin created by the demands of the military. An even worse spectre than the anticipated rise in the price of milk was the threat the fodder shortage posed to public sanitation. The secretary of the city's cleansing committee, Fred Allan, said that 'The members of the Council will be aware that during the present hot weather it is highly important that the portion of the City

28   *DCC Minutes*, 3 and 17 July 1916; *Irish Times*, 4 and 18 July 1916.

cleansing work which most vitally affects the public health, viz., the house to house removal of refuse must be efficiently maintained, and it would be extremely serious if, through either a deficiency of proper foodstuffs or the enforced use of inferior material, any large proportion of their stud were put out of action'.[29] The military did take steps to release some of its stock of fodder to ease these shortages, but the situation was not helped by the destruction of 1,400 tons of military hay stored on the docks. As four ricks of dried hay caught fire simultaneously spontaneous combustion was ruled out, leaving the Council to compensate the army for malicious damage to the tune of £11,200, along with £125 11s. for the loss of four lorries.[30]

The military authorities were also unhappy with the City Council for other reasons. Lt Colonel A. Welby, secretary of the Statutory Committee for the implementation of the Naval and Military War Pensions Act, wrote to the Corporation in the same month pointing out that it had neglected to devise a scheme to relieve hardship among soldiers' dependents awaiting separation payments or widows' pensions. Such schemes were already in operation in British cities, as well as in Belfast and Cork. Nor did an appeal by the Royal Dublin Fusiliers Advisory Committee for comforts to relieve hardship among prisoners in Germany elicit much support, although a proposal to give separation women in Dublin the same cost of living allowance as their counterparts in London was passed without a vote. The different responses by councillors to these issues may well have had to do with the membership of the RDF committee being overwhelmingly Protestant and unionist in composition. The Council's parochialism allowed it to be protective of Dubliners, while at the same time becoming increasingly hostile to the British war effort and its supporters in their midst.[31]

'the embodiment of British rule in Ireland'

The ambiguity that now characterised the Corporation's position was clearly shown at its meeting on 2 October 1916 when votes of sympathy were passed on the deaths of Land League veteran Andrew J. Kettle and his son, Lieutenant Tom Kettle. Tom Kettle's brother Laurence was a senior Corporation official and had been a founder of the Irish Volunteers, who had then suffered the humiliation of being taken prisoner by the ICA in the Rising. It was generally felt that the father had died on hearing of his younger son's death at the front, and the family had been a major pillar of the Home Rule project in Dublin city and county.

---

29   *DCC Minutes*, 7 August 1916.
30   *DCC Minutes*, 7 August 1916; *Irish Times* 4 Dec. 1917.
31   *DCC Minutes*, 4 September 1916; *Irish Independent* 5 Sept. 1916.

However this did not prevent the ubiquitous Alfie Byrne from calling on the Corporation, at the same meeting, to enter 'an emphatic protest' against the [British] Government for allowing Irishmen temporarily in England on war work to be conscripted, although they had been guaranteed that the Military Service Act would not apply to them. He had no difficulty getting it passed along with another motion calling for the release of all Irish internees.[32] Nor was such ambiguity restricted to the public sphere. Alderman Patrick Corrigan, undertaker, and staunch Redmondite, as well as one of Dublin's largest slum landlords, went to considerable personal risk to dispose of explosives belonging to his imprisoned colleague, Sinn Féin Alderman Tom Kelly. Corrigan was a business partner of Kelly's as well as a friend, and he removed the explosives on a handcart to his own business premises before disposing of them in small quantities in the Liffey over several nights.[33]

It was O'Neill's election as Lord Mayor in January 1917 that marked the most public demonstration by the city fathers of their anxiety to take cognizance of the changes being wrought in the city after Easter 1916. His rival, Sir Patrick Shortall, who would once have had a strong expectation of succeeding Gallagher, withdrew his nomination and Gallagher himself only secured the traditional vote of thanks by 24 votes to 19. Sinn Féin Alderman Tom Kelly denounced him as 'the embodiment of British rule in Ireland'. O'Neill was a potato merchant, auctioneer and minor slum landlord, but he had been one of the more radical nationalists close to Sinn Féin and Labour before the Rising. The fact that he had been arrested by the military briefly after the Rising gave him an air of martyrdom, if not its aura. By contrast, Gallagher's knighthood for saving Grafton Street from the worst excesses of the looters, with the help of the Trinity College defence force, now smacked of collaboration rather than civic heroism.

O'Neill proved an extremely skilled politician, treading a fine line between defiance of the British authorities and staying within the law when the risks outweighed the potential benefits. On Easter Sunday 1917 he attended a commemorative mass in the Pro-Cathedral in memory of the rebels who died a year earlier. In April 1917 he hosted the national conference called by Count Plunkett, father of the martyred Joseph Mary Plunkett, to harness radical nationalism at an event which proved a forerunner to the reconstituted Sinn Féin and Irish Volunteer movements in October 1917. Unlike Sinn Féin however, O'Neill would attend the Irish Convention established to seek a compromise settlement to the Irish

---

32   *DCC Minutes*, 2 October 1916; *Irish Independent* and *Irish Times* 3 Oct. 1916.
33   William T. Cosgrave, BMH WS 268.

question by the new Prime Minister Lloyd George. His attendance was sporadic, and was dictated by the public mood in the city.[34]

The main political crisis of 1917 was the death of 1916 leader Thomas Ashe on hunger strike in Mountjoy. O'Neill agreed to the dead leader's remains lying in state at City Hall in defiance of the authorities in Dublin Castle. Even as the body was being brought across the city from the Pro-Cathedral, O'Neill was at a heated meeting with Sir William Byrne, the Under Secretary, who was adamant that British troops would prevent Ashe lying in state virtually next door to his own offices in Dublin Castle. It was the military commander, Lt General Sir Bryan Mahon, who averted a serious confrontation with the Volunteers by withdrawing the troops on his own authority in defiance of Byrne. What is of interest is that O'Neill's fellow representatives at the meeting were Alderman Patrick Corrigan and Sir Patrick Shortall. It certainly symbolised the growing alienation from the British establishment of such staunch pillars of constitutional nationalism since the outbreak of the war.[35] Already in January 1917 the members of the City Council had overruled their own procedures and reinstated their three imprisoned colleagues. When they were eventually released Cosgrave was preoccupied with national politics, but still managed to remain a very active member of the Council; P. T. Daly took over from the late Richard O'Carroll as leader of the Labour group. Unfortunately William Partridge never recovered from the nephritis contracted in prison and returned home to his native Ballaghaderreen, where he died in the summer of 1917.

The nationalist majority on the council, men such as Corrigan and Shortall, now sought to reflect the more militant mood on the streets while defending the constitutional nationalist cause. Unlike in many parts of provincial Ireland, the Irish Party contested every Dublin constituency in the 1918 general election.[36] All four sitting M.P.s for Dublin, William Field, P. J. Brady, John Dillon Nugent and Alfie Byrne ran again. The latter two, Nugent and Byrne, were sitting councillors but all four lost their seats to Sinn Féin, with only Byrne offering a serious challenge to militant nationalism.[37] The real test of public opinion came in the municipal elections of 1920, the first since 1915. Sinn Féin won 45 per cent of the

---

34 Morrissey, *Laurence O'Neill (1864-1943)* , pp 76-7.
35 Yeates, *A city in wartime*, p. 207. W. T. Cosgrave gives a different but not contradictory account of events, see Laffan , pp 58-9.
36 Sinn Féin candidates were elected unopposed in 25 constituencies.
37 Byrne was defeated by fellow publican Phil Shanahan, a 1916 veteran but regained the seat in 1922. Yeates, *A city in wartime*, pp 288-95. Sir Maurice Dockrell was elected to represent Rathmines, the only unionist returned to Westminster outside of Ulster and the Trinity College constituency. Rathmines was an independent township outside the city boundaries in 1918.

first preference vote and 53 per cent of the seats, but the Irish Party, despite its rout in 1918 managed to garner more votes than Labour: 14.5 per cent as opposed to Labour's 12 per cent. However a third of the nationalist vote went to Alfie Byrne and only one other Redmondite managed to scrape in. Independent nationalists who had abandoned the Redmondite ship managed to secure as big a share of the vote as Labour, but again, half went to the Lord Mayor Laurence O'Neill. The former nationalist councillors who enjoyed the most success were those such as Dr McWalter who led the new Municipal Reform Association, an alliance that included former unionists whose candidates eschewed the cause of Ireland and the cause of the Union for the interests of the ratepayers.[38] It too secured 12 per cent of the vote and, through transfers from nationalist and unionist voters, won enough seats to become the main opposition to the new ruling bloc of Sinn Féin and Republican Labour.[39]

Whatever its image as 'rebel Dublin' the political reality in the capital was that Sinn Féin and Labour, the two parties most associated with the Rising had only won 57 per cent of the vote. There remained a large number of mainly middle class voters whose main concern was securing value for money as ratepayers rather than pursuing abstract political causes. Laurence O'Neill continued to serve as Lord Mayor until 1924 when the Free State abolished the Council after surviving over 750 years of foreign rule. But that is another story.

---

38 The unionist vote collapsed to 1.12 per cent but two unionists were nevertheless elected.
39 Dublin Labour split in the 1920 election between Trades Council Labour and Republican Labour. The former espoused traditional labour issues while the latter aligned itself with Sinn Féin and consequently enjoyed greater electoral success.

Councillor Richard O'Carroll, Councillor William Partridge,
the Labour Party and the 1916 Rising

Lawrence W. White

Richard O'Carroll
(Courtesy of Building &
Allied Trades' Union)

William Partridge
(Courtesy of SIPTU, *Fifty years of Liberty
Hall* (Dublin, 1959))

The early years of the 1910s witnessed the emergence of a small but tightly organised, articulate and disciplined bloc of Labour members on Dublin City Council. Among the most prominent were Councillor Richard O'Carroll (1876–1916), representing the Mansion House ward, and Councillor William Partridge (1874–1917), representing New Kilmainham. Both were skilled workers who became active members of craft unions early in their working lives, and both had already served on the City Council prior to the Labour Party presence of the early 1910s. The careers of these two nearly exact contemporaries, culminating in their participation as combatants in the Easter Rising of 1916, not only illustrate the fitful progress of labour representation in Dublin municipal government, but also embody the major questions with which the Irish labour movement grappled in the first fifteen years of the twentieth century: the competing claims of craft unions and general unions, of British-based and Irish-based trade unions and trade union congresses, of reformist labourism and militant socialism; the relative efficacy of industrial struggle or political activity; and the relationship between socialist internationalism and Irish nationalism.

Richard O'Carroll: early career

Born 29 February 1876 on Hanover Square in the Liberties area of Dublin city, Richard ('Dick') Carroll was a bricklayer by trade and an active member of one of Ireland's oldest trade combinations, the Ancient Guild of Incorporated Brick and Stonelayers Trade Union.[1] Attracted in early adult life to cultural nationalism, he joined the Gaelic League shortly after 1900 and affixed the patronymic 'O' to his surname.[2] In the aftermath of a bitterly divisive strike and lockout of Dublin bricklayers in 1905, he was elected general secretary of the bricklayers' union in February 1906, riding the crest of a rank-and-file revolt that ousted the old leadership. Revitalising the body, he rebuilt its strength in the Dublin region and extended its organisation outside the capital. By 1913 he had established fourteen branches throughout Ireland (in some instances by absorbing existing local societies), travelling to building sites and provincial offices on a motorcycle provided by the union, which also provided accommodation for him and his family in their imposing headquarters, the Bricklayers' Arms Institute, at 49 Cuffe Street.[3]

J.P. Nanetti, J.P., M.P. (DCLA)

From this base within a long-established and newly re-energised craft union, O'Carroll launched a career in Dublin local politics. Efforts by trade-union bodies to establish labour representation on local authorities had been stimulated by the extension of the franchise incumbent upon the 1898 Local Government Act. In the Dublin municipal elections of January 1900, labour candidates won one-fifth

1   Birth certificate (GRO, Dublin); Sarah Ward-Perkins, *Select guide to trade union records in Dublin* (Dublin, 1996), p. 26.
2   Richard O'Carroll, T. C. (1876–1916), 'Personal life' (https://richardocarroll1916.wordpress.com).
3   Ward-Perkins, *Select guide*, p. 26; *Thom's Dublin and county street directory* (Dublin, 1907–15 eds.); Dublin Corporation, *Diary* (Dublin, 1908–16 eds.).

of the seats. Within several years, however, this labour initiative disintegrated, in part discredited by jobbery and corruption practised by some of the elected councillors, but in large measure owing to an absence of discipline and cohesion: the labour councillors were not responsible to the bodies that had nominated them, nor were they unified around an agreed programme of objectives. Thus, there was a lack of coordination amongst the labour councillors themselves, and between them and the trades organisations that theoretically sponsored them. For the balance of the decade, Dublin city councillors who identified as 'labour' were largely labour nationalists ('lab-nats') endorsed by the United Irish League (UIL), the local organisation of John Redmond's Irish Parliamentary Party (IPP) at Westminster, and analogous to the 'lib-labs' of British local and national politics (labourites associated with the Liberal party). There was a smattering of Irish 'lab-nat' M.P.s, most notably J. P. Nannetti.[4]

During 1906 a small number of nationalists (including some trade unionists), disenchanted with the tactics of the IPP/UIL amid the refusal of the newly elected British Liberal government to adopt Irish Home Rule in its programme, gravitated to the more radical separatist policies being propagated by Arthur Griffith. Trade unionists were especially attracted to Griffith's espousal of national self-help and promotion of native industrial development.[5] In January 1907 O'Carroll stood for the first time in the Dublin municipal elections as a candidate in the Mansion House ward, one of seven official candidates of Griffith's National Council[6] (while abstention by Irish M.P.s from Westminster was a key plank of Griffith's programme, he encouraged participation by his supporters in local government bodies, in part to facilitate an eventual transfer of allegiance by such bodies to an abstentionist Irish national assembly). O'Carroll was also endorsed by the executive of the bricklayers' union and by the National Council's sister party, Cumann na nGaedheal[7] (the latter two were among the organisations that later that year coalesced to become Sinn Féin). Losing to the UIL candidate by only nineteen votes (out of nearly 1,150 cast), ten months later (October 1907) O'Carroll was elected to Dublin City Council in a special election to fill a vacancy;[8] he would represent the Mansion House ward on the council for the rest of his life. In January 1909 he was elected to a full three-year term by a substantial majority, 514 votes to 280, and thereafter enjoyed a safe seat, uncontested by any opponent in two subsequent elections.[9]

4   Arthur Mitchell, *Labour in Irish politics 1890–1930: the Irish labour movement in an age of revolution* (Dublin, 1974), pp 15–16, 19–21.
5   Ibid., p. 58.
6   *Sunday Independent*, 6 Jan. 1907; *Irish Times*, 7 Jan. 1907.
7   *Freeman's Journal*, 15, 16 Jan. 1907.
8   *Irish Times*, 17 Jan. 1907; *Irish Independent*, 22 Oct. 1907.
9   *Irish Times*, 6, 16, 23 Jan. 1909; *Freeman's Journal*, 18 Jan. 1909.

A member for a time of the Sinn Féin executive, O'Carroll resigned in 1909 over Griffith's increasingly hostile attitude to trade unionism, especially the militant 'new unionism' associated with James Larkin and the Irish Transport and General Workers' Union (ITGWU).[10] Larkin's activities in Dublin and the foundation of the ITGWU transformed labour politics in the city. The new unionism challenged not only the city's employers, but also the cautious reformism and sectionalism of the established craft unions, with its concerted organisation of the unskilled, militant and confrontational tactics, and ideology of syndicalist socialism. Larkin and his supporters vigorously promoted the establishment of independent, trade-union-sponsored labour parties at local and national level. Prior to this, the proponents of such Irish-based labour parties were a tiny minority within the Irish trade union movement, eclipsed by those who eschewed any political activity in favour of exclusive concentration on workplace issues; by others who argued that alliance with the cross-class UIL/IPP was the best way to pursue the interests of labouring people, and who feared that separate labour political action would divide nationalist Ireland and retard the movement towards home rule; and finally, by proponents, largely Belfast-based, of affiliation with British labour's emerging political movement. By forcefully advocating independent, Irish-based political activity, Larkin and the ITGWU rapidly popularised this idea within the labour movement, and did so at an opportune moment. The two British general elections of 1910 each produced a minority Liberal government dependent on IPP support, resulting in the government's adoption of Irish Home Rule in exchange for IPP support for its radical budget and virtual abolition of the Lords veto, thus portending the establishment of an Irish home rule parliament in the near future. This scenario strengthened the case for an Irish labour party sponsored by the Irish Trade Union Congress (ITUC), that would represent labour and working-class interests in the anticipated home rule parliament in Dublin without posing a threat to the IPP in Westminster.[11]

In this context, in January 1911 Dublin Trades Council (DTC) established a labour representation committee (LRC), of which O'Carroll was a founding officer. Though an official of a craft union, he embraced the tactical militancy and class consciousness of the new unionism, and for the rest of his career was described by a hostile mainstream press as a 'Larkinite'. Within months, Larkin supporters won control of the DTC, and thereafter directed the activities of the LRC and dominated its membership.[12] In summer 1911 O'Carroll was returned by the electors of the Mansion House ward to the board of guardians of the South Dublin Union (of which he was already an outgoing member), one of four LRC

---

10   Richard O'Carroll, T. C., website.
11   Mitchell, *Labour*, pp 22–4.
12   Ibid., p. 27.

candidates elected as poor law guardians in the Dublin area in the first election contested by the committee.[13] The LRC then fielded six candidates in the January 1912 municipal elections, of which five were successful; O'Carroll was returned unopposed, and the other four, including Larkin in North Dock, won contested seats. The following month they were joined by a sixth LRC-endorsed councillor, Thomas Farren, returned unopposed as the only nominee to fill a vacancy in Usher's Quay ward.[14] When in September 1912 Larkin was removed from his council seat by court order (due to a criminal conviction some years earlier arising from an industrial dispute), O'Carroll, as the senior serving councillor within the Labour group, who occupied their safest seat, was chosen to succeed him as leader of the Labour councillors.[15]

O'Carroll was elected to the parliamentary committee (soon to be restyled the national executive) of the Irish Trade Union Congress (ITUC) in 1911. At the June 1912 congress in Clonmel, he helped to secure passage of a motion authorising promotion of labour representation on all public bodies, leading to formation of a Congress-affiliated Irish Labour Party. (The introduction two months earlier of the Home Rule Bill in the Westminster House of Commons decisively influenced Congress's decision.) The party constitution, drafted by the executive and accepted at the 1914 congress, linked congress and party in a single organisation, styled the Irish Trade Union Congress and Labour Party (ITUCLP).[16] This combination of the industrial and political wings of the labour movement in a single entity underlined the dominance of syndicalist ideology among the leadership of Irish labour.

Labour politics and syndicalist ideology

Syndicalism was a variant of socialism that insisted upon the primacy, if not the exclusivity, of industrial action in securing working-class demands and supplanting the capitalist system with a socialist organisation of economic and social life. Since the economic system was the determining foundation of a society, syndicalists argued, the workers' strength lay in the economic power of their labour and their most potent and revolutionary tactic was the withdrawal of that labour. Syndicalists sought to organise workers into unions along industrial rather than craft lines, and in most anglophone countries aspired to achieve 'one big union' (OBU) of all workers (epitomised for contemporaries by the Industrial Workers

---

13   Ibid., p. 28; *Freeman's Journal*, 29 Apr. 1911.

14   Mitchell, *Labour*, pp 28–9; *Irish Times*, 6, 16 Jan., 17 Feb. 1912; *Irish Worker*, 6, 13, 20 Jan., 3 Feb. 1912.

15   Mitchell, *Labour*, p. 29.

16   Donal Nevin (ed.), *Trade union century* (Dublin, 1994), p. 444; Mitchell, *Labour*, pp 32–7; C. Desmond Greaves, *The life and times of James Connolly* (London, 1961), pp 58, 75.

of the World (IWW) of North America, of which James Connolly was a leading member); the ITGWU for a time aspired to be Ireland's OBU. The revolutionary trade union thus organised would not only achieve the final conquest of capital by labour through militant activity on the industrial front, likely culminating in a millenarian general strike, but would then supplant the bourgeois state as the administrative structure of the new socialist order (a process outlined by Connolly in his tract *Socialism made easy* (1908).)

In such a scenario, the conquest and wielding of state power by political means was both unnecessary and theoretically unsound. In most countries, syndicalists renounced any political activity, such as electioneering, office-holding, or the lobbying of elected representatives, as an unnecessary distraction, and at worst a corrupting and corrosive diversion, a perpetuation of the oppressive and bureaucratic state. Syndicalism in Ireland, however, took a more flexible and pragmatic approach to the question of political action. Led by Larkin, the movement's chief agitator, and Connolly, its chief theoretician, Irish syndicalism held that the industrial struggle was paramount as the field on which capitalism would ultimately be conquered, but it also allowed an important place for political activity, regarding it as an important weapon in the industrial struggle. Through political activity, workers could wrest short-term concessions, thus ameliorating to some degree their working and living conditions; the labour movement would gain in experience, confidence and support; class consciousness would be fostered, by providing workers with a labour alternative to bourgeois capitalist parties.[17] In a characteristically vivid metaphor, Larkin declared: 'I am an industrialist and at the same time appreciate the fact that labour can accomplish a great deal through the intelligent use of the ballot. Why use one arm when we have two? Why not strike the enemy with both arms – the political and the economic?'[18]

On foot of the 1912 resolution authorising the formation of a national labour party, the Dublin LRC was reconstituted as the Dublin Labour Party (DLP). Over the next several years, the DLP councillors established a reputation as an outspoken and disciplined group, arguing forcefully for reform within Dublin Corporation and for improvements in workers' wages and conditions, especially for Corporation employees. As leader of the group, O'Carroll denounced jobbery and corruption within the Corporation bureaucracy, and attacked the employment of child labour by businesses on municipal contracts. He charged 'seething' corruption in the

---

17   Mitchell, *Labour*, pp 26–7, 37–8; Emmet O'Connor, *Syndicalism in Ireland 1917–1923* (Cork, 1988), pp xiii–xix, 1–19; James Connolly, *Socialism made easy* (1908; reprint, Dublin, 1971), 33–48.

18   Mitchell, *Labour*, p. 26.

management of the South Dublin Union. While lacking Larkin's charisma, he was an able public representative and party leader.[19]

Notwithstanding their energy and outspokenness, the DLP councillors were a small minority on the City Council, and were powerless to enact much in the way of tangible reform. Over the next several years, the initial public enthusiasm for their candidates and programme waned, and the party made little electoral progress, managing to maintain their strength but not to increase it, their numbers on the council fluctuating at around a half-dozen. In the January 1913 election, only two of the DLP's seven candidates were successful, one of them being William Partridge in the ward of New Kilmainham. The DLP's representation stood at six councillors, Farren having lost his Usher's Quay seat.[20]

William Partridge: early career

(3) Next Lorcan, is Partridge, a bird we call "game."
He "grouses" a lot, but he's really quite tame.

Cartoon of William Partridge (DCLA, *Lepracaun Cartoon Monthly*, Dec. 1913, p. 245)

William Patrick ('Bill') Partridge was born 8 March 1874 in Sligo town.[21] His father, an engine driver on the Midland and Great Western Railway (MGWR), was an English-born Protestant of liberal and pro-labour opinion who was sympathetic to Irish constitutional nationalism. His mother was an Irish Catholic. In his infancy the family moved on his father's transfer to Ballaghaderreen, then in County Mayo, where Bill was educated in national school and at St Nathy's College. Baptised at birth in the Church of Ireland, under the influence of a teaching nun

---

19   Ibid., p. 29; Emmet Larkin, *James Larkin: Irish labour leader, 1876–1947* (London, 1989), pp 104–5.
20   *Irish Worker*, 11, 18 Jan. 1913; *Irish Times*, 16 Jan. 1913.
21   Birth certificate (GRO, Dublin).

he was baptised a Catholic at age 11; in adult life, a fervent Catholic faith coexisted with his radical socialist politics. After serving an engineering apprenticeship with the MGWR in Sligo town (1891–3) and in Dublin at the Broadstone workshops (1893–6), he worked first with the MGWR and then with other Dublin firms before being employed in 1899 as an engine fitter in the Inchicore works of the Great Southern and Western Railway (GSWR).[22]

Like his future DLP and City Council colleague Richard O'Carroll, Partridge first came to prominence within the trade-union movement and in his locale owing to his role in a particularly acrimonious and unsuccessful strike. Active from the late 1890s in Dublin No. 2 branch of the British-based Amalgamated Society of Engineers (ASE), which he represented on DTC, Partridge initially argued against strike action in pushing a wages claim by the ASE in Dublin railway workshops, but once a majority voted to strike, he was in the forefront of activity during the five-month stoppage (May–October 1902), serving as secretary of the strike committee.[23] Prominent in efforts to secure improved housing in the locality (Kilmainham and Inchicore), he was nominated by tenants' and labour organisations to stand for Dublin City Council in New Kilmainham ward in the January 1904 municipal elections, and was defeated by only six votes (546 to 540). Three months later, in April 1904, he successfully contested a by-election over a UIL candidate.[24] A founding member and treasurer of the Inchicore branch of the Gaelic League,[25] he was deeply influenced in his political thinking by Griffith's polemic *The resurrection of Hungary* (1904), and was among the first of several Dublin councillors to affiliate with the National Council, under whose auspices he was re-elected to a full term in January 1905.[26] His Griffithite associations were, however, reviled by some trade unionists as a betrayal of the movement. A hard-working and outspoken councillor, he often clashed in the chamber with Timothy Harrington, eminent UIL leader and former Lord Mayor; it was said that when they 'crossed swords it was a sight for the gods'.[27] His initial tenure as a city councillor would, however, be short-lived. Because of his energetic advocacy of Corporation housing to accommodate railway workers in his ward, Partridge was allowed time off work by the GSWR to attend City Council meetings. When he took up more radical pro-labour issues the permission was withdrawn, resulting in his resignation from the Council in March 1906.[28]

---

22   Hugh Geraghty, *William Patrick Partridge and his times* (Dublin, 2003), pp 15–36.
23   Ibid., pp 25, 59–79; Ward-Perkins, *Select guide*, p. 2; *Dublin Saturday Post*, 4 Aug. 1917.
24   Geraghty, *Partridge*, pp 85–9, 101–2.
25   Ibid., pp 44–5.
26   *Sligo Champion*, 18 Aug. 1917; Geraghty, *Partridge*, p. 106, 109; *Irish Times*, 16, 18 Jan. 1905.
27   *Dublin Saturday Post*, 4 Aug. 1917.
28   Geraghty, *Partridge*, pp 107–8; Pádraig Yeates, *Lockout: Dublin 1913* (Dublin, 2000), p. 86; Dublin Corporation, *Diary* and *DCC Minutes* (1905–6 eds.).

Patridge was initially sceptical of Larkin's militant tactics and syndicalist strategy, largely because of his first-hand experience of the hardships that strikes imposed on the families of striking workers. He was soon persuaded by the force of Larkin's arguments and became one of Larkin's staunchest supporters and ablest lieutenants.[29] Like O'Carroll, during 1909 Partridge broke with Sinn Féin over Griffith's hostility to Larkinite trade unionism.[30] In August 1912 he was dismissed from his employment by the GSWR after refusing to withdraw his accusation that the company was preferring Protestants over Catholics for promotion in the Inchicore works.[31] Blacklisted thereafter by many potential employers, while working on petrol engines in a motor garage in Carrick-on-Suir he lost part of a finger in an accident, which presented him with physical difficulties in practising his trade. Appointed as a full-time, paid official of the ITGWU in October 1912, he managed the newly opened Emmet Hall in Inchicore, which housed the union's insurance section and local branch.[32] The following year he organised for the union in Cork city and among farm labourers in rural County Dublin.[33] In the unusual position of being an employee of an industrial union (the ITGWU) while remaining an official of a craft union (the ASE), during 1913 Partridge was the latter's Dublin district president and represented the engineering union at the ITUC.[34]

Watercolour of Lutyen's proposed design for the Municipal Gallery (Courtesy Dublin City Gallery The Hugh Lane)

29   Geraghty, *Partridge*, p. 116; R. M. Fox, *The history of the Irish Citizen Army* (Dublin, 1943), p. 37; Larkin, *Larkin*, pp 159–60.

30   Geraghty, *Partridge*, p. 116.

31   Ibid., pp 141–3; C. Desmond Greaves, *The Irish Transport and General Workers' Union: the formative years 1910–23* (Dublin, 1982), p. 80.

32   Geraghty, *Partridge*, p. 147.

33   Ibid., pp 176–80, 184–8; Greaves, *ITGWU*, p. 90.

34   Yeates, *Lockout*, p. 34; Greaves, *ITGWU*, pp 88–9; Geraghty, *Partridge*, pp 154, 181.

With a strong, clear, resonant voice, Partridge was acclaimed as the best public speaker in Dublin apart from Larkin.[35] Re-entering local politics, he was defeated by twenty-three votes in a poll of nearly 900 as DLP candidate in an October 1912 by-election. His success in the January 1913 City Council elections, when he was easily elected to a full, three-year term (by 706 votes to 453), was secured despite vicious vilification by opponents and the mainstream press, and was based on a strong local Labour Party organisation centred on the Inchicore works.[36] Already a prolific contributor to the ITGWU organ, the *Irish Worker*, in which he authored a regular column of 'Inchicore items', after winning a City Council seat he also contributed 'Cork Hill items'. During 1913 the six Labour councillors joined the Sinn Féin members in supporting the proposal for a permanent Dublin municipal art gallery to house the Hugh Lane collection, in part because construction of the gallery would create employment, but also on the grounds that the arts were a fundamental component of workers' education. When a unionist alderman objected to Edwin Lutyens's design for a gallery located on a new bridge over the Liffey on the grounds that the view of the Four Courts from O'Connell Bridge would be obscured, Partridge replied with characteristic acerbity that the alderman must see around corners, as the Four Courts were not visible from O'Connell Bridge.[37]

The Lockout and its aftermath

Both O'Carroll, and especially Partridge, were prominent figures during the 1913–14 lockout. Dispatched by Larkin on 25 August 1913 to the Ringsend power station of the Dublin United Tramways Company to persuade workers there to join an all-out tramway strike in support of locked-out ITGWU members, Partridge reported favourably on the station workers' attitude, thereby fatefully inducing Larkin to call the strike. In the event, an insufficient number of powermen walked out – and were swiftly replaced by blacklegs – to force the expected power cut that would have comprehensively shut down the tramway network. Partridge later claimed to have personally stopped the first tramcar on the morning of 26 August.[38] Addressing the nightly lockout rallies in Beresford Place with fiery oratory, Partridge was twice arrested during the first week of the tram strike and both times released, firstly on an undertaking of good behaviour and secondly on bail.[39] On 31 August, O'Carroll addressed a workers' rally in Croydon Park, Fairview, that preceded the 'bloody Sunday' police baton charge of a Sackville Street crowd. That evening both O'Carroll and Partridge were badly beaten when police

---

35   Greaves, *ITGWU*, p. 82; Yeates, *Lockout*, pp 12, 294.
36   Geraghty, *Partridge*, pp 147–9, 157–9; *Irish Times*, 16 Jan. 1913.
37   Geraghty, *Partridge*, pp 167–9.
38   Yeates, *Lockout*, pp 12, 14, 16, 90.
39   Ibid., pp 33–6, 45; Greaves, *ITGWU*, 97–8.

invaded a meeting protesting against police brutality at the Emmet Hall.[40] Over ensuing months, both men vigorously argued the trade unions' case in bellicose exchanges at City Council meetings. As the most effective speaker within a special DTC delegation, Partridge addressed the British Trade Union Congress (TUC) on 2 September, graphically describing the violent events of the previous 'bloody Sunday'; his accusation that the Dublin police had been fuelled by drink was widely reported throughout Europe.[41] For the couple of weeks in September that Larkin and Connolly were both imprisoned, Partridge deputised as strike leader. When Connolly called on workers to vote against the Liberal government in three parliamentary by-elections in November to protest against the recent conviction of Larkin for seditious speech and the general handling of the situation in Dublin, Partridge campaigned successfully on behalf of a British Labour candidate in Reading. The initiative exacerbated tensions with the IPP owing to the latter's Liberal alliance, and Partridge was attacked in the City Council for supporting a 'socialistic' candidate against a home ruler.[42]

Contemporary press image of Bloody Sunday Sackville Street (DCLA, *Evening Telegraph*, 1 Sept. 1913)

Throughout the autumn of 1913 Partridge continued to speak on behalf of the locked-out Dublin workers in British cities and was instrumental in raising

40 Yeates, *Lockout*, 73–4, 90.
41 Ibid., 99–100; Greaves, *ITGWU*, 99–100.
42 Ibid., p. 109; Mitchell, *Labour*, pp 50–51; Yeates, *Lockout*, pp 385, 447.

financial assistance from British trade unionists. Nonetheless, with the unions and employers deadlocked, tensions emerged between ITGWU leaders and the crafts-dominated British TUC, whose leadership was alarmed by Larkinite syndicalism, and with the British-based amalgamated unions operating in Ireland (including Partridge's ASE) over their refusal to engage in sympathetic striking and blacklisting of goods.[43]

While O'Carroll was not actively engaged in the conduct of the strike (not being, like Partridge, an ITGWU officer), he frequently addressed support meetings, argued on behalf of the strikers in the City Council, and was involved in Trades Council initiatives on their behalf. He was one of eight Trades Council representatives to the Askwith Inquiry into the Lockout (September–October), whose recommended bases for negotiation were rejected by the employers.[44]

DEPORTING CHILDREN---DUBLIN CASES.

Children deported to Britian during the Lockout (DCLA, *Freeman's Journal*, 25 Oct. 1913)

The DTC approached the January 1914 municipal election as a potential show of strength, hoping that a large Labour poll might break the industrial deadlock. During the campaign, outgoing Lord Mayor Lorcan Sherlock attacked Partridge (whose seat was not being contested) for 'truculent and stupid speeches' that had frustrated Sherlock's efforts to mediate in the dispute.[45] The election results were a bitter disappointment: with the DLP standing ten candidates, the only one elected was in New Kilmainham, which was a testament to Partridge's success in having made the ward a DLP stronghold with a tight party organisation around the Inchicore engineering works.[46] Labour's disappointing showing was ascribed in part to the fallout from the controversial evacuation of the children of locked-out

---

43   Ward-Perkins, *Select guide*, p. 2; Yeates, *Lockout*, pp 101, 121–2, 258.
44   Ibid., p. 174; Greaves, *ITGWU*, p. 255.
45   Yeates, *Lockout*, p. 508.
46   Ibid., pp 500, 508–9; Mitchell, *Labour*, pp 51–3; *Irish Worker*, 10 Jan. 1914; *Irish Times*, 5, 10, 14, 16 Jan. 1914.

workers to host families in Britain, about which Partridge had publicly expressed reservations. Opposing Sherlock's re-election to a third term as Lord Mayor, the seven Labour councillors supported Sinn Féin's Thomas Kelly for the office: in the event, Sherlock was successful.[47]

The DLP fared even worse in the January 1915 elections. As party leader, O'Carroll avoided radical rhetoric and concentrated the campaign on such immediate issues as public housing, social services and educational reform. With the three-year terms won in the DLP's first municipal election contest of 1912 having expired, the party nominated five candidates for contested seats, and suffered a net loss of two seats; O'Carroll was returned unopposed once again.[48] The setback was largely attributed to the labour movement's opposition to the First World War, a principled position but one unpopular among the many working-class Dubliners with kinfolk in British uniform. The DTC had declared against the war at its outset, though (Connolly apart) the grounds for opposition were based more on Irish nationalism than socialist internationalism.[49] The *Irish Worker*, prior to its suppression in December 1914, inveighed against the potential of military conscription and the reality of the 'economic conscription' of employers inducing men to enlist by sacking them from their jobs.[50]

The graveside oration by Patrick Pearse at the funeral of O'Donovan Rossa (DCLA)

47   Yeates, *Lockout*, pp 270, 526–7.
48   Mitchell, *Labour*, 63–4; *Freeman's Journal*, 16 Jan. 1915; *Irish Independent*, 16 Jan. 1915.
49   Mitchell, *Labour*, 62.
50   *Irish Worker*, 5 Sept. 1914.
51   Richard O'Carroll, T. C., website.

Though he was described as a member from 1915 of C Company, 3rd Battalion, Dublin Brigade, of the Irish Volunteers, under the command of Éamon de Valera, during Easter Week O'Carroll was attached to the Dublin Brigade's 2nd Battalion, commanded by Thomas MacDonagh and headquartered in Jacob's biscuit factory in Bishop Street.[52] It appears that during the first few days of the Rising he delivered arms and ammunition to outposts in the 2nd Battalion's operational area in his motorcycle combination. On 26 April he was appointed a lieutenant by MacDonagh and assigned to lead a small force that seized Delahunt's public house at 42 Camden Street and established a battalion outpost there. The force soon engaged with a British army patrol from nearby Portobello barracks commanded by Captain John Bowen-Colthurst, the Irish-born officer who earlier that day had ordered the summary executions of three prisoners in the barracks, including the pacifist radical Francis Sheehy-Skeffington. The British patrol eventually drove the Volunteers from their position and captured O'Carroll. Disarmed and taken to the yard behind the building, O'Carroll was held at gunpoint with his hands raised. According to tradition, upon being asked by Bowen-Colthrust whether he was a 'Sinn Féiner', O'Carroll replied 'From the backbone out!', whereupon Bowen-Colthurst shot him with his revolver, the bullet piercing O'Carroll's right lung. Left lying in the street outside the building, O'Carroll was picked up by a passing bread van and brought to Portobello military hospital. After nine days of great suffering, he died there on 5 May 1916. He was survived by his widow Annie (née Power) and their seven children, the youngest of whom was born two weeks after O'Carroll's death.[53]

Bowen-Colthurst was court-martialled for the summary executions in Portobello; found guilty but insane and committed to an asylum, within several years he was released as sane. He was not, however, charged with the murder of O'Carroll. A parliamentary question requesting an inquiry into the circumstances of O'Carroll's killing was refused. Annie O'Carroll, like Sheehy-Skeffington's widow, Hanna, refused compensation from the crown for her husband's death.[54]

William Partridge enlisted in the Irish Citizen Army (ICA) on its formation in November 1913.[55] In the post-lockout reorganisation of the body he was elected to the first army council as one of five vice-chairmen (March 1914).[56] Some sources

---

52   Application for widows' allowance or gratuity under Army Pensions Act 1923, 5 Feb. 1924 (Military Archives, MSPC, Richard O'Carroll file, ID237).

53   O'Carroll file (MSPC); Desmond Ryan, *The rising: the complete story of Easter Week* (Dublin, 1949), pp 168–9; Max Caulfield, *The Easter rebellion* (London, 1964), pp 243–4; *Catholic Bulletin*, vol. vi, no. 7 (July 1916), pp 404, 406; ibid., vol. vi, no. 12 (Dec. 1916), p. 705.

54   Richard O'Carroll, T. C., website.

55   Geraghty, *Partridge*, p. 225; *Dublin Saturday Post*, 4 Aug. 1917.

56   Fox, *Irish Citizen Army*, pp 63–4.

attest that by Easter 1916 he held ICA officer's rank.[57] It has been claimed, but never confirmed, that he was in the IRB.[58] Appointed ITGWU travelling organiser in April 1915, he spearheaded an effort to rebuild the union's strength outside Dublin by reinvigorating provincial branches. Over the winter of 1915–16 he was especially active in Tralee and elsewhere in Kerry.[59] Owing to his familiarity with the area, on the Wednesday prior to the Easter Rising, 19 April, he was dispatched by Connolly to Tralee to supervise the handling of the anticipated arms shipment from Germany by ITGWU members on the Fenit docks, in coordination with the local Volunteers under Austin Stack. On returning to Dublin on Saturday 22 April, Partridge briefed the IRB military council on details of the abortive arms landing and the arrest of Roger Casement.[60] He appears to have commanded the ICA guard in Liberty Hall while the proclamation of the republic was being printed on Easter Sunday morning.[61]

19th century postcard of St Stephen's Green (DCLA, Postcard Collection)

During Easter Week, Partridge fought in the ICA contingent in St Stephen's Green and the Royal College of Surgeons, commanded by Michael Mallin. Veterans of the garrison remembered his efforts at maintaining morale, leading nightly recitations of the rosary and regularly visiting sentries and snipers posted

---

57 Variously described as a lieutenant (*Irish Times*, 7 Apr. 1966) and as a captain (Fox, *Irish Citizen Army*, pp 164, 229; Geraghty, *Partridge*, p. 269). Geraghty states that though a captain he fought in the rising as a private soldier. He is described as an ICA private in an application for widows' allowance or gratuity, 3 Apr. 1924 (MSPC, William Partridge file, ID303).

58 Geraghty, *Partridge*, p. 266.

59 Greaves, *ITGWU*, pp 145, 151–2, 155.

60 Fox, *Irish Citizen Army*, p. 141; Ryan, *Rising*, pp 78–9; Geraghty, *Partridge*, pp 261–6.

61 *Irish Times*, 7 Apr. 1966.

throughout the Surgeons building to offer encouragement.[62] On Wednesday 26 April he was part of a sortie down Harcourt Street intending to flush out a troublesome British sniper on the roof of the Russell Hotel. When heavy fire killed one man in the sortie and critically wounded Margaret Skinnider of the ICA (the most serious woman casualty among the Easter Week insurgents), Partridge carried her to safety under continuing fire.[63] After the surrender, Partridge was incarcerated in Richmond barracks next to Mallin, who in his last letter to his wife before his execution described Partridge as having been 'more than a brother' to him, and recorded that Partridge had held him close in his arms that he might have 'comfort and warmth' against the bitter cold.[64]

Court-martialled and sentenced to fifteen years' penal servitude (remitted to ten years), Partridge was imprisoned till December 1916 in Dartmoor, and then in Lewes prison. In January 1917 he was one of four imprisoned Dublin city councillors who were disqualified owing to six-months' absence from meetings, and were then co-opted to fill the vacant seats. Having suffered poor health for a year prior to the Rising (he had been ill during Easter Week), while being held briefly in Mountjoy Jail awaiting transfer to Dartmoor, Partridge was diagnosed with a kidney condition (Bright's disease). The condition being aggravated by the rigours of prison life, by April 1917 Partridge was seriously ill, and was released on health grounds.[65] Initially too ill to travel (in a letter to relatives he said he had been released when 'only fit for the scrap heap'[66]), after several weeks in a Brighton nursing home, he returned to Ireland, spending a short while in Dublin, then going to his brother's home in Ballaghaderreen, where he died on 26 July 1917. Countess Constance Markievicz, a fellow veteran of the ICA St Stephen's Green garrison, delivered the funeral oration before a large gathering in Kilcolman cemetery.[67]

A man of vivid contrasts, a deeply pious Catholic and a radical syndicalist, Partridge had a capacity for humane empathy that coexisted with a vituperative tongue prone to highly personalised invective. His celebrated piety was exploited after his death to help rehabilitate the public image of both the labour and republican movements. Markievicz attributed her conversion to Roman Catholicism to the

---

62 Geraghty, *Partridge*, p. 270; Fox, *Irish Citizen Army*, pp 164–5.
63 Caulfield, *Rebellion*, p. 268; Geraghty, *Partridge*, p. 271; Frank Robbins, *Under the starry plough: recollections of the Irish Citizen Army* (Dublin, 1977), p. 116.
64 Geraghty, *Partridge*, pp 274–6; Piaras F. Mac Lochlainn (ed.), *Last words: letters and statements of the leaders executed after the rising at Easter 1916* (Dublin, 1971), pp 122, 127–8.
65 Geraghty, *Partridge*, 278–92; Breandán MacGiolla Choille (ed.), *Intelligence notes 1913–16* (Dublin, 1966), p. 265.
66 *Dublin Saturday Post*, 4 Aug. 1917.
67 Geraghty, *Partridge*, p. 294; death certificate (GRO, Dublin); Greaves, *ITGWU*, p. 185; *Dublin Saturday Post*, 28 July, 4 Aug. 1917.

piety and selflessness she had observed during Easter Week in both Mallin and Partridge.[68]

The careers of Richard O'Carroll and William Partridge illustrate the relationship between the radical section of the Irish labour movement and 'advanced nationalism' in the early years of the twentieth century. Politically active within a Dublin working class that was imbued with nationalist sentiment, they each shunned alliance with mainstream bourgeois nationalism and entered local politics as adherents of the minority trend of Griffithite advanced nationalism. Breaking with Griffith on their respective conversions to Larkinite new unionism, they remained sympathetic to separatist nationalism – a position not inconsistent with the Larkinite commitment to separatist, Irish-based trade union bodies and labour politics – an outlook that set them each on a fateful course to armed insurrection at Easter 1916.

---

68   *Dublin Saturday* Post, 4 Aug. 1917; Fox, *Irish Citizen Army*, p. 165.

Alderman Tom Kelly

Sheila Carden

Tom Kelly, President of the
Old Dublin Society
(Gertrude O'Flynn)

Thomas Kelly's career in Dublin Corporation (later Dublin City Council) enabled him to contribute seriously to the wider political questions of his day and led him to play a significant role in national politics.[1] He was born in Dublin on 13 September 1868 into a Catholic working-class family. His parents, Isaac Kelly and Sarah Pitts, lived at the time at 31 Townsend Street, and he was baptised in St Andrew's Church, Westland Row. He attended school at the Christian Brothers' School next door to the church, where the records show that he first attended on 12 January 1874. In 1882 it appears the family inhabited the drawing room of 113 Cumberland Street, for which they were paying three shillings per week. From an early date Kelly displayed an aptitude for figures, and the school records show that he acted as a pupil-teacher at the school in 1884. [2]

The passage of the Local Government Act 1898, which reformed the structure of local government in Ireland, made it possible for Thomas Kelly to become a city councillor and then an alderman. Kelly had become involved in issues of social exclusion, especially those relating to the housing, health and education of the poor, during the 1890s, when he first joined the Total Abstinence and Workmen's Club, which nominated him as a candidate in the municipal elections of 1899. He was subsequently elected to Dublin City Council, topping the poll in the Mansion House ward in the election of January 1899,[3] and went on to serve on various committees such as the Finance, Libraries, and Housing Committees, where he and like-minded colleagues took a keen interest in servicing the city's needs, which ranged from housing and water services to the provision of new libraries. As chairman of the Public Libraries Committee, Kelly was also pivotal in the establishment of a Municipal Art Gallery in Dublin to house Hugh Lane's collection of paintings, a project which was brought to fruition in 1908.[4] He was closely associated with Arthur Griffith to whose newspapers, *The United Irishman*

---

1   Unless otherwise stated, all the material and references in this essay are drawn from Sheila Carden, *The Alderman* (Dublin, 2007) which gives a full account of Kelly's life.
2   Tom Kelly 'I Remember', *Capuchin Annual* (1942), p. 591.
3   *The Alderman*, p. 10.
4   *Irish Times*, 29 Sept. 1908.

and *Sinn Féin*, he contributed, inter alia, 45 articles under the heading *The Streets of Dublin* during the years 1910 and 1911.[5]

Faddle's Alley, off Dowker's Lane' from *Report to inquire into the housing conditions of the working classes in the city of Dublin* (London, 1914)

On 8 May 1911, Dublin City Council resolved to create a dedicated committee to deal with Dublin's notorious slum problems and, in the same year, a detailed report was submitted to the Council on the experience of town-planning and the provision of open spaces in Birmingham.[6] Following this report the Housing Committee was established on 14 February 1913 with the active participation of Kelly who served as its vice chairman and then chairman, occupying the latter post from May 1914 until December 1919. The new committee was charged with 'all matters relating to the selection of sites for, and the erection of Artisans' and Labourers' Dwellings".[7] From its inception, the Housing Committee had taken over several projects, which were already in hand from the General Improvements and Public Health Committees and had continued the work of clearing and preparing various sites which were deemed to be in immediate need of re-development and in developing ambitious building plans for the reconstruction of the most dilapidated areas of the city. The outbreak of the First World War, however, impeded progress in these areas as the requirements of the British war effort ensured the supply of money for Irish needs was very much diminished.

5   Thomas Kelly, *The Streets of Dublin* (Dublin, 2013).
6   *DCC Minutes.*
7   *The Alderman*, p. 114.

Meanwhile, through his friendship with Arthur Griffith and his work on the nationalist party within the City Council, Kelly became more involved with the development of Sinn Féin in 1905 and by 1906 was elected to its Organising and Press Committee.[8] During the following years, Kelly worked vigorously on issues of social equality and on workers' rights which were especially important in the Lockout of 1913. He also contributed to the debates on the Home Rule question that dominated Irish politics in the years leading up to the First World War.

In 1913, Kelly did not join the Irish Volunteers, explaining, in his reminiscences many years later, that he feared that this new military movement would mean 'the end of Sinn Féin as we knew it'.[9] However, in 1916, in his capacity as vice president of Sinn Féin, Kelly delivered a speech in City Hall during a meeting of Dublin City Council concerning the so-called 'Castle document', supposedly a British plan purporting to come from the British undersecretary, Sir Matthew Nathan, outlining a plan to intern all known nationalists prior to Easter week and to suppress all nationalist organisations as well as ordering the disarming of the Irish Volunteers.

Kelly later related how the first knowledge he had received regarding what came to be known as the 'Castle Document' came from Arthur Griffith as a result of a chance street meeting with him on the Tuesday of Holy Week 1916. They discussed what Griffith described as a provocative document, purporting to have been leaked from Dublin Castle. The contents of the document outlined government plans to arrest all members of nationalist organisations, together with instructions that all the inhabitants of Dublin remain in their houses. Various prominent buildings such as the Mansion House, the Catholic Archbishop's residence, and the homes of several prominent nationalists such as that of Eoin MacNeill were to be isolated and picketed by armed patrols.[10] Griffith took a very serious view of the nature of such a document being circulated and warned Kelly of the dangerous consequences that might arise if the information proved to be correct.[11] The following day Kelly was visited by Francis Sheehy Skeffington in his office in South William Street, who gave him a copy of the document and asked if Kelly would read it out at a meeting of the Corporation scheduled for that afternoon. It had been handed to Skeffington by the editor of *New Ireland* a well-known nationalist periodical, P.J. Little, who had been given it by a sympathiser working in Dublin Castle, who felt that its contents should be made known publicly as they were potentially so inflammatory.[12]

---

8   *United Irishman*, 9 Dec. 1905.
9   Tom Kelly, 'I Remember', p. 237.
10   Charles Townshend, *Easter 1916, the Irish rebellion* (London, 2005), pp 131-3.
11   Tom Kelly 'I Remember', p 591.
12   Townshend, *Easter 1916*, p. 132.

We know from Kelly's own account that his decision to publicise the document was one that he did not take lightly. He recounts that while walking to the City Hall for the meeting of Dublin City Council that day, and talking to a friend, that he was in two minds as to what he should do. He thought it might do more harm than good but he also formed the opinion that the motives for publicising it were peaceful ones. Later he expressed his doubts as to whether or not it was genuine and perhaps part of a military plan, justifiable in war, but probably a forgery.

Kelly's exposure of the 'Castle Document' almost certainly contributed to his arrest after the Rising. The exact date of his arrest is not known. What is known is that the Kelly family home was ransacked and that Kelly was certainly imprisoned in Kilmainham Gaol during the period when the executions of the leaders of the Rising took place. He was later to recount how he heard the sound of the shots from the stonebreakers' yard as the leaders were executed during the week following the Rising. Kelly was then moved from Kilmainham to Richmond Barracks and is listed as being there on 20 May, which would indicate that he spent at least 17 days in Kilmainham.

On 13 May the Lord Mayor, James Gallagher, together with E. W. Eyre, the City Treasurer, had called on the Archbishop of Dublin, William Walsh, to sign a petition that Alderman Tom Kelly should get a fair and immediate trial. The archbishop subsequently added his signature to the petition. Amongst those imprisoned in Richmond Barracks with Kelly was the future senator, Joseph Connolly, a well-known nationalist who had been arrested in his native Belfast, and who was taken with his associates to Dublin by train, thence to Richmond Barracks. Connolly recalled that Kelly occupied a single room on the same landing beside Connolly and his companions. This room had been previously occupied by Count Plunkett, father of the executed Joseph Mary Plunkett.

> There was neither food nor water and the latrine service was limited to a couple of buckets on the landing which served the room opposite. There was neither blanket nor mattress nor other furnishing in the room, so, as night fell we just huddled together to try to keep warm. Poor Tom, whom everybody loved and respected, suffered untold agonies not indeed at the hands of the enemy, but due to internal trouble. This left him quiet and morose but always infinitely patient.[13]

---

13   J. Anthony Gaughan (ed.), *Memoirs of Joseph Connolly* (Dublin, 1996), pp 107-9, 112-3.

While he was in jail, Kelly's public reputation as an individual who pursued democratic and peaceful means of conflict resolution contributed to his selection by the Supreme Council of the IRB as a potential candidate in the event of a successful outcome from the Rising.

> The revolutionaries had made some small provision for the day of victory, however unlikely. A provisional civil government, less abhorrent to the people than they were, had been selected – Alderman Tom Kelly, Arthur Griffith, William O'Brien, Mrs. Sheehy-Skeffington and Seán T. O'Kelly (Sinn Féin, Sinn Féin, Labour, Suffragette-socialist and Sinn Féin respectively). It is most unlikely that any of these prominent citizens knew of the august role for which they had been chosen … In case Tom Kelly refused the chair, Seán T. was to direct the civil government.[14]

> Kelly was never charged or tried, and was released on 7 June 1916. Although he undoubtedly suffered psychological damage during his captivity, he had recovered sufficiently from his ordeal to resume his responsibilities in the City Council on 4 September 1916. Kelly's eldest son, Isaac, had also been imprisoned after the Rising, and was sent to Knutsford Prison in England on 3 May, but was released before the end of May 1916.

After the Rising, Dublin City Council publicly stated its concerns for the well-being of Republican prisoners who were still held in captivity. An all-Ireland convention to establish a political prisoners' amnesty association was proposed with Kelly suggesting that three Council members be appointed to visit Frongoch camp to report to the Corporation on the conditions of some hundreds of Irish prisoners there.[15]

The Corporation was faced with the daunting task of reconstructing the city after the Rising. Some of the ruins were demolished by contractors working for their owners, but the most dangerous structures were dealt with by Corporation workers themselves. Over 240 premises had been damaged in the fighting. These included buildings on Upper and Lower Sackville Street, Eden Quay, Cathedral Street, Eden Place, Middle and Lower Abbey Street, Beresford Place, Moore, Henry and North Earl Streets and Sackville Place. The Presbyterian Church and Royal

---

14 Quoted in Ruth Dudley Edwards, *Patrick Pearse, the triumph of failure* (Dublin, 2006), p. 276.
15 Kelly, O'Neill and Sherlock were delegated to visit Frongoch on behalf of the Council. *DCC Minutes*, 1916, p. 548.

Hibernian Academy buildings, both in Lower Abbey Street, were destroyed, as were parts of Marlborough Street, Harbour Court, Princes Street, North Lotts, Coles Lane, Henry Place, Sampsons Lane, Usher's Quay, Clanwilliam Place and Lower Mount Street.

View from Nelson's Pillar to North Earl Street following the Rising (DCLA, BOR Collection)

An exhibition devoted to the subject of the reconstruction of cities and towns destroyed during the war was being held in Paris at this time. It was suggested that it would be useful for a delegation from the Corporation to visit it, in view of Dublin's pressing need for extensive reconstruction. Kelly was not part of this group, as he was still recovering from the shock of his imprisonment in Kilmainham Jail and Richmond Barracks in May and June. The delegation included C. J. MacCarthy, City Architect and Alfred Byrne. On their way to Paris, on 6 July 1916, the group were introduced to the Prime Minister, Herbert Asquith, in London by John Redmond. Dublin Corporation's appeal for financial assistance was for two objectives: (i) to lend money to citizens whose premises had been destroyed and to assist them to rebuild in accordance with the requirements of the Corporation; and (ii) to borrow money for the necessary street widening and improvements, and to purchase any sites on which the occupying tenants did not propose to re-build.

However, no funds were forthcoming for this essential rebuilding by the end of 1916. The First World War was continuing, with catastrophic losses, especially at the Battle of the Somme. Great Britain had a new Prime Minister (Lloyd George) who lacked interest in tackling Irish affairs, and who was undoubtedly distracted by ongoing wrangling over Home Rule that led to the 1917 Irish Convention.

Kelly had resumed his position as chairman of the Housing Committee from the beginning of September 1916, with ambitious plans for the redevelopment of derelict and ruined sites. By December 1916, the urgency of providing dwellings for the poor was so acute that the City Treasurer, Edmund Eyre, advised that the preparation and planning for housing schemes on the north-side of Dublin should continue unabated. Because of the war and the difficulty of obtaining money from Britain, serious consideration was now given to seeking out financial loans from America for the re-building of the city.

In February 1917, Laurence O'Neill was elected Lord Mayor, while Kelly continued to chair the Housing Committee. Kelly was thanked by the City Council for the very earnest, capable and impartial manner in which he conducted the committee business and the keen and unselfish interest he consistently took in finding a solution to the committee problems.[16] It will be remembered that he had only recommenced work after his term in prison in the summer of 1916.

In the early part of 1917, the business of Dublin Corporation was focused on the financial shortages resulting from the aftermath of the Rising and funds were finally being earmarked for the reconstruction of Dublin. A report from the Housing Committee on 19 April 1917 noted that the Fairbrothers' Fields, McCaffrey Estate, St James' Walk and Spitalfields sites were now in the hands of the Corporation, and recorded the good news that the necessary loans for their development were about to be made available by the treasury. The plan to obtain a loan from the US was abandoned in view of the prohibitive rates of interest required. Kelly summed up his own views regarding Corporation housing policy and the work of the committee in the course of a testy interview between the committee and P. C. Cowan, Chief Engineering Inspector of the Local Government Board, which took place on 19 October, 1917:

> The position of affairs is this. The Housing Committee was constituted at the beginning of 1913, and has continued its work ever since. All the officers are honorary officers; not one of them gets a penny piece. This is a very important point, and I want to get it into your head. The Committee is really doing the work for absolutely nothing. It doesn't cost the citizens a £100 a year. I am personally in favour of building entirely inside - that is inside the

---

16   *DCC Minutes*, February 1917.

old City before its boundaries were extended. Do not take that as the policy of the Housing Committee, but if I were the Housing Authority, I would allow no building outside until the slums were gone.[17]

During 1918, efforts continued to force the British Government to fulfil its commitments for financial assistance to Dublin Corporation for rehousing schemes, in response to multiple demands for housing assistance made to Dublin Corporation. Writing to both W. T. Cosgrave and Arthur Griffith on 28 August 1919, Kelly outlined the mishandling by the British of the housing situation in Dublin:

> The Rebellion of 1916, with the terrible loss of life, vast material waste, the re-birth of dying antagonisms, the creation of new enmities and the setting back of the clock in many most vital movements, might possibly have been prevented if the people of Dublin had been better housed. After the declaration of War, the English Government passed into law an Act granting £4,000,000 for Housing in Ireland, but not a single penny of this grant was ever spent in Ireland, and it is now clear that this Act was passed to popularize the War in Ireland. In 1914, £3,500,000 would have sufficed to solve the problem, now the cost could be £12,000,000 which is about the sum collected in Imperial Revenue from the citizens each year.[18]

Moreover, the cost of rebuilding so much of the city centre as a result of the Rising had greatly exacerbated the Corporation's financial situation. However, the Housing Committee, acting on promises given, went ahead with its plans for the various schemes, the selection of sites, and the types of houses to be built. C. J. MacCarthy outlined the nine developments in hand, the staff required, possible costs and schedules. Of particular note were the plans for the Marino Estate, which had been in abeyance for a number of years, and the land for which was now held by the Corporation. Mr. MacCarthy suggested a better type of housing for this scheme, and stated that 600 dwellings could be built at a cost of approximately £395 each. Kelly commented also on the various issues involved, and stressed the urgency of making decisions, so as to have everything ready should permission come through to proceed with the work.

---

17   *DC Reports* (1918), ii, pp 485-8.
18   Quoted in Cosgrave to Griffith, 28th August, 1919 (UCDA, De Valera MSS, 2, p. 150).

From the beginning of 1918, Sinn Féin was in election mode in anticipation of a general election and, concurrent with his Corporation duties, Kelly was a member of the Sinn Féin Standing Committee, which was charged with fighting the election to be held on 14 December 1918. 73 members of Sinn Féin Party were elected to Parliament, sweeping aside the Irish Parliamentary Party which was left with only 6 seats. It was a tragic end to the once powerful Parliamentary Party, which had long enjoyed so much loyalty and respect. Kelly was elected as M.P. for the St Stephen's Green ward on the first count, but in line with Sinn Féin policy declined to sit in Westminster and instead took his seat at the inaugural meeting of the new Dáil Éireann on 21 January in Dublin's Mansion House. In the absence of the imprisoned Countess Markievicz, Kelly served as substitute Minister for Labour from 19 March 1919 to end of October 1919.

VISITING PRISONERS IN RICHMOND BARRACKS.

Queue outside Richmond Barracks waiting for admission to see their imprisoned friends.
" Irish Independent " Photo.

Irish Independent 1916 (DCLA, 1916 newspaper scrapbook)

As discussed, following the 1916 Rising, many nationalists had been detained, deported and imprisoned in British jails for their political activities. In 1918, the British authorities reacted to the results of the general election by intensifying their repression of individuals active within the republican movement. W. T. Cosgrave was jailed for the second time in May 1918, and was imprisoned in Reading Jail. Seán T. O'Kelly was also jailed after the Rising, released and then rearrested. And, on the morning of 11 December 1919, Thomas Kelly was taken from his bed by the military, deported, and imprisoned in Wormwood Scrubs in London.

At this time of his imprisonment in Wormwood Scrubs, Kelly was in his early fifties and, as it did to so many others, imprisonment effectively ruined his health which had already been adversely affected by his imprisonment in 1916. On 15 December 1919 he had written to his wife, Annie, stating that he was not allowed to write anything about the treatment he had received but that he had found the prison officials he encountered to be courteous and obliging. He gave his wife instructions for the delivery, before Christmas, of cheques that he had prepared before his arrest for various needy families whose relatives were in prison for their

DOOMED AT LAST.

Dublin housing crisis as seen by S.H.Y. in *The Lepracaun Cartoon Monthly*, Jan. 1913

republican sympathies. He told her he would not be permitted to write to her again for a further fortnight, and that any food sent to the prison would be sent back, but that a small amount of tobacco might be permitted. He also asked for some shirts and collars, ties, and socks to be sent as quickly as possible. He concluded by advising that neither she nor the children should fret for him and that he believed that all would come right in the end.

His family received another letter from him in January 1920, saying that he had got through Christmas well enough. He requested them (his family) to send word to all his old '41' friends of the York Street Club that he wished them a Happy New Year. He complained that he had missed mass on New Year's Day due to an error. After that, however, his health deteriorated, and he became mentally unstable. Prison officials started to express concern about his frail condition as early as 7 January 1920, when a medical officer W. R. K. Watson, examined Kelly and noted that he was a man of rather poor physique, albeit without any signs of serious disease. He was offered a special diet, but refused to have anything different from the others. Watson noted that he was beginning to fret over his imprisonment, being worried about 'the indefiniteness of it'. He noted that Kelly was not as well as he had been, and that if this deterioration continued, the question of his fitness for further imprisonment would have to be considered. A memorandum to this effect was attached to the file and it instructed that a copy of the medical officer's report be sent to the Irish government in Dublin; if the prisoner's condition were to continue to such a degree as to endanger his reason, then he might have to be released. Another note follows:

> As this man's condition might become serious at any moment, I should be glad to have your instruction on two points: If the Chief Secretary asks you to decide on the question of release, shall we take the responsibility and release if he is certified unfit? And secondly, if the Chief Secretary or the Irish Government insists on his being detained at all risks, will you accept this at all risks? I do not know how dangerous he is, but if we keep him, will he become insane? It would, I think, do more harm than could possibly come of his release.[19]

A note in another hand, dated 12 January stated that 'His illness is not due to hunger striking. He should be carefully watched and if the MO so advises should be released.'[20]

---

19   The National Archives, Kew, , London HO, 144/1615/395988.
20   Ibid.

In January 1920, Kelly's seat in the Corporation was declared vacant and he thus was removed as chairman of the Housing Committee, as well as from his many other public and private responsibilities. His absence was keenly felt. Apart from being chairman of the Housing Committee, he had been a member of the School Meals and Scholarships Committee, the Electricity Supply Committee, and, as already noted, the Improvements Committee. He also represented the Council on the board of the Royal Hospital for Incurables in Donnybrook, as he had done for many years.

In his absence in prison, a vigorous campaign to elect Kelly as the future Lord Mayor of Dublin was mounted in late 1919 and in January 1920. At the mayoral election held on 30 January 1920, he was elected unanimously and the event was marked by the running up of the tricolour flag on the City Hall. Amidst great cheering from the crowd outside, Laurence O'Neill, the outgoing Mayor, presided over the Council meeting and described the arrest of Kelly by soldiers, who broke his windows, hammered on his hall door, and openly and grossly insulted his family and himself at the whim of some 'understrapper who pulled the wires in Dublin Castle'.[21] O'Neill referred to Kelly's work on the anti-conscription committee and in the Corporation for over twenty years, and said that on such a man the British government had placed their claws. [22]

Ironically, as Kelly's condition continued to worsen in Wormwood Scrubs, a letter dated 4 February 1920 addressed to Thomas Kelly M.P. arrived at his address in Dublin from 10 Downing Street, stating that: 'Sir: On Tuesday February 10th 1920, His Majesty will open Parliament in person. An address will be moved and seconded in answer to the Gracious Speech from the Throne. I hope you may find it convenient to be in your place. Yours faithfully, D. Lloyd George.'[23]

The newspapers had great fun with this. *The Freeman's Journal* published a cartoon showing Kelly in a prison cell regretting that a previous engagement with the King would prevent him from accepting the Prime Minister's kind invitation. *The Evening Telegraph* reproduced the envelope and commented that 'Similar invitations have been sent to other Irish representatives who are held in jails in similar circumstances. Is the incident an ill-conceived and unmannerly practical joke, or is it to be deemed merely an outstanding example of the crass ignorance – not to say stupidity – of those who assume the right to rule in Ireland. The English language knows no words to suit the situation.' [24]

---

21 *Irish Independent*, 31 Jan. 1920.
22 Ibid.
23 *The Alderman*, p. 168.
24 *Evening Telegraph*, 4 Feb. 1920.

On 9 February 1920, despite the two days in hospital for special treatment, Watson, the medical officer who had examined Kelly in the early stages of his incarceration, reported that Kelly's health showed definite signs of deterioration. 'The strain of imprisonment and uncertainty as to his fate are more than his mind can stand with safety. He complains of constant nightmares, of visions of executions and similar horrors. I therefore feel bound to record my opinion that further imprisonment and suspense are not without danger to his bodily and mental health.'[25]

On 12 February, 10,000 sympathisers gathered in the Albert Hall in London to protest against the imprisonment of the Lord Mayor of Dublin and 64 other Irish prisoners. This meeting, which was held under the auspices of the Irish Self-Determination League of Great Britain, was addressed by Arthur Griffith and Eoin MacNeill both of whom denounced the tyranny of the British army.[26] On 13 February the *Manchester Guardian* published a leading article on Kelly's imprisonment. It stated that the Chief Secretary for Ireland was asked on the previous day how the Lord Mayor had come to be shut up in an English jail. The reply was that he was 'a person suspected of acting, or being about to act in a manner prejudicial to public safety' ... 'Any adequate intelligence work in Ireland would have warned the Government that Alderman Kelly, if arrested under the discredited Defence of the Realm Act, would become a world figure that would further stultify British rule in Ireland.'[27]

Kelly was released from Wormwood Scrubs on Monday 16 February 1920. The British authorities stated that he had been conditionally released on health grounds and that the order of internment had not been revoked, but merely suspended. Furthermore, his release was conditional on his not returning to Dublin.[28]

Kelly was suffering from a severe mental breakdown – a not unexpected result of prison treatment upon on a man of his age and constitution. It was not clear in the circumstances whether or not he had signed the letter of acceptance of the Lord Mayoralty. On his release, Kelly was met by Arthur Griffith, Desmond Fitzgerald, William Sears M.P., and J. H. MacDonnell, his solicitor. He was put into the care of Dr Mark Ryan, a well-known Irish nationalist and sympathiser, and taken to a nursing home where he remained for some time, and where he was visited by his wife and eldest son.[29] He subsequently went to stay with his sister who was a nun

25   The National Archives, Kew, , London HO, 144/1615/395988.
26   *Manchester Guardian*, 13 Feb. 1920.
27   Ibid.
28   *Daily News*, 18 Feb. 1920.
29   Mark Francis Ryan (10 November 1844 – 17 June 1940), was an Irish revolutionary, a leading member of the IRB and author of *Fenian memories*, ed. by T. F. O'Sullivan, (Dublin, 1945).

at the convent of St Joseph of Peace at Grimsby, and who had promised to look after him. He remained there until 23 April 1920 when the internment order was revoked by the government.

Kelly finally arrived home on 28 April 1920. His presence in political life continued and he was re-elected unopposed to the 2nd Dáil in 1921 on the first count for Dublin South. He supported the Anglo-Irish Treaty but was too ill to attend the Dáil vote. He was again re-elected at the 1922 general election as a member of Pro-Treaty Sinn Féin but did not take his seat in the Dáil. He did not join Cumann na nGaedheal along with other pro-Treaty Sinn Féin T.D.s in 1923, nor did he contest the 1923 general election as his health had been impaired by his prison experiences.

Dublin City Council was dissolved in May 1924 and its functions were taken over by three commissioners who carried out the duties in running the city until October 1930. When, in October 1930, the Free State government decided to reinstate the Council, Kelly returned to active politics by putting himself forward as an independent candidate. He was returned to Dublin City Council in 1931 and found himself once again chairman of the Housing Committee where he continued to work vigorously for the re-development of the inner city. In 1930 he joined Fianna Fáil and was elected to the 8th Dáil as a Fianna Fáil T.D. at the 1933 general election for Dublin South, a constituency he continued to represent for Fianna Fáil in the 9th Dáil in 1937 and in the 10th Dáil in 1938.

Kelly actively pursued his work for Dublin Corporation until his death, his remaining years being mainly devoted to housing issues. He was also a very vigorous supporter of the opening of the new Art Gallery in Parnell Square that was to house some of the collection of Sir Hugh Lane. In addition to his political career, Kelly was acknowledged during his lifetime to be an expert on the history of Dublin and he became a founding member and first President of the Old Dublin Society. Over the course of 40 years, his work in Dublin Corporation was directed at alleviating poverty and social exclusion, and his contribution to the intellectual and cultural life of the city continues to enrich Dublin to the present day.

His last recorded speech was at a City Council meeting on 3 November 1941 when his focus, as always, was on the welfare of Dublin's poor following the German bombing of the North Strand.

Thomas Kelly remained a T.D. and councillor until his death on 20 April 1942. He is buried in Glasnevin Cemetery.

Patriot and Man of Peace:
Laurence O'Neill, 1864-1943.
Lord Mayor of Dublin, 1917-1924

Thomas J. Morrissey, SJ

Laurence O'Neill with his family (O'Neill Family Papers)

Laurence O'Neill was born Laurence Neill, on 4 March 1864, at 7 King's Inn Street, a Georgian residence on the north side of the River Liffey. His father, John Neill, was a potato and corn factor or merchant.[1] By the 1870s, however, the family had reverted to the original name, O'Neill.[2] John O'Neill had land and a residence in the Portmarnock area of North County Dublin as well as a business and accommodation in King's Inn Street. Little is known of Laurence O'Neill's youth. He attended the local Christian Brothers primary school, and subsequently attended Belvedere College. He is remembered at Belvedere as being a small athletic youngster, who won prizes as a cyclist.[3] Like most pupils in those times, he left school at 15 or 16 years of age. He went into his father's successful business,

---

1   Birth certificate (GRO, Dublin, Births, Deaths, and Marriages, vol. 2, p. 501). Laurence's birth was registered in the North Dublin City Union, on 14 March 1864.
2   Marriage certificate (GRO, Dublin, vol. Jan.-March 1886, p. 399).
3   *The Belvederian* (Summer 1919), "News of Our Past".

which was located near Smithfield Markets and the legal world of Kings Inns. He grew up surrounded by people from all walks of life.[4] He acquired an ease of manner with all classes of people, and exhibited a particular empathy with the poor and the less well-off.

He married, on 26 February 1886, Anne Fottrell, from St Doloughs, Balgriffin, the daughter of a local farmer, William Fottrell. Their marriage proved a close and abiding relationship. They had six children of whom four survived: Mary, John, William and Annie. Mary married John Carrig, a solicitor from Ballina; John went into his father's business; William became a doctor, serving in the British army and subsequently in England; and Annie continued to live at home.[5] Much of the family history and information on the public life of Laurence O'Neill comes from his papers, kindly made available to the author by Mrs Nuala O'Neill wife of Laurence's son, John, and of Laurence's grandson, also John O'Neill.

Moving towards public life

In the household in which O'Neill himself grew up there was a strong nationalist tradition.[6] He was proud that his father had been a Fenian. He joined the Land League at the age of sixteen years, had a great admiration for Parnell,[7] and became, until about 1913 or 1914, a devoted supporter of the Irish Parliamentary Party.[8] In his spare time from his business, he cycled in competition under the rules of the Irish Cycling Association. He made friends with competitors from Britain and all parts of Ireland. Subsequently, he sharpened his political and oratorical skills at club and national administration level.[9] He was elected as the Association representative to international conferences in Cologne, Copenhagen, Glasgow, Vienna and Paris between 1895 and 1899. Consequently, when elected to the Dublin City Council in 1910, he was more travelled than most members and was equipped to do well in local politics. He was elected for the Rotunda ward. Dublin Corporation had many critics, but O'Neill was conscious of its unique standing in Ireland. In the absence of an Irish parliament, the Dublin City Council sometimes served as a representative voice for the majority of the population.

---

4   Catriona Crowe (ed.) *Dublin 1911* (Dublin, 2011), p. 174; Moira Lysaght. 'Smithfield Side-Shows' in Kevin C. Kearns. *Streets broad and narrow, images of vanishing Dublin* (Dublin, 2000), pp 168, 137.

5   Census of Ireland 1901, Form A, the night of 31 March 1901; and Laurence O'Neill Family Papers, courtesy of Nuala and John O'Neill (ONFP).

6   Seanad Debates, vol. 19, p.1575.

7   O'Neill's speech at the Municipal Council, 24 Jan. 1916, *DCC Minutes* 1916, pp 82-4. Report of the speech in the *Daily Express* in a column entitled 'By the Man in the Gallery'.

8   L.O'Neill Family Papers (ONFP).

9   See Thomas J. Morrissey. *Laurence O'Neill (1864-1943). Lord Mayor of Dublin 1917-1924. Patriot and Man of Peace* (Dublin, 2014), pp 9-11.

The Irish Cyclists Fellowship at the Mansion House, June 1917 (O'Neill Family Papers)

During O'Neill's years in the Corporation, he was noted for his concern for the poor and the working man, and for support of women's issues.[10] In 1913 he was an almost solitary voice speaking in favour of Larkin and the workers. His greatest embarrassment prior to 1916, he indicated, was being 'pilloried by the press as a slum owner'. This arose following evidence at the Dublin Housing Inquiry that was set up by the Local Government Board for Ireland. He was one of a number of city councillors mentioned as owning slum property. Deeply upset at what he considered an unfair judgement, he appealed to the tribunal conducting the inquiry. He pointed to the history of the property, to the amount of money put into the reconstruction of the two houses in question, and to the very small rent being charged to the tenants. He was publicly assured by the inspectorate that his houses were in 'good structural and sanitary condition' and that he had nothing to be ashamed of.[11]

Another incident which caused shock and embarrassment was his arrest in the wake of the Easter Rising. Accused by an anonymous person of participation in the insurrection, he was escorted under armed guard to Richmond Barracks. The sense of shame turned into pride in the long term. The experience marked the beginning of his admiration for and friendship with Éamon de Valera. As the prisoners waited under armed guard, it was decided to conduct a theatrical trial of de Valera. O'Neill was picked with Seán T. O'Kelly to appear for the defence. De Valera's demeanour next morning, as he calmly saluted his fellow prisoners before being led away to an expected death sentence, made a lasting impression on O'Neill.[12]

10   Ibid., pp 25-7 and *passim.*
11   Ibid., pp 39-40; and *DCC Minutes*, No. 872, p. 528.
12   ONFP

With the protracted execution of the leaders of the Rising and the imprisonment of many innocent people, the popular mood towards the insurrection and its leaders changed. By October 1916, Dublin City Council was calling for the release of those imprisoned without trial, and that, pending release, all should be treated as political prisoners and not as criminals. Laurence O'Neill was to the forefront in expressing support for the prisoners.[13] His imprisonment, far from being an embarrassment was now a bonus politically. In January 1916 he had been nominated for Lord Mayor. He was defeated by the incumbent Lord Mayor, Councillor James Michael Gallagher, but he received many votes. It came as no surprise, therefore, when, in January 1917, Laurence O'Neill was elected unanimously as Lord Mayor of Dublin.

The Lord Mayor

O'Neill's lengthy vote of thanks was informative regarding his life and his political aims. It was described by the *Evening Herald* as 'a remarkable speech'.

In the course of it, he referred dramatically, in the third person, to a man who was arrested 'without any charge against him, without being brought before any tribunal … and subsequently was told to go home in the dark of a summer's evening not knowing whether he had a home to go to or a friend to receive him. Today that man stands before you in the unique position of being Lord Mayor of his native city.'(Applause) It was, O'Neill added, one of those episodes scattered through Irish history – 'one day a political convict, the next placed in the highest position of trust which his fellow citizens can bestow upon him'. He finished by asserting that the aim of his life was to represent Dublin and its people as a whole, irrespective of creed, politics or class.

The speech received much praise. The commentator in the unionist *Evening Mail* had feared that the art of oratory had fallen out of fashion but he was reassured on hearing Alderman O'Neill. 'He has a mastery of thought that breathes and words that burn; and he has the courage of his convictions.' The writer believed that he would make a good Lord Mayor. He had 'the reputation of being a straightforward and honourable man: a man of character and integrity'.

Among the many problems that faced the new Lord Mayor was widespread unemployment. He approached it in a very personal way. He offered to interview each one of the unemployed. Queues formed at the Mansion House to meet him. He enlisted the aid of the Chief Secretary, H. E. Duke, to obtain jobs for the

---

13   Morrissey, pp 54-55; *DCC Minutes*, 9 Oct. 1916, No. 726, pp 447-8.

men.[14] Despite criticism from many nationalists, he consciously developed contacts with Dublin Castle. It subsequently proved helpful when he negotiated on behalf of political prisoners.

The Unemployed outside the Mansion House, June 1917 (O'Neill Family Papers)

A further pressing and immediate problem soon after O'Neill's election was the condition of the poor. Their plight was worsened by the shortage of food supplies and a very cold winter. The Lord Mayor sought and rallied support from better off individuals and organisations, and he arranged with the Royal Irish Automobile Club to provide motor cars to convey the generous donations of food to people in need. Lord Mayor O'Neill was exhibiting qualities that would lead the historian of the Royal Irish Automobile Club to applaud him as 'a born diplomat with a gift for reconciling the opposing unionist and nationalist camps'.[15]

In June, as feelings ran high over the condition of prisoners in British jails, O'Neill negotiated with the Chief Secretary, Henry Duke, for the release of some 120 prisoners. Duke trusted the Lord Mayor, and wished to promote a peaceful situation in Ireland. On 18 June, the men were released and received an enthusiastic welcome in Dublin. The Lord Mayor received them in the Mansion House. In September, he availed of his office as Lord Mayor and Chief Magistrate to gain access to Sinn Féin prisoners in Mountjoy Jail. He won their confidence and managed to bring about improvements in their conditions. The leading figure among them, however, the influential Thomas Ashe, decided to go on hunger strike to oblige

---

14   Ibid., pp 73-4.
15   Cornelius F. Smith. *The History of the Royal Automobile Club, 1901-1991* (Dublin, 1994),
       p. 87.

the government to recognise him and his companions as political prisoners. Other Sinn Féin prisoners followed his example. Forced feeding was applied to the fasting prisoners. Ashe resisted strongly, and, on 25 September, died while being forcibly fed. There was a nation-wide outcry. His body was accompanied from the hospital to the Pro-Cathedral by a large cortege of laity and clergy. Even the ailing and elderly Catholic Archbishop, William Walsh, insisted on taking part in the demonstration. The intention was to subsequently move the body to lie in state in City Hall. The authorities placed a strong military guard around City Hall, with many other soldiers standing by. O'Neill realised that, in the current enflamed feeling against the government, the presence of the armed military guard could lead to confrontation and bloodshed. He and fellow councillors Patrick Corrigan and Sir Patrick Shortall appealed to the Under-Secretary, W. P. Byrne, to remove the armed guard. He refused. Fortunately, the commander-in-chief, an Irishman, Sir Bryan Mahon, entered the room. He listened to the deputation and had the military withdrawn. O'Neill became a life-long friend of Sir Bryan Mahon.[16]

Meantime the prisoners remained on hunger strike, led now by Austin Stack. O'Neill managed to negotiate terms with the Chief Secretary that satisfied the prisoners and ended the strike. During the rest of his time as Lord Mayor, Laurence O'Neill made himself available again and again, even on Christmas Day, to the needs of prisoners in Belfast and Dundalk as well as Dublin.

At the end of his first year in office, it was almost universally agreed that Alderman Laurence O'Neill, despite a less than imposing stature and appearance, had impressed people by his assured ease of manner, his interest in people, his facility with words, and his commitment to his office. On 23 January 1918, he was re-elected Lord Mayor.

During 1918 the biggest challenge for the City Council and Lord Mayor O'Neill was the government's introduction of compulsory conscription for Ireland. On 8 April, the Dublin City Council issued a warning to the government that if conscription were put into operation it 'would be resisted violently in every town and village in the country'. The Lord Mayor was requested to invite John Dillon, M.P., Éamon de Valera, M.P., Joseph Devlin, M.P., Arthur Griffith, and representatives of the Irish Trades Union Congress to meet him in conference in order to form a united Ireland opposition to conscription.[17] He added to the list T. M. Healy, M.P., and William O'Brien, M.P., believing that a conference without them would be incomplete. He also suggested that Labour be represented by a

16 ONFP and see Morrissey. op. cit., pp. 84-9.
17 *DCC Minutes*, 8 April 1918, No. 257, p. 228.

Copy of Telegram received in the Chief Secretary's Office, dated March 11th, 1919.

His Majesty's Government deny that any undertaking, verbal or in writing, was given that the lawfully convicted prisoners in Belfast should be removed to an internment camp in Ireland or anywhere else. The Government cannot entertain any representations accompanied by suggestions of reprisals.

[COPY.]

IRISH OFFICE,
OLD QUEEN STREET,
LONDON, 11th *March*, 1919.

DEAR LORD MAYOR,

I cannot find that my predecessor, Mr. Shortt, gave any definite pledge to remove the lawfully convicted prisoners from Belfast Prison to an internment camp, and he has confirmed this in a conversation which I had with him to-day.

I am advised that such transfer to an internment camp would be illegal, and it would be impossible to obtain Parliamentary assent to any measure legalising such a course.

I am,
Yours very truly,

(Signed)   IAN MACPHERSON.

THE RIGHT HON. THE LORD MAYOR OF DUBLIN.

[COPY.]

MANSION HOUSE, DUBLIN,
and,
CHICHESTER PARK, BELFAST,
19th *March*, 1919.

DEAR CHIEF SECRETARY,

As both of us were concerned in the settlement effected in Belfast Prison on the 31st December last, and both had conversations by telephone with your predecessor, Mr. Shortt, on that occasion, we hope you will allow us to send a joint reply to your recent letter in reference to the gist of the said conversations. In your letter you state, " I cannot find that my predecessor, Mr. Shortt, gave any definite pledge to remove the lawfully convicted prisoners from Belfast Prison to an internment camp, and he has confirmed this in a conversation I had with him to-day."

Now, Sir, in view of this statement of yours, and of Mr. Shortt's confirmation, we wish to repeat the statement which we signed and published some weeks ago. It was substantially this. On the occasion in question Mr. Shortt gave a distinct and definite undertaking to consider sympathetically the following three points : (1), the question of allowing Mr. Doran, one of the Belfast

The row over the transfer of prisoners from Belfast to internment in Ireland, June 1919 (O'Neill Family Papers)

Prisoners, to be treated as a political prisoner; (2), the question of letting all the Prisoners go unpunished for anything that had happened during the preceding week or so; and, (3), the question of having all the Prisoners removed within a short time from Belfast Prison to an internment camp. Both of us were and are quite clear upon the point, that on all three questions the undertaking was equally precise and definite.

We note that neither Mr. Shortt nor you deny that such an undertaking was given, even in reference to the removal of the Prisoners to an internment camp. But, you say you cannot find that Mr. Shortt gave any " definite pledge to remove " the Prisoners. Pray, excuse us, Sir, if we feel constrained to regard you and Mr. Shortt as playing with words. It cannot be unknown to either of you that a single Minister like Mr. Shortt is not likely to give an explicit pledge on such a matter. But what was his promise of sympathetic consideration, if not equivalent to a pledge? Coming from a Chief Secretary, and given at a crisis when anarchy reigned in Belfast Prison and riots were threatening in the streets outside, it was reasonably taken by us and by the Prisoners as practically equivalent to the most definite pledge; and, we are quite certain that if it had not been so understood by the Prisoners, no settlement would have been possible on the occasion. To say, as you now do, that no " definite pledge " was given, is simply to quibble about words, and to add something very like mockery to tyranny and perfidy.

You say you are advised that the transfer of the Belfast Prisoners would be illegal, and that it would be impossible to obtain Parliamentary assent to any measure legalising such a course. But is there any impossibility about releasing them? Have they not suffered enough already? They have been in prison for many months, in handcuffs for weeks, and for the past eight weeks all, without exception, have been in solitary confinement. Surely this might fairly be taken to have atoned for such offences as drilling or appearing in Volunteer uniform, or even for the heinous crime of wishing to see Ireland free. Or is there, after all, one small nation which must be allowed no rights, and whose aspirations, however legitimately and constitutionally asserted at the polls, must be defied and trampled upon? We hope, Sir, that you will not lend yourself to a course so disgraceful to the British Empire and so atrociously unjust to this small but ancient nation.

We have the honour to remain,
Sir,

Faithfully yours,

✠JOSEPH MacRORY,
Lord Bishop of Down and Connor.

LAURENCE O'NEILL,
Lord Mayor of Dublin.

THE RIGHT HON. IAN MACPHERSON,
Chief Secretary for Ireland,
IRISH OFFICE, LONDON.

The row over the transfer of prisoners from Belfast to internment in Ireland, June 1919 (Document courtesy of O'Neill Family)

THE BELFAST PRISONERS.

Scene.—Shows His Lordship the Bishop of Down and
　　Connor, with the Lord Mayor of Dublin, reminding
　　two quibbling Chief Secretaries of an unfulfilled
　　promise.

Macpherson.—I tell you, Shortt, between oursels
　　Hot water here against us wells,
　　A promise to a bishop made
　　Is hard to dodge, or to evade,
　　Unlike some pledges oft we make
　　With show of zeal and then forsake.
　　But Shortt, not Codlin—meaning Mac—
　　Must bear the brunt of this attack.

Shortt.—I thought when finer job I won
　　With Irish troubles I was done,
　　But in that hope, now sadly shaken,
　　This artful dodger was mistaken.
　　Ah, well, if charge I have to face,
　　With quibble I will meet the case;
　　And if perfidious I appear
　　I have a job to give me cheer.

Bishop.—I ask you, sir, in reason all
　　Your word of promise to recall,
　　And tell me why that Belfast Jail
　　Does still repeat inhuman tale,

And men consign to torture fell
Whose crime was loving Ireland well.
Now, sir, in view of what you stated,
Why are such horrors unabated ?

Shortt.—I fear your Lordship is mistaken,
　　No pledge by me was undertaken,
　　And nothing in their case I saw
　　To interfere with course of law.

Lord Mayor.—Not, though their torture in that spot
　　On human nature makes a blot.

Macpherson.—As well our power is much restricted
　　In case of men by law convicted.

Bishop.—Your power should meet restriction when
　　You overpunish Irishmen.
　　But quibbles have colossal might
　　To block and smother Ireland's right.

Lord Mayor.—An outraged nation's moral force
　　Must deal with this perfidious course,
　　And this small dole from rulers wrest
　　Who never give until they're pressed.

　　　　　　　　　　　　　　A. M. W.

hose who knew the facts it was difficult, he thought,
o speak with any calmness about the horrible and dia-
olic treatment that these unfortunate men had been
eceiving in Belfast Jail. If they wanted any proof of
t the bad consciences of their jailers were pretty well
roved by the fact that they were making, and success-
ully making efforts to keep the truth from the Irish
eople. In one part of the Lord Mayor's letter he spoke
f the Chief Secretaries as, playing with words, but as
ar as that meeting could go they demanded from the
Government the immediate release of those men. And
he Lord Mayor concluded his remarks by declaring:—
That meeting was non-political, and was held solely in
he cause of humanity. As one who had been closely

associated with the prisoners in the past 18 months, he
was almost afraid to let himself go when he brought to
mind the infamous sights he had seen, and the barbar-
ous treatment inflicted on his fellow-countrymen, not
only in Belfast, but in other Irish jails.

There were meetings in about twenty parishes in
Dublin. Amongst the parishes in which there was no
meeting held were Sandymount, Donnybrook, and Had-
dington Road. We make the matter the subject of our
cartoon this week. The treatment of the prisoners and
the action of Shortt and Macpherson as representatives
of English rule have roused to a very great pitch an
already roused and enraged country.

The Leader - March 1919 row over the transfer of prisoners from Belfast to internment in
Ireland. (O'Neill Family Papers)

member from the three main cities - Dublin, Belfast and Cork. To get such diverse personalities to come together proved onerous. In terms of a united front, O'Neill and other members of the conference were clear that the support of the bishops was very important. He arranged with the Archbishop of Dublin, Dr William Walsh, that the Conference Committee would meet on 18 April, when the hierarchy was in session at Maynooth.

The Anti-Conscription Convenant agreed at the Mansion House, April 1918, l-r - back: T.M. Healy M.P.; William O'Brien M.P.; M. Egan J.P. T.C.; T. Johnson; Right Hon. Laurence O'Neill, Lord Mayor of Dublin; John Dillon M.P.; front: Arthur Griffith; Eamonn De Valera M.P.; Joseph Devlin M.P. (O'Neill Family Papers)

The Mansion House Conference approved a defiant declaration on the lines proposed by de Valera. It proclaimed Ireland's separate and distinct nationhood, and the principle that the government of nations derived its just powers from the consent of the governed. Hence, Britain had no authority to impose compulsory conscription on Ireland against the expressed wish of the Irish people.

The Conference Committee designed a pledge to be taken by the public: 'We pledge ourselves solemnly to one another to resist conscription by the most effective means at our disposal.' A deputation from the conference travelled to Maynooth. After lunch with the bishops, the Lord Mayor presented the pledge to Cardinal Logue, Archbishop of Armagh, for consideration and he called on Dillon, de Valera, and Healy to speak. The bishops then withdrew. After some time Cardinal Logue returned and announced that the bishops would take the pledge, and that they had agreed on the statement – 'We consider the conscription forced upon Ireland, against the will of its people and in defiance of the protests of its leaders, is an oppressive and inhuman law, which the Irish people have a right to resist with all the means consonant with the law of God.' They called for a national novena of prayer to bring the country safely through the crisis.[18] O'Neill was elated. With the hierarchy's support he felt that conscription was killed.

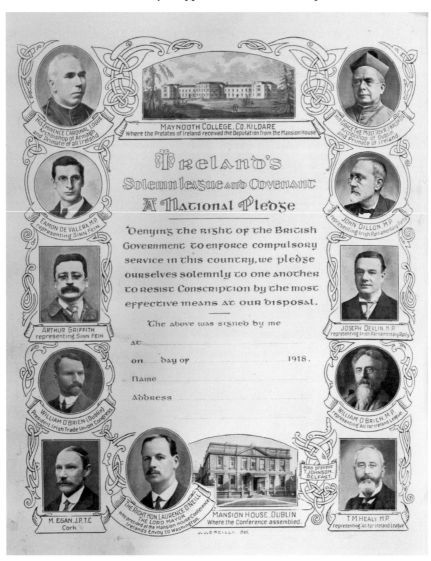

The Covenant Pledge (Document courtesy of O'Neill Family)

18   *Irish Catholic Directory* (ICD) 1919, for 1918. 18 April 1918.

The Evening Telegraph, April 1918 - Hundreds of Thousands Sign Conscription Pledge
(O'Neill Family Papers)

On the following Sunday, at every Catholic Church, the pledge was recommended
and a forthcoming collection was announced to support resistance to conscription.
A million people signed the pledge. There was no fanfare, just grim determination.[19]
Committees were set up in every parish. A National Defence Fund was inaugurated
with the archbishop and the Lord Mayor acting as trustees. The Central Committee,
which was now being termed the 'national cabinet', planned a detailed statement

---

19   Mgr. Curran Papers (NLI, MS 27,728 pp 264-7); Abp. Walsh's diary, 19 April 1918
      (Dublin Diocesan Archives).

for release to the world. The Lord Mayor was requested to present the statement in person to the President of the United States of America.[20] O'Neill at this stage had become a national figure. He applied to America for a passport and visa. After a delay this was granted. A. J. Balfour, the British Secretary of State for Foreign Affairs, also granted a passport but on condition that the documents carried by the Lord Mayor were first approved by the Lord Lieutenant. This had the effect Balfour desired. O'Neill and his committee refused to accept such a condition.[21] Determined, however, to have the manifesto statement sent to President Wilson, O'Neill arranged an appointment at the American Embassy in London, where he handed over the document for transmission to the president.

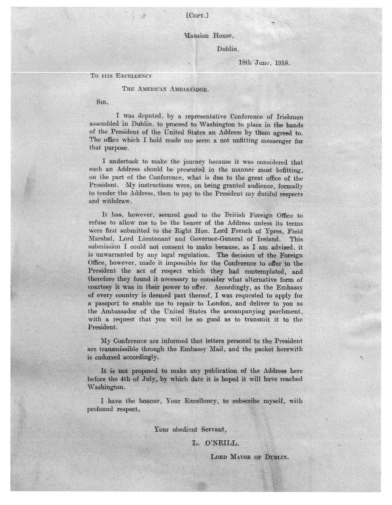

[COPY.]

Mansion House,

Dublin,

18th June, 1918.

To HIS EXCELLENCY

THE AMERICAN AMBASSADOR.

SIR,

I was deputed, by a representative Conference of Irishmen assembled in Dublin, to proceed to Washington to place in the hands of the President of the United States an Address by them agreed to. The office which I hold made me seem a not unfitting messenger for that purpose.

I undertook to make the journey because it was considered that such an Address should be presented in the manner most befitting, on the part of the Conference, what is due to the great office of the President. My instructions were, on being granted audience, formally to tender the Address, then to pay to the President my dutiful respects and withdraw.

It has, however, seemed good to the British Foreign Office to refuse to allow me to be the bearer of the Address unless its terms were first submitted to the Right Hon. Lord French of Ypres, Field Marshal, Lord Lieutenant and Governor-General of Ireland. This submission I could not consent to make because, as I am advised, it is unwarranted by any legal regulation. The decision of the Foreign Office, however, made it impossible for the Conference to offer to the President the act of respect which they had contemplated, and therefore they found it necessary to consider what alternative form of courtesy it was in their power to offer. Accordingly, as the Embassy of every country is deemed part thereof, I was requested to apply for a passport to enable me to repair to London, and deliver to you as the Ambassador of the United States the accompanying parchment, with a request that you will be so good as to transmit it to the President.

My Conference are informed that letters personal to the President are transmissible through the Embassy Mail, and the packet herewith is endorsed accordingly.

It is not proposed to make any publication of the Address here before the 4th of July, by which date it is hoped it will have reached Washington.

I have the honour, Your Excellency, to subscribe myself, with profound respect,

Your obedient Servant,

L. O'NEILL,

LORD MAYOR OF DUBLIN.

O'Neill's letter to the American Ambassador, June 1918 (O'Neill Family Papers)

---

20   ONFP. Printed document: 'Extracts from Official Reports of the National Conference, 18, 19, 24, 29 April, and 4 May'.

21   Ibid.

To The President of the United States of America

SIR,

When, a century and a half ago, the American Colonies dared to assert the ancient principle that the subject should not be taxed without the consent of his representatives, England strove to crush them. To-day England threatens to crush the people of Ireland if they do not accept a tax, not in money but in blood, against the protest of their representatives.

During the American Revolution, the champions of your liberties appealed to the Irish Parliament against British aggression, and asked for a sympathetic judgment on their action. What the verdict was, history records.

To-day it is our turn to appeal to the people of America. We seek no more fitting prelude to that appeal than the terms in which your forefathers greeted ours :—

"We are desirous of possessing the good opinion of the virtuous and humane. We are peculiarly desirous of furnishing you with the true state of our motives and objects, the better to enable you to judge of our conduct with accuracy, and determine the merits of the controversy with impartiality and precision."

If the Irish race had been conscriptable by England in the war against the United Colonies, is it certain that your Republic would to-day flourish in the enjoyment of its noble Constitution?

Since then the Irish Parliament has been destroyed, by methods described by the greatest of British Statesmen as those of "blackguardism and baseness." Ireland, deprived of its protection and overborne by more than six to one in the British Lower House, and by more than a hundred to one in the Upper House, is summoned by England to submit to a hitherto-unheard-of decree against her liberties.

In the fourth year of a war ostensibly begun for the defence of

Page 1 of the statement of the Central Committee to President Wilson (O'Neill Family Papers)

The bishops of the north of Ireland, led by Cardinal Logue, also sought O'Neill's assistance. At the end of November, with a general election approaching, they wished to ensure unity among nationalist parties, so that representatives of Sinn Féin and of the Parliamentary Party would not compete against each other for the one seat. Such a division of votes was likely to result in a unionist victory. O'Neill got in touch with John Dillon, on behalf of the Irish Party, and John McNeill for Sinn Féin. At his own expense, he travelled to Mayo to meet Dillon, and then got both men together. They agreed that instead of a contest, the seats should be equally divided – four for the Irish Party and four for Sinn Féin. They left the allocation of the seats to Cardinal Logue, who was, needless to say, loud in his praise of the Lord Mayor of Dublin.[22]

---

22   Laurence O'Neill Papers, Cardinal Logue-Ld.Mayor, 6 Dec. 1918 (NLI, Ms 35,294/4). For bishops request to O'Neill see *Freeman's Journal*, 30 Nov. 1918.

DEPUTATION TO PARIS

To Be Headed by the Lord Mayor

TO SEE PRESIDENT WILSON

DUBLIN CORPORATION at a special meeting to-day on the motion of the LORD MAYOR, seconded by MR. SEAN T. O'KELLY, M.P., unanimously decided to offer the Freedom of the City to PRESIDENT WILSON on the occasion of his visit to Europe.

ALD. T. KELLY, M.P., moved, and MR. DOYLE seconded, that, in order to give practical effect to the motion, a deputation should go to Paris to offer the compliment to the President in person. Ald. Kelly said the Lord Mayor should head the deputation, and there should be representatives of Sinn Fein, Labour, and the Nationalists.

The Deputation.

After some discussion the following deputation was appointed to wait on President Wilson in Paris to ask him to receive the Freedom of Dublin:—
LORD MAYOR.   HIGH SHERIFF.   SEAN T. O'KELLY, M.P.
ALD. CORRIGAN.   P. T. DALY.   LORCAN SHERLOCK.
THE LORD MAYOR said he had a hope—it might be a slender one—that President Wilson would come to Dublin.

The Deputation to Paris to offer the Freedom of the City to President Wilson (O'Neill Family Papers)

In spite of such additional activity to the normal workload of his office, O'Neill also came up with a likely way of improving Ireland's case at the international Peace Conference. There had been no response from the American president to the manifesto from the Conference. Now, O'Neill thought of inviting President Woodrow Wilson to Dublin to receive the Freedom of the City. To add to the attraction and solemnity of the occasion, he sought to make it a national invitation. A mass meeting was held at the Mansion House on Sunday, 22 December. Other meetings took place throughout the country. At the Mansion House, O'Neill was met with enthusiastic support. A voice shouted – 'The future president of the Republic'.[23] A letter in the *Irish Independent* spoke of the Lord Mayor as 'a genial and great man' whose 'energy is extraordinary'. Hopes were high of a favourable response from the president. After all, he was of Irish ancestry. As days passed into 1919, however, there was no reply from the United States. In retrospect, it is clear that the fever of Irish nationalism clouded perspective. President Wilson was not going to jeopardise relations with Britain, and as to his possible sympathy with

---

23   *Irish Independent*, 23 Dec. 1918.

Ireland it was likely to be with the Orange Ulster of his ancestors rather than with the Catholic republicans of the rest of the country.

O'Neill saw out the year working at conciliation in a Belfast jail. He seemed to be unable to turn down requests for assistance. It placed a great strain on his family. There was little scope for a united family life. His absence, together with the prevailing climate of pressure and danger, may have contributed to the declining health of his willing and supportive wife. She became progressively ill during 1919. The deleterious impact on O'Neill's own health was hidden under his remarkable reservoir of energy.

In January 1919, he was re-elected to the chair of First Citizen; and was hailed in ballad as 'the greatest man since Mighty Dan to ornament that chair'.[24] It proved a repressive year. In September Dáil Eireann was prohibited. In October Sinn Féin, the Irish Volunteers, Cumann na mBan, and the Gaelic League were suppressed. The final straw for the Lord Mayor was the last minute banning, on 11 December, of the *Aonach na Nollag*, which had been held at the Mansion House every year since 1906. It was an occasion for the sale and exhibition of the goods and output of Irish industry. Some 150 police and 500 soldiers turned up to enforce the ban. O'Neill publicly announced the closure of the Mansion House for public events until further notice, stating that it was no longer safe to hold even a children's fancy dress there under the present government.[25]

On 17 December, he was angered by the attempt by republicans to assassinate General Lord French, the Lord Lieutenant. He supported a motion at the meeting of the Port and Docks Board expressing thankfulness at the failure of the attempt upon the life of the Lord Lieutenant. His support of the resolution caught public attention. The *Evening Herald*, of 23 December, praised his courage in opposing murder irrespective of who the victim was. That night two young men called at the Mansion House to say that they had been sent 'to warn him that if he were not more careful in his language they would "plug" him'. O'Neill did not lose his nerve or his temper. Already he had received over twenty threatening letters and many verbal threats.[26]

Early in January 1920, several thousand British recruits, later dubbed the Black and Tans, were enrolled. This signalled a more ruthless government policy. Later in the

---

24   ONFP. Ballad 'Our Good Lord Mayor' by Michael O'Grady.
25   Calendar of prohibitions issued by the police. W. E. Johnstone-Ld. Mayor, 11 Dec. 1919 (NLI. O'Neill Papers).
26   ONFP . Typed pages –'The attempt on the life of the Lord Lieutenant, Lord French, Dec. 1919'.

year, with scant regard for the Lord Mayor/Chief Magistrate, the Tans raided the Mansion House, using vile language, pilfering and destroying items. During 1920, a curfew was imposed on Dublin city. The Lord Mayor was harassed by military, the police, and the Black and Tans. In Cork, Lord Mayor Tomás MacCurtain was murdered. O'Neill lived on his nerves, though he appeared outwardly calm. On 3 May 1920, the Corporation took sides, pledging its allegiance to Dáil Eireann. By order of the Dáil, no income tax was paid by the Corporation or its officials to the government, and its books were not presented for audit to the Local Government Board. The Government responded by withholding funds that were necessary for city services; thereby occasioning particular hardship to the poor, the sick and the unemployed.[27] On 20 December, the military authorities took possession of City Hall and other Corporation buildings. Thereafter, the City Council met at the Mansion House.

In October 1920, Lord Mayor O'Neill had travelled to Southwark Cathedral to pay his respects to the remains of Terence MacSwiney, who had died following his long hunger-strike. He accompanied the coffin on the mail train to Holyhead. There the Irish party learned that the remains were being brought directly to Cork rather than *via* Dublin as had been planned. O'Neill did not make it to the funeral in Cork. He was immersed in efforts to save the life of eighteen year old Kevin Barry, who had been sentenced to death for the killing of a young British soldier. He sent personal appeals for commutation of the death sentence to all members of the British Cabinet, and to several former ministers who disapproved of British policy in Ireland. When he received only an official acknowledgement from the Prime Minister's secretary, he determined to meet personally with Lloyd George. He travelled to London, then from one Welsh location to another, in an effort to meet the Prime Minister. Eventually he caught up with him at Chequers.[28]

Lloyd George apparently assured the Lord Mayor that he would do what he could. O'Neill waited in Dublin for news of the reprieve. He received a telephone call from Lloyd George on 31 October, the night before the date for execution: the government could not grant a reprieve.[29] Next morning, 1 November 1920, Kevin Barry was hanged. On that day scores of his fellow-students in University College Dublin enrolled in the IRA.[30]

---

27   ONFP. 'The Dublin Corporation and Dáil Eireann'.
28   *Irish Times*, the "Irishman's Diary", 29 July 1943.
29   *Dublin Evening Mail*, 1 Nov. 1920.
30   Dorothy Macardle. *The Irish Republic*, (Dublin, 1937), p. 361.

DE VALERA AND THE IRISH AMERICAN MISSION.

The Irish-American delegates to the Peace Conference arrived at the Dublin Mansion House from Kingstown in motor-cars flying the American and Irish Republican flags. They were welcomed by De Valera and the Lord Mayor.—(Daily Sketch Exclusive Photograph.)

The Irish American Relief Delegation at the Mansion House. (O'Neill Family Papers)

On 8 January 1921, O'Neill was requested by de Valera to chair an Irish Relief Committee known as the Irish White Cross, which was to liaise with the American Committee of Relief for Ireland and be the vehicle 'for the relief of those suffering as a result of the present British campaign'. O'Neill contacted numerous influential people, including Cardinal Logue, to serve on what would be a national committee. The government alleged that the White Cross was a front for the IRA. This caused concern among supporters in the United States of America. Lord Mayor O'Neill, accompanied by R. A. Anderson, a well-known Irish Protestant who was prominent in the Irish Co-Operative Movement, and by James Douglas, a business man and an Irish nationalist of the Society of Friends, travelled to America and met with the executive committee of the American relief organisation. It was composed largely of Quakers. The presence of Douglas, and the sincerity and charm of O'Neill, persuaded them to send relief for Irish people of all denominations who had suffered from the conflict. The relief was sent through Douglas.[31] It provided needed assistance to people in many parts of Ireland.

During 1921 the violence continued worse than ever. Through 1920-1921, de Valera had an office in the Mansion House. Collins and others visited regularly, in a variety of disguises. O'Neill carried the responsibility, though he was placing himself, and members of his family, in a precarious situation. His role as a constitutionalist and man of peace had been undermined by government policy and the excesses of its forces.

---

31   J. Anthony Gaughan (ed.), *Memoirs of Senator James G. Douglas, concerned citizen* (Dublin 1998), p. 10. See T. J. Morrissey, op. cit., pp 187-92.

IRISH PEACE DELEGATION—This is the first photograph to reach the United States of Eammon De Valera and other members of the Irish peace delegation taken in their hotel in London following their arrival from Dublin for the peace parleys. Front row, left to right: Eammon De Valera and Arthur Griffith; back row, left to right, Count Plunkett; Mr. Chuders, the Lord Mayor of Dublin; Mrs. Farnan, Miss O'Brennan, Robert Barton and Miss O'Connell. (© International.)

The Irish Peace Delegation in London (O'Neill Family Papers)

In June 1921, King George's appeal for reconciliation gave Lloyd George the opportunity to invite de Valera to a conference. De Valera and Griffith decided to consult first with representatives of Irish Unionists. The Lord Mayor hosted the meeting at the Mansion House on 4 July. And next day brought General Smuts from the boat to meet with de Valera and Griffith.[32] On 8 July, as a heat wave continued, General Macready faced de Valera across a table at the Mansion House and the principles governing a truce were agreed.

Next day, de Valera and his party, including the Lord Mayor, left for London. De Valera met with Lloyd George alone. A reporter for the *Star* newspaper described

---

32   ONFP. Unionist Conference and General Smuts arrival.

meeting with 'Mr Larry O'Neill, the picturesque Lord Mayor of Dublin. He is the "good fellow" of the party, and is in charge of all the members of the delegation'.[33] On the Sunday, after mass, de Valera and some other members drove out of London, stopping *en route* at St Anthony's Hospital, Sutton, where the Lord Mayor's son was resident surgeon.[34]

The conference between de Valera and Lloyd George led to proposals from the Prime Minister, which were turned down at a special meeting of the Dáil. Lloyd George issued an invitation to a further conference to see how differences could be reconciled. This led to the appointment of the five delegates who signed the Treaty: Griffith, Collins, E. J. Duggan, Gavan Duffy, and Robert Barton. Before they left for London, however, there was a hitch. In an exchange of letters with Lloyd George, de Valera insisted that the negotiations must be on the lines of an independent constitution. Lloyd George was ready to negotiate on anything except independence. He contacted the Under Secretary at Dublin Castle, Alfred Cope, who had been active in seeking a settlement, to contact de Valera and get him to modify his letter. Cope motored from Dublin late at night to O'Neill's home at Portmarnock. He received a warm welcome from Mrs O'Neill and family. Cope asked the Lord Mayor to use his influence to get de Valera to modify his letter. Next morning, O'Neill met de Valera at his office and explained the situation. Later at a Sinn Féin meeting in the Mansion House, de Valera agreed to modify his letter and the way was open for the plenipotentiaries to proceed to London.[35]

As the talks went on week after week and the members of the Irish delegation returned regularly to report on events, O'Neill became conscious of the tension between Collins and Griffith and the extreme republican members of the cabinet, Brugha and Stack, whose hostility to Collins was palpable. Eventually the Treaty was signed and the cabinet split. On this last, O'Neill claimed to have played an important incidental role.

At the highly charged meeting of the Executive Committee to decide on the acceptance or rejection of the Treaty, there were seven members: three were already for - Griffith, Collins, and Barton; three had already declared against – Brugha, Stack, and de Valera. The one member unresolved was W. T. Cosgrave. O'Neill was nearby in his study, together with Donald O'Callaghan, Lord Mayor of Cork. They could hear the raised voices, especially that of Brugha against Collins. The seventh man, Cosgrave, left the meeting a number of times. He was battling with

---

33   *Dublin Evening Mail*, 16 July 1921.
34   De Valera Papers (UCDA P 150/1466).
35   Reminiscences of L. O'Neill, written some 9 years after the event.

his conscience. De Valera expected him to vote against the Treaty. O'Neill could hear Cosgrave debating with himself: 'I can't leave Dev down. He stood by me when others were against me. My oath to the Republic haunts me'. Eventually, almost in despair, he asked his old friend, O'Neill, for advice. The Lord Mayor said to him: "Willie, I am in a different position to you by being for the Treaty and because I have not taken an oath to be true to the Republic.' Then, putting his hand on Cosgrave's shoulder, and knowing the deeply religious man he was, O'Neill said: 'If I were you I would be guided entirely by prayer'. Cosgrave went to the other side of the room, and after some minutes came back looking more serene. He returned to the Executive Committee and declared for the Treaty.[36]

The Lord Mayor and Dr Edward Byrne, Archbishop of Dublin, intervened to prevent a civil war. They held meetings with the leaders of both sides and also with some Labour leaders, but to no avail. A general election was held. The Pro-Treaty side, supported by Labour, had a majority to form a government. Laurence O'Neill went forward as a Pro-Treaty candidate and topped the poll. He served in the first Dáil under an Irish government. Civil war broke out. Soon O'Neill was mourning the death of two men he greatly cherished, Griffith and Collins. His former City Council colleague and friend, W. T. Cosgrave, became leader of the government.

By then the strain of years of pressure, the sight of his friends fighting and killing each other, and his city being destroyed, together with his wife's illness from which she now seemed unlikely to recover, all combined to result in a grave break-down in health, something like a massive 'burn out' marked by physical and psychological exhaustion. The *Irish Times* observed that he was 'almost a wreck in health' by the time the Treaty was signed.[37] Together with one of his daughters he left the country, probably to his doctor son in England.[38] His illness continued from September 1922 to September 1923. As a result, he did not contest the general election of August 1923, and forfeited his Dáil seat. He returned to office for the conferring of the Freedom of the City on the celebrated tenor, John McCormack. It took quite a while, however, to re-establish his authority in a City Council, in which a majority had been openly critical of the elected government. This attitude of the majority, plus the frequent public criticism over the years of corruption and waste of public money, led the government, in 1924, to dissolve the historic Dublin City Council and replace it with a commission. Cosgrave assured Laurence O'Neill that there was no suggestion of corruption where he was concerned, and he offered him the position of chairman of the commission and the retention of his current salary.[39]

---

36 Ibid., and see Morrissey, op. cit., pp 205-6.
37 *Irish Times*, 29 July 1943, obituary.
38 *DCC Minutes*, 27 Nov. 1922, No. 626, p. 482. Mary O'Sullivan - Town Clerk.
39 *Irish Times*, 22 May 1924; O'Neill Papers. O'Neill-Cosgrave, 16 May 1924 (NLI, MS 15,294/15).

O'Neill denied any corruption among his colleagues in the Council, and declared that he would be disloyal to those colleagues were he to accept Cosgrave's kind offer. It was a stance worthy of his high principles but it had dire effects for him and his family. During the years of turbulence his business had declined and he, besides, had neglected it during his long term in office. In January 1924, prior to the dissolution of the Council, his wife died at Bridge House, the family home, in Portmarnock. She was buried in the local St Marnock's cemetery. The funeral was attended by a large concourse of citizens, and messages of sympathy came from England and Ireland,[40] including one from de Valera, who was in prison. No member of the government appears to have sent messages of sympathy or attended the funeral.

In the 1920s, O'Neill became virtually bankrupt. He called on W. T. Cosgrave for a loan of £200.[41] He received the money but did not pay back the loan. His business finally closed down in the 1930s. In 1927 he put himself forward for the Dáil as an Independent, but failed to get public support. Two years later prospects improved. With the help, it seems, of Cosgrave, he was elected to a vacancy in the Senate, where he soon made his mark. As the Seanad Debates indicate, he spoke eloquently and in an inimitable style that combined wide knowledge, with wit and a folksy manner. In 1930 he stood for the re-constituted Dublin City Council , and led the vote in Electoral Area No. 3. His close friend Alfred Byrne was elected Lord Mayor. In that same year, Alderman O'Neill, who could scarcely afford to part with any possessions, contributed some of his land for the building of a church, requesting that it be known as 'St Anne's Church' in honour of his wife. It served the people of the area for almost fifty years, and was then replaced by a more modern building. Typically, earlier in his career O'Neill had donated land for the local golf course. In the 1931 Senate election, he stood as an Independent and once again headed the poll.

Under the Fianna Fáil administration, Laurence O'Neill supported the government in debate after debate. He even supported the suppression of the Seanad by de Valera in 1936. His attendance at City Council meetings declined noticeably between 1933 and 1936, perhaps for reasons of health, and he does not appear to have attended at all after 1936. With the closing down of the Seanad much of the attraction of life also declined. He was a man who loved the public arena and the sense of public service. Nevertheless, such anguish as there may have been was concealed, as ever, by a cheerful exterior and an almost debonair manner. He was

---

40   *Dublin Evening Mail*, 16 Jan. 1924.
41   O'Neill-Cosgrave, 10 Feb. 1927, 19 March, 2 May 1927 (NAI, Taoiseach's Dept. Taois/S 7474). Also Cosgrave-O'Hegarty, 25 May, 25 June, 1928.

the owner of Bridge House, where he lived, and of three other small houses in the locality which were let at a weekly rent. He also held 24 acres of land that were let out for grazing. Despite outward appearances, however, all his property was heavily mortgaged and practically owned by the bank.

A new Seanad was formed in 1938. O'Neill was nominated to the body by de Valera on 4 January 1940. He attended regularly into 1943, but is not recorded as speaking. He died on his own, sitting on a chair in his summer house attached to Bridge House. He was 79 years of age.[42] The funeral took place from Baldoyle parish church to St Marnock's cemetery, Portmarnock. The attendance included the Taoiseach, Éamon de Valera, Seán T. O'Ceallaigh and Oscar Traynor, W. T. Cosgrave, and a number of members of the Corporation, Seanad, and Dáil.[43] It was an impressive send off, but thereafter Laurence O'Neill was virtually forgotten, and his graveyard neglected.

Laurence O'Neill's most cherished memory was probably that which he mentioned in a Seanad debate on 4 March 1936: 'The time of Conscription, when each and every one of us took a solemn oath that Ireland was a nation separate and distinct'. He was proud of the unity achieved against conscription and of his prominent role in that achievement. He was conscious that it was a critical moment in modern Irish history.

It is appropriate in recounting the life of this unusual ordinary Irishman, who had friends across national and religious boundaries, to leave the final comment to an Englishman, a confidant of Lloyd George, and Under Secretary at Dublin Castle, Alfred Cope, who, on 1 April 1924, assured Laurence O'Neill:

> When the true history comes to be written ... your great work for moderation and the avoidance of hardship and bloodshed on all sides will be fully recognised ... I know of no other man, who in your exalted position, would have worked so strenuously or who could have overcome so successfully the almost overwhelming difficulties of your office in so perplexing a period. And yet at the same time you retained the full confidence of your people. It was a great accomplishment.[44]

---

42   Most newspapers got his age wrong, presuming he was 69 years.
43   *Irish Press*, 29 July 1943.
44   O'Neill Papers, A. Cope- Ld. Mayor O'Neill, 1 April, 1924 (NLI, MS 35,294/15).

William Thomas Cosgrave

Anthony J. Jordan

William T. Cosgrave (Courtesy of the Irish Capuchin Provincial Archives)

William Thomas (W.T.) Cosgrave was born on 6 June 1880 at the family home on 174 James Street, Dublin, opposite the South Dublin Union. The Cosgrave family ran a grocery and public house, and the young Cosgrave attended the local Christian Brothers primary school on Francis Street. His father died in 1888 and in 1892 his mother Bridget Nixon married Thomas Burke, a native of Seskin in Tipperary, who had been working in the Cosgrave business. Two children were born from Mrs Cosgrave's second marriage: Joan, born on 28 September 1892 and William Francis (Goban).[1] After primary school Cosgrave attended the O'Brien Institute in Marino. He finished school at sixteen and was to regret this for the rest of his life. He worked for his stepfather in the family business, as did his younger brother Phillip. The Cosgrave-Burkes had a good middle class standard of living and participated in a vibrant social life which included horse riding in the nearby Phoenix Park.

Like his own father, Cosgrave took an interest in public affairs. The Irish Parliamentary Party would have been the expected natural home of a man of Cosgrave's background. There was also a publican's group on Dublin City Council with which he would have some affinity. But he was influenced by advanced nationalism and the attendant cultural revival, and attended the founding convention of Arthur Griffith's Sinn Féin in November 1905, together with his uncle James and brother Phil. The Sinn Féin party policy, as devised and promoted by Griffith, broadly consisted of demands for reforms in a wide range of areas, along with a particular emphasis on Irish self-sufficiency through the protection and promotion of native Irish industry, and crucially, the advocacy of a 'dual monarchy' based on the model of the Austro-Hungarian empire, whereby Ireland and Britain would be equals under the rule of a shared monarch: a policy that was

---

1   Cosgrave papers (NAI, MSS 1194-15).

to be highlighted, according to Griffith, by the withdrawal of Irish representatives from Westminster to a parliament in Dublin.

In 1909, Cosgrave was one of seven victorious Sinn Féin candidates elected to Dublin City Council and led by Alderman Tom Kelly.[2] At the start of each year, the Corporation Standing Committees were elected to look after particular functions. In his first year on the Council, Cosgrave became a member of the Public Health Committee. In successive years he served on the Waterworks Committee, the Cleansing Committee, and finally as chairman of the prestigious Estates and Finance Committee. He took this work very seriously and was an assiduous attendee at all committee and general meetings. The seven Sinn Féin councillors opposed a motion of sympathy on the death of Edward VII in 1910, and in 1911 they succeeded in having Major John MacBride appointed to the position of Water Bailiff.[3] But there was little sympathy for 'advanced' nationalism on the part of many of their fellow-councillors. That same year saw the Council pass a motion, 'that the City Hall, Council Chamber, and Members Rooms, be placed at the disposal of the Gaelic League and the Gaelic Athletic Association Carnival committee, for the purpose of holding their Ceilidh, which had to be postponed because the Mansion House was not available'. The majority of councillors supported the Irish Parliamentary Party and John Redmond.

The outbreak of the First World War ensured that anti-German feelings ran high during the course of the war, and in 1915 the Council removed the freedom of the city awarded to the German linguist and Irish language scholar Professor Kuno Meyer in 1911. Cosgrave opposed it vociferously, writing that 'Perhaps the most pernicious influence which has effected this country is the denationalising of the Irish race by the absorption of the soul of the nation ... The proposal now before the Council is to remove the name of this eminent Celtic Scholar from the roll of Honorary Freemen; to negative a life of work of Celtic erudition. No Continental upheaval can affect the everlasting gratitude owed to German Celtic Scholars'.[4]

At the beginning of 1916 Cosgrave was again elected as chair of the Estates and Finance Committee. On 4 April he presented the Committee's Report to the Council, and on 19 April he moved that the Poor Law Rate be adopted. The

---

2   Kevin O'Higgins described Cosgrave as 'A Dublin Corporator' when he was chosen as chairman of the Provisional Government. The items of Corporation business referred to are taken from the *Minutes* of Dublin City Council meetings.
3   Anthony J. Jordan, Major John MacBride, 'MacDonagh and MacBride and Connolly and Pearse' *Westport Historical Society* (1991), pp 90-5.
4   *DCC Minutes* 1915, item 262, p. 128.

Corporation had this power to finance the expenses of the North and South Dublin Union workhouse.

Cosgrave and the Easter Rising

Taxi collecting guns from the landing at Howth (*Irish Volunteer* 24 July 1915)

Cosgrave had been on the platform at the founding of the Irish Volunteers in the Rotunda in November 1913. He was later appointed to B Company of the 4th Dublin Battalion with the rank of lieutenant. He was subsequently involved in the Howth gun-running taking guns by taxi to Alderman Kelly's house in Longwood Avenue by a circuitous route as the military patrolled the Howth Road. In early 1916 Cosgrave was informed by Thomas MacDonagh of a Rising that was being planned. Cosgrave responded that it would be little short of madness as they lacked men and ammunitions ... he was not interested in a moral victory. Cosgrave said that any action should leave the country in a better state than when it began, and they should press ahead only on that basis.[5] Cosgrave was never a member of the IRB, and therefore not part of the inner conspiracy that orchestrated the Rising.

On 23 April, Easter Sunday evening, Cosgrave attended a concert in the Fr Mathew Hall in Dublin, where his stepsister Joan Burke sang *The Minstrel Boy* and *The West's Awake*. He only became aware of the mobilisation on Easter Monday after his brother received mobilisation instructions. Éamonn Ceannt commanded the 4th Battalion: 120 members assembled at Emerald Square in Dublin's Liberties at 11 a.m., fully equipped, to occupy the massive site of the South Dublin Union.

---

5   Anthony J. Jordan, *W. T. Cosgrave (1880-1965): founder of modern Ireland* (Dublin, 2006), p. 25.

Cosgrave suggested that they should occupy the formidable three-storey stone Night Nurses' Home, on the west side of the main courtyard of the complex opposite his home at the James Street entrance, on the grounds that much of the area could be controlled from there.

They had 1,500 rounds of ammunition as Cosgrave set up a rota for sentry duty on one-hour sessions and 'an officer with some training or experience posted them'.[6]

The strategy behind occupying that location was to prevent soldiers from relieving Dublin Castle. At the initial time of occupation the Volunteers could hear an army band playing in the nearby Richmond Barracks.[7] Shortly after twelve o'clock a party of about 100 soldiers of the 3rd Royal Irish appeared marching towards the city, bayonets fixed. The Volunteers engaged them at the James Street entrance and received return fire. Cosgrave reports that 'Nurse Keogh, attached to the hospital, SDU, was killed by British fire – it was generally conceded – accidentally'.

The main group of Volunteers still held the Nurses' Home back on James's Street. But now they came under fire from the rear also. During this action one of the fatal casualties was Goban Burke, W. T.'s stepbrother. He was shot through the neck while firing from a window in the Union. W. T. was called but Goban had died instantly. It was a shattering experience, as he contemplated his own influential role in bringing Goban to that moment. This remained with W. T. for the rest of his life. W. T. described the death of Goban thus:

> One of the sentry posts was in the corridor of the Nurses' Home, commanding a view of the open space, the rectangle of the Protestant church and dining hall. He was a section commander, C/Company – Frank (Goban) Burke – and particularly keen on his work and duty as a Volunteer. Across the road from where he sat on duty, a wing of the hospital was on about the same level. An enemy soldier got into the hospital, saw young Frank Burke, took aim and shot him through the throat. He died immediately. R.I.P. ('Goban' Burke was brother of Joan Burke, the Irish contralto). He was one of the best Volunteers in the battalion, energetic, untiring and devoted to his comrades with whom he was most popular. This was the only fatal casualty we sustained since our occupation of the Nurses' Home.[8]

---

6   William T. Cosgrave, BMH WS 268.
7   *The Catholic Bulletin* (March, 1918), p. 153.
8   William T. Cosgrave, BMH WS 268.

Goban is commemorated at Mount Brown by the name of a road called Burke Place.

Cosgrave mentions that three officials in the South Dublin Union cooperated and rendered assistance to the garrison. He names them as Laurence Tallon, Smith and William J. Murphy. As night fell, the action stopped as each side tried to get some sleep. The Volunteers said the rosary. On Easter Tuesday morning a sentry heard suspicious noises coming from outside the boundary wall of a small yard, attached to HQ, and the noise of digging, which he had heard since 3 a.m. Cosgrave investigated and pointed out that the noise came from behind the window blind, caused by a broken window pane. The next morning, the Volunteers erected a flagpole out of a top window, bearing a flag with a gold harp on an emerald background. They stood to attention and sang *A Nation Once Again*. This drew intensive fire from the top of the Royal Hospital, which killed a woman in her home on James's Street and a visitor from Belfast on South Circular Road. There was little action on Wednesday. However they received a despatch from the GPO to say that there were 680 men 'out'. Ceannt was satisfied with this message, which Cosgrave believed came from Connolly. This was the sole message received by the garrison.

On Thursday however, the British launched an attack on the Nurse's Home from both front and rear. They were very careful, as they had little idea how many Volunteers were inside. In fact there were only 27. During the engagement, the plaster was shot off the walls and ceilings. Holes were breached in the walls from one room to the next, to permit more freedom of movement, when the attack increased in severity. Explosions went on repeatedly and every now and then a shower of bricks would fall from the Nurse's Home. Brugha was on the top floor, while Cosgrave occupied the ground floor. In the evening Captain French Mullen came down to tell Cosgrave that Brugha was wounded; that the British were in; that they were to retire. Cosgrave knew that the information was incorrect, but retreated as ordered along an outside passageway. They reached the point then being defended by Ceannt. Cosgrave informed him of the situation and Ceannt suggested that they return to the Nurses' Home. On the way they heard Peadar Doyle whistle or sing and they searched until they found him. Ceannt and Cosgrave each took alternate rooms, demanding surrender of anyone in possession. There was not a single soldier in the Home. An explosion at a barricade enabled the British to attack the Nurse's Home, but Brugha, though wounded, held them back with rapid fire. Volunteer Dolan and Cosgrave tended to Brugha's wounds for five or six hours, as he became delirious. The next day Rev. Fr Gerhardt, O. Carm., wearing a stole, led a procession carrying the Vice-Commandant to the Union hospital. Friday was an uneventful day apart from the sight of burning buildings in the city centre.

On Low Sunday, MacDonagh arrived under guard to inform Ceannt of the surrender at the GPO. James Foran and Cosgrave went out to meet them and escort them inside. After much discussion a surrender was agreed. Ceannt, accompanied by Cosgrave, then walked with General Lowe to the nearby Jameson Distillery on Marrowbone Lane to convey the news to the garrison there.

The men marched to St Patrick's Park and, together with the garrison from Jacob's Factory, onwards to Richmond Barracks, where they were detained. Cosgrave found himself in a barrack room, with no furniture and no ventilation, with sixty others.[9] For breakfast a bucket containing tea and a basket with hard biscuit rations were brought in. The biscuits were tumbled out onto the floor; empty corned beef tins were used as tea containers. Later, prisoners were marched to the gymnasium, and put sitting on the right hand side of the floor. Plain clothes DMP officers identified certain men, including Ceannt, John MacBride, the two Cosgraves, Corrigan, Hunter, Peadar Doyle, Downey. The Rev. T. W. Ryan, C.C. Golden Bridge visited the prisoners in the gymnasium. He heard confessions and blessed the men with the Blessed Sacrament. The prisoners were locked up at 8 o'clock. They then recited the rosary and settled down for the night. There were no beds or bedclothes, rugs, or blankets. Cosgrave and Major John MacBride spent a lot of time talking together at the barracks.

Cosgrave sent for a barrister, J. Roynane, himself an influential member of Dublin Corporation; Dr Lorcan Sherlock also arrived, together with the Lord Mayor, Sir James Gallagher. He got Ceannt and MacBride to discuss their defence with Roynane. Attorney General James Campbell had refused prisoners any right to have defence counsel. Cosgrave himself summed up the evidence against him as, 'of a policeman who saw him in uniform one hour before the Rebellion. Result – found guilty; sentence – death'.[10] The Prosecutor W. E. Wylie told the court that the accused wanted to make a statement and call evidence. Cosgrave's witnesses were James Gallagher, Lord Mayor, Surgeon McArdle and Lorcan Sherlock.

General Blackadder, the President of the Field Court Martial, was struck by the status of the witnesses called by Cosgrave. He later questioned Wylie about Cosgrave's position, asking, 'Is that a decent man and was he in your opinion

---

9   William T. Cosgrave, BMH WS 268.
10   Ibid.

rushed into this'. Wylie replied, 'Yes, sir'. Blackadder then replied, 'Thank you. We will recommend a reprieve'.[11]

Cosgrave and a number of others were then transferred to Kilmainham Jail where each prisoner was locked in a separate cell. Phil Cosgrave was on his brother's left and Major MacBride on his right. Cosgrave recalled that 'At daybreak on Friday morning I heard a slight movement and whisperings in the Major's cell. After a few minutes there was a tap on his cell door. I heard the word "Sergeant", a few more whispers, steps down the corridor, down to the central stairs. Through a chink in the door I could barely discern the receding figures; silence for a time; then the sharp crack of rifle fire and silence again. I thought my turn would come next and waited for a rap on the door, but the firing squad had no further duty that morning.'

The local curate, Fr Eugene McCarthy, later that day visited Cosgrave (he was a friend of the family) and told him that, with the exception of MacBride, the death sentences on his group with which he had been imprisoned had been commuted to imprisonment. They were subsequently sent to Lewes. The Cosgrave brothers' stepfather, Thomas Burke, was also arrested and interned with the others at Frongoch.[12]

After the Rising at Dublin City Council

After the Easter Rising, Dublin City Council passed resolutions dealing with the destruction and distress caused by what was widely dubbed the '*Sinn Féin rebellion*'. It expressed the Council's 'Deepest sympathy to relatives of those who lost their lives during the recent rebellion', and on 17 July demanded the immediate ending of martial law. On 2 August it voted for an inquiry on the shooting by British soldiers of prisoners in North King Street. On 4 September it demanded the release of interned Irish prisoners. On 8 January 1917 absent members co-opted back onto the Council included William Partridge, P. T. Daly and Cosgrave, with the latter elected to the Improvements Committee. On 2 July 1917 Cosgrave reappeared at the Council and on 13 August he is identified in attendance as councillor and M.P. He later seconded motions of sympathy on the deaths of Bishop O'Dwyer of Limerick and Thomas Ashe.

---

11   Leon O'Broin, *W. E. Wylie and the Irish revolution* (Dublin, 1989), p. 22.
12   Cosgrave papers (NAI, MS 1194).

Cosgrave campaiging in Kilkenny 1917 (BMHadmin / P11: (c) Sinn Féin Election group 1917, Military Archives, Ireland)

After the Rising the republicans sought to capitalise on the widespread public hostility to its suppression and the burgeoning public sympathy for the Rising itself. From 1917, as prisoners were finally released from detention, Sinn Féin candidates began to contest a number of parliamentary by-elections. In August 1917 Cosgrave was the Sinn Féin candidate in Kilkenny city; the *Kilkenny Journal* reported that 'Kilkenny turned out en masse on Thursday night in support of the candidature of Willie Cosgrave. The Irish Volunteers and Cumann na mBan numbering over 3,000 marched in procession. Arthur Griffith, editor of *Nationality*, was one of the speakers'.[13] Cosgrave won by 772 votes to 392 for Mr Magennis of the UIL. A celebration took place in the city centre. Cosgrave thanked everyone and said, 'Under the policy of the IPP pauperism and emigration had increased so much that in the city of Dublin, 80,000 people lived in hovels'.[14] The British authorities reacted to the Sinn Féin victories by more arrests and internments. Among those arrested was the 1916 veteran and Kerry IRB member Thomas Ashe, who subsequently died as a result of forced feeding while on hunger strike in Mountjoy Prison. His body lay in state at City Hall prior to the funeral in Glasnevin Cemetery. The Castle authorities refused permission as Cosgrave approached General Bryan Mahon who overruled the Castle and stood down the army for the duration of the lying in state and funeral.[15]

---

13   *Kilkenny Journal*, 28 July 1917.
14   Ibid., 15 Aug. 1917.
15   William T. Cosgrave, BMH WS 268.

KILKENNY RESULT

Sinn Feiner Returned by a Majority of 380.

SPEECH OF MR. MAGENNIS

Mr. W. T. Cosgrave, the Sinn Fein candidate, has been returned for Kilkenny. The poll was declared about noon on Saturday amid much Sinn Fein enthusiasm. The figures are:—

Cosgrave (Sinn Fein)	772
Magennis (Nationalist)	392
Majority	380

The result was announced by the Mayor, Councillor Slater, who acted as Returning Officer. There were 11 spoiled votes.

Mr. Cosgrave, proposing a vote of thanks to the Returning Officer and Assessor, said he had received from many sources testimony as to the orderly manner in which the election had been conducted. Kilkenny showed the world that however high their political feelings might be or their interest in the different sides taken, they could exercise their national self-restraint typical of the Irish race (applause). He was deeply grateful to the people of Kilkenny for the great honour they conferred on him, and to the Corporation of the city, to the Volunteers, Cumann na mBhan, the Fianna, and the many other personal friends who supported him in the contest (applause).

Mr. Magennis, in seconding, said that the victory of his opponent was a victory for tolerance, low, mean, lying, scurrilous abuse, terrorism, and intimidation of the grossest type. He had nothing to say against his opponent personally. He had met and talked to him in the streets many times, and they were on twitty terms.

Mr. Cosgrave—That is so.

The Mayor suitably acknowledged the vote of thanks.

SPEECH OF MR. COSGRAVE.

Mr. Cosgrave subsequently addressed a large crowd from the balcony of the Courthouse, and his appearance was the signal for enthusiastic cheers. He said that Kilkenny that day had expressed an opinion unmistakably for the absolute control by Irishmen of their own affairs here in Ireland (cheers). He thanked them as one of those who, whatever his shortcomings, held the belief that the Irish people were the only people to control the destinies of their business in their own way. One of the most remarkable features of that election was the great order at all times characteristic of the conduct of the people of Kilkenny (cheers).

SPEECH OF MR. DE VALERA.

Mr. de Valera said their watchword now was "Up, Kilkenny, and Kilkenny Abu" (cheers). If the people of Ireland stood with them as E. Clare, Longford, Roscommon, and Kilkenny, they would be able to achieve a final victory for Ireland free (cheers). Shaun Buidhe was already feeling like the lark when the farmer came to cut the corn (laughter). They were now going to reap the corn themselves, and not depend on Asquith, Lloyd George, or anyone else (cheers). The victory that day was a victory for a man who had gone out with his comrades, who showed that liberty was worth dying for, and worth all sacrifices (cheers). Nothing got was ever won without sacrifice, and that victory to-day showed that the country was ready to make sacrifices when called upon to win the freedom of Ireland (hear, hear). It would have been a disgrace to Kilkenny if it rejected the representative of the men who had died for Ireland's freedom. The Kilkenny victory was not a victory for anarchy. It was the victory of the government of Ireland by Irishmen. Sinn Feiners were not anarchists or Jacobins. They believed in the right

SCENES IN DUBLIN

Reception of the New Sinn Fein M.P.

EXCITING INCIDENTS

Mr. Cosgrave returned to Dublin last night. At Kingsbridge he received an enthusiastic welcome from several thousand persons. A procession was formed, and amidst much cheering and singing the crowd accompanying Mr. Cosgrave marched up Steevens' lane and into James's street.

Opposite the Irish Volunteer Hall, which was illuminated, and decorated with the tricolour, a halt was made to the surprise of the people, who were apparently unaware that the authorities had taken steps to prevent a demonstration in Westmoreland street.

A force of police, who were on duty at Kingsbridge, under Superintendents Bannon and Willoughby, proceeded with the crowd to James's street but attempted no interference with the proceedings, which passed off quietly. Mr. Cosgrave (scn.) presided at the meeting.

Mr. D. M'Carthy, who arrived from Kilkenny with Mr. Cosgrave, said the people of that city had sent a message to the bogus Convention that Ireland would have no patched up peace. Their demand was for a free and independent Ireland. That was the issue they had put before the electors, who had endorsed that claim. When Dublin got the chance it would do likewise (cheers). When the opportunity came they would sweep the members of the Irish Party from public life. Indeed they deserved to be swept out of the country altogether (cheers).

"An Outpost of the Pale."

Mr. Cosgrave, who was loudly cheered, said Sinn Fein had captured one of the outposts of the Pale, which was now in possession of the Gael. In that movement they were out for a free and independent Ireland. They had no quarrel with the English people, but the English Government had a quarrel against Ireland. Sinn Feiners denied the right of England to rule this country. They would fight against England until they had the same government as all other free nations had. They would fight against Germany if Germany sought to attempt domination in Ireland, or against any other foreign country which sought to do the same thing. A Convention was sitting in Dublin to settle the Irish question, but there could be no settlement of the Irish question except through the Irish people and what would be accepted by them.

The President of America, which was now the greatest country amongst the Allied nations, was using his influence and authority to settle the Irish question; but Sinn Fein would take no dictation from America in this matter. The settlement of the question must be a matter for the Irish people themselves. This fight had been going on for 700 years, and now Sinn Fein had taken it up, and they would carry it to a finish. The voters of Kilkenny had supported them because they knew they were earnest men, who meant to carry on the fight until they would succeed, and the example of Kilkenny would find expression in Dublin when the time came (cheers).

If the young men and young women had votes they would easily carry the country; but with the present franchise they were making good progress. In the near future they would have the North, which had been the centre of so many good national movements, with them (cheers).

No Trust in Promises.

They wanted no more broken treaties. Even the English Government had broken

---

Freeman's Journal, 13 August 1918 (DLCA)

In the December 1918 General Election Sinn Féin was enormously successful, winning 73 seats to 26 unionists of which 23 were in Ulster and the IPP getting 6. The Sinn Féin T.D.s not in jail assembled in Dublin's Mansion House on 21 January 1919 to declare the existence of an independent Irish Republic in the form of Dáil Eireann, and established a new republican 'counter-state' in direct opposition to the British authorities. Cosgrave subsequently became Minister for Local Government in the new revolutionary government.

ANOTHER REBEL LEADER SHOT·

MAJOR McBRIDE PAYS DEATH PENALTY

TWO GET LIFE SENTENCES, AND THREE 3 YEARS' PENAL SERVITUDE.

OFFICIAL.

5th May, 1916.

Trials by court-martial of rebels proceeded yesterday, and 36 men were tried. Confirmation has only taken place in three cases, namely, those of

THOMAS HUNTER. JOHN McBRIDE. WILLIAM COSGRAVE.

All three of these men were sentenced to death, but the General Officer Commanding-in-Chief

commuted the death sentence to penal servitude for life in the case of Hunter and Cosgrave. The death sentence on John McBride was carried out this morning.

The following men were tried on the 2nd May:—

EDWARD DUGGAN. PIERCE BEASLEY. JOSEPH MAGUINNESS.

These men were each sentenced to 3 years' penal servitude, and the sentence was confirmed by the General Officer Commanding-in-Chief.

(DCLA, 1916 newspaper scrapbook)

By January 1919 Cosgrave had been absent from the Council for over six months and as the Town Clerk told the Council 'ceases to be a member'. The clerk read a letter from Mr Cosgrave:

Place of Internment
Reading.

Dear Town Clerk,

Explanation due.

I was arrested by police and armed soldiers on or about midnight on 17th May 1918 and brought to Kingstown, and subsequently here, accompanied by armed military escort. I have therefore been forcibly prevented from discharging the duties of my public office.

In the event of retaining the office of Councillor, I should like to go back to the Estates and Finance Committee, if the Council is willing to allow me to do so …

W. T. Cosgrave

Cosgrave married Louisa Flanagan of Portmahon House, Rialto, in 1919. Her father was also on the Council as a member of the IPP. The Flanagans were wealthy. The couple bought a property called Beechpark in Templeogue. Liam, their first son was born on 13 April 1920.

As Minister for Local Government Cosgrave tried to persuade local councils across Ireland to transfer allegiance to the Dáil. Tom Garvin has observed that 'Cosgrave's role in the extraordinary achievement of taking over bodily the British local government in the south, was central and deserves more examination than it has hitherto had.'[16] At the same time Cosgrave was also chairman of the Finance Committee of Dublin Corporation, and felt that it was vital for Dublin Corporation to maintain public services in the capital. To ensure this he sought finance from the banks. The Bank of Ireland accommodated him and directors Henry Guinness and Andrew Jameson continued to support the emerging state with loans. Diarmaid Ferriter writes, 'Cosgrave and his assistant Kevin O'Higgins, presided over the new regime, one which was fraught with danger, but remarkable for its resilience and concrete achievements.'[17]

During this period Cosgrave had often to keep a low profile around Dublin as the British had offered a reward of £3,500 for his capture. David Neligan, who as a member of the DMP also acted as a vital republican spy in Dublin Castle, has written that Cosgrave found sanctuary with the Oblate Fathers in their house in the Wicklow Hills. In Cosgrave's absence his assistant Kevin O'Higgins was, however, critical of Cosgrave, writing to his future wife, Brigid Cole, 'when he does blow in he'll take up some work at random, give some wholly outlandish ruling on it and blow out again most complacently.'[18] Cosgrave had offices successively at Clare Street, Rutland Square and Exchequer Street. Among his staff were Kevin O'Higgins, Alderman Tom Kelly, Dr Hayes, Dr J. Ryan, J. J. Clancy, Frank Fahy, A. O'Connor, F. Lawless, J. J. Walsh, J. Dolan and J. McGuinness.[19]

Truce and Treaty

After the Truce of July 1921, and the subsequent decision to engage in full scale negotiations with the British later that year, Cosgrave was adamant that Éamon de Valera should lead the Irish delegation to London, and formally proposed this in the Dáil. Cosgrave said that the Irish team should not be 'leaving their ablest player in reserve'.

---

16   Tom Garvin, *The Birth of Irish democracy* (Dublin, 2006), p. 25.
17   Diarmaid Ferriter, *Lovers of liberty? local government in 20th century Ireland* (Dublin, 2001), p. 54.
18   Jordan, *W. T. Cosgrave*, p. 56.
19   Cosgrave papers (NAI, MS 1194).

The Irish delegation, led by Arthur Griffith, signed the Treaty on 6 December 1921. At the subsequent cabinet meeting Cosgrave 'interceded persistently' on behalf of the delegates in the face of great opposition to the Treaty from figures such as de Valera, Austin Stack, and Cathal Brugha.[20] He felt that it was vital to avoid a knee jerk reaction to the Treaty without giving the delegates a hearing. DeValera decided to be cautious, partially in order to keep Cosgrave on side, and agreed that Cosgrave's position was reasonable.[21] Ultimately, Cosgrave cast the decisive vote in the Executive Council's four to three decision in favour of the Treaty. De Valera issued a statement that same night rejecting the Treaty.

The subsequent debate on the Treaty in the Dáil was drawn-out and bitter. After the Dáil supported the Treaty, Arthur Griffith was elected president of the Dáil as de Valera and his followers withdrew in protest. The new Provisional Government that was formed to oversee the handover of power consisted of Collins as chairman, Cosgrave, Éamonn Duggan, Patrick Hogan, Fionan Lynch, Joe McGrath, Eoin MacNeill, and Kevin O'Higgins. A Sinn Féin Árd Fheis on 22 February agreed an adjournment to May. The army split on the Treaty as Cumann na mBan became anti-Treaty. Collins negotiated an election pact with De Valera to allow the necessary General Election to take place peacefully and agreed bizarrely to retain the numerical standings of the rival factions in Dáil post the election. This greatly annoyed Arthur Griffith who felt it was a betrayal of democracy by Collins.[22] The June election returned a clear majority for the Treaty as law and order broke down throughout the country. August saw the premature deaths of both Griffith and Collins. A hastily organised late night meeting to replace Collins had present: Cosgrave, Patrick Hogan, Joe McGrath, Kevin O'Higgins, Desmond Fitzgerald, Ernest Blythe, Michael Hayes, Hugh Kennedy, Kevin O'Shiel, assistant Law Officer, Richard Mulcahy, Commandant-General, Gearóid O'Sullivan, and Commandant-General Diarmaid O'Hegarty. Cosgrave, aged 42, emerged as the favoured chairman of the Provisional Government.

Cosgrave displayed utter ruthlessness in the vicious civil war to defeat the anti-Treaty forces. He told a neutral IRA group led by Donal Hannigan and M. J. Burke on 27 February 'I am not going to hesitate if the country is going to live, and if we have to exterminate ten thousand Republicans, the three million of our people is greater than this ten thousand.' He was of the view, as was Mulcahy, that the civil war was provoked by De Valera and he never renewed his earlier friendship with him.[23]

---

20   Frank Pakenham, *Peace by ordeal* (London, 1935), p. 262.
21   Ibid., pp 263-4.
22   Ibid., pp 76-7.
23   Anthony J. Jordan, *Éamon de Valera 1882-1975: Irish:Catholic visionary* (Dublin, 2010), p. 166.

Cosgrave told Archbishop Byrne on 17 November 1922: 'We are at a crisis in the history of our beloved Country when we, as the Government of Ireland, directly responsible to the Irish People for our administration of their affairs and for the very security of their Nation have most reluctantly and painfully been forced to a decision which may involve the carrying out of many stern but we hope, just actions. Before God and Man we must take responsibility for all these actions ...'[24]

The anti-Treaty side, with De Valera as titular head, eventually recognised defeat and dumped arms in April 1923.

Cosgrave as politician

Cosgrave saw his primary position as president of the Executive Council of the Irish Free State and as party politician second. He wanted the Dáil to be a forum for all kinds of community groups and not necessarily comprised of purely rival political parties. The new Senate was representative of all the diverse elements of Irish society with sixteen of Cosgrave's nominees representative of unionist supporters. Cosgrave refused to sign the Cumann na nGaedheal Party's appeal for election funds in 1923. This was an early symptom of a hands-off approach by the members, where on the other side, Sinn Féin had numerous voluntary workers. Cosgrave's attitude that the government was somehow apart and distant from the party, founded to fight elections, was common to the elite in the party. It was the reason why Cumann na nGaedheal did not become a mass party, with any popular enthusiasm among its members. It was a top down party, without any firm foundation, or policies, except those, which appeared from the government, on an *ad hoc* basis.

Michael Laffan writes of Cosgrave, 'He is honoured by Fine Gael as one the founders and the long-term leader of the pro-treaty party, even though he gave it only intermittent attention and viewed it without apparent warmth'.[25]

Religious conservatism

Cosgrave was a conservative Catholic, a friend of the clergy and a frequent visitor to Rome. On a visit there in 1924 as president of the Executive, Oliver Gogarty accompanied him.[26] He was made a Papal Knight of the Grand Cross of the First Class Order of Pope Pius IX in 1925, after he led the National Pilgrimage to Rome. Declan Kiberd has argued that the early governments not only had to

---

24   Archbishop Byrne Papers (Dublin Diocesan Archives).
25   Michael Laffan, *Judging W. T. Cosgrave: the foundation of the Irish state* ,(Dublin, 2014), p. 354.
26   Stephen Collins. *The Cosgrave legacy* (Dublin, 1996), p. 45.

secure the state against internal attack but also demonstrate to the British, and others, that they could govern successfully. This led to an extreme conservatism. Kevin O'Higgins declared that he and his colleagues were probably the most conservative revolutionaries in history. Declan Kiberd wrote, 'War and civil war appeared to have drained all energy and imagination away: there was precious little left with which to reimagine the national condition.'[27]

Diplomatic developments

The new state attended its first Imperial Conference in 1923 and established many international offices. In 1924 it registered the Anglo-Irish Treaty at the League of Nations. The 1926 Imperial Conference in the Balfour Declaration enabled the emergence of absolute co-equality of the member states of the British Commonwealth with Great Britain.[28] In January 1928, Cosgrave and Desmond Fitzgerald travelled on a semi-official visit to the United States of America and Canada. Cosgrave was received by President Coolidge and both Houses of Congress. He told the congressmen, 'I come to thank the American people for the part they have played in the achievement of our liberty.' The biggest breakthrough diplomatically, which lent credence to the Treaty being a stepping stone to greater independence from Britain, came in 1930-1, when Ireland was to the fore in having the Statute of Westminster enacted.[29] Fianna Fáil opposed the measure in the Dáil.

Fianna Fáil founded

Éamon de Valera realised that if he was to have a political future he had to have his own political party, enter the Dáil, and seek to win power. He resigned from Sinn Féin and launched his party Fianna Fáil on 16 May 1926 in the Scala Theatre in Dublin. Tom Garvin writes, 'In a strange and ironic sense the true founder of Fianna Fáil was Cosgrave, because he clearly offered DeValera a "middle way" between outright acceptance of the 1922 settlement and armed insurrection against it ...'[30] The government introduced a law requiring candidates for election to effectively accept the legitimacy of the state. This was intended to facilitate and put pressure on Fianna Fáil. On 12 August, de Valera led his T.D.s to the Dáil escorted by a large crowd of supporters.

1932 General Election

The prerogative of dissolving the Dáil and calling a general election rested with Cosgrave. This did not have to take place until October 1932. As in most elections,

27   Declan Kiberd, *Inventing Ireland* (London, 1996), p. 263.
28   Dáil Debates, Vol. 33, Col.2050-2167; 2195-2330.
29   Jordan, *W. T. Cosgrave*, p. 139.
30   Garvin, *Birth of Irish democracy*, p. 175.

tactics are very important and correct timing vital. The budgetary outlook for 1932 was poor, with cutbacks the order of the day. Cosgrave decided to go for a February election. John Horgan wrote, 'The Cosgrave government's approach to the 1932 Election was marked by an extraordinary tendency to embrace policies guaranteed to bring about defeat.'[31] Despite this the result, though quite close, was negative for the government. Before the new Dáil met, the *Irish Press* newspaper reported on rumours of a *coup d'etat* by disaffected army officers. But Cosgrave was absolutely intent on handing power over to the victor. When the new Dáil met, on 9 March, the Labour Party with two farmer T.D.s and one independent supported the election of De Valera as president. A vote was called when Cosgrave challenged the motion. The vote was 81 to 68. Cosgrave and his party then spent many barren years on the opposition benches as De Valera proceeded to dismantle aspects of the Treaty and introduce a new Constitution in 1937.

As Joe Lee so correctly writes, 'Cosgrave's place in history, does not ultimately depend on his performance as a vote-getter, but on his performance as a state builder.'[32] Michael Laffan writes, 'Cosgrave's long years in opposition must be considered a failure, although he helped prevent Fine Gael from slipping towards extremism.[33] John Regan characterises Cosgrave as an elusive political figure and very much a family man, where his home became as important as Dáil Éireann for political manoeuvring. He writes of him, 'as genial and witty, on even some of the dourest occasions in the Dáil he could be humorous.'[34]

Cosgrave resigned from politics before the 1944 election.

In retirement he devoted himself to bloodstock and dairy shorthorn cattle farming on his land. He became a member and later chairman of the Racing Board. Cosgrave kept in touch with his longtime friend Oliver Gogarty, who had moved to live in the USA. When he heard that Gogarty was thinking of retiring he wrote on 5 November 1956, advising, possibly from personal experience, ' …Don't! Everyone who does, steps over a canyon making it impossible to retrace; then they find it lonesome and are prone to lose interest in men and things.'[35]

In 1959, Cosgrave's wife Louisa died and was buried in Goldenbridge cemetery. He and his wife had earlier moved to a small house, and he now returned to join his son Liam in the family home, Beechpark.

---

31   John Horgan, *Seán Lemass* (Dublin, 1997). p. 60.
32   J. J. Lee, *Ireland 1912-1984: politics and society* (Cambridge, 1989), p. 171.
33   Laffan, *Judging Cosgrave*, .p. 354.
34   John Regan, *The Irish counter revolution 1921-1936* (Dublin, 1999*)*, p. 33.
35   J. B. Lyons, *Oliver St John Gogarty* (Dublin, 1980). p. 287.

W. T. Cosgrave died on 16 November 1965. At the request of his family the national flag was not draped over the coffin, which was carried on a gun carriage and received a twenty one gun salute. The cortege halted at the former South Dublin Union opposite his former home on James's Street. He was buried alongside his wife and parents at Goldenbridge.

In the Dáil, Taoiseach Seán Lemass said:

> Although William T. Cosgrave has left us, the work he has done for Ireland endures. The generosity of his youthful response to the call to serve Ireland, the privations and the sacrifices that he endured so that the national freedom might be ours, the capacity he displayed in presiding over the administration while responsibility was his, the grace with which he handed over responsibility when the people so willed ... and, finally, the exemplary character of his long life, these are elements of a legacy which we in Ireland and indeed the people who value freedom and democracy everywhere will forever cherish.[36]

---

36   *Dáil Éireann* official report, no. 218, 17 Nov. 1965, pp 1838-9.

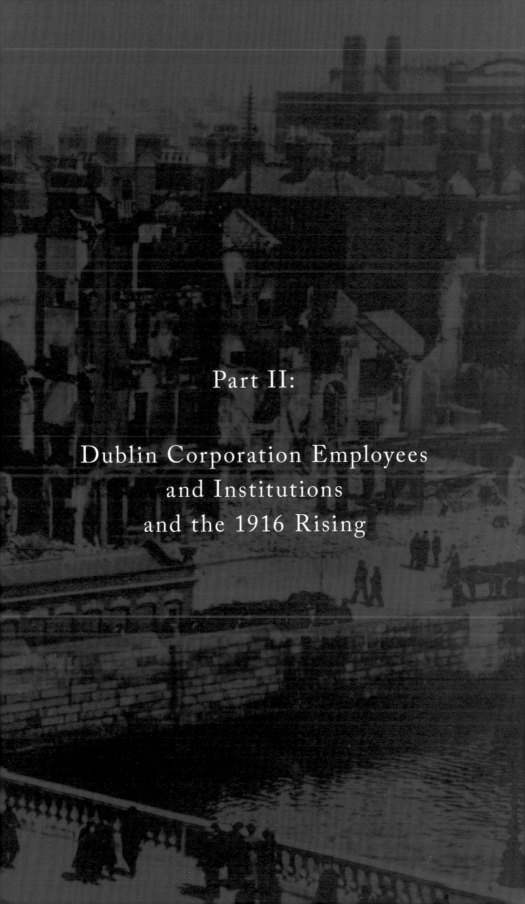

Part II:

Dublin Corporation Employees
and Institutions
and the 1916 Rising

Henry (Harry) Nicholls
(1889-1975)
Assistant City Engineer and Republican Revolutionary

Martin Maguire

Portrait of Henry Nicholls (Courtesy IMPACT Trade Union)

The surrender order that ended the Easter Rising on Saturday 29 April was communicated slowly and with difficulty to republican garrisons across Dublin city. One of the last to receive the order was the Irish Citizen Army garrison led by Michael Mallin in the College of Surgeons on St Stephen's Green.[1]

Their surrender was a disciplined affair. At 12.30 p.m., Captain H. W. Wheeler took the surrender of Mallin and Markievicz and the garrison of 109 men and ten women. After surrendering arms they were marched to Richmond Barracks in

---

1   Charles Townshend, *Easter 1916: the Irish rebellion* (London, 2005), pp 243-68; Fearghal McGarry, *The Rising Ireland: Easter 1916* (Oxford, 2010), pp 247-54.

Inchicore.[2] The detectives of the G Division of the Dublin Metropolitan Police (DMP) were brought in to sift through the prisoners and identify the leaders for courts-martial. As the 'G' men moved through the men at Richmond Barracks they were surprised to identify Henry (though always known as Harry) Nicholls amongst those brought in from the College of Surgeons.[3] Nicholls was an assistant engineer in Dublin Corporation, a graduate of TCD and a respectable professional man with a promising career ahead of him. Also, he was a Protestant, a member of the Church of Ireland. Appointed to the Dublin Corporation staff in a temporary capacity in 1913, he had, it seemed, sacrificed the prospect of a conventional and successful career in the Corporation by choosing to participate in the Easter Rising.[4]

It was also surprising that Nicholls had been brought in with the Citizen Army men and women as he was an officer in the Irish Volunteers. Nicholls was a captain in A Company, 4th Battalion of the Dublin Brigade of the Volunteers, based at Larkfield in Kimmage under the command of Éamonn Ceannt, a clerk in the Dublin Corporation Treasury Department, and Cathal Brugha. Another member of the 4th Battalion was W. T. Cosgrave, a Sinn Féin councillor in the City Council. Though he had no direct knowledge of the planned Rising on Easter Sunday morning, Nicholls had been preparing to mobilise as ordered at four o'clock when Desmond Fitzgerald called to his home to tell him that Eoin MacNeill's countermanding order, which had been published in newspapers that morning, was genuine and was to be obeyed. On Easter Monday morning Nicholls went to Brugha's house to discover what was happening, to be told that Brugha had already left to mobilise the 4th Battalion. Cycling back into the city in search of further information he saw an outpost being established at Davy's pub on the Portobello Bridge by the Citizen Army. Continuing down along Earlsfort Terrace he met Liam O'Briain of the 2nd Battalion Irish Volunteers, who also had lost contact with his company and was on his way home to collect his rifle.

Seeing the Citizen Army under Mallin taking control of St Stephen's Green, both men immediately decided that in a revolution it was best to fight where one

---

2   Seán Enright, *Easter Rising 1916: the trials* (Dublin, 2014), pp 190-3.
3   Nicholls' activism in the revolutionary movement can be tracked through the various sources in National Archives Ireland NAI, BMH WS 296, Harry Nicholls (MSPC, file MSP34REF15964 "Henry Nicholls"; NAI, Chief Secretary's Office Registered Papers (CSORP) 16628/1918 part II, 21699/Henry Nicholls; National Library Ireland 'personal narrative of events of the Easter Rising' (NLI, MS 10,915/11); Holmes/Nicholls papers (Military Archives, Cathal Brugha Barracks Dublin). Harry Nicholls was an occasional columnist in the newspaper and the Holmes/Nicholls papers in the Military Archives contains cuttings of many of these columns, a typescript memoir and other notes.
4   *DCC Minutes*, 1913, item 2682; Martin Maguire, 'Harry Nicholls and Kathleen Emerson: Protestant Rebels' in *Studia Hibernica* no. 35 (2008-2009), pp 147-66.

stood. Nicholls abandoned the search for his own Battalion (which at that moment was actually seizing control of the South Dublin Union) and joined in with the Citizen Army. Initially positioned in the garden of the park-keeper's house facing the junction of Cuffe Street and Harcourt Street, Nicholls then moved with the Citizen Army into the Royal College of Surgeons as the Green was abandoned early the following morning. In the College they discovered a store of Lee-Enfield rifles with ammunition, so while not well provisioned, the garrison was well-armed. With Mallin and Countess Markievicz he patrolled Harcourt Street and Camden Street as far as the area under the control of the 2nd Battalion of the Dublin Volunteers under the command of Thomas MacDonagh in Jacob's biscuit factory on Bishop Street. On Wednesday morning Nicholls, in command of a combined force of about sixteen Irish Volunteers and Citizen Army, took control of the Turkish baths on Grafton Street. Apart from some exchanges of sniper fire with British soldiers on the roofs of Mercer's hospital and the Shelbourne Hotel the position saw little action. Nicholls may well have had a chance for casual chats with a prisoner being held in the College, Laurence Kettle, who was an engineer in the Corporation's Pigeon House electrical power station. The nervous Citizen Army soldiers had arrested Kettle as a suspected spy.[5]

ROYAL COLLEGE OF SURGEONS WHERE COUNTESS MARKIEVICZ SURRENDERED, DUBLIN.

College of Surgeons, St Stephen's Green (DCLA)

On Saturday the Grafton Street post was evacuated and the men brought back to the College of Surgeons where, on Sunday morning, Mallin revealed the surrender order. He ordered Nicholls and the other officers to blend into the ranks pointing out that, though the leaders were certainly to be shot, there was no point in

5   Pádraig Yeates, *A city in distress Dublin 1914-18* (Dublin, 2011), p. 112.

others sacrificing themselves unnecessarily.[6] Nicholls was amongst those brought immediately to the North Wall for deportation, initially to Knutsford Prison on 1 May and then later to Frongoch Internment camp toward the end of June. He was elected leader of Hut 11 with Dick McKee as his deputy.[7]

There was little in his family background to make a rebel of Harry Nicholls. Harry's father, William (1837-1932), an inspector of national schools, was an Englishman from Shrewsbury and, as he described himself, an ardent imperialist.[8] A widower, he married a second time to Margaret Kelly in Tuam, County Galway. She was the sister of Richard John Kelly, owner and editor of the *Tuam Herald*. The *Tuam Herald* (which remained Parnellite in the split of 1890-91) was aimed at the provincial Catholic middle class of Connacht.[9] The Kellys were themselves a family of Catholic notables, so presumably Margaret converted to the Church of Ireland on marriage. Harry's eldest brother, William, had a long and honourable career in the imperial service, serving in the Sudan Civil Service (considered second only to the Indian Civil Service) from 1907 until 1932.[10]

Harry was born in Derry in 1889, making him twenty-seven years of age in 1916. As an unmarried younger son, in his mid-twenties, he was therefore typical of the first cohort of the Irish Volunteers.[11] His childhood was spent in Templemore, County Tipperary and in Dublin city.[12] He matriculated from Mountjoy School in 1907 with a mathematics sizarship and junior exhibition and entered TCD as a student of civil engineering, graduating in June 1911 with a gold medal in mathematics.[13] He was certainly unique in being the only graduate of Trinity College Dublin to be an active republican rebel in 1916.

Nicholls' initial introduction to separatism was through his brother George who gave him a pamphlet on Home Rule. Harry related that on reading the pamphlet he was instantly convinced that home rule did not go far enough and that Ireland needed complete separation from Britain, an opinion reinforced by reading John

6   Holmes/Nicholls papers, typescript memoir (Military Archives).
7   Eamon Markham, BMH WS 411; Joseph Good. BMH WS 388.
8   Letter W. Nicholls to H. E.Duke, 11 Dec. 1916. (NAI, Chief Secretary Office Registered Papers [CSORP], 1916 internees files, 16628/1918,ii, Henry Nicholls).
9   Patrick Maume, 'Richard Kelly' in *Dictionary of Irish biography*.
10   A. H. M. Kirk-Greene, *The Sudan Political Service: a preliminary profile* (Oxford, 1982); G. W. Bell and A. H. M. Kirk-Greene, *The Sudan Political Service 1902-1952*, a preliminary register of second careers (Oxford, 1989); additional information provided by Annabelle May, London, daughter of William Nicholls.
11   Peter Hart, 'Youth culture and the Cork I.R.A.' in D. Fitzpatrick (ed.) *Revolution? Ireland 1917-1923* (Dublin, 1990) pp 15-20.
12   1911 Census returns, Dublin 60/52, Church Avenue Rathmines (NAI).
13   Holmes/Nicholls papers, *Irish Times* cutting 13 June 1911; typescript memoir. (Military Archives).

Mitchel's *Jail Journal*. George also introduced his brother to the Gaelic League. George, who Gaelicised his name to Seoirse Mac Niocaill, was eight years older than Harry.[14] Both Seoirse and Harry were members of the gCúig Cúigí (Five Provinces) branch of the Gaelic League. Harry joined in 1910, when he was twenty years of age. This branch was popularly known as the Five Protestants branch, because of the number of Protestant members. It met at George Moore's house in Ely Place with classes being held in Estelle Solomon's studio, with Liam Shortall as teacher. Harry was also a member of the amateur dramatic group Na h-Aisteoirí (The Actors) and also Na Cluicheoirí (The Players), performing in the Padraig Ó Conaire's play *Banba Nua*.

Harry Nicholls' membership of the Gaelic League ultimately brought him closer to radical separatism. Nicholls, along with Seán Lester, Ernest Blythe and some other Protestant members of the league, formed *Cumann Gaelach Eaglaise na hÉireann* to demand that the Church of Ireland provide texts, hymns and services in the Irish language.[15] Early in 1912 Nicholls responded to Patrick Pearse's call, made in the pages of his short-lived newspaper *An Barr Buadh*, for Irish speakers to work to advance Irish freedom.[16] In response to this article Pearse, Michael (The) O'Rahilly, Éamonn Ceannt, Seán McCraith and Harry Nicholls met in the Moira Hotel to found an organisation that would spread the cause of Irish separatism amongst the Irish speakers, Cumann na Saoirse.[17] Cumann na Saoirse, though its business was conducted entirely through Irish, was mainly about getting guns. Nicholls founded the North Dublin Rifle Club. Rifle Clubs had gained popularity across Britain as part of the growing cult of male militarism. His Protestantism, Rathmines address and professional status provided a cover of respectability for the importation of rifles and ammunition.[18]

Harry Nicholls spent his holidays in the Dingle area to develop his Irish, and by his own account only began to attain fluency in the language after he spent a fortnight in the entirely Irish-speaking milieu of the Blasket Islands in 1913.[19] Nicholls, however, did not engage in the intense squabbling between the partisans of Munster Irish, led by Fr Patrick Dineen, and those of Connacht Irish, led

---

14   León Ó Broin, *Just like yesterday: an autobiography* (Dublin, 1985) pp 66-9; Diarmuid Breathnach and Máire Ní Mhurchú, *Beathaisnéis a dó 1882-1982* (Baile Átha Cliath, 1990), ii, 64-5, MacNiocaill, Seoirse.

15   Ristéard Ó Glaisne, *Dúbhglas de hÍde ceannróidaí cultúrtha 1860-1910* (Baile Átha Cliath, 1991), p. 174; Séamas Ó Maitiú, 'A spent force? *An Claidheamh Soluis* and the Gaelic League in Dublin 1893-1913' in Francis Devine (ed.) *A capital in conflict: Dublin city and the 1913 Lockout* (Dublin, 2013), pp 281-310, p. 289.

16   Joost Augusteijn, *Patrick Pearse: the making of a revolutionary* (Basingstoke, 2010), pp 229-30.

17   *Evening Press*, 3 Jan. 1964, article by Cathal O'Shannon.

18   Holmes/Nicholls papers, typescript memoir (Military Archives).

19   Ibid.

by Patrick Pearse.[20] Whilst spending time in the Dún Chaoin and Blasket area Nicholls came under the influence of Seán Óg Kavanagh (Seán an Cóta) who swore him into the IRB. He joined the Teeling Circle, which organised under the cover of the Bartholomew Teeling Literary and Debating Society with Bulmer Hobson (a Quaker) as its 'centre'; Hobson described it as the 'largest and about the intellectually toughest circle in Dublin'.[21]

Irish Volunteers Recruitment Poster (DCLA, BOR Collection)

Nicholls describes Hobson as the man who was the key influence on his own republicanism. In the winter of 1912-13 a meeting of all the Dublin IRB was held in the National Foresters Hall on Parnell Square, the only occasion on which the entire IRB membership was to meet. Speakers at the meeting were

20   Ó Maitiú, 'A Spent Force?' p. 305.
21   Quoted in Marnie May, *Bulmer Hobson and the Nationalist movement in twentieth-century Ireland* (Manchester, 2009), p. 101.

Denis McCullough, Ulster representative on the Supreme Council and later the president of the IRB, Diarmuid Lynch, Munster representative on the Supreme Council and Bulmer Hobson, chairman of the Dublin Centres Board. The meeting discussed the probability of war between Germany and Great Britain and the opportunity such a war might present to the IRB. It was at this meeting that Nicholls first met with Patrick Pearse. He joined A Company of the 4th Battalion of the Irish Volunteers' Dublin Brigade when it was formed in 1913, and was appointed engineering instructor to the 4th Battalion.[22] In the light of the events of 1916 it is interesting to note that his lectures concentrated on street fighting, erecting effective barricades and on the use of explosives. His company was largely comprised of lower middle class clerks, shop assistants, teachers, civil servants and a number of municipal officers including Ceannt, Cosgrave, George Irvine and Nicholls himself. A further radicalising influence on Nicholls was the 1913 Lockout, and the leadership of Larkin and Connolly. On the Friday 29 August he went to the meeting outside Liberty Hall where Larkin burnt the government proclamation banning the public meeting planned for the morrow. Caught in a baton-charge by the DMP on Eden Quay and beaten to the ground by constables 33B and 188B he made a formal complaint and received a grudging but formal apology from Inspector McKaig 'who didn't want the police to be at loggerheads with respectable people'. Nicholls promptly brought the letter of apology to the *Irish Worker* for publication.[23]

In June 1914 Nicholls paraded with the Irish Volunteers to the Wolfe Tone commemoration march to Bodenstown at which Pearse's graveside speech on the 'holiest place in Ireland' signalled the revival of republican separatism.[24] When war broke out in September 1914 Nicholls was again on holiday in the Dingle area. Along with Seán Kavanagh, Ernest Blythe and Desmond Fitzgerald he organised the local Volunteers to disrupt a recruitment meeting being held at Annascaul by 'The McGillicuddy of the Reeks' the local landlord.

In 1915 Nicholls was appointed as an Irish Volunteer member of the O'Donovan Rossa Funeral Committee. The O'Donovan Rossa funeral was a mass demonstration of armed Irish militant separatism organised by the IRB but including the Irish Volunteers, Irish Citizen Army, Sinn Féin, the labour movement and the women's movement. After the lying-in-state of the body in City Hall the militarised funeral procession was seen as a demonstration of a united front of advanced nationalism,

---

22   Captain Henry S. Murray, BMH WS 300; Seamas Murphy, BMH WS 1756.
23   Holmes/Nicholls papers, typescript (Military Archives); 'Henry Nicholls' in Donal Nevin (ed.) *1913 Jim Larkin and the Dublin Lockout* (Dublin, 1964).
24   Holmes/Nicholls papers, typescript (Military Archives).

bringing together the IRB, the Volunteers and the Irish Citizen Army.[25] Nicholls was appointed to the crucial 'Funeral and Cemetery' sub-committee in charge of organising the funeral procession and the graveside guard.[26] The graveside oration by Patrick Pearse extolling the 'Fenian Dead' signalled the resurgence of armed separatism and presaged the Rising.

O'Donovan Rossa Funeral Committee (*Evening Herald*, 17 June 1954. DCLA, BOR Collection)

The smuggling and storage of guns and ammunition was a key preoccupation of Nicholls between 1913 and 1916.[27] Of the 1916 leaders, Nicholls knew Patrick Pearse (though initially he was sceptical of Pearse's commitment to the republican ideal), Clarke, MacDiarmada and Ceannt, his commanding officer in the 4th Battalion. Nicholls was closest to MacDiarmada, who engaged Nicholls for both the Howth and the Kilcoole gun-running operations. At Howth Nicholls' role was to ground the telegraph line to Dublin to prevent Dublin Castle being alerted, and then to lead in the landing and in the dispersal of the guns.[28] The cutting of the telegraph line ensured the column of the now armed Volunteers got past the narrow isthmus at Sutton before the DMP could respond. In fact if the column had not rested at Raheny it would probably have got into the city before the DMP and military established a cordon at Fairview.[29] At the confrontation with the police and military at Fairview Nicholls organised a fleet of taxis to take the guns and also the dispersal of the Volunteers across the open countryside. The Kilcoole operation was, in contrast, a secret operation, taking place under cover of an outing to the Rocky Valley and Kilmacanogue. The guns were landed in the night and moved under darkness to safe houses.[30]

---

25   Augusteijn, *Patrick Pearse*, pp 268-9.
26   *O'Donovan Rossa Funeral souvenir programme centenary edition.*
27   Joseph Murray, BMH WS 254.
28   Patrick Egan, BMH WS 327; Harry Nicholls, 'With the IRB at Howth and Kilcoole' in F. X. Martin (ed.) *The Howth and Kilcoole gun-running: recollections and documents* (Dublin, 2014) pp 168-71.
29   Hay, *Bulmer Hobson*, pp 160-1.
30   Thomas McCarthy, BMH WS 307.

Irish Volunteers marching back from Howth with their guns, *Irish Volunteer*, 24 July 1915.

By 1916 the numbers in A Company were down to 56. To co-ordinate action across the depleted company ranks a Battalion Council was formed of Ceannt, Cathal Brugha, Seamus Murphy, Seamus Kenny and Harry Nicholls.[31] He, along with the other officers of the 4th battalion (including Cathal Brugha, William Cosgrave, Douglas ffrench Mullen, Seamus Murphy, Tom McCarthy, Con Colbert and George Irvine) were brought together some weeks before the Rising and made to understand that significant manoeuvres were planned for Easter, though no direct reference to the planned Rising was offered. The O'Rahilly gave Nicholls a list of the arms dumps in the Dublin area, though without any suggestion that they might be called on soon. Just before the Rising the officers of the 4th Battalion were subjected to an examination to 'ascertain the officer's capacity for higher and independent command'. In the examination, which required dealing with a tactical problem of a simple practical nature on the ground, William Cosgrave scored 'good to fairly good', Con Colbert was good as was George Irvine but Harry Nicholls was scored as 'very good, displays good grasp of tactical principles and sound appreciation of the ground'.[32] The examination was conducted by J. J. 'Ginger' O'Connell, one of the Volunteer commandants with military experience, having served two years in the US army (1912-14) in the 69th New York Regiment.[33] On St Patrick's Day 1916 the Irish Volunteers had held a large parade in Dublin city centre. Before the parade Nicholls, along with George Irvine, went to the early morning service in St Patrick's Cathedral in Volunteer uniform.[34]

---

31   Ibid.
32   Holmes'/Nicholls papers 'Further report on officer's examination 4th Batt., Dublin Brigade' (Military Archives).
33   Marie Coleman, 'O'Connell, Jeremiah Joseph (J. J., Ginger)' *Dictionary of Irish biography*.
34   Holmes/Nicholls papers, typescript memoir (Military Archives).

The secrecy that the planning of the Rising was shrouded in confused many of those not in the inner circles, such as Nicholls. Though his parents could not have been unaware of his involvement in the Volunteers, the elaborate excuses he devised to cover his more militant activities indicate his certainty of their strong disapproval. When Nicholls was interned in Frongoch, his parents wrote to the authorities to assert that their son had been either fooled or press-ganged into the 'insane enterprise' by the republicans, which was of course far from the truth.[35]

Prisoners at Richmond Barracks 1916 *(Irish Life record of the Irish rebellion 1916)*

At Frongoch he was part of a group of Protestant rebels that included Arthur Shields, Ellet Elmes, Sam Ruttle of Tralee and Alf Cotton of Belfast. He used his Protestantism to vex the authorities by insisting on access to a Protestant Minister and a Bible. The artist Micheál Ó Ceallaigh drew a fine pencil sketch of Nicholls, who now sported a beard. His contribution to the Frongoch autograph book was the well-known line from Byron's *Childe Harold's Pilgrimage*:

> Hereditary Bondsmen! Know ye not,
> Who would be free themselves must strike the blow.

Nicholls was not amongst those early releases approved by the Sankey Commission that investigated the internee's role in the Rising and assessed their suitability for release. He was taken to Wormwood Scrubs to be questioned by the Commission but his unapologetic account of his activities ensured his continued detention. He had to wait until Christmas 1916 to return to Dublin, even though the Chief Commissioner of the DMP objected to his release.[36]

---

35   Letter W. Nicholls to H.E.Duke, 11 Dec. 1916 (NAI, Chief Secretary Office Registered Papers [CSO], 1916 internees files, 16628/1918, ii, Henry Nicholl).
36   Report of chief commissioner (NAI, CSORP 21699 Henry Nicholls file; ' (File 22055)).

It might be expected that Nicholl's would have lost his job in the Corporation as a result of either his participation in the Rising or his lengthy absence. In fact, on his release from Frongoch and return to Dublin he enjoyed an immediate improvement in his position, when it was proposed and seconded by Councillors P. V. Mahon and John Foley that Nicholls, formerly a temporary appointment to the engineering staff, be moved to a permanent position.[37] Mahon, a councillor for Mountjoy ward, was a member of the IRB and the printer of the *Irish Volunteer* newspaper. Foley was a councillor for the more middle-class Clontarf ward. The motion to appoint Nicholls was passed 30 for and 9 against. Those against included the established nationalist councillors Keogh, Flanagan, Reigh, Moran, Cummins and Monks and the unionists Fox, Dinnage and Beattie.[38] Amongst the councillors who voted against Nicholls was Michael 'Bird' Flanagan of Usher's Quay ward, a prosperous market gardener and supporter of the Redmondite Parliamentary Party. (He was also the father of Louisa Flanagan, the future wife of W. T. Cosgrave).[39] The re-employment and promotion of Harry may well signal the shift in public opinion that was already visible on the streets and was now filtering through to the Corporation.

Nicholls remained active in the Irish Volunteers and the Gaelic League, organising a meeting in memory of Thomas Ashe at Dingle in September 1917. In the years after 1916, however, he was perhaps more prominent as a trade unionist then a republican.

Nicholls, like Éamonn Ceannt, was a member of the Dublin Municipal Officers Association (DMOA) founded in 1901 by a group of senior corporation officials.[40] The DMOA was traditionally a conservative association, but in early 1917 a group of activists, many of them IRB men and some of whom had participated in the Rising, took control of the DMOA, using it to launch the Irish Local Government Officers Trade Union (ILGOU) as a national trade union of local government officials that would support the new Dáil Éireann department of local government, founded in 1919 and headed by Nicholl's former Volunteer comrade W. T. Cosgrave, as the only legitimate authority of its kind in Ireland. At the head of this group was Harry Nicholls.

---

37   *DCC Minutes* 1917, 290; *DC Rerports*, i, 1917, no. 48, p. 373.

38   Ibid., Joseph V. O'Brien, *"Dear dirty Dublin" a city in distress 1899-1916* (Dublin, 1982) appendix C, pp 266-7.

39   Michael Laffan, *Judging W. T. Cosgrave: the foundation of the Irish state* (Dublin, 2014), pp 62-4.

40   Martin Maguire, *'Servants to the public: a history of the Local Government and Public Services Union 1910-1990* (Dublin, 1998).

Nicholls addressed the first annual conference of the ILGOU in November 1920. Local government had been transformed by the June 1920 County Council and Rural District Council elections. Sinn Féin, as the primary vehicle for republican political ambitions in the years after 1916, now controlled 208 of the 33 county councils and 172 of the 206 rural councils.[41] In this speech Nicholls drew together his labour and republican radicalism.

> Some years ago the formation of a trade union by public officials would have been regarded as a seven-day's wonder, but the world has grown considerably since then. The wonder now is that there should still be officials who are not members of our Union. The economic struggle has become so acute that the unorganised workers must go inevitably to the wall. People have come roughly under two heads, employers and employed, and those who do not stand with the section to the which they belong are in danger of being crushed between the two parties.

He then went on in his conference speech to firmly align the ILGOU and the local government officials with Dáil Éireann.

> Within the last twelve months there has been a revolution in the composition of the great majority of public boards in Ireland. Most of them have now acknowledged Dáil Éireann as its supreme authority and have repudiated the Local Government Board, and for us, as servants of the public through their elected representatives, the matter has a personal as well as a national significance ... We officials are, in the first place, servants of the public and as such, have a duty to the public. The majority of the people of Ireland have declared at the recent Municipal and Poor Law elections that they wish the local government of their country to be carried out in a certain way. It is therefore, I conceive, our duty to assist them in their work in every possible way ...

Given the nature of the Irish War of Independence by November 1920, with British paramilitaries behaving in an increasingly brutal fashion, this was a dangerous or even foolhardy speech to deliver.[42]

---

41   Michael Laffan, *The resurrection of Ireland: the Sinn Féin Party 1916-1923* (Cambridge, 1999), pp 326-9.
42   Maguire, *Servants to the public*, Appendix 1.

Though the Dáil could issue decrees and the Sinn Féin councils could pass motions, only the salaried officials could actually make a national local government system function. Nicholls' speech proposed that local government officials would act as administrators in support of a Sinn Féin revolution. Nicholls even persuaded the members to defer the pay increases recently won to prevent the collapse of Dublin Corporation. By the end of 1920 the Corporation faced bankruptcy as the British state withheld its funds. On behalf of the ILGOU, Nicholls agreed that the officials would loan money to the Corporation by allowing it to withhold a quarter of wages until the following April, thus ensuring its survival. When a dispute arose on sick leave entitlements Nicholls referred the case to the Dáil Éireann courts despite the protests of the official who had initiated the dispute. The official in question was fearful of attracting the attention of British forces if word got out that he had appealed to the underground courts. When the Kells town clerk queried the legality of an increase won for him at a Dáil Éireann arbitration court by the union, he got a frosty reply that the legality of a Dáil appointed body could not be questioned by the union. Nicholls also refused to allow the union represent or act on behalf of any official that continued to support or obey the British Local Government Board. The assistant town clerk John Flood was dismissed by Dublin Corporation for refusing to record votes in Irish and Henry Campbell, the town clerk, was also dismissed for maintaining contact with the British authorities. Nicholls had little sympathy for either man, though both were members of the union.[43]

Other assistance that Nicholls provided to the revolutionary Dáil was less public but no less vital. When the new union required a permanent general secretary Nicholls appointed Éamonn Price, a former civil servant dismissed for being active in 1916 and who had been interned in Frongoch along with Nicholls. His job as general secretary of the union was to travel the country setting up new branches. Price was an effective general secretary, bringing a new and refreshing lack of deference to meetings with the Corporation.[44] However Price was, in a sense, double-jobbing for he was also Director of Organisation of the IRA. His post as general secretary of the union was most likely nothing more than a convenient cover under which he could travel the country on IRA business. In 1920 he left the ILGOU and became a fulltime civil servant of the Dáil until he was captured and imprisoned. Price had acquired sufficient trade union consciousness of the value of his labour however to demand an increase in his Dáil salary of £270 per annum to bring him up to the £350 per annum he would have enjoyed had he stayed with the local government

---

43   Ibid., pp 43-50; Pádraig Yeates, *A city in turmoil: Dublin 1919-21* (Dublin, 2012), pp 155-7.
44   Ibid., pp 221-2.

officials trade union.[45] Nicholls employment of Price and the movement of Price from the ILGOU to the revolutionary Dáil, along with Nicholls alignment of the ILGOU with the Dáil government, strengthens the probability that Nicholls was part of Michael Collins' strategy of encouraging an IRB capture of the Irish trade union movement in support of the national movement.[46]

Harry Nicholls did not apply for the pension offered to 1916 participants by the first 1924 Military Service Pensions Act, but did under the Fianna Fáil 1934 amended Act. This suggests that he did not regard the Treaty settlement and the Free State as legitimate inheritors of the republican struggle but did regard the De Valera government as legitimate. For Nicholls it was not the money. As a public servant he would not have actually received any award granted. Rather it was about status and a measure of recognition for his part in the independence struggle. However, the verbatim notes of his interview convey the scepticism, poor understanding and often boredom of the assessors that reviewed his request. The response to his application, which was 'final, conclusive and binding', infuriated him as he was refused recognition for the period of his imprisonment in Frongoch and was also refused recognition of his rank as captain, being granted the lowest ranking 'E' allowance.[47]

Sometime around 1966, against the backdrop of the 50th anniversary of the Rising, Harry Nicholls wrote an account of what he and his fellow IRB men had hoped for in the Rising and what had been achieved. He writes that in the aftermath of 1916 the principles of republicanism came into open discussion within the IRB, 'many of us felt that this was a very conservative country and that in the early years of independence this conservatism would hold sway'. Nicholls had hoped for a republic that was Irish-speaking, egalitarian and liberal in its outlook. He then listed the disappointed hopes he had alluded to; an education system that remained conservative and elitist, the continued decline in the Irish language, the degraded condition of women in the state that was an insult to republicanism, and the stupidity of censorship. Yet he expressed no regrets and remained optimistic on the development of independent Ireland.[48] We may wonder if now, on the 100th anniversary of the Rising, Harry Nicholls, Dublin City engineer, Protestant republican and rebel, would recognise in today's Dublin City the egalitarian and liberal Ireland he fought for?

---

45   'Personnel file E. Price' (NAI, DE2/159).
46   Padraig Yeates, 'Craft workers during the Irish revolution, 1919-22' in *Saothar* 33 Journal of the Irish Labour History Society (2008), pp 37-56.
47   'Henry Nicholls' (MSPC, File MSP34REF15964).
48   Holmes/Nicholls papers, typescript memoir (Military Archives).

Under the Starry Plough:
The City Hall Garrison

Conor McNamara

Barbed wire around City Hall 1916 (DCLA, BOR Collection)

The Irish Citizen Army garrison who fought at City Hall during Easter Week was unique for a number of reasons. City Hall was (along with the GPO itself) one of the most prestigious public buildings seized by the rebels during Easter Week; the City Hall fighters comprised the smallest single insurgent garrison of the Rising; the first police casualty of Easter Week was killed by the rebels at City Hall; it was the only garrison completely composed of Irish Citizen Army fighters; and it had the largest percentage of women fighters of any of the Dublin garrisons, with women comprising ten of the fifty or so insurgents. City Hall housed the only garrison to lose its two most senior commanding officers while defending their position. It was also the first garrison to be completely overwhelmed by the military during the insurrection; and finally, it was the only garrison whose opponents were exclusively composed of Irish units of the British Army, with the Royal Irish Regiment, the Royal Irish Rifles and the Royal Dublin Fusiliers comprising the besieging forces.

The revolutionaries who fought in the City Hall garrison deserve particular recognition among the nationalist pantheon of heroes produced by the Rising. For a number of reasons, however, none of the insurgents who fought at City Hall received the popular acclaim awarded to other veterans of Easter Week, and the vast majority of the garrison lived out their lives in relative obscurity without popular, financial or political influence. Given the prominent role of the garrison during the Rising, the role of women in the fighting, and the symbolic resonance of City Hall, popular neglect of the garrison who seized the building reflected the wider priorities of a nationalist tradition that elevated the widows and wives of deceased Volunteer leaders (such as Margaret Pearse, Áine Ceannt and others) above the female fighters of Easter Week themselves, while simultaneously emphasising the role of the Volunteer leadership in the GPO at the expense of the Irish Citizen Army and its more radical political philosophy.

Background

O'Donovan Rossa lying in state at City Hall (DCLA)

Built between 1769 and 1779 by the Guild of Merchants as the Royal Exchange, City Hall was one of Dublin's most prominent public buildings, on a par with the Bank of Ireland (the old Parliament House) on College Green. An outstanding example of Georgian architecture designed by Thomas Cooley, who defeated the more illustrious James Gandon for the contract, the circular entrance hall and spacious dome supported by twelve columns was built as an ostentatious display of mercantile power. It became the City Hall in 1852, and became the home of Dublin City Council. The small group who seized the building in Easter 1916 were likely to have associated the building in more recent times with the funeral of Jeremiah O'Donovan Rossa whose body was laid out in the rotunda for public viewing before his funeral in August 1915. City Hall had both a symbolic and strategic value. The garrison at City Hall was commanded by Seán Connolly, and his small band were given the unenviable task of attacking, and pinning down, troops emerging from Dublin Castle – the centre of the British administration in Ireland - until various posts in the city had been successfully occupied by the insurgents.

Sean Connolly (DCLA, BOR Collection)

It has traditionally been regarded as a mistake on the part of the Citizen Army to occupy City Hall rather than Dublin Castle, the historic symbol of British occupation.[1] There was never an intention to try to occupy the Castle with so small a force, however, and by occupying the Castle guardroom and the vantage point over the Castle provided by the roof of City Hall it was hoped that any potential attacks from the Castle would be neutralised. The Castle itself was protected by a poorly armed skeleton force of troops, and was vulnerable to attack with a minimum of force. An anonymous source inside the Castle later revealed:

> The castle was almost empty. Police of assorted varieties were in the majority, and they were not too numerous. The place was practically denuded of troops - the garrison major and the whole lot had cleared out. Altogether there were only two officers in the place – a Colonel and a Major; there were about seventy wounded soldiers from overseas in the Castle Red Cross Hospital, and there was half a dozen disabled soldiers in the Ship Street barracks. That was all.[2]

---

1   R. M. Fox, *The history of the Irish Citizen Army* (Dublin, 1943), pp 144–55; 'Citizen Army posts', *Dublin's fighting story*, pp 55–60; Matthew Connolly, 'Dublin City Hall area', *Capuchin Annual* (1966), pp 193–201.
2   'Dublin Castle from the inside', *An t–Óglach*, 13 Feb. 1926, p. 3.

Thomas Kain led a detachment of six fighters that stormed the guard room of the upper Castle Yard, forcing the guards to retreat into the Castle. Kain was secretary to the ICA Army Council and director of mobilisation and had led several mock attacks on the Castle in the preceding weeks. Kain later recounted the atmosphere in the city among his fighters as they marched from Liberty Hall: 'We march up College Street and into College Green. Paces quicken and there is a hint of excitement in the rhythm of movement ... a few hundred yards more ... Heads rise and fingers subconsciously fiddle with triggers. People pause on the sidewalks. Some stare at us curiously but without an atom of interest.'[3]

The attack on City Hall commenced when Captain Seán Connolly of the ICA shot dead James O'Brien, an unarmed constable of the Dublin Metropolitan Police at the Cork Hill Gate at approximately 12 p.m. on Easter Monday. The sound of the shot was at first thought to be the result of an accidental discharge of a revolver by the military in the Castle; however, when the occupants of the Castle realised what was happening, 'at first there was general incredulity, this was followed by considerable indecision as to the best action to be taken for the defence of the Castle.'[4] With only a small detachment of troops, civil administrators and invalided veterans present, there was 'one thing they were very pleased about, and that was the manner in which the half-dozen disabled soldiers had managed to shut the gates of Ship Street Barracks in the nick of time.'[5]

Under Kain's command, six insurgents stormed the Castle guardroom, taking a number of guards prisoner.[6] With the building secure, the rest of the garrison were free to occupy City Hall without interference and Seán Connolly brought his unit of ten men and ten women into City Hall. Eight men were detailed for the Henry and James building on Parliament Street, four were stationed in the offices of the *Evening Mail* directly opposite City Hall, six in the Rates Office on Castle Street and three men were placed in the Huguenot graveyard in Nicholas Street. These were regarded as strategic points from which the garrison at City Hall could co-ordinate itself with the much larger garrison at Jacob's factory. Following the shooting of O'Brien, the rebels under Connolly's command were confused as to how to proceed. As Helena Molony later recalled:

3   Thomas Kain quoted in R. M. Fox, *Irish Citizen Army*, p. 148.
4   'Dublin Castle from the inside', *An t–Óglach*, 13 Feb. 1926, p. 4.
5   Ibid.
6   The members who stormed the guardroom were Tom Kane, Philip O'Leary, Tom Daly, George Connolly, James Seery and Christopher Brady.

The men behind Connolly did not really know they were to go through. Connolly said: 'Get in, get in' - as if they already did not know they were to go in. That guarded secrecy, not to let it look like anything other than the manoeuvres which were taking place for weeks before, may have been the reason; but certainly there was hesitation on the part of the followers. Seán Connolly shouted: 'Get in, get in'. On the flash, the gates were closed. The sentry went into his box, and began firing. I thought no one had succeeded in getting in. It breaks my heart - and all our hearts - that we did not get in.[7]

The arrival of the rebels came as a complete surprise to those in the Castle; as one later recounted, 'and then came the bolt from the blue and sunny sky! Whatever knowledge or suspicion others in the Castle possessed, I had not the remotest idea that anything so far fetched (to the official mind) as a Rising against the might of England was likely to be attempted. Even the best informed in the place, I think regarded such a happening as a remote possibility.'[8] A member of a Voluntary Aid Detachment (VAD) working in the Castle later wrote: 'It was now clear there was going to be trouble. The patients' blood was up, and they wanted to be out and in it, but of course this was impossible. Large numbers were at the windows when the policeman was carried across the yard, and the women, who accompanied him, shouted, "You call yourselves soldiers, and you won't come out and help". It was very unkind, for the men were dying to go, and it hurt.'[9]

The roof of City Hall provided a vantage point across the Castle Yard for rebel snipers: 'All the surrounding roofs seemed to be densely populated with snipers, and it became quite a common thing to hear the whistle of a bullet and see chips knock off a wall uncomfortably near to where you were standing.'[10] With the men taking up positions, the female fighters of the Citizen Army went about their duties, as Helena Molony recalled, 'My idea was to find out where there was a kitchen, and where there was a suitable place for a hospital. There was a kitchen upstairs. The building is like a pepper canister set on Cork Hill. In the kitchen we discovered a large dish of fruit - oranges and apples. I said: "Nobody is to touch these, because there will be wounded probably". We got ready for the wounded. We "sat pretty" for a couple of hours.'[11]

---

7   Helena Molony, BMH WS 391, pp 34–5.
8   'Dublin Castle from the inside', *An t-Óglach,* 13 Feb. 1926, p. 3.
9   'Experiences of a V.A.D. at Dublin Castle During the Rebellion', *Blackwood's Magazine,* 200 (Dec., 1916), p. 814.
10   'Dublin Castle from the inside', *An t-Óglach,* 13 Feb. 1926, p. 4.
11   Helena Molony, BMH WS 391, p. 36.

With the rebels securing their positions, military reinforcements relieved the Castle at around 2 p.m. with the arrival of a detachment of between two and three hundred soldiers.[12] Kathleen Lynn remembered that 'A regiment of British soldiers arrived at the Castle, I think in the late [Monday] afternoon. I did not see them, but I imagine the men on our roof and those on the roof of the *Evening Mail* and the tailor's shop opposite must have. I often thought afterwards that it was surprising that those soldiers were allowed to enter the Castle Yard unmolested by our men.'[13]

The arrival of the military led to heavy exchanges of fire between the two groups, with the military taking up a range of positions throughout the Castle complex. As Matthew Connolly of the ICA (and the brother of Seán) recalled 'Knowing that it was easy to get in the line of fire from military snipers from the clock tower of the Castle, I moved carefully up the slates of a roof slope nearby, in order to cut across to the opposite side of the building, to where I might have a word with Seán before it was too late, but, as I reached the top of the slope, a burst of rifle fire splintered the slates around me, and it was impossible to cross over the top without being hit'.[14]

The military managed to seize the crucial advantage at this early point, and as Kathleen Lynn later recalled 'It was a pity some attack was not made on them because immediately after their arrival the fusillade started. The bullets fell like rain. We had come down from the roof and were collected in the hall. The firing came from all sides and continued till after darkness fell. There was no way of escape although we discussed all possibilities.'[15] For the inpatients of the Castle hospital, the experience was horrifying, as one member of a Voluntary Aid Detachment later wrote:

> By this time many of the men were tired watching, and came back to the ward; and for the first time, or certainly more vividly than ever before, I began to realise what France had meant to them. One could hardly believe they were the same men who had been there in the morning. They were not excited as I should have expected; their faces were white, with horror and repulsion written on them; all their cheeriness was gone. I heard many of them say, 'We're in Hell again, we might as well go back to France'; and others said, 'I am so frightened, I am going home tomorrow'.

---

12   'Dublin Castle from the inside', *An t–Óglach*, 13 Feb. 1926, p. 4.
13   Kathleen Lynn, BMH WS 357, p. 5.
14   Matthew Connolly, BMH WS 1,745, p. 10.
15   Kathleen Lynn, BMH WS 357, pp 5–6.

It was not fear but the noise which reminded us of reviews and military tournaments, told them a very different story. They saw again their friends being killed, and all the horrors they had tried to obliterate from their minds.[16]

Seán Connolly was killed not long after taking possession of the roof by sniper fire from the Clock Tower of the Castle. With heavy sniper fire being exchanged between the two groups, the death of Connolly came as a heavy blow to the morale of the small garrison; Helena Molony recalled that 'After Connolly's death, there was nothing to do, only sit. The men in the main positions fired desultory shots all day. They fired at anything they saw'.[17] Kathleen Lynn, who arrived later, described the effect on the entire garrison. 'Seán Connolly's death had a demoralising effect on the City Hall men'.[18]

With so small a force of fighters defending such a strategic building, the garrison were keenly aware of their vulnerability; early in the afternoon Helena Molony had been dispatched with Molly Reilly to ask for reinforcements from the GPO. James Connolly told them that he could spare no further men but sent Kathleen Lynn to City Hall to help care for the wounded. The position at City Hall was now under continuous fire, was isolated and was rapidly coming under pressure as the military became fully mobilised. With the troops from various Dublin barracks pouring into the city centre by early afternoon, heavy machine guns were trained on City Hall around 4 p.m. and a mass slaughter of the garrison was prevented only by the unwillingness of the military to destroy such a prominent public building. By the late afternoon on, however, the Citizen Army's position was a hopeless one; surrounded and subject to continuous heavy fire, it was only a matter of what the military decided to do next.

On Monday evening, it appeared that some relief was on its way, as George Norgrove brought seven Citizen Army men from the GPO to bolster the garrison. A unit of Volunteers from Maynooth accompanied by a group of Hibernian Rifles also occupied the Exchange Hotel on Parliament Street on Monday evening. Within minutes of their arrival, however, Volunteer Edward Walsh of the Hibernian Rifles was mortally wounded. In intense pain, he was removed to Jervis Street hospital where he died on Tuesday. The small detachment in the Exchange Hotel were completely ill armed for such a perilous mission against overwhelming force; with just one rifle between the entire group. As a member of the Maynooth Volunteer

---

16   'Experiences of a V.A.D', p. 817.
17   Ibid., p. 37.
18   Kathleen Lynn, BMH WS 357, pp 5–6.

later recalled 'our bombs were absolutely ineffective and although we expended many scarcely any of them exploded. Our position towards evening had become absolutely untenable.'[19] After a heavy exchange of gunfire, the group evacuated the hotel and moved into Shortall's shop next door before making their retreat back to the GPO.[20]

The end came with a full bayonet charge by the military late on Monday night and by early on Tuesday morning City Hall and her defenders were in the hands of the Crown Forces. The attacking force was composed of the 3rd Royal Irish Regiment, the 10th Royal Dublin Fusiliers and 3rd Royal Irish Rifles.[21] Thus, like elsewhere in the city, Irishmen fought each other for control of the capital during the first two days of the Rising. Helena Molony recalled: 'At about half-past eight or nine o'clock, when nightfall came, there was a sudden bombardment. It came suddenly on us. On the roof level, on which were glass windows, and through the windows on the ground floor of the City Hall, there were machine gun bullets pouring in'.[22] Some rebels fled the building to evade surrendering and William Oman was chased through the streets by an angry mob. When British troops found the group of women fighters in the shell of City Hall, they mistook them for prisoners: 'The British officers thought these girls [Citizen Army members] had been taken prisoner by the rebels. They asked them: 'Did they do anything to you? Were they kind to you? How many are up here?'[23] Oman later wrote:

> They [Crown Forces] came down Christchurch into Little Ship Street in open formation. Of course, they saw us. I dropped one of the home-made bombs but it did not go off. They fired on us from the street. As I was under the impression that they would form an outer cordon around the Castle and so surround us, I decided to evacuate the position. In Werburgh Street the mobs were cheering the troops. I held a consultation with the others, and we decided that each man should take his chance individually in getting away. I decided that, on account of the mob, they should not take their equipment with them. The others left and I remained there by myself until about five o'clock.[24]

19 P. Colgan, 'The Maynooth Volunteers in 1916', *An t–Oglach*, 8 May 1926, p. 4.
20 Ibid.
21 R. M. Fox, *Irish Citizen Army*, p. 151.
22 Helena Molony, BMH WS 391, pp 37–8.
23 Ibid., p. 39.
24 William Oman, BMH WS 421, pp 7-8.

The military had been burying the dead from both sides inside the Castle compound on Monday and one civilian employee later recalled, 'Well it was so fine that it made it imperative to allow as little time as possible to lapse between death and burial. We buried them in what is known as "The Pound" – without coffin or shroud, in their habit as they lived. Before the end of the week, the pound was pretty full – British soliders, Irish republican soldiers, and civilians. It was a tough job, acting as an amateur gravedigger, but the graves were not dug very deep, as they were intended by be only temporary'.[25]

Rebels Killed During the Occupation of City Hall

Name	Occupation	Address	Details
Byrne, Louis	Cabinet Maker	23 Summer Hill	Died on Tuesday from gunshot wounds to the heart, elbow and thigh; married with five daughters; was sent as a reinforcement from the GPO
Connolly, Seán	Dublin Corporation Clerk in Motor Registration Dept.	3 Mountjoy Square	Shot dead on Monday on the roof of City Hall; left a widow, two sons and a daughter
Darcy, Charles	Worked in a department store	Gloucester Place	Aged fifteen, he was shot dead on Monday on the roof of the Henry and James Building on Parliament Street on Monday
Geoghegan, George	Boilermaker	27 Upper Dorset Street	Died on Wednesday from wounds received in City Hall; he left a widow and three children
O'Reilly, John	Carter	12 Lower Gardiner Street	Second in command to Seán Connolly; shot dead on Monday on the roof of City Hall; unmarried
Walsh, Edward	Carter	3 Ryders Row	Walsh was wounded in No 8 Parliament Street and died on Tuesday in the Hibernian Bank on O'Connell Street; he left a wife and two children; his only son Edward, was born seven months after his death and sent to an orphanage

---

25   'Dublin Castle from the inside', *An t–Óglach*, 13 Feb. 1926, p. 4.

Source: R. M. Fox's 1943 list of Citizen Army combatants approved by the ICA Old Comrades Association and published in Fox, *History of the Citizen Army*, pp 227-32, with additional biographical information provided by the Military Service Pension Records.

Aftermath

With both commanding officers, Seán Connolly and Seán (John) O'Reilly, having been killed on the roof of City Hall on Monday afternoon, the garrison was at least spared any executions by the military in the aftermath of the Rebellion. A small number of fighters in isolated outposts, such as William Oman, managed to avoid arrest, but the majority of the City Hall garrison were overwhelmed on Monday night and taken prisoner. Seán Connolly was one of the Citizen Army's most charismatic leaders, and his loss to the movement compounded the vacuum in leadership following the execution of James Connolly and Michael Mallin after the Rising. One of sixteen children, his father worked as a seaman, yet Connolly managed to transcend the rigid class structures of Dublin society through his involvement in drama, the Gaelic League and related cultural organisations. Active during the 1913 Lockout, he was prominent as an actor in the Liberty Players, along with fellow rebel, Helena Molony, and possessed of remarkable good looks and charisma. A committed revolutionary, he fought in City Hall alongside his sister Kathleen Barrett, and three brothers, Eddie, George and Mathew, along with a fourth brother, Joe, who fought in the GPO. He left a widow and three children.[26] Connolly had been due to play one of the lead roles in the Abbey that night in a performance of Yeats' *Cathleen Ní Houlihan*.

Seán Connolly and Countess Markievicz in *The Memory of the Dead* (Courtesy Connolly Family)

---

26   Lawrence W. White, 'Connolly, Seán', *Dictionary of Irish biography.*

Of the ten women who fought, Helena Molony and Dr Kathleen Lynn were among the small handful of women fighters that were deported in the aftermath of the Rising. Both women were among the most committed and remarkable figures of the revolutionary generation. Following the Rising however, the archetypical grieving mother and wife became a centrepiece of nationalist propaganda; it was role that was to be filled by figures such as Margaret Pearse and Áine Ceannt. The more politically sophisticated fighters such as Lynn and Molony, maintained a high profile in left republican circles while languishing in relative obscurity in wider nationalist society.

Helena Molony (1883-1967) had joined the women's nationalist organisation, Inghinidhe na hÉireann, in 1903. The daughter of a grocer, she became class conscious at an early stage and contributed widely to Inghinidhe's journal, *Bean na hÉireann*, advocating a blend of republicanism and feminism. She was subsequently involved with Bulmer Hobson and Countess Markievicz in the foundation of the republican boy scouts movement, Na Fianna Éireann in 1909. As general secretary of the Womens' Workers Union, Molony was heavily involved in relief work during the Lockout and was an enthusiastic supporter of James Connolly. Jailed in Aylesbury prison following the Rebellion, she remained politically active with various trade union organisations and republican prisoner groups throughout her life and was elected Irish Trade Union Congress president in 1936. She remained close to Kathleen Lynn and other republican women who took the anti-treaty side during the Civil War. She never married and frequently suffered from ill health in later life.

Dr Kathleen Lynn (1887-1955) was a most unlikely figure to be among the fighters of City Hall. From a comfortable Anglican background in south Mayo, Lynn transcended her social class to become a passionate and pragmatic advocate for social progress. A clinical assistant at the Royal Eye and Ear Hospital when the Rising broke out, the economic injustice under which the rural poor laboured in south Mayo had inspired in Lynn a deep rooted commitment to social justice. She offered her medical expertise to both the Volunteers and the Citizen Army in the years before the Rising and, despite her background, was regarded with reverence by the working class fighters of Dublin. Following the Rising she became vice-president of the Sinn Féin executive in 1917 and was interned in Arbour Hill prison in 1918. Along with her lifelong companion Madeline ffrench Mullen, she established St Ultan's Hospital for infants on Charlemont Street in the south inner city in 1919. The hospital provided much needed medical assistance and practical guidance to the impoverished mothers of the city. Like Molony and her wider circle, she was against the Anglo-Irish Treaty of 1921 and was elected as a Sinn

Féin T.D. for Dublin County in 1923. She faded from public life when she failed to be re-elected in 1927.[27]

For the families of those killed in the defense of City Hall, there was little financial reward. Edward Walsh's widow, Ellen, was awarded an annual pension of £90 per year in 1924 and her youngest son, Edward, who was born seven months after his father's death was placed in an orphanage in Dún Laoghaire. Ellen Walsh died prematurely in 1930.[28] Charlie Darcy was fifteen when he lost his life on the roof of City Hall. His father passed away prematurely in 1920, leaving his frequently ill mother to provide for three children. The family was given £120 by the Irish National Voluntary Aid Association, which had been founded to care for the families of prisoners and the deceased.[29] Similar payments were made to the families of the other dead often only after prolonged bureaucratic wrangling.

Conclusion

The occupation of City Hall was a hopeless mission, but the small band of revolutionaries who seized it displayed admirable tenacity in their refusal to surrender their position when outgunned and overwhelmed. The garrison had no chance of withstanding a concerted attack by the military due to their small numbers, limited firepower, their isolation from other outposts and the unwillingness of the Volunteer leadership to send meaningful reinforcements. Under these circumstances, their refusal to surrender, their willingness to engage the enemy at such close range and their brief but unremittingly hazardous occupation of City Hall was among the most daring endeavours of Easter Week.

The garrison was notable for its relatively high level of casualties; six of the forty or so defenders were killed; and the high number of women combatants, with ten female fighters participating. Rather than initiating a resurgence in the Citizen Army, however, Easter Week marked the beginning of the end of the Citizen Army as a meaningful and popular military force. In the absence of the emergence of new leadership on a par with the inspirational leaders such as James Connolly, Michael Mallin and Seán Connolly, and as it competed for working class and trade union recruits with the more glamorous Irish Volunteers, the ICA declined rapidly in the aftermath of Easter Week.

---

27 Margaret Ó hOgartaigh, 'Lynn, Kathleen', *Dictionary of Irish biography*.
28 MSPC, 1D124, Edward Walsh.
29 MSPC, 1D2014, Charles Darcy.

City Hall Garrison, Easter 1916

Name	Address	Details
Barrett, Kathleen, [née Connolly]	14 Lower Rutland Street	Released on 12 May; subsequently joined Cumann na mBan, fought in the Civil War on the anti-treaty side and interned
Connolly, Matthew	Raheny	Was released after one month due to his youth (he was fifteen); subsequently joined the Volunteers while in London during the War of Independence
Corcoran, Mary Teresa (Molly) [née O'Reilly]	45 Leix Road, Cabra	Worked as a republican spy in the United Services Club from 1918; took the anti-treaty side in the Civil War and was interned
Coyle, Thomas	8 Queens Square, Pearse Street	Wounded in Easter Week; his brother Henry was killed in the fighting near the GPO; later fought with the National Army in the Civil War
Farrell, Denis	Off Lower Rutland Street	Sent to City Hall from the GPO; interned until August; remained a member of the ICA; claimed to be involved in the removal of guns from US ship in 1918
Finlay, John (Jack)	5 Grenville Street, off Mountjoy Square	Received a serious gunshot wound in the shoulder during Easter Week; released in December 1916
Grange, Annie [née Norgrove]	12 Upper Rutland Street	Detained in Ship Street and Kilmainham; subsequently joined Cumann na mBan; took the republican side in the Civil War
Halpin, William	6 St Valentine Terrace, East Road	Interned until December; rejoined ICA and took some part in the Civil War during the occupation of Vaughan's Hotel where he was wounded
Hanratty, Emily [née Norgrove]	77 Eccles Street	Detained in Kilmainham following the Rising
Kelly, Elizabeth (Bessie), [née Lynch]	16 Kildare Road, Crumlin	Released after the Rising and moved to Glasgow in 1917
Lamert, Thomas	Unknown	Sent to City Hall from the GPO
Lynn, Dr Kathleen	Belgrave Square, Rathmines	Chief medical officer for the ICA; took the anti-treaty side in the Civil War; elected a Sinn Féin TD in 1923

Name	Address	Details
Molony, Helena	Larkfield Grove, Kimmage	Deported to Lewes and Aylesbury jail and released at Christmas 1916; served as a justice in the Republican Courts during the War of Independence
Murphy, Bridget, [née Brady]	12 Corporation Street	Imprisoned with her comrades in Ship Street Barracks and Kilmainham before release in early May
Nelson, Thomas	34 North Great Georges Street	Interned until December; subsequently served with ICA during the Civil War and fought in the Hamman Hotel and subsequently interned
Nolan, Shaun (John)	North Wall	Sent to City Hall from the GPO; Interned until August; fought with the anti-treaty IRA at Barry's Hotel and involved in the raid for arms on the Custom House
Norgrove, Alfred George	Strandville Avenue, North Strand	Sent to City Hall from the GPO; interned until December; quartermaster of the ICA during Civil War
O'Duffy, Bridgid [née Davis]	32 Mobhi Road	Briefly interned following the Rising; served alongside Kathleen Lynn during the War of Independence
O'Dwyer, James	76 Tolka Road	Released from Frongoch in December and resumed activities with the ICA
O'Reilly, John	5E Ross Road	Interned until July; subsequently joined the Irish Volunteers
Poole, John	25 Townsend Street	Sent from the GPO to City Hall; released from Frongoch in December; he subsequently joined the Irish Volunteers
Sexton, Michael	Unknown	Unknown
Shanahan, Jane (Jennie)	Larkfield Grove, Kimmage	Supported the Volunteers during the War of Independence and the took the anti-treaty side in the Civil War when she served in the makeshift field hospital in Cullenswood House; died prematurely in January 1936
Walsh, Tom	Unknown	Unknown

Henry and James Building Outpost, Easter Week 1916

Name	Address	Details
Byrne, John	31 Upper Wellington Street	Also served in the GPO
Connolly, Edward	58 Lower Gloucester Street	Released in October; rejoined the ICA; later emigrated to the US
Donnelly, James	62 Amiens Street	Released from custody on 8 May; joined the National Army during the Civil War
Elmes, Ellett	23 St Jarlath's Road, Cabra	Interned after the Rising; fought with the ICA at the outbreak of the Civil War at Barry's Hotel and the Hamman Hotel; subsequently interned
Halpin, William	Moore Street	Transferred from Frongoch to Richmond Asylum and died prematurely
King, Samuel	Drumcondra	Stationed in the Henry and James Building on Parliament Street before transferring to GPO at 8 p.m. on Monday; rejoined the ICA after the Rebellion

Evening Mail office, Parliament St, Easter Week 1916

Name	Address	Details
Kelly, Martin	16 Kildare Street, (Road?) Kimmage	Evaded arrest following the Rising; subsequently rejoined the movement and interned during the Civil War
King, Daniel	67 Aungier Street	Wounded on Monday; he reported back to the GPO before being taken to hospital; evaded arrest
McDonnell, Jim	unknown	Stationed in the *Evening Mail* Office, Parliament Street; hid out in the basement of 37 Parliament Street until Saturday after the surrender of the garrison; released after questioning by military
Winstanley, Henry	Windy Arbour, Dundrum	A member of the Irish Volunteers, he was posted to the *Evening Mail* Office, along with Jim McDonnell, he hid out in the basement of 37 Parliament Street until the end of the Week; evaded arrest

Name	Address	Details
Brady, Christy	Unknown	unknown
Connolly, George	13 Buckingham Terrace	Posted to the guard room of Dublin Castle; later fought with the anti-treaty IRA
Daly, Thomas	Unknown	unknown
Kain, Thomas	15 Old Camden Street	Led the party that captured the Castle guard room; interned in Frongoch
O'Leary, Philip	4 Middle Gardiner Street	Took part in the occupation of the guard room of Dublin Castle; interned until December; subsequently fought during the Civil War with the ICA during the defence of Barry's Hotel on 28/9 June and at Hamman Hotel on 30 June 1922
Seery, James	Benburb Street	Posted to guard room, Upper Castle Yard, he evacuated to the basement of 12 Castle Street around ten o'clock on Monday night; evaded arrest; later served as a cook in the National Army
Williams, Patrick Joseph	24 Stafford Street	A member of the Irish Volunteers but was posted to Dublin Castle Yard; interned until December; rejoined the Volunteers and was interned during the War of Independence

Synod House Outpost, Easter Week 1916

Name	Address	Details
Byrne, Patrick J.	60 Dominick Street	Posted to Synod House and received head wound during the fighting
Healy, Thomas	23 Lower Oriel Street	Evaded arrest after the Rising
O'Keefe, John	Unknown	Unknown

Name	Address	Details
Delaney, Michael	31 Patrick Street	Interned following the Rebellion; subsequently joined the Volunteers; served with the National Army during the Civil War
Oman, William	Joyce Road, Drumcondra	Released from Richmond barracks because of his youthfulness; fought with the Volunteers during the War of Independence and interned during the Civil War
Williams, Patrick	24 Stafford Street	Opened fire on the RIC in Lord Edward Street; subsequently joined the Volunteers

Source: R. M. Fox's 1943 list of Citizen Army combatants approved by the ICA Old Comrades Association and published in Fox, *History of the Citizen Army*, pp 227-32, with additional biographical information provided by the Military Service Pension Records.

Éamonn Ceannt,
Dublin Corporation employee, trade unionist and the 1916 Rising.

Shay Cody

Éamonn Ceannt (DCLA, BOR Collection)

Éamonn Ceannt was born Edward Kent in 1881 in Galway, the son of an RIC constable. A month after Éamonn's second birthday, his father was promoted to Head Constable in County Louth. On his retirement in 1892, the family moved to Dublin and Éamonn attended the Christian Brothers O'Connell Schools where he won a number of scholarships. While one of his brothers followed their father's career path into the RIC, Éamonn secured a clerkship in Dublin Corporation in 1900 following a competitive examination.[1]

---

1   Mary Gallagher, *16 Lives: Éamonn Ceannt* (Dublin, 2014), pp 15-21.

Compared with Connolly and Pearse, Ceannt remains a remote and shadowy figure. He was however a key figure in the genesis of the 1916 Rising and was one of the most committed to revolutionary violence. He was described as a man who believed in the logic of the pike and was more naturally a physical force man than any of the other leaders.[2] He was encouraged by Seán MacDiarmada to join the Irish Volunteers in order to advance the Irish Republican Brotherhood's infiltration of the force. He rose from Captain of A Company of the 4th Battalion of the Dublin Volunteers to the rank of Commandant after the September 1914 split with John Redmond's supporters, and then served on the Volunteers' Headquarters Staff as Director of Communications with Pearse and Plunkett.

Ceannt spent practically all of his life in Dublin. He was devoted to Irish language, music and dance and in 1899 he joined the Gaelic League. Besides teaching Irish he was an excellent uilleann piper. He founded the Dublin Pipers Club. His wife Áine recalled;

> In 1908 Éamonn accompanied the CYMS Pilgrimage to Rome. They were competing in the sports which were being held to mark the sacerdotal jubilee of Pope Pius X. Éamonn determined to speak no word of English outside of Ireland, so he spoke either French or Irish, or German at which he was not so proficient, and he had learned a few words of Italian. The costume which he wore was an eleventh century costume which created rather a stir in the streets of Rome. His holiness heard of the Irish piper and Éamonn was invited to play before him.[3]

Éamonn Ceannt (who continued to be recorded in Union and Dublin Corporation records by his anglicised name of Edward Kent) was first elected to the Executive of the Dublin Municipal Officers Association (DMOA) in December 1907. The DMOA, which was a forerunner of today's IMPACT Trade Union, had been established in 1901. The primary objective of the DMOA was 'to bring the officers into direct association and generally to promote their interests'.[4] The DMOA opened its membership to all professional and clerical staff appointed by the Corporation. Its immediate aims were enhancing the status of Local Government Officers, defending their positions and ensuring the security of their jobs. The first attempts to organise Local Government Officers had occurred in 1897 when the

---

2   Brian Barton *From behind a closed door – secret court martial records of the 1916 rising* (Belfast, 2002), p 182.
3   Áine Ceannt, BMH WS 264.
4   Martin Maguire, *Servants to the public: a history of the Local Government and Public Services Union 1901-1990* (Dublin, 1998), p. 9.

Local Government (Ireland) Bill was before parliament. The initiative faltered, as it emerged that the position of Local Government Officials, despite their initial fears, would be protected in the Act. However the election of 'Ratepayer' councillors in Dublin, pledged to ease the burden on ratepayers by reducing expenditure by the Corporation (including expenditure on the salaries of officials), led to the establishment of the DMOA. The DMOA was a moderate entity: it appointed the serving Lord Mayor as its Honorary President and marked its launch, not with a more traditional meeting but by holding an inaugural dinner.[5]

Following the enactment of the 1898 Local Government Act, Dublin Corporation decided that appointments to clerkships and similar offices should be made by public competition. Following this, Ceannt secured a position as a clerk in the City Treasurer's Office, working in the Rates Office in Castle Street. He was a diligent employee (apparently only missing work once in seventeen years, according to his wife Áine, when he fell off his bicycle). At the 1908 annual general meeting he was elected vice-chairman of the DMOA and in December 1909 was elected to the chairmanship of the DMOA for 1910. Ceannt continued to serve on the executive in 1911 and 1912, before resigning from the executive without explanation in July 1913. The swift rise of Ceannt in the DMOA reflected his energy and his commitment to the Association. However, though he was clearly a popular chairman and member, his radicalism was far in advance of the mass of the Corporation officers and his term on the executive was marked by a series of unsuccessful campaigns to radicalise the membership on key issues.

DMOA Annual Dinner 1908 (DCLA)

5   Maguire, *Servants to the public*, pp 27-8.

During the same period, Ceannt was also an organiser for Sinn Féin. The aim of Sinn Féin was to use the existing machinery of the elected local authorities to engineer unilateral independence by the creation of a parallel administration that would bypass the existing British one. This policy had been advocated by Arthur Griffith in his 1904 pamphlet *The resurrection of Hungary: a parallel for Ireland*, where he argued for the withdrawal of Irish M.P.s from Westminster and the formation of a national council based on the General Council of County Councils.[6] Most of the proposals he made foreshadowed subsequent Sinn Féin policies.

In 1908 Ceannt urged, again unsuccessfully, that the DMOA should give financial aid to the striking carters brought out by Jim Larkin. The membership rejected his proposal that the Association should amalgamate with the Civil Service Guild, in order to bring together all the permanent officials of the state, a proposal that Sinn Féin had adopted as its own. In rejecting the proposal it is likely that the membership was aware that Ceannt was advocating his own political party's policy. Nevertheless, Ceannt continued to work on behalf of the DMOA and his colleagues in the Corporation. John Monks, one of his colleagues in the City Treasurer's Office and an activist in the DMOA, later recalled that Ceannt, as chairman, had a genius for organisation and his year in office was characterised by the promotion of a number of successful schemes for the betterment of the officials. He credited Ceannt as 'a staunch believer in the need for organisation in defence of one's rights' and he initiated what would ultimately be a successful claim on behalf of First Class Clerks.[7]

Ceannt was held in high regard in wider Dublin Trade Union circles. As late as March 1916, the prominent trade unionist, William O'Brien, described him as a 'front rank man and a good one too'. Ceannt was familiar with the writings of Marx and Engels and was more sympathetic to socialist policies than most of his Sinn Féin colleagues.[8] O'Brien recorded that Ceannt had lectured for the Socialist Party of Ireland on a number of occasions.[9] The Socialist Party of Ireland had been established in 1904, drawing together a number of small socialist groups including former members of James Connolly's Irish Socialist Republican party. The SPI was propagandist in nature. Connolly joined the party on his return from the United States in 1910 and he established branches in Cork and Belfast.[10] As well as adopting a militant approach for the DMOA, Ceannt belonged to a group that directed

6   Arthur Griffith, *The resurrection of Hungary: a parallel for Ireland* (Dublin, 1904), p. 93.
7   Gallagher, *16 Lives: Éamonn Ceannt*, p. 82.
8   James Quinn, 'Éamonn Ceannt' in Lawrence William White and James Quinn (eds) *1916 portraits and lives* (Dublin, 2016), p 69.
9   William O'Brien, *Forth the banners go: reminiscences of William O'Brien as told to Edward MacLysaght, D.Litt* (Dublin, 1969), p. 259.
10   Arthur Mitchell, *Labour in Irish politics 1890 – 1930* (Dublin, 1974), p. 31.

their energy into the revival of the Irish language and other cultural activism. These cultural nationalists were later to form the core of the Irish Local Government Officers Trade Union, which helped to make control of local government the key political victory of Dáil Éireann in the later War of Independence. Among their ranks were Ceannt's colleagues in the DMOA, Harry Nicholls and Thomas Gay, who were both IRB members, and the national union's first General Secretary, Éamonn Price. Nicholls and Price both fought in the Easter Rising of 1916.

Ceannt, though increasingly preoccupied by the Gaelic League from 1909, worked with a few others to overcome the general conservatism of the DMOA executive. Though Ceannt's proposals to merge the DMOA with first the County Council Officers Association and later the Civil Service Guild were defeated, other, more assertive proposals were approved. The DMOA executive prepared a statement of the grievances of the municipal officers, and formed a vigilance sub-committee to reply to any critical reports in the newspapers. The chief demand put forward by the DMOA was for the extension into local government of the practices then being established as the norm for the civil service; namely, entrance by examination and the filling of higher grades by promotion, practices which incidentally, were supported by the Local Government Board. Ceannt was such a strong advocate of this policy that he even favoured the expulsion from the DMOA of all officers who had not entered the service by examination and were seen to have secured their position through favouritism or patronage.

By the time of his resignation from the DMOA executive, Ceannt was moving into the leadership ranks of the innermost circle of revolutionary nationalism: the IRB. At the launch of the Irish Volunteers in November 1913 the provisional executive, which included Ceannt, was dominated by the IRB. Operational control of the Volunteers had effectively passed to the IRB while the Irish Volunteers' titular leader, Eoin MacNeill, was seen by the IRB as a figurehead. In September 1914 the IRB Supreme Council decided that the outbreak of the First World War created an opportunity for an insurrection. The IRB secretary Seán MacDiarmada and the treasurer Tom Clarke were directed to form a planning committee to examine the possibilities for such a project and to report back. Clarke and MacDiarmada held a meeting with a select group of leading political activists in the library of the Gaelic League in Parnell Square. Present were the Irish Citizen Army leaders James Connolly and William O'Brien; Major John MacBride (also a DMOA member); Arthur Griffith and Seán T. O'Kelly of Sinn Féin, and the Gaelic Leaguers and Volunteer leaders Patrick Pearse, Thomas MacDonagh, Joseph Plunkett and Éamonn Ceannt. At this meeting of the main figures of 'advanced' nationalism, the intent to stage an insurrection before the end of the war was agreed.

Following John Redmond's support for enlistment in the British Army and the split with his supporters (who then became known as the National Volunteers), the residual Irish Volunteer executive established a military headquarters staff in December 1914 with Ceannt as director of communications. Ceannt was also appointed commandant of the 4th Dublin Battalion Irish Volunteers. In January 1916 a meeting of the Supreme Council of the IRB was held secretly in Clontarf Town Hall and a military committee was appointed. Ceannt, Pearse and Plunkett, as Volunteer leaders, formed an advisory committee to counsel on the military planning of an insurrection. The military council regularly held its meetings in Ceannt's house. After its first meeting in his house in January 1916, Áine Ceannt recalled the tensions that existed in the lead up to the Rising and, in particular the fear on the part of the Volunteers that Connolly's Irish Citizen Army would act unilaterally and independently. She described what became known as the kidnapping of Connolly prior to his assimilation into the IRB Military Council;

> Shortly after that meeting James Connolly disappeared. I remember – I would say it would be about the end of the month of January or February, pay time in the Corporation – saying to Éamonn jocosely. 'Give me some money before the Rebellion starts'. Éamonn replied, 'It may start sooner that you expect'. Then he added, 'James Connolly has disappeared'. Connolly had instructed his next-in-command that if at any time he disappeared and did not turn up within three days the Citizen Army was to go out and take Dublin Castle. Éamonn said, 'We can't let the Citizen Army go out alone, if they go out we must go with them. Three of us are going to see Mallin to ask him to hold his hand'… Éamonn said, 'I am going now to see what was the result of the deputation that went over to the Citizen Army, asking them to wait a few days. In the meantime I have ordered all the officers of the Fourth Battalion to report here, and on my return it will be either to give them orders for ordinary manoeuvres, if the situation has cleared, or, alternatively, to tell them their places for the fight'. When he returned, at about half-past ten, he dismissed the men rather quickly and told me that Connolly had re-appeared.
>
> At the next meeting of the Military Council, held at our house, Connolly was present and was a member of that body from that day forward.[11]

11   Áine Ceannt, BMH WS 264.

Ceannt spent the next few months preparing for the Rising. All this work had to be done at lunch hour, in the evenings and at weekends as his job in the Corporation Rates Department kept him fully occupied during office hours. St Patrick's Day saw a mass mobilisation of the Irish Volunteers and Citizen Army in Dublin and Ceannt was on the reviewing platform. He arranged to visit and inspect the Guinness Brewery and the South Dublin Union as potential sites for the Rising. He concluded that the Brewery was not a suitable site for an insurrection as it was impossible to garrison and had no food. By contrast, the South Dublin Union had a ready supply of food.[12]

As commandant of the 4th Dublin Battalion, Ceannt was in charge of operations during the Rising at the South Dublin Union workhouse (some of which survives in the St James's Hospital complex). The South Dublin Union had a special strategic importance, because it could command access to the city from the Richmond and Islandbridge Barracks, from the army headquarters at the Royal Hospital Kilmainham and from Kingsbridge railway station. Earlier, Ceannt had asked his IRB colleague in the Corporation, Harry Nicholls, to prepare drawings and get prints of a map of the South Dublin Union. Nicholls was also a member of the DMOA and as a Civil Engineer in the Corporation had access to the relevant papers. According to Nicholls, 'he did not say what it was for and I did not ask him'.[13] Seizing the South Dublin Union, a hospital in the ownership of Dublin Corporation, was probably the most controversial aspect of the Rising as on the morning of Easter Monday 1916 it had 3,282 residents (though at the time they were called 'inmates'). It would have taken a large number of volunteers to control its vast labyrinth of streets, courts and alleys and the scattered residences, wards, sheds and halls. Because of the confusion arising from the countermanding orders of Easter Sunday, Ceannt had no more than sixty-five men, limiting his ability to seize full control of the facility, never mind other strategic premises in the area.

William Murphy, a storekeeper in the South Dublin Union, later recorded his recollection of the events of Easter week in the South Dublin Union;

> At about 12 noon I saw a group of Volunteers enter the grounds by the front gate under Commandant Ceannt and Liam Cosgrave. Ceannt asked me for supplies. He first asked me if I had any corned beef or bacon. I told him that I had not, but could give him supplies of anything else he required, such as tea, sugar, condensed milk, butter, etc. He handed me a written order

---

12   Gallagher, *16 Lives: Éamonn Ceannt*, pp 205-8.
13   Harry Nicholls, BMH WS 296.

for these provisions. I asked Cosgrave what it was all about. He said all the Volunteers were out today in arms against the British. Ceannt took up his headquarters in a building called the Orchard shed adjacent to Basin Lane. It was a wooden structure. Later in the day he changed his headquarters to the Nurses' Home. Before this the Volunteers erected barricades in front of the main gate on the inside and they dismantled the telephone.[14]

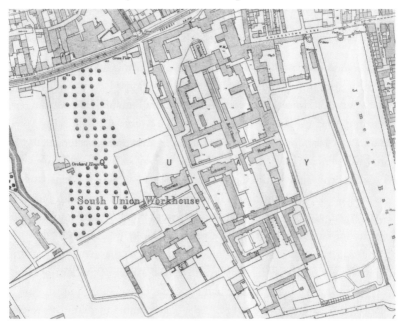

South Dublin Union, OS Sheet XVIII 65, 1908 (Courtesy of DCC Survey and Mapping Division)

Murphy was obliged to deliver supplies to the various departments of the Institution (even though, he recorded, it was not part of his normal job). He secured the agreement of the Volunteers. Accompanied by a work colleague, whom he subsequently married, he proceeded under cover of a white flag of truce and got through without being fired on. They had to give assurances that they would not pass on information to the other side. Before making a further round, they spoke with Ceannt. Murphy recalled that:

> Ceannt gave my wife a written message to take to the Commanding Officer of the British Forces within the Union asking for a cease fire for twenty minutes while they, the Volunteers, were collecting the dead and wounded. My wife delivered this note to the British Officer in command and his

---

14   William Murphy, BMH WS 352.

answer was 'No, they have shot our Major (Ramsay) and we will give them no quarter'. He tore up the note. My wife reported back to Ceannt and told him what the British Officer had said. The Volunteers cheered when they heard the news. By late on Monday night the British had occupied all buildings at the back of the institution while the Volunteers held all the buildings at the front overlooking James's St. until the surrender.[15]

The fighting in the South Dublin Union was intense. Buildings were often occupied by both the Volunteers and the British Army simultaneously, and the fighting was marked by sudden and bloody encounters, with hand-to-hand fighting in stairwells and corridors. A nurse, Margaret Keogh, who had remained with her patients, was killed in the fighting.[16] At night, the darkness added to the terror. Thursday saw a concentrated British attack as explosions shook the Volunteer held buildings. This attack was to provide cover for supplies of ammunition and escorting soldiers to reach the Royal Hospital in Kilmainham, proving the merits of Ceannt's judgement in choosing the South Dublin Union as a strategic location.[17] Ceannt and his second-in-command Cathal Brugha rallied their men by assuring them that the whole country was in insurrection and that the Germans had landed and were marching on Dublin. All the while the South Dublin Union staff tried to shelter the unfortunate residents, shepherding them from building to building as the fighting raged about them.

Unlike the rebels fighting in the city centre area, the Volunteers in the South Dublin Union were in a position to continue fighting beyond the end of Easter week and Ceannt had great difficulty coming to terms with the surrender order of Saturday 29 April. It was only after a meeting with Thomas MacDonagh, who brought Pearse's surrender order under a flag of truce, that the reality of the situation dawned and Ceannt acknowledged the surrender late in the morning of Sunday 30 April.

He was tried by court-martial in Richmond Barracks on 3-4 May. Ceannt's approach to the trial was that he would not deny anything that was proven, or admit what was not proven. He secured legal advice and sought to rebut the evidence of the only witness called by the prosecution, Major J. A. Armstrong, whom he cross-examined aggressively. He denied a charge of 'assisting the enemy' but refrained from using an argument he had prepared that the Republic had been

---

15   Ibid.
16   Gallagher, *Éamonn Ceannt*, p. 250.
17   Ibid., p. 268.

duly established, and that the British were the aggressors. Prosecuting counsel William Wylie described Ceannt as a 'brave man [who] showed no sign whatsoever of nervousness before the court. I would say, in fact, that he was the most dignified of any of the accused'.[18] He was found guilty and sentenced to death. However his wife was misled by an erroneous newspaper report that he had been sentenced to three years' penal servitude.[19] In his last statement, written on the night before his execution 'for the guidance of other Irish revolutionaries', he railed against the surrender, a view he shared with Tom Clarke who had been out-voted at a meeting of available leaders when the surrender order was agreed. Ceannt urged that in future there should be no treating with the enemy but a fight to the finish; 'I see nothing gained but grave disaster caused by the surrender which has marked the end of the Irish Insurrection of 1916'.[20] In one of his last notes to his wife, dated 7 May and written in Kilmainham Jail, he suggested that, in her now desperate circumstances, she should apply to the DMOA for a grant. Ceannt, aged 34, was shot at dawn on 8 May 1916 along with Michael Mallin and Seán Heuston.[21]

The reaction in the DMOA to the events of 1916 was muted, and almost shocked. The Executive recorded a vote of sympathy with Mrs. 'Kent' on the death of Mr. E. 'Kent', as well as on the death of another member, John MacBride. A proposal for a general fund for the relief of dependents in distress after the rebellion received no support. It was only at the December annual general meeting, following protests from the floor, that a fund was inaugurated to assist Ceannt's widow and children. Thomas Gay, the librarian from Capel Street Public Library, led these protests. Gay was an IRB member and later became a key figure in Michael Collins's intelligence network. He served for many years on the executive of the Irish Local Government Officers Trade Union.

For most local government officials their trade unionism was built on issues of pay and conditions and not on issues of nationality and freedom. Áine Ceannt, in her letter of thanks to the DMOA for their financial assistance acknowledged that the opinions of her late husband were not those of the vast majority of his fellow officials who were in the main, constitutional nationalists and in some cases, unionists.[22]

---

18   Barton, *From behind a closed door*, pp 188-9.
19   Áine Ceannt, BMH WS 264.
20   Piaras F. MacLoughlainn *Last words: letters and statements of the leaders executed after the 1916 rising at Easter 1916* (Dublin, 1996), p. 136.
21   Maguire, *Servants to the public*, p. 31.
22   Ibid., p. 39.

Mrs. Ceannt and her son Ronan,
(DCLA, Irish National Aid and Volunteer Dependents' Fund programme)

In Éamonn Ceannt's memory, the head office of IMPACT is named as Ceannt House.

John MacBride:
The making of the Major

Donal Fallon

John MacBride (DCLA, BOR Collection)

For many participants in the Irish revolutionary period, the Second Boer War (1899-1902) played an important role in their own political radicalisation. Seamus Robinson, a participant in the Soloheadbeg Ambush of 1919, recalled that:

> Heavens! What thrills we got out of that great struggle. Bonfires in the streets on the news of a Boer victory, complete disbelief in Boer reverses! The Irish Boer Brigade! How we wished we were old enough to be with them.[1]

In Ireland, the name of Major John MacBride became synonymous with the cause of the Boers, and his praises were sung in the nationalist press and at mass demonstrations. This chapter examines John MacBride's life from his middle class upbringing in Westport, his participation in the Second Boer War, his low-key return to Ireland following the disintegration of his marriage to nationalist

---

1   Seamus Robinson, BMH WS 1721.

campaigner Maud Gonne in the early twentieth century, and his subsequent employment with Dublin Corporation.

The development of a young Fenian:

John MacBride was born on 7 May 1868 in Westport, County Mayo. Writing years later in a brief autobiographical sketch penned for his legal team on the eve of his bitter and public separation from Maud Gonne in 1905, he recalled that:

> His great-grandfather took part in the insurrection of 1798; his grandfather followed the fortunes of the Young Irelanders who first struggled for the establishment of an Irish parliament and ultimately drifted into revolution; his father and uncles were members of the Irish Revolutionary Brotherhood of 1867 ... Irish patriotism was therefore, so to say, in his blood.[2]

If Irish patriotism was in his blood, it came from his maternal side. John MacBride's father, Patrick, was the captain of a merchant schooner who had settled in Westport and married into the Gill family in the mid-nineteenth century. Patrick was of Ulster-Scots Protestant heritage and hailed from Glenshesk in Antrim. Honoria Gill, John's mother was rooted in the county and the islands off its coast, and was one of nine children herself, from an Island More family. She was a much respected Westport shopkeeper, with relations who had devoted themselves to the Fenian cause. Éamon de Valera would praise her while speaking in the town at the unveiling of a plaque to John MacBride in 1963:

> There was a strong Fenian tradition in the Gill family. James Stephens, the Fenian, was a friend. Martin Gallagher who married a Gill was the Head Centre of the Fenians in Mayo; he made a spectacular escape to America and later took part in the Fenian invasion of Canada in 1870.[3]

When only thirty-five years of age, John MacBride's father Patrick died of typhus in 1868, leaving Honoria with both the raising of the family and the maintenance of the family business. With the help of her sons she continued to operate the commercially successful family wholesale grocery. John was the baby of the family, and at the time of his father's passing he was a mere six months old.

---

2   NLI, MS 29,817.
3   Éamon de Valera's 1963 Westport speech appeared in Westport Historical Society journal *Cathair Na Mart*, 10, no. 1 (1990).

All of the MacBride siblings were boys; all, to some degree, became involved with radical nationalism. Joseph, the eldest of the siblings, became a Sinn Féin TD in 1918 and remained active in Irish politics throughout his life, supporting the new Irish Free State following the Anglo-Irish Treaty of 1921. It is important to note there was no family consensus on that issue: Joseph's nephew - and Major MacBride's son - Seán, took up arms against that state as an Anti-Treaty IRA volunteer during the Civil War. Another brother, Anthony, became an important figure in the Irish republican movement in London, establishing himself as a medical doctor there before later returning to Ireland where he continued his medical career. He was a committed Fenian in his own right and an active member of the Amnesty Association in the late nineteenth century, a body which campaigned for the rights of imprisoned Fenians in British prisons. John's third brother, Francis, emigrated to Australia, while Patrick eventually assumed control of the family business in Westport.

John was initially educated by the Christian Brothers in Westport, before continuing his studies in the middle class surroundings of St Malachy's College, Belfast. After he graduated, employment opportunities came via his family connections, who helped arrange an apprenticeship for him with John Fitzgibbon, a draper based in Castlerea, County Roscommon. MacBride later claimed that as a young man of fifteen he 'took an oath to do my best to establish a free and independent Irish nation', and that by the time he had arrived in the capital he was 'associated with the party known as Advanced Nationalists.'[4] The oath he referenced was the famous Fenian Oath of the Irish Republican Brotherhood, the republican secret society. Michael J. Cassidy, a native of Castlerea and a contemporary of MacBride, would comment decades later that:

> I remember the late Mr. Fitzgibbon telling me during the Boer War that MacBride was an extreme nationalist when he worked as an apprentice in his shop. When I went to serve my time in Castlerea I met from time to time a number of the old Fenians and heard from them that MacBride, during his apprenticeship years, was very active organising the Brotherhood.[5]

MacBride spent some time working for Fitzgibbon in Castlerea, though by his own admission 'not finding that occupation congenial I left it and went back to St Malachy's for another year. After leaving St Malachy's I entered into the

---

4   NLI, MS 29,817.
5   Quoted in Owen Hughes, 'Major John MacBride', *Cathair Na Mart*, 6. No.1 (1986).

employment of Hugh Moore.'[6] Moore maintained a wholesale druggists and grocery in Dublin, and MacBride would spend several years with the firm, on and off. The move to Dublin offered MacBride new chances to engage with nationalist political organisations which he appears to have availed of. Certainly, he involved himself with a number of cultural nationalist bodies, like the Young Ireland Society (YIS), and the presence of a young MacBride is noted in its minute books. The authorities regarded the YIS as a front for the IRB, and its premises were raided by the authorities on the day after they opened, indicating that the authorities were deeply troubled by its existence.[7]

A central figure in such movements, and a man who would have an enormous impact on the young John MacBride, was the veteran Fenian John O'Leary. To a detective of Dublin Castle, O'Leary was 'an old crank full of whims and honesty',[8] but Roy Foster has suggested that for many idealistic young participants in the nationalist movements of the day, O'Leary represented 'a voice from the heroic past'.[9] In his autobiography, William Butler Yeats recalled of O'Leary that 'he had the moral genius that moves all young people and move them the more if they are repelled by those who have strict opinions and yet have lived commonplace lives'.[10] Years later MacBride would carry O'Leary's coffin at his funeral in Dublin's Glasnevin Cemetery in 1907.

The late nineteenth century brought years of stagnation for the Fenian movement, leading to turbulence as rival factions sought to revitalise and reclaim the Fenian tradition. MacBride would join the Irish National Alliance (INA) split in 1895, essentially a short-lived offshoot of the Irish Republican Brotherhood. It has been described as 'a radical organisation comprised of old Clan na Gael renegades, traditionalist Fenians, a resurrected cabal of Invincibles, and a London-centered association of regular IRB dissidents.'[11] MacBride recalled that he travelled as a delegate from Ireland to the Irish National Alliance Convention held in Chicago in 1895. One American newspaper noted that the following motion was 'submitted and met with instantaneous approval at the hands of the convention':

6   NLI, MS 29,817.
7   Owen McGee, *The IRB: The Irish Republican Brotherhood from the Land League to Sinn Féin* (Dublin, 2005), p. 85.
8   Roy Foster, *W. B. Yeats: a life, 1: the apprentice mage 1865–1914* (Oxford, 1997), p. 43.
9   Ibid.
10   William Butler Yeats, *Autobiographies* (Dublin, 1955 edition), p. 95.
11   Caoimhe Nic Dháibhéid, This is a case in which Irish national considerations must be taken into account: the breakdown of the MacBride-Gonne marriage, 1904-1908, *Irish Historical Studies*, xxxvii, no. 146 (November 2010).

That this convention recommends the formation of military companies wherever practicable, in order to foster and preserve the military spirit of the Irish race and to be prepared for action in the hour of England's difficulty.[12]

Afterwards a representative of the Irish National Alliance informed the press that 'the new organisation will concentrate the efforts of the Irish race and unite the Irish people all over the world for one object – Irish independence. It will become the ally of any power with which England may become involved, and will aid any such power with men and money in order to weaken England's prestige and curb her arrogance.'[13]

While the Alliance would ultimately be short-lived, its ideological approach of supporting those beyond Ireland's shores at war with England is certainly something which may have influenced John MacBride to go to South Africa. John's brother, Joseph, also appears to have involved himself in the activities of the Irish National Alliance. An 1896 police report on him noted that his mother 'is a grocer and publican in the town of Westport, and also deals in dynamite detonators. Until recently MacBride never took an active part in Secret Society work. He is now believed to be actively engaged in furthering the Irish National Alliance.'[14]

MacBride's South African journey:

J. J. O'Kelly, who knew the young MacBride, recalled that 'my feeling now is that John was a young chemist, and that the reason he went to Africa was that he did not care about Dublin and thought he would like to go abroad. I feel sure he told me more than once, but it made no lodgement in my memory.'[15] This seems at odds with the level of political activism MacBride involved himself with in Dublin, by actively participating in both cultural nationalist organisations and political separatist bodies. What we know for certain is that the young John MacBride left Dublin in 1896 and travelled to South Africa. Recalling the reasons for his own migration, MacBride would claim that 'shortly after the Jameson Raid, I resolved to go to the South African Republic as I knew that England had her mind made up to take the country, and I wanted to organise my countrymen there, so as to be in a position to strike a blow at England's power abroad when we could not, unfortunately, do so at home.'[16] The Jameson Raid that MacBride referenced was a disastrous invasion of the Transvaal in 1895, launched on the orders of Cecil

12 *Los Angeles Herald*, 27 Sept. 1895.
13 *Skibbereen Eagle*, 26 Oct. 1895.
14 Quoted in Anthony J. Jordan, 'Joseph MacBride 1860–1938', *Cathair na Mart*, 30 (2012).
15 J. J. O'Kelly, BMH WS 384.
16 NLI, MS 22,817.

Rhodes, a British mining magnate and Prime Minister of the British Cape Colony with imperial ambitions in the region.

It is important to note that there were two separate 'Boer Wars', pitting the British Empire against the Boer population of the region. The word 'Boer' is Afrikaans for farmer, and the Boers were descendent of Dutch settlers in the region. The Boers would ultimately establish the Orange Free State, or *Oranje-Vrystaat* in 1854, while the South African Republic was established in 1856.

The First Boer War was fought from 1880–1881, as the Boers of the Transvaal revolted against an earlier British annexation, which was deeply resented. In Afrikaans, the war is known as the *Eerste Vryheidsoorlog*, meaning the 'First Freedom War'. The conflict ultimately resulted in the British agreeing to complete Boer self-government in the Transvaal, though under British suzerainty. In Ireland, the first Boer War received very significant coverage in the nationalist press. In the United States, *The Irish World* proclaimed that the Irish should give thanks to God, as the Boers were 'fighting the battle of Ireland, although they don't know it.'[17]

Donal P. McCracken has noted that while there was no mass Irish migration to South Africa, Dublin Castle was aware from the mid-1890s that some 'advanced Irish nationalists' were making for the Transvaal. According to his research, 'by 1896 there were about 1,000 Irish living in the mining settlement of Johannesburg as well as others in Pretoria and in more far-flung corps, such as Middelburg.'[18] MacBride himself would later recall 'working on the Robinson Gold Mine outside Johannesburg and during my spare hours devoting my time, energy and money to organising my countrymen.'[19]

Young Irish nationalists arriving in the Transvaal in the late 1890s, such as the nineteen year old Thomas Byrne who would later participate in the Easter Rising, recalled the importance of MacBride to their small community. Byrne claimed MacBride to be 'the only outstanding Irishman in the Transvaal at this time.'[20] MacBride's name began to appear in nationalist newspapers in Ireland not long after he first arrived in South Africa. In *The Nation*, an influential Irish nationalist newspaper which had been founded by prominent Young Irelanders including Thomas Davis, it was reported in October 1896 that the Irish National Amnesty Association learned with 'extreme pleasure' that John MacBride, 'until lately an

---

17   Quoted in Joseph H. Lehmann, *The First Boer War* (London, 1972), p. 263.
18   Donal P. McCracken, 'MacBride's Brigade in the Anglo-Boer War', *History Ireland*, 8, issue 1, (2008) pp 26-9.
19   NLI, MS 22,817.
20   Thomas Byrne, BMH WS 564.

EN IRLANDE
Manifestation contre M. Chamberlain

Pro-Boer demonstrators at College Green, protesting the awarding of an Honorary Degree to Joseph Chamberlain. Demonstrations in sympathy with the Boers were commonplace during the conflict. (DCLA, BOR Collection)

MacBride and others successfully organised commemorative events in Johannesburg in 1898 to mark the centenary of the United Irishmen's rebellion. A commemorative march through Johannesburg was greeted with enthusiasm not only by Irish exiles but by other *Uitlanders*, the term of choice for foreigners in the Transvaal. At a commemorative banquet to the memory of Theobald Wolfe Tone and other United Irish leaders, the Boer general Ben Viljoen was in attendance. He would later tell his people to put their faith 'in God and the Mauser', something they got the chance to do the following year.

---

21   *The Nation*, 10 Oct. 1896.

The Second Boer War

The Second Boer War formally broke out on 11 October 1899, following an ultimatum issued two days earlier to the British government by Paul Kruger, President of the South African Republic. Kruger had given the British 48 hours to withdraw from the borders of both Boer Republics, stating that failure to comply would result in a declaration of war. The weeks and months leading up to this had seen heightened tensions in the region, and the emergence of a movement in sympathy with the Boer cause in Ireland, with a crowd of more than 20,000 gathering at Beresford Place in early October 1899. At that meeting, a letter was read from the Mayor of Kilkenny, who proposed that two maxim guns be sent to the Boers with which they could defend themselves. One could be called 'Parnell', and the other 'Wolfe Tone'.[22]

For MacBride and others in the Transvaal, active participation in the conflict was the only form of solidarity worth offering. Michael Davitt, the veteran political leader of the Land League and a committed radical who had taken the Fenian Oath himself, resigned his seat in Westminster in protest at British aggression in the Transvaal, and later visited South Africa. In his account of the Second Boer War, Davitt claimed that:

> The Irish Brigade was organised in Johannesburg chiefly by the exertions of Mr. John MacBride, a native of Mayo, who was at the time employed as assayer in one of the Rand mines. He was warmly supported by other prominent Irishmen on the Rand. A manifesto was issued appealing to Irishmen to remember England's manifold infamies against their own country, and on this account to volunteer the more readily to fight against a common enemy for the defence of Boer freedom.[23]

By September 1899 a proposal for an Irish Transvaal Brigade, numbering 700, was put to the Boer government and accepted. There had been earlier proposals to assemble an Irish force in readiness for conflict, though such offers had been declined. MacBride later wrote of the formation of the Irish Brigade that 'I never claimed to have done more than one man's part. The fact that Mr. Sol Gillingham came first to me with private news of the impending war, and a hint to get the Irish Nationalists together, and that the word, therefore, went around from me, I suppose, gave my name some prominence in the work.'[24] The Sol Gillingham

---

22   Donal P. McCracken, *Forgotten protest: Ireland and the Anglo-Boer war* (Belfast, 2003), p. 42.
23   Michael Davitt, *The Boer fight for freedom* (New York, 1902), p. 319.
24   *Freeman's Journal*, 5 Jan. 1907.

MacBride referred to was an important figure in the Transvaal, a man whom the London-based Fenian leader Mark Ryan recalled that 'he was a big businessman in Pretoria, and, when trouble was developing between the Boer Republic and England, he acted as agent for Kruger in London.'[25]

In Ireland, this body of men became known as MacBride's Brigade, thanks in no small part to the propaganda work of Arthur Griffith's *United Irishman*, which claimed at one point that as many as 1,700 men were actively involved.[26] Griffith had spent some time in South Africa, arriving there early in 1897, and editing a newspaper in Middleburg before finding dangerous work in the mines, not like MacBride. The newspaper published ballads and poems loaded with praise for MacBride, for example:

> In far-off Africa today the English fly dismayed
> Before the flag of green and gold borne by MacBride's Brigade.
> With guns and bayonets in their hands, their Irish flag on high
> As down they swept on England's ranks out rang their battle-cry:
> Revenge! Remember 98! And how our fathers died!
> We'll pay the English back today, cried fearless John MacBride.[27]

In reality, the Irish Brigade was led by John Blake, an Irish American native of Missouri. Blake was a war veteran, who had served in the American armed forces during the Apache Wars, a series of armed confrontations between American armed forces and Native American Apache nations fought in the Southwest between the late 1840s and 1886. Blake had graduated from the U.S. Military Academy at West Point in 1875, and was assigned to the 6th U.S. Cavalry, serving under the famed General Wilcox, who had served as a general in the Union Army during the American Civil War. Blake later penned an exciting, albeit propagandistic, account of the Second Boer War. He had arrived in South Africa shortly before the Jameson Raid, and Michael Davitt noted that he had 'a slight suggestion of Buffalo Bill in his general appearances and bearing.'[28]

How Irish was the Irish Brigade? Certainly, it was a diverse force. Of the 300 men who formed its backbone, it has been noted that they included 'a Catholic chaplain, some Gaelic speakers and about forty Protestants. There were two sets of fathers and sons. Only a few men, however, had fighting experience.'[29] MacBride himself

25   Mark Ryan, *Fenian memories* (Dublin, 1945), p. 187.
26   Robert Kee, *The green flag: a history of Irish Nationalism* (London, 2000), p. 444.
27   Ibid., p. 455.
28   Davitt, *The Boer fight for freedom*, p. 319.
29   McCracken, 'MacBride's Brigade', *History Ireland*.

recalled that the body included a number of Frenchmen, as well as a number of Americans. A second so-called Irish Brigade would enter the war at a later stage, led by Colonel Arthur Lynch, who would later stand trial for his actions. Born in Victoria, Australia, Lynch was a journalist who had been Paris correspondent of the London *Daily Mail* at the time war broke out in South Africa. He had travelled there as a war correspondent, but felt an urge to fight alongside the Boers. Ironically, he would later volunteer for the British armed forces during the First World War, and raise a private 10th Battalion of the Royal Munster Fusiliers to fight in it. Lynch's force in South Africa had small numbers of native Irishmen in its ranks, consisting largely of a mix of European fighters. One member of Blake's force described Lynch's force colourfully as 'fifty or sixty soreheads, greasers, half-breeds and dagos.'[30]

MacBride and the men he served with fought at some of the bloodiest battles of the conflict. At the Battle of Dundee, the men of the Irish Brigade encountered the Royal Dublin Fusiliers and the Irish Fusiliers, an ironic reminder that thousands of Irishmen were fighting in the conflict in the uniforms of British soldiers. MacBride claimed that soldiers from these Irish regiments 'were driven into a cattle-kraal and compelled to surrender. A number of the prisoners had been in school in Ireland with members of the Brigade, who naturally could not help feeling sad and humiliated at seeing their own countrymen and former schoolmates in such a humiliating position. Blake stated in his memoir that 'of the 196 Irishmen captured, eighty-five begged to join the Irish Brigade and fight with the Boers ... When first captured, all were half scared to death and the first thing they wished to know was whether the Boers would shoot them or not.'[31]

The military engagements of the Irish Brigade have been well documented.[32] While the Boers did succeed in achieving a number of stunning and unexpected victories in the early stages of the conflict, the tide gradually turned in favour of the British, who succeeded in lifting the Boer siege of Ladysmith, a key garrison town where the Irish Brigade were fighting, and in rooting Boer forces from many other areas of war. To MacBride, this period represented a new phase in the conflict, with the seemingly unconquerable Boers seeing 'darker days, bringing test and trial of every man in the splendid volunteer army.'[33] As the war turned, the Boers adopted guerrilla tactics, with MacBride recalling:

30   McCracken, *Forgotten protest*, p. 127.
31   John Blake, *A West Pointer with the Boers* (Boston, 1903), pp 64–5.
32   See Donal P. McCracken. *'MacBride's Brigade: Irish commandos in the Anglo-Boer War'* (Dublin 1999)
33   *Freeman's Journal*, 29 July 1907.

It will be easily understood that, especially at the closing stages of the war, men on foot were useless to the Boer army. The tactics of General Botha and his colleagues at that time were entirely in favour of rapid movements from point to point, harassing the enemy here today, and twenty miles off tomorrow, and in such circumstances we would be less an aid than an encumbrance.[34]

In September 1900, the Boer government provided a steamboat to America for the Brigade's subsequent departure, with MacBride recalling that they 'paid the passage of the men to America and gave each a present of a small sum of money.'[35] Just prior to leaving South Africa, MacBride received a letter of deep thanks from General Louis Botha, expressing his sincere gratitude for the role the Irishmen had played in the conflict. Botha stated:

> Hereby we have much pleasure in expressing our deepest gratitude to you and the Irish Brigade for all the military services rendered to us during the past twelve months, in which we were engaged in a war against Britain. We appreciated very highly the assistance which you have so sincerely rendered us during the war: and we wish you and your men a hearty farewell on your return voyage.[36]

While Britain ultimately succeeded in the annexing of the two Boer Republics, the cost of the conflict was great, both in terms of lives lost and finances. MacBride departed for Paris, where he received something of a hero's reception. His arrival in Paris in the aftermath of the Boer War marked his first encounters with Maud Gonne, the woman he later married.

After South Africa:

On arrival in Paris, MacBride encountered many familiar faces in the Gare de Lyon train station, including those of family members and his friend Arthur Griffith, but there was also a new face, in the form of the nationalist campaigner Maud Gonne. She recalled the first time she set eyes on Major MacBride, remembering 'a wiry, soldierly-looking man with red hair and skin burnt brick-red by the South African sun.'[37] She was clearly fascinated by a man who had physically taken the fight to

---

34   Ibid.
35   NLI, MS 29,817.
36   Quoted in Anthony J. Jordan, *Major John MacBride, 1865–1916: MacDonagh and MacBride and Connolly and Pearse* (Westport Historical Society, 1991), p. 45.
37   Maud Gonne MacBride, *A servant of the queen* (Gerrard's Cross, 1994), p. 308.

the British Empire, remembering that 'we sat up all night talking. MacBride said he had come back hoping there would be something doing in Ireland.'[38]

While MacBride and Gonne were both radical separatists, in many ways they were born worlds apart. The daughter of a British Colonel who had been presented as a debutante at Dublin Castle, her privileged upbringing was very different to that of the middle class MacBride. Unable to return to Ireland following his participation in the war for fear of arrest, MacBride instead sailed for the United States in December 1900 after his brief sojourn in Paris, where he lectured to sizeable Irish American audiences on the conflict. When he was interviewed at the Vanderbilt Hotel following his arrival in New York he made it clear to the press that while Winston Churchill and others were adamant that the Boers were a spent force, MacBride's view was that 'the Boers will fight just as long as there is a man, woman or child alive.'[39]

Maud Gonne, billed as 'Ireland's Joan of Arc', joined MacBride on his American speaking tour. She was a veteran of the circuit, having travelled to the United States during the conflict when the Irish Brigade was in action, lecturing audiences on the parallels between their cause and the cause of Ireland. MacBride was certainly taken by Gonne's abilities. Soon after her arrival he wrote to his beloved Honoria that 'Miss Gonne astonishes me the way in which she can stand the knocking about. For a woman it is wonderful.'[40]

Maud Gonne claimed that MacBride proposed to her in the United States, though he categorically denied this later, commenting to his legal team during his divorce case that:

> I was not anxious for the marriage as I knew we were not suited for one another … Then at last moved by her tears and thinking I was doing good for my country and good for herself I consented to marry her. It was a foolish thing to do. I gave her a name that was free from stain or reproach and she was unable to appreciate it once she had succeeded in inducing me to marry her.[41]

Maud Gonne and John MacBride were married on 21 February 1903, in the most unlikely of locations. A civil ceremony at the British Embassy in Paris was followed by marriage rites at the Church of Saint-Honoré d'Elyau. Of his incongruous

---

38   Ibid.
39   Nancy Cardozo, *Maud Gonne: lucky eyes and a high heart* (New York, 1990), p. 204.
40   Ibid.
41   NLI, MS 29,817.

embassy visit, MacBride remembered that: 'We had to go to the British Consulate to have the civil ceremony performed and I kept my hand on my revolver while the deed was being done as I was under the British flag while there and I was not going to allow them any tricks.'[42]

In July 1904, it was noted curiously in John MacBride's Dublin Castle intelligence file that:

> I beg to report that I have received information from a reliable source that Major John McBride is about to leave Paris, and is proceeding to the Seat of the Japan and Russian war – ostensibly as a war correspondent.[43]

In reality, by this time MacBride's relationship was crumbling around itself, and little did intelligence gatherers know that they would soon be following him on the streets of Dublin once again. MacBride arrived in Dublin prior to the commencement of the separation case in Paris, and from that point onwards clearly moved freely between Dublin, Westport and all other places. The marriage of Gonne and MacBride was deeply unhappy. Allegations of drunkenness, violence and sexual impropriety were later levelled against MacBride, though crucially, it was drunkenness alone that was found against him in court when the marriage was finally dissolved. MacBride meanwhile was angered by the emergence of evidence of Maud Gonne's affair with married French politician Lucien Millevoye years before their relationship, and was uneasy with her close relationship with the poet W. B. Yeats.

If there was any joy for both participants in the relationship, it was the birth of their son, Jean Seágan, later Seán MacBride. He was born on 26 January 1904, and his birth received considerable international attention. The *New York Sun* noted that the couple expressed hope little Seán would 'be the first president of the Irish Republic.'[44]

In the years following McBride's return to Ireland, he lodged primarily with Fred Allan, a veteran IRB member. In the 1911 Census for example, MacBride is listed as a boarder at Allan's household in Spencer Villas, Glenageary. Allan was born in 1861 into a politically unionist Methodist family, though he joined the IRB in 1880 and by 1883 was secretary of the brotherhood in Leinster. Allan was also a

---

42   Sinéad McCoole, *Easter widows: seven Irish women who lived in the shadow of the 1916 Rising* (Dublin, 2014), p. 49.
43   Dublin Castle Special Branch Files (NAI, CO904/208/258).
44   *Nenagh News*, 7 May 1904.

significant figure within Dublin Corporation, having served as secretary to the Lord Mayor of Dublin at the turn of the century. He later held a number of positions in the body, including that of secretary of Dublin Corporation's Electric Light Company in 1901. Dublin Corporation had become an increasingly nationalist body from the late nineteenth century onwards. In 1885, the Corporation voted by forty-one votes to seventeen not to take part in welcoming the Prince of Wales to Ireland, and indeed the 1903 royal visit to Dublin had included no loyal address from Dublin Corporation.

It was perhaps because of the nationalist ethos of the Corporation that MacBride became hopeful of gaining employment there. The authorities seem to have believed that the plan in nationalist circles was for MacBride to stand for election to Dublin Corporation. It was discovered, however, that it would be invalid for him to contest an election. An intelligence report in January 1905 noted that:

> It was at first intended that he should be nominated for municipal honours as a National Council candidate but it was discovered that his nomination would be invalid in so much as his name does not appear on the Burgess roll. He applied for a position in at least two city firms to the managers of which he had been previously known but in each case he was met with a prompt refusal.[45]

The report optimistically noted that he 'is looking for a situation under the Dublin Corporation and that when this has been secured very little will be again heard of him.'[46] Evidently, the authorities believed that if MacBride secured employment he would fade into obscurity.

In time, he did finally find work via Dublin Corporation. In 1908, it was reported in the press that John MacBride had become its Petroleum Inspector.[47] Later, he obtained the position of Assistant Water Bailiff and by January 1911 he had become the city Water Bailiff. Seán T. O'Kelly, himself a member of the Corporation at the time, remembered that 'this post had been secured for him through the influence of Alderman Tom Kelly, Councillor P. T. Daly and myself.'[48] Daly, a Dubliner by birth, had been a member of James Connolly's short-lived Irish Socialist Republican Party, and by the early twentieth century had become a senior figure in the IRB. He was elected to Dublin Corporation in 1903. That MacBride acquired

---

45 Ibid.
46 Ibid.
47 *Irish Independent*, 19 Oct, 1908.
48 Seán T. O'Kelly, BMH WS 1765.

his position in the Corporation owing to his political affiliations and actions seems highly likely, both from O'Kelly's recollections and police intelligence.

John McBride's ferry inspection log, week to the 1st April 1916 (DCLA)

Some years later, W. B. Yeats's sister Lily, when writing to her brother, joked that 'it must have been some humourist who got him the post of water bailiff to the corporation'[49]; presumably a reference to MacBride's drinking during his marriage. Allegations of drunkenness had been levelled against him by Gonne's legal team during the bitter separation, and Yeats was aware of this through his own correspondence. The job with the Corporation evidently gave MacBride a sense of purpose, as was clear in the recollections of Gearoid Ua h-Uallacháin (Gary Holohan), a prominent veteran of Na Fianna Éireann. He remembered MacBride's daily journey to the Corporation:

> I used to see Major MacBride every morning walking to his office. He always dressed smartly, and carried his umbrella under his arm like a walking stick or a rifle. When he would be passing the works I would say to Tom Kane, an ex-British soldier, 'There is the man who made you run in Africa', and Kane would boil

---

49   R. F. Foster, *The Irish story: telling tales and making it up in Ireland* (Oxford, 2001), p. 63.

with temper. Poor Tom Kane was blown up in the First World War.[50]

John MacBride remained an employee of Dublin Corporation until the time of his execution. While he did not join the Irish Volunteers, he remained a committed IRB man, briefly serving on its Supreme Council in 1911. A central part of MacBride's appeal to younger nationalists, and what he would repeatedly find himself lecturing on, was his time in South Africa. While the Irish Brigade had no significant impact on the outcome of the war in the Transvaal, they did inspire a generation of separatist nationalists at home.

---

50   Gearoid Ua h-Uallacháin, BMH WS 336.

'Siege mentalities':
the occupation
of Jacob's factory Easter 1916

Séamas Ó Maitiú

Major John McBride, (DCLA, BOR Collection)

It is unclear precisely how Major John MacBride ended up with the insurgents who occupied Jacob's biscuit factory in 1916. He was not a member of the Irish Volunteers, although he was a friend of many of those high up in the movement.[1] At Easter 1916 MacBride was lodging, as he had been for some years, with Frederick Allan of Dublin Corporation in Glenageary, County Dublin. John's brother, Anthony, a doctor in Castlebar, was to be married on the Wednesday of Easter Week and John was to be his best man. Anthony was to meet John for lunch in the Wicklow Hotel on Easter Monday, no doubt to discuss the forthcoming nuptials.[2]

By this it appears that MacBride had no exact knowledge beforehand of the Easter Week plans for an insurrection. He was seen in Thomas Clarke's shop in what is now Parnell Street, and in the headquarters of the first battalion of the Volunteers

---

1   Anthony Jordan, 'How Major John MacBride became involved in the 1916 Rising' in *Cathair na Mart: Journal of the Westport Historical Society* (2001), pp 45-50; Donal Fallon, *16 Lives: John MacBride* (Dublin, 2015), p. 231.
2   Brian Barton, *The secret court martial records of the Easter rising* (Port Stroud, 2010), p. 221.

on Easter Sunday morning. He may well have learnt that an insurrection was planned for Easter Sunday, and of its subsequent cancellation but was unaware that some intended to go ahead with a Rising the following day.

Thomas Clarke, outside his shop at 75 Parnell Street (DCLA, BOR Collection).

According to Frederick Allan's wife, Clara, MacBride left his lodgings for the appointment with his brother on Monday morning dressed in civilian clothes, stating that he would be back at around five or six o'clock. MacBride himself recounted that:

> In waiting around town I went up as far as St Stephen's Green and there I saw a band of Irish volunteers. I knew some of the members personally and the Commander told me that an Irish republic was virtually proclaimed ... Although I had no previous connection with the Irish volunteers I considered it my duty to join them.[3]

MacBride's appearance among the insurgents on the Sunday morning probably signalled a willingness to take part in any hostilities that might break out; it is not surprising that while he was on his way to meet his brother on Monday morning at least one effort was made to contact him. At 11.15 a.m. Seán MacDiarmada

---

3   Ibid., p. 222.

despatched a boy courier to the home of Ignatius Callender, who served under MacBride in Dublin Corporation, and who was to forward it to MacBride. [4]

Callender set off for 4 John Rogerson's Quay, MacBride's office as water bailiff for the Corporation on the 'off-chance' that he would find him there. MacBride was often there at weekends recording details of shipping activity on the quays. On the way Callender met Seán Heuston who was mobilising a small number of his men. Callender was requested to fall in. However, after showing Heuston the letter he was told to get it to MacBride if at all possible. Callender was disappointed to find that MacBride was not at the office. Neither he nor the caretaker at Rogerson's Quay knew MacBride's home address. Callender then decided to contact his brother John, an assistant to MacBride in the Corporation who had often been at MacBride's lodgings at Glenageary and so knew its location. He found his brother near the Mendicity Institute at Ussher's Quay and he agreed to take the letter to MacBride.

MacBride may have received word of the mobilisation through another channel. Molly Reynolds, whose father, John, and brother, Percy, were in the Volunteers, states that her family were mobilised:

> early at Easter Monday morning – about 5 or 6 a.m. – he [her father] got mobilisation orders and my brother Percy and I set out to carry them out. At that time we were living at the North Strand and Percy went citywards; among those whom he mobilised was Major Seán McBride [sic] 'by wire'. [5]

Volunteer Thomas Pugh at St Stephen's Green on Monday morning saw MacBride come along the street with John Reynolds. So it is possible that the Reynolds family got a message to MacBride. Pugh saw Reynolds and MacBride shake hands and part, Reynolds for the GPO, as it transpired. [6]

MacBride's natty civilian attire was noted by many. His immaculate blue suit, malacca cane and cigar were commented on; some even mention spats. Michael J. Molloy, one of the printers of the 1916 proclamation, had formed up under Captain Tom Hunter at St Stephen's Green awaiting orders and later recalled that 'A short time later a man came along wearing a large swinging cloak. "What are you standing here for? Get those men in their places." I learnt later that he was the

---

4   BMH WS 923, p. 4.
5   BMH WS 195, p. 4.
6   BMH WS 397, p, 4.

late Major McBride. He called us to attention. We then moved off.'[7] MacBride was now part of a detachment largely manned by the members of the 2nd Battalion of the Irish Volunteers under Thomas MacDonagh heading for Jacob's biscuit factory. They found themselves some distance from their home base on the north side of the city and their depot at Fr Mathew Park.[8]

The consequences of Eoin MacNeill's countermanding order were clearly seen. Most accounts put the numbers at the initial attack on Jacob's at less than a hundred. Vincent (Vinnie) Byrne put it at about ninety. At manoeuvres the week before Peadar Kearney reckoned that B Company alone had numbered close to two hundred.[9] The wide gaps in the ranks were a cause of concern. Michael Walker was at St Stephen's Green for about an hour and a half when he was approached by Dick McKee who asked him to cycle to Fr Matthew Park to see where the other companies were (he and his brother were champion cyclists). When Walker got there he saw Frank Henderson and a 'couple hundred men'. Walker asked Henderson why he had not gone to the Green and was told that there was a transport problem. He told him to commandeer cars, presumably to transport his men to the Green, and he agreed. Walker then returned to the Green but could not locate his colleagues. A civilian told him to try Jacob's.[10]

General view of Jacob's biscuit factory (W.& R Jacobs' archives, DCLA)

---

7   BMH WS 716, pp 5-6.
8   Charles Townshend, *Easter 1916: the Irish rebellion* (London, 1906), p. 179.
9   BMH WS 432, p. 2.
10   BMH WS 139, p. 4.

In the meantime Thomas MacDonagh and his men began to move down Cuffe Street towards Jacob's. According to John MacDonagh, Thomas's brother, MacBride was an object of curiosity once again:

> At twelve exactly, we set out to take up position in Jacob's biscuit factory in Peter Street. Tom asked me to march in front with him and, on the other side of him, marched an alert man well dressed in a blue suit, carrying a cane and smoking a cigar. I whispered to Tom, asking who he was, and he told me 'That is Major John MacBride.' We were followed by a lot of well-known G-men (detectives). Prominent among them was Hoey, who was afterwards shot in the street during the Black and Tan period. As we marched through Cuffe Street and Mercer's Street the separation women of the Irish soldiers in the British army became hysterical in their abuse of us. The mildest of their remarks was, 'Go out and fight the Germans'.[11]

The rather unexpected arrival of MacBride was greatly welcomed by Thomas MacDonagh and he was appointed second in command. Eily O'Hanrahan was given a message to this effect to bring to Pearse in the GPO. She was the sister of Michael O'Hanrahan, who up to this point was second in command and was now demoted behind MacBride.[12]

As it was a Bank Holiday there was only a small number of maintenance workers, such as fitters, boilermen and chimney sweeps, in Jacob's that morning. Also on duty was caretaker, Thomas Orr, and watchman, Henry Fitzgerald, no doubt enjoying a quiet respite from the normal hustle and bustle of up to three thousand workers.[13] There is some confusion as to how the attackers entered the factory. The building was so big – comprising a huge block fronting four separate streets – that more than one entry may have been made. According to Michael Molloy, when the rebels arrived at Jacob's some began to enter the building, while others waited in Bishop Street opposite the factory door for the arrival of a cab. It shortly came up laden with rifles and ammunition. Beside the driver was Pat Sweeny, an officer of F Company, 2nd Battalion, who began to unload the cargo.[14]

Other eye-witnesses recalled that a window about six feet from the ground was broken and the rebels climbed in. As one Volunteer entered, his rifle went off and

---

11   BMH WS 532, pp 9-10.
12   BMH WS 270, p. 9.
13   Séamas Ó Maitiú, *W. & R. Jacob: 150 years of Irish biscuit making* (Dublin, 2001), p. 41.
14   BMH WS 716, p. 6.

shot a hole in the ceiling. MacBride, who was already inside and helping others in, told them to be more careful, as he picked powder falling from the ceiling from his moustache. Other windows were also smashed on the orders of Tom Hunter.[15]

Doors on other sides of the huge building were now attacked. Vinnie Byrne saw a volunteer called Mick McDonnell with a big axe attacking the wicket gate on Peter Street. A very officious DMP man refused to leave the street when ordered to by Commandant MacDonagh. He was told that he would be shot if he did not immediately desist. John whispered to his brother recommending patience. Thomas replied that it might be necessary to shoot some of these policemen and detectives to show that they were at war.[16]

Thomas McDonagh (DCLA, BOR Collection)

Having gained entry to the factory Thomas Pugh recalled Hunter lining them up and telling them that they were no longer the Irish Volunteers but the Irish Republican Army. MacDonagh gave a speech and read the proclamation, accompanied by a cry of 'Long live the Republic' from MacBride.[17]

When Thomas Orr, the Jacob's caretaker, realised what was happening he immediately phoned George Jacob, the chairman of the company and one of

15   BMH WS 532, p. 10.
16   Ibid., pp 10-11.
17   BMH WS 423, p. 6: Shane Kenna, *16 Lives: Thomas MacDonagh* (Dublin, 2014), pp 215-6.

the managers, a man called Dawson, just before the telephone wires were cut. They managed to make their way to the factory through the chaos in the city but were powerless to do anything. The Jacob's workers were allowed to leave but the caretaker and watchman remained for the week, as Orr explained:

> The watchman came to me and asked me what he was to do; I advised him to go home with the others, I taking possession of his clock and keys. During his absence for his coat and hat, I was told to leave, which I at once refused to do. I explained that I was caretaker, and no matter what was the result, I could not leave (which they afterwards admired me for), and they moreover told me that in case of an invasion by the military, we were just in as dangerous a position as they were. Well, as I remarked, the watchman had gone for his clothes; when he arrived back the hall door was barricaded and he was detained a prisoner with myself. They then took possession of my apartments and remained there until Sunday 30 April.[18]

The watchman, Fitzgerald, was questioned by MacBride as to his name, address and religion. He was then requested to allow himself to be 'sworn in as a member of the Sinn Féin Volunteers'. He declined, saying he was never a member of any organisation. MacBride seemed disappointed.[19]

The building commandeered by the rebels was a forbidding one. It comprised the whole block bordered by Bishop Street, Peter's Row, Peter Street and Bride Street, which had been built up by the Jacob family since 1851. Its strategic position, adjacent to major arteries into the city from the south (especially that leading to and from Portobello Barracks) was the main reason for its capture. It was surrounded by a maze of small streets making it hard to assault. It was self-contained with two high towers overlooking the city. It was also next door to a major hospital, useful for tending to the wounded and perhaps inhibiting an attack by the government forces. A weakness was that the rebels, including Commandant MacDonagh, did not know the building very well despite a certain amount of reconnaissance beforehand. Peadar Kearney regarded Bride Street as a weak point from which the building could be attacked. British troops managed to occupy houses there so they had cover. The British also tried to set up machine guns in Digges Street but were 'blown out of it'.[20]

---

18 Ó Maitiú, *W. & R. Jacob*, p. 42.
19 Ibid.
20 Séamas De Búrca, *The soldier's song: the story of Peadar Kearney* (Dublin, 1957),p. 119.

As well as attacking the biscuit factory a rebel detachment was sent up New Street as far as Fumbally Lane to establish an outpost to control access from the south city, and then divided into two groups. One occupied Barmacks, a hop food providers in Fumbally Lane, while the other took over a block of four houses which commanded the approach down Clanbrassil Street. They were ordered to burrow through these to connect them. They also requisitioned milk carts from the many dairy yards on that street and made a barricade of them.[21] Some houses on nearby Camden Street, running parallel to Clanbrassil Street, were also occupied.

A number of DMP constables – six or seven – were taken prisoner in this operation. One, Patrick J. Bermingham, who was off-duty and captured while walking in St Patrick's Close, escaped, but the others were taken back to Jacob's. These were all released unharmed at the end of the week. However MacDonagh's belief that some policemen were in danger of being shot came true back at the factory. A plain-clothes officer who was taking copious notes on the activities of the rebels was warned to desist by MacDonagh. When he refused to do so he was shot by a rebel marksman.[22]

The local people, especially the women, reacted badly to the occupation of the factory. Many were workers or families of workers in the company. The area consisted of a tightly-knit community, very many of whom relied on Jacob's for a livelihood for generations. There was also the fear that any attack by the British would put their own homes at risk. Many were also 'separation women' whose income derived from the British army and felt that the Rising was a stab in the back to their menfolk. These women were to prove a problem for most of the week. One of them spat in Peadar Kearney's face and he reckoned that much of their bravado was fuelled by alcohol. He regarded this unsavoury reality as the 'worst feature of Easter Week'.[23] The local people in the tenements in the Fumbally Lane / Blackpitts area were particularly troublesome. Pugh describes the women as being in a 'in a terrible state. They were like French revolution furies and were throwing their arms around the police [those detained by the rebels, presumably], hugging and kissing them, much to the disgust of the police. I got a few kicks, and I think Twomey [another rebel] got some too, but somebody fired a shot to clear them off and they went away'.[24]

Volunteer Michael Walker described it as a more serious issue:

21 BMH WS 716, p. 6.
22 Kenna, *MacDonagh*, p. 211.
23 De Búrca, *Peadar Kearney*, p 116.
24 BMH WS 397, p. 5.

The inhabitants of Blackpitts were very hostile, singing and dancing to English songs of a quasi-patriotic type – [they] pelted stones at us and generally showed great opposition which eventually culminated in an attack on a Volunteer by a man who formed one of the crowd with the object of disarming the Volunteer. This man was shot and baynotted [sic], I believe, fatally.[25]

It should be noted that a young girl, Eleanor Warbrook of 7 Fumbally Lane, died in Mercer's Hospital, having been shot in the jaw on that day. Whether this was connected with the incidents recorded here is not known.[26]

At least one rebel tried to rationalise this attitude on the part of the people for whom they were fighting: 'Populace don't understand, execration and jeers. Free fight between themselves', recorded Seosamh de Brún in his rebellion diary. He also asks: 'Are these the people we are trying to free? Are they worth fighting for? The dregs of the population. They don't understand. Patience! They are the product of misrule. If fighting for them improves their condition that alone consoles. Maintenance money has changed them. Tomorrow they will cheer us'.[27]

At about one-thirty on Monday, having forced rebels out of Davy's public house at Portobello Bridge, about fifty men of the Royal Irish Rifles pushed towards the city centre with the intention of reinforcing Dublin Castle. A forward party advanced down Camden Street and the rebels occupying the houses here informed MacDonagh of their approach. He ordered his men to hold their fire until they came abreast of the factory. But they began to fire prematurely as the advance party came into view at the Cuffe Street corner. The rebels claimed that about seven were injured or killed at this point.[28] The main party eventually made its way to the Castle through Kevin Street. Another group of about a hundred men left Portobello Barracks at 1.50 p.m. to get to the Castle. They came under fire, again near Cuffe Street, and a James Calvert from County Armagh was killed and at least two others injured.[29]

The outposts in the Fumbally Lane / Blackpitts area were abandoned later that evening around dusk and the men, together with the prisoners, were recalled to

---

25 BMH WS 139, p. 4.
26 http://static.rasset.ie/documents/radio1/joe-duffys-list-of-children-killed-in- 1916-rising. pdf.
27 Mick O'Farrell, *The 1916 diaries of an Irish rebel and a British soldier* (Cork, 2014), pp 82-3.
28 Neil Richardson, *According to their lights: stories of Irishmen in the British army, Easter 1916* (Cork, 2015}, p. 145.
29 Ibid., pp 148-9.

Jacob's. 'Thank heaven', recorded de Brún. The displeasure of the local people was evident as they made their way back and attempts were made to knock their caps off. An exploratory party sent to probe the Ship Street area in the direction of the barracks and the Castle was also withdrawn. They had found themselves in engagements with British soldiers in that area, but it appears that all got back safely.

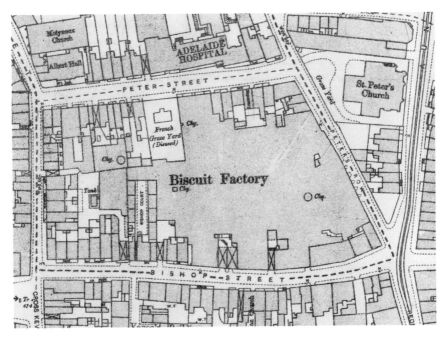

Jacob's Biscuit Factory, OS Sheet XVIII 67, 1909 (Courtesy of DCC Survey and Mapping Division)

One of the Volunteers' first tasks after seizing the factory was to bore through walls to connect the factory to Kelly's public house which commanded Camden Street and other streets at the Cuffe Street corner. Two stone masons among their ranks directed this work. The doors to the public bar were sealed and no-one was allowed near the alcohol. The Volunteers also took the opportunity to test one of about two dozen home-made bombs they had taken. These were cans filled with explosives fitted with a fuse which was lit before they were thrown. It was reported that they produced a loud explosion but no destructive effect.

Men were posted at various vantage points in the vast building from the flour loft down. Vinnie Byrne was posted to a window overlooking Peter's Row. As night fell on Monday, the rebels tried to sleep. They took some comfort in the fact that tins had been strewn around the building which would alert them if disturbed by enemy encroachment.

The hostility of the locals remained a problem. At one point they tried to attack the building, and indeed set it on fire with a lighted rag pushed under the door. MacDonagh ordered men to fire blanks to disperse them.[30] On the other hand, Peadar Kearney, who had a torrid time with some locals, claimed that others handed in milk and cigarettes to the insurgents.[31] The insurgents expected a siege; that they would be surrounded by British forces and attacked. This siege never took place; insofar as the Volunteers in Jacobs were besieged, it was by the local people around the biscuit factory.

On Easter Monday, and indeed in the succeeding days, Volunteers continued to arrive at the factory. When Joseph Furlong arrived late on Monday, having been blessed by a priest on the way when he informed him where he was going, he was welcomed by MacDonagh and given the commander's own new 'Peter the Painter' Mauser gun. They were soon joined by a young unknown Derry Volunteer who clamoured to get in; he was told to go to his lodgings for his rifle and stayed for the week.[32]

Martin Walton had an unforgettable experience as he tried to join the revolution:

> When I arrived then at Jacob's it was surrounded by a howling mob roaring at the Volunteers inside, 'Come out to France and fight, you lot of so-and-so slackers.' And then I started to shout up at the balustrade 'let me in, let me in.' And then I remember the first blood I ever saw shed. There was a big, a very, very big tall woman with something very heavy in her hand and she came across and lifted up her hand to make a bang at me. One of the Volunteers upstairs saw this and fired and I just remember seeing her face and head disappear as she went down like a sack. That was my baptism of fire, and I remember my knees nearly going from under me. I would have sold my mother and father and the Pope just to get out of that bloody place. But you recover after a few minutes.[33]

On Tuesday sniping began in earnest, both from Jacob's and at it from the government forces. The two towers emerging from the building back and front had a particularly commanding view over the city. Veterans of the garrison claimed

---

30 Kenna, *MacDonagh*, pp 214-5; BMH WS 822, p. 7.
31 De Búrca, *Kearney*, pp 120-1.
32 BMH WS 335, p. 6; WS 352, p. 12.
33 Kenneth Griffith and Timothy O'Grady, *Curious journey: an oral history of Ireland's unfinished revolution* (Cork, 2nd ed., 1998), pp 58-59.

that the soldiers as far away as Portobello Bridge whose buckles and bayonets were, improbably, seen glinting in the sun were hit. Apart from the bridge there was also firing from Portobello Barracks itself, the Castle and Wellington Barracks on the South Circular Road. For the rest of the week sniping took place between the towers of Jacob's and the British army on Portobello Bridge and elsewhere. A sentry on the bridge was hit at one stage. After this the army set up a machine gun there and began firing in the direction of the towers.[34]

The sniping from the Castle direction was identified as machine gun fire, but it hit only the top of the building. High windows overlooking the Adelaide Hospital in Peter Street were, according to Volunteer John Murphy, in view of the tower in Dublin Castle and came under this machine gun fire. Séamus Ó hAodha was one of those who took his turn to fire from one of the towers. This was limited due to lack of ammunition. Furlong, with his 'Peter the Painter', was the only one with a plentiful supply.[35]

Attempts were made to remedy the lack of arms and ammunition inside the factory. Michael Hayes entered Jacob's early on Wednesday morning. He was welcomed by MacDonagh and given a revolver and made a lieutenant. He was told that arms were in short supply and asked if he knew of any in the area. Hayes and Capt. Edward Byrne volunteered to go to certain houses in the vicinity. They went to three houses in Lombard Street West, Seán Campbell's, Patrick Maloney's and a family of O'Brien's. One of the O'Brien's, Liam, was fighting in the South Dublin Union. Thomas Atkin of Spencer Street was at home and would not give up his arms nor come to Jacob's. As far as he remembers they got two revolvers and some ammunition.[36]

Throughout the week the Jacob's garrison were plagued by rumours of what was happening in the rest of the city and country: that men were marching from Wexford to join the fight; that German prisoners held in Ireland had escaped and were on the way and even that the German army itself had landed. Some reliable information did come MacDonagh's way. Hayes, who had gone out collecting arms on Wednesday met Volunteer Larry Murphy who had come from Cork the previous day and he informed him that there was no Rising there. On his return to Jacob's he informed MacDonagh of this but he observed that he remained in a buoyant and talkative mood. Hayes says that while he was away a priest had been in to say that German prisoners were marching from Oldcastle.[37]

34   Richardson, *Irishmen in the British army*, pp 149–50; BMS WS 734, p. 26.
35   BMH WS 204, p.7.
36   BMH WS 215, p. 4.
37   Ibid.

A canteen and supply store was set up and was put in charge of Henry O'Hanrahan, Michael's brother, where food, tobacco, clothing and boots could be obtained, although some of the women, including Máire Nic Shiubhlaigh, the Abbey actress, took over cooking and tea-making duties. Volunteers were told to carry three days' rations when they mobilised and further rations were commandeered at places identified in reconnaissance before the Rising. When milk began to run low a new supply was identified and brought back in churns on carts. Potatoes were also requisitioned and a number of what Thomas Pugh termed 'corner boys' were dragooned into helping to carry them back. They also supplied the nearby garrison in the College of Surgeons with food.[38]

While nutritional food had to be sourced elsewhere the rebels began to tire of the rich fare of biscuits, crystallised fruit and chocolate which was readily available and some of them had gorged themselves on. As Thomas Pugh said: 'We were well-off as regards that kind of food, but we would have given a lot for an ordinary piece of bread.' If they had held out longer he might have got his wish as an oven was got ready for baking when the surrender came.[39] Although there was no doctor among the garrison a medical unit was set up under the supervision of Patrick Cahill, a chemist. Sorties for medical supplies were made to the Adelaide Hospital across the road in Peter Street and staff from the hospital were expected to come to their aid if required.[40]

Two requests made to MacDonagh by the caretaker, Orr, were granted. One was that for fear of fire all smoking by the garrison be stopped. Despite the unpopularity of this by men in an increasingly tense atmosphere, MacDonagh ordered it immediately. The other was that fourteen horses stabled nearby be fed and watered. This was also done by the insurgents sometimes at danger to themselves.

Fears of an impending attack on the building were never far away. An assault was expected on Wednesday night and work on new barricades continued until 1a.m. De Brún had a fitful night's sleep 'in equipment'. De Brún described the scene inside the factory as 'darkness and nervousness', the darkness the result of the electricity being turned off and candles used. He called the factory 'a vast place. A big place for a small number of men to hold'. The morning came as a relief. De Brún wrote in his diary that, although their volunteering days were over and they were becoming soldiers, the 'men of our section nervous. Officers also apprehensive'.[41] One man gave him particular concern. He confided: 'P. Callan nervous. Can't sleep

---

38   Kenna, *MacDonagh*, p. 210; BMH WS, 397.
39   BMH WS 397, p. 6.
40   Kenna, *MacDonagh*, p. 210,
41   O'Farrell, *1916 diaries*, p. 87.

and bad digestion. He was calm yesterday [Tuesday].' However on the Wednesday he reported: 'Paddy Callan is quite calm today. Poor Pat. Like me he did not expect to be engaged in Revolution, at least so suddenly.'[42]

The tension rose again on Thursday as sniping appeared to intensify. Another rumour that swept through the building was that incendiary bombs were being prepared by the British army to use on the factory and that local people had been moved from their homes for this eventuality. De Brún was on watch and there was heavy firing on his post. The staccato entries in his diary capture the atmosphere: 'expect to be riddled inside the building'. Also, 'darkness and silence save for the rattle of rifles and machine guns'. Pugh also experienced lack of sleep and found it difficult to know one day from the next. He had come under fire while resting in a room on the top floor which had a library, glass roof and glass windows. He thought the gunfire came from the direction of St Patrick's Park.[43] Peadar Kearney also felt the tension: 'Nerves were as taut as a violin at pitch, in addition to which physical exhaustion and lack of sleep had the men in such a nervous condition that rows of houses seemingly marching solemnly away was a usual occurrence.'[44]

This mental and emotional siege was a consequence of many factors. Wild rumours causing, by turns, sudden elation and fear, sleep deprivation, the first sight of blood and sudden death contributed. So did, perhaps, a ban (not always observed) on cigarettes and an imbalanced sugar-rich diet.

Some of those in the garrison found consolation in religion. A number of priests came and went into the building during the week, and many of the men, de Brún included, availed of the opportunity to have their confessions heard. John MacDonagh mentions a Capuchin priest to whom MacBride confessed. He told MacDonagh of the satisfaction he derived from confession as he had been away from the sacraments for some years – he 'just kept putting it off', he explained.[45]

Tension seems to have been most in evidence, naturally, at night time. Both that and boredom experienced during the day (due to inactivity) could have been damaging to *esprit de corps*. Attempts were made to alleviate this. A miniature céilí was organised. Music of a different kind was available. A gramophone and a piano were found on the premises and a stack of records. According to de Brún the piano could be heard being strummed occasionally on an upper floor to the accompanying rifle fire. De Brún enjoyed reading, including a copy of Shakespeare found in

---

42   Ibid., p. 86.
43   BMH WS 391, p. 5.
44   De Búrca, *Kearney* 120-1.
45   BMH WS 532, p.11.

the factory library, smoking (although it had been banned by MacDonagh) and listening to the records. Humour could also break the tension. Someone got their hands on a recording of 'God Save the King' and played it to see MacDonagh's reaction.[46]

MacDonagh himself began to show signs of indecisiveness as the week went on, sometimes countermanding his own orders or giving orders that mystified his men. On one occasion he ordered men, including Peadar Kearney, who had just gone to bed to go to the College of Surgeons with food and to collect rifles. When they returned they were reprimanded for not obtaining bayonets, which had not been mentioned before, and sent immediately back with great danger to themselves.[47]

It seems that the pressure of command was getting to MacDonagh.[48] In this regard it was fortuitous that MacBride had turned up on Monday morning as he played an important role in maintaining morale. But for the presence of MacBride, Michael O'Hanrahan as second in command would have been pushed more to the fore. However he sustained concussion in a fall while foraging for food in the factory and may have been incapacitated to a certain extent. He kept his fall a secret from MacDonagh.[49] John MacDonagh records that MacBride was 'useful in steadying our men'. One day an excited Volunteer, Dick Cotter, entered the HQ room to say there were hundreds of British troops advancing up the street. MacBride calmly replied: 'That's alright.' Thinking he did not realise the importance of his message, Cotter repeated it. MacBride said again 'That's alright and turned to MacDonagh and said 'So I played my King and won the game.' Cotter went away reassured that there was nothing to be worried about.[50]

Perhaps the greatest boost to morale came on Thursday, when a tricolour flag was raised over the building. It had been forgotten in the hurly-burly of the outbreak and one was improvised by a tailor, Derry O'Connell. It was made of 'green and white bunting … and some yellow grass cloth' and described as being 'very fine'.[51] Counter-intuitively the glow from the fires in the centre of the city which could be seen increasingly towards the end of the week did not dent morale, but the opposite. John MacDonagh observed that it showed them 'the magnitude of the rising and that it would have an effect in the country.'[52]

---

46   BMH WS 312, p. 9.
47   Kenna, *MacDonagh*, pp 221-2.
48   T. P. Coogan, *Michael Collins: a biography* (London, 1990), pp 44-6.
49   *Dictionary of Irish biography*, vii, pp 525-6.
50   Ibid., p. 10.
51   Kenna, *MacDonagh*, 225.
52   BMH WS 532, p. 13.

At least six women formed a permanent part of the Jacob's garrison. They were from Cumann na mBan and the Clan na nGael girl guides led by Captain May Kelly. De Brún, reflecting contemporary attitudes, was filled with praise for: '...those girls working so hard. Only in great moments like these does one get a true glimpse of Womanhood, patient, self-sacrificing and cheerfully brave.' On Friday he records: 'girls singing national songs dressed in green'.[53] Alongside the women who formed part of the garrison, messengers, many not more than girls, came and went all through the week. They took great risks and displayed remarkable bravery. Mary McLoughlin, who was only fifteen at the time of the Rising was in Clan na nGael. This was the female equivalent of the Fianna as the Dublin Fianna did not admit girls as the Belfast Fianna did. On Wednesday she was in the GPO and was asked to bring a message to MacDonagh in Jacob's. She was willing to go immediately. If stopped she was told to swallow it. Pearse put his hand on her head and said 'God bless you', as she left.[54]

When she got to Jacob's she met her group captain, May Kelly. MacBride asked her name. When he heard she was a MacLoughlin he said (in the mistaken belief that MacLoughlin is a Viking name) that it was strange that there were three Danes fighting for Ireland. She then returned to the GPO. She tried to get back to Jacob's again the following day with a message but failed to get through. She managed it on Friday and on leaving Jacob's this time she donned blue overalls to cover her uniform. Nellie Giffard, Thomas MacDonagh's sister-in-law, came to Jacob's and got messages to other commanders. MacDonagh also managed to get messages to his wife.

Due to the lack of activity at Jacob's re-enforcements were sent out to other garrisons, especially the nearby College of Surgeons. At the end of the week reports filtered in that Volunteers in the Lower Mount Street / Boland's Bakery area were under pressure. A detachment on bicycles was sent out on Saturday to draw off the attack there, the success or otherwise of which is not reported. Returning by Stephen's Green near the corner of York Street they were fired on by British soldiers. Volunteer John O'Grady was hit and was carried back to Jacob's. His injuries were serious and a doctor was sent for in the Adelaide Hospital across the road. Word came back that none would come but any casualty sent over would be looked after. A detachment was then sent to bring a doctor back by force if necessary. One came in bad humour and reported that there was little hope for O'Grady. He was sent over to the hospital but died almost immediately.[55] To Volunteer Joseph Furlong, perhaps not used to gunshot wounds, the injury looked

---

53 O'Farrell, *1916 diaries*, pp 87, 92.
54 BMH WS 934, pp 2-4.
55 BMH WS 532, pp 11-12.

like that caused by an explosive bullet, as O'Grady's stomach was 'practically ripped out'.[56]

Fr. Aloysius Travers
(Courtesy of the Irish Capuchin Provincial Archives)

Louise Gavan Duffy may have been the first to bring news of the general surrender on Saturday to MacDonagh. She got word of this and went to Jacob's shortly afterwards. She recalled: 'I remember he was not at all pleased with our news. I think that was the first intimation he got of the surrender. He did not believe that they had surrendered, and he did not believe that it was at an end.'[57] Confirmation of the surrender came around the middle of the day on Sunday with the arrival of Elizabeth O'Farrell carrying Pearse's signed order. MacDonagh's first reaction was to reject it as it came from a captive Pearse. He felt he should deal directly with Brigadier General Lowe, who was in charge in the city. Lowe sought the assistance of the Capuchin priests, Frs Augustine and Aloysius and asked them to intervene, letting them know that if a surrender was not forthcoming the factory would be stormed, leading to great loss of life.

Fr Aloysius and Fr Augustine were well aware of the situation as they had seen Pearse in Arbour Hill prison that Sunday morning. Fr Aloysius recalls their visit to Jacob's:

> We left the car near the last military barrier a little above Whitefriar's Street and Fr. Augustine and myself walked to the factory. We were admitted through a door in Peter Street, and brought through the factory to Commandant MacDonagh. He took us to a room where we met Major MacBride. Miss O'Farrell had already arrived with a copy of Pearse's letter similar to the one we bore.[58]

---

56 BMH WS 335, p. 7.
57 BMH WS 216, p. 12.
58 *Capuchin Annual* 1966, p. 283.

MacDonagh reiterated that the surrender order had no validity as Pearse was a captive; he was now in command of the republican forces in the city and would only enter negotiations with Lowe himself.

This message was brought back to Lowe who in turn consulted General Sir John Maxwell. Lowe agreed to meet MacDonagh at the corner of St Patrick's Park at 12 p.m. MacBride offered to accompany MacDonagh to this meeting, but it was felt that his record in the Boer War might hamper negotiations and he stayed behind.[59] Having met Lowe, MacDonagh agreed to advise his men to surrender, with Lowe granting him a ceasefire until 3.00 p.m.

MacDonagh returned to Jacob's for a consultation with his senior men in the staff room. Éamon Price recalled the tense meeting:

> A silent company awaited his report. Major MacBride sat calmly beside him at a table. Tomás announced that Pearse had surrendered and had issued an order to all units to do likewise. He read the order pointing out that we were not obliged to obey orders from a prisoner. He solicited the views of those present as to as to the most desirable course to be followed.
>
> Each officer spoke up in turn and though some were in favour of fighting it out the majority counselled obedience to the order. Outstanding amongst the former was, I remember Séamus Hughes [Ó hAodha]. He delivered a fiery speech pointing out that by surrendering we would, in fact, be offering our leaders as a sacrifice and that it were better to die with guns in our hand than to face the firing squad.[60]
>
> Michael O'Hanrahan advocated surrender and so did Price; in the end this view prevailed.

MacDonagh then summoned his men to parade in one of the lower rooms in Jacob's. They were informed of the surrender of Pearse and Connolly, that the GPO, Liberty Hall and O'Connell Street were in ruins and that their own leadership was advising that they follow Pearse's order. There was immediate consternation. The word of the surrender came as a surprise and a shock. Witnesses speak of anger and confusion with men close to insubordination and hysteria, shouting 'Fight it out! Fight it out!' - crying and some in rage breaking their rifles. Some of the men turned to MacBride seeking advice. He recommended surrender, saying 'Liberty is a sweet thing. If it ever happens again, take my advice and don't get inside

---

59   Kenna, *MacDonagh*, p. 233.
60   BMH WS 995, p. 9.

four walls.' He was presumably recalling the tactics of his Boer days. This calmed matters.[61]

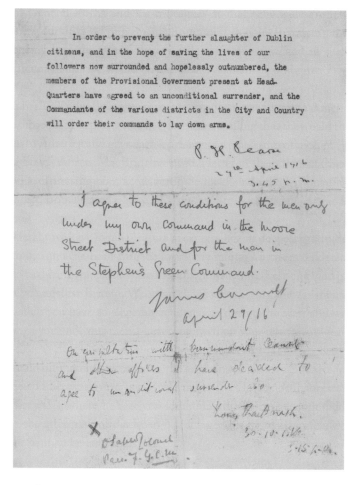

In order to prevent the further slaughter of Dublin citizens, and in the hope of saving the lives of our followers now surrounded and hopelessly outnumbered, the members of the Provisional Government present at Head-Quarters have agreed to an unconditional surrender, and the Commandants of the various districts in the City and Country will order their commands to lay down arms.

Pearse's surrender notice signed by Connolly and MacDonagh and mentioning Ceannt. (Margaret Skinnider, *Doing my bit for Ireland* (New York, 1917)).

MacDonagh was initially calm as he listened to his men, but he broke down, crying 'Boys, we must give in. We must leave some to carry on the struggle.' It was a poignant moment and one to remain indelibly in the memories of those present.[62]

With calm restored, MacDonagh left under British military escort to visit the garrisons in the South Dublin Union and Marrowbone Lane, to advise them to surrender. Fr Augustine sat in the car with MacDonagh. They carried a white flag made from an apron of one of the Jacob's workers attached to a brush handle. Near Basin Lane they encountered a barricade across the street and had to walk to the

61   O'Farrell, *1916 diaries*, p. 128.
62   BMH WS 995, p. 10

South Dublin Union. There they saw Éamonn Ceannt and he agreed to surrender. On leaving they were fired on by a soldier at the barricade. No one was hit and the British officers accompanying them apologised, saying they would put the soldier under arrest.[63]

Prisoners from Jacob's factory (*Irish Independent* photograph. DCLA, BOR Collection)

On their return preparations were made to evacuate Jacob's Factory just before 3.00 p.m. MacDonagh asked Price to lead the men out, which he did with some difficulty in single file by a narrow door. The writer, James Stephens recorded that on Sunday afternoon:

> It is half-past three o'clock, and from my window the Republican flag can still be seen flying over Jacob's factory. There is occasional shooting, but the city as a whole is quiet. At a quarter to five o'clock a heavy gun boomed once. Ten minutes later there was heavy machine gun firing and much rifle shooting. In another ten minutes the flag at Jacob's was hauled down.[64]

The men and women of the Jacob's garrison marched past the Adelaide hospital, with the doctors and nurses looking out the windows at them. They lined up beside St Patrick's Park, near Éamonn Ceannt and his men, who had already arrived.[65]

---

63   *Capuchin Annual* 1966, p. 285.
64   James Stephens, *The insurrection in Dublin* (Dublin, 1916).
65   BMH WS 397, p. 7.

The arrest of John McBride (DCLA, BOR Collection)

In his last public gesture John McBride laid down his personal revolver which had been presented to him by the Boers. An Irish sergeant in the British army picked it up and read MacBride's name on it. Realising its significance he brought it to his commanding officer. John MacDonagh overheard their conversation: 'Major MacBride, sir – he fought in the Boer war' 'With us or against us?' asked the officer.[66]

Shortly afterwards the Jacob's garrison was marched away. Three of them were executed: Thomas MacDonagh, Michael O'Hanrahan and John MacBride.

---

66   BMH WS 532, p. 14.

Dublin Public Libraries
and the 1916 Rising

Evelyn Conway

Great Brunswick Street (Pearse Street) Library (DCLA)

When the Easter Rising broke out, Dublin's citizens had been availing of public library services for more than three decades. Established by Dublin Corporation in 1884 for the education and recreation of the city's poor, the first of Dublin's 'free' libraries, as they were then called, were officially launched on 1 October 1884. On that day, amid great pomp and ceremony, two district libraries were opened one north and one south of the Liffey, in specially adapted Georgian houses on Thomas Street and Capel Street respectively.[1] Heavy public demand for the book borrowing and newsroom services ensued and by 1911, despite serious financial challenges along the way, the system had expanded to five district libraries.[2] Three new purpose-built libraries were opened in the early twentieth century; Charleville Mall in the North Strand (1900), Kevin Street (1904) and Pearse Street (then Great Brunswick Street, 1911) which was the city's first Carnegie-funded library. In 1901, the former Township of Clontarf was absorbed into the city boundaries and Dublin Corporation, through its Public Libraries Committee, set about

---

1   'Opening of the Dublin free libraries', *Irish Times*, 4 Oct. 1884, p.5.
2   Máire Kennedy, 'Civic pride versus financial pressure: financing the Dublin Public Library service', in *Library History*, ix, nos. 3 and 4 (1992), pp 83-96.

converting a section of the Clontarf Town Hall into a public library, which would be managed and staffed from Charleville Mall library and which opened in early 1902.[3]

More libraries created the need for additional staff to man them and by 1900, the Corporation's Public Libraries Committee had devised a new appointment system based on competitive examination, recruiting boys from 16 years as junior assistants.[4] Prior to this, the practice had been to employ adult men, selected by interview. Between 1900 and 1915, four young Dubliners entered the library service as junior assistants under this new scheme. All went on to play active and courageous roles prior to and during Easter week 1916.

The first was Thomas Gay, who took up duty in September 1900, serving initially at Charleville Mall library.[5] Twelve years later, Patrick J. Stephenson was recruited as an assistant at Thomas Street.[6] James O'Byrne started the following year, 1913, as an assistant at Charleville Mall Library.[7] The last was Thomas Dowling, who was assigned in 1915 as an assistant to Thomas Gay at Capel Street library, who had by then been promoted to head librarian.[8] By Easter week 1916, Gay, the eldest, was 32 years of age, Stephenson had just turned 21 years of age, O'Byrne was aged 20 and Dowling was still merely a boy of 17. Gay, Stephenson and Dowling all enlisted in separate companies of the 1st Battalion (under Edward Daly) of the Dublin Brigade of the Irish Volunteers, and so were located at various garrisons in Easter Week. O'Byrne joined F Company of the 2nd Battalion, under Frank Henderson. Gay did not actually engage in combat but was instead assigned to intelligence and external liaison duties, operating between the Jameson Distillery in Marrowbone Lane and Jacob's biscuit factory in Bishop Street.[9] Stephenson saw action at several sites, first at the Mendicity Institution on Usher's Quay, and subsequently at the Four Courts, the GPO and the *Irish Independent* offices in

3   *The Freeman's Journal*, 4 Sept. 1901; 18 May, 1901.
4   Stephenson, Patrick J., *Report on the origin, growth and development of the Dublin Municipal library service.* 29 November (1954), unpublished.
5   James Barry 'Death of Colonel Thomas E. Gay' *An Leabharlann: Journal of the Library Association of Ireland* (March, 1953), p. 3.
6   Dublin Corporation, 'Report of the Public Libraries Committee, breviate for quarter ended 31st December, 1911', in *DC Reports*, 50 (1912), pp 559-62.
7   James O'Byrne (MSPC application).
8   Dublin Corporation, 'Report of the Public Libraries Committee, breviate for the Quarter ended 30th June 1915, in *DC Reports*, II, 54 (1915), pp 441-2. There is also a reference in Garry Holohan's witness statement (BMH WS 328, p. 29) to a Brendan Gillan, who was a library assistant at Kevin Street library and was a member of Na Fianna, but there is no pension application or witness statement on file in his name. I wish to gratefully acknowledge the contribution of Mrs. Deirdre Ellis-King, former Dublin City Librarian, who directed me to Thomas Dowling's connection to the 1916 Rising.
9   Thomas E. Gay, BMH WS 780.

Middle Abbey Street.[10] O'Byrne served at Fairview and at various locations in the vicinity of the GPO area, while Dowling assisted in the defence of the Four Courts at Mary's Lane, Church Street and Bow's Lane.[11]

In 1901, the Clontarf Town Hall (which was sold in 1925 and reopened in 1927 as St Anthony's church; and from 1975 changed use again becoming a community centre, 'St Anthony's Hall') came within the Corporation's remit and by late 1901, they recruited a County Tyrone man, Michael McGinn, as caretaker.[12]

McGinn was married with three children and the family lived on the premises. The hall doubled as a public library and a cinema, from 1913, and his duties included tending to the library Reading Room.[13] McGinn was a veteran Fenian who had been a Tyrone IRB leader since the early 1870s, and was 65 years of age by the time of the Rising.[14] He was a close personal friend of both Thomas Clarke and Seán MacDiarmada and was very firmly aligned with key members of the IRB in the years leading up to the Rising.[15] It was through his auspices that IRB Supreme Council meetings were held at the Clontarf Town Hall 'which provided a fermenting ground for hatching the plot that produced the 1916 Rising'.[16] As McGinn became very ill and was bedridden by then, he was unable to play an active part in Easter week.

Meanwhile in Belfast, a young woman called Róisín Walsh had been working there as a college lecturer from 1914. A committed republican, originally from the Clogher Valley in County Tyrone, Walsh promptly became a member of the Belfast Cumann na mBan on its foundation in 1915. She was 27 years of age by 1916, and her family would collectively play an active role in the attempted mobilisation of

10   Patrick Joseph Stephenson, *Heuston's Fort: the Mendicity Institute, Easter week 1916* (Privately published, 1966).
11   Thomas Dowling, BMH WS 533.
12   I wish to gratefully acknowledge the contribution of Mrs. Deirdre Ellis-King, former Dublin City Librarian, who directed me to Michael McGinn's connection to the City Libraries and the 1916 Rising. Report of the Estates and Finance Committee, breviate for the quarter ended 1st January 1902, in: *DC Reports*, vol 2, 1902, p. 157.
13   Denis McIntyre, *The Meadow of the Bull: a history of Clontarf* (Dublin, 2nd ed., 1995), p. 103.
14   Owen McGee, *The IRB: The Irish Republican Brotherhood, from the Land League to Sinn Féin* (Dublin, 2005), p. 116. I wish to thank the Registrar of Cumann Gaolta 1916/The 1916 Relatives Association for facilitating the contact with both Brian McGinn (grandson of Mick McGinn) and Elizabeth Love (grandniece of Mick and Kate McGinn), both of whom provided details of their family history. The primary source of the information provided by Elizabeth Love was her late father, Patrick Love, nephew of Kate (Love) McGinn, who recorded this material in his unpublished memoirs written between 2000 and his death in 2011. Elizabeth also generously shared key sources uncovered in the course of both her own and her family's research, from which I have drawn heavily.
15   *The Fermanagh Herald*, 31 Jan. 1948.
16   McIntyre, *The Meadow of the Bull*, pp 102-5.

the Irish Volunteers in Tyrone during the Rising.[17] As she later relocated to Dublin, switching career to become a librarian, she crossed paths professionally with the four Dublin library staff who fought in the Rising in Dublin. By 1926 she had taken up the post of Dublin County Librarian, where Thomas Dowling, who had by then transferred from the city libraries, served as her deputy for five years. By 1931, the Corporation Public Libraries Committee (who had begun employing females from the 1920s), were seeking to recruit graduates with librarianship diplomas.[18] Walsh's outstanding credentials (a brilliant scholar, she held an honours B.A. and a library associateship of the UK Library Association) secured her the historic appointment of Dublin City's first Chief Librarian, and Walsh, Gay, Stephenson and O'Byrne now became colleagues. These are their Easter Rising 1916 stories.

Thomas Ernán (Tommy) Gay (1884-1953)

'Tommy' Gay was born in Dublin's inner city on 22 January 1884, the eldest of six children of Thomas Patrick Gay, a warehouseman, and his wife Catherine (née Coleman).[19] He was educated at the Christian Brothers School, Synge Street, and at the time of the Rising was living in Sandford Avenue on the South Circular Road. Gay's early life coincided with the political and cultural revival of the late nineteenth century and he became very active in a range of sporting and cultural organisations, including the GAA (he was a member of the Croke Gaelic Club) and the Gaelic League.[20] As Gay himself later explained it, these organisations 'gave impetus and new life to the revolutionary movement'.[21] By April 1916 he was already a mature 32- year-old man, established in his career as Capel Street Head Librarian and engaged to be married.

Within days of John Redmond's speech at Woodenbridge in September 1914, encouraging Irishmen to enlist in the British army - which led to a split in the Irish Volunteers - Gay joined the segment that opposed Redmond, enlisting at A Company of the 1st Battalion of the Dublin Brigade at the Columcille Hall in Blackhall Street, Stoneybatter. From that time he drilled regularly with his company and attended field manoeuvres near Swords under commanders such as Thomas MacDonagh and Piaras Béaslaí. By early 1916 Gay had learned from his company First Lieutenant, Denis O'Callaghan, that a Rising was to 'take place early in the year.' Under orders to parade in full kit on Easter Sunday, Gay, by his own account, turned out as instructed, but on learning of MacNeill's countermanding order he then returned home. Gay spent Monday 24 April at the

17   Nora Connolly, *The unbroken tradition* (New York, 1918).
18   Máirín O'Byrne, 'The Profession', in *Library Review* (Summer 1985), p. 109.
19   Census of Ireland 1901 and 1911 (NAI).
20   Sean M. O'Duffy, BMH WS 313, p.2.
21   Thomas E. Gay (MSPC, 24/SP/8332/2, (20/02/1925))

Fairyhouse races (where rumours of the fighting in Dublin reached him) and so had no way of knowing where his company was garrisoned. A pragmatic man, by Tuesday morning he decided to report to the post nearest to his home. This was at Jameson's Distillery in Marrowbone Lane under Captain Con Colbert, who decided that Gay, because of his keen knowledge of the area, should be deployed in an external liaison and intelligence capacity.[22] To all appearances Gay was 'a mild mannered and innocuous bookworm', and had a particular ability to make himself unobtrusive and so avoid suspicion.[23] This was therefore a role to which he was well suited and, as he later recalled, 'to which he was to become more and more attached' (his subsequent service up to 1924 was almost exclusively in an intelligence capacity).[24] He went on to provide vital assistance from the Tuesday right up until the surrender on the following Sunday. Reporting daily, he brought in crucial supplies of arms, ammunition, medical and other supplies, updating Colbert regularly on enemy movements. By the Thursday he observed the advance of a troop of the Nottinghamshire and Derbyshire regiment (the Sherwood Foresters) coming along the South Circular Road from the Harcourt Street direction, heading towards Rialto. This was most likely the 2/8th Sherwood Foresters who were 'detailed to escort a consignment of ammunition to the Royal Hospital in Kilmainham'.[25] Gay immediately forewarned Colbert who was able to alert neighbouring garrisons.

Colbert had instructed him to organise the urgent movement of food supplies from Jacob's factory; Gay went there on the morning of Sunday 30 April, when Thomas MacDonagh was already discussing terms of surrender. John MacBride instructed him to communicate this back to the Distillery where Captain Séamus Murphy was standing in for Colbert. Murphy ordered Gay back to Jacob's to request the order in writing. MacBride refused vehemently, stating that he had never and would never put in writing an order for an Irishman to surrender and that they would know when they saw the flag coming down from their building that the surrender had taken place. Gay avoided capture in the aftermath of the surrender and, heedless of personal risk, provided a safe house for his future brother-in-law 'Jack' (John) O'Shaughnessy (a Section Commander with B Company of the 4th Battalion) who was wounded in the South Dublin Union where he had fought all week from Easter Monday and escaped.[26] Gay married Eileen O'Shaughnessy in

22   Ibid.
23   J. B. E. Hittle, *Michael Collins and the Anglo Irish War* (Washington, D.C., 2011), p. 64.
24   Thomas E. Gay (MSPC, 24/SP/8332/2, (20/02/1925)).
25   Ibid. and Paul O'Brien, The battle for the South Dublin Union, online available http://www. paulobrienauthor.ie/436-2/, accessed 18/12/15.
26   Ibid.; John O'Shaughnessy (MSPC application, MSP34REF2372).

September 1917, a Cumann na mBan member who had been involved in the 1914 Howth gun-running.[27] The couple went on to have three children.

Patrick Joseph (Paddy) Stephenson (1895 – 1960)

Photograph of Paddy Stephenson (courtesy of his grandson, Jim Stephenson)

'Paddy' Stephenson (known to his family as 'Paddy Joe'), was born at 25 Upper Tyrone Street (now Railway Street) on 10 April 1895, the second eldest of nine children of Patrick Stephenson, a coachman, and his wife Alice (née Tynan).[28] He was educated by the Christian Brothers, to Junior Award level, at the O'Connell Schools, North Richmond Street, leaving in the summer of 1910, aged fifteen. By 1911, he achieved second place in the Dublin Libraries examination, and by January 1912 had begun his career as a library assistant at Thomas Street library.[29]

Stephenson was first drawn into the nationalist movement shortly after leaving school in 1910, when his older brother Samuel enrolled him in the Archbishop McHale branch of the Gaelic League in Dorset Street.[30] By 1915 he had joined the Irish Volunteers' Dublin Brigade, D Company, 1st Battalion, based at the Colmcille Hall at 5 Blackhall Street in Stoneybatter. There he encountered his childhood school friend Seán Heuston, whom he hadn't seen for over a decade. Stephenson was an 'enthusiastic Volunteer' and Heuston promoted him by late 1915 to the position of Company Quartermaster.[31] In this capacity, he had responsibility for procuring and smuggling the company's arms and ammunition, a meagre store that he stashed in the home of fellow Volunteer Patrick Kilmartin (his future brother-in-law) at Kane's greengrocery shop in Stoneybatter.[32] The nature of his shift work

27   Former Probate Officer of the High and Supreme Courts [Obituary] *Irish Times*, 18 Nov. 2000.

28   Eoin Cody, 'The story of PJ Stephenson: a rebel librarian', online: available http://www. storiesfrom1916.com/1916-easter-rising/paddy-joe/ Accessed 8/11/15; Census of Ireland 1901 and 1911 (NAI).

29   Dublin Corporation, 'Report of the Public Libraries Committee: Breviate for quarter ended 31st December *DC Reports* 1911 (1912), 559-62.

30   Patrick Joseph Stephenson, *Heuston's Fort: the Mendicity Institute, Easter week 1916*, privately published (1966).

31   John Gibney, *16 Lives: Seán Heuston* (Dublin, 2013), p. 93.

32   Stephenson, *Heuston's Fort*.

at Thomas Street library left him free until 2 p.m. one day a week and between 2 p.m. and 6 p.m. in the remaining afternoons, and he dedicated all of this spare time to his Volunteer duties.[33]

None of the rank and file Volunteers in D Company knew for certain that a Rising would take place on Easter Sunday 1916, but some suspected that action was likely due to increased activity in the lead up to Holy Week. Stephenson, with a group which included Seán McLoughlin of Na Fianna Éireann and Heuston spent Easter Sunday night on guard duty at Battalion HQ, where ammunition and explosives were being stored. Stephenson would subsequently go on to have a long and close association with Seán McLoughlin throughout the Rising and beyond.

Early on Monday morning, about 8 a.m., Stephenson and McLoughlin were among a small group sent by bicycle from Liberty Hall to deliver urgent mobilisation orders around the city. Later in the morning they mobilised with some of their company (no more than 13 turned out) at the assembly point at St George's church, Temple Street, where, led by Heuston, they paraded 'in speculative silence', stopping 'at ease' en route at Liberty Hall.[34] Marching four abreast they continued on to what turned out to be their final destination at the Mendicity Institution in Usher's Island, which they reached at around midday. Their uncertainty was abruptly ended when they were ordered to seize the building. Heuston had been ordered to hold the building for three hours only to hinder the movement of the Royal Dublin Fusiliers at the nearby Royal Barracks (now Collins Barracks) towards the city, giving the Volunteers at the Four Courts time to consolidate their positions.

In the event, the tiny Mendicity garrison managed to hold the building for just over two days. Reinforcements had arrived on Tuesday, but by Wednesday morning, with supplies of food nearly exhausted, Stephenson and McLoughlin were selected to make the hazardous journey back to the GPO, to brief Connolly and return with all speed with food supplies.

As the Mendicity fell in their absence, the deeply despondent men joined the defence of the Four Courts garrison. News filtered through about the fate of the Mendicity, and they learned that Heuston's deputy, Captain Richard (Dick) Balfe and 2nd Lieutenant Liam Staines (brother of Michael, who later became the first Garda Commissioner and T.D.) were 'stretcher cases' (Staines later died of his injuries).[35] By Thursday, now amid heavy bombardment, the resourceful duo managed by a

33 Sworn statement made before the Advisory Committee by Patrick Joseph Stephenson, no. 21748, 28th September 1936, p. 2 (MSPC, file MSP34REF21743).
34 Gibney, *16 Lives: Sean Heuston*, p. 92.
35 Stephenson, *Heuston's Fort*.

roundabout route to eventually re-enter the GPO, where McLoughlin was ordered by Connolly to lead an attempt to capture the *Irish Independent* offices at Middle Abbey Street, where his leadership abilities were noted by James Connolly.[36] They retreated back to the GPO on Friday morning until the evacuation to Moore Street on Friday evening. Unbeknownst to Stephenson, his father Patrick, aged 50, was shot dead shortly after 6 p.m. on Friday by British troops when he broke a curfew.[37] Stephenson's leadership abilities were also noted by Connolly, who ordered him to take charge of a number of men at the 'White House' facing Moore Lane, from where he retreated to Moore Street for the general surrender on Saturday afternoon.[38] He was brought to Richmond Barracks and was later deported on Sunday 30 April to Knutsford Prison in England; he was later transferred to Frongoch camp in Wales. He was released by September 1916.[39]

Paddy Stephenson married Mamie Kilmartin, whose family owned Kane's greengrocery in Stoneybatter, in September 1917, with his close friend Seán McLoughlin acting as his best man. Prior to and during the Rising, Maimie Kilmartin also played an active part as a Cumann na mBan member with the Colmcille branch, and was attached to the Four Courts garrison during Easter week.[40] The couple went on to have five sons.

36   Seán McLoughlin, 'The Boy Commandant of 1916', in *History Ireland*, xiv, no. 2 (Mar-Apr. 2006), pp 26-30.
37   Jim Stephenson, *Patrick Joseph Stephenson: 'Paddy Joe'* 1895-1960 (Sheffield, 2006), privately published. [Online version] Available from: http://1916-rising.com/1-introduction.html
38   Patrick Joseph Stephenson (MSPC, file MSP34REF21743).
39   Stephenson, *Patrick Joseph Stephenson: 'Paddy Joe'*.
40   Liz Gillis, *Women of the Irish revolution* (Cork, 2014), p. 49.

James O'Byrne, AKA James Byrne (1896 to 1947)

Formally named Byrne (the family later changed their surname to O'Byrne), James O'Byrne was born on 5 January 1896, the second youngest of eight children of Thomas Byrne, a farrier, and his wife Charlotte (née Howard).[41] The family lived at 44 Lower Mayor Street in the North Wall area. [42]

Details of O'Byrne's Easter week activities are sparse. O'Byrne was attached to the second Battalion, F Company of the Irish Volunteers Dublin Brigade.[43] F Company was small and under the command of Captain Frank Henderson and 1st Lieutenant Oscar Traynor. O'Byrne attended Fr Matthew Park on Thursday evenings for drilling and on Sundays for rifle practice.[44] In Easter week, he was engaged in combat across a number of sites - at Fairview, the Metropole Hotel, Eason's, the GPO, Moore Street and Henry Place.[45] After the surrender, he was arrested and interned first in Knutsford and later Frongoch Prison from where he was released 'about' 21 July 1916. [46]

O'Byrne had been working since 1913 at Charleville Mall Library under Patrick J. (Paddy) Fennelly, who was a well-known Gaelic Leaguer who had been appointed as Head Librarian there in 1907.[47] According to Hugo McGuinness, 'The IRB had infiltrated most of the GAA Clubs in the Fairview/Clontarf/North Dock area by 1910 and practically controlled the Gaelic language clubs'.[48] Fennelly was clearly sympathetic to the Volunteers during the Rising. According to Volunteer Harry Colley, about midnight on Easter Monday, Fennelly, who lived in nearby Cadogan Road, brought him out tea and sandwiches to where he was manning a barricade at Fairview corner (now Edge's corner), near Annesley Bridge.[49] As the Charleville Mall librarian was responsible for the management and staffing of the Clontarf public library, both Fennelly and O'Byrne clearly also had a lot of direct

---

41   Birth certificate of James O'Byrne (GRO).
42   Census of Ireland 1901 and 1911 (NAI).
43   James O'Byrne (MSPC, file 24SP2492).
44   Harry Colley, BMH WS 1687, p. 13.
45   James O'Byrne (MSPC, file 24SP2492).
46   Ibid.
47   Ibid.
48   Personal communication from Hugo McGuinness, local historian.
49   Harry Colley, BMH WS 1687, p. 13. Personal communication from Hugo McGuinness, local historian.

contact with Mick McGinn in the years leading up to the Rising. It would seem reasonable to speculate that this must have helped McGinn to provide a cover for the IRB Supreme Council meetings frequently held there. O'Byrne never married. He collapsed and died at his place of work on 13 November 1947 at the age of 51.

James Thomas (Tom) Dowling (1889 to 1966)

Tom Dowling was born on 5 February 1899 to Joseph Dowling, a carpenter, and his wife Margaret (née Archbold), a shopkeeper. The family lived at 148 North Strand Road.[50] He was recruited in 1915 to the Dublin Corporation Libraries as a junior assistant, having achieved second place in the Libraries examination.[51] Dowling recalled that it was 'about' September 1915 (then aged only 16 years) when he was enrolled in C Company, of the 1st Battalion of Dublin Brigade, based at 41 Parnell Square.[52] Prior to the Rising, he attended weekly arms drills, lectures and parades at that venue. He was armed by his company 1st Lieutenant Joe McGuinness who provided him with a shotgun, revolver and ammunition.[53]

On Holy Thursday, 20 April 1916, Dowling got his first indication that a Rising was imminent, when the company was mobilised and addressed by Commandant Edward Daly, who ordered them to 'hold themselves in readiness for further orders as they would soon have an opportunity to put their arms drills and military exercises into operation.'[54] While making his way to mobilise with his company at Blackhall Place on Easter Monday at 11 a.m., Dowling was stopped at Mary's Lane by Lieutenant Diarmuid O'Hegarty, who ordered him to join his unit who were in the process of erecting barricades in the immediate vicinity at Mary's Lane, Church Street and Bow Lane. Dowling remained there under fire for the entire week, retreating with the remainder of the 1st Battalion into the Four Courts on the following Saturday. He was then detained overnight at the Rotunda Gardens, and later Richmond Barracks where he was held for a week. Due to his youth, he was released on 5 May.[55] Dowling later married and had two sons.[56]

50   Census of Ireland 1901 and 1911 (NAI); Birth Certificate of Thomas Dowling (GRO).
51   Dublin Corporation, 'Report of the Public Libraries Committee, breviate for the Quarter ended 30th June 1915', in *DC Reports*, II, 54 (1915), pp 441-2.
52   Thomas Dowling, BMH WS 533.
53   Ibid.
54   Ibid.
55   James Thomas Dowling (MSPC application MSP34REF3801).
56   *Irish Times*, 9 Dec. 1966.

In an obituary notice following Dowling's death on 8 December 1966, fellow librarian Dermot Foley described him as exceedingly modest and reserved. Dowling was 'the least likely of us all ever to be remembered for a vigorous or noisy action', and it 'was not easy to associate this gentle man with the eager boy who saw active service as a volunteer in the Easter Rising'.[57] A few weeks prior to his death, Dowling occasionally drove around by the Church Street area 'to look once again at the high wall he scrambled along for dear life when his unit was at last blasted out of its positions in North King Street'. This, Foley stated, was the 'one touch of justifiable pride' he ever saw Dowling allow himself.[58]

Michael (Mick) McGinn (1851 to 1916)

Born in 1851 into a farming family in Omagh, County Tyrone, Mick McGinn's Fenian activity stretched back many years prior to the events of Easter 1916.[59] As a member of the Fenian Brotherhood he had spent a lot of his life in British jails.[60] By the late 1890s he was the Fenian Head Centre for County Tyrone, based at Dergmoney House in Omagh.[61] In May 1896, at the age of 45, he married Catherine (Kate) Love, a young woman from Enniskillen twenty-two years his junior. Their first child, a boy named Conway, was born in April of the following year.[62] At this time McGinn, who had a small farm in Omagh, was working there as a baker for a grocer called Dan Hackett.[63] In 1897 McGinn was elected deputy leader of the Ulster Executive of the 1798 Centenary Committee and in this role was busily promoting the establishment of '98 centenary clubs across Ulster. The Catholic clergy, who were traditionally hostile to the Fenians, were also forming their own 1798 centenary clubs and parish priests began undermining McGinn, warning their parishioners that 'a certain dangerous individual from Omagh is going from town to town' spreading the Irish Republican Brotherhood organisation throughout the country.[64] At one point a local parish priest in Omagh delivered a thinly-veiled denunciation of McGinn from the altar in which he almost pointed

57   Dermot Foley, 'Mr. James Thomas Dowling, (Obituary)', *An Leabharlann: Journal of the Library Association of Ireland*, xxv, Nos. 1 (March 1967), p. 9.

58   Ibid.

59   Marriage certificate of Michael McGinn and Catherine Love, 1896 (GRO).

60   Personal communication from Elizabeth Love drawn from the unpublished memoirs of her late father, Patrick Love, nephew of Catherine and Michael McGinn, obtained September 2015.

61   Ibid.; *Strabane Chronicle*, 8 Oct. 1960.

62   Personal communication from Elizabeth Love drawn from the unpublished memoirs of her late father, Patrick Love, nephew of Catherine and Michael McGinn, obtained September 2015. Personal communication from Brian McGinn, grandson of Michael McGinn, obtained September 2015.

63   Extracts from the Papers of the late Dr Patrick McCartan: Part Two, *Clogher Record*, vol. 5, no 2 (1964), p. 192.

64   McGee, *The IRB*, pp 252-3.

him out.[65] McGinn lost his job and, unable to find employment in Omagh, by 1897 he was forced to relocate with his wife and young son to Dublin.[66] The couple subsequently had a second son Patrick Romuald, known as 'Rommy', in 1900, followed by a daughter, Sheila, in 1901. By 1901 he had secured employment as a Time Keeper and was living at Paradise Place, Inns Quay.[67] His final family home was the Clontarf Town Hall, where in late 1901 he took up the position of caretaker.[68] According to Owen McGee, this was a job that was given to him by Fred Allan (Frederick James Allan), a fellow veteran Fenian of McGinn's who was at that time employed by Dublin Corporation as secretary of the Dublin Electric Light Co. and John Clancy, a republican and Councillor in Dublin Corporation who represented the new Borough of Clontarf in City Hall.[69] Presumably Allan had influence with Clancy and was able to exert 'pull' to secure McGinn the post.

McGinn was a close personal friend of Thomas Clarke, who was godfather to his son Romuald. Indeed, 'Clarke had joined the Tyrone IRB in 1878 at the request of both John Daly and Michael McGinn'.[70] Clarke had returned to Dublin from the United States in 1907, setting up his tobacconist shop at 75 Parnell Street (which acted as a front for his IRB activities), and he and McGinn had renewed their acquaintance. McGinn's seniority in advanced nationalism is strongly evident in his activities in the lead up to the Rising; in July 1915 he was identified as a senior member of the IRB by the DMP.[71] His importance is also testified to by his membership of the O'Donovan Rossa Funeral Committee at this time.[72]

Kate McGinn was also closely associated with the leaders of Easter week and was recalled as 'acting as hostess to every young fighter who came to Dublin' with the McGinn family home becoming known as a 'centre of resurgent nationalism'.[73] Mick McGinn provided a 'haven' for meeting of the IRB Supreme Council in the Clontarf Town Hall, and had a specific 'committee' room available in the hall for various revolutionary meetings'.[74] It was here that the IRB Supreme Council held their last vital meeting before the Rising on 16 January 1916, at which the IRB

65   'Extracts from the Papers of the late Dr Patrick McCartan, p. 192.
66   Address to Mr. Michael McGinn from the Nationalists of Omagh on his departure to Dublin, dated 9th November 1897.
67   Cenus of Ireland 1901 (NAI).
68   Report of the Estates and Finance Committee, breviate for the quarter ended 1st January 1902, in: *DC Reports*, vol 2, 1902, p. 157
69   Ibid.
70   Ibid., p. 350. This information was also provided by Michael McGinn's descendents, Brian McGinn and Elizabeth Love.
71   DMP, Movements of Dublin extremists, dated 31st Jul, 1915 (NAI, CSO/50/2/50(1)).
72   'The first O'Donovan Rossa Funeral Committee' (Photo), *Evening Herald*, 17 June 1954, p. 3.
73   *Strabane Chronicle*, 8 Oct. 1960
74   McIntryre, *The Meadow and the Bull*, p. 104.

'being a democratic body, voted to change its decision on the Rising in 1916 from one in principle to one in fact'.[75]

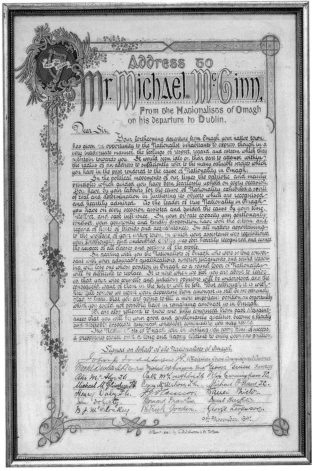

Illuminated address presented to Michael McGinn (Courtesy of Joan O'Hare and Michael Baldwin)

By Easter week 1916 McGinn had fallen ill with what was termed 'creeping paralysis' and therefore was unable to take part in the Rising.[76] Both of his sons participated; Conway saw action at various locations including the Imperial Hotel in O'Connell Street and his younger son Rommy played a smaller role. As recounted by Rommy's son Brian 'My father being then just 16 was involved in some skirmishes along the North Strand but most of the time he carried

---

75   Austen Morgan, *James Connolly: a political biography* (Manchester,1988), p. 169. McIntryre, *The Meadow of the Bull*, p. 104.

76   Eilis Nic Ionmhain, My uncle Michael Love', Cumann Gaolta 1916 /the 1916 Relatives Association 'http://www.1916relatives.com/#!Spotlight-on-history-My-uncle-Michael-online available, accessed 22 September 2015.

information to his father and cared for him with his mother Kate.'[77] Despite not participating in the rebellion, Mick McGinn was nonetheless arrested from his sick bed and held for a short time after the Rising, but was later released on health grounds.[78] He died shortly after on 28 July 1916.[79] By the end of 1916, Rommy McGinn had been taken on as a permanent library assistant at Charleville Mall library.[80] Kate McGinn retained her employment as caretaker/housekeeper at the Clontarf Town Hall until it was sold in 1925.[81]

Róisín Walsh (1889—1949)

Róisín Walsh was born on 24 March 1889 into a staunchly nationalist Catholic family, in Lisnamaghery, Clogher, Coounty Tyrone. She was the eldest child of a schoolteacher and farmer, James Walsh, and his wife Mary (née Shevlin); the couple had eight children.[82]

By 1914, due to the outbreak of the Great War, she had returned to Ireland from a teaching post in Germany. From that time she was based in Belfast as a lecturer in Irish and English at St Mary's Training College (then a primary school teacher training college for Catholic women).[83] From this time she was closely associated with James Connolly's two daughters, Nora and Ina, who were then based in Belfast, becoming a member of the Belfast Cumann na mBan on its foundation by Nora Connolly the following year.[84] Under the influence of Nora Connolly the Belfast Cumann na mBan was noted for its 'assertive' nature in that the women,

77   Personal communication from Brian McGinn, grandson of Michael McGinn, obtained September 2015.
78   Patrick Love, *Memoir*, (2011).
79   Death certificate of Michael McGinn (GRO); obituary notice in *The Fermanagh Herald*, 5 Aug. 1916.
80   Personal communication from Mr. Brian McGinn. Breviate for the quarter ended 31st December 1916, no. 36, p. 315, *DC Reports*, vol 1, 1917.
81   Michael Conway McGinn (MSPC application, file 24SP3001). Report of the Public Libraries Committee, breviate for the quarter ended 30th September 1916, p. 405, *DC Reports* vol 3, no. 219.
82   Census of Ireland, 1901 and 1911 (NAI).
83   Nora Connolly O'Brien, BMH WS 286, p. 7.
84   Ibid.

unusually, underwent regular practice in rifle marksmanship, with many becoming quite skilled.[85]

The dynamic nature of the Belfast Cumann na mBan is captured in this account which appeared in the *Irish Volunteer* shortly before the Rising:

> To add to their many activities they are now starting a class for semaphore signalling. They are making a minute study of the rifle, cleaning and using it. Their first aid classes are going vigorously. They have just held a rifle raffle, and the proceeds are sufficient to purchase an ambulance outfit into the bargain.[86]

Walsh was evidently already a good shot by late 1914, even prior to joining Cumann na mBan, as related in the following account by Ina Connolly (both of the Connolly sisters had been given rifles following their courier duties after the Howth gun-running earlier that year):

> By Christmas we had a shooting competition; for the winner we gave a turkey. It was won by Miss Róisín Walsh ... who made a present of it to our family as she had no need to take one home to the country. This was looked upon as a very generous act on her part.[87]

Recalling another incident that involved Walsh, Ina Connolly relates how one day in 1914 she was marching up the Falls Road with her Fianna Group: the Fianna was explicitly a boy scout group and the Connolly sisters 'founded the first and only girl's branch of the Fianna in Belfast which they named the *Betsy Gray*', (after a heroine from Antrim who was killed in the north in the United Irishmen Rebellion of 1798) singing the *Watch on the Rhine* in their imperfect German. Walsh happened to be passing (a brilliant linguist, she was fluent in German and had a repertoire of songs) and was highly amused at their German and put them right. She was also able to give them first-hand information about the state of things in Germany as she saw them.[88] Connolly singles Walsh out for her kind, gentle and helpful nature and as someone who was held in affection by them all.

---

85 Margaret Ward, *Unmangeable revolutionaries: women and Irish nationalism* (London, 1995), p. 104.

86 *Irish Volunteer*, 11 Mar. 1916.

87 Sinéad McCoole, *No ordinary women: Irish female activists in the revolutionary years, 1900-1923* (Dublin, 2004), p.152; Ina Connolly Heron, BMH WS 919, p. 92.

88 McCoole, *No ordinary women*, p.26.

Prior to the Rising, Róisín and her sister Bridget became friends with the charismatic Seán MacDiarmada on his travels as an IRB organiser around Ulster. Both women were in close contact with him prior to the Rising, with Róisín helping him with correspondence to the United States while Bridget provided the covering address for letters to MacDiarmada from John Devoy, the Clan na Gael leader in the United States.[89]

One of the key IRB members in County Tyrone was none other than the Clogher parish priest, Fr James O'Daly who was one of two 'militantly nationalist clerics' who were considered 'vital in promoting the spread of revolutionary nationalism in County Tyrone' (the other was Fr Coyle of Fintona).[90] Both clerics were, in turn, closely associated with the Tyrone doctor Patrick McCartan, who was a member of the IRB Supreme Council and a 'mainspring of the Irish Volunteer movement in County Tyrone.'[91]

At home in Clogher in Easter week, Walsh received advance knowledge of the Rising on Good Friday from Fr O'Daly.[92] Due to the confusion that followed MacNeill's countermanding order on Easter Sunday, the Northern Volunteers' mobilisation in Tyrone was short lived and they dispersed. In Clogher, the Walsh family awaited news from Nora and Ina Connolly. The sisters had returned to Dublin on Easter Sunday to report to the Military Council on the situation in Ulster, and had subsequently been sent back to carry dispatches from Pearse for the Tyrone men to commence hostilities. The Walsh family, collectively and in close collaboration with Fr O'Daly, the Connolly sisters and Archie Heron, played an active role in the concerted but ill-fated attempt to implement Pearse's orders and bring about a remobililsation.[93] They carried out a range of activities, including providing a safe house for the Connolly sisters. Walsh's younger siblings, her sister Teresa (Teasie), along with Ina Connolly, and her brother Joseph carried despatches around the county throughout the week. On the Wednesday of Easter week, Róisín, her youngest brother Tom and Teasie helped to smuggle ammunition and supplies in a pony trap to the Volunteers Clogher Company which had assembled on Tuesday at Ballymacan on the orders of Fr O'Daly.[94]

---

89 *Irish Press*, 28 June 1949; 24 Apr. 1951.
90 Eamon Phoenix, 'Nationalism in Tyrone, 1880-1972', in Charles Dillon and Henry A. Jeffries (eds), *Tyrone: history and society* (Dublin, 2000), p. 77.
91 James O'Daly, BMH WS 235, p. 1.
92 Róisín Walsh, Statement regarding Ina Connolly's (Mrs. A. Heron) part in the 1916 Rising in County Tyrone, 1938 (Military Archives, IE/MA/MSPC/MSP34REF21565- Ina Connolly Heron).
93 Nora Connolly, *The unbroken tradition*, (New York, 1918); Archie Heron, BMH WS 577.
94 James O'Daly, BMH WS 235, pp 3-4.

Róisín Walsh was identified in 1947 by the Bureau of Military History as a potential witness and is on file as having 'information regarding events in County Tyrone prior to and during Easter Week'. Unfortunately as she died in 1949; her sworn statement corroborating Ina Connolly's role is the only documented account of her own participation.[95]

Conclusion

While Mick McGinn died shortly after the Rising, all four of the Dublin library staff and Róisín Walsh, who was based in Ulster until late 1922, remained active in the Irish revolution. Tommy Gay became an Intelligence Officer on the General Headquarters staff of the Irish Volunteers, reporting directly to Michael Collins. Interrupting his library career for a time, in 1922 Gay joined the National Army, rising by 1923 to the rank of Colonel, again in an intelligence role.[96] Paddy Stephenson re-joined his company following his release from Frongoch, transferring to Na Fianna from 1917 to 1919 and rising to the rank of Adjutant General of the Fianna Éireann Headquarters staff. His activities, such as raids for arms and the campaign against conscription brought him into clashes with the authorities. He also smuggled instructions from Michael Staines into the republican prisoners in Mountjoy in 1919 in relation to an escape. He left Na Fianna and re-joined D Company of the Dublin Brigade of the Volunteers in 1919, remaining active until late 1921, from which time he was engaged mainly in arms trafficking (he did not take part in the Civil War).[97] James O'Byrne rejoined his company following his release from Frongoch and was active in the War of Independence, where he was engaged in armed patrols, raids for arms and was mobilised for the attempted rescue of Kevin Barry. O'Byrne joined the National Army in 1923 and consequently had to resign his library job. He rose to the rank of Captain and was reinstated in the library service after his demobilisation in 1924.[98] Dowling also re-joined his company and was also highly active throughout the War of Independence, carrying out a range of activities, participating in ambushes at Granby Row and Lower Dorset Street corner, as well as armed guards and patrols and anti-conscription duties. As he went out of Dublin on holiday about a week before the outbreak of the Civil War in June 1922, he did not play any part in it.[99] His obituary recounted Dowling's involvement in the 'cloak-and-dagger' adventures of the War of Independence, when Tommy Gay, his librarian, operated

95   BMH WS 726; Róisín Walsh: Statement regarding Ina Connolly's (Mrs. A. Heron)
       part in the 1916 Rising in Co. Tyrone, 1938 (Military Archives, IE/MA/MSPC/
       MSP34REF21565- Ina Connolly Heron).
96   Thomas E. Gay (MSPC, 24/SP/8332/2, (20/02/1925)).
97   Patrick Joseph Stephenson (MSPC application, MSP34REF21743).
98   James O'Byrne (MSPC application 24SP2492).
99   Thomas Dowling (MSPC application, MSP34REF3801).

a centre for military intelligence from the upstairs office of the library [in Capel Street], and found willing accomplices in young Tom and the rest of his staff'.[100] Róisín Walsh left her lecturing post in Belfast in 1919 and returned to Clogher, where in 1921 she took up a position as a Rate Collector with Tyrone County Council.[101] In 1922, she was dismissed from this post following her refusal to sign a mandatory declaration of allegiance to the King and the Northern Ireland Government.[102] She was forced to move to Dublin in late 1922 to avoid arrest and prosecution following an RUC raid on her family home in Lisnamaghery, in which alleged seditious literature was found and an exclusion order was issued against her.[103] The following year the Walsh family relocated to Cypress Grove Farm and House in Templeogue, Dublin.[104]

James O'Byrne went on to become Head Librarian at Kevin Street Library in 1946. He died suddenly in late 1947. When Róisín Walsh left the Dublin County Libraries in 1931 to take up the Chief Librarian post for the city libraries, Thomas Dowling succeeded her as Dublin County Librarian. Walsh died in office as Chief Librarian in 1949.[105] Thomas Gay went on to serve as the Capel Street librarian until 1940, from which time he became Private Secretary to the Dublin City Manager, retiring in 1947.[106] He died in 1953. Patrick Stephenson in turn succeeded Róisín Walsh, going on to become the city's second Chief Librarian from 1950 until his death in 1960, just days before retirement. Tom Dowling continued to serve as Dublin County Librarian until his sudden death in office in 1966.

---

100 Dermot Foley, 'Mr. James Thomas Dowling (Obituary)', *An Leabharlann*, xxv, No. 1 (March 1967), p.9.
101 Cumann na mBan mural wall http://www.ul.ie/wic/content/cumann-na-mban-mural-wall, accessed September 2015; *Ulster Herald*, 14 May 1921.
102 *Ulster Herald*, 28 Jan. 1922.
103 PRONI: HA/5/283, File relating to the prosecution of James Walsh 1922-23; *Irish Press*, 25 June 1949.
104 *Ulster Herald*, 10 Mar. 1923.
105 Herbert A Frew, 'The passing of a Librarian: an obituary of James Byrne' *Irish Library Bulletin*, new series (1948), ix, p. 24.
106 James Barry 'Death of Colonel Thomas E. Gay' *An Leabharlann* (March, 1953), p. 31.

Three Castles Burning:
Dublin Fire Brigade and the Easter Rising.

Las Fallon

*I stood on the rooftops in the gathering gloom, Dublin Burning! What
a sight! Gruesome, awe-inspiring. Man's inhumanity to man – there
is nothing so brutal and callous in all creation. Columns of deep black,
evil looking smoke spiralled up into the darkening sky. Flames leaped,
twisted, curled and danced fantastically and the glow of this inferno
tinted every object with a lurid redness. The face of a volunteer, as he
looked towards me, took on this horrid tinge. It was as if all the evils
that had tormented our people through the ages were now gathered in
our metropolis and were having a witches frenzy of ritual and grim
stalking death.*[1]

In April 1916 Dublin Fire Brigade (DFB) was a professional fire service under
the command of Captain Thomas Purcell.[2] The municipal brigade, under the
jurisdiction of Dublin Corporation, had been founded in 1862 under Captain
James Robert Ingram and had replaced the previously fragmented firefighting
system of parish brigades, insurance company fire brigades, the small police fire
service provided by the DMP, and the Corporation Waterworks fire brigade which
itself had roots back to the origins of a city fire service in 1711. Purcell was Dublin's
third chief officer, having replaced Captain John Boyle in 1892. Purcell was an
engineer and was intensely interested in the science of firefighting. He also had
practical experience as a volunteer firefighter in his native Kilkenny, where he had
been awarded a medal for saving the life of a young woman trapped in a burning
building at a fire in the city in December 1875. In his years as chief of the fire
brigade he travelled widely to study advances in firefighting techniques in Europe
and the United States. In Purcell's time in Dublin he had overseen the expansion
of the city fire service and added new equipment to its fire-fighting armoury, some
to his own design and invention. The city was protected by four fire stations. Purcell
had moved away from the original small cramped headquarters in the Waterworks
depot in Whitehorse Yard which he had inherited from his predecessors, and had
divided the city into quarters: A, B, C and D districts. Each district, by 1916, was
equipped with a modern fire station. The city stations were at Thomas Street (A),

---

1   W. J. Brennan Whitmore. *Dublin burning: the Easter Rising from behind the barricades*
(Dublin,, 2013), p. 121. Reproduced by kind permission of Gill & Macmillan, publishers.

2   The chief officer of the Dublin Fire Brigade was known as the 'captain' until 1938. His
second in command carried the title of 'lieutenant'.

Tara Street (B) which was also the brigade headquarters, Buckingham Street (C) and Dorset Street (D).

Fire Brigade Tender in Brunswick Street (Tara Street) Fire Station (Dublin Fire Brigade Museum)

The brigade strength in 1916 stood at forty-five men. Purcell and his lieutenant, John Myers, were stationed at brigade headquarters in Tara Street. The headquarters and district stations each had a station officer, with a foreman to deputise for the station officer in his absence. The remainder of the thirty-six men of the brigade were assigned to headquarters or the district stations where they all 'lived in'. The men with families lived in married quarters in the station, and the single men in dormitories. The brigade was equipped with two modern motor fire engines, both built to Purcell's own design. The first, RI 1090, was stationed at Tara Street with the second, RI 2080, at Thomas Street. In addition, the brigade had three horse-drawn turntable ladders which could be used for firefighting or rescue work. Again, they had been designed by Purcell and had been introduced in the late 1890s to deal with the difficulties of getting the old style street fire escape ladders under the overhead wires of the new electric tram system. Their design had been patented by Purcell and his turntable ladders were in use throughout the United Kingdom. Other equipment consisted of hose carriers and hose carts designed to fight fires using standpipes from street hydrants, or to carry additional supplies of hose to major fires. The brigade also maintained three horse-drawn Shand-Mason steam driven pumps, but by 1916 these had been relegated to reserve status.

Dublin Fire Brigade also provided the city's ambulance service. In 1898, following a visit to Belfast where he had observed that city's fire brigade ambulance, Purcell designed a horse-drawn ambulance for Dublin. The firemen were instructed in first aid by Dr McAuley, the brigade's doctor. By 1916 the brigade had three ambulances in service. The first two were horse-drawn, and a motor ambulance had entered service in 1912. For the two years prior to the Rising these ambulances, along with the ambulances from the township fire brigades in Pembroke and Rathmines, had been involved in removing wounded soldiers from the hospital ships which regularly docked in Dublin. The wounded were then taken to the various hospitals within the city, including the George V Military Hospital (now St Bricin's), and the new military hospital set up within Dublin Castle.

The First World War had had little impact on the running of the brigade. Only two firemen, Patrick Bruton and John Murphy, volunteered for military service in spite of incentives from Dublin Corporation which included a promise to hold their jobs open for them on return, payment of half pay while in the military, and an undertaking to accept military service as Corporation service for pension purposes. In all, 169 Corporation staff had left for service with the British Army or Royal Navy, but the fire brigade provided one of the lowest levels of recruits from within the Corporation's various departments.[3]

The brigade had been unionised since 1892 with its members forming the Dublin Fire Brigademen's Union (DFBU). This was the first firefighters' trade union in the world and indicated the degree to which the men, often drawn from the ranks of the heavily unionised craft workers, were very much a part of trade union life of the city. As a public service union they had not been directly involved in the Lockout of 1913, but their trade union sympathies were well known to the DMP; as one policeman noted: 'The Dublin Fire Brigade also was unfriendly to the police, they too were on the radical side and always surly to the force'.[4]

The day on which the Rising broke out, 24 April 1916, began as all days did in Dublin Fire Brigade, with the reading of the 'slate' for the day.[5] This involved each fireman being detailed to specific duty as a crewman on a particular vehicle, and also included telephone duty as each man did his turn in the watchroom. Men were detailed to fire or ambulance duty, checked their allotted vehicles to make sure that all the equipment needed was carried, and made good any shortages which came to their attention. If members of the crew were on leave, that was

---

3   *DC Reports* 1916, Report no. 67.
4   David Nelligan, *The spy in the Castle* (London. 1968), p. 512.
5   To this day the detailing of individual duties for each firefighter at the start of a shift is known as 'reading the slate'.

noted as well. This would be a 24 hour period free from duty. In the Tara Street occurrence book Firemen Byrne and Collins were recorded as being on leave on 24 April.[6] In the daybook for Dorset Street station, Fireman McSweeney is listed as being on leave.[7] In Thomas Street, the officer in charge, Station Officer Martin Lambert was on leave and the station was in the care of Foreman Michael Fox.[8]

S. O'Barry and his son (Tara Street) Fire Station (Dublin Fire Brigade Museum)

For Dublin Fire Brigade, the first indication that anything out of the ordinary was happening in the city that day came between 11 o'clock and noon when a detachment of the Irish Citizen Army stopped at Tara Street and the officer in charge, Seán Connolly, sent for his brother Joseph, a fireman stationed there.[9] Joe

6   Tara Street fire station logbook (DCLA, 1916.02). The logbook covers the period 21 January to 6 May 1916.
7   Dorset Street fire station daybook 1916 (Dublin Fire Brigade Museum).
8   Notes on Thomas Street fire station – 24 April to 7 May, submitted to Captain Purcell by Station Officer Lambert (DCLA, 1916.03).
9   The incident is mentioned in a number of BMH witness statements, including those of Rosie Hackett (WS 546) and William Oman (WS 421) and also in unpublished documents held by the Connolly family.

Connolly had joined the DFB in 1915 and was still in his probationary year. Like his brothers Seán, George, Mattie and Eddie and his sister Kate, Joe Connolly was also a member of the Irish Citizen Army. Seán told Joe that he was needed at Liberty Hall, not just to supplement the numbers turning out after the disastrous effect of Eoin MacNeill's countermanding order over the previous weekend, but also because Joe was a motor driver, a rare skill amongst the ranks of the Citizen Army. Joe changed out of DFB uniform and returned to his family home for his rifle. On his way to Liberty Hall he commandeered a motor car which was used to ferry supplies to the GPO. He spent the first night of the Rising there, and on Tuesday morning was told to report to the ICA garrison at Stephen's Green. He arrived there in time to take part in the occupation of the Royal College of Surgeons. Under Michael Mallin the garrison had originally based themselves within the Green, but early on Tuesday morning they came under heavy fire from positions held by the Royal Dublin Fusiliers in the Shelbourne Hotel and the United Services Institute.

Joe Connolly formed part of the garrison in the college and is mentioned in several accounts. He was engaged in sniping from the roof and, using his skills as a fireman, was also in a position to help with treating the wounded. He rescued Michael Doherty under fire after Doherty was hit by a burst of machine gun fire, and treated him before he was removed by DFB ambulance to Mercer's Hospital where his life was saved despite the fact that he had received twelve bullet wounds. Connolly also helped to treat Margaret Skinnider after she was shot and wounded in a sortie to Harcourt Street. After the surrender Joe Connolly was taken to Richmond Barracks. He was sent to Wandsworth prison on 9 May, and then to the internment camp at Frongoch in Wales.

As units of the Irish Volunteers and Citizen Army moved into their allotted positions, the fire brigade became aware of the battle beginning in the city. In one of the first actions of the Rising members of Na Fianna Éireann and the Volunteers had hoped to capture and destroy the Magazine Fort in the Phoenix Park, the main magazine for holding spare weapons, ammunition and explosives for the British Army garrison in Dublin. Having taken the fort, they were unable to gain entrance to the main store rooms as the keys were missing. They removed rifles and ammunition and set a fire to try and ignite the main explosives storage area. The fire ignited some charges left by members of Na Fianna but failed to set off the explosives themselves. It did, however, start a serious fire and a crew from Thomas Street Station was despatched to deal with it. They later called for assistance from Tara Street. While the Tara Street crew were on their way to the park at around 4 p.m., they were turned back at a Volunteer barricade on the quays. While the Chief

Officer, Captain Purcell, described a threat from the Volunteers to fire on his men in a piece he later wrote for the *Sinn Féin Rebellion Handbook* produced by the *Irish Times*, the man on the spot, Lieutenant Myers, contradicted him in a letter to the *Irish Times* which was also reproduced in the Handbook, in which he denied that he or his men had been threatened. The crew were driving into an area of active military operations, and had been directed to a less dangerous route.

Brunswick Street (now Tara Street) Fire Station (Dublin Fire Brigade Museum)

In other parts of the city the fighting had started in earnest. The busiest fire brigade vehicles were the ambulances, which would work non stop for the coming week. An ambulance returning to Tara Street just before 2 p.m. on 24 April reported that they had left three soldiers of the 5th [Royal Irish] Lancers dead in Jervis Street hospital as well as two wounded soldiers. These men were part of a patrol from the 6th Reserve Cavalry Regiment (which included elements of the 5th Lancers) which had been ordered on a foolhardy patrol down Sackville (O'Connell) Street, apparently to find out what was happening in the area. They were fired on from the GPO and other garrisons on Sackville Street and retreated, leaving their dead and wounded behind to be picked up by a DFB ambulance. Another dead soldier from the 5th Lancers would later be left in Jervis Street, as would John Keely, a Volunteer officer in E Company of the 4th Battalion killed at the GPO in what may have been either the accidental discharge of a weapon or fire from British troops in Upper Sackville Street.[10]

As the afternoon went on the ambulances became busier, and one wonders at the stories which lay behind entries such as these:

> Alexandra Wilson age 18 of North Brook Ave [left] in Jervis St. bruised shoulder struck with Rifle
> or
> 'James Hoare age 13 in Jervis St. of 25 Nth Cumberland St. Cut on nose plate glass fell on him[11]

Later that afternoon an ambulance reported that it had left:

> Two 5th Lancers in Stephens[sic] Hospital, two R[oyal] I[rish] Regiment in Richmond Barracks.
>
> One P[olice]. Con[stable] in Meath [hospital] one unknown male dead in St. Vincents Remainder suffering from gunshot wounds.

The policeman was DMP Constable Michael Lahiff, shot dead by the Citizen Army at Stephen's Green. The details of the other casualties indicate how the battle in Dublin was spreading, with actions at the Mendicity Institution, the South Dublin Union, the Four Courts, City Hall and elsewhere.

---

10   Ray Bateson, *They died by Pearse's side* (Dublin, 2010) pp 191-5.
11   Tara Street logbook, 1916.

We are largely reliant on the evidence of the Tara Street log to trace incidents as they happened. The ambulances were based there, and it is the only complete log to survive (though events in Thomas Street can be traced from an account of the station's activities during Easter Week prepared for Captain Purcell by Station Officer Lambert). The Tara Street log book records in stark detail the work being done by the city's firemen. The wounded lieutenant and three wounded privates of the Royal Irish Regiment, as well as the dead British soldier and the dead Volunteer left in Steevens' Hospital later that day, were no doubt casualties of the savage fighting going on in and around the South Dublin Union, where Éamonn Ceannt's 4th Battalion were holding their own against vastly superior forces. The log recalls a litany of ambulance cases, but at 10.14 p.m. there is the first call to a fire. The section from Buckingham Street station were dealing with a fire in the Cable Shoe Co. in Sackville Street. Within ten minutes they had requested help from Tara Street and an engine was dispatched. Within an hour there was a second serious outbreak, again in a shoe shop on Sackville Street, as the Trueform Shoe Company was burned.

Since shortly after noon, when the GPO was initially seized, crowds had gathered on the streets to view the spectacle of an armed uprising and to try and find news of what was happening in the city and countrywide. As the afternoon wore on and in the absence of police on the streets, some within the crowds began to realise that an opportunity for looting offered itself. Efforts to subdue it by the Volunteers were unsuccessful as they had to concentrate on strengthening their positions. One of their tactics, which was militarily very effective, was to burrow or 'mousehole' between buildings to allow them freedom of movement without being seen by British snipers or machine gunners. However, these same holes allowed fires to spread easily from building to building later in the week.

As the evening wore on the looting of clothes shops was followed by the looting of shoe shops, as some who had never owned a decent pair of boots in their lives now found themselves able to pick from the finest stock. Fires were started by looters in these buildings: the fires in the Cable and Trueform shoe shops were the first ones in the area the brigade that the brigade responded to.

Date *April 24th* 1916. *Mon* day ~~No.~~ *B* Station.

	A	M	OCCURRENCES	Left	Returned
	10	66	Byrne on leave		
	10	3	Collins on leave		
	11	4"	Rochells fire signal correct		
X	12	5	Ambulance to 72. Cadogan Rd. by phone. 1480		
	12	33	Do. returned Male refused to be removed		
X	12	39	Ambulance to 40 ams St. by phone 2256		
X	12	40	Do. to 20 Benburb St. by phone . 2307.		
X	12	41	Do. to Kildare St. by phone. 3182.		
X	12	57	Do. to Merchants Quay by phone 3618		
X	1	5	Ambulance to Grand Canal St. did not attend		
Kildare St	1	8	Ambulance returned left male unknown age about 30 in Vincents Hospital Dead		
X X	1	21	Ambulance to Earlsfort Terrace by phone 1063 also to Harrington St. did not attend by phone 3519		
X	1	25	Ambulance to Island Bridge by phone 7227		
X	1	28	Do. to Mount Brown by phone 236 did not attend		
X	1	37	Ambulance to North Earl St. by phone 2173		
X	1	38	Do. to Stephens Green by phone 1459. not available.		
Charles St.	1	52	Ambulance returned left Three Soldiers of the 5th Lancers Dead in Jervis St also left 2 wounded Soldiers in Jervis		
Abbey St.			St. Left John Reilly of Rathfarnham in Jervis St wounded in Stomach		
Sackville St.			left 1 Soldier of 5 Lancers Dead in Jervis St		
1th Earl St	1	55	ambulance returned left alexandra wilson age 18 of 23 north Brook in Jervis St Bruised shoulders done by 1 inch rifle also left James Hoare age 13 in Jervis St of 26 1th Cumberland St cut on nose plate shrapnel or this		

April 24th 1916 Fire Brigade Ambulance Logbook (DCLA)

The fires were recorded by Captain Purcell and were later included in his annual report for 1916:

'April 24th
10.06 pm. 31 Sackville street. -Extinguished fire in 'Cable' boot shop (previously looted)
11.59 pm. 18 Sackvile Street. -Extinguished fire in basement of 'Trueform' boot shop (previously looted)

April 25th
11.56 am. 32 Sackville Street. -Extinguished fire in rear of Dunnes Hat shop (previously looted).
4.11 pm. 5, 6, 7 upper Sackville Street.-Extinguished fire in Lawrences fancy goods warehouse ... The place was being looted and in complete disorder, two persons trapped in an upper room by fire and taken down by fire escape proved to be looters.

April 26th
12.59 pm. 47 Henry Street – Extinguished fire in Williams and Co.'s store at rear of shop ... building saved but stock looted.
5.14 pm. Called again to same building and saved it.
8.07 pm. 8 Sackville Street. H. E. Taffe, outfitter. Did not attend (within the firing lines). Burned down, but fire did not extend.
8.40 pm. 1 and 2 Clanwilliam Place – Did not attend as the houses were being shelled by the military.

April 27th
5.07 am. Harcourt street – Extinguished fire in shop of four storied building ... stairs and part roof destroyed.
9.30 am. Linenhall Barracks. Could not attend under conditions prevailing in that section of the city. Barracks burned down and fire which lasted two days and nights unchecked extended to and burned the extensive adjoining oil and drug stores of Hugh Moore and Alexander Ltd., also Leckie and Co.'s printing works and three other business houses in Bolton Street.
12.32 pm. Abbey Street Lr. – As this, the GPO district, was then under continuous rifle fire and being shelled by field guns and mortars we could not approach it, consequently this was really the commencement of the conflagration which wrought such havoc on the Sackville Street area. In twenty minutes the

fire ... had extended to both sides of the thoroughfare, through
a printing office on [the] north side into Sackville Place and
through Wynnes Hotel on the south into Harbour Court,
gradually spreading by Hoytes Corner to the DBC building
and by Hamilton and Longs stores to Eden Quay. At 7.20
pm. The 'May Oatway'[12] detector in Scotts, 2 Lower Sackville
Street, indicated in our station that fire had reached that
point. During the night the fire extended to [the] Imperial
Hotel and Cleary's Warehouse, and caught the new bakery
and restaurant of Sir Joseph Downes in Earl Place.[13]

This latter fire would prove to be the start of what Purcell would call 'the Great
Fire'. This conflagration would consume whole blocks of buildings and continue
to spread unhindered until after the ceasefire of 29 April, when the brigade could
devote its resources to tackling it.

Apart from the Tara Street log book, the only other intact account of a fire station
during the Rising comes from the material submitted by Station Officer Lambert
of Thomas Street to Captain Purcell. This took the form of notes from the station
log detailing the day to day events throughout the week. It goes into the detail of
what duties were assigned to each man on each day down to the hours of telephone
duty, but it also tells the story of what those men were dealing with in the Thomas
Street area and the remainder of the district that they covered. These notes record
the Thomas Street section being dispatched to the fire in the Magazine Fort on
24 April at 12.7 p.m. They tell of being dispatched to Upper O'Connell Street
on Tuesday afternoon, 25 April, and to Henry Street on Wednesday 26 April.
Perhaps the most significant entry refers to a major fire at the junction of Bridge
Street and Ushers Quay on the morning of Friday 28 April. The previous night
two Volunteers from the Four Courts garrison, Lieutenant Peader Clancy and
Volunteer Tom Smart, had crossed Church Street Bridge under fire and used cans
of paraffin or petrol which they had brought from the Four Courts to start a fire
in a building at the corner of Bridge Street and Ushers Quay. The upper floor was
being used by a detachment of the Royal Dublin Fusiliers to fire into the Four
Courts and the accurate fire from their position was a serious hazard to those in
the complex. Clancy and Smart broke into the ground floor of the building being
used by the Fusiliers and started a fire which forced the troops to evacuate the
building and lose their vantage point.[14]

---

12   The 'May Oatway' was an automatic fire detection system linked to a control panel in the
     Central Fire Station in Tara Street.
13   *DFB annual report* 1916, p. 8.
14   Las Fallon, *Dublin Fire Brigade and the Irish revolution* (Dublin, 2012), p. 60.

Control Room Great Brunswick Street (Tara Street) Fire Station (Dublin Fire Brigade Museum)

In mentioning this fire and the response to it S/O Lambert also tells us that

> On the previous night Captain Sleigh of the 5th Lancers who was in charge of Thomas Street told me he would not allow any lights in the stn + to keep all doors closed, that his men would fire on any light or at any stir they hear.[15]

In the face of these threats from the military S/O Lambert could not turn out to any fire without the permission of the British military. He sent word to Captain Sleigh. In Lambert's own words:

> He told me that he would have to get permission from Headquarters. After some delay he gave me permission + I turned out with motor engine + 5 men + the whole time that we were working we were in the line of fire with the military in upper Bridge St. and the volunteers at Bridge St. Bridge.[16]

This fire involved a direct threat to British military lives yet the brigade had to wait for permission to attend from British Army headquarters. In his account of the fighting in O'Connell Street, Irish Volunteer Commandant W. J. Brennan-Whitmore of the Dublin Fire Brigade offered further proof of how the military treated the DFB:

---

15   Notes on Thomas Street fire station (DCLA, 1916.03).
16   Ibid.

214

I cannot let the recording of these events pass without paying a well-deserved tribute to the Dublin fire brigade. All that evening and night they were being called to fires in O'Connell Street and they uncomplainingly responded to every call. They continued to render this service until some time on Wednesday when we had occasion to call them to a fire which had broken out rather mysteriously in our vicinity. When the call went through the fire brigade replied that they were prohibited from answering any more calls from O'Connell Street and that the British authorities had told them that there would be many more fires in O'Connell Street before they were finished with us.[17]

It would certainly appear to have been a deliberate British policy to let the fires in central Dublin burn unhindered. At this point buildings were being shelled by artillery on the city streets, and machine guns had also been mounted on vantage points including the Rotunda Maternity Hospital.[18] The tactics seemed designed to burn out the rebels and force them out into the streets where they could be annihilated by machine gun and artillery fire. In the densely packed tenements and slums of Dublin, ordinary civilians, men, women, and children, would pay the butcher's bill for these tactics.[19]

By the time of the Ceasefire order on 29 April, there were a number of major fires burning in the city. Two were particularly dangerous. Jervis Street Hospital was in extreme danger from burning material being blown from the huge fires in Sackville Street and Henry Street and landing on its roof and verandahs. On the other side of Sackville Street the fire was rapidly spreading from North Earl Street towards the Pro-Cathedral in Marlborough Street. Within minutes of the ceasefire

---

17 Brennan Whitmore, *Dublin burning*, p. 88.
18 Paul O'Brien, *Battleground: the battle for the General Post Office, 1916* (Dublin, 2015), p. 104.
19 The author, at the time the curator of the DFB Museum, handled material relating to the DFB in the Rising in the Adams & Mealy's auction of April 2008 in the Adams showroom on St Stephen's Green. Lot 398B in that auction related to the DFB and the Rising and included a copy of the very scarce 1916 annual report as well as other documents. The most significant pieces, in this author's opinion, were a series of letters, four in all, between Captain Purcell and a Colonel Portal at 'the Lower Yard, Dublin Castle' in which Purcell pleaded for a ceasefire to allow the fire brigade to fight the fires burning in central Dublin and prevent a conflagration. The requests were refused until the Saturday. Following the ceasefire a note was sent from Colonel Portal giving the brigade permission to operate in the city centre. It carried a covering note to his officers telling them to open fire regardless of the presence of the firefighters in the event of a resumption of hostilities with the 'Sinn Féiners' I was unable to transcribe or copy the material under the (very reasonable) rules of the auction house and the brigade were outbid on the day of the auction. The items are believed to be in a private collection and hopefully will re emerge someday for the benefit of scholars of the period. Adams & Mealy's Independence Auction Tuesday 15th April 2008, p. 111 of catalogue.

order Purcell concentrated his forces to stop the spread of the Henry Street fire. The brigade were in danger as shots were fired in their vicinity and Purcell again withdrew his men. It is unclear who was firing but word of the ceasefire had not spread widely at this time and isolated snipers were still operating. Realising the imminent danger to Jervis Street Hospital, where the authorities had appealed to him to help evacuate the patients in the face of the approaching inferno, Purcell split his small force. He sent Lieutenant Myers and one small crew to stop the North Earl Street fire and save the Pro-Cathedral, while he took the rest of the brigade, augmented by a small number of firefighters from the private fire brigades of both the Guinness Brewery and Power's Whiskey Distillery, to stop the Henry Street fire and save Jervis Street. By 7 a.m. the next morning Purcell could declare that the fight had been won. His exhausted crews had worked throughout the night stopping the spread of the fires. They were forced to watch as buildings which had already ignited burned to a shell, but they were able to set up fire stops and fight the blaze to prevent it spreading beyond the area already involved at the time of the ceasefire. They did so while being exposed to dangers from collapsing buildings and the regular detonation of ammunition and explosives left behind within the former fighting area.

In the aftermath of the Rising the centre of the city lay in ruins. The cost of the damage ran to over £2,000,000, but the DFB had prevented further damage and saved the lives of many citizens. The work of the fire brigade in both its firefighting and ambulance roles was recognised, and the brigade received tributes from all sides. Dublin Corporation were requested to recognise the bravery and devotion to duty of the firemen in some concrete way, and granted the award of a chevron for bravery to each man on duty that week. The chevron carried a one shilling pay rise for the men to whom it was awarded. Captain Purcell himself was awarded a bonus of £50, as was Lieutenant Myers. In addition, Purcell was awarded the bronze medal of the British Fire Prevention Committee 'as a token of regard for the splendid work done by him and his brigade during most trying circumstances during the Irish Rebellion of 1916'.[20]

---

20   Tom Geraghty and Trevor Whitehead, *The Dublin Fire Brigade: a history of the brigade, the fires and the emergencies*, (Dublin, 2004), p. 154.

One of the poets of the period, the composer Arnold Bax, writing under his pseudonym of 'Dermot O'Byrne' in his poem 'A Dublin Ballad -1916' captured the destruction of the city centre :

> *Well, the last fire is trodden down,*
> *Our dead are rotting fast in lime,*
> *We all can sneak back into town,*
> *Stravogue about as in old time.*
>
> *And stare at gaps of grey and blue*
> *Where Lower Mount Street used to be*
> *And where flies hum round muck we knew*
> *For Abbey Street and Eden Quay.*[21]

---

21 Arnold Bax (writing as Dermot O'Byrne), 'A Dublin Ballad – 1916' from *A Dublin Ballad and other poems* by Dermot O'Byrne (Dublin, The Candle Press, 1918), pp 6-7.

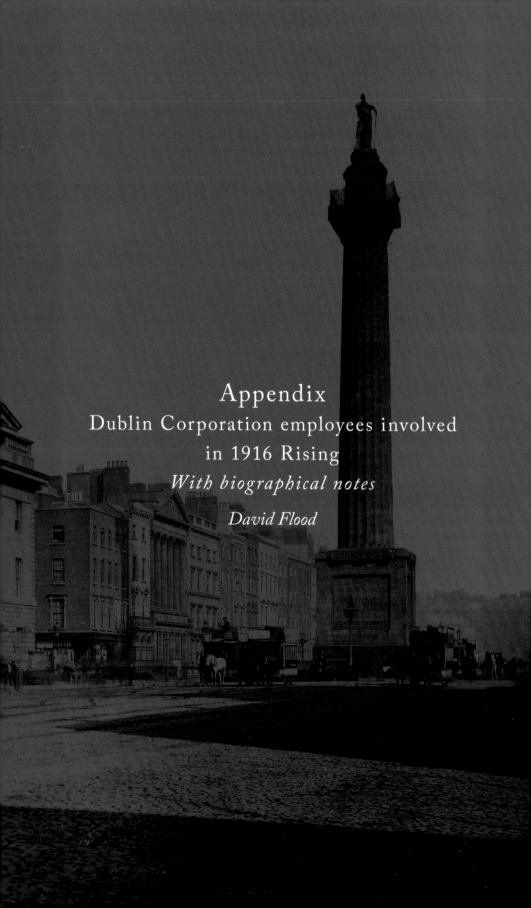

Appendix
Dublin Corporation employees involved
in 1916 Rising
With biographical notes

David Flood

Name	1916 Rank / Unit /Garrison	Sources
Allan (Allen), Frederick J.	One BMH statement has him as 'Captain' Fred Allan. In any case claimed by people such as Laurence Nugent to have been in charge of the Kingstown/Dún Laoghaire Company, Dublin Regiment, Irish National Volunteers. [South County Dublin].	BMH WS 409 (Val Jackson), WS 907 (Laurence Nugent); IE UCDA P17b/88 (Ernie O'Malley Papers), Laurence Nugent; McGee, Owen, 'Frederick James Allan (1861-1937), Fenian & civil servant', *History Ireland*, 10.1 (Spring 2002); Kelly, M.J., *The Fenian ideal and Irish nationalism, 1882-1916* (Woodbridge, 2006).

Corporation Service

First, secretary to Lord Mayor Pile and then from 1901 secretary to several committees (Lighting, Cleansing and Electricity) of Dublin Corporation.

Other Notes

IRB member from 1880. Fred Allan rapidly rose within the Brotherhood to make it onto the Supreme Council by 1883. By the 1900s he was one of the IRB's most powerful men. Manager of John Redmond's Parnellite newspaper the *Irish Independent*, he was dismissed and then found employment as Mayor Pile's secretary. He later became secretary to no less than three of Dublin Corporation's committees (and was credited with the creation of Fairview Park). He was deposed from the IRB Supreme Council and expelled from the IRB in the early 1910s in favour of the new generation which would plan and carry out the Easter 1916 Rising. Some testimony claims that the INV companies controlled by Fred Allan and Thomas Cullen were ready to come out in Easter Week if arms promised by Éamonn Ceannt had arrived via the *Aud*. However they were told by Rory O'Connor not to mobilise due to shortage of weapons. Later, Allan became involved with the 1916 rebel dependents' fund, and was interned by the British during the War of Independence for having 'seditious' literature.

Name	1916 Rank / Unit /Garrison	Sources
Ashton, William Francis	Volunteer, D Company, 1st Battalion, Dublin Brigade IV North King Street, Church Street, King's Inns Quay, Four Courts.	MSPC 24SP2848.

Corporation Service

Temporary employment working on Corporation Electoral Register, 11 December 1925 to 7 January 1926.

Other Notes

Escaped arrest and internment after the Rising. Attacked British armoured car in Phibsborough during the War of Independence, among other operations. Arrested and interned in Ballykinlar Camp (from December 1920 to December 1921). As a National Army officer (Comdt), was later involved in Army Mutiny of 1924.

Name	1916 Rank / Unit /Garrison	Sources
Banks, Henry T.	Volunteer, A Company, 3rd Battalion, Dublin Brigade IV. Railway works at Grand Canal Street, Boland's Mills.	MSPC MSP34REF228; BMH WS 1637 (Henry T. Banks); *DC Reports* Vol I, 1915, p. 582; *DCC Minutes*, 1916, p. 261.

Corporation Service

Employed from 2 November 1906. Storekeeper, Tara Street Public Lighting depot. Denied his recommended pay increase after the Rising. In 1935 became a gas meter tester.

Other Notes

IRB member from 1910 (sworn in by Seán Mac Diarmada). Joined the Irish Volunteers at the Rotunda. Involved in the Howth gun-running. By his own account, 'While I was in the 1st Battalion, I bought my rifle, and paid £4.5.0 or £4.10.0 for it, not in a lump sum but on the easy payment system. I owed £1.0.0. on the rifle when I transferred to the 3rd Battalion, and the 1st Battalion tried to claim it, but they did not get it. I paid the £1.0.0. for it. These rifles, I think, were got through the IRB, and it was IRB men who got preference when they were given out. They were long Lee Enfields [...] We had manoeuvres all over in the county, around the hills. We had target practice in Camden Row, where we paid a penny for five shots. De Valera used to come in, the same as myself, and pay his penny for five shots.' Acted as bodyguard to Captain O'Connor before the Rising. Encountered Alderman Tom Kelly in Stamer Street while mobilising, who wished him luck in the Rising. Encountered Elizabeth O'Farrell when she arrived at Boland's Mills with the surrender orders. Interned in Wakefield and then Frongoch. Had been recommended for a pay increase on account of 'the manner in which he has improved the storekeeping', but may have been penalised for having been in the Rising (*DCC Minutes*). Henry Banks put away 'cases of grenades, revolver ammunition and revolvers' in his Corporation stores, which also functioned as a drop for Battalion intelligence reports and orders during the War of Independence. 'I was working in the Corporation, and when things got bad I could get in touch with [Comdt Joe O'Connor] at dinner time and again at five o'clock, if he wanted me.'

Name	1916 Rank / Unit /Garrison	Sources
Boland, Gerald/Ó Beoláin, Gearóid	Volunteer, B Company, 2nd Battalion, Dublin Brigade IV. Jacob's Factory.	BMH WS 586 (Kathleen Boland), MSPC MSP34REF15471; *DC Reports* (II), 1921, No. 220; ElectionsIreland. org http:// electionsireland.org/ candidate.cfm?ID=1417, http://electionsireland. org/candidate. cfm?ID=2415 (accessed 28/09/15); Houses of the Oireachtas Dáil Éireann Member's Directory http://www.oireachtas. ie/

Corporation Service

Employed in Main Drainage (Clontarf Pumping Station) from October 1907 as a fitter. Land Steward (and subsequently Resident Engineer) at Crooksling TB Sanatorium, Brittas, Co. Dublin from January 1916 until June 1922.

IRB member. Brother of Harry Boland. Son of Jim Boland, who was a very prominent Dublin Fenian of the late 1800s (originally from Manchester, and involved as a boy in the jailbreak of Captain Thomas Kelly); also a member of Dublin County Board of the GAA who controlled the paviors in Dublin Corporation and was associated (rightly or wrongly) with the Invincibles, also with the Parnellite faction of the Irish Party. On hearing of the Rising on Easter Monday made his way in by bicycle from Crooksling to join the Jacobs' garrison. Interned after the surrender. Gerald was again arrested and imprisoned from May to December 1918. In 1919 or 1920 took over the Brittas Company (i.e. the Volunteers in the vicinity of Crooksling). Commandant, 7th Battalion, Dublin Brigade at the Truce. Fought on the anti-Treaty side in the Civil War, being captured at Blessington on 7 July 1922 and imprisoned until 19 July 1924. Supposedly known as 'Trotsky' for his left-wing views. Elected as TD for Roscommon in the 1923 General Election. Founder-member of Fianna Fáil, and re-elected for Roscommon until the 1961 General Election, being a Minister 1936-48 and 1951-4. His attempt to withdraw his MSP application in 1942 caused consternation among officials over the bureaucratic mess (there was no provision for this), not least when Boland in the Fifties decided to withdraw his withdrawal. Member of the Seanad 1961-9. His son, Kevin Boland TD, famously resigned on 4 November 1970 during the Arms Crisis (father Gerald also resigned as vice President of Fianna Fáil).

Name	1916 Rank / Unit /Garrison	Sources
Brady, Francis	Volunteer, E Company, 2nd Battalion, Dublin Brigade IV. Jacob's Factory, Delahunt's pub on Camden Street.	MSPC MSP34REF1512.

Corporation Service

Casual labourer on Clontarf Sea Wall in 1938. Variously employed in Lighting, Cleansing and Housing Departments (labourer and lamplighter) from late 1938.

Other Notes

In Delahunt's public house during the Rising. Escaped arrest and internment afterwards – he was cut off from his unit on the night of Thursday 27 April and couldn't rejoin at Jacob's. No further service.

Name	1916 Rank / Unit /Garrison	Sources
Brady, James Joseph	Volunteer, C Company, 3rd Battalion, Dublin Brigade IV. Jacob's Factory, Merrion Square.	MSPC 24SP12927.

Corporation Service

Employed as porter by Dublin Board of Assistance in late 1930s/early 1940s.

Other Notes

Joined the Irish Volunteers in 1913. Interned at Knutsford and Frongoch. Internment number 1514C. During the War of Independence got leave of absence from the Volunteers to undertake political work for Sinn Féin (particularly electioneering). In the Civil War involved in pro-Treaty 'Citizens' Defence Force', then joined the National Army as Military Police. Discharged in 1924.

Name	1916 Rank / Unit /Garrison	Sources
Breslin, James	Volunteer, D Company, 1st Battalion, Dublin Brigade IV. North King Street, Church Street, North Brunswick Street, Red Cow Lane, Four Courts.	MSPC MSP34REF20849.

Corporation Service

Lighting Department from 1 October 1934.

Other Notes

Interned at Stafford and Frongoch. Resident caretaker of Colmcille Gaelic League Hall at 5 Blackhall Place used by the IRA during the War of Independence, and in charge of the secret armoury there in the basement. Took part in the Thomas Ashe funeral from City Hall. Involved in many activities, and escaped over the roof of No. 5 during a Black and Tan raid. During the Civil War was arrested and a prisoner in Wellington Barracks, but received compassionate early release because of his wife's bad health. His brother Peadar was shot while 'escaping' from Mountjoy during the Civil War, brother Christy (Kit) was kidnapped and shot by plain-clothes Free State forces. Paddy Holohan statement in MSPC notes that that Breslin 'was [in bad health at this time] – his two brothers had been murdered [...] and it probably did play the deuce with his nerves.'

Name	1916 Rank / Unit / Garrison	Sources
de Búrca, Aoife (Eva Burke)	Member, Cumann na mBan Central Branch. 'Nurse in Charge GPO' according to J.J. Doyle. Reis's, Hibernian Bank, GPO.	MSPC MSP34REF53445; BMH WS 359 (Aoife de Búrca).

Corporation Service

Public health nurse from (at least) 1934, Dublin Corporation.

Other Notes

Private nurse in 1916. Mobilised on Easter Sunday and then again on Easter Monday, being sent home both times. On Tuesday she went into O'Connell Street and stayed that night at Reis's, attending to a wounded volunteer. On Wednesday she went into the Hibernian Bank, which was evacuated about Wednesday noon to the GPO. That evening she was sent by Pearse on messages around the city, spending her night at home in Drumcondra. She returned to the GPO on Thursday and was there until Friday night, when she accompanied the garrison wounded into Jervis Street hospital. 'She was most capable and cool and untiring in her efforts to give relief to the wounded' (Máire Mapather statement in MSPC file). She was allowed home on Saturday after the surrender, and had no further activities.

Name	1916 Rank / Unit / Garrison	Sources
Burke, Edward	Private, ICA. St Stephen's Green, Leeson Street, College of Surgeons.	MSPC MSP34REF1199.

Corporation Service

Corporation labourer in Streets Department, 'quasi-permanent' from 1920s. 'Continuous service from 3 December 1928 [...] about 5 ½ years' previous broken service'.

Other Notes

Carried out the usual ICA activities (drilling, route marches, manufacturing munitions, guarding Liberty Hall) before the Rising. Interned at Stafford and Frongoch afterwards. Helped defend Liberty Hall during the Armistice Night, 1918 riots by loyalists and British servicemen in Dublin. Served right up until the Civil War (usual activities such as getting arms, etc.), fought in the city with the ICA and was taken prisoner by the Free State after the Battle of the Bridges. Released in October 1923.

Name	1916 Rank / Unit /Garrison	Sources
Byrne, Alphonsus	Volunteer, A Company, 4th Battalion, Dublin Brigade IV. Dolphin's Barn, Marrowbone Lane Distillery, South Dublin Union.	MSPC MSP34REF88; CSORP, 1916 Index of Internees, NAI.

Corporation Service

Temporary timekeeper on Sewers Relief Works Scheme, 10 December 1934 until some point in 1939.

Other Notes

No. 501 on the War Office's 'Dangerous List'. The Marrowbone Lane Distillery garrison was a rearguard for the South Dublin Union position. After the surrender he was interned in Lewes Prison and then Frongoch. Released on 27 July 1916. Having lost his job after the Rising he went to London to get work, where he had an accident which removed four fingers of his left hand. Because of this he resigned from the IV in March 1918.

Name	1916 Rank / Unit /Garrison	Sources
Byrne, Christopher	2nd Lt, F Company, 4th Battalion, Dublin Brigade IV. Ardee Street (Watkin's) Brewery, Marrowbone Lane, South Dublin Union, St Stephen's Green.	MSPC MSP34REF101; BMH WS 167, WS 642 Is present as 'Christopher O'Byrne', labourer, with both Irish and English, boarding at 16a in the 1911 Census, aged 27.

Corporation Service

Possible reference in BMH WS 280 (Robert Holland), 'was at that time [1915] a fitter's helper in the Dublin Corporation'. Appears in SFRH: '16a (169) Upper Basin Street, Corporation labourer, sent to Knutsford on 3rd May 1916'. 26 May 1910 recruitment to Cleansing Department. Promoted into Housing as clerical worker on 26 November 1934. Retired on 1 October 1949.

Other Notes

IRB member from 1908, and at some point became a Centre (Lord Edward Circle in 41 Parnell Square, referred to as the 'Sodality'). Prisoner no. 1545B. Gaelic League. Raided a house in Celbridge before the Rising to try to find a Howth cache. Close friends with Con Colbert, who stayed at his house from the aftermath of an IRB Centres' meeting on Good Friday until Easter Monday, and was his commander in Watkin's Brewery until they were ordered by James Connolly to reinforce Seamus Murphy at Marrowbone Lane. Their contingent was cheered by the locals when marching out to surrender. Received Con Colbert's watch, sent just before his execution, with an inscription in Irish. Interned in Knutsford and then Frongoch. Armed attacks, anti-conscription, election campaign, drilling and arms gathering activities. Promoted out of the Company to the Battalion. Got a 'Jimmy Donnelly', ex-BA and his replacement as Company commander, a temporary job in the Corporation. Involved in Bloody Sunday and Kilmainham jail break. Interned. Active on anti-Treaty side during the Civil War, at Marrowbone Lane and on O'Connell Street, then interned. Ended as Vice-Commandant of 4th Battalion, Dublin Brigade IRA.

Name	1916 Rank / Unit /Garrison	Sources
Byrne, John (Seán)	Battalion Medical Lt, 3rd Battalion (formerly in C Company, of same Battalion) Dublin Brigade IV. Camden Row, Grand Canal Street Dispensary, GPO, Boland's Mills, City Hall, Grand Canal Street, Four Courts.	MSPC MSP34REF2281; BMH WS 422; WS1768 Andrew McDonnell; *Irish Volunteer*, 8 Feb., 26 Feb. 1916.

Corporation Service

Messenger at Tara Street Fire Station before Rising, Lamplighter from September 1916, then labourer in Paving Department until mid-1930s at least.

Other Notes

Joined IV in March 1915. After passing John J. Doyle's first-aid course (100 per cent score), gazetted in the 'Irish Volunteer' as Battalion Ambulance Officer, 3rd Battalion, on 26 February 1916. His commanding officer de Valera was reluctant to mobilise Byrne by ringing at the Fire Station on Easter Monday, so he received a couriered note in summons during the morning: 'Don't fail me. E. de V.' Battalion first aid officer (i.e. medic) and instructor before and during the Rising. Among the lives he saved was John O'Keefe's: '[...] for gunshot wound in right arm. There was an artery severed and it was some job to stop the flow of blood. And the doctors in Sir Patrick Dunn's Hospital remarked that whoever gave me the First Aid Attendance knew this job'. States in MSPC that regarding his medic skills 'I got it in the Movement. I was previously engaged in the Fire Station and I studied it there'. During the week a priest was brought in via Fire Brigade ambulance to hear confessions, and the rebels got bad news about the tide of battle from the sympathetic firemen. Carried the flag of surrender for Boland's Mills garrison (and is present as he describes at the head of the marching surrendered Boland's garrison, in the well-known photograph). Interned in Frongoch. Resigned from the IV later due to illness.

Name	1916 Rank / Unit /Garrison	Sources
Byrne, Joseph	Unknown. Unknown –likely not in Boland's Mills, though (he was deported from Richmond Barracks, not the RDS, according to the SFRH).	SFRH, 1911 Census, Electoral Roll.

Corporation Service

Labourer

Other Notes

No sources, apart from: SFRH as Corporation labourer, mention in BMH WS1686, electoral rolls and 1911 census (for 99 Marlborough Street, married labourer born in Manchester and forty years of age), sent from Richmond Barracks on 2 May to arrive Knutsford on 3 May 1916, according to SFRH. There are four 'Joseph Byrnes' on the 1916 Roll of Honour: B Company, 3rd Battalion (Boland's), C Company, 2nd Battalion (Jacob's), and C and D Companies, 4th Battalion (South Dublin Union).

Name	1916 Rank / Unit /Garrison	Sources
Byrne, Thomas F. ('Boer')	Captain, Maynooth Company and also O/C B Company, 1st Battalion, Dublin Brigade IV. Maynooth, GPO, Parliament Street (Exchange Hotel), Liffey Street.	MSPC 24SP9369; BMH WS 564.

Corporation Service

Clerk 1917-19, then Inspector of Night Watchmen during War of Independence – 1919/20 (according to reference statement).

IRB member. Joined John MacBride's 'Irish Brigade' in the Boer War. Later with the Irish evacuation to the USA by ship (along with the Irish-American 'Red Cross caravan' who had joined the Brigade). Miner in the Transvaal before the Boer War, miner in the US afterwards, supported by Clan na Gael. Returned on a visit to Ireland in 1913 and stayed to join the Irish Volunteers at their inauguration. Sent by Tom Clarke to be organiser-instructor of the Galtee Brigade of the pre-split IV. Member of the O'Donovan Rossa Funeral Committee. Was involved in a 1915 IRB raid to steal INV rifles held in Customs. Assigned under the improvised IRB orders for Monday's Rising (as a miner) to destroy bridges from Kildare back into Dublin, an echo back to the Irish Brigade days. He was at this time lodging with the Sheehans in Phibsborough. Brought a Volunteer contingent from Maynooth into Dublin, cheered by the college students, and they camped overnight in Glasnevin Cemetery. He and his men (including some deserters from the Royal Dublin Fusiliers) saw constant action throughout the week. Escaped to go on the run after the Rising. In 1918-19 he was interned by the British. Involved, as commanding officer of 1st Battalion, in planning many War of Independence operations. Asked to resign as O/C 1st battalion by GHQ after the Customs House attack of May 1921 and then on Brigade staff. Interned for a second time in the Rath Camp in the Curragh, until the Truce after which he escaped and was re-appointed O/C 1st Battalion. Taking the pro-Treaty side, was involved in organising the new National Army and operations like occupying Bolton Street Technical School until discharge in September 1922. He then took charge of the guard on the Dáil for many months, until that duty was relieved by the National Army. Officially Captain of the Dáil Guard (i.e. sergeant-at-arms in Leinster House) from 1 October 1924 until retirement in 1947.

Name	1916 Rank / Unit / Garrison	Sources
Caldwell, Patrick	Volunteer, Kimmage Garrison, Dublin Brigade IV (after the Rising joined F Company, 1st Battalion IV). GPO.	MSPC 24SP1495; BMH WS 638.

Corporation Service

Clerk. As per his witness statement 'obtained employment in the Dublin Corporation through the influence of Alderman Tom Kelly' three months after being released (which happened at Christmas 1916). By this timing, he served from early 1917 until sometime in 1920 or so, when he left to take up full-time intelligence duties.

Other Notes

Having emigrated to England in search of work, he joined a Liverpool company of the Irish Volunteers. Returned to Ireland and joined the Kimmage Garrison in order to avoid conscription. Got temporary employment with four others at the De Selby quarries at Jobstown – handy for the IV raid there for gelignite on Easter Sunday. Joined the IRB sometime in early 1916. With the rest of the Garrison marched to Harold's Cross and then got two trams (fares paid by Captain George Plunkett!) to O'Connell Street, from where they marched to Liberty Hall. Garrisoned the Ship Hotel on Abbey Street, then the GPO and was in Moore Street prior to the surrender. Regarding employment in Dublin Corporation in early 1917, notes that 'Two very prominent officers in similiar employment with me at the time were Commandant Joseph O'Connor of the 3rd Battalion and Commandant Thomas Byrne of the 1st Battalion.' Ended up in the Engineer Battalion, Dublin Brigade. During 1919 was extensively involved in IRB reorganisation in Monaghan and Tipperary. Afterwards he was involved in intelligence work full time, being arrested and imprisoned for a few months in 1920. Later joined the National Army (Coastal and Marine Service). He was discharged in September 1925.

Name	1916 Rank / Unit /Garrison	Sources
Callender, Ignatius Calaindear, Eighneochan	Volunteer, D Company, 1st Battalion, Dublin Brigade IV (appointed Intelligence Officer by Comdt Daly of the Four Courts garrison). Four Courts.	MSPC MSP34REF20252; BMH WS 923; *DC Reports*, Vol II, 1910, p. 958.

Corporation Service

Weigh Clerk, Weights & Measures Department, from June 1900. Retired in [1949].

Other Notes

Gaelic Leaguer. Joined the IV in 1913. Stored Battalion and Brigade automatic pistols in Dublin Corporation Weigh Office on Eden Quay, which also functioned as a message drop. In his Corporation job worked under the direction of Major John MacBride (the Water Bailiff's office was separate at 4 Rogersons Quay). Sent by Seán MacDiarmada with urgent message for MacBride there on Easter Monday (also later conducted Dáil Éireann loan account for St Michan's Division from this office). Collected a cache of automatic pistols (likely C96 Mausers) from the Weigh Office that day. Intelligence Officer under Edward Daly's command in 1916. Worked with Nicholas Lennon in gathering and hiding arms at Colmcille Hall, No. 5 Blackhall Street. John Callender, brother, was assistant to MacBride in Water Bailiff duties. Saw British troops using Red Cross ambulances for transport at Blackhall Place. Witness to proposed rebel attack on lancers holed up at Charles St (Ormond Quay). P.J. Stephenson lecture in 1934 to Old Dublin Society quoted from interview with Senator Michael Staines: 'No history of Ireland from the founding of the Volunteers in 1913 up to the Treaty is complete if it does not bring in Callender and the Eden Quay weigh-house, and for that matter Columcille Branch as well. Some of the most important activities of the period were carried out from the weigh-house. In fact it was used for every purpose.' (Quoted in Callender's MSPC statement). Both a 'J.P. Callender' (recruited by the Corporation in January 1900) and a 'J. Callender' (employed as 'life buoy carer' in April 1905) were employed in the weigh-house. His memoirs of the Rising were published in the *Dublin Brigade Review* (Dublin, 1938). Had severe difficulties getting his 1916 military service officially recognised.

Name	1916 Rank / Unit /Garrison	Sources
Carrigan, James (Seamus)	Volunteer, C Company, 1st Battalion IV (Roll of Honour says E. Coy, 2nd Battalion). Hibernian Bank, Abbey Street, GPO.	MSPC 24SP2477; BMH WS 613; Roll of Honour.

Corporation Service

Carter with Dublin Corporation from sometime post the Rising up until service with the Dublin ASU in 1920-21? Employed from June 1925, first as a labourer in Paving Department, then by 1941 a motorman in Sewers Dept. (absent that year for eighteen days due to a Corporation strike, but his pension was still abated for this period). Pensioner from 3 August 1966.

Other Notes

Involved in Howth gun-running as member of Na Fianna Éireann (which he joined between 1911 and 1913). Member of C Company, 1st Battalion from early 1916 but ended up fighting with E Company, 2nd Battalion. Part of the Moore Street surrender. Was imprisoned for a week, then released. Involved in the 1920 raid in which Kevin Barry was captured and in Bloody Sunday as getaway driver (he had been transferred to the Dublin Brigade Transport on account of his driving licence), as a member of the Active Service Unit from December 1920 involved in the attack on the Custom House. Later in the National Army (but not commissioned). According to his MSPC file, after demobilisation, he 'found it very hard to get work, and did not succeed in getting any work, until the Government Road Scheme came along, when I got a job using a pick and shovel, at the moderate salary of £2-10-0 per week, and when you take into consideration, the fact, that I am the only one at home, who is working, and also the fact, that out of my meagre salary, I have to keep my Aunt and my Brother (who can't find work) and Myself. I feel that you will now agree, with me, when I say that it is a very hard struggle'.

Name	1916 Rank / Unit / Garrison	Sources
Ceannt, Éamonn	Commandant, 4th Battalion IV Member of Military Council, IRB, member of the Provisional Government, signatory to the 1916 Proclamation. Member of the Central Executive, IV. South Dublin Union.	MSPC 1D330, Áine B. E. Ceannt in BMH WS 264, extensive references in BMH WS 511, WS 99, WS1756, WS 186, WS 304. *DC Reports*, Vol II, 1910, p. 974; *Irish Volunteer*, 20 Mar. 1915.

Corporation Service

Joined the Corporation in 1900, Clerk in City Treasurer's.

Other Notes

Member of the IRB Military Council, Gaelic League governing board member; noted piper who played for Pope Benedict XV as part of a Dublin Corporation delegation to Rome; trade union activist and one-time chair of the Dublin Metropolitan Officer's Association (the DMOA., forerunner of Dublin City Branch of IMPACT). In 1911 was involved in arranging the erection of a protest banner across Grafton Street against a British royal visit: 'Thou art not conquered yet, dear Land.' Member of the O'Donovan Rossa Funeral Committee. Gazetted as Commandant of the 4th Battalion on 20 March, 1915. Involved in the Howth and Kilcoole gun-running, and Director of Communications for the Irish Volunteers. Executed after Rising. Despite being a member of Sinn Féin, had a running public dispute with party leader Arthur Griffith throughout the 1913 Lockout (Ceannt supported the strikers, unlike Griffith). Wife Áine was also prominent. His son Rónán later worked in the Law Department, Dublin Corporation.

Name	1916 Rank / Unit / Garrison	Sources
Christie, Peter (Peadar)	Volunteer, E Company, 2nd Battalion IV. St Stephen's Green, Fumbally Lane, Jacob's Factory.	MSPC 24SP12822.

Corporation Service

Casual labourer with Paving Department from 6 August 1916. Permanent from March 1924.

Claimed to have been on several patrols during the Easter Rising. Was arrested and interned in Knutsford and then Frongoch. Transferred from his company 'much against his own will' in order to organise F Company (Artane), 3rd Battalion in the Fingal Brigade as Captain. Was involved in various armed operations in his area throughout the War of Independence. Later on, as a member of Brigade staff, went on the run while still being employed by the Corporation. Had a 'serious accident' before the 1922 election while travelling on a military vehicle, breaking his hand. Undercover intelligence work around 'Coolock, Artane and Raheny' during the Civil War with National Army, while ostensibly in Dublin Corporation service. Letters in his MSPC file note that 'It is not desirable that his connection with the Army should be made known, and any further enquiries which may be raised regarding his Army service, I would ask to have forwarded to the minister for Defence or Director of Intelligence'; 'The above named never formally attested in the Army. About the time of the outbreak in the Four Courts he was convalescent after being in Hospital, and when living in Artane was approached by Lieut. Peppard and myself to aid us in Intelligence work in that district. He is an old Volunteer and knew all the Irregulars in the District, and agreed to help us. For about a month he engaged himself wholly on this work without any remuneration and in a purely civilian capacity, i.e. with no apparent connect to the Army. He then obtained work in Dublin while we kept in touch with him up until about April or May in 1923. During all this time he rendered every assistance in his power to us and was instrumental in effecting the arrest of some wanted men and in forestalling the activities of others'; 'Christie was employed or rather utilised by the Intelligence Dept.' The latter detail only came to light in the MSPC file after Dublin Corporation (reasonably enough) flatly contradicted the Department of Defence's assertion that, to them, Christie had no apparent National Army service for his pension, having been employed by the city all through this period.

Name	1916 Rank / Unit / Garrison	Sources
Coates, Peter	ICA St Stephen's Green.	MSPC MSP34REF615.

Corporation Service

Employed from 14 June 1921 in the Corporation. In the 1930s was a Stationary Engine Driver (Boilerman), Public Health Department at the North Circular Road abattoir. Worked until October 1947, then retired on medical grounds.

Other Notes

Member of ICA from 1915. Member of the armed guard at Liberty Hall, 1916. Interned at Stafford and then Frongoch. Involved in a public demonstration on Easter Monday 1917, also in attempts to obtain weapons from the USS *Defiance* in Dublin port and Portobello Barracks. Present at Thomas Ashe's funeral. Involved on a raid on the TSS *Helga* in dry dock, involving an attempt to set it on fire (he was also tasked with getting engineering tools from the ship yards when needed). Also involved SF public events and in the 1918 General Election. Protected Liberty Hall on Armistice Night, 1919. Part of the armed guard on safe house at Shanahan's pub, Foley Street for several years. Was with a detachment of six ICA in Liberty Hall who, by chance, came to be part of the picket around the burning of the Custom House, and engaged Black and Tans arriving on the scene. Sent to get Joe Connolly from Tara Street Fire Station, as they were concerned that Volunteers might be trapped inside the building; they smuggled some arms away. Belfast Boycott. Fought on the anti-Treaty side in the Civil War first at O'Connell Street, later taking part in the 'Bridges' operation, in which the anti-Treaty IRA attempted to destroy bridges leading into Dublin in August 1922, and in subsequent patrols and attacks around Amiens Street. Like many other former comrades in a similar situation, was distressed at what he saw as the delay and reluctance of bureaucrats to offer him the correct recognition for his service. A union delegate to the Dublin Trades Council from 1933 onwards, possibly for the Municipal Workers' Union.

Name	1916 Rank / Unit / Garrison	Sources
Cole, Thomas	Volunteer, A Company, 1st Battalion, Dublin Brigade IV (joined during Rising) Four Courts.	MSPC MSP34REF8801.

Corporation Service

Labourer 1919-29. 1930-42 (at least), motorman, Waterworks Department.

Other Notes

As a youth he joined the Easter Rising when he just happened to be passing by the Four Courts on Easter Monday. During the Rising was involved in an arms raid on Keegan's gun shop, and assisted during the heavy fighting with British troops on the opposite side of the Liffey. After the Rising, his complete illiteracy made him unsuitable for use as a soldier so he was engaged mainly as a trusted man for arms gathering, movement and storage work with his 'jennet and cart' but also armed street patrols, police work. He was involved in some mêlée fighting with Crown Forces on Capel Street on two occasions. Arrested in November 1920 when arms were found in his house, badly beaten and detained for thirteen weeks – released when his brother (also in A Company) took sole responsibility. Fought on anti-Treaty side in the Civil War.

Name	1916 Rank / Unit / Garrison	Sources
Colley, Henry (Harry) Edward/ Ua Collaigh, Enrí	Volunteer, F Company, 2nd Battalion IV. GPO, Imperial Hotel.	MSPC MSP34REF20060; Directory of Members of the Oireachtas; BMH WS1687; *DC Reports*, Vol II, 1918, No. 125.

Corporation Service

Clerk under the Electrical Supply Committee from 1912. Appointed Rate Collector, 1921 to at least 1952.

Other Notes

Joined the IV in 1914. Recorded great confusion in the 2nd Battalion at Father Matthew Park on Easter Monday due to attempts to countermand the Monday Rising mid-mobilisation. Colley fought at Ballybough Road and Annesley Bridge, was part of a party under the command of Vincent Poole who attempted to blow up a railway line with gelignite, and after the withdrawal to the GPO at the Imperial Hotel, he and his companions outfitted themselves with boots and overcoats for an anticipated breakout to the country. Evacuating their position, the garrison carried out a bayonet charge on the British cordon in an attempt to break out and he was wounded six times, including a serious lung wound. He was then placed on the same British barricade at Seán McDermott Street (former Gloucester Street) and his body was used as a rifle rest by a British soldier in the fighting. He was brought to Dublin Castle hospital afterwards for three months of recovery, then interned in Frongoch – on his march through the city, he and his comrades were cheered by the crowds. Recovering eventually from his wounds, he was heavily involved in several major IRA operations in the War of Independence, rising to Dublin Brigade adjutant. One night, having left work in the Corporation, he was held up by Auxiliaries and narrowly escaped death. Interned during the Civil War, he was released early owing to his vital position in the Corporation as a Rate Collector. On another occasion, as a former Custom House employee, he aided the IRA in scouting the building before the plans to burn it were finalised. Received a disability pension also. Fianna Fáil TD from 1944 until his seat was taken by Charles Haughey in 1957. Senator 1957-61. Father of George Colley T.D, whom Charles Haughey defeated for the leadership of Fianna Fáil.

Name	1916 Rank / Unit /Garrison	Sources
Conlon (Conlan), Martin	Volunteer (temporary promotion to Medical Lt. for the Rising) F Company, 1st Battalion IV. Four Courts, Church Street, North King Street.	MSPC 24SP10720, *DC Reports*, Vol II, 1910; BMH WS 798, WS 419 (Mrs. Martin Conlon (Peig)); 'The "Secret Service Unit" of Michael Collins's Operation in Irish Craft Unions', *Fusion (Official Magazine of the Technical, Engineering & Electrical Union (TEEU))*, Jan. 2015; Directory of Members of the Oireachtas.

Corporation Service

'Either in the Sanitary Office or in the Rates Office' as per BMH WS 419. Employed from May 1903 as Sanitary Sub-Officer in Public Health Department. Became Rate Collector sometime in 1921 or thereabouts. Again employed 1924-30, when he was pensioned.

Other Notes

IRB member and Centre (and eventually a member of the Supreme Council). Member of the O'Donovan Rossa Funeral Committee. Bulmer Hobson was lured to his house and put under arrest there by the IRB on the eve of the Rising (though Conlon wasn't directly involved in this). Lieutenant in charge of medical post at Father Mathew Hall during the Rising. Never arrested, went on the run afterwards and returned to work in August. One of Michael Collins's key men for intelligence and other work (and his designated replacement on the Volunteer Executive in case of emergency). 'Martin was very quiet; he was not a talker and in that way he was not so much known to the authorities. He was friendly with the detective, getting them to do things for the IRA, such as getting the numbers of the police cars and what the police were doing and where they were going. He was seen a good deal with the police and, therefore, the authorities did not suspect him.' (BMH WS 419). This came to an end when Michael Collins showed Conlon a letter informing on them, which had been intercepted in the post. Conlon was in charge of the so-called 'Labour Board', an IRA unit which infiltrated and influenced the trade union movement. Though never formally attested (or paid), he joined the National Army at City Hall and then was stationed at GHQ in Portobello (now Cathal Brugha) Barracks on staff work. Left in September 1922 at rank of Lieutenant. Was in addition a Cumann na nGaedhael TD for Roscommon from 11 March 1925 until 1933, and then a Fine Gael Senator from 1938-43.

Name	1916 Rank / Unit /Garrison	Sources
Connaughton, Patrick	Volunteer, B Company, 1st Battalion IV (later a member of C Company). GPO.	MSPC MSP34REF20064.

Corporation Service

Possibly working as a Dublin Corporation labourer from arrival until the Rising: 'I got a sort of temporary job in the Pigeon House, making artificial manure, just to keep myself going.' (MSPC). Messenger for Main Drainage and City Architects, January 1917 to December 1935 at least. By 1938 working for Finance Department, City Hall.

Joined the Irish Volunteers in March 1916. He returned from Scotland seven weeks before the Rising and was introduced by his brother to Tom Clarke, who enrolled him in the Irish Volunteers (and gave him a .22 revolver). Returning by train from a week in his home town of Longford on Easter Monday, he went to the GPO and was in that garrison until the surrender at Moore Street. After the Rising was interned in Stafford and then Frongoch. Previously resident in Scotland (and therefore liable for conscription) he got permission to sign an early release form. On release, involved in the re-organisation work, training and election work in Longford, then dropped out in 1918.

Name	1916 Rank / Unit /Garrison	Sources
Connolly, George	Private, ICA City Hall	MSPC MSP34REF1284.

Corporation Service

Dublin Fire Brigade from 1923.

Other Notes

Brother of Seán Connolly. Former member of Na Fianna Éireann. Prior to the Rising involved in the armed ICA guard on Liberty Hall, on Easter Sunday night and Easter Monday morning was carrying messages around the city. Returning to find Liberty Hall about to be abandoned, he fell in with his brother's group going to Dublin Castle. There he witnessed the confrontation with the policeman on duty and was part of the section who took the guardroom and remained there under heavy fire until later that night. Seperated in the withdrawal, on Tuesday morning he found City Hall filled with British soldiers and made his way to Liberty Hall. Took no part after that, and wasn't arrested. Involved in drilling and the Thomas Ashe funeral, along with the arms raid on the transport ship USS *Defiance* in Dublin port in 1918. During the Truce he joined 2nd Company 5th Battalion (Engineers), IV and fought on the anti-Treaty side in the Four Courts, helping to mine the building. Imprisoned in Mountjoy until late 1922.

Name	1916 Rank / Unit /Garrison	Sources
Connolly, Joseph W.	Private, then promoted to Sergeant during the Rising, ICA. GPO, St Stephen's Green.	MSPC MSP34REF56783.

Corporation Service

Dublin Fire Brigade from October 1915 until retirement (1938?) as Chief.

Other Notes

Brother of Seán Connolly. Former member of Na Fianna Éireann. Joined the ICA in 1914. Prior to the Rising involved in the armed guard on Liberty Hall. On Easter Sunday he was on duty as a fireman at Tara Street Fire Station. Mobilised at noon on Easter Monday, found himself in demand as a driver transporting arms, supplies and dispatches using a commandeered car. Was also involved in constructing barricades. Interned at Wandsworth and then Frongoch. Released in July 1916, he re-joined the DFB and became busy 'drilling and preparing for another fight'. (MSPC). Took Thomas Ashe by ambulance to hospital after his hunger strike. During the War of Independence his ability to assist as a DFB fireman proved useful during the Custom House attack of May 1921. In the Civil War fought on the anti-Treaty side at Hammam's Hotel on O'Connell Street before being ordered to evacuate. Ended his service as a Captain in the ICA. Might possibly have been in IRB along with his brother Seán – there's a curious reference in his MSPC interview to 'the Organisation'.

Name	1916 Rank / Unit /Garrison	Sources
Connolly, Matthew	Leader of Boys' Section, ICA Private in the ICA. City Hall.	MSPC MSPREF341750, BMH WS1746.

Corporation Service

Carpenter in City Architects' Department from 24 August 1937 until 1939 at least.

Other Notes

Joined the Boys' Section of the Irish Citizen Army in 1914, having been in Na Fianna Éireann for about three years previously. Brother of Captain Seán Connolly. Took part in various ICA activities pre-Rising – armed guard at Liberty Hall, making weapons and printing. Bugler on Easter Monday, part of the ICA party which attacked Dublin Castle and then took occupation of buildings on Cork Hill, including City Hall (part of a planned encirclement of Dublin Castle). From his account, Seán Connolly wasn't the first rebel to die. Also includes an account of a fight with an armoured car at that garrison. Fell asleep during the night, and captured with the rest of the City Hall garrison on Tuesday 25 April. Arrested and detained at Ship Street Barracks for a month, then released because of his age (15). Took part in electioneering and drilling, then went to London in February 1920. While there, took part in an IRA campaign of sabotage against telegraph communications and took part in protests outside Wormwood Scrubbs until June 1921.

Name	1916 Rank / Unit /Garrison	Sources
Connolly, Seán	Acting Commandant (substantive rank of Captain), ICA. Commanded the City Hall garrison. City Hall.	MSPC 1D205; numerous BMH statements such as WS 733. *DC Reports*, Vol III, 2016, p. 87.

Corporation Service

Clerk in charge of motor registration. Employed from April 1906 (office attendant and messenger) by the Paving Department.

Other Notes

Member of IRB and Gaelic League. Also Abbey Theatre actor, a Pioneer and a devout Catholic. According to James O'Shea's account of the sudden March 1916 ICA mobilisation in response to an attempted DMP raid, 'the only one respectably dressed was Seán Connolly who came from City Hall.' (BMH WS 733). On guard at Liberty Hall on Easter Sunday, he remarked to Maeve Cavanagh that he would be 'going to a regular death trap, but the risk has to be taken.' (BMH WS 258). Led the abortive attack on Dublin Castle and then killed in action at City Hall. The 'John Connolly' who joined the Corporation in April 1906 as 'office attendant and messenger' was highly thought of there. A report of the Paving Committee in 1916 states: 'We regret exceedingly to have to report the death, during the recent rebellion, of Mr. John Connolly, one of the staff of the Secretary's Office. He had charge, under the Secretary's directions, of all the work pertaining to registration and the issue of licences under the Motor Car Acts, and in all his work he gave the utmost satisfaction. He was a young man of excellent abilities, and in his death the Corporation have lost the services of a most valuable and efficient officer.'

Name	1916 Rank / Unit /Garrison	Sources
Corbally, Richard	Private, ICA. GPO.	MSPC MSP34REF208, BMH WS 7333.

Corporation Service

Hired from December 1938 by Streets Section for horse, cart and driver.

Other Notes

Before the Rising he was employed by the ICA in transporting arms. On Easter Monday he brought munitions from Liberty Hall to the GPO, then fought with the garrison all week. Interned in Stafford and Frongoch. After, involved in raids for arms at the Portobello Barracks and from the freighter USS *Defiance* and other related activities. Interned at Arbour Hill during the War of Independence. Took the anti-Treaty side in the Civil War, but didn't take part in fighting.

Name	1916 Rank / Unit /Garrison	Sources
Coyne, Thomas	Volunteer, D Company, 3rd Battalion IV. Boland's Mills, Ringsend Road.	MSPC 24SP7620, BMH WS 160.

Corporation Service

Dublin Fire Brigade from March 1924 onwards.

Other Notes

Joined the IV in 1915. Evaded arrest after Rising. Mention in Joseph Byrne account in MA/IE/ MA/MSPC/MSPC/RO/14 Dublin Brigade, Easter Week, 3rd Battalion. From 1918-19 with the 2nd Battalion. His duties mainly consisted of maintaining and driving motor cars. In February 1922 he joined the National Army. Demobilised in March 1924 as a 2nd Lieutenant from the Mechanical Transportation Corps, joined the DFB on 29 October 1924. His employment in the latter only came to the attention of the Department of Defence in 1942, when they calculated that he owed £335-16-7 in repayment because of the requirement to abate pensions if recipient was in receipt of other public monies (as per Military Service Pensions Act, 1924). A flurry of correspondance followed, but the judgement was that an acquittal was likely if a public prosecution was pursued, which would only encourage others.

Name	1916 Rank / Unit /Garrison	Sources
Cullen, John Christopher/Ó Cuillin, Seán	Section Commander (i.e. Sergeant), D Company, 3rd Battalion IV. Boland's Mills.	MSPC 24SP11651, BMH WS 160.

Corporation Service

Clerk in Dublin Corporation from at least 1917 or so, up until he joined the National Army.

Other Notes

Used his Corporation office to store IRA documents during the War of Independence. Promoted to Captain and O/C of D Company, went on the run in 1920-21. Was on the Quartermaster General's staff until July 1921. Retired from the National Army in 1928 at the Curragh Camp, and posted to the Reserve of Officers. He died later that year in a motor accident.

Name	1916 Rank / Unit /Garrison	Sources
Cullen, Patrick	ICA St Stephen's Green, Harcourt Street.	MSPC MSP34REF1724.

Corporation Service

Lamplighter with Street Lighting Department. Worked for two months at this in 1917, then from 1923 or 1925 onwards.

Other Notes

Joined the ICA in January 1916. Involved in the typical ICA activities pre-Risng – route marches, drilling, the armed guard on Liberty Hall. Interned after the Rising at Stafford and then Frongoch. After release involved in the Thomas Ashe funeral and the reception at Westland Row (now Pearse Station) for Countess Markievicz on her release. Helped guard Liberty Hall from a loyalist mob on Armistice Night, 1918. Various service up until the Truce on 11 July 1921. Took no part in the Civil War.

Name	1916 Rank / Unit /Garrison	Sources
Daly, Frank	Engineer Captain (i.e. Staff Captain) of 1st Battalion IV, simultaneously 2nd Lt in B Company, 1st Battalion IV. Ashbourne, Cabra, GPO and Four Courts.	MSPC MSP34REF20270; BMH WS 278.

Corporation Service

Worked on Roundwood Reservoir before the Rising, up until late (Nov.?) 1915 –then asked by IRB to change jobs to go work at an IRB-controlled brickworks, to study more about explosives.

Other Notes

IRB member. Gained his knowledge of explosives while managing the rock boring at Dublin Corporation's Roundwood reservoir. Engineer Captain to 1st Battalion IV, Director of Munitions on GHQ Staff IV, and involved in the manufacture of munitions before the Rising in Cluny House in Clontarf. Also involved in the Howth and Kilcoole gun-runnings. Worked through the Easter weekend at Liberty Hall on preparations for the Rising. During Easter Week constructed or inspected various barricades around the Four Courts and Church Street, then was sent on unsuccessful demolition mission from North Dublin City (with Thomas Byrne) to obstruct the arrival of British artillery from Athlone. He discovered that Bill Sheehan had panicked and disposed of the gelignite stored at Cabra for this work. Daly then fought at Ashbourne, capturing an RIC carbine. Arrested and interned a few days after, having been tasked with clearing Volunteer dumps in the city of evidence, sent to Wakefield then Frongoch. Very active afterwards with electioneering, training and attacks. Took part in Civil War in Dublin on anti-Treaty side, was captured and interned.

Name	1916 Rank / Unit /Garrison	Sources
Daly, William Joseph	Started in C Company 2nd Battalion IV going on to be 2nd Battalion Lieutenant of Engineering (gazetted on 14 August, 1915). Prior to the Rising became Brigade Signalling Officer (possibly also appointment as in charge of signalling at IV HQ), Dublin Brigade IV. During the Rising was a staff officer on the GHQ to Thomas McDonagh in Jacob's Factory. Jacob's Factory.	MSPC MSP34REF20275.

Corporation Service

Electrician, 21 June 1937 onwards in Public Lighting, Tara Street, late 1937 in Portobello Barracks, for Corps of Engineers, and again 8 August 1938 to 10 August 1950.

Other Notes

Joined the IV in early 1914 'from inception'. Signalling instructor to 2nd Battalion from January 1915. Appointed Battalion Lieutenant of Engineers on 15 August 1915. Two or three months later appointed in charge of the Brigade/GHQ signalling staff and gave signalling classes at 2 Dawson Street until the Rising (the IV had been trying to work out a separate scheme of Morse to that used by the British). 'Staff officer' in Jacob's, where he also set up the internal telephone system for communications between posts and Thomas MacDonagh's office on the first floor. He 'usually accompanied' MacDonagh and John MacBride on their rounds, and escaped after the surrender. After the Rising was involved in various activities until 1920, due to being employed in 'country work'. Service until 30 September 1923. Married his fiancée, Marianne/Mary Anne Brady on 15 November 1916. His place of residence from at least 1935, Oak Lodge (No. 23 Oak Terrace, later No. 340 North Circular Road) was William Sheehan's house in 1916 – coincidence? Daly certainly knew both William and Ted Sheehan (the latter was senior Engineering Officer according to Daly: 'Sheehan was supposed to be Brigadier, Ted Sheehan'). Daly had the hundredweight of gelignite in his house on the Saturday; according to Frank Henderson, there were 'two loads of explosive stuff […] On the Sunday I handed it over to Sheehan'. Daly's house was 'one of the call houses for collection of stuff'. Henderson, in his MSPC statement on behalf of Daly, also went on to say that Teddy Sheehan 'is not available, I suppose' to certify Daly's pre-Rising service in the IV. In 1936 'This poor fellow is in bad circumstances. He is elderly' (MSPC).

Name	1916 Rank / Unit /Garrison	Sources
Derham, Michael	Volunteer, C Company, 1st Battalion Dublin Brigade IV. From 1918 with K Company (Engineers), 1st Battalion then No. 1 Company, 5th (Engineers) Battalion. Church Street, Four Courts.	MSPC MSP34REF2413; *DC Reports*, Vol. I, 1916, No. 164.

Corporation Service

Assistant Timekeeper (before the Rising) and then Timekeeper in the Waterworks Department.

Other Notes

Joined the Irish Volunteers on their formation in 1913. Involved in the preparations for the Rising, such as mounting armed night guard on Volunteer headquarters in Dawson Street, and Tom Byrne's operation to steal a shipment of Martini Henry rifles from the INV. After the surrender held in Richmond barracks, then deported to Stafford Gaol and then Frongoch. His father, also Michael Derham, was a Dangerous Buildings inspector and one of a group of Corporation staff (including the crew of the SS *Shamrock)* who made overtime claims for making safe ruins after the Rising. After the release, was involved in the Company re-organisation, intelligence work on postal and telephone services, cutting communication wires from Cabra to the Vice-Regal Lodge and other armed activities. He provided a place in Fishamble Street – the Waterworks office – for the Company to meet and for 'special purposes' such as making guncotton. 'It was absolutely [a dangerous thing], so much so that they all got scared that night when they saw the fumes going up and they cleared out' (MSPC). Derham was taken prisoner in an Auxiliary raid on the Corporation Waterworks office on 2 December 1920 and kept prisoner in the North Dublin Union ('I got a good hammering') until 21 February1921. From then until March 1922 (when he resigned) he was Intelligence Officer for the Company. Like other 1916 and War of Independence veterans, he attempted to claim a pension under the 1924 Pensions Act but was refused on the basis of having no National Army service.

Name	1916 Rank / Unit /Garrison	Sources
Derrington, John Joseph/Seán	Brigade Armourer, Dublin Brigade IV (sometime a Lieutenant with D Company, 1st Battalion, Dublin Brigade IV). Mendicity Institute.	MSPC MSP34REF20923.

Corporation Service

Foreman (mechanic) in Dublin Corporation Municipal Workshop until 1925.

Other Notes

William Derrington's father. Joined A Company 1st Battalion of IV in 1913, then D Company in 1914, and was appointed musketry instructor and company armourer. Later made Brigade armourer in order to teach Brigade-level classes: 'The men in the employment were very good to me, I could get work done with the smiths and others there, I had a free hand, in fact I was brigade armourer instead of battalion armourer, men out of the different battalions came to me, I gave them instructions [in the daytime] I was employed in the Municipal Workshops, Stanley Street. [Spending most of my working hours doing arms repair] many times in the morning my wife said what time did you go to bed at.' (MSPC). During the Rising, fought in the Mendicity Institute, that garrison surrendering on Wednesday afternoon and initially being held in Arbour Hill prison. He was sentenced to death after the Rising, commuted to three years' penal servitude. 'He was sentenced to penal servitude [because] they put up such a fight. There was only a handful of them, and they put up a fight, and they played havoc – in the Mendicity Institute. [Heuston] was a man who knew military tactics.' (MSPC). Seán Derrington was imprisoned in Portland, Lewes and Pentonville until the general release in 1917. Became battalion armourer on his return, also making grenade pins and repairing weapons: 'He was cock of the walk himself in the shop in Stanley Street – he was foreman there. He was able to do a lot of work there. He was a fellow, I know personally, who used to buy a lot of stuff from the fellows bringing in bins – anything he could turn into use for repairing the guns, such as springs of clocks, pieces of brass etc.' (MSPC). Later on was on the HQ Munitions Section staff. Dropped out of the movement after the Treaty.

Name	1916 Rank / Unit /Garrison	Sources
Derrington, William P. (Liam)	Volunteer, D Company, 1st Battalion, Dublin Brigade IV. Mendicity Institute.	MSPC MSP34REF40124.

Corporation Service

Wood machinist, Stanley Street Workshops, from 14 May 1914 until 1921 at least.

Other Notes

Seán Derrington's son. Had been in Na Fianna Éireann, and transferred from it to D Company at its inception. Before the Rising helped bring arms in from St Enda's. During the Rising fought in the Mendicity Institute, that garrison surrendering on Wednesday afternoon and initially being held in the Royal (now Collins) Barracks. He carried out a reconnaissance to the GPO on Tuesday which brought in the Ashbourne reinforcements for the Mendicity Institute. William Derrington was sentenced after the Rising by British court-martial to two years' imprisonment with hard labour, one year commuted. Imprisoned in Kilmainham, Mountjoy, Wormwood Scrubs and then Lewes. Active after the general release, especially helping his father as armourer. Arrested on 29 April 1921. Dropped out of the IRA after the Truce.

Name	1916 Rank / Unit / Garrison	Sources
Doolan, Joseph	Battalion Ambulance Officer, A Company, 4th Battalion IV (later transferred to the ICA). South Dublin Union.	MSPC MSP34REF62059; BMH WS 199; *Irish Volunteer*, 8 Jan. 1916 (as 'J. Doulan'); 26 Feb. 1916 (as 'J. Doutan').

Corporation Service

Disinfector, Health Section, 6 Marrowbone Lane from at least June 1949 (during his MSP application) until at least 1953.

Other Notes

Sworn into the IRB by Éamonn Ceannt shortly after the Howth gun-running; member of the Teeling Circle. Joined the Irish Volunteers in 1914. Prior to the Rising, was involved in munitions work at Kimmage (which was in the Battalion area). Doolan was a 4th Battalion medic who gave a series of first-aid lectures to the Battalion on Éamonn Ceannt's orders immediately before the Rising, and during same ran a Red Cross station in the South Dublin Union, treating the seriously injured Cathal Brugha among others. His account of the fiercest day of fighting claims that Cosgrave had abandoned the wounded Brugha to die, before a rescue led by Ceannt. Interned in Knutsford, Wormwood Scrubs and then Frongoch. Involved in the IV re-organisation afterwards (later under cover of the Gaelic League in Rathmines), and the Thomas Ashe funeral, drilling, arms gathering and political activities for SF. During the War of Independence transferred to the South County Dublin group of ICA. Involved in patrolling, raiding, the Custom House burning and the Belfast Boycott. During the Truce period involved in drilling at a camp in Sutton. Mobilised with the ICA to fight the Free State. Did not apply for a pension until 1951. When asked why he delayed doing so, replied: 'I fought for the Republic, and as the Republic was not declared until before [the pensions application deadline] I did not apply. The Republic is now declared and so this application.' (MSPC). His reasoning was accepted.

Name	1916 Rank / Unit / Garrison	Sources
Doyle, John J.	Dublin Brigade Medical Officer (Captain or Commandant?) and Director of Medical Services GHQ, IV. GPO, Fairview.	MSPC MSP34REF975; BMH WS 738 John J. Doyle; *Irish Volunteer*, 30 Oct. 1915.

Corporation Service

Painter in the Housing Department since 11 June 1942 until 1946 (?). Before that, a painter for the Army Corps of Engineers in March and April.

Gazetted as Surgeon-Lieutenant, 2nd Battalion staff on 30 October 1915 (and Captain shortly after, if his MPSC and BMH statements are correct). His father's Land League activities forced the family to leave Bray and move to Kingstown. Joined the Irish Volunteers in June 1914 (C Company, 2nd Battalion), bringing twelve men of the St John's ambulance service in with him. As Dublin Brigade medical officer and Director of Medical Services GHQ, was involved in organising and training Volunteers. Was mobilised in Fairview Park on Easter Monday and was to proceed to St Stephen's Green (they commandeered a lorry for this purpose). Attacked en route at Ballybough Road, they fought British troops around Summerhill Bridge until ordered to the GPO early Monday evening to establish his medical HQ there. His medical staff was joined by some volunteers with medical training and Cumann na mBan. The most important casualty was James Connolly, who was injured by a round in the biceps, and later by a round which caused a complicated fracture. Claimed that there were thirty-five British military prisoners held in the GPO. Evacuating from the GPO they gave up their thirty or thirty-five wounded at the British lines at Jervis Street Hospital. Afterwards he was arrested but let go after a couple of days, and then went on the run. Treated several wounded volunteers in the War of Independence, including Dan Breen for a gunshot wound at a residence on the Botanic Road following the Ashtown ambush, 21 December 1919. Involved in the Civil War on the anti-Treaty side, present at the Four Courts and Hamman's Hotel. Attempted to carry on medical services at his own house. Arrested and interned September to October 1922. His MSPC file includes letters from the National Army's Director of Medical Services, attempting to recruit him (and to bring trained medics) in February 1922 into that force.

Name	1916 Rank / Unit /Garrison	Sources
Drennan, William	Volunteer, G Company, 1st Battalion IV. Four Courts, North King Street.	MSPC MSP34REF29864.

Corporation Service

Temporary labourer, Cleansing Department, from 6 February 1935 to 17 August 1942, went out sick without pay, died in 1946 (aged 67).

Other Notes

Joined the Irish Volunteers in 1914. During the Rising, was in the Four Courts garrison, occasionally on outpost and barricade duty. Deported to Knutsford. Lost his job because of the Rising, and dropped out of IV on release from internment.

Name	1916 Rank / Unit /Garrison	Sources
Dunne, Thomas	Volunteer, B Company, 1st Battalion IV. GPO.	MSPC MSP34REF3799; CSORP Easter Rising, 1916 Index of Internees.

Corporation Service

Employed by Waterworks from 3 July 1911. In 1935 a Turncock.

Other Notes

Joined the Irish Volunteers in 1914. C49 on DMP watchlist as a 'taxidriver' (CSORP). Tom Byrne recalled Thomas Dunne being one of the men on the ground floor facing O'Connell Street on a particular night in Easter Week (Byrne was doing his rounds as an officer, in order to keep sentries awake). Interned in Stafford and Frongoch. Involved in anti-conscription activities. Also, 'I was working in the Corporation. There was a plant there and we were going to dismantle the water machinery.' (MSPC). In 1935 he was anxious to get the pension in order to be able to get two of his children vocational training.

Name	1916 Rank / Unit /Garrison	Sources
Fagan, Patrick	Volunteer, F Company, 1st Battalion IV. Four Courts, North King Street.	MSPC MSP34REF59081.

Corporation Service

Casual labourer, City Architects (including Dangerous Buildings section) and Sewers, 30 September 1934 to 1944 at least.

Other Notes

Joined a couple of weeks before the Easter Rising. Involved in distributing bread from Monk's Bakery, and putting up barricades at North King Street, Cuckoo, Mary's and Bull Lanes, armed with a .45 Webley. Wounded at Mary's Lane by British machine-gun fire from Finnegan's in Capel Street on Friday 29 April at a barricade on Mary's Lane. Taken to the first aid post in Father Mathew Hall and then to Richmond Hospital on the day of surrender. Escaped arrest afterwards, and resumed activities with his Company.

Name	1916 Rank / Unit /Garrison	Sources
Finlay, John (J.J.)	Private, ICA. City Hall.	MSPC MSP34REF1635; CSORP Easter Rising, 1916 Index of Internees.

Corporation Service

From 16 December 1943 to 17 May 1953 employed first in City Architects and then Housing Maintenance as a labourer.

Other Notes

Joined the Irish Citizen Army in 1913. Received gunshot wound (shoulder) in Rising on Easter Monday, 24 April, shot from and treated at Dublin Castle. Deported first to Knutsford and then Frongoch. On release, involved in the Rising anniversary demonstration in 1917 and then Thomas Ashe's funeral. Took part in the defence of Liberty Hall from a mob of loyalists and soldiers on Armistice Night, 1918.

Name	1916 Rank / Unit /Garrison	Sources
Fisher, John	Volunteer, C Company, 1st Battalion, Dublin Brigade IV. Four Courts, Church Street Bridge, Bridewell.	MSPC MSP34REF59669.

Corporation Service

Rent Collector, Housing Department, 1934-47 at least.

Other Notes

Joined the IV in 1914. Involved in distributing arms and ammunition in the Four Courts area in the week preceding the Rising. Avoided capture after the Rising, under orders from Commandant Daly at the surrender for any Volunteers in civilian clothing to get away; spent the Sunday night sheltering in a restaurant near St Michael and John's Church. Played no further role in IV.

Name	1916 Rank / Unit /Garrison	Sources
Fitzgibbon, Seán	Vice-Commandant, 3rd Battalion Dublin Brigade IV. Member of the Central Executive, IV. None.	BMH WS 130 (Seán Fitzgibbon), WS 0006, WS 007 (Liam Ó Bríain), WS 409 (Valentine Jackson), WS 141 (James Kenny), WS 497 (Éamon Bulfin), WS 264 (Áine, Bean E. Ceannt); *DC Reports*, Vol II, 1916, p. 911; *Irish Volunteer*, 20 Mar. 1915.

Corporation Service

Employed from May 1905. Clerk in Engineering Department.

Other Notes

'J.P. Fitzgibbon' taken on by Dublin Corporation in 1905. In 1911 he was involved, with Corporation colleague and fellow Sinn Féiner Éamonn Ceannt, in arranging the erection of a protest banner across Grafton Street against a British royal visit: 'Thou art not conquered yet, dear Land.' He was invited by Éamonn Ceannt to come to the meeting which set up the Provisional Committee of the Irish Volunteers in late 1913. With Val Jackson, Fitzgibbon was heavily involved in planning the second arms-landing for the Volunteers in 1914 at Kilcoole. Notice given of his appointment as Vice-Commandant of the 3rd Battalion, Dublin Brigade on 20 March 1915. Member of the O'Donovan Rossa Funeral Committee, but never in the IRB. In 1916 he was sent on what was effectively a decoy mission to Kerry (in order to keep him away) by the members of the Military Council at the start of the week before the Rising. Following the loss of the *Aud* he was involved in disseminating Eoin MacNeill's countermanding order. Both he and MacNeill countermanded in person the E Company, 4th Battalion mobilisation at Rathfarnham Roman Catholic Church on Easter Sunday.

Name	1916 Rank / Unit /Garrison	Sources
Fitzpatrick, Denis	Volunteer, B Company, 1st Battalion IV. Four Courts.	MSPC MSP34REF816.

Corporation Service

Dublin Fire Brigade from 1932.

Other Notes

Escaped after the Rising to his sister's house on Blackhall Place. From March 1919 was active in Scotland for about a year. On arrival back in Ireland, involved in intelligence work and some armed operations. Was in the Dublin ASU for a period, from just before the Truce. Resigned from the National Army after four months and joined the Four Courts garrison. Claimed that he was shot by Emmet Dalton and other National Army members in April 1922. Involved in some fighting, a tunnelling attempt into Mountjoy and was interned from about August to September 1922 until the end of the Civil War.

Name	1916 Rank / Unit /Garrison	Sources
Fox, Michael	Volunteer, F Company, 4th Battalion IV. GPO.	MSPC 24SP199.

Corporation Service

Waterworks Relief Projects in 1925.

Other Notes

Member of the IRB. Joined the Irish Volunteers in 1914. Deported to Stafford and then Frongoch. Was a coach painter with the Great Southern and Western Railway at Inchicore but lost his job after the Rising. Involved in various activities such as armed patrols and attacks on police. Joined the National Army in February 1922 before the Civil War broke out 'Company with very few exceptions followed Captain (die-hard).' (MSPC). Demobilised from the National Army in 1924 as a private.

Name	1916 Rank / Unit /Garrison	Sources
Gahan, Tadhg	Volunteer, C Company, 2nd Battalion IV (in the Roll of Honour as B Coy, 2nd Bn.) St Stephen's Green, Jacob's Factory.	MSPC MSP34REF1127; Roll of Honour.

Corporation Service

13 December 1916 - 28 March 1929 (transferred to ESB). Appears in Corporation records as 'Timothy' Gahan. Started in Rates; later transferred to City Engineer's Office.

Other Notes

University student. Joined the Irish Volunteers in 1913. Distributed arms before the Rising (about forty automatic pistols, which had been stored in his own house). Interned in Frongoch. After some further activities, dropped out of the IRA in 1920 after moving to Co. Dublin.

Name	1916 Rank / Unit /Garrison	Sources
Garland, Patrick (Paddy)	Sergeant, Hibernian Rifles (from March 1917 1st Lieutenant, then from May 1918 Captain and O/C of E Company, 1st Battalion, Dublin Brigade IV From December 1921 I Company, 1st Battalion). GPO.	MSPC MSP34REF20509; Jimmy Wren, *The GPO Garrison Easter Week 1919* (Dublin, 2015), pp 107, 415

Corporation Service

Bricklayer, Sewers Department

Other Notes

Member of Hibernian Rifles in March 1915. At the start of the Rising, their Commandant J.J. Scollan gave a free choice to his men and women on whether to be involved. Those involved mobilised at No. 28 North Frederick Street on 23 April, before being ordered by James Connolly to the GPO on Easter Monday morning. The Hibernian Rifles fought as part of the GPO garrison until the surrender on Moore Street. Interned first in Stafford Gaol then in the Frongoch concentration camp. On release in 1917, transferred with the rest of the Hibernian Rifles to the Irish Volunteers as E Company, 1st Battalion, where he held the rank of Lieutenant. The usual activities up until the outbreak of the War of Independence. Interned in Ballykinlar Camp from November 1920 until 9 December 1921. During the Truce, also served as Captain of the guards on Fowler Hall and then No. 44 Parnell Square. Took the anti-Treaty side in the Civil War, and commanded in O'Connell Street during the initial fighting in Dublin. Interned again, from 5 July 1922 onwards. Joined the Defence Forces during the Emergency (commissioned on 4 December 1940). Served with the Construction Corps until he was demobilised on 31 March 1946.

Name	1916 Rank / Unit /Garrison	Sources
Gay, Tomás Érnan	Volunteer, A Company, 1st Battalion IV. Jameson Distillery, Jacob's Factory.	MSPC 24SP8332; *DC Reports*, Vol II, 1910, p. 983; BMH WS 780.

Corporation Service

Joined September 1900; transferred to Thomas Street as Senior Assistant Librarian in April 1904.

Other Notes

IRB member. Thomas Street Public Library, where he worked, was used as a key intelligence drop and communications hub by Michael Collins's network. Was on 'Special Intelligence' duties for GHQ during the War of Independence. MSPC notes that 'He was in constant touch with Michael Collins and other members of Volunteers HQ. His house was used by Michael Collins for meetings practically every week,' and 'his work must have been considerably interfered with as he had to go all over the metropolitan area at all hours of the day with important despatches. He had frequently to be out after midnight on these errands also.'

Name	1916 Rank / Unit /Garrison	Sources
Hayes, Dr Richard	Commandant, 5th (Fingal) Battalion, Dublin Brigade, IV. Co. Dublin, Co. Meath, Ashbourne.	MPSC MSP34REF63430; BMH WS 097 (Richard Hayes); *Irish Independent*, 20 May 1918, p. 4; *DCC Minutes* 1920, No. 319.

Corporation Service

Appointed as Medical Officer to the South Dublin Union (which later became the Dublin Union) circa 1918, an appointment strongly resisted for the next number of years by the Dublin Castle-controlled Local Government Board. Retired from the Dublin Board of Assistance (successor to the Dublin Union) as an MO in November 1941.

Other Notes

Part of the 5th Battalion, Dublin Brigade mobilisation under Thomas Ashe (to whom he had given up his command) which captured RIC barracks in Donabate, Swords & Garristown; involved in the battle at Ashbourne. Hayes acted as Medical Officer, and was in command at Garristown. Sentenced by court-martial after the Rising to twenty years' penal servitude. In the general release in 1917, but imprisoned again in Reading Gaol May 1918 to March 1919 under pretext of the 'German Plot'. Interned in Ballykinlar from November 1920 to July 1921. During the War of Independence carried out medical duties around Dublin city, as required.

Name	1916 Rank / Unit /Garrison	Sources
Henderson, Leo/ MacEanruig, Leomhan	Acting Captain, B Company, 2nd Battalion, Dublin Brigade, IV. Also Director of Equipment on the GHQ staff of Na Fianna Éireann. Fairview, GPO.	MSPC MSP34REF60142.

Corporation Service

Appointed Assistant Secretary from 12 May 1931 to the Dublin Board of Assistance (successor to the Dublin Union).

Mobilised at Father Matthew Park, Fairview on both Easter Sunday (23 April) and Easter Monday (24 April). On 23 April he accompanied other senior officers of the Battalion on a last reconnaissance of the positions to be occupied. Henderson was part of the column which set out for the GPO later on Monday and was in command of the rearguard which fought at Annesley Bridge. He was then placed in charge of a position on Henry Street which saw heavy fighting from Thursday. Rejoining the GPO garrison, he was present at Moore Street for the surrender. Interned first at Wakefield and then Frongoch. In early 1918 he became Acting Commandant, 2nd Battalion, and then was appointed Vice-Commandant. Taking the anti-Treaty side, he was appointed director of the Belfast Boycott, but was arrested and detained by the National Army prior to the Civil War.

Name	1916 Rank / Unit /Garrison	Sources
Henderson, Thomas	Volunteer, A Company, 1st Battalion, Dublin Brigade IV. Four Courts, North King Street, North Brunswick Street, Church Street.	MSPC MSP34REF20865.

Corporation Service

'Joined in 1867 (apprenticed) 1893' according to *DC Reports*, Vol II, 1910; Pension application claims Corporation service from 1902 until his death in 1947. Overseer, North Paving.

Other Notes

Erected barricades and occupied and fortified houses in North Brunswick Street during the Rising. Interned in Stafford and then Frongoch. Had little involvement in the War of Independence, apart from moving weapons. He was arrested after Bloody Sunday, 21 November 1920, and detained at both the North Dublin Union and then at Arbour Hill, for three to four weeks. At the latter location he saw his father, who had been lifted in his place, and despite his protests that his parent had nothing to do with the conflict, Henderson Sr was sent to Ballykinlar internment camp.

Name	1916 Rank / Unit /Garrison	Sources
Hendrick, James	Volunteer, B Company, 1st Battalion IV. North Circular/Cabra Road bridge barricades, then Four Courts.	MSPC MSP34REF20867.

Corporation Service

Labourer employed in Streets Section, Waterworks Department, Housing Department, Sewers Department and the City Abattoir from 1932-40 at least.

Other Notes

IRB member, 1914-21. Member of the Irish Volunteers from inception until 1917. During the Easter Rising was part of Captain Seamus S. O'Sullivan's party defending barricades at the North Circular Road and Cabra Bridge, and then reported to Church Street on Tuesday night with news that British forces had destroyed these with artillery fire and forced the Volunteers back. Detailed by Edward Daly to establish communications with Seamus O'Sullivan, he was denounced by a woman to British soldiers and had go into hiding, and was unable to return to Church Street. After the Rising he was involved in the usual parading and electioneering during the 1918 Election. Ill health forced him to drop out of the IRA, although he stored arms and ran an anti-Treaty safe house until the end of the Civil War.

Name	1916 Rank / Unit /Garrison	Sources
Henry, James/ Seámus Mac Énrí	Volunteer, B Company, 1st Battalion (he was attached to B Company, 3rd Battalion IV). Boland's Mills, railway line Westland Row (now Pearse) Station to Lansdowne Road.	MSPC 24SP9209; *Irish Press*, 26 Mar. 1991.

Corporation Service

December 1947-52 (at least) as foreman carpenter in City Architect's Department, Dublin Corporation.

Other Notes

Originally trained as a carpenter and joiner. Joined the Irish Volunteers at inception. During Easter Week was with the Boland's Mills garrison, then interned. During the War of Independence was on some armed street patrols until starting full-time on munitions manufacturing as Battalion adjutant, 1st Battalion Dublin Brigade IRA from October 1920. Was arrested by the British in June 1921, then released after the Truce in December 1921. Later a Captain in the National Army based in the Ordnance Office, Collins Barracks, Dublin. Left the regular Army for the Reserve in late 1920s. Retired from the Irish Army (post-Emergency) on 1 April 1946 as a Commandant. In 1991 he was interviewed in an article in the *Irish Press* concerning the 75th anniversary commemorations.

Name	1916 Rank / Unit /Garrison	Sources
Holahan/ Holohan, Gerard (Garry)/ Ó hUallacháin, Gearóid	Lieutenant in Na Fianna Éireann, attached to 1st Battalion, IV Na Fianna Éireann service 1910-22, IV service 1913-24. Four Courts, Magazine Fort.	MSPC MSP34REF1385; BMH WS 328, WS 336.

Corporation Service

Employee of Dublin Corporation since September 1920. 'I gave one week's holidays in charge of [Na Fianna Éireann officer training] I was never a full time man. I was in the Corporation and always available [...] sometimes four hours a day. the meetings were held in the pumping station during work hours. From '20 on I could get out at any time. The Republicans controlled the Corporation. I had a telephone at my hand. I was always available.' (MSPC). He also arranged an IRA raid for needed plant and equipment on the pumping station in 1920. Lost his Corporation service for at least part of the Civil war period. Finally was able to start a five-year college course to become an engineer after the Civil War ended. Became an electrical engineer in the Electrical and Public Lighting Section, City Engineers Department, from where he eventually retired.

Joined Na Fianna Éireann in 1910, and was one of those who drilled the IRB before the IV were formed (became IRB Centre of the Fianna and a member of the Dublin Centre Board from 1918). Involved in the Howth and Kilcoole gun-runnings. During the Rising was involved in the attacks on the Magazine Fort (he apparently killed the twenty-three-year-old George Playfair), Broadstone and Linenhall Barracks. Afterwards fought at Red Cow Lane and Church Street. Interned at Knutsford and then Frongoch. Lost his job as an electrical fitter in Dublin Port and Docks power station as a result of participating in the Rising. Appointed Fianna Quartermaster General in 1917. In November 1919 was appointed as Captain in 2nd Company, 5th Battalion (Engineers) Dublin Brigade. Involved in activities such as the December 1919 raid on the *Irish Independent*, instruction in military engineering, and carrying out an engineering survey on the Custom House of its surrounding communications cables prior to the May 1921 attack. Was on the run from early 1920 until the Truce, never sleeping at home (but did take a week's honeymoon in February 1922). Arrested by the Black and Tans at work in Clontarf pumping station at December 1920 and was badly beaten. Court-martialled but acquitted, he was re-arrested and detained. Part-time O/C training for Fianna officers – he used a week of his holidays in training them. Was on the Fianna executive and O/C Dublin Brigade Fianna. Taken on as engineer on a ship sailing to London in August 1920, to gain experience for gun-running purposes and to evaluate the practicality of closing the mouth of the Liffey against the Royal Navy at need. Later involved in an attack on Auxiliaries at North Wall, and various arms-smuggling schemes involving shipping. After September 1920 he was working directly for Rory O'Connor, Director of Engineering, on special assignments (such as the November 1920 plan to destroy the Stuart Street power station and the Clayton Vale pumping station in Manchester). He was the electrical, mechanical and civil engineering expert; O'Connor was only on the civil side and 'academic'. The plans he drew up after an engineering survey were subsequently captured. After the Treaty was signed, they discussed the use of the city sewers system (which he inspected) if the Four Courts were attacked. Afterwards was involved in the Civil War fighting around O'Connell Street (he had charge of taking, fortifying and holding part of the street), Cabra and Fairview. He was second-in-command to Cathal Brugha in the rearguard and was wounded by machine-gun fire and surrendered after the burning of the Gresham Hotel. Interned from 5 July 1922 in Mountjoy. Went on a thirty-five-day hunger strike ending in final release on 22 December 1923. Awarded a disability pension in the 1940s for persitent ill health due to ill treatment and hunger strike he underwent through the period. Retired from the Corporation as an electrical engineer.

Name	1916 Rank / Unit /Garrison	Sources
Holahan/ Holohan, Patrick (Paddy) Hugh	1st Lieutenant in Na Fianna Éireann, attached to F Company, 2nd Battalion IV. Later F Company, 1st Battalion, Dublin Brigade IV. Magazine Fort, Church Street, Four Courts.	MSPC MSP34REF380; *DC Reports*, Vol 1, 1920.

Corporation Service

Employed as carpenter in Dublin Corporation from 31 May 1920 to July 1935 (when he worked as such in the Sewers Department), resigned at that point to become an overseer in the OPW.

Other Notes

Joined Na Fianna Éireann in 1910. Involved in the Howth gun-running. On the formation of the IV was selected to attend officers' classes at Larkfield and the Tara Street Baths. During the Rising was at the Magazine Fort and then at Church Street and North Brunswick Street (ended in charge of this area, from which he marched his men at the surrender). Involved in a diversionary attack on Broadstone Station to relieve positions on the North Circular Road. Imprisoned in Knutsford and then Frongoch. After release, was involved in re-organising the Fianna. Joined F Company, 2nd battalion IV in 1917 and was also appointed South Dublin City Fianna Director of Training. Arrested again but resigned from the Fianna and concentrated on the IV. Was part of the firing party for Thomas Ashe's funeral, and did armed election protection work in Crossmaglen, Armagh. Was involved in taking over Buckingham Street Fire Station during the Custom House attack in May 1921, and other operations such as the arms raid on Collinstown Aerodrome (where he worked at the time), general street patrolling and ambushes, and police work catching criminals who were posing as IRA. Became Commandant of 1st Battalion IRA. Commanded the anti-Treaty troops who seized the Four Courts on 22 April 1922, but was not involved in the subsequent fighting there. Involved in the August 1922 attempt to destroy Dublin bridges, and was arrested and imprisoned in Kilmainham Gaol. During the Emergency was involved in organising and training the 26th Battalion Old IRA (later 26th Battalion F.C.A.) as a reservist officer and then returned to the regular army as a Commandant commanding the 1st Battalion, Construction Corps and then with No. 1 Depot Construction Corps, Curragh Camp. As he had died in 1946 of a haemorrhage after returning to the Reserve, his widow was granted a pension as it was judged that his Emergency service had been responsible, as too great a strain for a man of his age.

Name	1916 Rank / Unit /Garrison	Sources
Howard, George	Civilian boy, aged about twelve years, attached to B Company, 1st Battalion IV. Four Courts, Church Street, North King Street. Came to defend the convent in North Brunswick Street from rumoured British seizure (per brother's MSPC file).	MSPC MSP34REF43172.

Corporation Service

In 1925 was an apprentice motor mechanic, as per his brother Seán's MSPC file. His father was a fitter in the Corporation; his brother Seán was in Stanley Street before his death (possibly George was in Stanley Street too at some point). In 1942 at least employed by Dublin Corporation. In 1935, and from 1943 onwards lived in Ipswich, Queensland, Australia (he might be an emigrant through unemployment mentioned by his mother in the other MSPC file).

Other Notes

Brother of Séan Howard. Despatch carrier for Edward Daly and other senior officers during the Easter Rising between different posts. Only joined the IV after the Rising, in 1917. Took part in anti-recruiting and anti-conscription activities, and police work during the 1918 Election; also some armed patrols (including attacks on armoured cars) and a raid on the *Irish Independent*. Fought on the anti-Treaty side around Dublin city during the Civil War, in 'armed defence of the Republic'. Captured by the National Army during the IRA attack on Dublin bridges in August 1922 and was subsequently interned.

Name	1916 Rank / Unit /Garrison	Sources
Howard, Seán Bernard	Volunteer, B Company, 1st Battalion IV from 1915. Former member of Na Fianna Éireann from its formation to May 1915. Four Courts, Park Road Cabra, shot near junction of North King Street and Church Street.	MSPC 1D440, BMH WS 393 (Seamus O'Sullivan), SFRH.

Corporation Service

Resigned after two years from the British Civil Service (Clerk first in the Land Commission and then in the Congested Districts Board) in January 1916, rather than be transferred back to London and be conscripted. Early in 1916, started in Stanley Street as an apprentice fitter (where his father George Howard was also a fitter).

Other Notes

On Easter Monday he was part of Captain Seamus O'Sullivan's B Company 1st Battalion, Dublin Brigade, and was detailed to hold the bridges at the North Circular Road, Cabra Road and Cross Guns Bridge. With insufficient numbers and ammunition, and the non-appearance of William Sheehan with the needed gelignite to blow the bridges, O'Sullivan sent Howard back to the Four Courts that evening with a report and a request for reinforcements. Seán was shot in action (in the thigh) at dawn at the junction of King Street and Church Street on 29 April 1916, and died in the Richmond Hospital that evening. The eldest of twelve children, his mother received compensation from the National Aid in 1916 and 1917. The Cumann na nGaedheal government refused his parents a claim for compensation under the 1923 Army Pensions Act: 'I was not aware I was begging money for the loss of my son Seán who went Out on Easter Monday 1916 to make it possible for the people to live [...] Is this the way the Free State Government treated all the mothers of the 1916 Boys. Had he gone to France from london to fight for Britain, instead of coming home to Dublin to fight for Ireland his mother and the other Children would be well looked after today.' His case was taken up again by the '1st Batt Economic Committee' with the Fianna Fáil government in 1938, and was still being pursued in 1969.

Name	1916 Rank / Unit /Garrison	Sources
Hughes, Patrick	Volunteer, C Company, 1st Battalion Dublin Brigade IV. GPO, Henry Street, Liffey Street.	MSPC MSP34REF21151.

Corporation Service

Caretaker, Corporation Buildings, Foley Street (Housing Dept). '23 years' service' in 1935 – so started in 1912 (assistant in October 1914).

Joined the Irish Volunteers in October 1914. On 8 September 1915 appeared in court charged with stealing a rifle left behind in a room by a British soldier on leave from the Western Front. While the judge accepted that there was no evidence of theft – Hughes claimed that the door was open and he took it only for safe-keeping, as caretaker in Corporation Buildings – Hughes's Howth rifle was ordered to be confiscated. This became the basis of a scheme of purchasing British weapons from Portobello Barracks that Hughes followed from October 1915 until the end of 1918, with the room's occupant who turned out to be a deserter. His office was used as a dump for purchased weapons before they were moved on. On the Tuesday of the Rising formed part of a party sent up Henry Street to clear out looters. Wounded on Thursday – 'while defending the post at O'Neills' Corner of Liffey St and Henry St I was wounded in the neck,' according to Leo Henderson this was during an attack by one of the British improvised armoured vehicles. Helped erect barricades at Princes Street and Moore Street. Was in Hanlon's of Moore Street at the surrender. Interned in Knutsford and then Frongoch. Under arms during the South Armagh by-election. Other than that, drilling and grenade and revolver practice until the outbreak of the War of Independence. After that, patrolling and outpost duties. Served until 11 July 1922: 'I asked Capt. Prendergast what was up. He told me. I said I told him a fortnight before that I was not going to take part in the Civil War. I said that publicly in front of the company a fortnight before in the Orange Hall.'

Name	1916 Rank / Unit /Garrison	Sources
Hyland, James	ICA. St Stephen's Green, Mount Street.	MSPC MSP34REF22258.

Corporation Service

Employed by Dublin Corporation from 1921 to at least 1938.

Other Notes

Member of the Irish Citizen Army 1914-17. Served as guard on Liberty Hall and involved in munitions manufacturing before the Rising. In the Rising fought at St Stephen's Green, was part of the party who bored through walls of houses to Mount Street before the surrender on Sunday. Interned in Stafford Gaol and then Frongoch. In his MSPC file, in reply to the form question asking if he applied for a pension under the 1924 act, wrote: 'I did not serve in the National Army at any date. Did not apply for a pension under the 1924 Act. The reason I did not apply was I was hostile to the Cosgrave Regime and the then Free State Army.'

Name	1916 Rank / Unit /Garrison	Sources
Jackson, Ralph (Raphael)	IRB. South County Dublin.	BMH WS 409 (Valentine Jackson), WS 332 (Joseph Kenny), WS 328 (Gearóid Ua h-Uallacháin); MSP34REF11867 (John Joseph Twamley); *DCC Minutes* 1927 No. 461; 1928, No. 53; 1930, Nos. 329 & 402; *DC Reports*, 1927, No. 226, pp 660-1

Corporation Service

Employed by the Waterworks department at Stillorgan Reservoir from about 1911. Temporary timekeeper from about 1919 and then temporary Superintendent from 1925 (replacing his brother Valentine in both cases). Permanent Superintendent from 1 January 1928.

Former IRB member. Brother of Valentine (and therefore likewise related to James Stephens). Ralph was asked on Good Friday by P.J. Farrell, IRB Centre in Bray, to join on Easter Sunday with a party ordered to cut the telegraph wires on the Killiney-Bray railway line, some of which led to Kilcoole and from there undersea to London (possibly, from other descriptions of this group, sabotage of the railway line was intended as well). While Jackson, Farrell and the Bray contingent were preparing their weapons in a secluded spot on Saturday evening a messenger arrived to call the Sunday Rising off. In the confusion of Easter Monday's mobilisation, both Jackson and Farrell travelled to each other's homes at the same time and therefore never met up for the intended sabotage at noon, which Farrell then proceeded to carry out. During the War of Independence, the Jackson brothers stored arms and ammunition for the IRA in underground valve chambers at Stillorgan Reservoir.

Name	1916 Rank / Unit /Garrison	Sources
Jackson, Valentine (Val)	No longer an active member of the IV at the time of the Rising due to becoming an invalid. N/A	BMH WS 409; *Irish Independent*, 27 Sept. 1923, p. 5; *DCC Minutes*, 1927, No. 461; 1928, No. 53; 1930, Nos. 329 & 402; *DC Reports*, 1927, No. 226, pp 660-1.

Corporation Service

Employed from 1897 in Stillorgan Reservoir, becoming timekeeper and then, from about 1919, Superintendent. From about 1925 became a draughtsman in Waterworks Section, City Engineer's Office, Castle Street.

Other Notes

IRB Centre, relative (and acquaintance) of James Stephens. His first IRB Circle had as Centre P.T. Daly, and he encountered both James Stritch and Seán O'Casey in the IRB. Involved in the Howth gun-running. Saved from falling out on the march back (he had gout in his foot) by 'Providence' – the stand-off with the RIC and King's Own Scottish Borderers, and a friendly householder nearby. For the Kilcoole gun-running was involved with Seán Fitzgibbon in an abandoned scheme to use the Stillorgan reservoir as a transportation depot. Visited at home by British column, led by improvised armoured vehicle (employing dismounted naval gun from Kingstown as armament) and armoured cars, at end of week in the subsequent round-up – but not arrested. Scathing about the confusion of Easter Week. Afterwards involved in electioneering and anti-conscription activities, schemes with Rory O'Connor around cutting off the water supply to the various barracks, stealing the maps of the city water mains (returned in 1922), testing explosives in 1920 on the Roundwood upper reservoir site, storing arms at Stillorgan and being a member of a Dáil court. Remained neutral in the Civil War.

Name	1916 Rank / Unit /Garrison	Sources
Kavanagh, James Joseph (J.J.)	Volunteer, C Company, 1st Battalion Dublin Brigade IV. Four Courts.	MSPC MSP34REF15024.

Corporation Service

Painter, Housing Department from (at least) 1934 until his death in 1948.

Other Notes

A Volunteer for some time previous to Easter Week. During the Rising stationed in the Records Office, from which he sniped at random with his Mauser rifle during the week. Imprisoned in Richmond Barracks, Knutsford and then Frongoch. On his release in July 1916 he reported back to his Company, but after a couple of months went to work in Tipperary and took no further part in revolutionary activities. Emigrated to the UK for some years but returned in the 1930s.

Name	1916 Rank / Unit /Garrison	Sources
Kavanagh, Seán (John)	There was a Captain Seán Kavanagh commanding H Company, 1st Battalion Dublin Brigade (per Christopher McGrane's MSPC). Unknown.	*Irish Independent*, 12 Oct. 1945, p. 3; *DCC Minutes*, 1930, No. 135; *DC Reports*, Vol. I, 1930, No. 70.

Corporation Service

Clerk of Works (Engineer) in the Streets Section and then the Housing Department from 1930 until his death in late 1945, apart from a period during the Emergency when he re-enlisted.

Other Notes

According to his 1945 obituary, Seán Kavanagh (who lived at 27 St Alban's Road, South Circular Road) was originally from Arklow in Co. Wicklow and had fought in the Easter Rising. He took the pro-Treaty side in the Civil War, and was demobilised later from the National Army, joining the Corporation. At the beginning of the Emergency he re-joined the Defence Forces and served in the 4th Infantry Battalion, returning to Dublin Corporation service in 1944. He died in October 1945.

Name	1916 Rank / Unit /Garrison	Sources
Kearney, Thomas (Tom)	Volunteer, E Company, 4th Battalion, Dublin Brigade IV. GPO.	MSPC 24SP5327.

Corporation Service

Plumber in City Architects' Department from at least April 1952.

Other Notes

During the Rising, sent from the GPO to Annesley Bridge, where he helped with efforts to blow the railway line. Ordered back to the GPO on Tuesday night with the rest of the rebels at that location, he was on Friday in the attempted break-out through Moore Street and then in the surrender. Held first at Richmond Barracks, then deported to Stafford Gaol then Frongoch. After the release he found himself unable to finish his plumbing apprenticeship due to his Volunteer activities, so had to take work as a handyman. Involved in drilling, electioneering and running dance and dramatics classes to raise funds. As a Section Commander (Sergeant) and then 2nd Lieutenant during the War of Independence he took part in arms raids, the burning of Rockbrook RIC barracks, ambushes, etc. He joined the National Army on 21 August 1922 and fought on the Free State side in the Civil War. Discharged from the National Army on 3 March 1924, with rank of CQMS in the Corps of Engineers, Collins Barracks.

Name	1916 Rank / Unit /Garrison	Sources
Kelly, Patrick J.	Volunteer, G Company, 1st Battalion IV Four Courts.	MSPC MSP34REF457, MSP34REF18103 (Patrick J. O'Brien); BMH WS 781, WS 726.

Corporation Service

Dublin Fire Brigade. 'Fire Station Dorset St', as per N. Laffan list in MSPC RO/12.

Other Notes

Referee for Patrick J. O'Brien. Active in the 1913 Lockout, hostile to DMP afterwards. Involved in fighting at North King Street. Involved in confrontation with British Army at City Hall before Thomas Ashe funeral.

Name	1916 Rank / Unit / Garrison	Sources
Kenny, James	Volunteer, D Company, 4th Battalion IV. South Dublin Union.	MSPC MSP34REF20937; BMH WS 174 (James Kenny).

Corporation Service

Employed as a saddler in Dublin Corporation from 1932, labourer from 5 June 1940 in the Streets Section until 10 January 1945, when he was sacked (as a casual worker) because of becoming too ill to work.

Other Notes

IRB member from 1903, in the Lord Edward Branch: 'There was no fixed address for any of the IRB branches at that time, the reason being to keep the authorities "in the dark" regarding the meeting places and the activities of the organisation. [A member of his Circle] was a '67 man and shot an informer in Skipper's alley'. In the IRB 'for many years and was one of those responsible for winding up of same'. (MSPC). Joined the Irish Volunteers in the Rotunda at inception, being a steward at the meeting. Involved in both the Howth and Kilcoole gun-runnings. During the Rising, fought hand-to-hand at the South Dublin Union and gives a witness account of seeing heavily-armed RIC who had been training at an NCO school in Portobello Barracks and were dressed in half-military, half-RIC uniform. Interned in Knutsford and then Frongoch. Post-Rising, involved in election work (1918) and a series of arms smuggling trips from Liverpool (before the re-organisation in 1917), and operations such as the attempted destruction of the RIC Barracks at Crumlin, raiding Broadstone Station for material for munitions. Involved in Bloody Sunday as part of a guard picket, and was involved in intelligence work such as shadowing: 'was personally interested in the welfare of D.O. Dan Hoy'. In hospital by 1949, died in 1952.

Name	1916 Rank / Unit / Garrison	Sources
Kettle, Laurence J. (L.J./Larry)	Joint National Secretary to the INV. Involuntary guest of the St Stephen's Green garrison.	BMH WS 130 (Sean Fitzgibbon); Brian Barton, *From behind a closed door: secret court martial records of the 1916 Rising* (Belfast, 2002), pp 272; 278-9.

Corporation Service

May 1906 as Works Superintendent. Deputy City Electrical Engineer, Electricity Supply Dept.

Other Notes

Brother of UCD lecturer and Home Rule MP Thomas Kettle. Invited to become part of the Provisional Committee of the Irish Volunteers in 1913 at the suggestion of Éamonn Ceannt, fellow Dublin Corporation employee. Kettle was heckled by members of the ICA at the meeting in the Rotunda which established the Irish Volunteers, as his farming family had allegedly employed 'scabs' during the 1913 Lockout. After the 1914 split in the Irish Volunteers, he was joint Secretary of the Irish National Volunteers (INV). Held prisoner by St Stephen's Green garrison (which included Harry Nicholls). Kettle appeared as a witness for the prosecution in Michael Mallin's trial, to testify that Mallin was in command at St Stephen's Green (while confirming that Kettle had himself been well treated).

Name	1916 Rank / Unit /Garrison	Sources
Lawless, J.V. (James Vincent)/ Seamus Ua Laoidhleis	Captain of St Margaret's/ Santry Company, 5th Battalion IV (appointed as Battalion Adjutant in Easter Week). Co. Dublin, Co. Meath, Ashbourne.	MSPC MSP34REF818; BMH WS1043, WS 727.

Corporation Service

Staff officer in Dublin County Council during the revolutionary period, but mentions of temporary employment as Registration Inspector with Voters' Registration, Dublin Corporation, 1934-39 at least.

Other Notes

From a Republican family; his brother was County Centre in at least the War of Independence, and others in the family were 'involved'. Joined the IRB in 1907. Became a member of the Na Fianna Éireann in 1909. Joined the Irish Volunteers in 1913, and in 1914 organised the Santry Company. During Easter Week mobilised the Battalion at Knocksedan on Easter Monday and was involved in various operations such as the attack on the barracks at Swords and the battle at Ashbourne. His picket at Finglas village captured thirty returning British officers, but he was ordered to release them. Was sentenced to death but this was commuted to ten years of penal servitude. Interned in Dartmoor, Parkhurst, Pentonville and Lewes. On release had lost four stone and his position as Assistant Secretary in Dublin County Council. With the assistance of Michael Collins was re-appointed. Carried out intelligence work for Collins from September 1917 (including monitoring British motor car and lorry registrations, and temporary registration of IRA vehicles) and 'made arrangements with overseers and other[s] on the outdoor staff of the County Council to keep in touch with enemy activities over the whole County Dublin area, my well known sympathy with Labour helped very much in this direction, and having saved many of the RIC in the area from rough handling in 1916, I was able to secure co-operation from many of the force in obtaining very important information'. Active with Department of Local Government during the War of Independence, not least as Secretary to the County Council Officials' Association. As one of the Dublin Corporation representatives to the Dáil Commission on Local Government he moved the motion (on Collins's instructions) to break with the Local Government Board. Interestingly, he claims W.T. Cosgrave voted against this move. Arrested and interned again from December 1920 to December 1921. Took an anti-Treaty position and did intelligence work for the IRA. His pension claim was held up as the secretive Collins had Lawless reporting to him alone, and so corroboration was nearly impossible; getting wind of this, and in difficulties, he tried to expedite the award by withdrawing his War of Independence claim.

Name	1916 Rank / Unit /Garrison	Sources
Lemass, Noel	Volunteer, C Company, 3rd Battalion IV Later a Captain. GPO, Imperial Hotel.	Various BMH statements such as WS813, WS953, WS1053; 'Noel Lemass and his commandeering of a Dublin tram' http://comeheretome.com/2014/02/12/noel-lemass-and-his-commandeering-of-a-dublin-tram/ (accessed 05/05/15); *Irish Press*, 9 Jan. 1947, p. 1; Yeates, *A city in turmoil*, pp 222-3.

Corporation Service

Started employment as apprentice fitter by the Works Committee in Stanley Street in 1916, having lost his previous apprenticeship after the Rising). Was a draughtsman (or perhaps an engineer) in the Cleansing Department at his time of death after the Civil War.

Other Notes

Elder brother of Seán Lemass. Noel Lemass was wounded while escaping from the Imperial Hotel during the Rising. Escaped capture afterwards. Involved in the Dublin fighting against loyalist mobs on the night of Armistice Day 1918, and captured arms from British officers. Involved with Irish Volunteer engineers, lecturing on hand grenades, destruction of bridges and use of explosives. For at least part of 1919-20 was held in Derry Gaol. Both Noel and Seán were present in the Four Courts at the start of the Civil War, having taken the anti-Treaty position. Still on the run in July 1923 (after the end of Civil War), he was kidnapped at the corner of Exchequer and Drury Street in broad daylight, while in the company of John Devine (Superintendent of City Cleansing) and executed by Free State forces. His remains were found a year later in the Wicklow Mountains, which seriously embarrassed the Free State government, with at least one minister having close ties to the reputed killers. The City Council passed a motion condemning the death of this 'esteemed and worthy officer of the Council who had been foully and diabolically murdered', and adjourned for one week as a mark of respect to the Lemass family.

Name	1916 Rank / Unit /Garrison	Sources
Lennon, Michael John /Ó Leannáin, Micheál	Section Commander (i.e. Sergeant) B Company, 3rd Battalion IV. Boland's Mills	MSPC MSPC34REF1776; *DC Reports*, Vol I, 1917, No. 224; Vol I, 1920, No. 26.

Corporation Service

From his MSPC file 'He is a clerk in the Corporation'. Appointed from 23 June 1910. Working in the City Engineer's Department by at least Easter 1916, and certainly under the Waterworks Committee at the time of going on the run during the War of Independence.

Other Notes

Possibly the 'Lennon' given as being absent by M.J. Buckley in same 1916 report as Fitzgibbon. 'The City Engineer reported that Messrs. Fitzgibbon and Lennon, Clerks in his Department, had not resumed duty since the Easter holidays, and that he required temporary clerks until their return.' p. 158 *DC Reports* 1916 Vol II. 'In Jan. 1921, he was forced to leave his job in the Corporation and from this time until the Truce he was engaged on the compiling of a large brochure dealing with acts of aggression by British Crown Forces on members of Local Govt. bodies and on local representatives. This was done at the request of Mr. Cosgrave who was then Minister for Local Government.' 'They had raided the Corporation for me and the men were very loyal to me. There was one spy there. He is since dead. And the men told me just as I got in. And then as I could not work I took this on by arrangement with Mr. Cosgrave and got assistance from others to do the research; and did in fact compile an enormous brochure [...] It was a big thing. It was on the acts of aggression throughout the country. Nobody knows better than you gentlemen what sort of a thing that was. And so I had to dodge around from library to library, so as not to get labelled' '[...] Publication of this brochure was abandoned upon the truce.' Was wounded and sent to St Vincent's, warned by a wounded Tommy of the impending raid and got out in time, but was captured on South Circular Road shortly after escaping due to his bandaged wound. 'From that date [12 December 1919] until 11th July 1921 I did not sleep ever in my house save on three or four occasions, each of which took place during the week of the strike of the Corporation staff.' Home was raided many times by Auxiliaries, and his parents beaten. Wasn't militarily active in War of Independence, but police tried to arrest him for 'murder'.

Name	1916 Rank / Unit /Garrison	Sources
Lennon, Nicholas (Nick)/ Mac Giolla Fhinnéin Nioclais	Volunteer (acting Lieutenant), A Company, 1st Battalion, Dublin Brigade IV (References in the MSPC file to his having had a rank of officer in the ICA). Four Courts, Church Street.	MSPC 1P774. Mistaken for 'Michael' Lennon in BMH WS 259.

Corporation Service

Bricklayer, 1 Jan 1913 to late 1920s or so, according to MSPC. Appears in DC Reports 1924, No. 120, as 'Assistant Foreman Mason, Sewers Department. 14 years' service'. Widow claimed he was in the Corporation. Also claimed he had '3 years record from the Corporation before 1916', 'my husband was also victimised in the Corporation during the Commissioners time for his Republican views'. In November 1925 Commissioner Heron was critical about 'above the normal' sick leave.

Other Notes

IRB member from 1907. Joined the Irish Volunteers in 1913-14. Shot and wounded in the abdomen by a British sniper on the roof of Ganley's Woollen Merchants, Usher's Quay, at Church Street Bridge, he was removed first to the Father Mathew Hall medical aid post and then to Richmond Hospital where he spent two months (therefore escaping capture and internment). Got forty-one days' sick pay from Dublin Corporation from 26 April 1916 for 'gunshot wounds' (released from Richmond in the middle of June 1916), and received £10 from the National Aid. Got stuck in on the re-organisation in 1917, being closely associated with Peadar Breslin's squad in procuring (from British soldiers in Portobello Barracks and Wellington Barracks). 'Mainly responsible' for designing and building the hidden armoury beneath Colmcille hall. Arrested at an engineering class in 28 North Frederick Street in 1918 and interned, went on thirteen-day hunger strike in Mountjoy prison. In Crooksling sanatorium for six weeks with Phthisis in February to March 1919 to aid recovery. Later unsuccessfully tried to claim pension for chronic bronchitis (or TB) from his service (he died in 1931). His almost destitute wife struggled to get help (in lieu of unsuccessful further attempts at a wounds pension, after his health was broken during hunger strike, and while on the run) in a cleaner job in Government buildings in the late 1930s. Lennon was in the IRA until at least 1924 and at latest 1931 (date of death). His disability pension claim in 1929 repeatedly asked witnesses: 'Why did he not join the National Army?' (Real answer: he took the anti-Treaty side, but was too unwell to fight). By 1925 was Secretary of the 'Seán Heuston' Sinn Féin Club; later both he and his wife appear to have joined Fianna Fáil.

Name	1916 Rank / Unit /Garrison	Sources
Love, Michael	Volunteer, F Company, 2nd Battalion, Dublin Brigade IV. Jacob's Factory.	MSPC 24SP11754.

Corporation Service

He gained employment as a night watchman after the Easter Rising and during the War of Independence. Later in charge of Corporation stores at Annesley Bridge (the Sloblands) – Charles Saurin reference from Love's MSPC file.

Other Notes

Joined the Irish Volunteers in 1914. Escaped after the Rising. Post-Rising, active member of his Company, later becoming a Section Commander. Involved in intelligence work, raids for arms, ambushes and Bloody Sunday. Arrested 23 November 1920 and interned until 17 May 1921. Captured, inside and armed, at the Custom House burning on 25 May 1921 and re-interned. Joined the National Army in February 1922 and went to the Dublin Guards. Retired in March 1927 as Commandant in the Defence Forces. Re-commissioned as a Reservist Officer during the Emergency (Lieutenant, then Captain). Fine Gael candidate in the Dublin North-west constituency in the 1943 General Election.

Name	1916 Rank / Unit /Garrison	Sources
Lynch, Michael Joseph (M.J.)	Volunteer, B Company, 4th Battalion, Dublin Brigade IV. South Dublin Union.	MSPC RO/14; Mentions in BMH WS 511, WS 371, WS1446 and others.

Corporation Service

Clerk in Rates Office from April 1913, then in Accountants Office. On 16 June 1920 appointed Superintendent of Dublin City Abattoir.

Other Notes

Peripherally involved in the operation to hold up and steal British armoured car at the abattoir in an (ultimately) failed attempt to get the condemned Seán MacEoin out of Mountjoy, by IRA Volunteers posing as British soldiers. Ended as Vice-Brigadier, Dublin Brigade.

Name	1916 Rank / Unit /Garrison	Sources
Lyons Thornton, Dr Brigid	Member, Cumann na mBan. GPO.	MSPC 24SP13615; BMH WS 259 (Dr. B. Thornton); http://www.ouririshheritage.org/page/dr_brigid_lyons_thornton, (accessed 22/01/16); Gillis, Liz, *Women of the Irish revolution* (Cork, 2nd ed., 2016), p. 155.

Corporation Service

Paediatrician with Dublin Corporation's Public Health Service from 1929 or so.

Other Notes

Joined Cumann na mBan in late 1915. Headed the Cumann na mBan section in the O'Donovan Rossa funeral. Was a medical student in Galway in 1916, when along with her uncle and another man, she drove up to Dublin during Easter Week on news of the Rising in order to take part. They made their way into the Four Courts via Church Street. On her second day in the Four Courts, while lying down upstairs to rest, wrapped in judges' ermine robes '[…] Barney Mellows came in and woke us – this is my most vivid recollection – and said that Lt. Clancy had take over a post […] and two girls were required to go over to him and his men. Somebody said "call that fat girl that came up from the country". I resented the slight, but my patriotism asserted itself'. (Lyons's BMH statement). The two Cumann na mBan members went over to No. 5 Church Street, which was Michael Lennon's house, and used this as their post. After the surrender, was detained along with most of the rest of the women at Richmond Barracks, being released on 9 May. Involved in the Longford and Clare by-elections, the National Aid and various arms procurement and transport activities. She took the pro-Treaty side and was commissioned on 13 November 1922 as a Lieutenant in the Army Medical Services of the National Army, where she was responsible for female Republican prisoners interned in Kilmainham. She was demobilised due to TB in 1924. She applied for and received a military service pension from the Free State, in contrast to the official attitude taken towards other women veterans such as Margaret Skinnider who had been anti-Treaty or neutral in the Civil War.

Name	1916 Rank / Unit /Garrison	Sources
MacBride, Major John	Possibly in J.R. Reynolds's 'special unit', Dublin Brigade IV (commissioned as Vice-Commandant during Rising by Tomás MacDonagh). Jacob's Factory.	MSPC DP6639; BMH WS 328, WS 317, WS 564, WS1765 Part 2, WS 150 (Gregory Murphy); *DC Reports*, Vol II, 1910, p. 958.

Corporation Service

6 Oct 1909, appointed Assistant Water Bailiff and Oil Inspector, Water Bailiff's Office. Involved in the DMOA. 'Major McBride was at this time an employee of the Waterworks Committee of the Dublin Corporation. This post had been secured for him through the influence of Alderman Tom Kelly, Councillor P.T. Daly and myself' – Seán T. Ó Ceallaigh (BMH WS328).

Other Notes

IRB member, but only briefly on the IRB Supreme Council in 1911. Commissioned as Major in the Transvaal during the Second Boer War, was an Irish war hero (on the Boer side, a cause popular back in Ireland) with his Irish Brigade – whose flag, sent from Ireland, of a harp on a green field, is in the National Museum. His horse with the Commando was famously named 'Fenian Boy'. Husband of Maud Gonne in a tempestuous and unhappy marriage. 'I remember Major MacBride gave a lecture to the Fianna in the hall at 34 Camden Street on his experiences in the Boer War, and I was greatly impressed by it. It was very interesting, and we gave him a great reception. At that time he was employed as a Water Bailiff by the Dublin Corporation and in charge of the weighing scales and weights used by the various merchants at that time for weighing coal and grain as it was unloaded from the boats. The coal was weighed in small tubs and the grain by the bag. This gear was given over to the Public Lighting Department after Major MacBride's execution and is still in the Tara Street depot. I used to see Major MacBride every morning walking to his office. He always dressed smartly, and carried his umbrella under his arm like a walking stick or a rifle. When he would be passing the works I would say to Tom Kane, an ex-British soldier, "There is the man who made you run in Africa", and Kane would boil with temper. Poor Tom Kane was blown up in the first world war.' (BMH WS328). Member of the O'Donovan Rossa Funeral Committee. He lived as a lodger in Fred Allan's house, whom he had known well in Dublin IRB circles even before the Boer War. His relationship with Allan's wife, Clara, has been the subject of hints and speculation for a century. It is likely that claims of his accidentally joining the Rising are untrue and intended to try to give him a fighting chance in his court-martial after the surrender. Gregory Murphy, J.R. Reynolds and others strongly suggest from the sum of their BMH statements that MacBride instead mobilised on Monday morning as part of an Irish Volunteers 'Special Unit' at No. 41 Parnell Square. Later that day, he made his way first to the GPO and then to St Stephen's Green in the company of J.R. Reynolds, before joining in with McDonagh at Jacob's.

Name	1916 Rank / Unit /Garrison	Sources
MacCarthy, Thomas/Mac Carthaigh, Tomás	O/C C Company, 4th Battalion IV. South Dublin Union.	MSPC MSP34REF59024; BMH WS 307, WS 327, WS1697; *DC Reports*, Vol III, 1916, p. 238; Oireachtas Directory of Members.

Corporation Service

The MSPC metadata claims that he had been employed by Dublin Corporation, but there is no evidence of this in the uploaded files. There is, however, a Thomas McCarthy, Clerk in the Electricity Supply Department, Fleet Street in 1915 (employed from August, 1905).

IRB member. Brother of Dan McCarthy. Thomas MacCarthy arranged the escort to get a smuggled Liam Mellowes back to Athenry in time for the Rising. In command at Roe's Distillery, but 'evacuated' on Tuesday due to loss of contact with the main South Dublin Union garrison (two of his men had disappeared already). Subsequently on the run for three months. Some of his garrison wanted to sign the Roll of Honour and were denied permission – but maybe signed later. Claims he was court-martialled by the IRB after the Rising.

Name	1916 Rank / Unit /Garrison	Sources
McCormick (McCormack), Richard	Captain, ICA. St Stephen's Green, Harcourt Street, Davy's Pub.	MSPC MSP34REF2186.

Corporation Service

Labourer, Sewers Dept 6 April 1926-41 at least.

Other Notes

Former British soldier and veteran of Boer War. In charge of ICA outposts to protect the St Stephen's Green position while it fortified, then withdrew. Dispute over who was senior at the Green – McCormick or Christy Poole. Interned at Knutsford, Frongoch and Reading. Afterwards involved in raiding and buying arms, and Thomas Ashe funeral. Fought in Dublin on anti-Treaty side in the Civil War. Involved in the Night of the Bridges, etc.

Name	1916 Rank / Unit /Garrison	Sources
MacDowell, Cathal (Cecil Grange)/ MacDubhghaill, Cathal	Volunteer, D Company, 3rd Battalion IV. Boland's Mills.	MSPC DP25533; mentions in BMH WS 258 Maeve MacDowell, WS 129, WS 160, WS 328, WS 889, WS1768; *Irish Press*, 15 Dec. 1932, p. 1; 7 Mar. 1934, p. 6, 27 May 1935; *Irish Independent*, 19 Aug. 1926, p. 8; *DCC Minutes*, 1924, Vol I, p. 261; 1926, Vol I, p. 9; *DC Reports*, Vol I, 1925, p. 546; Roll of Honour; *Irish Volunteer*, 9 Jan. 1915; 6 Nov. 1915.

Corporation Service

Wife claimed engineer, but other sources (such as BMH WS 129) claim 'city architect'. Letter from Corporation in file 'took up duty as temporary draughtsman on the North Side Housing Survey on 5.3.17 […] appointed to the permanent staff […] 1.12.25'. 'Architect and engineer' according to one account (*Irish Press*, 1935). *DCC Minutes* of 1917 (no. 545, p. 373) claim McDowell to be a draughtsman in the Drawing Office, appointed by the Housing Committee for the North City Survey from February 1917.

Other Notes

Joined the Irish Volunteers in 1915. At that time employed in the City Engineer's Department, Dublin Corporation, according to his disabled pensions claim. Was organist and choirmaster in the Church of Ireland St John's Church, Sandymount and was a composer of popular Volunteer songs such as 'We'll crown de Valera King of Ireland', 'The Pig Push', 'Pop goes the Peeler' and 'The Rocky Road to Berlin'. Also played at the large Volunteer concerts. A delegate for D Company at the Volunteer Convention on 31 October, 1915. Coverted to Roman Catholicism during the Rising. Sent to Stafford Gaol and Frongoch after the Rising. While there, he heard some of his future wife Maeve Cavanagh's poetry being read out, and asked for an introduction whenever they were released. 'There were two vast oak vats in the distillery buildings. These were broken down and provided the material for wood-carving. We had a number of artists who drew the designs – Cathal Mac Dubhghall, Murray, Michael Kelly brother of the President, Seán T.), and Frankie Kelly, to mention a few [...] In the meantime we were getting on all right in the camp. We had frequent sing-songs, there being some grand singers amongst us and a few very fine musicians. Cathal McDowell, whom I have already mentioned as an artist, was also an accomplished musician.' (WS 889). Became ill after the general release, treated by Dr Kathleen Lynn, needing frequent sick leave from Dublin Corporation. Some of his paintings and drawings were in the Municipal Gallery and/or the National Museum. Involved with design of reconstructed Upper O'Connell Street. Had a reputation as a composer and songwriter, and was responsible for the musical arrangement to Amhrán na bhFiann. Early in 1920 became associated with the South County Dublin part of the ICA and was involved with them in various War of Independence and Civil War activities (on 'special duty' in the latter conflict). On armed duty during attack on the Custom House, had been asked to get maps of Dublin Castle, and also the Dublin Corporation sewer network as a get-away in emergency, using his access to maps as an 'engineer'. Went to Nice, France in 1926 (meeting Seán MacBride) with advanced TB and died there after accident while in high fever. His wife, Maeve Cavanagh MacDowell whom he married in 1921, was a noted poet, writer and activist; she was a member of the O'Donovan Rossa Funeral Committee and the ICA, and was the sister of the political cartoonist Ernest Kavanagh who was shot dead on the steps of Liberty Hall during the Rising.

Name	1916 Rank / Unit / Garrison	Sources
McGinley, Conor/ Mac Fhionnlaoich, Conchubar	Volunteer, E Company, 4th Battalion, Dublin Brigade IV. GPO.	BMH WS 694 (Feargus (Frank) De Burca), WS 497 (Eamonn Bulfin), WS 907 (Laurence Nugent), WS 370 (Fintan Murphy), WS1043 Joseph V. Lawless; *DC Reports*, Vol. I, 1924, p. 783; http://www.dia.ie/ architects/view/4354/ MCGINLEY-CONOR MICHAEL(CONCHU BHARMACFHIONN LAOICH (downloaded on 3 March 2016).

Corporation Service

Appointed as temporary Assistant City Architect (subject to having or acquiring Irish) in early 1922. Appointed as permanent Assistant City Architect in 1924. Acting Dublin City Architect from 1945, promoted to the post in 1947.

IRB member (Fianna Circle). Eldest son of Peter T. McGinley, President of the Gaelic League 1923-25. A secondary education student at St Enda's, he was from 1914 one of a number of former pupils (including his brother Eunan) who continued to lodge there while now going to college in Dublin. Early on Good Friday morning, both he and Fintan Murphy were given messages from Patrick Pearse for other members of the Military Council, which led to a day of cycling around Dublin city in search of them. Mobilising at Rathfarnham Church on Easter Monday, E Company made their way to Liberty Hall and from there marched to the GPO. On Thursday he was detailed (along with others) to help with attempted tunnelling operations along Henry Street. After the surrender on Moore Street, McGinley was court-martialled and sentenced to ten years' penal servitude, with seven years remitted. He was interned first in Dartmoor and then Lewes. McGinley's architectural studies at UCD were cut short by the Rising, and were only finished in 1920, having worked in (Irish Volunteer Captain) Thomas Cullen's architectural practice since 1918. He was involved in counter-intelligence work (under Cullen, a senior operative for Collins's network) in at least a daring 1920 operation to trap and expose a British spy named Hardy. Later in 1920 McGinley was arrested again and interned at Ballykinlar for a short period. On his release he resumed work at Cullen's practice before being appointed to the City Architects' staff in Dublin Corporation. On the morning of the 28 June 1922, the day of the Free State attack on the Four Courts, McGinley had a conversation with J.V. Lawless which decided him to take no side in the Civil War.

Name	1916 Rank / Unit /Garrison	Sources
McGinn, Michael Conway (Con)	Section Commander (i.e. Sergeant) F Company, 2nd Battalion, Dublin Brigade IV. Fairview, Imperial Hotel, GPO.	MSPC 24SP3001; BMH WS 288 (Lieut.-Col. Charles Saurin), WS 249 (Mr. Frank Henderson), WS 510 (Frank Thornton); Fermanagh 1916 Centenary Association, *Fearless but few: Fermanagh and the Easter Rising* (Fermanagh, 2015), pp 88-92.

Corporation Service

His MSPC file includes a statement by a referee that Conway was employed by Dublin Corporation at some point in the War of Independence.

Other Notes

Son of Michael (the Fenian caretaker of the Clontarf Town Hall), brother of Patrick Romuald. Joined the Irish Volunteers in 1914. Lost his job with the Customs & Excise in 1915 because of his Volunteers association. Conway fought at Fairview and the Imperial Hotel, and was interned in Wakefield and then Frongoch. He took the pro-Treaty position and resigned on 31 January 1924 as a captain in the National Army.

Name	1916 Rank / Unit /Garrison	Sources
McGinn, Patrick Romuald (Rory/ Rommy/Ronnie)	Volunteer, F Company, 2nd Battalion, Dublin Brigade IV. Liberty Hall	BMH WS 693 (Patrick Maguire), WS 721 (Nicholas Smyth), WS 458 (Sean Corr); Fermanagh 1916 Centenary Association, *Fearless but few: Fermanagh and the Easter Rising* (Fermanagh, 2015), pp 88-92.

Corporation Service

Worked in the Housing Department of Dublin Corporation.

Other Notes

Son of Michael (the Fenian caretaker of the Clontarf Town Hall), brother of Michael Conway. Rommy mobilised for the Easter Rising but was injured in the first hours in an accident at Liberty Hall, and had to be sent home. During the War of Independence he was sent to Tyrone in 1918 or 1919 to take charge of the local Volunteers. After raising a Flying Column, he was arrested while back in Dublin looking for explosive supplies. In the Civil War, he took an anti-Treaty position.

Name	1916 Rank / Unit /Garrison	Sources
McGowan, Séamus (James)	Captain, ICA. GPO, Liberty Hall.	MSPC MSP34REF4289; BMH WS 542; http://comeheretome. com/2013/06/17/ raiding-the-defiance/ (as of 10 August 2015).

Corporation Service

Employed as ganger on the Crumlin Housing Scheme, 1934-38 at least.

Other Notes

Involved with Na Fianna Éireann from 1910 as a staff officer. Joined the ICA in 1913. ICA Quarter Master General and a captain from circa 1914 , McGowan lived in Liberty Hall for a month before the Rising, working on munitions through the daytime. During the Rising, he was in charge of the Citizen Army stores in Liberty Hall until their evacuation that afternoon. On moving to the GPO was appointed with James O'Neill as Quartermaster in charge of munitions. Was in charge of the ICA men at Moore Street who were to take part in the aborted plan to tunnel through the houses. Interned in Stafford, Reading and Frongoch. Continued very actively in charge of ICA munitions and equipment after the release. McGowan was centrally involved in the raid on the USS *Defiance* in Dublin port in late 1918. Along with the rest of the ICA took the anti-Treaty position and fought at Findlater's on O'Connell Street. Surrendered and was interned from 4 July 1922 until 16 December 1923.

Name	1916 Rank / Unit /Garrison	Sources
McGrane, Christopher	Member of Sluagh Emmet, Na Fianna Éireann (from 1917 a Volunteer in E Company, 2nd Battalion, Dublin Brigade IV and then from 1918 H Company, 1st Battalion).	MSPC MSP34REF23344; Jimmy Wren, *The GPO Garrison Easter Week 1916* (Dublin, 2015), p. 415.

Corporation Service

Painter

Other Notes

Brother of Thomas McGrane. Joined Na Fianna Éireann in 1912, and was involved in the Howth gun-running. In the run-up to the Rising was attending special officers' classes in the Dawson Street Volunteer HQ on subjects such as street fighting. Like his brother, received no mobilisation order on Easter Monday but ended up going to the GPO once he heard that the Rising had started. On Wednesday he was on a work detail boring through walls. He was captured in Henry Place on Saturday night, and then used as a hostage by British troops in clearing houses in the area. On Sunday he was let go on account of his youth. Mobilised for two separate proposed attempts to storm Mountjoy and rescue Kevin Barry. Arrested in November 1920 and held in Ballykinlar until December 1921. Took no part in the Civil War.

Name	1916 Rank / Unit /Garrison	Sources
McGrane, Thomas	Na Fianna Éireann, attached to C Company, 2nd Battalion IV during the Rising (but on the C Company, 1st Battalion roll). Later in H Company, 1st Battalion, Dublin Brigade IV. St Stephen's Green, Jacob's Factory.	MSPC MSP34REF14735.

Corporation Service

After 1916, lost his job. In the Corporation during the War of Independence. 'The majority of [his time was taken up with Volunteer activities…

Between us he was not sent to certain areas […] He was definitely full time truce service. As I explained before, with McGrane, who was a Corporation employee, it was just a matter of going in and signing the book and then doing whatever I told him, or Tom Byrne told him […] While he received his wages he was not actually working. It was simply saving me from paying him. If the Corporation did not pay him then I would have had to pay him [He wasn't doing Corporation work at all] I was foreman in the Corporation and then I had a very friendly engineer. The same applied to Garry – when he went on the run he did not lose his job although he did not do a day's work from 1920.' (MSPC). Painter, Sewers Department, Dublin Corporation 1934 (at least)-49 (date of death).

Brother of Christopher McGrane. Member of Na Fianna Éireann from 1911 or so. Joined the IV in 1915, and became a Section Commander. Took part in the Howth gun-running and the mass IV parade in Limerick in 1915. Took part in the mass Volunteer parade in College Green on St Patrick's Day, 1916. During the Rising joined in with the 2nd Battalion IV. Was involved in marking of the anniversary of the Rising in 1917, postering the city with copies of the Proclamation and running up a Tricolour at 28 North Frederick Street. Became a Lieutenant in the new H Company in 1917, an auxiliary company from surplus C Company bodies. Involved in the Thomas Ashe funeral. His H Company was to take part in an attempted rescue of Kevin Barry. On the run from October 1920. Was involved in the Custom House attack in May 1921. Was part of the party responsible for holding and instructing on a Lewis Gun (given to a Volunteer by a Ship Street Barracks British soldier) in special classes. Transferred to battalion staff in August 1921, officer in charge of special police duties during the Truce. 'He used take charge of police patrols for all the big foot-ball matches when they would not recognise the DMP My battalion used [to] patrol Dalymount Football Club Grounds, and Croke Park, and he also took part in the round-up of some of the motor-car thieves at that period. I regraded him as a most honourable and reliable man.' Patrick Holohan, MSPC). As per other testimony from the same source, DMP detectives would transfer a list of robberies to the IRA who would deal with it through investigation, interviewing pawn shops and setting up special courts. Took anti-Treaty side and fought at Capel Street and Parnell Square, until capture on 24 December 1922. Interned first in Wellington Barracks and then Mountjoy.

Name	1916 Rank / Unit / Garrison	Sources
Macken, Patrick	Volunteer, C Company, 1st Battalion IV. Four Courts.	MSPC MSP34REF820.

1919 onwards with Paving Department.

Not to be confused with Peadar Macken who had been an elected member of Dublin City Council. Made very emotional appeals for pension in the 1930s, while suffering greatly from TB.

Name	1916 Rank / Unit / Garrison	Sources
McKeon, William	Volunteer, C Company, 1st Battalion IV. Four Courts, Church Street Bridge, North King Street.	MSPC MSP34REF9310; DC Reports, Vol I, 1921, No. 61.

Employed as labourer (and occasionally as timekeeper or chainman) by Dublin Corporation in the Sewers Department from at least 1921 until 1940.

Joined the Irish Volunteers in 1913. Escaped under orders from the Four Courts at the surrender and went on the run 'for several months' after the Rising, rejoining his unit in 1917. Ill from September 1917 so took no further part in IRA.

Name	1916 Rank / Unit /Garrison	Sources
Maguire, Tomás (Thomas)	Volunteer, A Company, 1st Battalion, Dublin Brigade IV. Cabra, Church Street, Four Courts.	MSPC MSP34REF24358; 'Irish craft workers in a time of revolution' Pádraig Yeates, *Saothar* 33, Journal of the Irish Labour History Society.

Corporation Service

From circa 1917 working in Dublin Corporation's Pigeon House power station as a stationary engine driver. By 1938 working in the Sewers Department.

Other Notes

IRB member since 1902. Working in the Great Western Railway (GWR) as a locomotive engine fireman, he was in J.R. Reynolds' special unit (part of the Volunteer Auxiliary, 'railwaymen and Post Office men and old men and men on night work and all that class. Some could not parade') on account of his employment, which he used for intelligence work. Ordered on Easter Sunday to remain in Dublin; he did so and on Easter Monday was at Broadstone station when he received the order to help direct a party in blowing up Cabra Bridge. On Tuesday morning he was ordered by Captain Seamus O'Sullivan to find out if there were British troops at Broadstone and report on to the Four Courts, which he did. Fighting at a barricade in the Four Courts for the rest of the week, he was interned after the Rising in Knutsford and then Frongoch. Lost his job in the railway. During the War of Independence was involved with the Collins 'Labour Board' intelligence operation to break the grip of British trade unions in Ireland. In connection with the latter he was ordered to get on to the executive of his union, which he did and then was on the executive of the breakaway IEIU. His house in Broadstone was also the point for staff from Dublin Corporation waterworks department to drop off arms, which were picked up by sympathetic railwaymen and distributed around the country (disguised as GWR consignments to their own works). Apparently M. J. Lennon had some connection with this smuggling scheme. No involvement after 1921.

Name	1916 Rank / Unit /Garrison	Sources
Mahon, Thomas Christopher	Volunteer, IV (joined IV during Rising on 24 April). Afterwards a Volunteer with F Company, 2nd Battalion Dublin Brigade, IV. GPO.	MSPC MSP34REF1176.

Corporation Service

Employed by Dublin Corporation's Waterworks Department as an Inspector in 1935.

Other Notes

Released shortly after the Rising on age grounds. Involved in the attack on the Custom House and other operations in War of Independence.

Name	1916 Rank / Unit /Garrison	Sources
Malone, Robert	Volunteer, D Company, 3rd Battalion, Dublin Brigade IV. Boland's Mills.	MSPC MSP34REF21431 Mention in Joseph Ml. Byrne account in MSPC RO/14 Dublin Brigade, Easter Week, 3rd Battalion.

Corporation Service

Dublin Fire Brigade, Tara Street from 1920. 'This job in the Fire Station became vacant, and he asked me to help him, and we succeeded in getting him in.' –Joseph O'Connor in Malone's SMPC file. Died on duty with DFB at a fire on Pearse Street, on 6 October 1936.

Other Notes

Joined the Irish Volunteers around the start of April 1916, having previously been in the 'boy scouts' (presumably Na Fianna Éireann) and then the National Volunteers. Interned in Wakefield and then Frongoch. After release, was engaged in drilling, munitions manufacture (hand grenades), instructing recruits in the use of firearms, etc. Appointed Lieutenant from 1918, but resigned in 1920 due to 'business reasons'. Joseph O'Connor claims in an interview in the MSPC file that it was due to Malone's job changing (to becoming a fireman) and also his getting heavily involved in 'Church work'.

Name	1916 Rank / Unit /Garrison	Sources
Martin, Joseph P.	Volunteer, C Company, 3rd Battalion, Dublin Brigade IV (from 1918 or so Lieutenant on 3rd Battalion Staff in charge of munitions). Boland's Mills.	MSPC MSP34REF28301.

Corporation Service

From April 1913 a brass fitter in the Waterworks Department. Transferred as caretaker to Waterworks House, Kilcroney, Bray, Co. Wicklow in 1923 while on the run during the Civil War.

Other Notes

Joined the Irish Volunteers in December 1915. Part of the guard on the Dawson Street Headquarters of the Irish Volunteers in the week preceding the Rising. Deported to Wakefield afterwards. In 1918 or so was placed in charge of organising factories to manufacture munitions such as grenades for the 3rd Battalion. 'I made them and I had men to help me […] my work in the daytime was for the republicans as I worked in the Corporation - seven out of eight hours.' (MSPC). Involved in the destruction of cameras at Lord French's propaganda parade through Dublin city in 1919, and the setting up of munitions factories in the captured Masonic Hall and Kildare Street Club during the Truce. Took the anti-Treaty side in the Civil War, was captured and kept in Portobello (now Cathal Brugha) Barracks, was threatened with being shot by 'Ginger' O'Connell but escaped with the help of a sympathetic ex-comrade. He was on the run during the Civil War period, and unable to work in the Corporation.

Name	1916 Rank / Unit / Garrison	Sources
Meehan, William	Volunteer, Lusk Company, 5th Battalion, Dublin Brigade IV (later Lusk Coy, 2nd Battalion, Fingal Brigade). Finglas, GPO, Mendicity Institute.	MSPC MSP34REF11744.

Corporation Service

In 1921 he was a 'farmer' on his marriage certificate. Labourer, Cleansing Department (street sweeper?), from at least 1934-38 in Dublin Corporation.

Other Notes

Joined the IV in 1913. Took part in fighting around North County Dublin, before volunteering to go on Tuesday in a party of reinforcements needed in Dublin city. Sent from the GPO to the Mendicity Institution, he was taken prisoner there at the surrender on the Wednesday. Sentenced to death after the 1916 Rising, but this was commuted to three years' penal servitude and he was released in the June 1917 amnesty. Moderately active in the IRA up until 1921, including an attack on Rush RIC barracks in 1920, and service in the Republican Police.

Name	1916 Rank / Unit / Garrison	Sources
Mooney, Patrick	Volunteer, B Company, 2nd Battalion IV (later C Company, 3rd Battalion, and then B Company, 1st Battalion, Scottish Brigade). GPO, Ballybough.	MSPC MSP34REF21279.

Corporation Service

1934-37 employed on casual relief work, Sewers Department. Working in Clondalkin Pumping Station 1938.

Other Notes

Initially part of GPO garrison during Easter Week; was sent to Ballybough Road Monday evening and returned on Tuesday. Lost his job in the DSER after the Rising. Arrested in 1917, went on hunger strike and was released. Involved in armed patrolling, election (protection) work, moving arms, etc. Was involved in activities such as procuring explosives, protective duties, arms raids and helping smuggling in Scotland from 1920 to 1921 after going on the run and moving to Glasgow (under the name 'Sean Watters') when his house was raided and arms discovered there.

Name	1916 Rank / Unit / Garrison	Sources
Mullen, Martin	Volunteer, A Company, 3rd Battalion, Dublin Brigade IV. Jacob's Factory.	MSPC MSP34REF21467, BMH WS 328.

Corporation Service

'Dangerous Buildings Inspector in the Corporation' per MSPC. Appears in DC Reports 1924, No. 120, as 'Bricklayer'. Same report recommended him for appointment as temporary Assistant Inspector of Dangerous Buildings.

Other Notes

Joined the IRB pre-1913, and was in the 'Emerald Section' (had been drilling at the Foresters' Hall, No. 41 Parnell Square before establishment of the IV). Member of both the Na Fianna Éireann and the Michael Dwyer National Club. Having breakfast at 11.30 at home on Easter Monday while waiting for orders, heard shots outside in the street (New Row) and asked his mother if anyone had called for him (the answer was 'no'). Going outside, he encountered Tom Hunter, who told him to come in at Barmac's Factory in New Street. Later transferred to Jacob's. Arrested and interned in Knutsford, Wormswood Scrubs and then Frongoch.

Name	1916 Rank / Unit /Garrison	Sources
Mulvey, Dominick	Volunteer, E Company, 4th Battalion, Dublin Brigade IV. GPO, DBC and Moore Street.	MSPC MSP34REF11820.

Corporation Service

24 February to 29 July 1942 (unknown occupation). 17 July 1945 to 21 January 1950 in the Sanitary Department (died 22 January).

Other Notes

Member of Rathfarnham Company; proceeded to Liberty Hall by tram. They briefly worked on putting this place in a state of defensive readiness when they were ordered to the GPO – arriving in time to see the Lancers coming down Sackville Street. Slightly wounded in Easter Week by machine-gun fire during the evacuation of the GPO, arrested and interned in Knutsford. Used his occupation as an insurance agent (before the Rising was an agent for Singers) for occasional intelligence work. Briefly arrested and interrogated by the British Army in 1921, and was released the same day.

Name	1916 Rank / Unit /Garrison	Sources
Murphy, Gregory/Ó Murchadha/ Gríogóir	Acting Captain, 'Special Unit' (part of the Volunteer Auxiliary?), 1st Battalion/F Company, 1st Battalion, Dublin Brigade IV. GPO, Four Courts, Church Street.	MSPC MSP34REF10228; BMH WS 150 (Gregory Murphy).

Corporation Service

Employed by Dublin Corporation 1 April 1921 to 11 July 1921 in the Art Gallery. Casual employment with Dublin Corporation as Voters Registration Officer, 1934-51 or thereabouts. Inspector (Housing Department) 11 April 1939-9 May 1939 Presiding officer, municipal elections on 19 August 1942.

Other Notes

IRB member from 1903 or 1904, Teeling Circle. Expelled from his Gaelic League branch (with others) in a dispute about an ex-British Army member hoisting a Union Jack on a field trip to Bray. Became a Centre and Secretary to the Leinster IRB. Joined the Irish Volunteers at inception, being attached to the 1st Battalion but parading with the 'Special Unit'. The Special Unit was of 'principally Civil Servants and older men [...] who could not very well attend public parades and that sort of thing' (MSPC). Involved in arms purchasing (had control of the IV funds at some stage), and preparations for the Rising, and in general IV organising around the country for months. Ended the Rising having been instructed by Edward Daly to 'remove all war material from the Father Mathew Hall and to get the wounded and hospital staff away' to the Richmond Hospital, so escaped arrest and internment. Member of the Provisional Executive of the Irish Volunteers from July 1916 to October 1917, also involved in the Prisoners' Dependents' Fund. Was later in the GHQ Intelligence Section of the IRA after reporting to Michael Collins (and occasionally Martin Conlon).

Name	1916 Rank / Unit /Garrison	Sources
Murphy, John	Volunteer, E Company, 2nd Battalion, Dublin Brigade IV. St Stephen's Green, Four Courts, Magazine Fort.	MSPC MSP34REF1301.

Corporation Service

Employed by Dublin Corporation from June 1927 until at least mid-1930s, as a labourer in the Streets Section, Paving Department.

Other Notes

Joined the Irish Volunteers in July 1914, involved in Howth gun-running and various raids for weapons. As a blacksmith by trade (in Thomas Lenihan's of Capel Street, who also helped with purchases), was appointed Company Armourer, and was also involved in the bomb and bayonet manufacture at Cluny House in Clontarf. In charge of ten men in the attack on, and capture of, the Magazine Fort in the Phoenix Park. Arrested after the Rising and interned in first Stafford and then Frongoch. After release was involved in Thomas Ashe's funeral, and various other activities such as munitions manufacture, armed patrols and street ambushes and stewarding at Dáil meetings. Left IRA after the 1921 Truce because of recurring sickness.

Name	1916 Rank / Unit /Garrison	Sources
Murphy, Seamus/ Ó Murchadha, Seamus	Captain, A Company, 4th Battalion, Dublin Brigade (also 4th Battalion Adjutant). South Dublin Union, Marrowbone Lane Distillery	MSPC/RO/14, MSPC/RO/15; *Irish Volunteer*, 14 Aug. 1915; BMH WS 167, WS 1756, WS 300, WS 601; Dáil Éireann Debate Vol. 86, No. 9 (1942).

Corporation Service

Chair of Dublin Union Commissioners in 1923. Dublin City Commissioner, May 1924 to October 1930.

Other Notes

Member of IRB Teeling Circle, inducted by Éamonn Ceannt at some point before the Volunteer split of 1914. Had already joined the Gaelic League aged fourteen. Present at the Rotunda as a steward and joined the Irish Volunteers. Gazetted as Captain of A Company on 14 August, 1915. During Easter Week Murphy commanded the garrison at Marrowbone Lane. Interned in Frongoch. Like several participants, Murphy's future wife was also a 1916 veteran (and was in Marrowbone Lane). In 1917 became Commandant of 4th Battalion IV. He transferred to Galway at the end of 1917 until 1920 as Galway Brigade Commandant.

Name	1916 Rank / Unit /Garrison	Sources
Murphy, Thomas	Squad Leader, F Company, 4th Battalion, Dublin Brigade IV. Rialto Bridge, Watkins Brewery, South Dublin Union.	MSPC MSP34REF294.

Corporation Service

At least 1934-47 Inquiry Officer, Finance Section.

Other Notes

One of two Volunteers arrested under arms by the British at Rialto Bridge at 12.45 pm on Easter Monday, while trying to join the Chapelizod IV who were nearby (his companion got a 'terrible beating that night in Kilmainham [...] nearly blind since'. (MSPC). Imprisoned in Wakefield. Had been a labourer in Guinessess, lost his job due to involvement in the Rising. Excused further duties because of his health problems. Claimed to have picked up TB while interned after the Rising, and to have passed it on to his a wife and six children, causing their deaths.

Name	1916 Rank / Unit / Garrison	Sources
Murray, James (Seamus)	Volunteer, Battalion Transport (assigned to A Company, during the Rising) 3rd Battalion, Dublin Brigade IV. Boland's Mills.	MSPC MSP34REF21495; BMH WS 308.

Corporation Service

Employed since at least 1918 until 1952, for use of his horse and cart by Paving Section, City Engineer's Department.

Other Notes

Engaged in moving 3rd Battalion supplies before the Rising. Interned in Wakefield and Frongoch. First Company, then Battalion, Quartermaster post-Rising (buying, storing, transporting arms) and eventually appointed to IRA Quartermaster General's staff – hired another man with a cart to cover for him in his Corporation work when appointed full-time to the QMG staff. Arrested again in 1921 and sentenced to ten years for possession of arms. Fought in Civil War on anti-Treaty side.

Name	1916 Rank / Unit / Garrison	Sources
Nicholls, Harry (Henry)/Mac Niocail, Aonrai (according to Martin Maguire's sources. But given as Enrí Mac Niocaill in a letter in his MSPC file).	Captain (Battalion Engineer) 4th Battalion, Dublin Brigade IV (formerly of A Company, same battalion). St Stephen's Green.	BMH WS 296; MSPC MSP34REF15964; Annual Report 2003-04 of the Institution of Engineers of Ireland; *Irish Volunteer*, 14 Aug. 1915; CSORP Easter Rising, 1916 Index of Internees.

Corporation Service

Appointed as temporary Dublin Corporation Assistant Engineer in December 1913.

I.R.B. member from 1911 or so, in the Teeling Circle - which was under cover as the 'Teeling Literary Society'. Member of the Gaelic League. Nicholls witnessed internal I.R.B. opposition to membership for P.H. Pearse because he was such a well-known Home Ruler. Harry was one of those younger I.R.B. members who started military drilling under Fianna instruction in early 1913 in the Forester's Hall to the rear of No. 41 Rutland (now Parnell) Square. On behalf of the I.R.B., he was involved in setting up and running the North Dublin Rifle Club in Father Mathew Park and in purchasing arms through same; 'I had a respectable unionist looking address that it worked well from, Rathmines'. Sick at the time of the Rotunda meeting, Nicholls joined the Irish Volunteers a month later. Centrally involved in Howth and Kilcoole gun-running, and anti-recruiting activities. Member of the O'Donovan Rossa Funeral Committee. A notice in the *Irish Volunteer* notified his appointment as 2nd Lieutenant, A Company (and extra appointment as Battalion Lieutenant of Engineers) on 14 August, 1915. Nicholls also assisted Peadar Slattery in giving military engineering classes leading up to the Rising. Again involved in arms purchases and smuggling for the O'Rahilly. NC 139 on the DMPs watchlist before the Rising. Nicholls prepared drawings and got prints of a map of the South Dublin Union for his Battalion commandant (and Dublin Corporation colleague) Éamonn Ceannt. Not getting mobilisation orders on Easter Monday, and having difficulty re-joining the 4th Battalion, Harry Nicholls ended up with the St Stephen's Green garrison. 'In Easrlfort Terrace I was overtaken by a friend of mine on a bicycle, Harry Nicholls [...] He was damning and blasting - like a good engineer - because he had not been mobilised [...] and Harry Nicholls said at once: "I am with you, boys," threw away his bicycle, and started to climb over the railings' - Liam Ó Briain account in the 1966 *Capuchin Annual*. In charge of Turkish Baths outpost to the College of Surgeons garrison, late in Easter week. Interned in Knutsford then Frongoch. Dropped out of the Volunteers in May 1917 in order to concentrate on undefined important Local Authority work for the cause in the War of Independence, which was likely related to Michael Collins' 'Labour Board' intelligence operation to take control of and direct Irish trade unionism during the struggle. Harry Nicholls would be centrally involved in Irish trade union activism, first as chair of the Dublin Metropolitan Officer's Association (D.M.O.A.) and later as founder and first president of successor union, the Irish Local Government Officials' Union or I.L.G.O.U. (which in time became the IMPACT trade union). Later a member of Fianna Fáil, and started the first Trinity College cumann in the mid-thirties. Secretary of the Contemporary Club, an influential Dublin debating society which lasted until the late '40s. President of the Institute of Civil Engineers of Ireland in 1953 and '54. Martin Maguire reports on the speculation as to why such a prominent Protestant professional never became Dublin City Engineer - namely, a stranglehold of the (Catholic) Order of Columbanus within Dublin Corporation at the time (Maguire, 2008).

Name	1916 Rank / Unit /Garrison	Sources
Norton, James	Volunteer, F Company, 1st Battalion, Dublin Brigade IV. GPO, Abbey Street.	MSPC MSP34REF1414; CSORP Easter Rising, 1916 Index of Internees.

Corporation Service

'Apprentice' in CSORP. Chauffeur at Crooksling Sanitorium from 1921 or so, up until end of Civil War. Labourer, Waterworks Department up until 1937 at least.

Other Notes

I.R.B. member from 1911 or so, in the Teeling Circle - which was under cover as the 'Teeling Literary Society'. Member of the Gaelic League. Nicholls witnessed internal I.R.B. opposition to membership for P.H. Pearse because he was such a well-known Home Ruler. Harry was one of those younger I.R.B. members who started military drilling under Fianna instruction in early 1913 in the Forester's Hall to the rear of No. 41 Rutland (now Parnell) Square. On behalf of the I.R.B., he was involved in setting up and running the North Dublin Rifle Club in Father Mathew Park and in purchasing arms through same; 'I had a respectable unionist looking address that it worked well from, Rathmines'. Sick at the time of the Rotunda meeting, Nicholls joined the Irish Volunteers a month later, . Centrally involved in Howth and Kilcoole gun-running, and anti-recruiting activities. Member of the O'Donovan Rossa Funeral Committee. A notice in the 'Irish Volunteer' notified his appointment as 2nd Lieutenant, A Company (and extra appointment as Battalion Lieutenant of Engineers) on 14th August, 1915. Nicholls also assisted Peadar Slattery in giving military engineering classes leading up to the Rising. Again involved in arms purchases and smuggling for the O'Rahilly. NC 139 on the DMP's watchlist before the Rising. Nicholls prepared drawings and got prints of a map of the South Dublin Union for his Battalion commandant (and Dublin Corporation colleague) Éamonn Ceannt. Not getting mobilisation orders on Easter Monday, and having difficulty re-joining the 4th Battalion, Harry Nicholls ended up with the St Stephen's Green garrison. 'In Easrlfort Terrace I was overtaken by a friend of mine on a bicycle, Harry Nicholls [...] He was damning and blasting - like a good engineer - because he had not been mobilised [...] and Harry Nicholls said at once: "I am with you, boys," threw away his bicycle, and started to climb over the railings' - Liam Ó Briain account in the 1966 *Capuchin Annual*. In charge of Turkish Baths outpost to the College of Surgeons garrison, late in Easter week. Interned in Knutsford then Frongoch. Dropped out of the Volunteers in May 1917 in order to concentrate on undefined important Local Authority work for the cause in the War of Independence. - which was likely related to Michael Collins' 'Labour Board' intelligence operation to take control of and direct Irish trade unionism during the struggle. Harry Nicholls would be centrally involved in Irish trade union activism, first as chair of the Dublin Metropolitan Officer's Association (D.M.O.A.) and later as founder and first president of successor union, the Irish Local Government Officials' Union or I.L.G.O.U. (which in time became the IMPACT trade union). Later a member of Fianna Fáil, and started the first Trinity College cumann in the mid-thirties. Secretary of the Contemporary Club, an influential Dublin debating society which lasted until the late '40s. President of the Institute of Civil Engineers of Ireland in 1953 and '54. Martin Maguire reports on the speculation as to why such a prominent Protestant professional never became Dublin City Engineer - namely, a stranglehold of the (Catholic) Order of Columbanus within Dublin Corporation at the time (Maguire, 2008).

Name	1916 Rank / Unit /Garrison	Sources
O'Brien (Ó Briain), Liam	1st Lt, D Company, 4th Battalion, Dublin Brigade IV. South Dublin Union.	MSPC MSP34REF1443; BMH WS 168; SFRH.

Corporation Service

Employed in Dublin Corporation from November 1915 onwards, according to description on MSPC record. According to Thomas J. Doyle's BMH WS, he was in the 'Architects section' – possibly before becoming a referencer in the Borough Surveyor's Department, which is where he was in 1935/36.

Other Notes

Probably the 'William O'Brien' who was the brother of 'Patrick V. O'Brien'. Appointed as 1st Lieutenant just before the Rising. Interned in Knutsford and Frongoch. Undertook parades, training and reorganisation, the Thomas Ashe funeral and election work. Became Captain of D Company before dropping out due to illness. As he was sick from TB, the effort of attending an interview for his military pension in the mid-1930s probably caused his death shortly afterwards.

Name	1916 Rank / Unit /Garrison	Sources
O'Brien, Patrick V.	Unknown. Quite likely Boland's Mills.	SFRH, 1901 and 1911 Censuses for '43 Lombard Street West'.

Corporation Service

'Corporation employee' in 1916.

Other Notes

In SFRH as Corporation employee, living at 43 Lombard Street West and confirmed in 1911 Census (aged 24, 'cabinet maker'). He was held in the RDS, Ballsbridge before being deported to Knutsford on 6 May – which suggests that he may have been part of the Boland's Mills garrison. His brother William O'Brien, of the same address (and likely to be the Liam O'Brien above), was deported from Richmond Barracks to Knutsford on 3 May. A 'Patrick Vincent O'Brien' was released between 13 and 22 May, again according to the SFRH.

Name	1916 Rank / Unit /Garrison	Sources
O'Byrne, Hugh	Squad Leader, C Company (attached to A Company before the Rising, which may have originally been intended for Guinesses's) 4th Battalion, Dublin Brigade IV. South Dublin Union, Marrowbone Lane.	MSPC MSP34REF20549.

Corporation Service

February 1921 appointed Rate Collector to Dublin County Council (which brought 'special attention from the military') – but was still free for full-time IRA duty. 'Only had to report once a fortnight. We attended a couple of times a week or oftener to collect any letters that might be there just.' Transferred to Dublin Corporation April 1931.

Other Notes

IRB member from 1912. Joined the Irish Volunteers in the Rotunda in November 1913. Quizzed on the Guinness layout at the start of Easter Week. Post-Rising, interned in Knutsford then Frongoch. Lost his job in Guinness because of his part in Easter Week. Subsequently involved in Thomas Ashe funeral, election work, anti-conscription, Dáil guard, armed raids and patrols. Took active part in Bloody Sunday, November 1921. On anti-Treaty side and involved in fortifying Four Courts in Civil War. Captured by the Free State forces while collecting rates, and interned in Mountjoy.

Name	1916 Rank / Unit / Garrison	Sources
O'Byrne, James	Volunteer, F Company, 2nd Battalion, Dublin Brigade IV. GPO, Fairview, Moore Street.	MSPC 24SP2492.

Corporation Service

Temporarily employed assistant librarian at Charleville Mall from 12 March 1913 to 26 November 1923, 1 June -31 December 1924, 9 February -13 March 1925, then permanent from 14 April 1925.

Other Notes

Part of the group who engaged the British at Fairview and later were in the Metropole Hotel. Imprisoned at Knutsford and Frongoch. Was active in armed patrols, etc. Interned during the War of Independence. Took pro-Treaty side and saw fighting in the National Army in the Civil War. Had to resign his position in Dublin Corporation during this period, and was refused reinstatement.

Name	1916 Rank / Unit / Garrison	Sources
O'Connor, Joseph	Captain, A Company, 3rd Battalion, Dublin Brigade IV. Boland's Mills.	MSPC MSP34REF54; BMH WS 157, WS 487, WS 544.

Corporation Service

Employed by Corporation February 1917 to March 1929. Rates Collector.

Other Notes

Father of IRB and had been (as a Fenian inmate in 1865 in the Richmond Bridewell) involved in the escape of James Stephens. Also member of Gaelic League. Involved in Howth gun-running and guard of honour on O'Donovan Rossa at City Hall. Worked in City Rates Office.

Name	1916 Rank / Unit / Garrison	Sources
O'Connor, Rory	Engineering officer, GHQ, IV (later Director of Engineering, GHQ). GPO.	MSPC DP6664; BMH WS 527 (Norbert O'Connor), WS 680, WS 865, WS 907, WS 1043, WS 1769; *DC Reports*, Vol II, 1920, No. 116.

Corporation Service

Corporation engineer, Paving Deparment, from July 1917 onwards.

Other Notes

Returned to Ireland from Canada in October 1915; according to his brother this was at the request of Joseph Plunkett. Wounded in the Rising. Involved in much of the Department of Local Government's work during War of Independence. In charge of the Four Courts anti-Treaty garrison in 1922 and executed on 8 December 1922 in a Free State reprisal during the Civil War.

Name	1916 Rank / Unit / Garrison	Sources
O'Donohoe (Donoghoe/ Donohoe), Robert	Volunteer, B Company, 1st Battalion, Dublin Brigade IV (from April 1919 Captain and O/C of No. 1 Company, 5th (Engineers) Battalion IV/IRA until March 1920, when he was ordered under protest to take up trade union activities instead.) Four Courts.	MSPC MSP34REF20487; SFRH, p. 71; obituary in *Irish Press*, 11 Jan. 1938, p. 12; 'Irish craft workers in a time of revolution', Pádraig Yeates, *Saothar* 33, Journal of the Irish Labour History Society.

Corporation Service

Electrician and cable joiner who transferred from the Electricity Department of the Corporation (employed there with 26 years' service per his obituary) to the ESB in either 1927 or 1929, where he worked until his retirement in May 1937.

Other Notes

The 1911 Census shows a Robert Louis Donohue, aged 25, electrician, living with his family at 26 Hardwicke Street. According to his obituary, O'Donohoe joined the Emerald Isle Circle of the IRB in 1913. O'Donohue joined B Company, 1st Battalion on its establishment. An 'R. Donohoe' of 2 Eccles Street was sent from Richmond Barracks to Knutsford on 30 April (the MSPC file says Stafford Gaol and then Frongoch). After his release, was involved in the usual activities until the start of the War of Independence, then grenade manufacture (in J.V. Lawless's shop), engineering lectures, armed guards, etc. Founder member of the breakaway union the IES and FTU (later the Irish Engineering Industrial Union, the IEIU) and secretary of its electrical section. Here was part of Michael Collins's 'Labour Board' intelligence operation during the War of Independence, to weaken the influence of the British trade union leadership. After the Truce he took no position on the Treaty, and was not involved in the Civil War.

Name	1916 Rank / Unit / Garrison	Sources
O'Donovan, Cornelius (Con)	Volunteer, F Company, 1st Battalion, Dublin Brigade, Irish Volunteers (later Captain of the Brittas Company, Dublin Brigade). Four Courts.	MSP34REF52585, BMH WS1750 (Cornelius O'Donovan), BMH WS 131 (George O'Flanagan), BMH WS 162 & BMH WS 669 (John Shouldice), BMH WS 328 (Gearóid Ua h-Uallacháin), BMH WS1043 (Joseph V. Lawless), FourLives (IMPACT trade union pamphlet, 2016), *DCC Minutes*, 1924, No. 424.

Corporation Service

Had employment at Crooksling TB Sanatorium as Land Steward from July 1917 until October 1924 (working under Gerry Boland, who was also his Volunteer commanding officer during this time).

Other Notes

Member of the IRB and of the Keating Branch of the Gaelic League. Brother of Seán O'Donovan. Joined the Irish Volunteers in 1913. A scholarship agricultural student in the Royal College of Science, Dublin in 1916, he was on holidays in Easter Week, but stayed in Dublin instead of returning home to Cork because of the imminent Rising. Was on duty Easter Sunday at North Frederick Street and Liberty Hall. Mobilised on Monday and was in North King Street, North Brunswick Street and the Four Courts. After the surrender, he was court-martialled in Richmond Barracks; O'Donovan was sentenced to death but this had been commuted to penal servitude for eight years. He was then deported to Dartmoor Prison, thence to Lewes. Released on 15 June 1917, his re-admittance to the College was refused because of his part in the Rising (he eventually was allowed resume his studies in 1924). He then got a job with the Corporation, working and living at Crooksling TB Sanatorium, as Land Steward from July 1917 until October 1924. Active in Sinn Féin after 1917. Arrested during German Plot in May 1918 and interned in Usk in Wales until early 1919, when he was released having suffered from the Spanish flu while in prison in Britain. After two weeks on an officers' training camp at Glandore in Cork, he returned to Dublin and took charge of the Brittas Company, South Co. Dublin Battalion, which he had helped to organise. Arrested in November 1920 while coming back from Terence McSweeney's funeral and interned in Arbour Hill (where he was elected the prisoner's O/C) and then Ballykinlar (released 8 December 1921). Active in Civil War, having opposed the Treaty. 'Nominally' working all through this time. In 1934 he finally succeeded, and worked there first as an Agricultural Instructor and then as an Inspector. He was a stalwart on the Executive of the IPCS (Institute of Professional Civil Servants), one of the public sector union forebears of IMPACT, and was president of that union between 1945 and 1947. During the Emergency he served as an NCO with the 26th Infantry Battalion.

Name	1916 Rank / Unit /Garrison	Sources
O'Dwyer, James	ICA. City Hall, Dublin Castle.	MSPC MSP34REF1604; CSORP Easter Rising, 1916 Index of Internees

Corporation Service

Temporary cleaner, Cleansing Department in the Corporation (in part of the War of Independence?) and later 1933-38

Other Notes

Participated in occupation of City Hall in 1916. Arrested, deported and interned in Wandsworth and then to Frongoch and Wormwood scrubs. Active during War of Independence and took anti-Treaty side in Civil War.

Name	1916 Rank / Unit /Garrison	Sources
O'Flaherty, Liam (William)/ Ó Flaithbheartaigh, Liam	Volunteer, B Company, 4th Battalion, Dublin Brigade IV. South Dublin Union.	BMH WS 248, WS 371; DC Reports, Vol II 1910 p. 986; CSORP Easter Rising, 1916 Index of Internees.

Corporation Service

Rates Department from October 1904. 'Clerk' according to index card in CSORP.

Brother of Martin O'Flaherty. Member of Gaelic League, and secretary of a branch on the South Circular Road which welcomed the Kimmage garrison to Ireland and was one of their main recreational outlets. Joined the Irish Volunteers in November 1913. During the fight at the SDU he was sent to contact Thomas MacCarthy's command at Roe's Distillery but just missed their evacuation. Interned at Knutsford.

Name	1916 Rank / Unit /Garrison	Sources
O'Flaherty, Martin	Volunteer, B Company, 4th Battalion, Dublin Brigade IV. South Dublin Union.	MSPC MSP34REF57457; BMH WS158 (Seamus Kenny).

Corporation Service

Fired from Guinness's after 1916. Subsequently employed by corporation. Housing Department Rent Collector and Storekeeper, at least from 1937 to 1939.

Other Notes

Brother of Liam O'Flaherty. He and Seamus Kenny of B Company, on tips from W.T. Cosgrave who was a publican, would search for and steal British soldiers' rifles hidden outside pubs while they were drinking. Deported to Knutsford, then Frongoch. Collector of Dáil Bonds during War of Independence. Full-time official on Dáil loan collection duties 1919-20. MSPC statement during part on Civil War claims that he was on the run and that, although supposed to be working for the Corporation, was in a position to give his time to IRA activities. Early in 1923 was obliged to give up his job (reinstated at some point).

Name	1916 Rank / Unit /Garrison	Sources
O'Gorman, Joseph	2nd Lieutenant, F Company, 4th Battalion, Dublin Brigade Irish Volunteers (later in D Company). South Dublin Union, Marrowbone Lane Distillery.	MSPC MSP34REF1544; BMH WS 167 (Christopher Byrne), WS 186 (Thomas J. Doyle), WS 280 (Robert Holland).

Corporation Service

Sacked from his job as Locomotive Foreman in the GSW Railway for having taken part in the Rising (told that he and others were to be 'never taken back'); Fitter in Main Drainage from 1919.

A member of the Lord Edward Circle at 41 Parnell (then Rutland) Square. Military drilling there under Na Fianna Éireann instructors before the formation of the Irish Volunteers – the 'North City Gymnasium Club'. Joined the IV on the first night, i.e. the meeting in the Rotunda. Drilled first under Peadar Macken and The O'Rahilly in Tara Street Baths, then at 41 Parnell Square. O'Gorman was involved in the Howth gun-running, the massed Irish Volunteers parade through Limerick in 1915, and in the three weeks before the Rising was involved full-time in preparations for the Rising. Initially he was at Kimmage on armourer's duties, working under Harry Nicholls to repair 'Howth' Mausers and other tasks, but in the days immediately before the Rising he was involved in moving arms and armed guards. On Easter Sunday carried dispatches from Ceannt to Connolly in Liberty Hall. On Easter Monday he was delegated to round up stragglers to the 4th Battalion mobilisation point. Acted again as a dispatch bearer on bike, between there and the South Dublin union, with Thomas J. Doyle as his escort. Ended up in the Marrowbone Lane distillery outpost. Accidentally wounded by another Volunteer at the surrender on Sunday. O'Gorman spent two months recovering in Dublin Castle Red Cross post, before being imprisoned first in Kilmainham Gaol, then Kuntsford and finally Frongoch. On release was involved in the East Clare, Kilkenny and South Armagh by-elections. In 1919 went on the run after hiding fugitive Volunteers. In 1920 elected for the South Dublin Rural District, and participated in the Bloody Sunday attacks. Took the anti-Treaty side in the Civil War.

Name	1916 Rank / Unit /Garrison	Sources
O'Hanlon, Bernard	Volunteer, Dublin Brigade IV (joined in Easter Week). Four Courts, Church Street, King Street.	MSPC MSP34REF43513.

Corporation Service

Labourer, Corporation from 1907 in Paving Department. Broke service in 1921, continuous from 1922 on.

Other Notes

Son of the caretaker of the Colmcille Hall, Blackhall Place. Active in and around Four Courts and Church Street, but avoided arrest after the Rising.

Name	1916 Rank / Unit /Garrison	Sources
O'Keeffe, John (Seán)	Acting Lieutenant, B Company, 3rd Battalion, Dublin Brigade IV. Boland's Mills.	MSPC 24SP82; BMH WS 188 (Seán O'Keeffe); 1911 Census.

Corporation Service

Electricity Supply Department, Fleet Street, returned there in 1924 from the National Army service (had been granted leave of absence, with 'several years' of service). On 28 March 1929 it became part of the ESB.

Other Notes

Joined Irish Volunteers in November 1913. Assigned to command the party cutting cables at Lombard Street East to break the telephone link between Dublin and London. Seriously wounded in arm and ended up in Dublin Castle Hospital. Interned in Frongoch. Active in IRA in War of Independence. Arrested but released following hunger strike. Fought in Civil War on pro-Treaty side.

Name	1916 Rank / Unit /Garrison	Sources
O'Keeffe, Michael	Volunteer, B Company, 3rd Battalion, Dublin Brigade IV. Boland's Mills (railway).	MSPC 24SP6677; 1911 Census.

Corporation Service

'Corporation worker on cables' during the Rising and after, according to MSPC file. The only break in this was six weeks with the National Army. In 1927 working in the Electricity Supply Department, had been there for 'about 28 years'.

Other Notes

Probably brother of Seán O'Keeffe. Was detailed in the Rising to cut telegraph cables between Dublin and London. Allegedly had operation for ulcer and perforated intestines on 29 April in Sir Patrick Dun's Hospital, though allegedly he deserted. Active in IRA during War of Independence and interned. Served in National Army during Civil War.

Name	1916 Rank / Unit /Garrison	Sources
O'Kelly, Fergus Francis/Ó Ceallaigh, Feargus	Volunteer, B Company, 2nd Battalion, Dublin Brigade IV. Appointed Staff Lieutenant in April 1916 for Volunteer GHQ as director of wireless communications (which lasted until 1918 or 1919. Then attached to G Company, 4th Battalion as a Volunteer. From 1921 as Captain with G Company, 2nd Battalion. In the Civil War rejoined the 4th Battalion). Reis's (Wireless College), GPO.	MSPC MSP34REF14627; *Irish Press*, 27 June 1979, p. 3.

Corporation Service

Electrical engineer. From 1919 he was employed (shift work) in an office in the Corporation electrical generating station at Pigeon House, in Ringsend. Was then in the ESB for eleven years.

Other Notes

Joined the Irish Volunteers in 1913. Prior to the Rising, during April 1916, was sworn into the IRB and then involved in an attempt at Kimmage to fashion an illegal (under DORA) wireless transmitter: 'He was a student in the National University (College of Science), and for the first few weeks in April was constantly at Larkfield with the Plunketts. During Holy Week he spent from 12 to 16 hours a day in the camp trying to get in touch with the "Aud"' (from MSPC file). Claimed to have been appointed as a staff Lieutenant (to Joseph Plunkett) on April 1, 1916, and to hold that rank right up until 1918. Responsible for reassembling a Marconi wireless set in Reis's wireless school during Easter Week to broadcast news of the Rising. Interned in Stafford and then Frongoch. Active in IRA in War of Independence. Also in charge of wireless communications under Director of Engineering Rory O'Connor until the start of the Civil War and claimed that he set up a receiving station in Dublin which was used to intercept British signals. During the Civil War he was active on the anti-Treaty side but was arrested on his way into work in the Pigeon House on December 6 1922, and imprisoned until March 1924.

Name	1916 Rank / Unit / Garrison	Sources
O'Kelly (Kelly), Michael	Volunteer, F Company, 1st Battalion, Dublin Brigade IV (later Company Quartermaster). Four Courts, Church Street.	BMH WS 925 Mairéad Ní Cheallaigh, WS 699; CSORP Easter Rising, 1916 Index of Internees; SFRH; *Irish Press*, 3 Apr. 1933, p. 7.

Corporation Service

Served his architectural apprenticeship with Vincent Kelly. Architect or draughtsman.

Other Notes

Brother of Seán T. Joined the Irish Volunteers in November 1913, and was involved in the Howth gun-running. Acted as a messenger to Liberty Hall and to Rathfarnham for the Pearse brothers (their guests in the house just before the Rising, as a precaution against arrest). Wounded by a shell that exploded near a barricade in the North King Street area. Deported to Stafford Jail, then Frongoch. Active in War of Independence and Civil War. During Civil War was in a flying column with Liam Clarke around Rathfarnham, Glenmalure, Blessington until being wounded and captured. Died from an aneurism at age thirty-five. O'Kelly's 'best-known work was the reconstruction and decoration of the Municipal Art Gallery in Parnell Square, Charlemont House.' (WS 925). Much of his sketchwork is still to be found in the 'autograph books' popular with Republican prisoners through the period. He was the artist who drew the original masthead for the *Irish Press*, depicting a phoenix.

Name	1916 Rank / Unit / Garrison	Sources
Bean Uí Cheallaigh, Phyllis (Phyllis O'Kelly, neé Ryan).	Had not joined Cumann na mBan at this point (later on Captain in the Ranelagh Branch and on the CnamB Executive. From November 1920 CnamB General Secretary. Later appointed Director of Organisation). GPO.	MSPC MSP34REF22412; *Irish Examiner*, 25 Nov. 1972, p. 26; *Sunday Independent*, 5 June 1966, p. 1.

Corporation Service

From 1920 or 1921 worked in Dublin as a public analyst (i.e. as contract chemist to local authorities). After four years working out of UCD's laboratory, in 1925 she set up an all-female laboratory practice on Dawson Street which she ran until at least the 1950s. Appointed Dublin City Analyst at some point before the late 1930s.

Phyllis Ryan, UCD undergraduate and youngest member of the well-known republican Ryan family from Wexford (and not at that time formally a member of Cumann na mBan) served under Miss Gavan Duffy in the GPO. Phyllis was actually in the GPO for about twenty-four hours, Tuesday/Wednesday, then sent with her sister Min to deliver messages for British military prisoners and to make themselves available for questioning on events by Monsignor Curran in the Archbishop's Palace, Drumcondra. Returned to the GPO on Thursday and were then sent back out again with messages. Afterwards the two sisters couldn't return to the GPO, so they stayed in their home (and incidental arms dump) at 19 Ranelagh Road. After the Rising she finished her degree that October (the only woman that year, and the fifth ever, to do so in science in the National University) with her post-graduate studies going on for another four years. She was also involved in activities such as carrying dispatches, running safe houses, collection and redistribution of the National Aid (NVAADF) funds for 1916 veterans and their families, and in the work of the Ranelagh Branch, CnamB (formed in Autumn 1917) which co-ordinated with the 4th Battalion, Dublin Brigade IV. Took the anti-Treaty position, but while in CnamB headquarters during the Dublin fighting took no active part. Ceased active service with Cumann na mBan in Autumn 1922, but kept on with prison committee work and helping men on the run. Phyllis became Seán T. Ó Ceallaigh's second wife in 1936, following her sister Cáit (Mary-Kate) who had died in 1934. Bean Uí Cheallaigh applied for a military service pension in the late 1930s; after lengthy back-and-forth about the need to see details of her gross income as a Public Analyst, she withdrew her application until the 1950s when the 'public monies' provision (of abatement on a state pension if in receipt of other public remuneration) was rescinded. In 1972 she was a member of the RTÉ Authority sacked and replaced by the Fianna Fáil government of Jack Lynch, RTÉ having breached the Section 31 prohibition in interviewing a member of the Provisional IRA.

Name	1916 Rank / Unit /Garrison	Sources
O'Reardon, Michael	Volunteer, B Company, 1st Battalion, Dublin Brigade IV.	MSPC MSP34REF2011.
	Four Courts, North King Street, North Brunswick Street.	

Corporation Service

Inspector, weights and measures (from about 1920).

Other Notes

Fought in and around Four Courts. Assigned on Monday morning to cut communications at Parkgate Street (telegraph poles, etc.) but couldn't get near them, then the fighting started. Released on account of youth (seventeen years) after two weeks in Richmond Barracks. Thomas Ashe funeral, drilling, Coleman funeral, anti-Conscription, armed patrols (his section commander was Lieutenant Seán Lemass), etc.

Name	1916 Rank / Unit /Garrison	Sources
O'Reilly, John	ICA (transferred to IV after release).	MSPC MSP34REF1470.
	City Hall.	

Corporation Service

Electrician in the Electricity Supply Department, Dublin Corporation from at least prior to the Rising up to 1928, afterwards in the ESB. 'I was paid by the Dublin Corporation during my Period of Internment.'

Joined the ICA 'six or seven months' before the Rising. Fought at City Hall, and subsequently interned in Wakefield, Wormwood Scrubs and then Frongoch. Transferred to B Company, 1st Battalion after release but took little part in War of Independence. Brother of Patrick O'Reilly and Thomas O'Reilly.

Name	1916 Rank / Unit /Garrison	Sources
O'Reilly, Patrick	Private, ICA. St Stephen's Green.	MSPC MSP34E139, 1D291; CSORP Easter Rising, 1916. Index of Internees; Roll of Honour.

Corporation Service

Apprentice pavior from 25 July 1911 until at least the Rising. Night Inspector of watchmen, Street Section (Paving Department), 1923 onwards. Brother Thomas's MSPC claims that (at least in May 1924) he was a Night Inspector in Water Works. Worked in the Corporation until retirement in 1958 on medical grounds.

Other Notes

Active during the Easter Rising, then imprisoned. Appears to have dropped out of the ICA afterwards. Brother of John and Thomas O'Reilly.

Name	1916 Rank / Unit /Garrison	Sources
O'Reilly, Thomas	ICA. City Hall, GPO, Liberty Hall.	MSPC 1D291.

Corporation Service

Apprentice electrician in Fleet Street, Dublin Corporation at time of the Rising. Aged twenty at time of death.

Other Notes

Wounded in action (shot in the stomach) at Liberty Hall on 25 April carrying a dispatch for James Connolly from City Hall, and died of his wounds on 27 April in Jervis Street hospital. His mother received £104 from the National Aid. Brother of John and Patrick O'Reilly.

Name	1916 Rank / Unit /Garrison	Sources
O'Shea, James	ICA. St Stephen's Green.	MSPC MSP34REF150; BMH WS 733, WS 585; CSORP Easter Rising, 1916 Index of Internees.

Corporation Service

Cleansing Department. Labourer/street cleaner from 1917.

Joined a boy scouts movement in opposition to the Baden Powell scouts – and organised by Michael Mallin – in 1909, one of the precursors to Na Fianna Éireann. Organiser for the ITGWU in Inchicore Works during the Lockout period, facing not only the brutal union-busting of the DMP and RIC but also 'UIL Ward Heelers' and the Freemasons. Started an Inchicore Works group (Emmet Hall) of the ICA. Close confrontation with the INV at a meeting in Rutland Square (Parnell Square), when Larkin was prevented from speaking on stage. 'We had also something that was worth more than anything else since or before – a peculiar comradeship that had no limits. It meant that you stood by your mates against all comers, friend or foe. We were like a big family when you got the swing of it. Home or nothing else mattered. I stress this as I have felt it and sensed it among ICA of the period. It made for a carelessness in danger and a happy-go-lucky devil-may-care comradeship that I had never experienced before.' WS 733. Involved in armed ICA intervention to picket a B & I dispute, facing off against the DMP. Encountered Desmond Fitzgerald in Mountjoy in 1915, O'Shea having been sent there following a farcical trial. He was C 166 on the DMP's watch list. Was at one stage about to be ordered to infiltrate the IRB by Connolly and Mallin. Gives a lengthy and dramatic account of the emergency March 1916 ICA mobilisation in response to an attempted DMP raid: 'The only one respectably dressed was Sean Connolly who came from City Hall.' (this was the start of the armed guard on Liberty Hall). Interned at Knutsford and then Frongoch. Involved in various activities after release. Arms raids/purchases, training and several attacks. On the run after shootings at banned concert commemoration for James Connolly in the Mansion House. Joined on Intelligence staff of A Company, 3rd Battalion IRA in May 1922. Arrested and interned. Went on hunger strike. Left the IRA in 1929 and later joined the Volunteer Force.

Name	1916 Rank / Unit /Garrison	Sources
Poole, Christopher (Kit).	Staff Captain, ICA. Claimed to be second-in-command at St Stephen's Green to Michael Mallin as 'Senior Captain'. St Stephen's Green, College of Surgeons.	MSPC MSP34REF10145; mentions in BM WS 328, WS 585, WS 779 Section 2, WS1693, http://comeheretome. com/2013/06/17/ raiding-the-defiance/ (as of 10 August 2015); National Archives CSORP DMP: MFA 6/1.

Lost his job as a docker in the Lockout (1913). For 1936 and 1937 at least, employed by Dublin Corporation, position unknown.

Former British soldier, who may have served in Boer War. Brother of Vincent. Their brother Joe Poole, a member of the Invincibles, had been executed in 1883; the circumstances of this formed a story told by Arthur Griffith after the Soloheadbeg attack of 1919 'to illustrate the evils of physical force' (BMH WS 779 Section 2). During the 1913 Lockout, Poole 'followed a [scab] home with another fellow and I heard that they hit him on the head with a pot, with the result that he never returned to the power station'. (BMH WS 328). C169 on the DMPs watchlist. Interned first in Stafford and then Frongoch. Involved in reorganising the ICA after his release. He was involved in the raid on the USS *Defiance* in Dublin port.

Name	1916 Rank / Unit / Garrison	Sources
Poole, Vincent	See note. Certainly led men in the Easter Rising and was previously associated with the ICA. GPO, Fairview, Annesley Bridge.	MSPC MSP34REF460; BMH WS 340, WS 384, WS 585, WS 660, WS 733, WS 779 Section 2, WS1687; *The Hibernian*, Vol II, No. 38, Saturday 26 Feb. 1916; CSORP; DC Reports, Vol I, 1919, p. 974; David Fitzpatrick, *Harry Boland's Irish revolution* (Cork, 2004), p. 42; 'Dublin family claims mustachioed mystery man on stamp' http://www.irishtimes.com/culture/heritage/dublin-family-claims-mustachioed-mystery-man-on-stamp-1.1667660 (downloaded on 31/01/2016).

Corporation Service

From February 1910, according to MSPC. 'Paid by Dublin Corporation as sewer worker at present and at any time I was not in prison'. (MSPC, in 1935). In 1919 reported as being a painter in Main Drainage with 'over fifteen years' service' (including absence for sixty-five weeks from Easter 1916 until 26 July 1917).

Other Notes

Former British soldier who served in Boer War. Brother of Christopher. 'Vincent Poole ceased to be a member of the ICA either late 1914 or early 1915 because of his turbulent nature.' (BMH WS 585). Before the Rising, 'I was [active]. I got six months for making a speech, and for holding up police at the Custom House with Molloy and Skeffington. I came out in November, 1915.' (MSPC and 'Ireland's Roll of Honour' in *The Hibernian*, where he is in the group labelled 'Imprisoned' with Francis Sheehy-Skeffington). During the Easter Rising attacked a military train in a mixed group co-led by Harry Boland. Retreating back to the GPO, he seems to have been accepted back into the ICA once more. He was later involved in fighting around the GPO as a sharp-shooter. While in the Metropole, accused Harry Boland of being a deserter, a situation only resolved when he was reminded of a promise he had made to James Connolly to obey Oscar Traynor's orders. Court-martialled after the Rising, sentenced to death but commuted to five years' penal service. Imprisoned at Portland, Lewes, Parkhurst and Pentonville until June 1917. In bad health on release. '[…] Vincent Poole seemed to think that the Citizen Army section of the dependents were not getting fair play, and he came into the committee room with a pistol in his hand. Michael Collins was secretary at the time. William O'Brien sprang to his feet and said boldly: "Poole, put that gun away. I know you and your methods well." That practically ended an episode which upset some of the members for the moment.' (BMH WS 384). Joined 2nd Company, 5 (Engineers) Battalion, Dublin Brigade IRA, in 1920 as Company captain, his Battalion CO was Rory O'Connor. Taught musketry among other drilling. In the Four Courts during the Civil War (laid mines, fixed up the 'Mutineer' captured armoured car), captured and interned by the Free State. Allowed out after two months because of sickness, and returned to his job with Dublin Corporation. In 2014 the 'turbulent' Poole had a fitting postscript in Irish public life, as the ICA member mis-identified for Captain Jack White by An Post in a commemorative stamp issued that year.

Name	1916 Rank / Unit / Garrison	Sources
Redmond, Patrick	Volunteer, F Company, 2nd Battalion, Dublin Brigade IV. St Stephen's Green, Jacob's Factory, Fumbally Lane.	MSPC MSP34REF59866.

Corporation Service

Travelling overseer (northside) during the War of Independence, in Drainage Department at some point, retired as foreman.

Other Notes

Was involved in the 'North City Rifle Club' (see Harry Nicholls) and the running of Volunteer arms and ammunition stores as caretaker of Father Matthew Park before the Rising. Also involved in the Howth gun-running. Deported to Knutsford and Frongoch. Involved in the Ashe and Coleman funerals, election and anti-Conscription work, the seizure of pigs meant for export to Britain, etc. Was part of the armed guard on the inaugural Dáil meeting in the Mansion House. Used his Corporation position to secure suitable arms dumps during War of Independence, and also in extensive intelligence work. His own house was used: 'men called to the house for the arms and his wife handed them out'. Also used as Cumann na mBan post. Gave over his remaining arms to the anti-Treaty IRA in the Civil War, but took no other part.

Name	1916 Rank / Unit / Garrison	Sources
Roe, Patrick Joseph	Volunteer, C Company, 3rd Battalion, Dublin Brigade IV. Boland's Mills, 25 Northumberland Road.	MSPC MSP34REF21792.

Corporation Service

With the ESB from February 1930 (employed at the Pigeon House Generating Station), as he was employed in the Dublin Corporation Electricity Supply Department when it was taken over.

Other Notes

Former member of Na Fianna Éireann. Was at 25 Northumberland Road. Detailed by Lt. Malone on the Wednesday to go to his (Malone's) house on the SCR. Was on the run after the Rising. Active in training, policing meetings, election work and on the anti-Conscription campaign. On duty the night of the Armistice Day riots, 1918. Involved in disarming RIC at Ticknock. Took part in the Coleman funeral and armed guards and went on hunger strike after being arrested at Whitehall in a raid. Did Munitions work. On the Mansion House armed guard in 1919 for the first meeting of the Dáil. One of those involved in Bloody Sunday, and other intelligence work. Interned until the Truce, and then active during the Civil War on the anti-Treaty side. After a debate between them, his brother left the National Army for the anti-Treaty side.

Name	1916 Rank / Unit / Garrison	Sources
Saurin, Charles James	Volunteer, F Company, 2nd Battalion Dublin Brigade IV. Fairview, GPO, Metropole Hotel.	BMH WS 288; MSPC MSP24SP12094.

Corporation Service

'From the time of his dismissal from the Public Record Office in 1916 he was studying for an exam for post of Sanitary Sub-Officer in the Dublin Corporation. He commenced his service in the Public Health Department along with me on 25 April 1917.' Charles Saurin, giving John Stafford's MSPC testimonial. Later resigned from the Corporation.

Interned in Knutsford, Wandsworth and Frongoch. After release, involved in election work, drilling, etc. In 1918 started doing intelligence work. Arrested and interned December 1920 to December 21. Joined the National Army and held various staff positions. Second in command at Wood Quay during the bombardment of the Four Courts. Later involved with the Irish Sweep Stakes. In 1947 was a (regular) Lt. Col serving on the Staff Directorate, An FCÁ. Later served in the BMH. Retired from the Army on 7 August 1953.

Name	1916 Rank / Unit /Garrison	Sources
Scullin, Frank	Volunteer, Kimmage Garrison (formerly with A Company, Irish Volunteers in Glasgow. After his release in December 1916 joined B Company, 1st Battalion Dublin Brigade, then from 1918 transferred to F Company). GPO, Hibernian Bank.	MSPC MSP34REF60223, BMH WS 156 (Seamus Robinson).

Corporation Service

Labourer in the Corporation from April 1917 to 1929 in Public Lighting Section and/or the Electricity Supply Section (then transferred to the ESB).

Other Notes

From 1913 to 1916 was an Irish Volunteer in Glasgow (taking part in arms raids, and boxing instructor to both Fianna and Volunteers). Brother of Leo Patrick (Paddy) Scullin, likewise a 1916 veteran and probably a one-time Corporation employee too (as he ended in the ESB). He was centrally involved in bringing back a large package of gelignite (probably spoils of Volunteer raids on Bothwell Park and Uddington Collieries in Scotland) in January 1916 which was stored at Bill Sheehan's house, where he would be (like Tom 'Boer' Byrne) a lodger: 'I know Scullin; I was in Kildare for a week before the Rebellion; he left gelignite at my digs to be taken down to Kildare, a big, heavy case of it [...] he was a wild type & would be in everything. He was a friend of the people I boarded with [...] I don't know that he had any special qualifications; he was in the Lighting Department of the Corporation and was used by GHQ I believe.'(Tom Byrne reference in Scullin's MSPC records). In March he joined the Kimmage garrison, where he helped in their munitions work in the weeks before the Rising. During the Rising he was with the GPO garrison, involved in bringing provisions from Henry Street on Tuesday, on the same day capturing a British officer and also leading Richard Coleman's 5th Battalion reinforcement party from the GPO to the Mendicity Institution. On Thursday he was wounded in the back on the Reis's corner of Abbey Street/O'Connell Street by machine-gun fire (see above) during the attempt to re-occupy the Hibernian Bank and the DBC. Imprisoned from April to December 1916 (in Sir Patrick Dun's, the Dublin Castle Hospital, Richmond Barracks, Kilmainham Gaol then sent to Knutsford and finally Frongoch, where he was for a few days on hunger strike). Was involved in the Richard Coleman and Thomas Ashe funerals. During the War of Independence was a machine-gun (Lewis gun) and musketry instructor, and occasionally took part in armed actions. He had the usual active duty (on account of his injury) as the 'Lights Man' in extinguishing Dublin street lighting (as a Corporation employee) in order to facilitate Volunteer operations: 'I looked after arc lamps as a Corpn. employee – Collins told me I was to take orders from any officer who told me to put out arc lamps in any area.' In the Civil War fought on the Republican side at Fowler Hall and O'Connell Street as a Lewis gunner, and afterwards elsewhere in Dublin including the 'Night of the Bridges'. In March 1923 he was involved in an attempt on W.T. Cosgrave at Herbert Park. Arrested and interned April 1923 to May 1924 in Mountjoy and then the Curragh Camp (in Tintown and then Hare Park). Again went on hunger strike in Tintown internment camp (thirty-five days), and from then on until release was very ill in bed after getting wet during a transfer march to the Hare Park internment camp. From then on he suffered constant ill health. Applied for a military pension in 1935, which still hadn't been processed by 1944.

Name	1916 Rank / Unit / Garrison	Sources
Scully, Michael	Volunteer, C Company, 1st Battalion, Dublin Brigade IV. Four Courts, Mendicity Institute.	MSPC MSP34REF13744, MSP34REF20252.

Corporation Service

Was working in the Cleansing Department at the time of the Rising. In Oct 1935, was working in the Housing Department with '39 years' Service'.

Other Notes

IRB member. Involved in Howth gun-running. Pre-Rising, had been delegated to be on 'that thing in the magazine' by his superiors, but rejected by Thomas MacDonagh as 'too old it was a younger man they wanted'. On first day of Rising sent to cut telegraph wires down a manhole beside the Mendicity. Mention in BMH WS1511. Holding up traffic (trams, etc.) on Queen Street on first day of Rising with a revolver, per Ignatius Callender (noted also in Scully's MSPC, and that Seán Heuston had asked him to do this 'for a while'). Sentenced by court-martial to ten years (seven years remitted). Sent to Kilmainham, Mountjoy, Portland, Lewis and Pentonville. Was an armed guard at the inaugural meeting of the First Dáil in the Mansion House, also involved in Ashe and Richard Coleman funerals, the Volunteer Convention on Jones' Road in October 1917 and various other protection duties, etc.

Name	1916 Rank / Unit / Garrison	Sources
Seery, James	Private, ICA. City Hall (Roll of Honour claims St Stephen's Green).	MSPC MSP34REF2279.

Corporation Service

Dublin Union relief work 7 December 1936 to 14 January 1937.

Other Notes

Involved in the usual pre-Rising duties and activities with the ICA. Was part of Seán Connolly's group that went to City Hall, and was in the guardhouse after it was captured, until evacuation on Monday night. Sent from the 12 Castle Street outpost on Tuesday evening for food and information but was unable to return. Evaded arrest afterwards. No subsequent service until he served as a cook in the National Army during the Civil War.

Name	1916 Rank / Unit / Garrison	Sources
Sexton, James	Volunteer, C Company, 2nd Battalion, Dublin Brigade IV. GPO, Father Matthew Park.	MSPC MSP34REF1432.

Corporation Service

Labourer in Paving Department from 1 October 1934.

Other Notes

On the roof of the GPO, etc. Involved in tunnelling through the walls of Moore Street after the evacuation of the GPO. Interned in Knutsford and Frongoch. Involved in the funerals of Mrs McDonagh and Thomas Ashe, also armed patrols and raids when the War of Independence started. Intelligence officer during the War of Independence; interned. On release involved in the Belfast boycott and took some part in the Civil War (left in September 1922). Was at Croke Park on armed duty during Bloody Sunday.

Name	1916 Rank / Unit /Garrison	Sources
Shannon, Martin Joseph	Private, ICA. St Stephen's Green, Harcourt Street Station.	MSPC MSP34REF1397.

Corporation Service

Employed in Main Drainage as a sewer worker from 1921 onwards.

Other Notes

Pre-Rising was involved in the usual ICA activities – drilling, making munitions and guarding Liberty Hall. Interned in Knutsford and then Frongoch. Involved post-Rising in drilling and training, went to Scotland to find employment from March to July 1917, and again for same reason from February 1919.

Name	1916 Rank / Unit /Garrison	Sources
Shaw, John (Jack)	Section Commander (i.e. Sergeant), A Company, 1st Battalion, Dublin Brigade IV. Imprisoned by the British on Volunteer-related offences during the Rising.	MSPC 1924A60, BMH WS 350 (Peter Reynolds).

Corporation Service

City Marshall from 2 July 1923 until 1940.

Other Notes

Took part in Howth gun-running, was arrested but imprisoned in a highly-publicised case for buying arms from British soldiers from Marlborough (now McKee) Barracks before the Easter Rising. As a result he missed the fighting (along with his fellow prisoner Thomas O'Reilly, later a Dublin City Alderman). Their friend Percy Reynolds narrowly escaped being caught for being in with them on the same activities: 'They were told they could go home if they told who the motor cyclist was. They laughed and said "don't make us laugh". "All right," said the magistrate "I'll have a laugh; 6 months' hard labour." They went down the stairs still laughing.' (per Peter Reynolds). Took part in armed election work in Longford, Thomas Ashe's funera and guard duty at 18 October Volunteer Convention. Was in the B & I raid in 1920. Arrested and went on hunger strike. Released after Treaty, and then fought on the pro-Treaty side.

Name	1916 Rank / Unit /Garrison	Sources
Sheehan, William (Bill)/Ó Síothcháin, Liam	Lieutenant Engineer, 1st Battalion, Dublin Brigade IV (from 4 March 1916). Supposed to mobilise on the North Circular Road to take charge and with Seamus S. O'Sullivan blow the bridges in the area; didn't turn out.	1888 and 1908 Ordnance Survey Sheet XVIII-26; *Irish Volunteer*, 20 Feb. 1915; 20 Mar. 1915; BMH WS 510, WS 278, WS 1686, WS 393, WS 564, WS 1637 'He was employed by the Dublin Corporation' via BMH WS 393 – this text is unclear, but I believe that William is the 'Sheehan' referred to, based on Oak Lodge (23 Oak Terrace, later 340 North Circular Road when occupied by William Joseph Daly) confirmed as being his residence according to the 1915 Electoral List. There's also a 'William Sheehan', electrical engineer, living at 43 Patrick Street in the 1911 Census. *Irish Volunteer*, 4 Mar. 1916. National Archives **CSORP DMP: MFA 6/1.**

Corporation Service

Electrician in the Electricity Supply Department.

Other Notes

Very possibly the same 'William Sheehan, Volunteer' praised for his baritone solo of 'A Nation Once Again' in the *Irish Volunteer* on 20 February 1915 and was heavily advertised through the year in the same publication to sing at a Manchester Martyrs Commemoration Concert on 22 November 1915 (other artistes included Séan Connolly and Éamonn Ceannt on uilleann pipes). On the eve of the Rising William Sheehan panicked and disposed of the two hundred weight of gelignite stored at his house (this was No. 23 Oak Terrace (Oak Lodge), in which Sheehan and both a brother and sister lived, and Thomas Byrne and Frank Scullin as lodgers), and which had been intended in the rebellion plans for use in blowing three key bridges along the northside (Cabra Road, North Circular Road and Cross Guns). This loss, and Sheehan's failure to mobilise (he was assigned responsibility to blow the bridges on the northside, with the help of Seamus S. O'Sullivan) led in turn to O'Sullivan and Frank Daly's parties being unable to hold those bridges in the North Circular Road/Cabra/Phibsborough area. This was in spite of constructing barricades –a combination of British artillery shrapnel and machine-gun fire forced the Volunteers to retreat. O'Sullivan had, from his passing motorbike, seen William Sheehan at the Mater Hospital on Monday morning and thought it strange that Sheehan wasn't already at his task. This setback allowed British lancers, troops and eventually artillery to move down towards the city centre, dooming the GPO garrison. On Tuesday Thomas 'Boer' Byrne called to Oak Lodge and discovered that the Sheehans had disposed of his Volunteer officer's uniform, too. William's brother was Commandant Ted Sheehan, Brigade Engineer, who was ordered to take charge of occupying the Crown Street Exchange and cutting all wires from Dublin Castle via a manhole on Dame Street, but he didn't show up either, allowing this vital point to be seized by the British. (Ted Sheehan was for some reason visited at his home in Stamer Street by Alderman Tom Kelly that morning, as witnessed by Henry Banks).

Name	1916 Rank / Unit /Garrison	Sources
Sheridan, James	Volunteer, A Company, 1st Battalion, Dublin Brigade IV (had been in the ICA). Four Courts and Church Street.	MSPC MSP34REF10155.

Corporation Service

Carter in Dublin Corporation employ as contractor/employee from 28 November 1934 (from 1 April 1945 carters were treated as employees only). Carrying 'materials to garden staff of Paving Dept'.

Other Notes

Had been in the Citizen Army 1913-15. Owned a horse and cart. Involved in moving munitions prior to the Rising; during the Rising had charge of a barricade on Church Street, as well as delivering messages, escorting prisoners, and watching the suspected location of a British armoured car for an opportunity to attack it. Escaped and went on the run for two weeks. During the War of Independence was involved in similar transportation duties in support of arms manufacture, purchases and seizures (assisting Peadar Breslin), including the big Collinstown Aerodrome raid. Also took part in arms manufacture and occasional armed patrols. Interned and released on the Truce. Took the anti-Treaty side in the Civil War. Ended as Company Quartermaster.

Name	1916 Rank / Unit /Garrison	Sources
Slater, Michael	Volunteer, B Company, 2nd Battalion, Dublin Brigade IV. St Stephen's Green, Fumbally Lane and Jacob's Factory.	MSPC MSP34REF21845; mentions in BMH WS 165, WS 1687.

Corporation Service

Employed by Public Lighting Department, Tara Street from May 1920 (fitter) up until at least the late 1930s.

IRB member. A year prior to the founding of the IV, was involved with Harry Nicholls and other IRB men in setting up a rifle range and club at Father Matthew Park, and was responsible for running this, storing the arms and ammunition at his own house. Took part in Howth and Kilcoole gun-running, also buying .303 ammunition. Member of the O'Donovan Rossa Funeral Committee. Escaped after the Rising and went on the run. Post-Rising, involved in buying arms from soldiers in Portobello Barracks and in the reorganisation of the IV. Transferred to 2nd Company, 5th Battalion, Dublin Brigade (Engineers) from 1919. Assigned to trade union infiltration work during the War of Independence, as member of a key IRA intelligence unit which was set up for this purpose (euphemistically called the Labour Board) and led by Martin Conlon. The aim was to influence unions towards supporting the national movement, to establish contacts with union members in key employments, and to organise breaking away from the control of British unions. Slater was one of the founders of the Irish Engineering Union, and arranged for the Dublin Brigade HQ to be accomodated at the union's new Gardiner Row HQ, an arrangement which lasted until the Truce. Also involved in various armed activities during the War of Independence and ended up on the run.

Name	1916 Rank / Unit /Garrison	Sources
Slattery, Peter 'Sla' (P. J.)/ Ó Slatora, Peadar	Captain or Commandant, GHQ Staff IV ('Director of Engineering'). E Company, 4th Battalion, Dublin Brigade IV. GPO.	MSPC 24SPP8004, a BMH WS listing exists for Slattery but no hyperlink to a document (as per BMH website in early 2015). BMH WS 725, WS 157; Roll of Honour.

Corporation Service

Temporary appointment as Assistant to the Surveyor, Rathmines and Rathgar UDC 6 or 11 March 1929 to 2 March 1931, when he was re-employed by Dublin Corporation as Temporary Engineer (question over whether his service should have continued over uninterrupted on suppression of the UDC in October 1930). Corporation service ended on 30 November 1931.

Other Notes

Gave an (open to the public) course in 'industrial explosives' at the Royal College of Science, TCD for the hidden benefit of IV members. Teacher at P.H. Pearse's school of St Enda's (and later headmaster). 'Very early in 1915 I was instructed to attend at a special class which was formed. The instructor was a man whom we knew as Slattery [...] The classes were of a very advanced nature in the destruction of bridges and barricades. He gave us a lot of instructions in the use of high explosives, how to handle them, and their power when properly used. The attendance at those lectures was very select.' WS 157. Claimed to have been gazetted 'Director of Engineering (combined forces)' as a Captain on the GHQ staff, IV and to have held that position during the Easter Rising. Sentenced to death after the Rising, commuted to penal servitude. Again involved in a variety of activities and schemes – smuggling, intelligence, organisation, elections, Dáil Department of Local Government.

Name	1916 Rank / Unit /Garrison	Sources
Smart, Thomas	Volunteer, C Company, 1st Battalion, Dublin Brigade IV. Four Courts, Bridewell, North Brunswick Street.	MSPC MSP34REF1556; BMH WS 255.

Corporation Service

Lost his job because of 'activities'. Also temporarily employed at Pigeon House Fort in 1918 (possibly in the Electricity Supply Department of the Corporation). Dublin Fire Brigade from 1920.

Other Notes

Joined IV circa March 1915. Active in Four Courts garrison during the Rising. With the Bridewell garrison at the time of the general surrender, they slipped away and were helped by friendly locals. Talked his way out past the British cordon and escaped arrest and internment to go on the run (but lost his job). Afterwards, was an armed driver for Éamon de Valera and Laurence Ginnell. Attended Thomas Ashe funeral. On armed street patrols. He was later excused ordinary duties for 'special services' (driver to 1st and 2nd Dáils). Gave shelter to armed Volunteers at Tara Street Fire Station during curfew hours; firemen also covered for wounded Volunteers by disarming them. Had a narrow escape when he was temporarily arrested at the Custom House attack while smuggling arms under his tunic. Took IRA dispatch bearers to Blessington during July 1922 in the Corporation ambulance. Many other examples Smart of using the DFB as opportunity and cover for activities.

Name	1916 Rank / Unit /Garrison	Sources
Stafford, John (J.J. or 'Jack')	Volunteer (Squad Commander, i.e. Corporal), B Company, 2nd Battalion, Dublin Brigade IV. Later a member of the ASU (Active Service Unit), was attached part-time on special duty to 'the Squad'. GPO, Hibernian Bank.	MSPC W24SP13630, MSP34REF2609; BMH WS1687, WS 818.

Corporation Service

'From the time of his dismissal from the Public Record Office in 1916 he was studying for an exam for post of Sanitary Sub-Officer in the Dublin Corporation. He commenced his service in the Public Health Department along with me on 25 April 1917.' (Charles Saurin, MSPC testimonial). Joined the National Army in June 1922. Later again a local government employee – see his father Mathew Stafford's MSPC file.

Other Notes

Member of the IRB from about 1910 (joining the Holt Circle, of which he was secretary from 1917 until 1922). His father Mathew Stafford was a veteran Fenian. Jack Stafford joined the Irish Volunteers on formation in 1913 at the Rotunda Rink. Involved in the Howth gun-running. During the Rising fought at the Hibernian Bank outpost of the GPO garrison, which moved first to the Imperial Hotel and then to Marlborough Street to avoid the burning flames. Charles Saurin saw him 'posted on balcony of Bank at corner of Lower Abbey Street & O'Connell Street replying to enemy fire, to which he was greatly exposed. He was very daring.' (MSPC). Escaped after the Rising. Under suspicion, he was dismissed from his job as a clerk in the Public Records Office in the Four Courts, so joined the Corporation in 1917. Promoted to Section Commander, but then reverted back to Volunteer by his own request. Bought five Lee-Enfield rifles off a member of the UVF in 1916 or 1917. Active in IRA in War of Independence. 'Owing to my position as Sanitary Officer [in Dublin Corporation] I was made Intelligence Officer and was always on duty in that capacity, and obtained very useful information on various occasions.' (MSPC). Also generally engaged as the drill and musketry instructor in B Company. Joined the National Army in June 1922, bringing a number of his company with him as 2nd Company, 2nd Battalion Dublin Brigade. Took part in fighting in Dublin in the Civil War. By 1926 was a Captain in the Eastern Command Ordnance Office, Defence Forces. Retired on 15 June 1929, and became an employee of the Co. Kildare Health Board.

Name	1916 Rank / Unit / Garrison	Sources
Stephenson, P.J. (Patrick Joseph)	Company Quartermaster, D Company, 1st Battalion, Dublin Brigade IV. Mendicity Institute, GPO, Four Courts.	MSPC MSP34REF21743; mention in BMH WS 251.

Corporation Service

Working in Thomas Street Library at the time of the Rising, and Assistant Librarian, Kevin Street Library in 1934. Later Chief City Librarian.

Other Notes

In the weeks just before the Rising he was working '[…] in Thomas Street Library. I would be free between 2 and 6 in the afternoons and in the morning time, one morning free until 2. All my spare time was taken up. I did not report for duty in the Library on Thursday, Friday or Saturday, I was engaged for the full three days.' (MSPC). During the Rising was initially in the Mendicity Institution, then sent out for supplies to the GPO but unable to return to the Mendicity (ended up staying with the Four Courts garrison). Returned to the GPO and was in the evacuation. Interned in Frongoch. MSPC states that he was in Na Fianna Éireann as its Adjutant-General after 1916 and during the War of Independence. After release, involved in organisation workdrilling, arms raids, election work, clashes with police and buying arms and ammunition off British soldiers. Also kept some of this in the Thomas Street Library, which was raided on 2 November 1920 by the British, but with nothing found. From the MSPC: 'Q. You were evading arrest but you were still able to carry on your job at the Library? A. Yes'.

Name	1916 Rank / Unit / Garrison	Sources
Stritch, James	Volunteer, B Company, 1st Battalion, Dublin Brigade IV. GPO ('Jim Strich' misspelling in some sources).	*DC Reports*, Vol II, 1910, p. 912, DC Reports, Vol III, 1916, p. 69; BMH WS 409, WS 1765, WS 280.

Corporation Service

Joined Dublin Corporation in 1882. Street Inspector, Paving Department in 1916.

Other Notes

IRB member, member of both the Wolfe Tone Memorial and O'Donovan Rossa Funeral Committees. His arrest is noted in a report of the Paving Committee in 1916 (also the confiscation by the British of his Corporation-issued bicycle, which then went missing). Also involved in Irish National Foresters. Stritch is listed on the Roll of Honour for the GPO, and appears in the list of deportees to Wakefield on 6 May 1916. Later took the anti-Treaty side, was in Fianna Fáil and was a founder of the National Graves Association.

Name	1916 Rank / Unit / Garrison	Sources
Tannam, Liam (William)	Captain, E Company, 3rd Battalion, Dublin Brigade IV. GPO.	MSPC MSP34REF797; DC Reports, Vol II, 1910, p. 905; *DCC Minutes*, No. 298, 1920; BMH WS 242, numerous other WS.

Corporation Service

Joined Corporation as Boy Messenger in March 1910, permanently appointed to Sanitary Staff in 1926, Sanitary Sub-Officer/Inspector by (at least) 1937, Sanitary Officer by 1951, Public Health Office, Municipal Buildings, Dublin City.

IRB member from July 1915, sworn in by Éamonn Ceannt. Joined the Irish Volunteers in 1914, after being convinced by Ceannt, whose office was next to his in Municipal Buildings, that the Irish Volunteers would fight for independence. Spent his fortnight's annual leave in 1915 organising for the IV in Tallaght, Glencullen and Enniskerry. Commanded the guard on O'Donovan Rossa's remains in City Hall. Before the Rising, organised a guard on Volunteer HQ in Dawson Street and was told by Ceannt on Holy Thursday that in the event of conflicting orders, he was to follow the IRB chain of command. His Company was assigned to the GPO to help make up the HQ Battalion, but went instead to Boland's Mills on conflicting orders. Gave the order in the GPO to fire on the charging Lancers. Sent to take charge of Reis's and the Dublin Bread Company. Was a member of Connolly's stretcher-bearer party and officer escort in the escape from the burning building. Interned in Frongoch. Commanded guard on Thomas Ashe's body in City Hall in 1917. Arrested and interned during the War of Independence, he subsequently escaped, was re-captured and then tried on the charge of escaping once his prison sentence was up. His wife had become very ill, so he was granted permission to recognise the court and defend his case (the then-Lord Mayor, Laurence O'Neill, went bail), and was given leave from the IV for a period because of the controversy over his recognition of a British court. Arrested and interned again during the Civil War, 'got a bad time' in Mountjoy (MSPC reference, Andrew McDonnell), 'he was in a shocking state – they nearly killed him' (MSPC reference from Michael Chadwick).

Name	1916 Rank / Unit / Garrison	Sources
Walsh, Róisín	Unknown, possibly CnamB (or Fianna, i.e. the Belfast Girls' Branch) in Tyrone and/or Belfast. Tyrone.	MSPC MSP34REF21565 (Ina Connolly Heron); BMH WS 179 (Elizabeth and Nell Corr), WS 919 (Ina Heron); *Irish Press*, 3 Nov. 1931, p. 3; 27 June 1949; 'The Bell and the Blanket: Journals of Irish Republican Dissent', http://thepensivequill. am/2012/09/the-bell-and-blanket-journals-of-irish.html (downloaded on 05/05/15).

Corporation Service

Rathmines & Rathgar UDC and County Dublin as a librarian up until the restoration of Dublin City Council; thereafter Dublin Corporation Chief Librarian 1931-49.

Made a statement in support of Ina Connolly Heron's pension application, even though she herself never applied. Won a turkey in a shooting competition in Belfast at Christmas 1914 among the CnamB, but gave it to the Connollys. 'It was won by Miss Roisin Walsh, our late city librarian, who made a present of it to our family as she had no need to take one home to the country. This we looked upon as a very generous act on her part. We were all very fond of her, she was so kind and gentle and never tired of trying to enlighten us on a number of things that were always turning up unexpectedly due to war conditions. She had just returned from Germany and was able to give us first hand information about the state of things as she saw them. She had a number of German songs and one day she stopped us – a group of Fianna – marching along the Falls Road singing 'The Watch on the Rhine'. She was very amused at our German and put us right, saying: "It is just as easy to say the words in the correct German if you take your time and learn. You don't know when you will need it; some day perhaps the Germans may come here and then they will feel at home when they hear you sing."' BMH WS 919 (Ina Heron Connolly). Walsh was told about the Rising on Good Friday by a priest in her native Clogher, Co. Tyrone. With Ina Connolly and other members of the Walsh family, she was involved in moving ammunition around that week, and visited a group of Volunteers who were preparing to mobilise. Later was on the editorial board of *The Bell*, a 'committed republican activist […] and moved in the same circles as Hannah Sheehy Skeffington, Mary Kettle, and Maud Gonne MacBride. Her involvement with Peadar O'Donnell goes back at least as far as the formation of Saor Éire, where the IRA General Army Convention met in her kitchen in 1931 to underline their commitment to radical socialist republican politics.' (*The Pensive Quill* blog, 2012). Her funeral in 1949 drew distinguished guests such as Éamon de Valera, Richard Mulcahy, as well as former Cumann na mBan member such as Nancy Wyse-Power.

Name	1916 Rank / Unit /Garrison	Sources
Williams, Patrick	Private, ICA (after the Rising Volunteer B Company, 3rd Battalion, Dublin Brigade IV, see note). Boland's Mills.	In the SFRH as labourer, Corporation and living at 25 Stafford Street; MSPC MSP34REF60455.

Corporation Service

Labourer (Paving Department) in 1916 at least. Dublin Corporation pensioner from 25 May 1938.

Other Notes

IRB member. During Easter Week he was with Seán Connolly's party, then was detailed under William Oman's command to Ship Street/St Werburgh's graveyard. Then went to Boland's Mills, where two nephews were in B Company, 3rd Battalion IV. Dug a grave for Peadar Macken in 'the yard near Boland's stables' according to BMH WS 422. Interned in Wakefield then Frongoch afterwards. Later joined B Company, 3rd Battalion IV. Arrested again and interned in the North Dublin Union. At the time of his pension application in the 1940s he had become senile, so his old comrades (including Christy Poole and Seán O'Keefe) came in to testify to his service.

Name	1916 Rank / Unit /Garrison	Sources
Wren, James	Volunteer, Dublin Brigade IV (joined during Rising). GPO.	MSPC MSP34REF1392.

Corporation Service

Rent Collector, Housing Department from at least the mid-1930s onwards and employee at time of death in 1953.

Other Notes

Sentry and messenger duties during Easter Week, and sent as an armed scout to the Custom House and Westland Row. Joined F Company, 2nd Battalion IV after the Rising. Involved in War of Independence activities.

Contributors

Sheila Carden spent most of her working life in the programmes division of RTÉ. She decided in 1997 to devote herself to writing the biography of her grandfather Thomas Kelly, a project which long fascinated her, and which took nine years to complete. It involved extensive research both in the Dublin libraries and in the National Archives, Kew, and she based some of her work on various family papers, hitherto unavailable. The biography of Kelly, titled *The Alderman,* was published in 2007 and was made possible by the sponsorship of Dublin City Council. She followed this work by publishing a collection of Kelly's writings on the history of Dublin, titled *The Streets of Dublin,* which had been originally printed serially in Arthur Griffith's newspaper *Sinn Féin* in 1910 and 1911. This collection in its modern form was published in 2013 by the Dublin Civic Trust.

Shay Cody is General Secretary of the IMPACT Union which is a successor organisation to the Dublin Municipal Officers Association. He is a member of the Executive Council and General Purposes Committee of the Irish Congress of Trade Unions. Previous historical publications include co-authoring *The Parliament of Labour: 100 years of the Dublin Council of Trade Unions* and *May Day in Dublin 1890-1986.* He recently published *Four Lives: IMPACT Union's roots in the 1916 rising* and has completed *The Dublin Trades Council: reactions to the Easter Rising of 1916* for publication in *Saothar* 41, the Journal of the Labour History Society.

Evelyn Conway is a librarian with Dublin City Public Libraries. A native Dubliner, on leaving school she began her career with the city libraries as a library assistant. She later obtained her professional qualifications in librarianship and holds a BSc Econ ILS (hons) from the University of Wales, Aberystwyth, and a DLIS from UCD. She has worked extensively around the city library network and managed the Dublin Prison Library service as a Senior Librarian from 2000 to 2006. She currently holds the post of Adult Fiction buyer for Dublin City Public Libraries.

Donal Fallon is a historian based in Dublin with a particular research interest in the social history of twentieth-century Dublin. He is editor of the Dublin history blog 'Come Here To Me' (www.comeheretome.com) and author of *The Pillar: the life and afterlife of the Nelson Pillar* (New Island, 2014) and a biography of Major John MacBride (O'Brien, 2015). His academic publications include a detailed study of the 'Animal Gang' phenomenon in 1930s Dublin in *Locked out: a century of Irish working class life* (Irish Academic Press, 2013). He is currently researching republican commemorative practice in 1930s Dublin as a PhD candidate of University College Dublin.

Las Fallon is a firefighter with Dublin Fire Brigade since 1985. As a fire service historian and writer he has published two books: *Dublin Fire Brigade and the Irish revolution* (Dublin, 2012) and *The Firemen`s tale: the burning of the Custom House 1921* (Dublin, 2015). He has also published a number of articles in magazines and on-line. He is a member of The Fire Service Trust, the Fire Heritage Network, and the Fire Mark Circle. He holds a certificate in Local History from NUI Maynooth. Originally from Ballyfermot, he lives in Palmerstown with his wife Maria and has two sons, Donal and Luke.

David Flood (Daithí Ó Maoltuile) is from Ashford, Co. Wicklow, and is at present C.A.D. manager in the Information Systems Department of Dublin City Council, having joined Dublin Corporation Engineering Department in 1998. He volunteered to join 'C' Company, 21st (Dwyer) Infantry Battalion F.C.A. in 1993, and is currently serving with the R.D.F. Platoon, 2nd Field Engineer Group, 2nd Brigade of the Defence Forces and based in Custume Barracks, Athlone. He is also a member of the executive of the Dublin City Branch (modern successor to the D.M.O.A.) of the IMPACT trade union.

John Gibney holds a doctorate in history from Trinity College, Dublin. He has been a research fellow at the University of Notre Dame and NUI Galway, was a contributor to the Royal Irish Academy's *Dictionary of Irish biography* (Cambridge University Press, 2009), and in 2012 produced the acclaimed RTÉ Radio One documentary, *The Animal Gang*. He worked in heritage tourism with the highly rated 'Historical Walking Tours of Dublin' between 2001 and 2015. He co-developed and edited the official 'Decade of Centenaries' website (www.decadeofcentenaries.com) created by *History Ireland* magazine in partnership with the Department of Arts, Culture and the Gaeltacht and is the author of *Ireland and the Popish Plot* (Palgrave Macmillan, 2008), *The shadow of a year: the 1641 rebellion in Irish history and memory* (University of Wisconsin Press, 2013), *Seán Heuston* (O'Brien Press, 2013), and *A history of the Easter Rising in 50 objects* (Mercier Press, 2015). He is currently Glasnevin Trust Assistant Professor in Public History and Cultural Heritage at Trinity College Dublin.

Anthony J. [Tony] Jordan is a graduate of Maynooth University, St Patrick's Drumcondra and UCD. He is an historian and biographer. His biographies include Major John MacBride, Éamon de Valera, W. T. Cosgrave, Arthur Griffith, Seán MacBride, Winston Churchill, Conor Cruise O'Brien, W. B. Yeats, Christy Brown, and John A. Costello. He has edited a collection of the writings and speeches of John MacBride called *Boer War to Easter Rising*. He has also written two books, *Yeats/Gonne/MacBride triangle* and *Willie Yeats & the Gonne MacBrides* on the interaction between Yeats/Gonne/MacBride. His autobiography is called *The Good Samaritans*. His most recent book is *A Jesus biography 2015*.

Dr Conor McNamara is the 1916 Scholar in Residence at the Moore Institute at NUI Galway. He has written extensively about the history of the Irish revolution, food shortage and minor famine, and the intersection between criminality and political violence in twentieth-century Ireland. In 2011, he was awarded the National Library History Studentship and catalogued the Mahon Papers, one of the largest collections of estate papers in Ireland. He is the joint editor of *The West of Ireland: new perspectives on the nineteenth century* (History Press, 2011) and *The Easter 1916: a new illustrated history* (Collins Press, 2015). He was the senior researcher on the Notre Dame University, 1916 Project.

Dr Martin Maguire is Senior Lecturer in the Department of Humanities at Dundalk Institute of Technology. He has published many articles and essays on Irish Protestant history. His books on the history of civil and public service trade unions, *Servants to the public: a history of the Local Government & Public Services Union 1901-1990* and *Scientific service: a history of the Union of Professional and Technical Civil Servants 1920-1990* are published by the IPA. His most recent book *The Civil Service and the revolution in Ireland, 1912-38 "Shaking the blood-stained hand of Mr Collins"* is published by Manchester University Press.

Dr Thomas J. Morrissey is a Jesuit priest, an educationalist, historian and author. Former headmaster of Crescent College Comprehensive, Limerick, and Director of the National College of Industrial Relations, Dublin, he has taken his degrees in History from N.U.I., the B.A. and M.A. in UCD, the PH.D in UCC. He has written some sixteen historical works. These include: *Towards a national university* (1983); *The social teaching of James Connolly* (ed. 1991); *Peter Kenney, S.J., 1779-1841: his mission in Ireland and North America* (1996); *William J. Walsh, Archbishop of Dublin, 1841-1921* (2000); *William O'Brien, 1881-1968: Socialist, Dail Deputy, Trade Union Leader* (2007); *Jesuits in Hong Kong, South China and Beyond* (2008); *Edward J. Byrne, 1872-1941: the forgotten Archbishop of Dublin* (2010); *Laurence O'Neill, Lord Mayor of Dublin, 1917-1924 (2013); and From Easter Week to Flanders Field: the diaries and letters of John Delaney SJ, 1916-1919* (2015). During 2016, he will publish *A secular liberal or a Christian state? The Ireland of Edward Cahill, 1868-1941.*

Dr. Séamas Ó Maitiú was a secondary teacher in CBS Westland Row Dublin for many years. He has also lectured on local studies and Irish history in UCD, Maynooth University, St Patrick's College, Drumcondra and Marino Institute of

Education. He currently teaches the annual Lord Mayor's Certificate in Local Studies in the Dublin City Library & Archive, Pearse Street. He has published widely in Dublin and Wicklow history and is editor of *Dublin Historical Record.*

Lawrence W. White is research assistant and copy editor of the Royal Irish Academy's *Dictionary of Irish biography* (*DIB*). A graduate of the University of New Hampshire, USA, he has done postgraduate work at Salem State University, Massachusetts, and Trinity College Dublin. His chief research interests are Irish political and cultural history of the twentieth century, especially the history and ideology of the trade union movement and other leftist movements and organisations. He has written over 330 *DIB* articles, largely on persons active in these fields, and is co-editor of *1916: portraits and lives*, a selection of *DIB* articles pertinent to the Easter rising.

Pádraig Yeates is an author and journalist whose books include *Lockout: Dublin 1913; A city in wartime: Dublin 1914-1918; A city in turmoil: Dublin 1919-1921* and *A city in civil war: Dublin 1921-1924.* He previously edited the *Irish People* and worked for the *Irish Times* as Community Affairs and as Industry and Employment Correspondent. He is a member of the 1913 Committee, which organised events to mark the centenary of the Dublin Lockout and is now involved in events to mark the 1916 centenary, particularly aspects involving SIPTU, the Irish Citizen Army and the role of the Labour movement.

Select Bibliography/Further Reading

Augusteijn, Joost, *Patrick Pearse: the making of a revolutionary* (Basingstoke, 2010).

Barton, Brian, *The secret court martial records of the Easter rising* (Stroud, 2010).

Bateson, Ray, *They died by Pearse's side* (Dublin, 2010).

Brennan-Whitmore, W.J., *Dublin burning: the Easter rising from behind the barricades* (2nd ed., Dublin, 2013).

Carden, Sheila, *The Alderman: Alderman Tom Kelly (1868-1942) and Dublin Corporation* (Dublin, 2007).

Caulfield, Max, *The Easter rebellion* (London, 1964).

De Búrca, Séamas, *The soldier's song: the story of Peadar Ó Cearnaigh* (Dublin, 1957).

Devine, Francis (ed.) *A capital in conflict: Dublin city and the 1913 Lockout* (Dublin 2013).

Dublin's fighting story, 1916-21 (2nd ed. Cork, 2009).

Dudley Edwards, Ruth, *Patrick Pearse: the triumph of failure* (London, 1977).

Enright, Sean, *Easter Rising 1916: the trials* (Sallins, 2014).

Fallon, Donal, *John MacBride* (Dublin, 2015).

Fallon, Las, *Dublin Fire Brigade and the Irish revolution* (Dublin, 2012).

Ferriter Diarmaid, *Lovers of liberty: local government in 20th century Ireland* (Dublin, 2001).

Fitzgerald, Mairead Ashe (ed.), *A terrible beauty: poetry of 1916* (Dublin 2015).

Foster, R.F., *The Irish story: telling tales and making it up in Ireland* (London, 2001).

Fox, R.M., *The history of the Irish Citizen Army* (Dublin, 1944).

Gallagher, Mary, *Éamonn Ceannt* (Dublin, 2014).

Gaughan, J.Anthony (ed.), *Memoirs of Senator Joseph Connolly (1885-1961), a founder of modern Ireland* (Dublin, 1996).

Gaughan, J.Anthony (ed.), *Memoirs of Senator James G. Douglas, concerned citizen* (Dublin, 1998).

Geraghty, Tom and Trevor Whitehead, *The Dublin Fire Brigade: a history of the brigade, the fires and the emergencies* (Dublin, 2004).

Geraghty, Hugh, *William Patrick Partridge and his times* (Dublin, 2003).

Gibney, John, *Seán Heuston* (Dublin, 2013).

Gillis, Liz, *Women of the Irish revolution* (Cork, 2014).

Griffith, Kenneth & Timothy O'Grady, *Curious journey: an oral history of Ireland's unfinished revolution* (Cork, 1998).

Greaves, C. Desmond, *The life and times of James Connolly* (London, 1961).

Greaves, C. Desmond, *The Irish Transport and General Workers' Union: the formative years 1910–23* (Dublin, 1982).

Hay, Marnie, *Bulmer Hobson and the Nationalist movement in twentieth-century Ireland* (Manchester, 2009).

Jordan, Anthony J., *Major John MacBride, 1865 –1916: MacDonagh and MacBride and Connolly and Pearse* (Westport, 1991).

Jordan Anthony J., *W.T. Cosgrave, 1880-1965: founder of modern Ireland* (Dublin, 2006).

Jordan, Anthony J., *Arthur Griffith with James Joyce and WB Yeats: liberating Ireland* (Dublin, 2013).

Kee, Robert, *The green flag: a history of Irish nationalism* (London, 1972).

Kenna, Shane, *Thomas MacDonagh* (Dublin, 2014).

Kiberd, Declan, *Inventing Ireland: the literature of the modern nation* (London, 2015).

Laffan, Michael, *The resurrection of Ireland: the Sinn Féin party, 1916-1923* (Cambridge, 1999).

Laffan, Michael, *Judging W. T. Cosgrave* (Dublin, 2014).

Larkin, Emmet, *James Larkin: Irish labour leader, 1876–1947* (London, 1989).

Levinson, Leah, *With wooden sword: a portrait of Francis Sheehy-Skeffington, militant pacifist* (Boston, 1983).

Litton, Helen, *Thomas Clarke* (Dublin, 2014).

Lyons, J.B., *Oliver St John Gogarty* (Dublin, 1980).

MacGiolla Choille, Breandán (ed.), *Intelligence notes, 1913–16* (Dublin, 1966).

Macardle, Dorothy, *The Irish republic* (London, 1937).

Maguire, Martin, *Servants to the public: a history of the local government and public services union, 1901-1990* (Dublin, 1998).

Martin, F.X. (ed.), *The Howth and Kilcoole gun-running: recollections and documents* (2nd ed., Sallins, 2014).

McCoole, Sinéad, *No ordinary women: Irish female activists in the revolutionary years, 1900-1923* (Dublin, 2004).

McCoole, Sinéad, *Easter widows: seven Irish women who lived in the Shadow of the 1916 Rising* (Dublin, 2014).

McCracken, Donal P., *Forgotten protest: Ireland and the Anglo-Boer war* (Belfast, 2003).

McGarry, Fearghal, *The Rising Ireland: Easter 1916* (Oxford, 2010).

McGee, Owen, *The IRB: The Irish Republican Brotherhood, from the Land League to Sinn Féin* (Dublin, 2005)

MacLochlainn, Piaras F., *Last Words: letters and statements of the leaders executed after the rising at Easter 1916* (Dublin, 1990)

Mitchell, Arthur, *Labour in Irish politics, 1890-1930* (Dublin, 1974).

Morgan, Austen, *James Connolly: a political biography* (Manchester, 1988).

Morrissey, Thomas J. *Laurence O'Neill (1864-1943). Lord Mayor of Dublin (1917-1924), patriot and man of peace* (Dublin, 2014).

Murray, Peter, 'Electoral politics and the Dublin working class before the First World War', *Saothar*, 6 (1980), pp 8-25.

Nelligan, David, *The spy in the Castle* (London, 1968).

Nevin, Donal (ed.), *1913: Jim Larkin and the Dublin lock-out* (Dublin, 1964).

Nevin, Donal (ed.), *Trade union century* (Cork, 1994).

O'Brien, Joseph V., *"Dear, Dirty Dublin": a city in distress, 1899-1916* (Berkeley, 1982).

O'Brien, Paul, *Battleground: the battle for the General Post Office, 1916* (Dublin, 2015).

Ó Broin León, *W.E. Wylie and the Irish revolution, 1916-1921* (Dublin, 1989).

Ó Maitiú, Séamas, *W. & R. Jacob: 150 years of Irish biscuit making* (Dublin, 2001).

O'Connor, Emmet, *Syndicalism in Ireland, 1917–1923* (Cork, 1988)

O'Farrell, Mick, *The 1916 diaries of an Irish rebel and a British soldier* (Cork, 2014).

Regan, John M., *The Irish counter-revolution, 1921-1936* (Dublin, 1999).

Richardson, Neil, *According to their lights: stories of Irisjmen in the British army, Easter 1916* (Cork, 2015).

Ryan, Desmond, *The rising: the complete story of Easter Week* (Dublin, 1949).

Townshend, Charles, *Easter 1916: the Irish rebellion* (London, 2005).

Ward, Margaret, *Unmanageable revolutionaries: women and Irish nationalism* (London, 1995).

Yeates, Pádraig, *Lockout: Dublin 1913* (Dublin, 2000).

Yeates, Pádraig, *A city in wartime: Dublin 1914-1918* (Dublin, 2011).

Yeates, Pádraig, *A city in turmoil: Dublin, 1919-1921* (Dublin, 2013).

Index

Compiled by Julitta Clancy

Note: unless otherwise indicated, buildings and streets listed are in Dublin city.

Page references in *italics* denote illustrations; references in **bold** denote principal sections

'A must-read counterblast to the investment industry's marketing millions. It gives invaluable City insider knowledge.'

Tony Levene, personal investment author, journalist and scambuster

'Alexander Davidson acts an informed guide for the not-yet-fully-seasoned investor. In a wide ranging exploration of the factors that drive shareholder value, he shines his torch beyond company financial results to look at reputation, risk and most of all the interdependent relationships of those working within the square mile and its supporting industries.'

Jane Wilson, Chief Executive Officer,
Chartered Institute of Public Relations

'Ideal bedtime reading for the novice investor, this book demystifies the jargon of financial markets, alerts the neophyte to the many pitfalls and honeytraps and debunks many of the best-known myths about how to make money.'

Professor Laurence Copeland, Cardiff Business School

'This wise little book takes the reader on a journey into the mysterious caves of finance and investment, to discover the monsters and puppeteers who control the market and either make our money or lose it for us. By linking the current field of financial markets with the age old myths and philosophy of classical antiquity, Davidson helps us to see perennial patterns in human society, the opportunities for greed and manipulation, and the ways in which we in our small boats sail past hazards that tempt us on every side. These timeless truths are put to good use in charting the specific territory of the current financial seas.'

Catherine Osborne, Professor of Philosophy, University of East Anglia

'It takes confidence to take on the market and put your money where your mouth is. And as *The Money Myth* makes clear, it is human emotions such as confidence that will in large part determine your fate. This book is engaging and well written, covering the basics of investing as well as some fascinating perspectives on the City.'

Anthony J. Evans, Associate Professor of Economics,
ESCP Europe Business School

'I was delighted to read a business book which highlights the critical importance of risk management and the value of effective insurance. Airmic research shows that risk is an essential board agenda item and many of the most dramatic corporate failures over the last decade have been evidenced ... y the board. *The Money Myth* provides excellent e essential management disciplines.'

CEO, Airmic

'This shrewd handbook reveals how regulation and compliance, among other things, can drive share prices as well as City behaviour, and how you should take account of such factors as an investor.'

Joanna Page, partner, head of the corporate and commercial litigation group, Allen & Overy

'Alexander Davidson opens his new book with a "Wealth Warning" but at least there is no call to issue a health warning – this is no rogue trader's manifesto but a soberly argued guide to the labyrinthine maze that is today's globalised world of investment opportunities. His text is moreover enlivened and enlightened unusually by references to Classical myths, such as that of Er at the end of Plato's *Republic*. These are not mere window-dressing. His occasional use of ancient mythology is intended to illuminate the workings of human nature, as expressed in financial markets.'

Paul Cartledge, A.G. Leventis Professor of Greek Culture, Cambridge University, and Honorary PhD (Economics), University of Thessaly, Greece

'Recent history has shown us how easily reputations can be damaged. Technological advancement poses enormous opportunity for growth but also introduces reputational risks. It was great to see Alexander Davidson cover these important dimensions and his book will help investors who want to understand the potential impact of risk management practices, for better and for worse, on their shares and other savings.'

Ryan Rubin, UK security and privacy director, Protiviti

'There is plenty for private investors to ponder over in this punchy and easy-to-read book. Alexander Davidson is forthright in his opinions and his analysis is sound. You don't need to be a classics scholar – in fact, you don't need to know much about investing to gain a stack of knowledge from this insight. I welcome any book that helps to demystify the stock market and encourages the public to gain a share of the wealth that the City offers.'

Rodney Hobson, financial journalist and author

'For those who wonder where the financial system is taking us but cannot resist the temptation to get involved themselves, Alexander Davidson's book takes the reader on an invigorating romp of markets and the whole panorama of the financial status quo. Woven throughout is the imagery of Greek mythology which also bears much of the same characteristics of moths being drawn into flames, but the Greeks were not – and indeed are not – so fortunate as British investors in that the latter now have Alexander Davidson as a guide.'

Gavin Oldham, Chief Executive, The Share Centre

The Money Myth

A classic introduction to the modern world of finance and investing

Alexander Davidson

PEARSON

Harlow, England • London • New York • Boston • San Francisco • Toronto • Sydney
Auckland • Singapore • Hong Kong • Tokyo • Seoul • Taipei • New Delhi
Cape Town • São Paulo • Mexico City • Madrid • Amsterdam • Munich • Paris • Milan

PEARSON EDUCATION LIMITED

Edinburgh Gate
Harlow CM20 2JE
Tel: +44 (0)1279 623623
Fax: +44 (0)1279 431059
Website: www.pearson.com/uk

First published in Great Britain in 2012
© Alexander Davidson 2012

The right of Alexander Davidson to be identified as author of this work has been asserted by him in accordance with the Copyright, Designs and Patents Act 1988.

Pearson Education is not responsible for the content of third-party internet sites.

ISBN: 978-0-273-75520-3

British Library Cataloguing-in-Publication Data
A catalogue record for this book is available from the British Library

Library of Congress Cataloging-in-Publication Data
Davidson, Alexander, 1957–
  The money myth : a classic introduction to the modern world of finance and investing / Alexander Davidson.
     p. cm.
  Includes index.
  ISBN 978-0-273-75520-3 (limp)
1. Investments. 2. Finance. I. Title.
  HG4521.D129 2012
  332--dc23
                              2012002451

10 9 8 7 6 5 4 3 2 1
16 15 14 13 12

Typeset in 10pt Galliard by 30
Printed and bound in Great Britain by Ashford Colour Press Ltd, Gosport, Hants

Contents

Dedication

I am dedicating this small book to a group that had a major impact on me, and which inspired me, even many years later, to use classical mythology to explain financial markets. This is the classics department at St Benedict's School, Ealing, 1972–76, its teachers, Denis Costello, the late Gill Harrison, Andy Hardman, Basil Nickerson and Vaughan Irons, and my fellow sixth-form pupils, Derek Barretto, Simon Kolka, and Anthony Agius.

Wealth warning

You will find in this book my experience of financial markets. The views expressed are entirely my own and do not necessarily coincide with those of any parties for whom I work or have worked. The text is for educational purposes only. Do not use it as a definitive source. Above all, this book is no substitute for investment advice. Some of the coverage in the book will date, but the essential truths remain the same.

Acknowledgements

My thanks to the Association of Investment Companies for some help on understanding some finer points on its industry. I am obliged to ShareScope for providing, at my request, some of its excellent charts for this book. May I also offer thanks to Denis Peters, director, corporate communications, at Euroclear, for helping on the section in Chapter 10 concerning back office infrastructure. I am grateful to Professor Catherine Osborne at the University of East Anglia for giving me some useful perspectives on relevant ancient philosophy, which have helped to inform various parts of this book, but were particularly useful for Chapters 19, 25 and 26. I would like to thank Chris Cudmore, my editor at FT Pearson, for giving me the chance to write this book on a subject important to me. Last but not least, I thank Aigulia, my wife, and Acelia, my daughter, for maintaining the home while I was busy on this latest project.

Alexander Davidson

Abbreviations

When I use the name of an organisation for the first time in a chapter, I spell it out in full. Subsequently, I usually abbreviate it. For example, you will find the Financial Services Authority referred to subsequently as the FSA.

Introduction

We all believe in the money myth. Our society could not function without a fundamental belief in the value of money, but it is fuelled by blind faith, sometimes far more than we all care to acknowledge.

The money myth dictates that, if you have money, it is something solid, and that if you invest it, it is tied to the value of the underlying assets, which can rise or fall in value. What is far less appreciated is the power of perception. Investors' emotions can so influence the price of money that it takes on a life of its own.

If you hold some money in shares, the value may fluctuate wildly. If you cash in, how much you get depends on factors beyond fundamentals. This is not just about shares. In the investment and money game, we live in a world where a guarantee may not be what it says on the tin. Your money handed over is your money gone, exchanged for a promise to repay a similar amount that relies on availability.

It is not all bad. Shares go up as well as down. Reputable banks will typically pay up on demand and compensation schemes are in place. If you invest carefully, you can win, sometimes spectacularly, but you need to understand how the money myth works. As part of the game plan, financial markets close ranks, the respectable alongside the dubious.

The interconnections run deep, and to understand this is an essential step towards dispelling the money myth, perpetuated as it is by the noise of governments and regulators, and the mantras of stockbrokers that encourage you to buy and hold for the long term and to suffer your losses stoically.

The more the money is kept, and moved round, within the system, the greater are the profits for traders and corporate financiers. The communication experts give it all a positive image. In this way, investment demand is largely created, and its level at any given time drives security prices.

Selling the dream

The money myth says that you can trust a company, a stockbroker, the regulator, the system, and the claims of ethical standards. The City encourages us to tolerate the investment risk and conflicts of interest, and to buy the dream.

It is part of the complexity that, much of the time, the game works. When a motivational speaker has encouraged his followers to walk on red-hot coals it is only the ones who do not keep walking fast enough that are likely to get their feet burnt.

Confidence in the system keeps investors in the market, and there is no industry that makes more use of the friendly handshake. If you trust in the bonhomie, however, you may be let down. The UK financial regulator has found that financial services firms have been unwilling, even over years, to grasp the concept of Treating Customers Fairly.

Recognise your limitations and capitalise on your advantages.

The reality is that, behind the scenes, there are battles. To succeed as an investor, you must join the fray, and your first task is to recognise that it exists. Your second is, like any fighting solider, to recognise your limitations and capitalise on your advantages.

Most retail investors cannot invest in the same quantities as the City institutions or afford to take the same risks, and it is their own money they are using. By way of compensation, as US investment guru Peter Lynch has made clear, you can operate much more flexibly in this position. Unlike the institutions, you do not need short-term targets. When it suits you, you can take the longer view.

As a medium- to long-term investor, you should not, however, ignore important immediate events such as takeovers, or changes in strategic direction. You must separate the significant, which may have influence on the longer term, from market noise.

The underlying driver here is the profit motive. This gives rise to risk-taking, not just by quoted companies but also the financial markets that trade the securities. The money myth is a weapon. To demonstrate it in action, we will delve deeper into myths.

Myths, money and the money myth

At first glance, you may be surprised that in a book focused on financial markets and investing, we draw parallels with ancient Greek and Roman mythology. We are using the old myths, however, to cast light on a big modern one, the money myth, and how it works, as well as its assumptions and fallacies.

You may not have come across ancient Greek and Roman mythology since school, and perhaps not even then, but these tales have survived for well over two thousand years and remain fresh today.

You should not be put off any dry encounters you have had with these stories in the classroom because, for the purpose of illuminating the workings of financial markets, they are paramount.

The old fables shine the torch on greed, ambition and intrigue, those characteristics that drive financial markets in such a concentrated way. The continued financial crises are proof of the damage they can do. Markets create enormous value, hope, prosperity and jobs, but illusions as well, and the money myth has undoubtedly failed us.

To invest successfully, we need guidance in these areas, and I am not talking here of technical analysis, although, as this book makes clear, the charts have something to offer if used selectively. Many investors prefer with good reason to be focused on fundamentals, including interest rates, investment ratios, profits and cash flows.

Sadly, this too is not enough. It is a truism of financial markets that even amid tightening accounting standards, the profit figures can be manipulated. Statistics have the same spurious accuracy they always have. Some analysts' forecasts could be plucked out of thin air.

Not to accept the limitations of all these numbers is to buy into the money myth. What counts at least as much is human nature, because that is what markets are about. To demonstrate these eternal truths, we will draw on the ancient mythology in a way you never learnt at school.

It is part of the money myth that as we invest on the stock market, we listen to the reassuring noise of our stockbroker, perhaps lulled into complacency as we enter investor territory, with predators in our path. Let's not heap all the blame on the City. We find that many of our fellow investors are victims of their own folly and greed.

This book helps you to see the perils ahead by comparing financial markets with the dark underworld portrayed by Virgil, the ancient Roman poet, in his masterpiece *The Aeneid*. The descent of Aeneas into these realms, with the Sibyl as his guide, is a powerful analogy for the investor's journey, guided by his or her broker.

Forecasts, risks and confidence tricks

The Sibyl could foretell the future and, as such, is a mythical forerunner of today's stock market analyst. In financial markets, prediction can become a self-fulfilling prophecy. Investors rush to put their money where they are told it is best invested.

We are too prone to believe what we want to believe, and stock market analysts exploit this weakness in human nature, much as did the oracles of ancient Greece. As an investor, by understanding the limitations of analysts' research and forecasts, including the same ambiguities and salesmanship the ancient oracles used, you can perhaps use the research to your advantage.

The old fables and other experience from the ancient world enable us to understand not just forecasting but business risk. Today's researchers into systemic risk fumble and bluster, much as did the pre-Socratic philosophers in their theories about the universe. To understand the vast potential for interconnected risk, without being able to quantify it, is as far as we have been able to get in two and a half thousand years.

The investment pitfalls echo the ancient warnings no less. As retail investors, we can fall victim to the investment banks, which fail to give us priority in their share issues. The institutions rape some of us, much as Pluto, god of the underworld, whisked away Persephone from her flower-picking into the bowels of the earth.

Still worse, we may fall prey to the boiler rooms, which, like Circe, the witch in Homer's *The Odyssey*, can lure us with sweet blandishments. Just as Circe turned her guests into pigs, the boiler rooms ruin many investors. After falling victim to these outfits at least, it is usually too late to retrieve your money. If the lessons of Circe, as presented in this book, do not stop you falling victim to the share sharks, perhaps nothing will.

More integrated into the City than the boiler rooms are the banks, and they immediately use money deposited on the assumption they will never have to repay it all at once. This is comparable with the black arts of Medea, the sorceress of ancient Greek mythology, who enjoys the support of Helios, an immortal god who happens to be her grandfather. In comparison, our banking system is government-backed, with all the moral hazard it has engendered.

Perpetual self-invention

Most importantly of all, the City operates in cycles, which enable it to reinvent itself. Companies merge, investment banks change structures, and players with a shoddy reputation wipe the slate clean. This is a version of the metempsychosis that Greek philosophers such as Pythagoras promoted. On the grander scale, Plato's myth of Er tells of how human sinners pay any due penitence in an afterlife and will then be reborn, starting afresh with a new identity. So it is with the City.

The developments are invisible to outsiders, except through shaded representations, packaged by PR experts. The media distribute the message, and rarely question it. Plato's famous myth of the cave, in which prisoners are chained, seeing only shadows of reality, describes most investors.

The secrets of the financial markets, hidden as they are, are as old as time. On this basis, old fables are all we really need to crack them. Even as technology advances and the City's trading power multiplies, human nature stays the same. As an investor, you cannot hope to change what goes on behind the scenes, but in so far as this book gives you extra perspectives and knowledge and stimulates your vision, you can ask the right questions and invest with know how.

> Even as technology advances and the City's trading power multiplies, human nature stays the same.

If your stockbroker recommends a bargain stock based on a low price–earnings ratio, your first right approach can be as simple as querying why the stock has been overlooked by the market. When banks have to raise more capital, you should at least assess the impact on the sector and its share prices.

You can still profit from the conventional approach to investing, and this book gives you the tools as one part of the investing framework it offers, but, as the old wisdom demonstrates, you need to be wily. Not to put too fine a point on it, the old values, from numerical analysis to trust in brokers and financial experts, and much of the new investing wisdom, and the regulatory trust in efficient markets, have proved untrustworthy, unless backed by the deeper understanding.

Timeless investment wisdom

We can love financial markets, flaws and all. The City propaganda experts continue to wheedle and charm others, including their own kind, but let us give them their due. It is they who have brought back the City from the brink of collapse, making their big talk a reality. They have much in common with the politicians who are their close collaborators.

It is in our interests that the City stays a world leader in financial markets. Rest assured that the City, government and regulators will ensure, as far as they can, that the game continues. They use such techniques of rhetoric and persuasion that the sophists of ancient Greece peddled to the rich because these have never been bettered.

By illuminating such practices, and the markets in which they flourish, *The Money Myth* offers you classic investment guidance. You cannot stop the pervasiveness of the money myth, but you can join the few investors who see through it. Luck happens here and there, but, if you are to take steady profits from financial markets, and some deserved, more spectacular gains, you need the understanding this book gives you.

That's enough of our enjoyable preamble. Together we are launching on a journey into the darkest corners of the City and financial markets to discover what is really going on and how to invest successfully.

Give this book a little of your time, and I promise you the truths of eternity that you may apply to your investing. And if, in reading the following pages, we find that the money myth evaporates, let us find strength from our discomfort. We are replacing it with timeless investment wisdom.

PART ONE

The investor's journey

1

The rational stock market investor

Introduction

To win in the stock market over the medium to long term is largely about self-discipline and money management.

In this chapter, we will look at how you should go about investing successfully in today's turbulent markets. With a sound investing system and some patience, you can make money even amidst significant share price volatility.

We are looking here at investing. For a focus on short-term trading, see Part Two.

Irrational forces

Irrational forces sweep through stock markets. Stock markets, or individual shares, tend to soar on good news and plummet on bad, overreacting before they revert to equilibrium. This process goes on continually.

In this way, markets reflect the hopes and fears of investors. In the short term, the share prices are thus driven by sentiment. If a telecoms company in difficulty becomes a takeover target, or is rumoured to be, the share price may soar, falling back if the talk is scotched.

Particularly in volatile market conditions, the stock market is not for the faint-hearted. It is not right for everyone.

Be prepared

If you are to invest in the stock market, you should first have enough cash to pay for your home, life insurance, your home and contents insurance, to pay off your credit cards, and for emergencies.

Beyond this, you need cash that you can leave in the markets. In Book 6 of Virgil's epic poem *The Aeneid*, the Sibyl, a priestess, tells Aeneas to pluck a golden branch before he enters the underworld as an offering to its queen. This is the prerequisite. So in the stock market, without enough money to have a balanced portfolio and to cushion your losses, and to leave your investments untouched for a while, you are at a major disadvantage.

You need enough money to spread eventually across a portfolio of at least several shares, and, for that matter, other investments. If you cannot afford to broaden your exposure in this way and build a portfolio, you should in most cases avoid investing directly in the stock market. You would be better off investing in an investment fund as a way to spread your risk, even if the amount you had put up small.

> If you cannot afford to broaden your exposure, you should avoid investing directly in the stock market.

Your investment portfolio

Your portfolio should be diversified, which means that you avoid putting your eggs in one basket. You should hold non-correlated assets; if one investment goes down, another should rise. This process reduces potential losses but also the gains.

As part of the process, you should split your investments across asset classes, with some money in riskier investments, commodities and shares, and, at the cautious end of the scale, some in government bonds and cash. You may also invest in corporate bonds, slightly riskier than the government type, and in property assets.

As a rough guide, investors should hold the equivalent of their own age as a percentage of their investment in bonds, so a 25-year-old will have a quarter of his portfolio in bonds, but a 60-year-old 60 per cent. The rest of the portfolio could contain equities and other investments.

Within each asset class, you should similarly have diversification. In shares, for example, you might hold a mix of solid blue-chip stocks, including defensive stocks such as pharmaceuticals, and some risky stocks, such as in the gambling sector, and some cyclical stocks, which are correlated to the business cycle, such as in mining or house-building.

In addition, you should have some geographical diversification across the entire portfolio. In shares, this could mean having US, European and perhaps emerging market stocks as well as some from the UK.

Successful diversification is all about balance. If you invest a lot in a few stocks without diversifying your portfolio, it can pay off if you get it right, but if you get it wrong, it can be a disaster. At the other extreme, research shows that there is a saturation point. Once you spread your risk over more than about 10–12 stocks, the extra diversification does not provide further risk-spreading benefits.

Your stockbroker

Your choice of stockbroker, and constantly reviewing that choice, are part of your investment strategy. Your transaction costs, which vary across brokers, are one factor that will have an impact on the profitability of your investment strategy.

Even more significantly, the stockbroker you choose will affect how far you must rely on your own resources, for which some investors are better equipped than others. Clearly, if you rely on your stockbroker's advice, it needs to be good and tailored to your needs. Let us look at the stockbroker options.

Discretionary

The discretionary stockbroker makes decisions on your behalf. To use such a firm is an option available only to those with significant sums invested, and the service can sometimes be outrageously incompetent, particularly in a bear market. Many a person sufficiently wealthy to use such a firm ends up losing out to such an extent that his or her reduced wealth is no longer sufficient for such a service. I urge you to keep a close eye on the broker's decisions. Do not hesitate to ask questions or intervene.

Such involvement, I know, goes against the whole purpose of using a discretionary broker, which is to leave your affairs in the firm's hands. The active approach is better, however, than losing a great deal of money with a firm that, you find out too late, could not care less about safeguarding its clients' money.

Execution only

Execution-only stockbrokers are readily available to investors. The usual way to access their services is through their web sites. From such a broker, you will receive no advice and so will pay much lower charges than to a traditional private client broker.

If you are able to make your own investment decisions entirely, without anybody to blame or to hold your hand if things go wrong, this could be a good deal, but you need to choose the firm carefully. The cheapest are not all the best.

Most of the execution-only brokers are manned by only a skeleton staff, but some have more reliable telephone access than others. The web sites vary in sophistication. The speed of transactions can vary. The very cheapest services may bundle transactions and trade them at specific times in the day, meaning that the price could move against you in the meantime.

Many online brokers offer not just stock market trading but other financial services, ranging from pensions to investment funds and contracts for difference.

Advisory

Some investors should not dream of getting involved in the stock market without access to an advisory broker, costly as it can be. It is as in *The Aeneid*, where Aeneas uses the Sibyl as his consultant as he enters the underworld, and would be lost without this informed assistance.

Make sure that you fully understand the risk involved in buying and selling shares.

Your stockbroker should make sure that you fully understand the risk involved in buying and selling shares, and how you can position yourself best in the market in relation to your risk profile. The Sibyl warns Aeneas that it is easy to enter the underworld, but hard to leave it. The same can be true of the stock market, where collapsing prices can make you feel locked into your portfolio because it might be impossible to liquidate it at a price reflecting value.

The advisory stockbroker is not, like the Sybil, divinely inspired and unerringly accurate in foreseeing the future. Market talk, however, is valuable, and brokers are in the market, with access to gossip, analysis and sentiment that they can pass on to you.

At the same time, any stockbrokers who ply their trade successfully have their stock of insights and information that provide a basis for trading stocks. This is the most impressive part of the expertise the broker displays, and, at the very least, it can trigger ideas or reactions.

Not all stockbrokers are equally proficient in this area, but even the most incompetent or stupid advisory stockbrokers will be able to steer you gently past the most obvious horrors lurking in the markets for the unwary or inexperienced investors. They can protect you from losing all your money due to beginners' mistakes. On a worst case scenario, they are somebody whom you can blame if they give you poor advice. This adds to the case for using an advisory stockbroker.

Even with your hand held, you will find many unknowns in the stock market. Things are rarely what they seem. Your stockbroker cannot know all that is going on, but, if he or she is any good, can assess what might be and when it is best to buy, or to run and hide.

The will to provide the best service is not always there. Some advisory stockbrokers, it has to be said, are not over concerned what stocks they trade or whether they make clients money. Their main aim is to generate commission for themselves.

The half-commission advisory stockbrokers in particular need watching. These are individuals working for an authorised stockbroker but who have their own client books and may be self-employed. They will split commissions earned on trades with the employing broker. A significant number of such brokers are ex-boiler room salespeople (see Chapter 4).

On a practical level, any stockbroker knows how to put through a deal and advise you of the settlement procedures. In the vast majority of cases, the shares will be held electronically in a nominee account, and settlement is T+3, meaning that money is credited to your trading account or taken from your bank account within three days of placing the trade. For trades involving transfer of paper certificates, which involve extra administration, settlement is T+10.

The culture

There is one enormous script to which the stockbroker works, and it is written without much leeway for change. It is set in the tradition of the City and other financial markets, the output of the regulator, the attitude and mindsets of the institutional investors, and in the interests of those who influence City behaviour, including policymakers and politicians.

We cannot blame the stockbrokers for not deviating too far from this script. If they did, they would find themselves out of a job, even perhaps out of a career. The script is stabilised by an emphasis on appearance and reputation, particularly in international terms.

Like the Sibyl, who went into a trance before she took Aeneas into the underworld, the broker is mesmerised by the financial interests that gave him or her the chance to make a comparatively modest income from the markets.

In the underworld, the shade of Anchises singles out the future Augustus Caesar, the emperor who was supportive of Virgil's poem, describing him as a god. He compares him favourably to Hercules and Bacchus. Stalwarts in financial markets have no less admiration for the successful deal makers, fund managers and investors who have contributed to their reputation.

Rational investing

Once you hold shares, you have a piece of the underlying company, and, even when using an advisory stockbroker, you have to take responsibility for your investment decisions.

In the long term, share prices tend to reflect fundamental value. As an investor, you can invest for the medium to long term, ignoring market fluctuations. If this is your strategy, it is important to avoid knee-jerk reactions to market moves. Leave that to the day traders. They play a difficult game.

Many treat the long term as a series of short terms, buying and selling continuously. They sell a stock as it falls, and later, think about re-buying. This can make sense at the right price, but timing the markets in this way is notoriously difficult. Even if you call the share price movements correctly, you can run up a fortune in transaction costs.

Stay emotionally detached

The markets move on emotional buying and selling. In the short term, you can make money following the crowd. If you are investing for the longer term, however, you should consider the value of the stock, or its growth prospects.

In *The Aeneid*, Aeneas is guided by reason, in the form of pietas, against all irrational forces. He thus fulfils his goal and destiny of laying the foundations of Rome. You too as an investor must find in yourself the strength to overcome market irrationality. It is achievable, with experience and self-discipline.

Cut your losses and run your profits

One of the secrets of success is to cut your losses and run your profits. Investment is a numbers game. You cannot realistically expect every stock that you buy to be a success. Do not get so angry about losses that you prefer to hang onto the dud stocks in the forlorn hope of regaining profits. No less importantly, do not become so impatient to crystallise your paper profits that you sell winning stocks far too early.

To use a stop loss is an effective way of implementing this money management strategy. See Chapter 5, p. 54, for how this technique works. I recommend it there for short-term trading, but it also useful for investors.

To cut losses is easier said than done. The less experienced you are as an investor, the easier it is to fall in love with stocks, as Aeneas did with Dido for a period before he wrenched himself away from the doomed relationship. Stocks are only paper representing an investment. Your decision whether to stay invested should be based on whether, based on your time horizon, this is the best you can be doing with the money.

> **Stocks are only paper representing an investment.**

One of the biggest mistakes investors make is to hang on to losing stocks for too long, fuelled not just by familiarity and fondness but by human reluctance to admit an investing mistake and crystallise a loss.

Conquer the irrational

By leaving Dido and later killing the warrior Turnus, Aeneas defeats the symbolic forces of the irrational, and you should do the same in the stock market.

Do not overinvest or put more money on the stock market than you can afford. To use a credit card for investing or trading in the stock market when you do not have the hard cash is near madness. It can amount to taking risks with money you do not have, at an interest rate that is higher than you need to pay.

Be prepared for the unknown

Pockets of intransparency, including, but not confined to, dark pools (see Chapter 10), can create a cover for transactions large enough to move markets. Some parties illegally profit from prior knowledge of such transactions.

The regulators do not have the resources to address this problem as thoroughly as it needs. The lake at the entrance to Virgil's underworld has breath streaming from its black throat so deadly that no bird can fly over it, and dark pools can be similarly impenetrable.

At the same time, the investor should not fear every bit of bad news in markets. Many of the scare stories prove ephemeral or unreal. The good stockbroker can distinguish 'market noise' from anything more ominous. If it had not been for the Sibyl's warnings, Aeneas would have rushed at the empty shadows with his sword.

Your investing system

Know your fundamentals

Over the medium term, you will profit more often than not from investing in stocks that are good value on fundamentals. There are risks. You may extrapolate too much from the numbers because you do not know the full story. A company's revealed circumstances are always changing, and so are economic conditions. Even a few weeks can make a difference.

As a fundamental investor, your first step is to assess the financial status of a company in comparison with its peers, and the quickest way is through ratios. In Chapter 2, we will discuss the most important ratios, and how to calculate them. There are services such as Hemscott (www.hemscott.com) and ShareScope (www.sharescope.co.uk) that do the calculating for you.

As a rule of thumb, you should seek a five-year track record of steady growth in earnings per share, and in return on capital employed, a measure of management activity. You should ensure that cash flow is strong, irrespective of earnings. If the company's borrowings exceed 50 per cent of shareholders' funds, ask why.

Prospective ratios, based on analysts' consensus forecasts, are important because we invest for the future. The present or past ratios have the certainty of being based on reported figures, but are much less useful to you because they are historical.

Value investing

Value investing is about finding stocks where the price is low on fundamental value. Benjamin Graham, the stock analyst and guru who invented this concept in 1934, took the view that investment should be made only when the market value of shares was 40 per cent lower than the business value, the difference between the two being the 'margin of safety'.

Except in extreme bear markets, this is difficult to find today. Many experts are monitoring markets closely and will detect any value, which, once known, leads to buying from investors, so closing the value gap. If a blue-chip company seems significantly underpriced on fundamentals against its peers, be wary. Institutional investors will have shunned the stock for a reason.

As was true for Graham, it can be easier to make value investing work by investing in suitable small companies. It is this sector that the institutional investors are most likely to have overlooked. It is also, however, a highly risky sector and not worth investing in unless you take the trouble to acquire some specialist knowledge.

Small company investing is, indeed, more often a field for speculators, dangerous and exciting and pretty well guaranteed to lose you money if you invest in the field without specialist knowledge. On this basis, it is the very opposite of the value investing that Graham advocated. See the box below.

Investing in penny shares

In penny shares, the first rule is that you must select your own stocks. Take advice or follow tips if you must, but make your own buying and selling decisions. Be as informed as possible before you do so.

In these stocks, I prefer to see *earnings*, although I can make an exception if the growth story is strong. If the stock trades at a substantial discount to net asset value, this gives it a defensive backbone and makes the company an attractive take-over target. Corporate borrowings should ideally be low. If the management has a good track record, this is a better bet than if it consists of budding entrepreneurs straight out of university.

Regardless of fundamentals, a penny stock needs a trigger to set the share price moving. In recovery stocks, the turning point is often when new management moves into the underlying company, and starts implementing changes. My advice is to avoid recovery shares unless there is a significant and confirmed catalyst for change. When in the underworld Aeneas meets the shade of Deiphobus, his body mangled and his face cruelly torn, it is too late to repair this damage.

In any penny shares, do not necessarily expect a dividend. Any young company with fire in its belly will instead reinvest earnings in the company to fund growth. Instead, concentrate on stocks that are likely to achieve a good capital gain.

Given the speculative nature of penny shares, diversification is particularly important and I advise you to invest only up to 15 per cent of your equity portfolio in this sector. Invest in several stocks rather than one, and you will not be hit so hard should one of the companies collapse.

In the penny share business, vested interests are at work. Watch for rigged promotions of dud stocks. The share price will soar, but only temporarily until the promoters see fit to sell out of their own large holdings acquired at a very low price.

It is safest to buy penny shares in listed companies. Avoid penny shares touted from abroad unless you really understand what you are buying. A listing on the US pink sheets market or the Vancouver exchange, for example, is no guarantee of respectability. Unproven high-tech or oil companies in particular can be suspect.

Growth investing

Growth investing is to invest in companies with growth prospects, even if the price is, or becomes, high against fundamentals. You will buy into a stock with a trigger story, perhaps a change in management or direction, and hope to profit from a rise in the share price as investors pile in.

The City most often recommends growth stocks to institutional investors, and stockbrokers encourage retail investors to jump on the same bandwagon. It can go well when markets are booming and there is a sense of euphoria.

The share prices of growth stocks are often far above fundamental value, and, when markets crash, so do these investments. If you invest in overpriced growth stocks, it is often something of a short-term trading situation, and you need to be ready to sell out quickly if the price begins to drop, just as everybody else is rushing for the exit.

> If you invest in overpriced growth stocks you need to be ready to sell out quickly if the price begins to drop.

Momentum investing

Momentum investing is about timing. It is not the same as growth investing, but there can be some overlap. Momentum investors aim to take advantage of upward or downward trends in the share price. The theory is that the stock price will continue to head in the same direction once it has started to move because of the momentum behind it – if upwards, driven by the presence of a large number of investors in the market who will buy a stock that is moving up.

The buying trigger may be a change in analysts' forecasts, or in relative market strength. Momentum addicts will continue to buy as long as everybody else does but will sell when the turnover slackens. The trick is to do the same.

A key component is volume of shares traded, which should be rising to provide depth to the momentum.

Copycat approach

If, as a value or growth investor, you follow the choices of a guru or other investors, you can sometimes do well, assuming you get in early enough. The copycat approach means experts have done all the work for you, but you should still conduct your own research to ensure that the stock seems sound, and that it is right for you. No two investors have exactly the same resources, time horizons and expectations. For example, a fund manager can afford to take a loss more easily than retail investors.

The way forward

Choosing the right stockbroker, running a diversified portfolio and selecting shares carefully are the basics of successful stock market investment. To run profits and cut losses are essential to maintaining your portfolio.

The current trend is towards more independent investing. To invest without advice is fine if you know what you are doing. Otherwise, it can lose you money.

A good advisory stockbroker can help you, just as the Sibyl helps Aeneas, but select the firm carefully as there are a lot of dubious operators. Whether advised or not, you must conduct research of your own, and not be afraid to ask awkward questions, whether of your broker or of the companies in which you are considering investing.

2

Magic numbers

Introduction

In this chapter we will assess the use of numbers and accounting in financial markets, and how that language can be misused. We will assess the role of analysts and other market professionals in the process.

The numbers game

Pythagoras and some of the other pre-Socratic philosophers had a mystical reverence for numbers. There was talk of a link between mathematics and music, or between numbers and the soul. In the same way, financial markets revere numbers, finding them to be of greater significance than mere figures. They attribute concrete value to ratios such as turnover, as well as comparability with other companies. They attribute to them a validity that sadly can prove misguided.

For the salespeople and propagandists of financial markets, numbers are the patter, the wand waved to distract the audience's attention while the sleight of hand goes on. The problem is about not just creative accounting, a phenomenon that the accounting authorities and the regulators, try as they may, cannot get rid of, but also the touching faith in the power of numbers.

The regulators have worked at eliminating creative accounting over the years, and the accounts have become much more transparent. Even so, two plus two does not always equal four under every accounting system used in the world today.

There is something that seems serious about firm numbers, just as, in the epics of Homer, it is a fixed number of oxen slaughtered that constitutes a solid sacrifice to the gods.

Fundamental analysts present their forecasts in numbers, typically discounted cash flows, which clothe wild ideas in quantifying language.

As one professional examination course on investment analysis teaches, forecasting is, in principle, a game. When I was studying for this qualification at one of the main training colleges, the lecturer taught us to think of a profit figure that sounds sensible for the company on which we were making forecasts and to slot in appropriate percentage growth or loss in business segments over the previous year, making sure that they balanced out to reach the forecast profit. Real analysis works in almost as crude a way, my lecturer told me on this course, and he was right.

In the manipulation of numbers, to shift gear from the human calculation to machines is not in itself a gateway to accuracy. Models operate on the basis of numbers in, numbers out.

Key numbers and ratios

The ratios used for investment are no more solid than the numbers that make them up. The ratios enable investors to assess, in broad terms, the message that the accounts give. Ratios can be based on past figures but the most useful are predictions based on forecast figures, and they can also be the most dangerous. Like the pronouncements of the oracles, they are unreliable. This does not matter if the limitations are understood. Let us take a look at some of the key numbers and ratios.

Cash flow

Cash flow is the life blood of a company. Earnings can be greater than cash flow because they can include items other than pure cash and, as the City saying has it, profit is a matter of opinion and cash is fact. To compare cash flow with earnings, the ideal approach is to compare the cash flow statement with the income statement in the annual report and accounts.

> **Profit is a matter of opinion and cash is fact.**

Discounted cash flow analysis translates future cash flows into a present value, and analysts manipulate the numbers mercilessly. This is the most relied on method of analysis used in the City.

Discount cash flow calculation

Discounted cash flow analysis translates future cash flows into a present value. It starts with the net operating cash flow, which is the company's earnings before interest and tax, deducting corporation tax paid and capital expenditure, but adding depreciation and amortisation, which do not represent movements in cash, and adding or subtracting the change in working capital. This can be calculated for future years, reducing its value to the present day by a discount rate, often the weighted-average cost of capital to the company, which includes equity and debt.

The cost of equity is the expected return on equity, most often measured by the Capital Asset Pricing Model. The CAPM finds the required rate of return on a stock by comparing its performance with the market. It expresses this return as equal to the risk-free rate of return plus the product of the equity risk premium and the stock's beta. The beta measures the sensitivity of a share price to movements in the general stock market.

The CAPM has the premise that the market does not reward investors for taking unsystematic (company-specific) risk because it can be eliminated through diversification. The model is theoretical and is based on various assumptions, including no taxes or transaction costs. Share buyers require a higher return than debt providers to compensate both for the investment risk, and for the fact that the company must give priority to debt repayment over paying dividends.

The cost of debt is more transparent. It is commonly estimated as the redemption yield on the company's bonds, and interest rates on loans and overdrafts.

To make an accurate forecasting scenario more likely, analysts may plot DCF models using different discount rates and different cash generation scenarios to present alternative valuations. It is, of course, a flexible tool. Users need only to change one or two of the parameters, and this will change the outcome.

Earnings per share

You need to understand the earnings per share, as it is the ratio that City professionals follow most widely. In addition, it is part of the price–earnings ratio (see below). The EPS is the company's profits after tax divided by the number of shares in issue. Institutional investors look for an EPS that rises consistently every year to give the reassurance of constant growth.

In the past, creative accounting has enabled the numbers to be adjusted to create this impression. Nowadays under International Financial Reporting Standards, this is more difficult as the accounts, taken as a whole, are required to give you the full picture. However, where there is a will, there is a way. PR can distort the truth, whether by accentuating sales growth and ignoring profits, or by downplaying one-off payments.

P/E ratio

The price/earnings ratio shows how highly the market rates a company. It is useful when comparing a company against its peers, or the sector, or the market. The comparison is only valid, however, when the ratio is similarly calculated. A prospective P/E ratio must be compared with a prospective one, or the historic figure with a historic.

Let us look at the basic calculation. The ratio is the current share price, divided by the earnings per share in the most recent twelve-month period. It moves in the opposite direction to the yield (see below). If a stock has a P/E ratio higher than its peers, the market rates it highly. The shares may be overpriced but could shoot higher, based on demand exceeding supply. If the company, sector or market has a setback, the crowd euphoria can reverse and the share price could revert to a level closer to or below fundamental value.

If the P/E ratio is low, the market is not attaching much value to the stock's prospects. This is often for a good reason, but, in the case of a less widely followed stock, a low P/E ratio suggests the possibility of over-looked value. The ratio does not always exist. If a technology company, for instance, should have no earnings per share because it has not yet broken into profit, it has no P/E ratio. Other methods will then have to be used to value the shares, such as price-to-sales ratio.

In the case of small growth companies, a P/E ratio is more useful when considered in conjunction with profit growth. If a stock has a P/E ratio of 20 and is growing at 20 per cent a year, this may represent good value, but if the annual growth rate is only 5 per cent, it could look expensive. The P/E/growth ratio, known as the PEG ratio, is the P/E ratio divided by earnings growth and has been widely used in this sector.

EBITDA

For capital-intensive companies with large borrowings, as in telecommunications, a useful figure is earnings before interest, tax, depreciation and amortisation. In this type of company, EBITDA arguably presents a more realistic valuation than conventional earnings, which are calculated after interest and tax.

However, EBITDA is not recognised by accountants. Because it excludes tax, there is an obstacle in comparing stocks based on this valuation method across international borders when the respective countries' tax regimes differ, although this also avoids a distorting factor in the comparisons.

Analysts value companies using the enterprise multiple, which is enterprise value, consisting of a company's market capitalisation less cash plus debt, divided by EBITDA. The EV/EBITDA ratio takes debt and cash into account, which the P/E ratio does not, and it is used to filter out attractive takeover candidates, showing how much debt the acquirer would have to take on. As in the P/E ratio, the lower the enterprise value, the better the value of the company. The ratio tends to be higher in high-growth industries, and comparisons should be made against the sector.

Relative strength

If a stock has relative strength, this means that it has outperformed against its sector or the market. You can calculate relative strength manually, although software will produce a line for you. Take the share price, and divide it daily or weekly by the FT All-Share index. The result is the stock's relative strength. Plot this on your chart against price and volume.

If everything is right about the stock, good relative strength is a confirming signal that you should buy. On precedent, shares that have outperformed the market consistently over the last month and year often continue to outperform, and the reverse is also true.

Changes in relative strength can lead to obvious trading opportunities, including taking a short position, perhaps through contracts for difference (see Chapter 6), to take advantage of a perceived likely decline in the share price. If relative strength falters, the share price is likely to decline.

Return on capital employed

The return on capital employed evaluates how effectively the company's capital is used to generate a return. This is a measure of management performance. It is calculated as profit before interest and tax, divided by year-end assets less liabilities, expressed as a percentage. If the company's ROCE is higher than in peer companies and rises steadily every year, analysts will see it as a favourable factor in their valuations.

Share price/net asset value

To value property companies, investment trusts or composite insurers, the share price/net asset value per share is in common use. This is the company's total assets less its liabilities, debentures and loan stocks, divided by the number of shares in issue.

The yield

From an income perspective, investors should focus carefully on the yield, which is the dividend divided by the share price, multiplied by 100. The higher the yield, the higher are the income payments to investors as a proportion of the current share price. Some sectors such as utilities are high-yielding, but growth companies typically have a low yield.

Dividend cover

Dividend cover says how easily a company can pay a dividend from profits. The figure is made up of earnings per share divided by dividends per share. The ratio applies only to those stocks that pay dividends, which excludes some of the small-growth stocks.

> **A company in good financial health should be able to pay its dividend comfortably from current earnings.**

A company in good financial health should be able to pay its dividend, assuming it has one, comfortably from current earnings. If not, it may have to use its reserves to keep up the payments. As a rule of thumb, when dividend cover is less than one, there may be cause for concern.

Gearing

Gearing represents a company's level of borrowing, or the relationship between debt and equity in its capital structure. It is most commonly expressed in debt capital as a percentage of total capital funding (that is, of debt capital plus equity capital). The higher the gearing, the greater the risk.

Let us now take a look at the professionals at work who interpret and juggle with these numbers, and produce some of their own in their forecasts.

The professionals

Fundamental analysts

The City takes analysts' forecasts seriously because the process makes money from them. When something goes wrong, the fall guys will be the investors, and the firm will stand by the numbers it had provided. In the same way, the oracles of ancient Greece gave ambiguous prophecies that could be interpreted as right, no matter how events had turned out.

The majority of analysts, and the ones with which we are most concerned in this chapter, are fundamental analysts. This means that they base their share price and other market recommendations on the company's financial status, as well as on qualitative factors such as strategy, senior management experience and industry factors.

Analysts are informed by the companies on which they put out recommendations, and they tend to be influenced by their own investment banking departments, which may have, or hope to have, the companies as a client. Understandably, analysts provide far more 'buy' than 'sell' recommendations.

The damage is minimal as the analysis is aimed at institutional investors who understand how it is concocted. Changes in recommendations by leading analysts are picked up by the news wires and will move the share price of a listed company, perhaps by a few per cent. Reporters cover analysts' recommendations on stocks in their news stories. There are many analysts, particularly the less distinguished ones, who will talk to the press because the resulting publicity brings business to their firms.

An analyst follows a sector in which he or she specialises, watching closely developments in perhaps five or six companies. The task of fore-casting adds mystique to the otherwise quite routine observing role. Brash salesmanship is now part of the analysts' role and imbues it with further authority.

In the final analysis, investors seek, and need to believe, in an intui-tive quality in the analyst's forecasts. If this exists, it is encapsulated in the analyst's understanding reached from liaison with companies, corpo-rate finance, clients, salespeople and others in the market, and something besides. It is the harnessing of experience to make leaps in judgement, using flair. It is the grasp of a person who, young as he or she typically is, spends his waking hours in the market, coupled with some stubborn inde-pendence of thinking, regardless of commercial pressures from his or her employer. Analysts are often wrong in their forecasts, but they stand more of a chance than others.

Technical analysis

Technical analysis can encourage buying at ever higher prices, regardless of fundamental value. It is, in my view, of more value to traders than to inves-tors, and so we cover it in Part Two. See Chapters 7 and 8.

Credit rating agencies

The credit rating agencies have a stranglehold on companies' abilities to borrow, or to meet some regulatory requirements for solvency purposes. Their job is to rate the ability of bond issuers, corporate or government, to service the debt. Their ratings really matter. The higher the rating, the better the credit terms a borrower will receive.

The process has proved less than clean. When highly rated structured products proved, in reality, toxic, a major factor in the 2007–09 financial crisis, the agencies' claim to independence of their ratings was exposed as a whitewash.

The agencies are paid by those that they rate, and this turned out to have wielded some influence. The conflict of interest became the main focus of reform discussions, and the European Commission has proposed to regulate the rating agencies.

The agencies remain as powerful as they ever were. It is a measure of the industry's continued importance that global panic arose in August 2011 when Standard & Poor's, one of the largest agencies, lowered its long-term sovereign credit rating on the United States from its highest AAA rating to AA+.

Strategists and economists

The numbers in statistics are no more reliable than those in the financial statements of companies. The strategists and economists, who focus on trends in inflation, interest rates and currency movements, understand that statistics are approximate. As in investment ratios such as EPS, a one-off figure could be a temporary blip. What counts is the trend. For example, a rising trend in Gross Domestic Product in a strong economy gives rise to inflation fears, but it may be only if it rises more than 3 per cent in each of four quarters in succession that the Bank of England would raise interest rates to restrain it.

The way forward

Just as the ancient Greeks consulted more than one oracle to obtain a consensus forecast, sophisticated investors view several analysts' forecasts. The ratios are constantly changing, and each presents a picture from one particular perspective. In addition, they can be calculated differently, and on different forecast numbers. They could be based on a consensus forecast or, alternatively, on the forecast of an individual analyst, which could differ from another's, although often not by much.

What is probably more important is to obtain an understanding of the thinking behind the forecasts, which is at least largely based on what the company told all the analysts at once, but may have some unique insights.

Obtain an understanding of the thinking behind the forecasts.

The numbers may have errors, or, in a long tradition, may be used for subterfuge. In *Prometheus Bound*, a play attributed to ancient Greek playwright Aeschylus, Prometheus, the Titan, explains that he is chained to a rock at the world's edge as punishment for, among other things, inventing for mankind, numbers, which he describes as chief of the stratagems.

Numbers may of course be used legitimately. Whichever way, they are the language of business and, as a market observer and investor, you must have respect for their power.

3

Safe havens

Introduction

It is a truism of investment that there are no absolutely safe places to keep your money. Even cash, after all, is exposed to erosion from inflation.

With that proviso, we can look to the best 'safe havens' available for your money in times of market turbulence.

Defensive stocks

Defensive stocks are not exactly a 'safe haven', but they are likely to prove more resilient than most other stocks in volatile or falling markets. Investing in such stocks is not about taking huge risks to make fast money. It is rather about parking your money in a resilient stock, hoping it will do well or at least stay above water in uncertain times. The price to pay is that, over the long term, the reduced risk can mean a reduced reward.

The defensive stocks such as utilities or pharmaceutical companies provide stable earnings and a good, sustainable dividend whether the broad stock market is up or down. They have strong balance sheets, and are non-cyclical, which means they are supposed not to be hit too hard by an economic downturn.

They can fall in value, and suffer unexpectedly, as did stocks of some transport companies when train seats were lost in the recession. Well-selected defensive stocks, however, can do well if you get the timing right as an investor, and are resilient if you don't. In our dangerous equity markets, it is about as close as you get to having your cake and eating it.

One fund manager with a big reputation who has stayed committed to favourite defensive stocks is Neil Woodford, manager of the investment funds Invesco Perpetual Income and Invesco Perpetual High Income. He has retained a loyal following even in periods when such stocks underperformed and other fund managers dismissed them as too expensive.

Of the most reliable defensive stocks, assuming you can get them at a reasonable price, pharmaceutical companies such as GlaxoSmithKline, a Woodford favourite, generate good cash flow and dividends. Companies in this sector can put a lot of time and money into developing new products, with uncertain results. They can bypass some of this process by acquiring other companies.

Tobacco companies such as Imperial Tobacco or British American Tobacco are defensive stocks that usually have a reliable market for their products in or out of a recession, particularly in emerging markets. Drinks companies such as Diageo do not suffer unduly from fluctuations in broad economic conditions. Utility companies such as water, electricity or gas, have some appeal because of their cash flows, but their return on equity can be hampered by regulation.

Investing in defensive stocks should be part of a broader strategy.

Investing in defensive stocks should be part of a broader strategy. You should, from a risk perspective, have a balance of equities in your portfolio, as well as other investments.

Looking beyond shares in this way, your investment portfolio should include bonds, a more cautious form of investment than equities, and widely viewed as a 'safe haven'.

Bonds

The widely publicised debt problems in euro countries are one symptom that government bonds in developed countries are not as secure as they were. In Europe, the quality of government bonds varies greatly, from junk status, as in Portugal, to the highest credit ratings, as in the United Kingdom, where this form of security remains an excellent defensive investment.

Index-linked bonds pay a coupon and make a capital redemption adjusted for inflation, and are for risk averse investors. However, bonds tend to move in the opposite direction to interest rates and this can mean risk. If you sell out of long-dated bonds before maturity, you could incur a loss.

Corporate bonds are riskier than government issues, and, of these, high-yield or junk bonds are the most likely to fail. They have, however, attracted investor interest in volatile markets due to their high returns combined with the bond status. In some cases, this is misguided because these bonds are not the 'safe haven' that investors suppose. Careful selection can minimise, but by no means eliminate, the debt exposure.

Since the crisis there has been a clear influx of money into emerging market bond funds, far more than equity funds. As the International Monetary Fund and other commentators have noted, emerging markets have now much less government debt than developed countries. The political risk remains, however, and things can go wrong. Emerging markets are, by nature, uncertain.

Gold and silver

Gold has boomed in times of market turbulence. The metal is money without counterparty risk, and its price is driven by supply and demand. Gold is perceived as likely to hold its value.

When the gold price is rising, the question is always how much this is a speculative bubble and how much it is based on solid demand from buyers.

The securest exposure to gold is to hold the metal itself. Buyers may store gold at home, or, more securely, but at a cost, in vaults.

Shares in mining companies are another way to gain exposure to gold, but such investment will not hedge against an overall fall in equities, as could a holding of the pure metal.

Silver is cheaper per ounce than gold, and the metal is much more volatile. It has the reputation of being gold's poor relation. This is not just another precious metal with 'safe haven' status but is also an industrial metal, exposed to the economics of production. Silver can profit from a recovering economy.

Speculators may want to buy gold or silver exchange traded funds as a means of exposure to the gold price. This is really a trading strategy, but it does offer exposure that, short term, or in limited sums, can be a cheaper and more flexible exposure to the metal than holding it physically, given storage costs and issues.

In this and other ways, exchange-traded funds can be part of a defensive strategy. For details of how this product works, see Chapter 14. Let us now look at a type of fund that aims to reduce risk through its structuring.

Absolute return funds

Absolute return funds aim to smooth out returns to above the level of a cash savings account, but do not always succeed. The fund takes positions in a variety of investments, and manipulates derivatives, with the aim of making money in falling as well as rising markets. Such funds aim at absolute returns every year, and the fund manager has a fairly free hand in how he achieves this.

In recent years, investors have rushed to invest in these funds to avoid market volatility, and the number of funds available has risen accordingly. The funds tend to underperform rising markets, but aim to offer some protection when markets fall. It does not always work.

Some of the absolute return funds market themselves as a potential core portfolio holding, but this can be dangerous. There is a strong argument for avoiding this type of investment.

It is partly that the fees on absolute return funds are high, although the extra part above the usual initial and annual fees comes only if the fund outperforms. A bigger problem is the product's complication.

The investment across asset classes is nothing special, but the use of sophisticated derivatives tools, including futures contracts, enables the fund manager to take short positions for hedging or trading purposes. In the right hands, this can work well, and some of these funds have put in an impressive performance, but too many have underperformed. Some have closed down or have been renamed and given another strategy.

If you want to invest in such funds, check out the track record of the fund manager, and the fund strategy. Some funds look only to beat cash funds, or the London interbank lending rate, by 2 or 3 per cent, but others have far more aggressive strategies, with the greater risk and reward potential involved.

Let us now turn to a type of product that can have still more appeal for the risk averse, if, as it has sometimes turned out, mainly because of how it is marketed.

Structured products

Structured products are often linked to stock market indices or a basket of shares. They have typically claimed to guarantee high levels of capital protection, which made them popular until the financial crisis exposed the fallacies in the case. Some such products were backed by Lehman Brothers, which went bust in September 2008, proving that the concept could be far riskier than its promoters had led people to believe.

The doubts have since multiplied, and mis-selling of complex structured products is a main focus of concern. A major contributor was the criticism around Keydata, a structured product provider put into administration in June 2009 by the Financial Services Authority after it sold products that it had incorrectly claimed qualified for ISA status. The firm sold policies, offered by two companies in Luxembourg, based on packages of second-hand life policies, designed to provide an income and return of capital. Following the firm's collapse there were concerns about cash flow, commissions paid out, and the ultimate security of the money invested.

The Keydata events led to a special £236 million levy made on fund managers to compensate those who lost money when Keydata collapsed, and there were subsequent concerns about how the FSA had conducted its investigation. Even so, there was some industry feeling that, next time a sales operation was headed for trouble, it would be helpful for others in the industry to volunteer to provide information about it to the regulator so it could take preventive action earlier.

Structured products are still on offer, and they are not all suspect. The complexity can remain, however, and nothing is risk free, no matter what is claimed.

> **Nothing is risk free, no matter what is claimed.**

If you invest in such products, it is important to check the claims very thoroughly, and to ensure that you are buying from a UK-based regulated firm, meaning that you would have access to the Financial Services Compensation Scheme, if something should go wrong. This is the UK's compensation fund of last resort for customers of authorised financial services firms, and it may pay compensation if a firm cannot pay claims against it.

Another product you may consider, although it has lost credibility in recent years, is the money market fund.

Money market funds

A money market fund invests in short-term securities such as government bonds or commercial paper, and has traditionally been seen as an alternative to bank or building society deposits, giving you a slightly higher return on preserved capital.

This 'safe haven' reputation for these vehicles suffered, and has since not recovered, since a fund 'broke the buck'. In September 2008, Reserve Primary Fund, a US money market fund, wrote off debt issued by Lehman Brothers, with its shares falling below $1 a share in net asset value, so inflicting losses on shareholders.

The event triggered panic selling. Similarly in January 2009, Standard Life's sterling money market fund suffered a loss through investment in asset-backed securities linked to the mortgage market.

Financial outflows from money market funds have continued since the 2007–09 financial crisis, and this could ultimately reduce their liquidity and drive investors away.

The way forward

So there you have it, a collection of 'safe haven' investments in which you can park your money in turbulent markets. They are far from perfect. In the underworld of Virgil's *The Aeneid*, Aeneas realises that even the friendlier shades, such as those of his former lover Dido and his father Anchises, are insubstantial, and the same is true of safety for investments. Some of the 'safe haven' assets are, however, often a safer home for your money in turbulent times than the alternatives.

4

Charm trap

Introduction

The dubious investment advisers appear plausible, until they have snatched your money. Even then, they keep up the façade. We will see in this chapter how you can recognise their sales techniques and protect yourself.

The boiler rooms are the worst offenders. They operate like Circe, the sorceress in Homer's epic *The Odyssey*, who entertains visitors, drugs them so they lose their memories, and turns them into pigs.

In this chapter, we will see how to detect and resist dubious investment promoters, just as Odysseus did Circe. We will consider how boiler rooms operate.

Tricks of salesmanship

One can buy shares in companies that give every promise of growth. The catalyst may be lucrative mergers, revolutions in management, and recovery from past misfortunes. Unfortunately, the promises may not materialise.

In reaction to changing events, large institutional investors buy or sell in such bulk that it can create market turmoil.

The resulting confusion is a convenient cover used by boiler rooms for the illiquidity or lack of performance of the stocks they have pushed. These outfits typically are based abroad but sell into the United

> **Boiler rooms typically are based abroad but sell into the United Kingdom.**

Kingdom, masquerading as *bona fide* stockbrokers. Some shady stockbrokers, financial spread betting firms, derivatives and commodities dealers, and financial advisers are playing a similar game on a smaller scale.

The more dubious firms take money from investors and give them little or nothing of value in return. Like Circe, they make victims of those whom they have appeared to serve. It is a formulaic procedure. If a pusher of penny shares – a nebulous concept referring to low priced shares – persuades investors to spend thousands, or tens of thousands, of pounds on shares in a small risky company, it may have misled them, selling a dubious stock to those who cannot afford the loss. The client may have been a willing victim, however, due to his or her greed.

The dealer may persuade the investor to acknowledge the risk, saying, 'Of course this is a high risk stock and there are no guarantees. You do understand that, don't you, although I would highly recommend the stock?' The client, if captured by the dealer's enthusiasm, may not listen to the words but say 'yes' and sign something to that effect.

If a major loss becomes apparent, the dealer may insist that a dud investment had been the client's choice and this may have been made clear in the sales process, which may have been tape-recorded. In the event of a dispute on what was said when there was no such recording, it may simply be the client's word against the dealer's.

Investors seeking redress will find it notoriously hard to prove that the salesperson used a sales pitch that misrepresented the truth. The dealers are canny. The technical words, processes and paperwork can be right, but what sways the investor is the broker's enthusiasm and persistence, the tone of voice on the phone.

When it comes to pinpointing blame, confusion arises because stock market failure can arise from gambling, bad luck and market conditions as well as fraud. It can be difficult for outsiders to prove skulduggery. The regulator has the job of making these calls and, in the UK, has managed to 'pick off' and penalise a few of the worst operators in the country, even when the paperwork has been right. This has, however, typically taken enormous time and resources, including working with police forces across Europe, and is limited. Regulatory action has had a few big successes, but has left most dubious operators selling into the UK from abroad untouched.

The firms typically target the vulnerable and the elderly, and there is usually little chance of them retrieving much of the money they have sent to unregulated boiler rooms in the belief they were investing it for high returns.

The Madoff fraud

There are occasional big catches but, due partly to inadequate resourcing and lack of cooperation and partly to incompetence and laziness, regulators across the globe have a poor record of detecting fraud. One such investor was Bernard Madoff. He sweet-talked investors into putting billions of dollars into his Ponzi scheme, which, true to its kind, paid out investors' returns with investors' own money.

Madoff is serving a 150-year sentence in a federal prison in Butner, North Carolina, but this does not return the money to investors that he swindled from them over the years. Madoff was a master of self-serving propaganda, and he had managed for years to dupe investors, others in his industry, and regulators with claims that he could generate consistent returns using options.

Many 'respectable' professionals had turned a blind eye to indicators that something was not right with Madoff's operation. Madoff was respected on Wall Street and his credibility facilitated the sales. It is image and reputation, more than truth, that enable financial markets to function.

In Madoff's case, whistle-blowing had failed to achieve decisive action. See Chapter 24, p. 219 for details.

Circe at large

It is important to understand that dubious firms, particularly when regulated in the United Kingdom, as some are, can be connected with the 'respectable' City of London. The penny share pushers serve the 'respectable' firms as a dustbin for stocks they do not want.

The regulated penny share dealing firm sometimes buys up small company stocks in bulk from sellers, which may be other City firms, and offloads them at an inflated price to investors. The price keeps rising entirely as a result of artificial demand generated by the outfit's sales team, which represents itself as dealers, or otherwise brokers or advisers.

Investors are entrapped by the firm without fully understanding the underlying process. Some investors in the know may acquire shares early at a low price in nominee names and be tipped off to sell before the bubble bursts, which happens when the sales team has punted out all the available stock. If a mis-selling scandal arises, the original off-loader of the stock, and some early large investors, may stay incognito.

The contagion spreads. Staff cross the bridges between the 'bad' City and 'good' City, and in between, in either direction. They may use false names when working for the boiler rooms and their real names at regulated firms. In personality, as in names, they may switch between Jekyll and Hyde.

There is a ghastly logic to it. A man who honed his craft in the boiler rooms of Marbella or Madrid will bring in business quickly to a respectable stockbroker. Men do it more often than women, but both are in the game. In this way, financial markets are bad at the same time as good. The mix perhaps reflects human nature. As the pre-Socratic philosopher Heraclitus says, doctors take fees from the sick, producing good and illness at the same time.

This can provide a loophole for fraudsters, and uncertainty where the dividing line comes. If an investment bank is taken over, changes its name and reinvents itself, is it the same bank? As Heraclitus says, we step into the same river, and we don't step into it; we are and we are not.

Lessons in love

One of the absolute lessons of financial markets, and one that is never learnt, is not to fall in love with Circe. In *The Odyssey*, she is one mother of sweet words to her targeted victims before she takes her horrific actions.

When Circe turns her human guests into swine, who retain the minds of humans, it is an ultimate humiliation. In the same position are investors who have been persuaded into dud shares and cannot sell them because they are illiquid or worthless.

Few investors have advisers as savvy as Hermes, winged messenger of the gods, who instructs Odysseus on how to get the better of Circe. Heed, however, this chapter's winged advice.

Salesperson is king

The markets are essentially about selling, and the interests of the customer never have priority.

This is Circe in action, and there are times when she is all too obvious. Retail investors who prove willing to deal with the bottom end of the financial markets – the boiler rooms, the crooked fund managers, the advance fee fraudsters, the sellers of dubious modern art and similar – are going to lose out.

The dubious firms are inexorable. If one is closed down, another starts up, perhaps in another jurisdiction, using a new name sounding very like a respectable firm. They are like the Lernaean Hydra, a serpent-like water creature with many heads. When one head is severed, two more grow.

> Dubious firms are like the Lernaean Hydra, when one head is severed, two more grow.

If clients pay money to such a firm, they will usually never see it again. It is important not to throw good money after the bad. This is easier said than done.

Occasionally, the dubious dealer will show a client a small profit with the aim of lulling them into investing more. Even then, the paper profit will never involve cashing in the investment.

The boiler room proposition

The boiler rooms sell shares in companies that typically exist only in formation, if at all. Salespeople typically hype up the company's prospects, take investors' money and run. The outfit may operate from a concealed office in, for example Marbella, and give targeted clients the telephone number of a switching office, perhaps in Paris, so giving the superficial impression that the operation is based there.

The salespeople have 'sucker lists' of targeted victims, often taken from share registers, or who have previously bought from the boiler rooms. Many boiler rooms may use the same list simultaneously. As the Financial Services Authority found in a 2005–06 survey, boiler rooms tend to prey on older people.

Investors have been deterred by regulatory warnings from sending money overseas to the boiler rooms. They are up against new tactics instead. They are sometimes now asked to transfer money to UK bank accounts. It is a boiler room ploy aimed at reassuring them. When the UK bank account reaches a certain balance, the crooks shift the money overseas.

Black-listed

The FSA now publishes on its web site a list of unauthorised firms. The outfits on this famous but never up-to-date black-list have a knack of cashing in on fashionable investment crazes.

At the time of writing, one outfit is tapping into a craze for gold as a safe haven in the market turmoil. The firm presents visitors to its web site with a popup window asking them for their full name, email and telephone number. Circe likes to know about her guests.

The site claims to be pioneering the sale of gold bullion through the network marketing industry. The gold bullion pictured glimmers against a pure white background. The web sites of all dubious investment firms are bold and simple in their presentation style as well as in their claims, a giveaway sign of potential fraud.

Another boiler room on the FSA's black-list offers carbon credits sales operations to UK private investors. The web site, with a green-coloured theme, is full of talk about the risks of climate change, and operates from a serviced office in a City location.

Some boiler rooms promote land banking schemes. This is the plausible scenario where a firm buys a field that does not yet have planning permission, splits it into plots and sells the land to investors on the basis that it might get planning permission. Often, this hope is ill-founded and the scheme is a fraud. In recent years, the FSA has dealt with 130 such schemes, and has 40 on its books, the current crop being more criminal and aggressive in nature.

A favourite trick of the boiler rooms is to hijack the identity of an FSA-registered firm, using the same or a similar name. They can then capitalise on the reputation of the real firm. Many such firms are at this game even as you read this.

Recovery rooms

When the boiler rooms have stolen investors' money, they do not stop there. There comes a point when the punters will not part with more money. This is where the recovery room comes in to fleece them further.

The recovery room, typically set up by boiler rooms, contacts victims of a boiler room scam, often when the firm has closed down or stopped trading, offering to recover their money. The victim pays an upfront fee for the 'service' and probably hears from the recovery room again only if it is trying to extract further fees.

Keeping Circe beautiful

When criminals make money fraudulently or illegally in any part of the world, the next step is to legitimise it, or launder it through the global financial system, so that the dirty money becomes clean.

Outside conventional banking, some launderers may use the *hawala* system, where, for example, a person pays dollars in the United States to a broker, who informs his or her partner in another country, who makes an equivalent payment in the local currency. No physical transfer of funds will have taken place, and the broker and its partner will settle amounts owed through fake invoices of, for example, the firm's ostensible import–export business.

All the money laundering efforts are spadework invested in keeping Circe looking beautiful. To achieve the process typically requires international coordination, from London and other big financial centres, and offshore and via the internet. The skilled launderer is permanently one step ahead of the authorities.

> The skilled launderer is permanently one step ahead of the authorities.

The FSA has not yet caught any money laundering, although it has penalised financial institutions with systems and controls failings.

The government's anti-fraud initiatives and new bribery legislation will technically make life harder for the crooked operators, but, so far, nothing has stood in their way. Lawyers have queried whether there is in the UK a real will to tackle money laundering and white-collar crime, as opposed to be seen to be doing it.

In the United States, a plea-bargain culture prevails. Parties to be convicted of money laundering or other crimes can reduce their sentences if they give useful information to the authorities. This sets a standard that the UK's Serious Fraud Office seeks to follow. Things are moving in that direction, but for its investigators to have the resources of their counterparts across the Atlantic remains yet a dream.

The Bribery Act

The Bribery Act 2010, in force from 1 July 2011, has had enormous publicity impact. Many large firms, in financial services and other sectors, are running scared. The act, applicable to United Kingdom companies operating anywhere in the world, makes facilitation payments illegal.

Of the four offences under the Bribery Act, the general ones of paying and receiving bribes are not dissimilar to those under previous law. In addition, it is now an offence to bribe foreign officials. A controversial new offence is when a commercial organisation fails to prevent bribery. This puts the onus on companies to ensure they have adequate anti-corruption procedures.

The court will decide what procedures are adequate. Parties associated with a company may include its local agents, as used in some Middle East countries, and the pressure is on the company to conduct thorough due diligence.

Before implementation, industry lobbyists had a vested interest in delaying implementation of the act. They presented a case for it being so strict that it would make UK companies uncompetitive overseas. Lawyers have been keen to highlight the legal uncertainty and so win business. The media has printed countless articles raising concerns.

Transparency International, the anti-corruption organisation, has fought back, publishing refutations of any suggestion that the act is anti-competitive or makes unreasonable demands.

The way forward

There is, and always will be, a thin line between the legitimate and the shady, with many apparently respectable firms crossing the barrier. Financial markets are by the standards of other industries quite crooked, and once, as an investor, you realise this, you will be better equipped to protect yourself.

PART TWO

Trading to win

The disciplined share trader

Introduction

As a share trader from home, you can make or lose thousands of pounds within minutes. The more volatile the market, the bigger the rewards, and risks.

In this chapter we will examine some of the basic rules of share trading, which requires a more immediately reactive approach than investing (as covered in Part One).

Getting started

The debate on whether traders are born or made is not entirely resolved, but it is clear that you will need the right attitude to succeed. Trading is a business, and serious traders treat it that way.

To trade in shares or other financial instruments, you will ideally have a dedicated office, with computer terminals and telephone to hand. The cheapest and most convenient way is from home, although it can be lonely. You will need some capital to get started, but not a small fortune. You can trade in modest amounts, setting tight stop losses so you prevent the risk of initial losses extending into major ones.

As in every business, there are costs. Before you break into profit, you will need to cover dealing expenses, including the spread on shares. Another expense is stamp duty, which is a 0.5 per cent tax that the government levies every time that you buy shares, although not when you sell them.

You will pay a stockbroker's commission on the purchase or sale of stocks. The lower this is, the better, provided that the standard of service does not lapse. If you are a prolific trader, there are often discounted rates available. One UK online broker has even introduced a single annual fee for frequent traders, with no ceiling on the number of trades, which can be cost-effective after they have traded about eight times a week over the year.

Such frequency of trading, and more, is for the dedicated. Not everyone has the luxury of working full time as a trader. Some do it while working in other fields. I know of some stock market traders who use their work computers to access news, analysis, stock prices, charts and statistics. This is obviously easier if your job requires access to such information, as in the case of financial journalists or researchers or, with particular privileged access, City professionals.

> **Not everyone has the luxury of working full time as a trader.**

Of course, restrictions may be imposed for legal or other reasons by your employer or profession. Even if you are allowed to trade as an employee, be warned that if you have half an eye on your job and half on your trading activity, it can be all too easy not to do either properly. On the other hand, the balancing act can be managed in many cases and, if so, it is a way to trade without putting too high stakes on fast success, given you still have a regular income from your job.

Types of trading

If you have other major demands on your time in the day, such as for earning a living, you may want to avoid 'day trading' and go for a more time-flexible method, whether swing or position trading. You can operate in more than one of these categories and they can overlap.

As a day trader, you close out your position every day. This way, you can easily keep stock of your financial position. You will avoid the risk of holding shares overnight, but will also limit time for retrieving a position that has gone wrong.

As a swing trader, you hold shares for between two and five days, which gives you more, sometimes too much, flexibility. As a position trader you will hold shares for between one and two months, which makes it less important to watch the market minute by minute.

Develop a system

To trade successfully, you will need a system. This is the rock on which you will build your future profits.

Your system will be based on rules that all successful traders follow, but it can develop its own extra techniques and quirks. No two traders operate in exactly the same way. Your system should adjust to market conditions. It will reflect, for example, that in bull markets, you can trade long positions (for example, buying shares) more readily than in bear markets.

You must risk your capital only when the system allows it. The odds must be in your favour. Gambling may make a few fluke gains, but will ultimately fail.

If your first attempts at building a trading system fail, take heart because trial and error are part of the price to be paid. Work at refining your system or creating an alternative. Once you have a workable system up and running, stick with it. No system works on every trade, but the secret is to have one that succeeds for you significantly more often than not, enough to make a profit after all expenses.

Information flows

Trading is about following price movements, not value. In the short term, share prices do not reflect fundamentals although, in the long term, the story is very different. As a trader, you will find that trading on technical analysis and on news flow may be of much more use than fundamental analysis. You must, however, attend to analysts' forecasts and comments because these alone can move markets instantly.

In tracking charts, news and forecasts, be selective, however. Do not expose yourself to a 'noise' of information excess. Do not be too influenced by bulletin boards on financial web sites. The parties posting messages often have ulterior motives, and their gossip and reported rumours, very possibly fabricated, may have temporary influence, or none.

You should, however, watch directors' dealings, available from some online news and data services. If a director buys shares in their own company for more than their annual salary, this can be a positive sign. Watch particularly in the two months before a listed, or Alternative Investment

Market-quoted, company releases its results, as this is the directors' last chance to buy or sell shares before they enter the close period when they are barred from it.

Keep an eye on macro-economic forecasts. If the reality turns out different, the stock market will overreact, at which point, before it corrects itself, you will have an excellent trading opening.

Surprises around interest rate changes are one source of such an opportunity. Interest rates are a macro-economic weapon. The Bank of England can raise them to combat inflation, but this is *detrimental* to the stock market, because the return on shares compared with on bonds will fall, and companies will find borrowing more expensive. In addition, a company's future cash flows will be discounted at a higher rate, and so seem less favourable.

Conversely, a reduction in interest rates, like a decline in the value of a country's currency, is, in theory, good for the stock market. Other factors may, however, prevail.

Macro-economic analysis aside, your trading positions will be affected, probably every day, by unexpected variables. Events such as terrorist attacks or war can create extreme uncertainty, which the market punishes more than anything.

Money management

Not least because of all these uncertainties, you cannot expect every trade to be successful. Speculators who hope for this are precisely those who hold on to a losing trade for too long. If you get it right four times out of ten, but run your profits and cut your losses quickly, you will make money. You will increase your chances of success by only trading positions where the rewards can be high in relation to your risks, perhaps three times the potential loss.

You can get rich by repeating this formula *ad infinitum*, assuming that you have the right trading system. This is about money management.

Let us get more specific. If you are cautious, you could commit 10 per cent of your savings as trading capital, which should overall be at least £10,000–£20,000, to each trade. On these figures, it means £1,000–£2,000 per trade, which is a very small amount, but enough for meaningful profits to mount up.

Experienced traders may have a much larger capital base of £100,000 plus, in which case they may commit only 1 to 2 per cent of this to every trade. Some have £500,000 plus in trading capital, and commit only 0.25 per cent to a trade.

Do not make the mistake of risking too much of your capital on a single trade. I have known traders risk 25 per cent of it at a time, and when they have taken a few big hits, they are wiped out.

> **Do not make the mistake of risking too much of your capital on a single trade.**

On share trading in the United Kingdom, unlike across the Atlantic, to buy on margin, as when trading derivatives, is almost never allowed. You will have to put up the full amount invested.

Buying shares

When you buy shares, the simplest way is to place a market order, meaning at the market price, which, as we have seen, you will pay in full. However, the market price at any given time is not within your control and may be too high to allow you a good trading profit later as the share price can change rapidly, and you may have paid too much.

The better tactic is to control what you pay by setting a limit order, as professional traders do. If it is not fulfilled at the price that you have specified, it is cancelled.

You can use a broker that accepts your limit order and will cancel this only if it is not fulfilled on the day. Some brokers operate the less flexible fill-or-kill strategy, by which they execute your limit order immediately, at the price specified, or cancel it.

If you have access to Level 2 data, as provided through sophisticated investment software, you will be able to see orders ahead of yours in the queue with market makers, and so assess their impact on the share price before your deal is executed. Using this service makes placing a limit order less imperative. Be warned, however, that some orders in the queue are placed to mislead, and are withdrawn before they actually take place.

Selling shares

When you sell shares, you could also place a limit order, so specifying the lowest price that you will accept for your shares.

I advise against this, particularly in a fast-moving market. I have known traders place one sell limit order after another, and none goes through because the share price keeps spiralling downwards.

Instead, place a market order to sell. Your share sale will be carried out immediately, even if the market price is lower than you would like. You can then use the proceeds for a more profitable trade.

Stop loss

Unless you have extraordinary self-discipline as a trader, you will find that the easiest way to cut your losses is by using a stop loss. It is useful also for medium- to long-term investing, for which see Chapter 1. Set your stop loss *before* you enter your trade. If the stock declines below your cut-off point, sell automatically. Taking a small loss this way is not too painful.

If you use a *standard* stop loss, this is set at a percentage below the price that you paid for the stock. You are usually better off using a *trailing* stop loss, which is established against the previous day's (or more recent) closing price.

I suggest that you set the stop loss percentage at 15 or 20 per cent for medium-sized to large stocks. If it is less, it will require you to sell out on temporary dips. If you are trading small stocks, these tend to be volatile, and I favour a 30 or 40 per cent stop loss.

Some traders set two trailing stop losses. If the stock hits the first stop, this serves as a warning. At this point, you may choose to sell half your shares. At the second stop, the system will require you to liquidate your holding.

If you are finding that you are always using your stop losses, switch to buying Put options (see Chapter 6). This is an option contract giving the owner the right to sell a specified amount of an underlying security at a specified price within a specified time. I know of traders who have made this switch very profitably.

Run your profits

You should run your profits and so benefit from occasions when the share price soars beyond expectations. This compensates for losses at other times.

Unfortunately, most traders cannot easily do this. They have a set idea of what constitutes a normal profit and feel uncomfortable if their position overreaches this. You need to think flexibly.

Scalping

For those who hate running their profits too far, the technique of scalping often appeals. As a scalper, you will aim to snatch plenty of small profits rather than to ride a few large ones. You may be in and out of the same stock several times a day.

It is hard work, as you will need to do a lot of trades, and it is only rarely a full-time job. You will be trading in small sums, which limits the size of your gains, but also of your losses. If you are diligent, it can work well.

Pyramiding and averaging down

To pyramid means that you will keep buying more of a stock as it rises in value, although never as much as you did first time.

You will end up with a position that you have acquired piecemeal at various stages and prices. Pyramiding is a risky strategy, but it can be immensely profitable in a bull market.

Averaging down is to buy extra shares in a company than you paid earlier, reducing the average price paid. This can work well, but if a stock is declining in value, you are often better off selling out of it completely.

Trading rules of thumb

Set goals and keep records

As part of your system, set flexible trading goals. Have broad goals for the next three to five years, broken down into each individual year, month and day respectively.

Keep meticulous records of your trades and review them to assess your successes and mistakes. Also, keep a trading diary.

Keep meticulous records of your trades

When you have achieved some significant goals, reward yourself. If you fail, remember that this is part of the learning process, but you must take responsibility and learn from your mistakes. Tweak your system and adjust your goals as appropriate.

Avoid boredom trading

Never trade for the sake of it. Traders typically do 10 or 20 per cent of their trades because they are bored. As star fund manager Peter Lynch has advised, if you can't summarise why you should own a stock in four sentences, you probably should not own it.

Should you be having a bad trading run, take a break. Do the same after you have achieved success. In either case, obviously make sure that you have first closed out your trading positions.

Special techniques

Trading volatility

As a trader, you must recognise that volatility takes different forms, depending on market conditions. If the market trends up or down without a break for enough time for you to get in and out at a decent profit, you have ideal trading conditions. There is, however, another type of volatility when markets switch direction before the trader has time to ride the trend, and you should leave such a market alone.

In volatile markets, it can be a good idea to increase your stop loss so that you don't get stopped out quickly by the volatility. You need a tight trailing stop loss that follows gains closely.

Mergers and acquisitions

When a company is subject to rumours of a takeover or a merger, the prospect can give a fillip to the share price. If you get into the shares early and – just as importantly – out in time, you can secure a fast profit.

Likely takeover targets are asset-rich companies, those with plenty of cash, or under-performers. Look also for synergy between a takeover target and its potential acquirer, as this can be a compelling reason to proceed. A company's rationale for taking over another can be simply to compete more effectively against European rivals.

In most cases, takeover talk will come to nothing. But the share price of a potential target company rises on anticipation, and you can make a lot of money buying on the rumours. The trick is to sell out after the bubble has almost reached a peak, or has started subsiding, but before the share price has fallen back dramatically because traders holding the shares realised that the mooted deal would not happen and sold them.

You can make money out of trading shares in predatory companies, but it is a tougher game. Make sure that your chosen company has a broad acquisition strategy and does not focus only on a single deal. Its management should be experienced in merger and acquisition activity.

Hit and run – a dividend-based trading strategy

You can profit from companies about to release end of year results that will pay out a dividend of more than 5 per cent gross. You will trade the stock and receive the dividend without ever paying for your shares.

First, negotiate a 20-day trading period with your stockbroker. This is known as T+20 and it is easier to arrange if you already have a reliable trading track record.

Look for companies that are about to announce a final dividend and when it will be paid, as well as the ex-dividend date. Buy your shares at the latest on the announcement as the pending dividend means that the company's share price should rise. The movement, if you have bought the shares in time to catch it, will probably cover your broker's fees and stamp duty on your purchase.

The shares are likely to continue to rise on the strength of a pending large dividend, although less so as the XD date approaches. Because you bought the shares, you will qualify as a shareholder on the XD date, which means that you will receive the dividend.

Once the share price gain and the dividend have together surpassed the costs, creating a profit, it is your cue to sell. This may be on, or shortly after, the XD date.

In some cases, it is worthwhile paying for the shares in full so that you can hold them for a short period beyond the T+20 period.

Emerging markets

If you trade shares in emerging markets such as India, China, Brazil or Russia, the risks are high, but so are the potential rewards. The stakes can be similar if you buy these shares as a medium- to long-term investor. Emerging market shares, more than most, can rise or fall quickly, typically regardless of fundamentals.

> Emerging market shares, more than most, can rise or fall quickly.

I am keen on the Russian stock market, which is volatile, something that can work for or against you as a trader, depending on your approach. In recent years, the most popular way to invest in Russian equities has been to buy into the large oil companies. Oil is Russia's largest and most important industry, enabling the country to negotiate how far it will cooperate with requests for price and quota restrictions, with consequent geopolitical implications. The oil price affects oil futures and has a knock-on effect on broader financial markets.

Other emerging markets have some different specific features. There can be some discriminatory treatment of foreigners investing directly in the local market. If you plan to invest in Russian or other emerging markets shares, it is safest to choose a company with a listing in New York or London. To achieve such a listing, the company will have needed to have achieved certain standards of disclosure and accounting. Corporate governance may be far less than the company claims and there may be other whitewashing. The internationally listed shares are, however, less of a pig in a poke than those listed on a local emerging market, even in some cases when in the same company.

The way forward

Stock market trading requires more ongoing time and attention than long-term investing. You will be similarly competing against professionals.

The trend is for amateur day traders to proliferate in bull markets, and do well while shares continue to rise. Investment software companies benefit, as do trainers, stockbrokers, and parties renting out office space with trading facilities. When the market falters into either a correction or a bear trend, as it eventually will, many of the new traders fail to sell out in time to avoid huge losses.

Money management is, and always will be, the most important aspect of share trading. In volatile markets, and in crisis, as well as in a clear bull trend, there are plenty of opportunities for traders, in shares and in other instruments, but it is easy to be wiped out unless you practise rigorous money management. The implementation of stop losses will help you to preserve your gains and avoid ruinous losses. Work your system without panicking or succumbing to greed and you will last the course.

6

Bear market toolkit

Introduction

When used in the right way, derivatives, as general trading instruments based on an underlying asset, can be profitable, but I urge caution. I have seen many amateur traders lose money on them every time, typically as speculators. In bear markets, however, derivatives come into their own because of their flexibility, enabling you to profit from declining as well as rising markets.

The aim of this chapter is to provide you with a few derivatives strategies to keep up your sleeve for when market conditions become bearish, or very volatile.

First we will look at short selling and pairs trading, using contracts for difference. Then we will look at various hedging and defensive strategies using options. The variety of methods can serve as a bear market toolkit with proven value.

Derivatives in bear markets

Derivatives can be a way of making significant money quickly from declining or volatile markets, but also of losing it. They are geared, meaning that you stand to gain or lose much more than the cash you put up.

You will trade on margin, which is the cash you will have deposited with your dealer as a proportion of the sum you are trading. Your margin must cover any ongoing losses for as long as you hold the position open. The margin is typically between 10 and 25 per cent of the amount traded. The gains or losses on the margin deposited will be geared, and on this basis directly proportionate to your full position. If your position moves against you, your dealer will require you to add to your margin accordingly. To play it safe, you may close out a declining position before the need for such a top up arises.

You can trade derivatives most cost-effectively through a broker, but the easiest access, particularly for small traders, is through the spread betting firms. These outfits typically offer contracts for difference, and bets on options.

Spread betting firms

The spread betting firms are user friendly, but they can be expensive. That is not to say that you cannot make good use of them for the bearish strategies outlined in this chapter, and others, but please keep your eyes open. Their charges are not always transparent, wrapped up as they are in the spread, in overnight lending charges and in the use of customers' margin as interest-free money.

To succeed in trading derivatives is difficult. It does not help if the charges are stacked against you, which is sometimes the case. In their many promotional presentations, the spread betting firms omit to discuss the success rate of traders. Sadly, this is so low that spread betting firms often do not bother to cover their positions. This chapter, helped by this book generally, aims to help you to narrow the odds.

> **To succeed in trading derivatives is difficult.**

Trading contracts for difference

Short selling

Short sellers sell shares that they do not own in the hope of buying back later at a lower price and profiting from the difference. You cannot easily sell shares short through your stockbroker, due to the functioning of the rolling settlement system.

With contracts for difference, or spread bets, you can, however, trade on a short position for as long as you like, based on putting up only margin, but, as we have seen, subject to topping up your account with extra margin if things go wrong. Out of the two types of instrument, like almost any market professionals, I prefer the CFDs, which are widely available to you through brokers or, including in very small amounts, through spread betting firms. Not only can they be more cost effective than spread bets, but, due partly to institutional investor involvement, they tend to be more transparent, and less vulnerable to price manipulation.

Let us look at how the CFD works. The product is a contract between two parties to exchange the difference between the opening and closing price of a contract, as at the contract's close, multiplied by the specified number of shares. It is a way to have exposure to the price movement in, among other things, a stock or index without ever owning the underlying instrument. As the current value rises or falls, you will make or lose money on the difference.

If you plan to sell short, a useful rule of thumb is only to do so when both the market and the stock that you are shorting are on a downward trend. This way, the chances of a sustained decline in the stock are higher.

You stand to make more money selling short as a speculator than when hedging your main portfolio, which is to take an opposite position to compensate if, for example, your shares lose money. There is, however, a time and place for either strategy.

To make prompt decisions on whether to take a short position, and for how much, you will benefit from access to Level II prices (see Chapter 5, p. 53).

Start off gently, and take just one short position. You need to watch it carefully. The more short positions you hold open at once, the more demanding on your time and concentration it is.

In taking short positions, you are often best off concentrating on large liquid companies. Small companies tend to be too risky. They can fluctuate in value quickly on thin trading, and the price may have little to do with market conditions, let alone fundamentals. They have wide spreads, and are dangerously illiquid.

News flow can warn you of shock disasters hitting any size of company, but, as a short seller, you need to act quickly to get some advantage. One cue to take a short position is when the company has issued a first profit warning. If you move earlier enough, the share price will usually have further down to go from the level at which you traded. Another cue for shorting is if analysts revise earnings expectations downwards.

When you have made some profits as a short seller, consider taking a break as you may then maintain a balanced perspective and continue trading without losing your cautious instinct. Do not make the mistake of becoming overconfident. I have seen many a short seller give all that they have made and more back to the market.

Above all, never feel guilty about short selling. It is a legitimate and legal market activity, whatever your fellow investors may say. Regulators abroad have banned short selling at crisis times, in recognition of its power, but it has such benefits as creating market liquidity and facilitating price discovery. It happens to be where many professionals have made most of their money in recent years.

Some short sellers are bear raiders. They try to persuade others to sell out of stocks, often by posting messages under a false name on the message boards of financial web sites. Be wary of such manipulation.

Pairs trading

You can use contracts for difference (or spread bets) for pairs trading. This is when you invest in the performance of one stock against a correlated stock. It is a form of arbitrage enabling you to profit from the divergence.

For example, you may take a long position (profit from the rise) on a stock likely to outperform, and simultaneously take a short position (profit from the decline) on a stock likely to fall in value. You are hedged. If the market goes in one direction, you will gain on the long investment, but lose on the short.

The two stocks should be from the same sector, which makes them highly correlated, and should react to the same industry events. They should be trading outside their historical range. You could, for example, go long on BP and short on Shell in the hope of making a profit no matter how the FTSE-100 performs.

You must treat the two transactions as one trade, investing the same money in each stock, and opening and closing both trades simultaneously. If, as you expect, the long stock outperforms the short stock, you will have gained. Your profit comes, however, only after you have paid two sets of commissions.

Trading options

Options are a long established form of derivative offering some opportunities for high-risk trading. In the retail investing context, the relevant derivatives are traded on an exchange, which provides transparency and liquidity.

Through an option, you have the right to buy or sell a security at a pre-determined price, the exercise price, within a specified period. The market price you will have paid for the right to exercise the option is the premium, which is a small percentage of the option's size. It means the option is geared.

For every buyer of an option, there is a seller, also known as a writer. On completion of your purchase, you will pay an initial margin, which goes to the writer and works, including top ups, as discussed earlier in the chapter. If you exercise the option, the writer must provide the underlying financial instrument at the exercise price. If you do not exercise it, the writer will have your premium.

You may buy a *Call* option, which gives you the right, but not the obligation, to buy the underlying security at the exercise price. If the asset price is more than the exercise price of the option, the difference represents the option's value, and the option is *in the money*. Alternatively, you may buy a *Put* option, which gives you the right, but not the obligation, to sell a security at the exercise price.

The options traded on Euronext.liffe, the pan-European exchange with a London presence, have expiry dates grouped three, six or nine months ahead. When a contract expires, for instance, in March, a new one is created for expiry in June.

Let us now look at some options trading strategies that are useful in bearish or volatile market conditions.

Buying a Put option

Buying a *Put* option is your simplest strategy when you think that a share price or index will plummet. Such a likelihood could arise in a bear market. If the share price falls below the level of the exercise price plus your premium (plus dealing costs), you will make a profit from selling the option.

Writing a Call option

As a parallel bear strategy, you could write a *Call* option. If so, you will take a premium from the buyer, and will retain it only if the option is not exercised. This should happen only if the share price fails to rise above the exercise price plus premium (and dealing costs) before the option expires.

If you write a *naked* Call option, you do not own the shares that you are selling. This carries additional risk. If the option is exercised against you, you will have to buy shares at the prevailing market price to sell them at the lower exercise price.

Under these circumstances, your loss will be the difference between the exercise price and the prevailing share price, plus all dealing expenses. This is offset by the premium that you will have received, and will keep.

In theory, as a naked Call writer, your risk is theoretically unlimited. In practice, the risk is limited by time, and also by the fact that stock prices do not soar to infinity.

The 'buy write' strategy

To implement the 'buy write' strategy, you will buy a stock and simultaneously either buy or write an option on it. By this strategy, you can reduce or increase your risk, and, with it, your reward potential. For example, if you buy a stock and a Put option on it, and the share price falls, you will make money on the option as compensation.

The straddle – a volatility strategy

Use a straddle if you expect the underlying stock to move significantly, but do not know in which direction.

In a long straddle, you will simultaneously buy a Call option and a Put option each at an identical exercise price and expiration dates. If you are to make a profit on the trade, the share price will need to move up or down enough to exceed the expense of two premiums as well as the high commissions payable on a straddle.

The way forward

In bearish or volatile markets, there are, as we have seen, derivatives trading strategies you can use profitably. Some of the strategies are complicated, but, once you master them, can be useful. If you do not have the time or the interest to focus on a given strategy, and suffer the practical learning curve this entails, avoid it. In bear markets, you can and should, as a default, convert your assets to cash and hold until conditions improve. Sometimes, it is best to do nothing, and this can be one of the hardest lessons for traders.

> Sometimes, it is best to do nothing, and this can be one of the hardest lessons for traders.

For trading derivatives or shares, some knowledge of technical analysis is helpful, and we will cover some basics in the next two chapters.

7

Charting dreams

Introduction

Technical analysis and the charts are about market movements, and the decisions of buyers and sellers. They are not about company fundamentals. This is a controversially grounded, but thriving industry, the subject of endless seminars from software manufacturers and spread betting firms, who stand to profit from converts.

The technicians often have a cult-like dedication to this uncertain craft. Many amateurs have started using charting, the practical application of technical analysis, typically without success. Technical analysis haphazardly followed can, of course, lose you money.

The uncertainties around technical analysis require us to take extra care in applying its rules. In this chapter, we will take a practical look at the two basic charting techniques: support and resistance, and trend following. We will see how technical indicators may be used as a back-up to the charts, so please read this chapter in conjunction with Chapter 8, which covers indicators.

My initial word of warning is that it is easy to get carried away with the dream that technical analysis can do more than it does, but, at the other extreme, it is tempting to dismiss it as nonsense. Both of these positions are mistakes. In this chapter, I will point out what technical analysis can do for you, while stressing its limitations and debunking the wilder theories.

Overview

Technical analysis aims to forecast future price and index movements based on past chart patterns. At its purest, technical analysis ignores the underlying company and focuses on share price movements, basing future forecasts on the past. The pure chartist is the man who knows the price of everything and the value of nothing. The market-driven nature of short-term share prices lends credibility to this approach. Share prices can be out of kilter with fundamentals for long periods.

Some traders prefer to combine technical with fundamental analysis. If the charts say one thing and fundamentals another, this can stimulate fundamental analysts into looking at their reasoning more closely. The two are, however, different beasts.

The cornerstone of technical analysts is trend theory, which claims to be rooted in crowd psychology. If the share price is rising, everyone tries to buy at once, which establishes an uptrend. Crowd selling, conversely, can establish a downtrend. The technical analyst believes that the trend will stay in force until it is unequivocally broken. Wishful thinking can get in the way of the true analysis. Some assume a trend is stronger than it is, or is continuing when it isn't.

Wishful thinking can get in the way of the true analysis.

Technical analysis can be applied rigorously, but that does not in itself mean usefully. There is not much in the way of academic studies to back the discipline, although there are pockets of support. This has not deterred technical analysts from hiring university premises to run their sometimes expensive training courses, suggesting a link with the institution. Occasional presentations and courses in technical analysis have filtered onto the university syllabus. One large firm of technicians gave itself a name that suggested it belonged to a top collegiate university, although it later changed this under pressure.

Such marketing tactics are not confined to technical analysis. Let us focus rather on the practical validity of the method. Many fund managers and traders deride technical analysis, but a few set some store by it.

Anthony Bolton, president, investments, at Fidelity International, is a distinguished fund manager who has a firm foot in the supporters' camp. As he has made clear in his writings and presentations, he uses technical analysis to complement fundamental analysis, on the grounds that it keeps him informed about mass investor behaviour and what the market is saying. When he looks at a new share, he checks the price chart first to see what investors have already recognised. He uses the charts for screening shares.

Even for the sceptics, technical analysis does provide a quick and dirty view of how markets have performed in recent or long history. As one Chinese proverb on a streetcar advertisement has noted, a picture's meaning can express ten thousand words.

How far technical analysis can make or save money for investors is the main issue, and it is subject to disagreement. The more that traders place positions based on technical analysis, the more likely it is to become a self-fulfilling prophecy, and that is a factor to be taken into account. The concept is popular with traders of commodities and foreign exchange, not least because the type of fundamental analysis available to equity traders does not exist in these sectors. The charts can work for them, if only because everyone uses them in their trading decisions.

Types of chart

Technical traders have their favourite type of chart, often depending on how long-term their approach is. The chart can be plotted on a semi-logarithmic scale, which shows the share price or index movement in percentage terms, putting it in perspective. This is good for an overview. Otherwise, the chart can be plotted on an arithmetic scale, emphasising absolute share price movements and so presenting a more sensitive picture, which is useful in short-term trading and, generally, when the share price moves only slightly.

Trading volume shows how many shares are traded, with buyers balanced against sellers. Charting software typically presents trading volume on the lower part of the chart as vertical bars in a histogram, enabling easy comparison with the share price or index movement above. The higher the trading volume, the more weight there is behind a trend. On the same logic, if trading volume contradicts price movements, a trend reversal is likely. In sideways trading, however, the market is indecisive and volumes tend to be low.

Line chart

The line chart is the simplest type. The closing price is plotted on the vertical Y axis against time on the horizontal X axis. The focus on the bigger picture makes it easy to spot the trend.

Bar chart

The bar chart has the closing prices, like the line chart, but also the opening prices, on ticks either side of every bar, and it has the high and the low. Unlike on a line chart, you can see how volatile the share price has been through the highs and the lows.

You can vary the time covered in the bar on your chart, with each bar representing perhaps ten minutes or perhaps an hour. The scale is most often arithmetic.

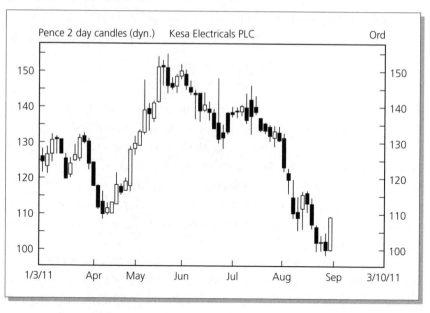

Figure 7.1 ◆ **Candlesticks at work**

Candlesticks

Candlesticks, a Japanese type of chart, have much in common with the bar chart, but in the last 15 years seem to have surpassed it in popularity. They are most useful for examining share price movement over a short period, which is helpful to traders but not so much to medium- or long-term investors.

Unlike bar charts, candlesticks focus on the gap between the opening and closing price, and the relationship between the two. The high and low are not considered important. As part of the presentation, candlesticks give more priority to reversal than continuation signals. They have in the past ignored volume and trend lines, but charting software now includes these.

It is part of the appeal that candlesticks make a visually powerful form of chart. The difference between the opening and close price is blocked into a 'real body',

> **Candlesticks make a visually powerful form of chart.**

which is white, if the closing price is higher than at opening, or is black, if the close is lower. Some software uses green and red instead. Running through the real body is a vertical line from the high to the low of the share price. Any parts of this line extending above the body are called the upper shadow and, where below the body, are the lower shadow.

If the price is the same at close as at opening, the candle is called a *doji*. This flat 'real body' appears as a horizontal line, and arises in trendless markets, showing investor indecisiveness. The 'battle' between bulls and bears on the day more often ends, however, with a winner. If the real body of a candlestick ends up longer than its predecessor, it is an engulfing sign, which can signal reversal.

Point and figure

The point and figure chart, unlike candlesticks, is not for short-term traders. This type of chart shows crosses marking share price rises and zeros marking falls, in each case a measure known as the 'box'.

The size of the box varies, and the reversal, registered where the share price breaks the trend and changes direction, is often larger than the box size. The count is a method of forecasting share prices based on the premise that the more the reversals showing on the chart, the greater the anticipated breakout.

This type of chart can initially appear confusing because it does not show time. As a consequence, it is not accompanied by volume. By cutting out this 'noise', the chart enables us to concentrate on pure price movement. The drawback is that it is not very good for short-term trading.

Practical charting

Some traders make money by sticking to the basic charting techniques of support and resistance and trend following. If you master these as a technical trader, you may never want more. Let us take a look.

Support and resistance

The support level on a chart is where investors have continually stopped selling and buyers move in. The share price does not go down below this line, but bounces up again. At the other end of the chart, resistance is the highest level a share or index reaches before investors continually refuse to buy further and sellers move in. The share price does not move above this line.

Support and resistance lines do not exist until they have been tested a few times, the price or index hitting the line but failing to get past it.

The longer support or resistance lines last, meaning the more they are tested, the more effective they will be. Three or four times should be the minimum. The lines are sooner or later breached as a function of market volatility.

I have found round numbers for shares, such as 100p or 500p, often prove to be support and resistance levels. The same applies to main stock market indices, but less often. If the FTSE-100 drops below 5,000, this can breach a support line, and if it rises above 6,000, this can penetrate a resistance line. Sometimes, however, the indices can slip across these 'round number' barriers without enough resistance or support to constitute lines.

For practical purposes, support and resistance lines showing on the chart are not infallible, but are an excellent basis for identifying buying and selling signals. If a share price rises through the resistance line, you buy. If it drops through the support level, you sell. As a rule of thumb, buy or sell soon after penetration of the trend.

You can reduce, but not eliminate, the risk of being caught by a false signal if you ensure that the penetration is significant, at least 3 per cent, and that trading volume is heavy. If the share price move was instigated by important news such as takeover interest, this increases the odds of a genuine penetration.

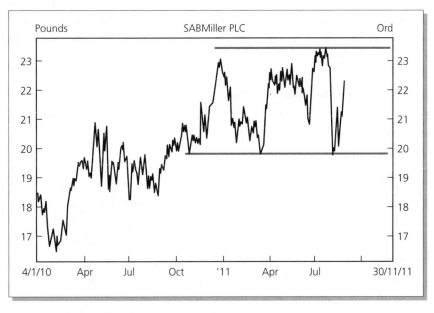

Figure 7.2 ◆ Support and resistance in the making

Trend following

If, like some US sceptical traders, you query whether the trend exists, do not bother with technical analysis because it is clearly not for you and, therefore, you are unlikely to be motivated to follow its rules. For the believers, crowd behaviour in buying or selling shares is observable, forming a trend that continues until it stops. It is a mantra of technical analysis that 'the trend is your friend'. This lasts 'until the bend at the end', but it is extremely difficult to detect that turning point. As a technical trader, you have, of course, made the detection of both the trend and its reversal your mission.

A trend may be long, medium or short. You may follow one or more of these trends at once. In assessing the broad market, you should watch the primary trend, which could be as short as five months, but is usually at least a year, as Dow Theory, the main foundation theory of technical analysis, would have it.

As a trader, you may let the primary trend reverse into what Dow Theory terms a secondary reaction. This is a retracement of between one and two thirds of the previous gain, followed by a rally in a medium trend lasting typically one to eight months. Catch this medium trend early and you can make money, trading in the direction of the primary as well as medium-term trend.

In fact, if you jump on the bandwagon of any trend that still has a way to go, you can make money, but the most difficult thing is to catch a short-term trend, the minor trend of Dow Theory. This lasts only three to seven weeks and may arise from market manipulation.

Trend lines

Your game as a technical trader is to detect trends after they have started; it is not to predict them. It is trend lines that enable this detection. They are sloping support and resistance lines, and you can use your charting software to produce them.

You can draw a line between any three tops rising or falling together, and call it the trend line, and a similar line for three bottoms in the same direction, which you can call the return line. When the tops and bottoms rise, there is an uptrend and, when they fall, a downtrend.

You will get the most realistic trend lines if you start at the bottom point for a rising trend (the top point for a declining one), and include those points you might otherwise ignore. Your trend line will be less steep, but you will be looking more at what the market is telling you.

Between the trend line, which indicates resistance, and the return line, which indicates support, runs the trend tunnel. For volatile stocks, this will be large, enabling you to trade on fluctuations within it. The trend tunnel may be divided along the middle, with a horizontal line. As a generalisation, when the share price is below this line, the shares are cheap and it is your cue to buy. When the share price is above the line, you should sell.

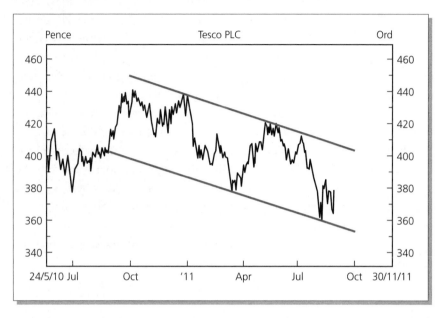

Figure 7.3 ◆ Trend line formation

Trend changes

To identify a trend change early, you should see a reversal signal, and, once this has been confirmed, act on it. Like every assessment in technical analysis or, if it comes to that, in investing, this is about probability, not certainty.

> Like every assessment in technical analysis or, in investing, this is about probability, not certainty.

A trend reversal comes on an uptrend, for instance when the uptrend line has been broken by a significant percentage closing price, traditionally 3 per cent. As further conditions of the uptrend being broken, a downtrend line must have appeared – with a high, a low, a lower high, and then a lower low. The previous significant low close on a rising trend must have been broken three times.

Patterns

A pattern on the chart indicates indecision in stock prices. In its completed form, it can resemble, for example, a triangle or head and shoulders. The pattern, depending on its form, can be a reversal, or a continuation signal. A pattern shows fluctuation over a period, representing a struggle between buyers and sellers. Eventually, one side of the pattern will have got the upper hand, and broken out. This indicates not more buyers or sellers, but that more existing players, on balance, made the decisive move.

The breakout may be upwards or downwards. Reversal patterns indicate that the trend is *changing* and continuation patterns *confirm* the trend.

The breakout is typically at least as far as the depth of the pattern behind it. Beware of false breakouts. Normally, you might consider a move to be a breakout if it achieves 3 per cent of the share price but, when assessing long-term trends, 5 per cent is a better measure. High trading volume is a corroborating force.

Following the breakout, there is often a temporary retracement, perhaps extending back to the original pattern, or nearly so.

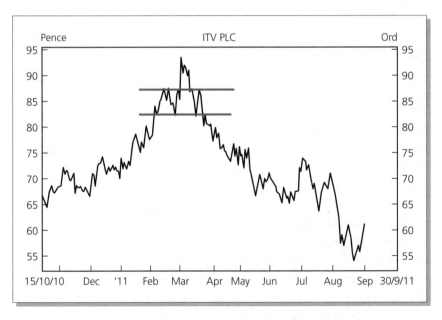

Figure 7.4 ◆ Head and shoulders breakout

Let us run through a few of the most common patterns, first reversal then continuation. Of reversal patterns, the best known is the head and shoulders, which can indicate a downturn in the share price or index, at the end of a bull market. The pattern develops as the share price moves up and back, forming the left shoulder, on higher trading volume than usual. The price then rises to a new high, again on substantial volume, and falls, on lower volume, to a 'neckline' support level, creating the head. The level to which it has dropped back in forming the pattern is known as the neckline.

There is also a reverse head and shoulders, serving as a bullish reversal signal, sometimes at the end of a bear market.

Technicians make the head and shoulders sound precise, but, in practice, it is not. The pattern slopes in any direction, and no head and shoulders formation is exactly like another. Sometimes it forms, and the unexpected happens. The price may move only slightly below the neckline or not as far as that. Next thing, buyers may pile in, encouraged by the temporary weakness in the share price, and short sellers may rush to cover their position. As a result, the share price may soar, with trading volume also up enormously.

Among other reversal patterns, the broadening formation happens occasionally, when a market is at its peak and out of control, with investors reacting to wild rumours. In this pattern, the price fluctuations become broader. This will enable you to join the tops, of which there should be at least three, with one line. You can similarly join the bottoms. The two lines will diverge. A sharp decline often follows the broadening formation, with a temporary retracement.

The diamond is a rare bearish reversal pattern that can arise in highly active markets. It is a broadening formation that converts into a symmetrical triangle. Another rare bearish reversal pattern is the double top, formed from a share price that rises and falls in two tops, one after another. The process usually takes several months. The double bottom is a double top in reverse, and is a bullish sign, reliable only if the second bottom is accompanied by rising volume.

Flip test

If you think you have spotted a pattern in the charts, it is worth putting it through the flip test. Jeremy du Plessis, a seasoned technical analyst, has recommended this technique. If a chart seems to show a buy signal, flip it upside down, and if the reversed pattern shows a sell signal, this corroborates it. Similarly, the chart showing a sell signal, when reversed, should seem to show a buy signal. Of course, a pattern, even when fully confirmed, will not invariably play out in a textbook way.

Prominent among continuation patterns is the rectangle, which consists of two approximately parallel lines on the chart. The top line indicates resistance, the lower one support. The share price will reach peaks and troughs as it fluctuates within these boundaries, creating a rectangular trend channel. The breakout will typically take months.

The triangle, like the rectangle, is mostly a continuation pattern, less trustworthy than the rectangle, and it sometimes instead signals a reversal. Reliability is increased when it is a right-angled triangle or when the price frequently touches the sides, or if the breakout arises after half, but before three-quarters, of the length of the triangle, between its start and its point.

The flag is a more obscure continuation pattern. This is a brief consolidation in the share price, and resembles a bent rectangle. In an uptrend, the flag forms after a steep upturn in the share price, on rising trading volume driven by profit takers. A pennant is similar to a flag, but its boundary lines converge rather than run parallel. It is similarly formed after the share price has moved up or down fast, and is completed in less than three weeks.

Saucers arise infrequently when a stock, with a large market float, is rising in value from a low point. Eventually, the share price will move away from the saucers. It is hard to detect the breakout point. Rounding tops are the reverse shape of saucers and arise when a stock falls from a high point.

The wedge is a pattern with boundary lines that both slope either up or down. This makes it different from a triangle, whose symmetrical version has the top line slanting down and the bottom one up, and whose right-angled version has the top line either up or down, and the bottom one horizontal. The wedge takes more than three weeks to finish, failing which it is better classified as a pennant.

A gap arises when the share price opens above the highest level that it had reached on the previous day. This creates a physical gap on the chart. Less significant are *intra-day* gaps, which arise when the share price has jumped more than one point during the day's trading. This can happen frequently. It is the infrequent gaps in the share price of heavily traded stocks that have the greatest significance in technical analysis.

Two theories to avoid

We have looked at some basic ways to make technical analysis work for you. Let us finish this chapter with a brief focus on two theories, which, in my view, you should avoid.

Elliott Wave

Enthusiasts apply Elliott Wave Theory not just to the Dow Jones Industrial Average but also to other stock market indices, as well as to commodities, currencies and bonds. How far it works on this broad application – or, indeed, at all – remains open to debate.

In essence, Elliott Wave is a theory of waves. A simple wave is likely to be followed by a complex one, and vice versa. Given this variety, it is often difficult to assess where one wave ends and another begins. A market cycle starts with five waves that broadly rise, and are followed by a three-part corrective wave. The waves have a proportional relationship linked to Fibonacci numbers. This gives the theory a spurious precision.

The late Bob Beckman, a very successful trader, always believed in Elliott Wave, but always considered it so complex that few understood it. Many traders have found it does not work for them. A professional colleague of mine who has worked for some years as a technical analyst at a spread betting firm considers Elliott Wave a con, and I incline to his view.

> Bob Beckman always believed in Elliott Wave, but considered it so complex that few understood it.

William Gann

Here are another guru's methods that I would shun. Gann made money from writing and selling courses, but not from trading stocks and commodities. When he died from stomach cancer in 1955, Gann was not wealthy.

Gann's system has some sensible bits, such as support and resistance and trend following, but there is too much that is ridiculous, all imbued with a misleading precision. The theory is based on geometrical and other mathematical principles, and their relationship with an intuitive market.

This trader put his faith in the significance of particular numbers, not just on share prices, but also on share price movements, and dates. One year was a watershed after which a future key point could be broadly identified. The same applied to eighteen months and two years.

On Gann's theory, seven is important because it represents the number of days in the week, and so are its multiples, particularly 49. Anniversaries of highs and lows are important. Percentages are seen as significant. If a price rises 100 per cent, the move is probably complete, and any fall will stop at zero per cent. An only slightly less important percentage is 50 per cent. Others that are significant include 12.5, 25, 37.5, 62.5 and 75 per cent, as multiples of one-eighth, into which Gann divided price action. He used a third in a similar way, making, for example, 33 and 67 per cent significant.

This pioneering trader found the 360 degrees in a circle significant, comparing this with the 365 days in a year. Turns of 30, 90 or 120 degrees and similar indicate a potential change in market conditions. Gann theory sometimes represents the degrees of a circle in pence. On this basis, 90 p or 360 p are *natural* levels of resistance and support.

Gann's most significant trend line is at 45 degrees, which represents an absolute balance between price and time. If prices are above the line, there is a bull market, and if below it, a bear market. To breach the line means to reverse the trend.

Gann was a closet astrologer, and, at one point, he had studied Indian sidereal astrology in India. He believed that share prices moved in cycles according to universal laws, including astrology. This hardly enhances his credibility.

The way forward

My suggestion is that you should forget Elliott Wave, and most of Gann. Focus on the simpler proven techniques of technical analysis, support and resistance, and trend following, and you can make the charts work for you.

You can profitably use technical indicators as a backup to the price and index charts. In Chapter 8, I will focus on a few useful ones.

8

Technical indicator secrets

Introduction

In this chapter, we will look briefly at some useful technical indicators to supplement the use of price and index charts covered in Chapter 7.

The use of technical indicators

Technical indicators offer a useful backup to analysis of share price trends, but never an alternative. Let us look now at those that, in my experience, are the most useful.

Moving average

The moving average is a popular indicator that represents changes in the *average* share price over a specified period. It lags rather than leads the action. You may use the moving average to indicate the end of an old trend and the beginning of a new.

The simple moving average is the most popular kind and is accessible through any technical software. It is calculated as the sum of closing prices (i.e. the total added together) for a given stock over a selected period, divided by the number of days included.

This version of the moving average has the advantage of not responding too quickly to signals that may turn out false. But if they turn out real, the indicator may have worked too slowly, causing you to miss out on profits from the early part of the trend change.

The weighted moving average gives more weight to recent share prices, and so is linearly weighted. As a third alternative, the exponential moving average similarly attributes more significance to recent prices, but it includes additional price information that precludes the period of the moving average.

The length of a moving average is linked to cycles, and is typically 5, 10, 20 or 40 days. If, for example, your moving average covers 10 consecutive days, it is a 10-day moving average. The shorter the period, the more sensitive the moving average is and the more suitable for short-term trading.

> You should buy shares when the price is below the moving average, but has started to rise.

As a rule of thumb, you should buy shares when the price is below the moving average, but has started to rise. Conversely, you should sell when the price is above the moving average, but has started to fall.

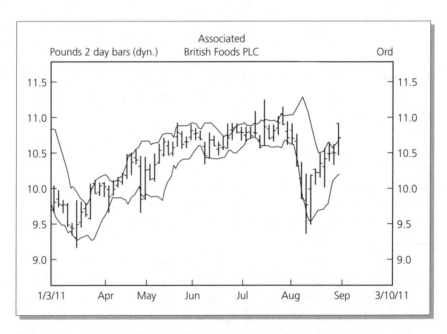

Figure 8.1 ◆ Bollinger bands. The battle of the bulge

Envelopes

The Envelope has two lines that are plotted a fixed amount (typically 3 to 4 per cent) both above and below a moving average. If the share price touches the upper band, this indicates that enthusiastic buyers have driven it relatively high. If the price touches the lower band, it is a sign that sellers have pushed it relatively low.

Of the envelope family, Bollinger Bands are the best known, and are available on even basic charting software. An upper band and a lower band are plotted at standard deviation, a volatility measure, both above and below a simple moving average. The Bands are normally constructed on closing prices.

When share prices are volatile, standard deviation becomes high and the Bollinger Bands bulge. When prices are stable, the reverse is true and the bands tighten. If the share price moves outside the bands, the trend is said to be likely to continue.

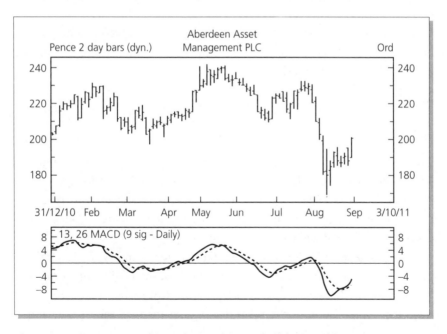

Figure 8.2 ◆ MACD and its relationship with the signal line

MACD – combining momentum and moving averages

One of the most popular oscillators is the moving average convergence/divergence indicator or MACD (pronounced MacD).

The MACD is constructed from the 12-day exponential moving average of the security or index being charted, less the slower 26-day one, based on closing prices.

The MACD rises above or below a zero line. If it rises above the line, this means that the faster 12-day EMA has crossed the 26-day one, and, the more it diverges in this direction, the greater the upward momentum. The reverse process works similarly.

A nine-day exponential moving average of MACD, known as the signal line, is plotted alongside the MACD, trailing it. When the MACD is above the signal line, it is a bullish sign, and you should take long positions. When the MACD is below it, it is a bearish sign, and you should take short positions. On a similar basis, when the MACD crosses above the signal, this is bullish, and, when it crosses below it, this is bearish, and you should trade accordingly.

In addition the MACD less the signal line can be viewed in a histogram, which consists of vertical bars. If the MACD histogram diverges from the price movement, it suggests a significant reversal and is a strong buying or selling signal.

ROC indicator

To explain how a momentum indicator such as the Rate of Change, or ROC, indicator, works, let us suppose that you are riding a toboggan down some snow slopes. The further down you travel, the faster your ride, and the momentum increases accordingly. Once the slopes flatten, your journey is slowed, which reduces the momentum.

The momentum indicator measures the momentum change in markets, meaning the rate of change, or velocity of prices, the equivalent of the percentage speed change of your toboggan ride from when you started the ride. This type of indicator tends to lead rather than lag the market, but is not infrequently simultaneous.

The ROC indicator plots the closing price less the opening price against a zero line. This is over, for example, 15 days. If the closing price is higher

than 15 days ago, the momentum line will be above the zero line. If it is
lower, the line will be below zero, and, if it is the same, the line will be flat.
Every 15 days, the line will be reassessed.

One valuable use of this indicator is when it contradicts the share price,
if the stock is rising in value but the ROC slopes downwards. This suggests
a pending share price decline. Nothing, of course, is certain, but many traders have found the ROC a good indicator of probability.

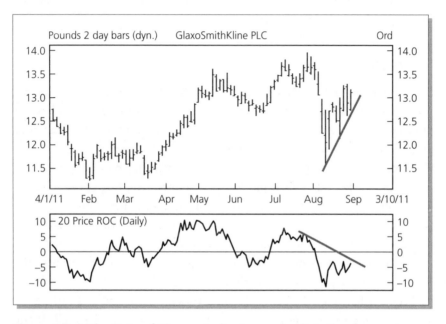

Figure 8.3 ◆ The Rate of Change indicator contradicts the share price

The RSI

The Relative Strength Index, known as RSI, is a less volatile version of the
ROC indicator. It is sensitive and so best used in a trendless market.

The RSI is simple to calculate, and this is usually done over a 14-day
period. First, focus on the RS, which is the average of the *up* closes over the
period, divided by the average of the *down* closes. The RS should be added
to 1 to create 1+RS. Divide the number into 100, and the resulting figure
should be subtracted from 100. This gives you the RSI.

The index creates a constant range, which is between 0 and 100 by an indexing adjustment. Against this range, the overbought and oversold levels are predetermined, whereas, on the ROC indicator, you need to decide the range. If the RSI is 50, this is neutral. Technical analysts normally consider the 70 level overbought, and the 30 level oversold.

If the RSI has breached 70 or 30 respectively in more than one move, and diverges from the price line, this suggests a future change in the current (probably strong) price trend. Wait, however, for signs of a trend reversal on the price chart before you take action.

Stochastics

Stochastics, created by Dr George Lane in the 1960s, is a popular indicator that shows when the market is overbought or oversold. Its underlying principle is that, in an uptrend, share prices close nearer the top of the price range and, in a downtrend, nearer the bottom.

Stochastics shows the last closing price as a percentage of the price range over a chosen period. This is plotted as two lines. The first is the solid %K line, which represents the share price. The second is the dotted %D line, which is a three-day moving average of the first, and, although less sensitive, is considered the more important of the two.

The two lines oscillate between 1 and 100 on a scaled chart. As with the RSI, the overbought/oversold perimeters are usually 70–30.

When either line falls below 25 then rises above it, this is a *buy* signal. When the line overreaches 75, then slips back, this is a *sell* signal. If the moving average falls below the price line, this is often another *sell* signal.

Nowadays, the slow Stochastic is used more often than the original. This excludes the %K (solid) line on the grounds that it is too sensitive. The former %D (moving average) line becomes the slowed %K line. The slowed %D is a moving average of this.

These are the main indicators that I have found the most useful. There is one other to which I would draw your attention.

Stop and reverse points

Stop and reverse points, known as SARs, offer you a trading system that keeps you in the market. They are plotted as dotted lines that define a trend. SARs will stop you moving out of a long position and tell you to go short, or the reverse.

> **Stop and reverse points offer you a trading system that keeps you in the market.**

A popular version of SARs has been the Parabolic SAR indicator, created by J. Welles Wilder. It is so named from the parabola that the indicator forms in a fast upward move. The indicator is sensitive to time as well as price movements. It works best when the market is trading up or down, but not sideways.

The stop loss incorporated in the Parabolic indicator follows the price trend, but accelerates should the price have reached a new extreme. If, at this point, the trade should falter even slightly, you will be stopped out.

The way forward

Some of these indicators perform nearly the same purpose, but the perspectives shown vary. If you have the time and commitment, it is worth using several at once in your own trading, as a backup to your main charts.

PART THREE

The professionals at work

9

Investment banking power

Introduction

Investment banking makes its money from mergers and acquisitions, issuing securities, sales and trading, and other financial activities.

In the rush to make profits, investment banking has to some extent raped the investment community by foisting on them dud investments. It happens quickly, as when Pluto, god of the underworld, pricked by Cupid's arrow, falls in love with Proserpine on first sight, and snatches her from her innocent flower-picking, carrying her down into hell.

There is some backlash on private investors. They are useful, as one investment banker once put it to me, for propping up the secondary market after a dud IPO when institutions have sold out. They bring liquidity to the market.

In this chapter, we will look at how investment banking works, its current status and its culture.

The rape

Investment banking can abuse its power and get its comeuppance, as the 2007–08 financial crisis has demonstrated. The industry rapes some investors with dubious investments that it represents as sound.

In his *Metamorphoses*, the ancient Roman poet Ovid describes how Proserpine is picking flowers when Pluto, god of the underworld, abducts her, whisking her away in his chariot to his domain. It is represented as a rape, which in archaic language means kidnapping. In a similar style, the banks are in the game of raping clients with their sales pitches to get their money. Interestingly, Pluto is also god of wealth.

It is in capital markets that the investment banks make most of their money. The issuing of securities and the mergers & acquisition activity are more lucrative than trading, research and sales, and can subsidise them.

Investment bankers have traditionally sought help from analysts in their firm, leaning on them to write research reports favourable to corporate clients. The reports must be justifiable in content, with full disclosure of potential conflicts of interests.

> **Banks raise capital for companies either as a secondary placing or in an international public offering.**

Banks raise capital for companies either as a secondary placing, which means the securities are already listed elsewhere, or in an inital public offering, which is the first time the company is listed. The issuance is of equities, or of bonds, a much larger market, or there may be a syndicated loan.

Equities

The stock market IPO is a major event, with shares ahead of a flotation allocated to institutional investors in a book build, and typically available in limited quantities to the public. When the company that is coming to the market is famous, there is press comment, the spread betting companies may run a book on the future price, and everybody gets excited.

The mandate to launch the IPO must be won and banks compete for this. The winner will run the book of orders. Sometimes, the banks compete on the basis of how easily they can gain indicative support from investors for the proposed flotation. An obstacle is any unresolved conflict of interest as, for example, when the bank is launching the IPO of a rival company.

In practice, many IPOs and secondary placements are handled by banks that have a corporate relationship with the issuing company. If there is a prospect of two banks becoming joint book runners, any historic conflicts come under scrutiny.

Placing shares

Once appointed to an IPO, the book runner takes lead responsibility for placing the newly floated shares with investors and, in a sizeable deal, will organise backup from other banks. The bank at the top of the syndicate may be global coordinator, and others may have lesser key roles such as lead manager or manager. As the classical underworld relies on defined delegation to its ferryman, its guard dog, and its shades, the banks work as partners for profit.

As Pluto aims at abducting Proserpine, the banks seek investors for their IPO. In a pre-marketing phase, the book runner pitches a case to investors. Unlike Pluto, it must negotiate, setting parameters for the subsequent pricing of the new issue.

There is room for opinion on the right pricing. The book runner's salesmanship presents the best case for the deal, but press opinion, fuelled by the often anonymous comment of analysts in rival firms, can tell a different story. The analysts may say that the price range is too high or too low against company fundamentals or peer ratings.

The book runner sometimes moves the indicative price range up or down, blaming market conditions, but it will be reluctant to take this measure as it could be accused of having misjudged the pricing.

The IPO process

The investment banks throw money lavishly at their IPO promotional activity. They conduct road-shows, with presentations across Europe and the United States. The company's chief executive and finance director and head of investor relations, alongside the book runner's corporate financiers and analysts, address potential investors. For *tier one* clients, meaning the largest and most important, the banks may organise one-to-one presentations.

A traditional book build lasts two to three weeks, or longer if market conditions are difficult. The institutional investors targeted often try to hold out on making a decision. They may play a waiting game, not committing themselves on subscription to the deal until close to the deadline.

On this basis, most orders are confirmed only one or two days before the book closes. Not every deal offered by an investment bank is good. The impact on subscribing investors depends, however, on what they pay, and at what stage they buy, and sell out.

For everybody's peace of mind, it is as well that most deals coming to the market are underwritten, which is where the bank guarantees the issuer a given price for a given number of securities. This ensures that the deal gets done, but at a price. The riskier the deal, the larger the underwriter's fee.

Pricing the deal

The deal is priced usually within the indicative price range that has been set. In good market conditions, a deal will typically reach a small premium, perhaps 10–15 per cent, over the issue price in early secondary-market trading. If the free float is small, with the shares tightly held by company directors and only a few available to the public, demand may quickly exceed supply and the share price may soar.

Institutional investors who bought shares during the IPO process may choose to snatch a profit by selling the shares early in the first days or weeks of secondary-market trading. Such 'flipping' is often the best way to make money quickly from new issues. Retail investors may hesitate to follow suit, especially if, as is likely, the book runner recommends that they should continue to hold the shares.

With retail investors involved, a book runner may have set a higher IPO price, partly due to the extra take-up, but also because the price will be more sustainable in early secondary-market trading. This helps to stabilise the price and to safeguard the book runner's reputation.

Accelerated book build

An accelerated book build, unlike an IPO or traditional secondary placing, is a rush job. The bank takes a selling company's shares in a listed company on to its book, and offers them to its investor clients. It will sell the shares in the course of one day or, exceptionally, over two or three days.

This compares with several weeks for a conventional book build and, for issuers, it has the major advantage of allowing less time for market conditions to deteriorate. Part of the genius is the speed, as in Pluto's abduction of Proserpine.

Rights issues

A rights issue gives shareholders the opportunity to acquire new shares without paying their stockbroker a commission. The company issues new shares to existing shareholders who subscribe, *pro rata* to their existing holdings. In a 'one for five' rights issue, shareholders will have the right to buy one further new share for every five they hold. The process takes perhaps six to eight weeks, twice the length of a conventional share offering.

As with IPOs, the issuing company will usually appoint an underwriter, generally a major bank, which, if the issue fails, will take up the rights. Some rights issues are not fully underwritten, which can be a high-risk strategy for both the issuer and the underwriter, although in practice, there may be a sound reason, such as near certain subscribers.

A rights issue can be enticing for shareholders who think it worth investing further in the company. Unlike Proserpine, they make the choice whether to elope with their abductor into a realm of darkness. This requires some assessment. If the issue is aimed to pay off debt, shareholders should assess the chances of success before they subscribe. A rights issue to fund expansion may be positive, depending on the potential benefits to the business.

Once the rights issue is under way, the share price can fluctuate, particularly in uncertain markets or if the issue is for a purpose that may not benefit shareholders, or if it is not fully underwritten. Hedge funds may then trade the underlying shares, adding to the volatility.

The new shares issued will be priced below the market value of the existing shares. In difficult markets, the discount might be as high as 40 to 50 per cent, a 'deeply discounted' rights issue which is more likely to attract subscription because the new shares are significantly cheaper than the existing shares.

After the rights issue, the share price evens out to a level slightly below that of the original shares. Shareholders may sell any rights to which they have not subscribed, known as nil paid rights, to other investors. Once they have sold the rights, after receiving the proceeds and seeing the share price adjusted down as a result of the rights issue, they will be cash neutral.

The book runner will later sell unsubscribed rights, known as the rump, to new investors in an accelerated book build.

Placing

In a placing, the broker issues a company's shares privately to institutions, at least some of which are its own clients. The process is often used to raise small amounts, through a broker or investment boutique rather than an investment bank. Retail investors are not given the opportunity to buy.

A placing may be done simultaneously with an open offer to existing shareholders to place shares in already quoted companies. The shares are placed provisionally with institutions, but subject to claw back by shareholders, should they exercise their right to take up shares under the open offer. Sometimes key shareholders will have undertaken to take up some shares.

This dual approach can be a quicker and more reliable way to raise cash than a rights issue, particularly in difficult markets. It tends to be for small capital raisings, typically under £50 million.

Corporate bonds

Companies can raise money cheaply by issuing bonds. If a company issues bonds, it may have to pay a coupon of, let us say 6 per cent, which compares favourably with the 10 per cent return it may have to pay on equities. In addition, interest payments made by bond issuers are tax deductible against the issuing company's profits. Companies sometimes issue bonds and use the cash raised to buy back shares from investors.

Companies sometimes issue bonds and use the cash raised to buy back shares from investors.

In issuing bonds, however, companies face the downside risk of taking on too much debt in relation to equity. Such high gearing gives the issuer a riskier profile with the credit rating agencies. The bond issuer cannot skip paying the coupon, as is possible with dividends on shares. It must repay the principal on maturity, although it can refinance by issuing new bonds.

Issuers of bonds usually offer a fixed rate of return, which is what investors prefer. But if the bonds fall in value, investors may feel they have lost out by not seeing an accompanying rise in the return as a percentage of the reduced bond value. This is why investors often swap fixed for floating rates using interest rate swaps, so benefiting if interest rates rise, but at a price.

Mergers and acquisitions

Mergers and acquisitions are where investment banks are often compared and judged. The game is to advise a company that plans a takeover, and help it to raise capital, or to help a bid target.

The prospective buyer of a quoted company can be another quoted company, or a private equity firm, which can acquire a listed company and take it private. Private equity has more resources to make acquisitions than quoted companies, and does not have a similar need for merger synergies.

The acquirer may use capital markets to finance its acquisition, paying for a target company's shares with cash, its own shares or both. The acquirer may appoint an investment bank as M&A adviser, or, for smaller transactions, may use in-house advisers. A bank's fee for M&A advice is up to 2 per cent of the deal's value, diminishing as the deal becomes bigger, but payable only if it proceeds.

Should the bank be acting for a target company, it may fend off the bidder with the intervention of a white knight, a rival bidder, or may block the deal with a white squire, a significant minority shareholder. As a next option, the bid target may then make a counter bid for the bidder.

If ultimately a takeover is to go ahead, the predator must obtain more than 50 per cent of the target company's voting shares. Once its stake has reached 30 per cent, it must make a formal offer to all shareholders. If some shareholders decline to take up the offer, a buyer can acquire their shares compulsorily once holders of 90 per cent of the voting shares have accepted.

The Panel on Takeovers and Mergers, an independent body with statutory powers, supervises and regulates takeovers with the aim of ensuring fair treatment for all shareholders. The Panel has a good reputation but doubts have arisen whether it is consistent in its handling of cases, for example, in its use of investigatory powers.

The way forward

The 2007–09 financial crisis annihilated large-scale investment banking as a standalone proposition. It encouraged a move to universal banks, which combine clearing with investment banking under one roof, and led to a flourishing of small investment banking boutiques.

Market conditions play a part in events. Investment banking is never popular because of the huge money it makes, but it is useful to the economy. In bull markets, it thrives and, in bear markets, it keeps a lower profile and dismisses staff. The market cycles will continue.

The super traders

Introduction

The algorithmic traders with their speed and buying power can make markets move quickly and unpredictably. These are the super traders.

This chapter is about their activities today, and is to be distinguished from Chapter 5, which is for home-based traders and similar, perhaps just starting up. All traders are, however, in the same game. There are important overlaps, such as the use of a consistently workable trading system.

In this chapter, we will examine the role of super traders today, the trading infrastructure, and the impact of regulation.

Technology drivers

We may feel nostalgia for the old City, much as ancient Greek mythology glorifies an earlier golden race of mortals who lived free of toil and grief.

In October 2006, computerised trading was introduced to the London Stock Exchange. The world was then less connected and systemic collapse not seen as a threat.

Since then, there has been further evolution. Algorithmic trading was initially designed to minimise the ripple in the market from major institutional orders placed separately. Now it drives markets and is enhanced by advanced use of technology.

> Algorithmic trading now drives markets and is enhanced by advanced use of technology.

High frequency trading, in which proprietary traders transmit many orders quickly into the market, is a powerful, and much used, form of algorithmic trading. The order execution can be in microseconds, and there are plenty of cancellations. Market participants can locate their trading engines next to the infrastructure of market operations, reducing latency – the time taken to process an order after execution – and so increasing competitive advantage.

The algorithms used in high frequency trading have become capable of adapting the trading strategy to market activity. The trader may provide liquidity when it suits, acting as a market maker but without the obligation to provide continuous pricing. Traders withdraw liquidity when it suits, which cause significant market volatility. They make many of their price quotes available only briefly before cancelling.

The 'high frequency' traders, which include hedge funds, stabilise markets. There are always some such traders in the market. Many trading firms went out of business in the 2007–09 financial crisis, but some have bounced back. Banks trade substantially but, where they have been unable to survive, have taken government bailouts. Trading firms are not likely to be rescued in this way, but have created their own strength.

By the speed and geographical reach of their transactions, the traders have smashed some barriers of time and space. The more sophisticated the technology, the more it is capable of thought processes, and the less is the need for traders' input.

Systems at work

The soul, says Socrates in Plato's *Phaedrus*, is like a chariot with two winged horses, a good one, and an unruly one that must be subdued. On a similar basis, traders must subdue their greed and fear. Computerised trading removes much of the struggle from the exercise.

Committed traders are invariably watching their screens. Their trading is typically based on a system, which applies consistent rules on when they buy and when they sell securities, regardless of emotional factors. The discipline overrides greed and fear. Traders typically keep their system confidential, so that others do not rush to copy, thereby diluting the impact, or even making the methodology ineffectual.

Within the discipline of their system, traders exploit downs as well as ups in the financial markets, taking short positions ahead of likely downward movement in share prices, and long positions when the movement seems up. They trade across asset classes and geographies.

As professionals, they see trading opportunity from adverse market reactions to unexpected human tragedy. When, for example, in March 2011, a quake and tsunami, with nuclear energy problems, hit Japan, some traders sold the yen. Traders at such times can exploit price or currency declines, by taking short positions. They also exploit unexpected good news.

When markets panicked in August 2011 as a result of the European debt crisis and concerns around the downgrading of US bonds by a rating agency, automatic securities trading was triggered, and the markets went into free fall, but the same traders could eventually buy again.

In a short stock market crash of 6 May 2010, the Dow Jones Industrial Average, a US index, fell 998.5 points in seconds, the largest single intraday decline in the index's history. On investigation, the Securities and Exchange Commission found that high frequency traders had not directly caused the crash. The incident however, alerted supervisors globally to the risks of computerised trading.

The systemic risk (see Chapter 19) that could arise from high frequency trading is based on knock-on effects. A fall in share prices could trigger panic selling elsewhere, and a drying up of liquidity. So far the case is unproven but it does not mean it couldn't happen.

Testing the waters

Traders use arbitrage strategies to seek to exploit pricing variations in the same security, or between a derivative and the underlying.

In addition, they use dark pools, which are electronic trading venues where institutional investors can buy and sell large blocks of shares without the user's order being displayed publicly. It is a way to keep competitors from muscling in on their area of trading activity, and so affecting its profitability.

They use 'gaming', which can include sending many buy or sell orders into a dark pool. If they hit it right and get an execution, this can indicate the price of some of the larger orders in the pool.

Another technique is sub-penny pricing, where non-exchange venues, including dark pools, quote and execute orders priced in very small increments. A sub-penny order placed in an anonymous dark pool can trade before orders in displayed markets, and this may give a distorted impression of buying or selling demand.

Trading venues

The Markets in Financial Instruments Directive, implemented in November 2007, opened up exchanges to competition. Trading venues in Europe compete for business on speed of execution, fees and flexibility.

Multilateral trading facilities have emerged since the MiFID's implementation to compete with exchanges, offering often a leaner trading operation, faster and cheaper than the exchanges with their legacy technology. The MTFs focus only on trading, however, while the exchanges have a business model that typically also includes listings, and sales of information and data, as well as other activity.

In addition, there are systematic internalisers, firms that execute orders from their clients against their own book or against orders from other clients. Under the MiFID, they are treated as mini-exchanges.

Back-office stability

In every dream, there are constants in the background, whether a bedside clock ticking or a partner's snoring. For traders operating in the dream-like fluctuations of markets, it is the back-office infrastructure that serves as the market's bedrock.

Clearing and settlement are necessary steps in the lifecycle of any trades transacted. Clearing defines the obligations of the parties to a securities transaction and assigns accountability. Settlement, in contrast, is the process where the assets are actually exchanged. This post-trade infrastructure has to be reliable if financial markets are to have credibility, not least because providers of clearing services are increasingly taking on the role of central counterparties, standing between the buyer and seller of securities to eliminate counterparty risk.

> **Post-trade infrastructure has to be reliable if financial markets are to have credibility.**

So far, the European post-trade infrastructure has stood firm in the midst of market gyrations, but inefficiencies resulting from fragmentation among the different providers linger. This poses some systemic risk, although the current arrangements proved stable after Lehman Brothers' collapse in September 2008.

Cost issues, however, still need to be tackled. Settlement of cross-border transactions is far more expensive than EU domestic or US transactions, due primarily to a lack of harmonised legal, fiscal and operational market practices. There have been attempts to address such inefficiencies, but there has been resistance.

The slowness of reforms suggests that some key market participants are unwilling to give up lucrative services that aim to bridge the inefficiencies of fragmented and disharmonised markets, however much they might like the idea in theory.

In 2001–03, a high level expert group chaired by Professor Alberto Giovannini, identified 15 barriers to an efficient market for post-trade services in the EU, and these have not yet been fully removed. There is now a voluntary Code of Conduct for Clearing and Settlement to stimulate open competition, and this has achieved more transparency and service unbundling, but open access and interoperability have not yet been properly achieved.

The European Commission is now looking to develop Central Securities Depository legislation to address the diversity in EU settlement practices.

Efficient market theory discredited

The failure of the efficient markets hypothesis is a major lesson from the 2007–09 financial crisis. Regulators and policymakers entrusted with safeguarding our financial system relied on efficient markets, which market practitioners had always dismissed.

Believers in market efficiency see benefits in more financial markets liquidity, enabling trading to take its natural course. In theory, markets should find their own level this way, but the problem is that liquidity can be illusory, and the high frequency traders can withdraw it instantly.

It was a belief in efficient markets that led to a hands-off approach by regulators in the run-up to the 2007–09 financial crisis, which in turn enabled traders to operate without transparency. There is now some feeling of disillusionment. Exchanges have had no rules requiring that traders should submit algorithms for testing before their systems are connected with the exchange, but this issue is now under discussion by regulators.

The way forward

Computerised trading is no longer just a market development, but it sometimes *is* the market. Such trading is the source of regulators' fears and other investors' nightmares, but it contributes as much to market stability as to havoc; it creates as well as removes stability.

In this area, regulators seek more transparency and control, although, as always, at some cost to free markets. How markets perform in the next few years will have some influence on how freely computerised trading is allowed to continue, and also the reverse.

Even so, because of certain technology advances and commercial demands, computerised trading will surely only become more powerful and more sophisticated, increasing the power held by the few.

Derivatives chaos

Introduction

Derivatives are geared trading instruments. Investors may use them for hedging risk, which is about protection, but speculators can grab them and make fortunes from their fluctuating values. It is speculation rather than hedging with derivatives where the unquantifiable chain-effect risk lies.

In this chapter we will consider how derivatives work. See also Chapter 6 for some practical techniques for trading derivatives in bear markets.

The derivatives paradox

Derivatives are instruments derivative of an underlying security, index, commodity or other product. There are synthetic versions of derivatives. The product is highly geared, meaning it can make significant profits or losses on very little money put up, and it can be used for speculating.

Derivatives can also be used to hedge profits, which is a protective role. Partly on this basis, the derivatives traders have disputed Warren Buffett's famous comment in a 2003 letter to shareholders that derivatives were 'financial weapons of mass destruction, carrying dangers that, while now latent, are potentially lethal'.

The 2007–09 financial crisis proved Buffett's concerns, one-sided as they may have been, well founded. Speculative derivatives trading had been a main factor in the near or full collapse of some financial institutions. The speculation was like the unrestrained behaviour of followers of Dionysus, the ancient Greek god of wine. The market still feels the repercussions.

> Speculative derivatives trading had been a main factor in the near or full collapse of some financial institutions.

The crisis made public the fact that derivatives would tend to be linked to other financial instruments in a chain of protections, stretching across financial institutions. The losses can have systemic impact. The Group of 20 finance ministers and bank governors, the Financial Stability Board, and regulators across the world are concerned about it. See Chapter 19 for more on systemic risk.

The current view, unsurprisingly, is that the risks of speculative trading in derivatives or other instruments must be acknowledged and respected. Regulators are looking to transfer some of the over-the-counter derivatives into exchanges, which would then be the counterparty to any transaction. This would produce greater transparency, although the exchanges are not without risks.

The industry, along with its regulators, is now showing some respect for the destructive power of derivatives arising from Dionysian speculation. To counterbalance the speculative effect, derivatives have the Apollonian hedging role, and these two opposite roles underpin the paradox defining this product.

Hedging brings investors peace of mind, for the price of a premium paid for a derivative. If the large trade wins, as planned, the derivative that hedges it will not be needed and the premium will be lost. Such hedging is considered economically viable because the premium payable is low in absolute terms compared with the potential profit on any pay-out that might be triggered.

The City is heavily dependent on the use of derivatives for hedging purposes, although this is far less publicised than the speculation. Farmers protect against bad crop seasons through buying commodity derivatives, just as, in financial markets, traders protect their main positions with financial derivatives.

It is not the case, as the thinking of some European supervisors suggests, that the speculators are evil and hedgers good, but rather that both are interdependent. In the financial crisis, nevertheless, derivatives speculation ruined some firms.

Power failure

In an October 2008 Congressional hearing, Alan Greenspan, chairman of the Federal Reserve until 2005, admitted that in his role he had put too much faith in free markets and their ability to correct themselves. He had not anticipated the damage that irresponsible mortgage lending could cause.

It was credit derivatives in particular that had played their role in the crisis. Large banks had used credit default swaps, a form of credit derivative, to insure financial institutions against losses on collateralised debt obligations that were, in some cases, backed by subprime mortgages and proved loss-making on a huge scale.

If a bank sells a credit default swap to another bank as protection on a bond it bought from a company, which then defaults, the seller will pay the amount of protection bought, and will in its turn claim on a credit default swap it bought through another bank, which will in turn have hedged its own risk. In such ways, a daisy chain links parties into the transaction.

As it turned out, a collapse in value of subprime mortgages in the financial crisis triggered a ripple through the daisy chain. Amounts payable and receivable were netted off, and this considerably reduced the impact. However, as the September 2008 bankruptcy of Lehman Brothers demonstrated, the unravelling of obligations can be horrendously complicated.

In retrospect, governments were as much to blame as regulators for having shown no respect for the power of derivatives. The US government had encouraged the lending of mortgages to disadvantaged buyers. There was an obvious risk that the borrowers could struggle with repayments, and the outcome was the collapse of the subprime mortgage market. The investment banks assumed that risk, believing that they could manage it by slicing the mortgage-backed securities, so that risk-free tranches at the top would be severed from the riskier tranches below. As it turned out, the risk could not be sliced and diced away.

The crisis showed that the idea of extra safe securities, so labelled by the rating agencies, was an illusion, although it had fuelled the market and, in doing so, the further sales of US mortgage sales to those who could not afford it, thereby triggering the near collapse of our financial system, from which we have not recovered today.

The victims emerging from the subprime mortgages and derivatives scandal in the crisis were across the chain, including buyers of property on mortgages they cannot afford, the retail investors and savers who trust in banks not worthy of it, and the taxpayer who took on the risk of bailing out financial institutions.

Regulation

Since the crisis, the European Union has put in process regulatory reform of derivatives markets through the European Market Infrastructure Regulation and the Markets in Financial Instruments Directive, each with different timetables. The regulations were timed roughly to coincide with those planned under the Dodd–Frank Wall Street Reform and Consumer Protection Act in the US, signed into law in July 2010.

> **There have been attempts to iron out some differences but some remain.**

There have been attempts to iron out some differences in the two sets of rules to avoid regulatory arbitrage, but some differences remain. Ministers for the group of 20 leading industrialised countries have pushed for implementing derivatives regulatory changes quickly, but this has since seemed optimistic.

The mandatory first time central clearing of some OTC derivatives, as proposed by regulators, should reduce the risks of a default, with the risk spread among many market players. The concerns are real. Lehman Brothers, which defaulted, and AIG, which nearly defaulted, in the financial crisis were both counterparties on substantial derivatives contracts.

The new regulations, as proposed, will require any authorised derivatives clearing house to accept trades from any trading revenue. From a competition perspective, there have been concerns that this could strengthen the monopolies in vertical silo structures of some large exchanges, where trading and clearing take place under the same roof. This is in light of global exchange mergers underway.

The Commodity Futures Trading Commission in the US has suggested that members of planned clearing houses for swaps should have to hold only US$50m of capital. This could open up the market to competition given that, currently, some clearing houses require as much as US$5bn of capital. There are concerns that this could lead to increased risk. In the past, not all clearing houses across the globe have proved resilient.

The way forward

The professionals in derivatives markets have mostly survived the crisis. Subsequently, the UK has even enhanced its dominance as the global centre for OTC derivatives trading, with its share of OTC interest rate derivatives up from 44 per cent in April 2007 to 46 per cent in April 2010, according to research by the Bank for International Settlements. The considerable freedom from regulation has been a feature of this success story.

It is my guess that derivatives speculation will survive the onslaught of regulators, and will be little affected in the long run. The risk-taking works more often than not, although the few major failures tend to have catastrophic potential. Derivatives trading can be highly profitable, establishes markets, contributes to the country's GDP, and ultimately helps to pay the salaries of everyone involved, regulators included.

12

Currency markets miasma

Introduction

Foreign exchange is a dangerous, as well as exciting, marketplace, particularly for retail traders. The market's huge volatility provides the potential for enormous trading profits, and losses.

With the increase in electronic trading, the potential illusion has arisen that there is more liquidity than there actually is. The market is not completely transparent. The carry trade, for example, as discussed in this chapter, is frequently off balance sheet.

In this chapter, we will focus on how foreign exchange trading works, and some of the potential uncertainties and concerns.

Comfortingly big

Foreign exchange is the largest of all financial markets. According to the Bank for International Settlements 2010 triennial survey of foreign exchange, it is getting bigger. In April 2010, the average daily turnover of global foreign exchange was US$3.9 trillion, up from US$3.3 trillion three years earlier. Foreign exchange trading is increasing long term, partly due to the increasing use of related financial derivatives and the growing importance of foreign exchange as an asset class.

The enormous size of this market means liquidity, although not always as limitless as it appears, and the comfort of a narrow spread (difference between buying and selling price), although this has widened during crisis, partly due to perceived greater default risk, making foreign exchange more profitable for banks. Trading is active for 24 hours a day, five days a week.

London is the major location, with 37 per cent of the global total in April 2010, followed by the United States at 18 per cent, the BIS survey records. This market share partly reflects that London is uniquely placed across the time zones.

> **London is uniquely placed across the time zones.**

Trading activity is highest when major markets overlap, as in the early morning in Europe or at the opening in North America, according to a TheCityUK report, Foreign Exchange 2010.

Traders

There are some 2,000 dealer institutions worldwide on the interbank market. Dealers trade foreign exchange on the phone, or through electronic brokerage, among themselves or directly with customers.

Foreign exchange traders include banks, and other financial institutions as well as companies and governments. In April 2010, activity with 'other' financial institutions – such as hedge funds, pension funds, mutual funds, insurance companies and non-reporting banks – surpassed transactions between reporting dealers, according to TheCityUK.

The increasing concentration of the dealers, partly due to the closure of some large investment banks in 2008, puts large-scale trading in fewer hands. In April 2010, the ten most active dealers accounted for 77 per cent of trading volume, as revealed by the Euromoney FX survey, as discussed by TheCityUK. In May 2010, Deutsche Bank, UBS AG and Barclays Capital accounted for more than 40 per cent of trading, compared with a 22 per cent share of the top three dealers in 2000, the survey found.

Moths to a flame

The range of execution venues and development of electronic platforms has facilitated access to this professional market – and at good tight spreads. Retail investors are drawn to the comfort of size and strength like moths to a flame. They account for 5 per cent of all trading, and growing, according to TheCityUK.

The punters place bets on foreign exchange movements between two currencies, as is the usual way, and they typically lose money. They lack the facilities and experience to read the markets, and trade part time. In short, they are not professionals.

The UK spread betting firms give retail traders exposure to foreign exchange, complete with risk warnings that, in their leveraged bets, they can lose more capital than they put up. In foreign exchange, traders can come in and out of profit quickly and one big loss can wipe out several weeks of gains.

Reading markets

The competent traders understand that monetary policy, currencies and stock markets are interconnected. By taking into account the knock-on effect, they make better informed trading decisions.

When interest rates are flat, exchange rates are driven substantially by psychological factors, including fear of sovereign defaults, as in Greece or Ireland. Other concerns are of credit rating downgrades for countries, or the likelihood of a collapse in the euro.

To forecast foreign exchange rates is, however, notoriously difficult. Purchasing power parity is the concept that exchange rates will converge to a level at which purchasing power is the same internationally, so countering infla-tion. It is the oldest theory of how exchange rates are formed, but, as analysts and traders tend to agree, it rarely works in the short term.

> **To forecast foreign exchange rates is notoriously difficult.**

Potential disruptions

Carry trade

The prospect of rising interest rates brings likelihood of a recurrence of the carry trade, which is where the trader sells, or borrows against, low-interest currencies, particularly the Japanese Yen. The trader converts the capital so released into a higher yielding currency such as the US dollar, and buys bonds such as US Treasuries for the same amount.

For as long as the bonds yield more than the Yen, this is a profit for the trader. By carrying out highly geared transactions, the trader who gets it right can make huge profits, but the risk is that exchange rates or interest rates move against this position. The trader is exposed to these and other fundamental factors.

The carry trade comes into favour when interest rates rise in some currencies but not in others. The practice can melt down, as happened in 2008, when borrowers had been forced to recall capital to pay off bad debts.

Carry trades are largely off balance sheet and, without more consolidated information on derivatives positions, there is no way to track them directly. As the May 2010 BIS paper, *Towards a global risk map*, by S.G, Cecchetti, I. Fender and P. McGuire, found, the size of the carry trade has eluded analysts for more than a decade partly because the term is used to refer to several types of financial activity.

The potential for a disruptive unwinding of such positions has been a long-standing policy concern, according to the paper.

Liquidity mirage

Generally, the increasing trend towards electronic trading means that supply and demand no longer entirely dictate exchange rates, according to analysts. There is a new *liquidity mirage* by which some large banks promise at any time to trade a given amount of currency at a given price. The risk is that this commitment could mean banks end up holding currency they cannot sell.

Default risk

Default risk arises in foreign exchange. Parties should exercise due diligence in checking out the counterparty. There are settlement and pre-settlement risks.

In the past, settlement risk has been greater than now. Straight-through processing has replaced manual and paper-based processing, and has considerably reduced costs and errors. The journey from trade inception to settlement is now electronic.

In general, netting, by which two parties offset trades, making it necessary to pay out only net amounts, has greatly reduced risk. If, however, one of the parties defaults, a liquidator could challenge the netting agreement, leaving the non-defaulting party among creditors claiming for losses.

There may be a requirement to put up collateral, otherwise known as margin, for trades, particularly the large ones. Traders will add to their margin where necessary to cover their open positions.

Some credit risk remains, particularly pre-settlement, and participants in foreign exchange markets must have reciprocal credit agreements in place.

The way forward

Foreign exchange trading is as rich in traps as it is in opportunity, and the sheer size of the market has its risks. At the same time, this market thrives on volatility, and is one of the few that does well in times of turbulence.

Retail investors seem likely to gain more market share in this growing market. Even for those who do not partake, the foreign exchange market usefully reflects global economic fluctuations. Investors in stocks and bonds, for example, will find this market worth watching.

PART FOUR

Your money

13

Bank tricks

Introduction

Banking is in crisis. The industry has lost public confidence and regulators have foisted on it. This will prove temporary. Public sentiment about banking fluctuates, but the industry remains indispensable to our economy.

In this chapter we will look at how banking works, and how it relies heavily on public confidence.

Image

When you use a UK bank, you are buying into a tradition which has a mainly clean reputation. The major banks benefit from their longstanding reputation for reliability even in times of crisis. They offer the security of backing from the Financial Services Authority and the Financial Services Compensation Scheme. The products on offer may not offer very exciting returns but are considered solid. The bank's name and the regulator's name, together, count for much in customers' eyes.

The bank gains and keeps its customers by projecting the right image. It is a combination of security consciousness, conservatism and competence, which often belies the uncertainties of those running the show. The image has the power to influence customers, just as in ancient Greek mythology, Jason has a magic unguent, given to him by his lover,

> The image has the power to influence customers.

the sorceress Medea, and this protects him against fire-eating bulls with whom he had to plough a field before being given the Golden Fleece that he seeks.

A major part of banks' image is ritual, and banks make extensive use of it in a gesture to the past. Cashiers, sometimes as young as in their late teens, may recommend the bank's investment services vaguely but enthusiastically to customers with spare cash in their accounts. They will refer them to the bank's financial adviser.

From the bank's perspective, the FSA requirements to know their customer are part of the ritual and, in themselves, a commercial weapon. The regulator comes down hard on rule breaches, but its stamp of authority, with its status as regulator included prominently on all the bank's sales literature, certainly reassures customers. Here is a major instance of financial institutions and the regulator working in cooperation.

On this basis, the customer who comes into the bank, for example to withdraw cash, may well walk out with an appointment made with the financial adviser. The bank promotes its products to customers in person or, on a more cost-effective basis, via the internet. In either case, potential customers must fill in forms and undergo identification and suitability checks. Money launderers typically operate without getting caught, but the banks at least play by the rules.

Confidence trick

As has become clear, the problem is that the rules can be too lax. The bank conveys the image of competence and reliability, as if deep rooted in hard cash, when a limitation on that cash supply is the biggest trade secret of the industry. The banks use money deposited to lend out at higher interest rates or to lend on the money markets. The money is sometimes exposed to significant risk.

If too many customers should seek all at once to withdraw their cash deposits, the bank would not have enough to pay them. Customers are not kept informed of this risk. Nor are many aware that when they save money in deposit accounts, the bank could never repay the amounts all at once. This is the system of fractional reserve banking at work. It is a *confidence trick*.

In the 2007–09 financial crisis, the trick was starting not to work. The UK government bank rescues in the crisis came at a potential cost to the taxpayer, and many saw this as a nasty surprise, just as Medea, estranged from her husband Jason, arranges delivery of a robe and a golden coronet to his new wife Glauce, and the gifts turn out, contrary to appearance, to be deadly poisonous.

The UK banks got away with it, this time, and have survived. Similarly Medea, in the version of Euripides, escapes the consequences of her revenge crimes by riding away in the chariot of Helios, the sun god. It is no exaggeration to say that banking trickery and reckless trading nearly brought down our financial system.

Cost to the customer

So far, some banks have been mis-selling some products, spoiling the track record of substantial solid selling. There have been some dud products sold, such as guaranteed bonds that fail, and some reasonable products sold that were, however, unsuitable for their buyers, such as payment protection insurance or some investment funds. There have not been outright frauds on any scale.

The reputation of banks is at a low now, but will revive. The banks are more trusted purveyors of financial services than most, although they are typically restricted in the range of products they sell. In return for the security of their name, the banks tend to offer products that have not very good terms or, at least, are not the best on the market. It is the price that they demand of their customers, just as Medea wants Jason as a future loyal husband if she is to help him with her magic to retrieve the Golden Fleece.

There is a school of thought that the names of the big banks are a diminishing asset, as customers are becoming increasingly savvy about the range of available products, most of which they can buy directly on the internet. So far, however, the big banks remain big and their names, even with all the problems, are well known and trusted.

Grey power

The names do not come much bigger than that of Barclays. When the FSA fined Barclays £7.7 million in January 2011 for failure to take reasonable care to ensure suitable advice in certain fund sales to customers, it sent out a warning message to the rest of the industry. Many of the customers in this case were retired, or near retirement, and the FSA regarded the breaches as particularly serious because Barclays had identified early some concerns with the funds, but had not acted properly to mitigate them. Subsequently, however, the bank undertook a business review to ensure that customers did not lose out as a result of the failings, and improved its processes, factors that the regulator took into account in assessing the seriousness of the breaches.

When a well-known UK bank breaches the rules, it can come as a shock, but, as in this case, the mechanisms are in place for remedy as well as punishment. Outside regulated banks, even among regulated firms, there can be far worse mis-selling than happened at Barclays, and it too often goes unpunished. In unregulated firms particularly, there can be outright fraud.

Older people may have money to invest and can be easy victims. A comfortable retirement can be wiped out in one fell swoop by unscrupulous financial services salespeople.

There is also phishing. Outfits that masquerade as the major banks and other financial institutions send emails to individuals everywhere instructing them, in the claimed name of the bank, to provide sensitive account information for administrative purposes. Individuals who fall for this scam, as planned by the perpetrators, will see money stolen from their account.

> Corporate identity theft continues and could be doing significant damage to their brands.

The big banks and other financial institutions act rigorously to differentiate themselves from the fraudsters who have hijacked their names, but the corporate identity theft continues and could be doing significant damage to their brands. Sadly, the misbehaviour of the real big banks may well be casting further doubt on who is the perpetrator of the phishing frauds using their names.

Big dreams, small returns

The banks have the unspoken aim of continuing in the comfortable position of taking in money from the sale of not very competitive products without making the game too obvious. This compromise in standard of product is a proven way to maximise profits. The display of a caring service, filling in all the relevant forms, with a warm handshake to seal the deal, can become for customers the most important aspect of the investment experience. They are in the weaker position. In the Greek mythology, what chance does Jason have, mere mortal as he is, of outmanoeuvring his powerful wife Medea, whose mother is the infamous sorceress Circe, and whose grandfather is Helios, the sun god?

Just as Medea has the ultimate support of Helios, in whose chariot she escapes from the consequences of her retributive crimes, so banking can call on the backup infrastructure of central banking, regulators and government. The emergency support has so far not been withheld from clearing banks, and has made it easier for them to cast their spell on the public, adding to the sense of security felt in dealing with them.

If a bank fails, there is sentiment that the government will step in and notice it, as it did in the crisis, and there are regulatory moves towards 'living wills' implementation, by which banks must prepare a plan in the event of their own demise to avoid being dependent on taxpayer funds. The 'moral hazard' concerns thus remain, and, on this basis, when markets are in an upturn, it is hard not to envisage the banks taking such chances as they legally can to maximise returns in the full knowledge that if things go wrong, they will be bailed out.

Heroes

In the aftermath of the 2007–09 crisis, the large banks that, in some cases, had misbehaved recklessly and disgracefully are coveted as lenders in the reviving economy. It is because of their indispensability to the workings of business and personal finance that the government had rescued them. The bank leaders, ever the opportunists, now harness the media to represent them as heroes. Their mantra is that it is time that everyone put the crisis behind them, that pay cuts in banking have already been dealt with, and that the imperative is to move forward.

The banks exploit their role in the economy as a negotiating tool with government bodies. They warn the government, which is under political pressure to impose regulation on them, not to burden the industry too much or else banking services will be restricted. They threaten, if over pressed, to move their headquarters abroad. They pretend to be aggrieved with proposed regulatory burdens that, as they well know, are a light let off. A prime example was Project Merlin.

Project Merlin

There is an element of the magician's showmanship about the Project Merlin deal, implemented between the banks and the Treasury in February 2011, and not just in the name. This was a microcosm of the entire relationship between government, banks, and the public. The deal was a sop to the public, suggesting that the government was taking serious action to force the banking industry, which had received bailouts putting the taxpayer at risk, to lend more to business. The biggest banks in the United Kingdom, RBS, HSBC, Lloyds TSB and Barclays, had committed themselves to committing £190 billion in gross lending to business, up from £179 billion in 2010, and the Spanish bank Santander signed up to the deal.

As a compromise in favour of the banks, the deal had a rationale. The banks are vital to the functioning of the economy. What is disconcerting, however, is that appearance here, as in other such agreements, became more important than reality.

The banks present the case of their contribution to the economy largely behind closed doors, to government bodies and regulators, to avoid attracting further public criticism. The government and regulators do not want to quash banking too much, in the interests of recovery of the economy, and so they concoct solutions such as Project Merlin. The banks put on a show of finding such solutions uncomfortable, and this can appease the public.

What is missing from the mix is not ethics, nor fairness, which is a complex assessment, but transparency in the negotiations. This is convenient for the negotiating parties but, when the entire banking system has been propped by the taxpayer, we need more openness.

Towards new customer relations

With concerns about their exposure to the Eurozone in 2011, banks were still playing a game of waiting, for the negative perceptions of their industry to disappear as much as for the economy to improve. The two go hand in hand. It is a matter of time and the banking leaders know it. The public has short memories. Bank–customer relations will be sweet if customers have, or believe that they have, the service they need. The resulting equilibrium should stay until the next crisis.

Managing the risk

Modelling issues

The banks model risk using Enterprise Risk Management, which takes a holistic approach. Unfortunately, model indications do not necessarily have any correspondence with reality. They are known for coping with business as usual but not with a 'black swan' event. The regulatory drive requires that everyone looks at broadly similar models, meaning that when the model is wrong, so is everybody.

Ring-fencing

The risk that the clearing banks face, exacerbated by their links with investment banking, is endogenous. If anything goes wrong in one area, it can have a domino-like effect on others. The idea of ring-fencing retail operations from others in the banking group, including investment banking, has come under regulatory consideration. The proposals would be a UK version of the separation between retail and investment banking enshrined in law by the Glass–Steagall Act 1933 in the United States, which had mixed results and was repealed in 1999.

Ring-fencing, as under discussion, would not be an easy fit for the banking model. The concept has superficial appeal and some high-level political advocates, but it would not, for example, have prevented the Lehman Brothers' collapse in September 2008. Retail banks lend more than they borrow, which can make them dependent on wholesale funding and so exposed to it. If retail was separated from investment banking within a group, it would come at a cost. Another problem is that where interconnections exist across a broad banking group, to unravel them may be difficult.

More capital

The main proposed solution to banking failure underway is the requirement for the banks to hold more capital. The global Basel III capital requirements, to be phased in from 2013 and completed by 2019, are considerably more stringent than the old Basel II ones. Political pressure has been a major driving force, and to some extent this is beyond common sense.

Under Basel III, the banks need top-tier capital that is 7 per cent of risk-bearing assets, considerably higher than before. In practice, the major UK banks already hold more than this. There is a capital surcharge of up to 2.5 per cent for large global banks, which the industry has understandably not welcomed.

Under the requirements, banks will have capital buffers on which they can draw in times of stress. Because letters of credit are defined as off-balance sheet, they will become more expensive, and banks are likely to shun them, using cheaper financing methods and so focusing more on counterparty risk. There will be an adverse impact on world trade.

The beneficiaries of Basel III will be shadow banking entities, such as hedge funds and asset managers, which can pick up some of the lending business dropped by the banks. These entities may not be as restricted in their capital requirements as banks and so may lend more cheaply, which poses a risk to the system.

The governments express determination not to bail out banks again, but, as we have seen in this chapter, there is a widespread belief that they would do so if necessary. Such triggering conditions might be systemic risk to the system and if the institutions' recovery and resolution plans should prove inadequate. As seen in the crisis, the governments are much less likely, however, to bail out the shadow banking players.

Cross-border banking

Cross-border banking brings special challenges, some of them out of the United Kingdom's control. Memories linger of Landsbanki, the large bank in Iceland, part of the European Economic Area. In October 2006, the bank had launched Icesave, an internet bank operation, which had attracted many deposits from the United Kingdom. When the group collapsed in October 2008, there were major concerns whether UK depositors could get their deposits back.

Unfortunately, as host country supervisor of Landsbanki's UK branch, the FSA had only limited power. In this case, depositors did not lose out, but the vulnerabilities around cross-border banking remain. The FSA has pressed for a review of bank passporting rights, and the Government has taken up the issue at European level.

Vulnerabilities around cross-border banking remain.

Further concerns

The conflict between short-term profit and consumer interest lurks under the surface of banking like a cancer. In the post-crisis environment, when wholesale funding is expensive and retail custom competitive, the banks seek out new sources of income.

One route is to sell wealth management products, an area that does not always require the same investment in systems and technology as others. In this area, the FSA has noted that banks might encourage private banking clients to take inappropriate risks on savings by selling them complex or illiquid products.

The way forward

There is plenty of scope in our banking system to increase Medea's type of sleight of hand and magic, and we can expect this. To keep a check on the excess, the regulator seeks a free flow of information from the banks. They will cooperate but tactically.

Everyone will have an eye to the public and political mood. On a temporary basis at least, banking can behave well. The waiting game is part of its time-honoured agenda. How to retain a functioning and globally competitive banking system while squeezing out mis-selling and subterfuge on a permanent basis remains unresolved.

14

Collective investments unmasked

Introduction

Investment funds may have good recent track records, but the projections can be very different. The fund that did well last year may do badly this year. A star manager may have departed for another job, and fund charges can hit your returns.

The fund managers can make a mediocre or inconsistently performing fund sound enticing.

In this chapter, we will look at how funds work, and issues around performance, charges and sales techniques. We will consider exchange-traded funds and also investment companies.

Financial services in flux

If you are to sort out financial affairs for long-term security, you must defer current pleasures for future benefits. Many are not in the habit of saving through investment, however, and opt for cash deposits, if anything. They are discouraged by market volatility, as well as uncertainty over where to invest and across what asset classes.

Another negative factor is the financial services industry's reputation for ripping off the public, which, unfortunately, is partly deserved. As an investor in funds, you must conduct some research of your own and understand what you are buying, if for nothing else to check up on the advice of your financial adviser.

You must recognise and block your ears to the sales pitches and selective statistics masking a patchy track record in a fund. It is true that a past track record can mean something, despite the investment fund industry's formal mantra that past performance is no guide to the future. Funds that have outperformed their peers for years may continue to do so. It is the exciting funds without much track record that should make you most wary.

> **Exciting funds without much track record should make you wary.**

The line can be thin between selective presentation of facts to sell funds, even if the risk warnings are provided on paper, and misrepresentation. Salespeople or fund operators can lapse into fraud. There are universal lessons in Homer's *The Odyssey*, where Odysseus, on his voyage, blocks his crew's ears with wax and ties himself to the mast to prevent them from being lured by the sweet-singing Sirens to a certain death.

The financial services industry never seems to learn from unethical behaviour. In a June 2011 conference about the Financial Conduct Authority, Hector Sants, chief executive, Financial Services Authority, said that consumer treatment had not improved over the regulator's lifespan, and that this was his biggest disappointment.

Your choice of funds

For most investors, collective investments such as funds make more sense than investing in shares. You can buy into a well-diversified fund, across shares or broad asset classes, and achieve the benefits of spreading your risk on a very small financial investment. You can drip-feed money into your fund investment over a period, averaging out returns across fluctuating market conditions.

You may diversify risk not just within a fund but also across funds. You may, for example, have some money in a balanced fund across asset classes, another amount in an emerging markets fund and the rest in a bond fund. Multi-manager funds can switch from one fund to another, a flexibility which can make or save money in fast changing market conditions. These funds have high fees, however, and the concept is as yet unproven.

The active versus passive fund debate

Most funds are actively managed. The fund manager personally selects stocks and other securities, and follows his own asset allocation strategy, buying and selling when it seems fit.

The job is about as skilled as the fund manager chooses to make it, which is sometimes not very. Many an investor, on a financial adviser's recommendation, has invested in an actively managed fund whose manager, being cautious, effectively tracks the benchmark index. This produces a market-average performance but is weighted by management charges.

Fund managers that follow this strategy take some comfort in the likelihood that they will not be personally held responsible if the fund should fall in value, and, given that the decline will be in line with the market, there will probably not be a disproportionate exodus from the fund. If the market is down, they can argue it is the same for everybody who invests broadly in the market, beyond the individual fund manager's control.

On the flipside, in a rising market, the fund's gain will be in line with the market's but not substantially more. Again, this is playing safe.

An index tracker fund, passively managed and simply tracking a recognised index such as the FTSE-100 index of Britain's largest shares, achieves an average market investment outcome but with much lower charges, which, over the long term, can make a significant difference to the returns for the investor. According to the Investment Management Association, index tracker funds now represent about 6 per cent of industry funds under management.

Financial advisers have not recommended tracker funds mostly because they generate little or no commission, and some do not believe in trackers under any circumstances. Actively managed funds can, if their remit allows it, sell out of hard hit sectors in a falling market, such as banking. This can make the actively managed fund's price hold up better than that of an index tracker fund, which must maintain a proportionate holding in every sector. The index tracker may also have tracking error, meaning it slightly underperforms the market.

Among actively managed funds a few have very low charges, comparable to those of trackers. These tend not to be the top performers. Some actively managed funds, typically among those with higher charges, can substantially beat the market, although, sometimes, this can still mean losing money in absolute terms.

The comparative high fliers are often in niche sectors, taking high risks, such as in emerging markets or small select UK companies or recovery stocks. There are, of course, plenty of ineffectual niche funds.

A top fund manager who consistently achieves above-average results may move from one fund to another, every three or four years, affecting performance in the funds from which he has departed.

Given the many ways of representing a fund's performance even without distorting the figures, mediocre funds often appear better than they are through clever marketing tactics. If they are disastrous, they may be given a new strategy and merged into another fund, changing their name, but not always their fund manager.

Investing strategy

Investors without the time or interest to spend continually checking investments may seek funds that they can buy and hold in the medium to long term, regardless of changing market conditions. Fund managers favour this approach because they do not want to see money leaving their fund. Their argument is that it is beneficial to stay the market to benefit from sudden upturns and in the realisation that downturns will not last for ever.

> **Reassess the portfolio regularly, sell out of funds that underperform, reinvesting elsewhere.**

This approach can work, but in the short term it can lose investors money. The better tactic can be to reassess the portfolio regularly, and sell out of funds that under-perform, or have become less promising, reinvesting elsewhere. This incurs switching costs, of course, and judgement.

The move can be simply to switch from a long fund into a better performer, or it can be to rebalance across asset classes and so maintain exposure proportionate to your risk profile.

If as an investor you hold a portfolio of several funds, it makes sense to get your money out of the losers into new funds before the losses become much bigger. In the same way, Odysseus loses six of his men to the voracious Scylla as the price to pay for passing through waters exposed to attacks from this cannibalistic monster. By sacrificing the few, he saves most of the crew and himself.

Exchange-traded funds

An exchange-traded fund is an investment fund, holding assets. This type of fund combines the valuation features of a unit trust, which can be bought or sold for net asset value, with the tradability of an investment trust, which sells at prices that may be more or less than its net asset value.

The ETFs are mostly index funds, which makes them low cost, although some are actively managed. They invest in, among other things, equities, commodities, bonds, or currencies. If used to invest in gold or silver, they can be part of a defensive strategy. They are also among those securities that may be conveniently used to hedge an opposite position.

Some ETFs have counterparty risks, including those that use derivatives. Leveraged ETFs, rising and falling at a higher rate than an index, are risky.

At European level, the European Securities and Markets Authority (see Chapter 21, p. 198) has raised discussion calling for communication and transparency on ETFs, and a possible limit on distribution on some of them to retail investors. The authority has said that safeguards on selling the products are inadequate and the more complex products pose a stability risk to the broader financial system. There are concerns, shared with the Financial Stability Board, about synthetic exchange-traded funds, based on derivatives.

Some have suggested that ETFs were used for market manipulation and short selling, including ahead of the 2007–09 financial crisis.

Quality of advice

Independent financial advisers these days are cautious with their advice. In the current regulatory climate if they get it wrong, they could end up being sued, or at the very least have to justify their actions in a job where reputation can mean survival.

Diversification across asset classes is important for most investors as the way to spread risk. As the 2002 Sandler Review found, investment theorists agree that the asset allocation decision is usually far more important in determining investment performance than security selection. This is the bit that IFAs can most easily get right.

In Chapter 1, we discussed asset allocation for direct investing and the same principles apply for funds. The exposures to different types and geographies of asset class should be mixed according to the investor's risk profile. A young investor who has time to regain losses can afford more equities exposure than the person approaching retirement, who should have more money in cash and bonds.

The pricing structure

Research by the Association of British Insurers has shown that a majority believe that financial advice is worth nothing. Until the Retail Distribution Review, in force from 31 December 2012, the cost of such advice has been hidden in commissions that cut into the product returns, a procedure that not everybody has understood.

Under the pre-RDR regime, an investor in a fund through an IFA has paid an initial fee of up to 5 per cent of the investment as well as 0.5 per cent a year in trail commission. Let us take an example of the individual savings account, which protects cash or investments from income and capital gains tax.

If the investor wants, for example, to transfer a £50,000 cash ISA into a stocks and shares ISA, he may give his adviser up to £2,500 as an initial fee just to set it up. The trail commission of £250 a year, paid to the IFA, will be deducted from charges of perhaps 2 per cent taken from the investment by the fund manager. In the first year, the adviser will have cleared £2,750.

> Some IFAs provide a good service for the money, and profits can eventually overcome the commission paid.

Let us be fair. Some IFAs provide a good service for the money, and the profits from the investment can eventually overcome the commission paid. In addition, not every adviser will charge the maximum 5 per cent initial charge. Discount brokers should cut this charge right back but they will not give advice.

Retail Distribution Review

The RDR will increase the professional standards of financial advisers and improve the clarity with which firms describe their services. Customers will know if they are getting independent or restricted advice. There will be a fee structure rather than commission paid for advice and so there will be no incentive for the adviser to recommend one product over another. Trail commissions, which are annual income paid to the IFA, will be paid by fund houses only on investments made before the RDR was implemented.

Advisers will need to hold a statement of professional standing if they want to give independent or restricted advice to retail investors after June 2013. The SPS will provide customers with evidence that the adviser subscribes to a code of ethics, is qualified and has kept knowledge up to date.

There are extra qualification requirements to meet the RDR standards. In addition, advisers will have to complete at least 35 hours of continuing professional development a year. In these ways, the RDR puts a lot of emphasis on paper qualifications, although it does not exclude experience.

The post-RDR world

Based on such changes, there is a widespread expectation that the RDR will work as a stamp of respectability, making the industry more like such professions as accountancy and law.

There is a price to pay, however. Many in the industry doubt whether the public, particularly at the lower end of the earnings spectrum, will be willing to pay upfront fees for financial advice. Advisers may target only wealthier customers. Ahead of the RDR, talk of industry consolidation has been rife, and some advisers have planned to leave the business.

Certainly, there is less incentive for misleading sales tactics. The RDR puts pressure on those financial salespeople who, in a long tradition, maximise commission earnings at the customer's expense. It is as in *The Odyssey*, when Odysseus returns home to Ithaca after 20 years to kill those many profligate suitors of his wife who have been living lavishly as unwelcome guests of his palace.

Investment companies

Investment companies, also known as investment trusts, are funds listed as companies on the London Stock Exchange to invest in shares of other companies. Investors buy shares in the trust. The investment companies are closed-end, which means they raise money once by issuing shares at launch. They may issue new shares subsequently if demand is strong, but only with shareholder approval. Demand for the shares does not increase the fund size, but should have positive impact on the share price.

Investment companies tend to trade at a discount to the value of their assets, but popular funds can trade at a premium. Discounts and premiums can be a reflection of market sentiment, and may be affected by such issues as past performance, and share ownership profile. In funds bought at a discount, investors have more assets working for them, hopefully to produce capital and income. However, for an investment company trading on a wide discount it is not necessarily cheap. Conversely, if the company trades at a premium, it is not necessarily expensive.

As quoted companies, investment companies are regulated by company law and by the UK Listing Authority, as overseen by the FSA. They are not, however, directly regulated by the FSA as investment funds are, and so they are not subject to the Financial Services Ombudsman, the independent dispute settling service, or the Financial Services Compensation Scheme. Wrapper products involving investment companies such as ISAs or savings schemes are regulated by the FSA, however. The financial adviser's advice is subject to FSA regulation.

New rules being introduced in 2013, under the Alternative Investment Fund Managers Directive, are likely to bring many aspects of investment company regulation directly within the scope of the UK regulator.

Further regulation of investment companies has already been introduced as a result of scandals. In 2002, some split capital investment companies, which, by definition, had several classes of share, collapsed. The companies had been investing in each other, and there had been a knock-on impact from problems affecting individual companies. Some 50,000 private investors lost an estimated £600 million from the large-scale failure, exacerbated by the contagion. In November 2003, changes to the listing rules and conduct of business rules were introduced. The investment circularity from split capital investment companies investing in each other is no longer possible.

As a much later regulatory development, the RDR levels the playing field between investment companies and funds. In the pre-RDR era, investment companies have been unable to pay commissions to advisers except at launch, a major reason why they have not often been recommended.

The RDR, by abolishing commissions as a means of remuneration to financial advisers, gives investment companies, an industry with £97 billion of assets under management, the opportunity to gain market share from the much larger investment fund sector. In addition, financial advisers now need to demonstrate they have looked at the whole market, including investment companies.

> Financial advisers now need to demonstrate they have looked at the whole market.

Over the long term, investment companies have outperformed investment funds particularly in mainstream sectors, due to gearing, lower than average charges, particularly for the mainstream sectors, and an independent board of directors to oversee shareholder interests. The closed-end structure means that managers can take a long-term market view without the worry of having to sell stock to meet redemptions.

The way forward

Now more than ever, investors and regulators alike are challenging misrepresentation of prospects for collective investments. In the post-RDR world, there is likely to be less of it. Even so, the vast majority of investment funds will continue to underperform the market, once all charges are taken into account.

Current investor demand is for flexible fund products, even when they are more expensive, in the hope that they can adjust to volatile conditions. Multi-manager funds are a growth area (see also the discussion on absolute return funds, in Chapter 3). In the post-RDR world without commissions, tracker funds and investment companies stand to gain market share.

15

Pensions crisis

Introduction

Old age can be uncomfortable if there is not enough money to support it. Saving money regularly into a pension is the main way our population saves for old age.

In this chapter we will look briefly at our pension system, how it works, why the public has lost faith, and at some of the changes under way in the industry to smooth the crisis.

Savings gap

People are not saving enough into their pensions. It is partly a government problem. If people cannot support themselves in old age, they will fall back on social security benefits, which cost the taxpayer.

Many are relying on other sources of money in old age. According to a May 2011 survey by YouGov for the National Association of Pension Funds, of some three million people who are not retired, 8 per cent of those surveyed rely on a lottery win to pay for their retirement and a similar number, 9 per cent, count on an inheritance. Fewer than half of those surveyed rely on a workplace or private pension.

How much people need to retire comfortably is open to discussion. The Scottish Widows seventh annual UK pensions report, published in June 2011, found that people wanted on average £24,300 a year at 70 years old.

This is a sizable drop from the £27,900 figure before the recession in 2009, but unobtainable if the number of people failing to save remained at current rates. Such an income would require a pension pot of several hundred thousand pounds, which most people will not have.

The government is always encouraging people to pay more into their pensions. The major incentive is the tax relief allowed on your contributions, but, unfortunately, you are taxed on the income you later draw from your annuity. The tax relief comes when you pay in, but not when you draw out.

Tax relief comes when you pay in, but not when you draw out.

On top of any pension you take out, there is the state pension. Let us take a look.

Different types of pension

State pension

The state pension is made up of the basic state pension and the additional state pension. How much you will receive as a regular payment on reaching the state pension age depends on for how many years you have paid National Insurance contributions.

You will need to have paid contributions for 30 years to get the full amount, but even this pays only for bare necessities. On top of this, you should have made other provisions for retirement. There are two types of pension: defined contribution and defined benefit.

Defined contribution

The 'defined contribution' pension is where contributions of the employer and employee are invested in a fund that, on retirement, is used to buy an annuity. The employee is exposed to the performance risk of investments in the fund. This is the most usual type of scheme in the private sector.

Personal pensions are a form of 'defined contribution' scheme that can be offered by employers as group personal pensions, and, outside the workplace, individual personal pensions work much in the same way. An employer may offer an occupational pension as a main alternative.

Specialist forms of personal pension include the self-invested personal pension. This is a flexible pension wrapper for those who like to choose their own investments. At the other extreme is the stakeholder pension, which has a cap on charges, and limited funds in which one may invest. This is aimed at low to moderate earners.

The National Employment Savings Trust, known snugly as NEST, is similarly aimed at the lower end of the saving market, and it inculcates a far more widespread savings culture in the workplace. From October 2012, employees are automatically enrolled in their company pension scheme if one exists or, if not, into a form of occupational pension aimed at low to moderate earners provided by NEST.

Individuals can opt out of NEST, but for those who stay in, employers will contribute 3 per cent of an employee's salary, and employees will pay in 4 per cent, with 1 per cent tax relief from the government. The scheme will operate using the services of third-party asset managers. The idea generally is to restore public confidence in savings. It is a basic system only, however, setting limits on the amount that can be invested in it, and, if started late in life, will certainly not be enough to enable a comfortable retirement.

Some are concerned that too many will opt out of NEST. One suggestion is that employers should pay the 3 per cent contribution for employees, even if they opt out. The pensions industry has expressed concern that employers could use NEST as a cheaper alternative to company schemes.

The system clearly has major deficiencies, but it is a move in the direction of helping people to save for retirement, and avoiding some of the burden that might otherwise fall on the state.

Defined benefit

'Defined benefit' schemes are the main alternative to 'defined contribution'. They remain in only a few private sector companies, having been phased out by many as uneconomical for the employer. This is the type of scheme commonly available in the public sector, to civil servants, nurses, police, firemen and others.

Because it offers a guaranteed pension with no investment risk, the 'defined benefit' scheme is more advantageous for employees than the 'defined contribution' scheme. The way the scheme works is that members make regular contributions out of their salaries and are given a level of pension based on years of service, the proportion of salary received for each year of service, and final or average salary. The employee's contributions are added to those of other members and the employer, and the trustee invests the money for members.

The framework for the public sector 'defined benefit' scheme, unlike for the others, is set up by an act of parliament which stipulates the scheme rules. Until now, the majority of state employees have enjoyed 'final salary' pensions, which are the best form of 'defined benefit' scheme, based on final rather than average salary.

Pension apartheid

With the two main types of pension provision in the workplace, we have, as some newspaper journalists have dubbed it, pension 'apartheid'. Employees in the public sector enjoy a far better pension, in the form of 'final salary' schemes, than many in the private sector, where schemes are often, although not invariably, 'defined contribution'. Employees who have spent their working lives in the public sector have often been able to retire far more comfortably than their counterparts in the private sector.

It is the taxpayer who subsidises the public sector pensions, and this has led to some resentment among those in the private sector. There is some truth in the conspiracy theory that, for decades, ministers and civil servants with a vested interest in protecting their own lucrative pension arrangements have kept the system going.

This is all changing, although, in the view of some, it is too little, too late. The government, battling with a huge deficit, is 'discussing' with the unions some proposed reforms to the public sector pensions. The reforms will increase payment contributions of employees and raise the retiring age to beyond 60. Another proposal is to switch the typical 'defined contribution' pension from final salary to average salary, so the pension is calculated on the average salary over the period of employment, rather than, as now, on the higher final salary.

Teachers, civil servants and other public sector workers have vigorously protested against the proposed reforms, which mean they have to work for longer, pay more into their pensions, and enjoy a reduced standard of living on retirement. Some protest that they cannot afford the extra pension payments. Teaching unions argue that the proposed reforms could drive teachers from the profession. Another argument, no longer as convincing as it was, is that public sector employees earn less than those in the private sector.

The near collapse of the Greek economy, highly publicised in mid-2011, is one of several cases from the euro zone from which the clear message is that no country indefinitely subsidises what it cannot afford.

> No country indefinitely subsidises what it cannot afford.

War of words

Even after reforms in line with the proposals, the public sector pension scheme will be far better for employees than the 'defined contribution' type of scheme typically available in the private sector. There is a feeling here that the state sector has had it too good for far too long, with no thought given as to how the pensions will be funded. Some press comment has dubbed the public sector pension arrangements as a giant Ponzi scheme.

Some of the unions have protested that the government is only going through the motions of negotiation with them because it has clearly decided on the reforms. That is probably right. Many in the private sector applaud the government's purpose.

The future of pensions, and the lifestyle of the old, have for a long time been, like everything else in financial markets, a war of words, a battle between different parties with their own vested interests. A pensions crisis is in full swing.

Crisis truths

The crisis is all about having a large enough retirement income. For many, pension provision is not nearly enough. One reason why people do not save enough for their old age is that they cannot afford it. According to the Association of British Insurers, the single most important factor that people say would increase their pensions savings is a pay increase. However, other research suggests that many people fit their spending to their income level. For some, this never leaves much for pension saving.

Another problem is that, in 'defined contribution' pension pots, stock market volatility can have impact on the value of the fund. If this comes just as a person is retiring, it means there is less cash available in the pension pot to buy an annuity. This means less retirement income. To cope with this, many people reckon on working for years longer than they had planned.

Some pension investors will have avoided this problem by de-risking their pension funds, shifting the money from equities into bonds and cash equivalents, a few years before retirement. Others will have failed to do this, not least because it can be difficult to say when they will retire.

From the perspective of financing retirement, an overall demographic concern is that people are living longer and, for that reason, the annual income paid by annuities has drastically declined. The message is always that we should work for longer and save longer, but it is not a complete solution. Two problems remain. First, the public is not well educated about investment risk, and how pensions work. Second, mis-selling scandals have contributed a poor reputation to the pension industry.

> **The public is not well educated about investment risk and how pensions work.**

Pension education

Pension education should be about facts, your choice of pension, for how long you need to save, and the fund investment options. The Pensions Advisory Service (www.pensionsadvisoryservice.org.uk) is an independent, government-backed, voluntary service, with experts available free of charge for answering your questions on pensions. I would recommend this service. It is also worth visiting Moneymadeclear, another government-backed service, at www.moneyadviceservice.org.uk.

In addition, you can obtain useful information and perspectives from investment authors and journalists, and industry examination courses. None of these is perfect, but they are a more independent source of education than the salesperson's mouth or the industry's 'free' assessments. That is not to say that your financial adviser cannot sometimes give you useful information, but many do not understand pensions, and I urge you to conduct your own research as well.

Bear in mind that if you take out a pension, it is a long-term investment and there are risks involved. There are often poor returns, and the tax advantages of investing in a pension may not always compensate.

In a July 2011 CII thinkpiece, Balancing Risk and Return, Barry O'Dwyer, deputy chief executive of Prudential plc UK and Europe, says that consumers must be brought to understand the risk of investing in pensions or real assets, and to accept risk as a necessary part of the deal.

The risk is not just from investment but is also political, and, O'Dwyer notes, it is hard to persuade people to commit money long term to pensions when politicians might change the rules. Risk taking requires knowledge and understanding to stand the best chance of success but it is fundamentally about temperament. Some people have an in-depth knowledge of how stock markets work, and may even be stockbrokers, but they cannot stomach investment risk personally, even in a pension where their money is invested long term beyond their reach.

Mis-selling

Pensions suffer from a dreadful reputation. The product has been subject to mis-selling scandals, and these are now deeply engrained into the industry, a major reason why people are reluctant to commit money to pensions in the first place. The history of pensions mis-selling is littered with switches from company to private pension schemes, now a problem of the past. Poorly designed and opaque products as well as hefty upfront charges have been further problems.

Robert Maxwell's plundering of his employees' pension funds at Mirror Group Newspapers, revealed as far back as 1991, triggered positive changes in pension legislation, but limitations have remained. The longstanding problems from the near collapse of Equitable Life in 2000 took years to reach resolution.

If the industry wants to understand why people are wary, it should look in the mirror. People do not want to pay heavy costs for poor pensions advice and maybe poor products. They will not entrust their money to a financial institution that takes investment risks out of their control and that may even go bust.

The regulators are at last intervening in a radical way. As we saw in Chapter 14, the Retail Distribution Review, effective from 31 December 2012, bans commissions paid on pension sales. This is a major blow to the advisers and not just the dubious ones.

The independent financial advisers will receive trail commissions from earlier pensions sales, typically 0.5 per cent a year, even after the RDR's abolition of commissions. Not all IFAs give much service in return for this, according to a 2011 Consumer Focus report.

The report noted problems in high costs and charges and opaque pricing, as well as in churning, where the IFA switches the customer from one pension to another to generate commission.

Pension solutions

The National Association of Pension Funds believes that NEST is a good step forward in the encouragement of saving into pensions, but would like to see further reform. The association has advocated super trusts. These would be large-scale, not-for-profit, multi-employer pension schemes, managed by trustees who would put members' interests first.

In a controversial contribution to the debate, the Royal Society for the encouragement of Arts, Manufactures and Commerce advocated in a December 2010 report moving to a Dutch-style collective pension operation in this country on the grounds that it would be much more cost-effective.

The Association of British Insurers has publicly opposed the introduction of such a scheme, partly because it would have much less flexibility than our present pension scheme, but also because it leaves nothing for family members if a saver dies, and, as the Dutch scheme has shown, it can be hit by financial crises.

Alternatives

There are options besides pensions for retirement planning, from saving in tax-free ISAs to buy-to-let and equity release. The apparent opportunities can provide a false sense of security. Many who rely on the options of downsizing their own residence or on equity release in retirement, for instance, have not assessed all the difficulties.

The way forward

Flawed as it is, our pension system is set to stay. Clearly, auto-enrolment and NEST will benefit some who would not otherwise save for pensions, and the public sector reforms will reduce the pension 'apartheid'.

Self-evidently, the reputation problem of the pensions industry is not resolvable overnight. The RDR's abolition of commission payable on pension sales stops commission-based mis-selling of pensions, but also some of the incentive for IFAs to sell pensions at all. The way forward must be a combination of government support and industry cooperation, with consumers, as always, taking risks other than from investment performance.

PART FIVE

Safety first

16

Insurance comfort

Introduction

Insurance is about putting safeguards in place, in case the worst happens. This enables people to go on living their lives and running businesses in the full knowledge that they are covered against risks. They seek insurance protection for peace of mind, just as, in ancient Greece, people sacrificed to the gods as a safeguard against future misfortunes.

In this chapter, we will look at how insurance works, and the tripartite relationship between insurers, broker and client. We will look at regulatory developments, particularly Solvency II, and the reputational problems that the industry faces.

Insurance

Companies buy plenty of insurance. For example, banks take large amounts of errors and omission insurance to cover them against the risk of giving wrong advice. They buy directors' and officers' liability insurance to protect the company, its officers and its directors against corporate liability claims, and insure against property damage risk.

The insurance must be precisely tailored to the firm's needs for cover. The wrong insurance is useless. Similarly in *The Odyssey*, Odysseus's men sacrificed to the gods after they had killed the sun god's cattle but this did not save them from divine retribution.

In a soft market, rates are low. When a hard market comes, rates rise.

The profitability of business varies, according to rates and the incidence of claims. The rates are impacted by cycles shifting from soft to hard markets and back again. In a soft market, rates are low, based on supply and demand, and underwriters prefer to take on really good risk. When a hard market comes, rates rise, and underwriters become more relaxed.

Let us now take a look at how the London insurance market works.

The London market

Insurance or reinsurance programmes have to be multifaceted and expertly crafted to meet the needs of buyers. The London market concentrates mainly on non-life insurance and is famed for covering a high proportion of very large or complex risks. The range includes marine, aviation and transport, home–foreign; and some treaty reinsurance (covering a class or classes of business) for general risks, meaning non-transport.

The unique structural elements of the London market are the cause of some misunderstandings in the US, Europe and beyond. London is split approximately 60:40 between Lloyd's and the London company market.

The overall London market is worth about £40 billion, some £10 billion more than the traditional figure given, according to new statistics from the Insurance Underwriting Association.

It is a subscription market where various underwriters, from Lloyd's syndicates and insurance companies, together underwrite a single risk, subscribing to percentage lines of the risk on a several, not joint, basis. Lloyd's consists uniquely of around 80 syndicates, each consisting of individuals and companies that have agreed to join together to underwrite insurance risks at Lloyd's.

Lloyd's and reputation

Lloyd's insurers are seen as the best in the world at what they do. The Lloyd's underwriters share a public-school type of camaraderie, addressing each other as 'old boy' or 'squire'. There is a reputation to keep up. Lloyd's has never failed to pay a claim, and its security has so far proved impregnable. Members of Lloyd's have 'several liability', which means they are not responsible for each other's losses.

As part of this security, the Central Fund is available, at the discretion of the Council of Lloyd's, to meet the underwriting liabilities of any member. It operates on the basis of some mutualisation of risk. All members are required to pay an annual contribution to the Central Fund, part of the Lloyd's chain of security. It is as in Homer's Olympus, where the gods compete with each other in love and war, but, in times of crisis, offer mutual support.

Like Olympus, Lloyd's has a strong brand, and it takes vigorous efforts to defend this, including against those who hijack the Lloyd's name abroad to sell dud policies or services. It is with the same zeal as, in Greek mythology, Zeus punishes Prometheus for stealing fire from the gods and bringing it to humankind.

Lloyd's now stresses its careful risk management but this was lacking in the past. More than three decades ago, London Market Excess of Loss (LMX) was used to reinsure catastrophe risks, and this led to the LMX spiral, prominent in the 1980s. In 1991, several thousand of these Names resigned from Lloyd's, and others reduced or stopped their underwriting commitments. Many refused to pay cash calls. Some took legal action against members' agents alleging, among other things, negligent advice and negligent underwriting.

Lloyd's had to reinvent itself, a pattern in financial markets. In 1996, David Rowland, Lloyd's first full-time paid chairman, completed a market-wide Reconstruction and Renewal settlement plan. Lloyd's made Names a £3.2 billion settlement offer that, ultimately, about 95 per cent of Names accepted. Equitas Reinsurance, a company formed to reinsure past liabilities, brought affordable finality to Names.

Some market observers at the time had thought that Lloyd's would not emerge from this crisis but it did, with its reputation intact. There was work for Lloyd's to do, not just in tightening up its control of underwriting standards, but also in recovering from the bad publicity it had suffered over the years.

Lloyd's implemented its franchise performance directorate in 2003 specifically because of poor past underwriting, and this has enabled the corporation to review the business plans of syndicates, and to do risk management. These days, Lloyd's is regulated under the UK financial services regime, but, under the Lloyd's Act 1982, it remains responsible for the management and supervision of the Lloyd's market. In practice, Lloyd's is often one step ahead of the Financial Services Authority.

How insurance is placed

Insurance underwriting is an art as much as a science.

Insurance underwriting is the lifeblood of insurance. The underwriters assess risk, deciding whether to take a piece of it, and on what terms. It is an art as much as a science.

In one recent case, a client sought terrorism cover for a hotel in the Middle East, and this seemed a bad proposition to one underwriter, based on his own loss experience, but good to another, who had visited the hotel and considered that it had good security and that the area's perceived riskiness was overrated. Neither of the underwriters was wrong.

Underwriters have in common that they live with risk. On writing business, they hope that there will be no claims, but cannot know until the year is up. Next are the annual renewals of insurance coverage, and the risk restarts.

Actuaries make a useful contribution to forecasting the long-term exposures. They focus on statistics, but underwriters, with their practical experience, get a better feel for risk. The two are perpetually in conflict.

It is as well that underwriting need not always be profitable. An insurer may well plan to break even on underwriting, paying out premiums taken in over the long run, but to make a profit on having invested those premiums in the shorter term.

When it comes to allocating capital against risk, the regulatory trend is towards greater caution. Individual underwriters are not free to write risk as they like. In line with Enterprise Risk Management, which requires a holistic approach to risk assessment and capital allocation (see Chapter 13, p. 127, on its application to banking), Lloyd's syndicates and insurance companies have underwriting guidelines in place. These set coverage limits and other requirements. They are dynamic and can change instantly, as for example, in early 2011, when they often included a ban on writing any Middle East business.

The broker is the middleman between the client and the insurers. Technology is replacing the simpler negotiations. Face to face transactions are still needed to arrange complex risks, as in cover to be placed piecemeal with different underwriters, and it is hard to see that they could be replaced by machines.

The broker will gather facts about the risk before he approaches the underwriter, and, to make the best case, will impress with his expertise. Brokers are sometimes deservedly tainted with the reputation of being salespeople, more interested in closing a deal than being open.

The underwriting firms are cautious. It is common for several underwriters in a syndicate or company to assess complex business risk on the grounds that a consensus opinion is more likely to be right. Some guidelines require two signatures for every piece of business written, including one from a senior underwriter or executive.

When the insurance risk is unattractive, much arm twisting goes on. Underwriters sometimes take on some symbolic risk to help out a broker. They understand that brokers are paid only on deals, and sometimes give them borderline business in return for effort or an on-going relationship. Because they carry the risk, they do sometimes reject business, of course.

In such ways, the relationship between underwriters and brokers has its ups and downs. Sometimes, underwriters will take only a small slice of the risk, not feeling comfortable with the whole, and the broker may need to place the risk with a large number of underwriters.

The broker may also arrange fronting, where a local insurer is paid a fee to insure the business locally, without taking risk on its books, and the business is reinsured into the London market. As an example of the procedure, London market brokers are currently asking insurers in Kazakhstan that want, but do not know how, to write directors' and officers' liability to let them arrange fronting. When the insurers later understand how the underwriting is done, they may do it directly.

Reinsurance

The insurers lay off their risk with their reinsurers. The reinsurance could be proportional, with reinsurers taking on a proportion of the risk and paying the same proportion of valid claims. Otherwise, it may be excess of loss, where the ceding company, as the insurer that places reinsurance is known, pays the initial layer of every valid claim, and the reinsurers pay the balance of losses up to a set figure. This form of reinsurance is popular because the risk is capped.

Reinsurers in their turn place their risk with retrocessionaires, who are the last line of defence, and have to be big enough to take it. They are like the major gods in the Greek pantheon, although all the gods are immortal. The 'reinsurance of reinsurance' process may continue until the initial cedent receives back some of its own business, a spiral. Very large reinsurers reinsure each other's balance sheets through finite reinsurance, which does not involve transfer of risk.

London market insurers generally have become less inclined to use reinsurance as a substitute for their own good underwriting of long-tail business, where the liability may be discovered and claims made many years after the loss was caused.

They have learned self-reliance, rather than passing on the risk, just as the ancient Greek gods never rely on mortals. If they do reinsure risk, they increasingly rely on downgrade clauses in the contract. This way, if a reinsurer's rating falls below a trigger level, the primary insurer may void the contract or require collateral to be posted.

The insurance buyer

Most insurance buyers have no interest in, for example, which Lloyd's syndicate, or insurance company, is used or even what a syndicate means. They are concerned about costs and appreciate transparency in broker remuneration.

This apart, the buyers want to know only that solid cover is in place. Contract certainty – the issuing of insurance contracts on a timely basis – remains a concern. If insurers pay claims quickly, this creates trust. The reinsurer must generally – but not invariably – 'follow the fortunes' of the insurer covering the policyholder.

Buyers can be insufficiently aware of the meaning of the policy they have signed and, as a result, what insurance is in place. If the insurer legitimately refuses to pay a claim, it can come as a shock. According to a March 2011 report, *Corporate Risk & Insurance: The Case for Placement Reform*, by Mactavish and PwC, the insurance placement process between buyers, brokers and insurers is not working well. Many inexpert insurance buyers fail to scrutinise the paperwork or provide enough information to the underwriter.

The UK looting and riots that took place in August 2011, for instance, led to many businesses making claims, and there was some scrutiny of insurance policies. There were fears that small businesses might be lacking in business interruption coverage, and renewed warnings that insurance buyers needed to be very aware of what their insurance policies covered.

It is not always the insured that is in the wrong. Some insurers among those less highly rated by the rating agencies are not always prompt to pay out. There are also cases of insurance fraud and of reckless underwriting culture. Many buyers reject brokers' proposals to provide insurance cover from poorly rated insurers.

Regulation

In 2011, insurers saw regulation as the biggest of their top ten risks, according to the CSFI/PwC Insurance Banana Skins report. Concerns focused on, among other initiatives, Solvency II, as well as the Retail Distribution Review and international financial reporting standards. There was some perception that new capital requirements were on such a scale that the industry could end up hindered rather than helped by them.

Solvency II

Solvency II, the biggest regulatory change in the European insurance industry ahead, should help to protect insurance buyers, but comes at a price. Under the directive, with its risk-based approach to capital adequacy, insurers will, on balance, hold more capital than before. For modelling risk, the directive uses the value-at-risk approach. This was discredited in the banking crisis, and there are now some modified versions. Models tell you more than they did, with an input of higher quality data, as required under Solvency II. They are, of course, not infallible. The use of several models and a multitude of scenarios can provide a broader view.

For Solvency II purposes, insurers may choose between a standard model, which is simplified, and an internal model, which is built to the insurer's individual specifications. It is the larger insurers that tend to seek an internal model, for which the process of obtaining regulatory approval is demanding. The internal model, once approved, has the major advantage, however, of enabling insurers to fine-tune, and more often than not reduce, their capital requirement, freeing up cash. In addition, there are other ways to enhance capital efficiency under Solvency II such as use of reinsurance.

In preparations for the directive, groups face the challenge of maximising capital efficiency. Some have been looking at converting subsidiaries into branches to enable the group as a whole, under the new rules, to gain access to centrally held capital, reducing overall capital requirements.

The smaller insurers are hit hardest by Solvency II, although the directive, within such limitations as exist, is proportionately applied. Captive insurers – entities ensuring the risk of their parent company – are afflicted, and it seems likely that some will close down because they are no longer economically viable.

The jurisdictional commitment to slightly different treatment of captives has emerged as a supervisory concern in the Solvency II equivalence assessment of Bermuda for one, although this may prove just teething problems. Equivalence does not require an exact match. The United States has a different solvency regime from that of Solvency II, and there are constant discussions about how to coordinate the two.

Some larger insurers claim long-term business benefits from Solvency II, which is as it is supposed to be, and so a commercial incentive for embedding the directive's requirements in the business's day to day practice, a supervisory imperative. The large insurers are better able to handle the implementation costs than their smaller brethren. The costs are huge for everybody, however, and the shortage of actuaries and IT contractors has sent the costs of hiring such specialists spiralling.

Some reputable insurers believe that the costs of Solvency II outweigh the benefits, and that there is a serious risk of the requirements becoming a mere tick-box exercise. However it is regarded, Solvency II is the way of the future and is setting an international agenda, not just in the European Union where implementation is a requirement, but beyond.

The lobbyist battle

One of the problems in the global insurance and reinsurance industry is that there are disparate regulatory and legislative approaches in different countries, a problem not so affecting banking with its globally applicable Basel capital adequacy standards (see Chapter 13). The International

Association of Insurance Supervisors is addressing the global fragmenta-tion with its 'Common Framework for the Supervision of Internationally Active Insurance Groups' project, but this may take years before it achieves a full outcome.

Some supervisors in local regimes where insurance regulation is working well do not see a need to iron out the global discrep-ancies. Generally supervision of insurers has not met with the same problems as of banks. The insurance industry had a 'good crisis', meaning that it emerged from 2007–09 relatively unscathed. The industry has since battled to avoid the stringent supervisory measures aimed at banks, the sector that caused the crisis.

> Supervision of insurers has not met with the same problems as of banks.

The mantra of the insurance industry in its lobbying efforts against excessive regulation is that the insurance business model is different from that of banks and is inherently less risky. Insurers are pre-funded and have to pay only when a claim is made, but bankers lend more than they have and can be required to return their depositors' money overnight.

How far such detail is appreciated publicly is at least partly down to the lobbying. There is a lot of feeling that supervisory regimes and politicians do not understand insurers as well as banking, and take much less interest in the industry.

The way forward

The business of risk assessment, which is what insurers do, is becoming increasingly complex, with new risks emerging (see Chapters 17, 18 and 19). With this come unprecedented business opportunities, but also new exposures.

The insurance industry is becoming better capitalised and supervised, and cooperation across borders is improving. Solvency II is likely to benefit the large insurers, but not so much the small ones. Industry consolidation may be expected in the long term.

The comfort provided by insurance will remain in demand, provided that the industry fulfils its promises. So far, it has done a fair job.

17

Risks without frontiers

Introduction

Businesses today push past conventional frontiers, incurring cyber risk on the internet and political risk in foreign countries. Epidemics and climate change are among other prominent new risks.

Reckless risk taking can fail. Some business leaders act like Phaethon, a young man in ancient Greek mythology, who drives the chariot of his father, the sun god, against his advice, and crashes it, causing nations to burn.

In this chapter we will consider some of the new risks, and how insurers are providing related protection products.

The nature of the new risks

Financial services firms, and listed companies, have to incur certain new risks if only to keep up with their competitors. If they do not use cloud computing, with its cost savings but related risks, others will.

Our understanding of the risks cannot keep up with the pace of progress, and it has always been thus. We capture cyberspace but cannot stop the hackers. We sail through treacherous waters, but our laws cannot stop the local pirates from kidnapping our crew for ransom and our insurance cannot always cover the risk.

Risk managers strive to protect the business, as board level support

_____ has not always been as strong as it should

The regulators are demanding high standards of risk assessment.

be. The regulators are demanding high standards of risk assessment, including business continuity planning and security in such areas as technology, particularly to protect customer data.

Insurance

Uncertainties and misconceptions

For some new risks, insurers do not explain the coverage of their policies properly. One area where this has arisen is in environmental insurance, where traditional insurance policies fail to cover some new exposures.

For certain risks such as tsunami, insurers are on very uncertain ground because there is not enough past data to extrapolate patterns. Modelling such risks, if it happens at all, can be, in current industry speak, garbage in, garbage out. Insurers are in the business of risk and, where they lack data, they will compensate by raising the premium level. They do not knowingly gamble, but, in entering the unknown, there are always unquantifiable elements.

Terrorism

Terrorism is another area where insurers have major problems in assessing risk. Lack of loss data is a reason for this, but there is also a lack of intelligence on the ground. There is randomness in terrorism risk. For example, if terrorists target building A, but there is a police car in front of it, they may attack building B instead.

Even so, underwriters follow established practice in assessing terrorism risk. Based on experience, they think of transport, hotels and airlines as high-risk targets. Events such as games or high-profile conferences are of concern. The insurers use blast zone analysis on insured assets to model the risk and make underwriting decisions. In the US and UK this technology relies partly on the established postcode system to assess the potential impact of an attack on buildings. In some countries, such as Russia, postal codes are less defined and so the risk is harder to model.

In light of such discrepancies, underwriters seek a good spread of terrorism risk, from high-risk to benign countries. The demand for standalone terrorism insurance has become higher since the 11 September 2001 attacks on the United States. In recent years, against the backdrop of a soft insurance market, some insurers have started to include terrorism cover in 'all risks' policies in low-risk territories.

Coverage is not ubiquitous. Events in Thailand and Egypt have demonstrated that a property damage policy is different from a terrorism policy. There is a potential gap where risks could fall, not covered by either type of policy.

Cyber risk

Cyber risk is another new area where sufficient past data can be missing and there are potential coverage gaps. Traditional insurance policies provide only limited cover. There is now specialist cyber liability insurance available, where, underwriter feedback suggests, setting the premiums is more of an art than a science due to the lack of loss data. Governance structure around processes and the attitude to data security are considered important for this assessment.

Cloud computing is a new area of risk in this arena. The underlying concept is that the risk of 'downtime' on the system is contracted out to the service provider. Having a tight contract with the provider, however, does not necessarily compensate for the damage to the client company's business that could arise in the event of a system failure.

From a regulatory perspective, if a financial institution's technology arrangements are compromised, the security of client data can be at risk, and the Financial Services Authority has imposed hefty fines on some prestigious financial institutions for such failings. For some discussion on the reputational risk arising, see Chapter 18.

Piracy

There are some areas where insurers have great difficulty in providing any cover. One is piracy risk. According to the Financial Action Task Force July 2011 report, *Organised Maritime Piracy and Related Kidnapping for Ransom*, piracy at sea has now become a financially lucrative criminal activity. The average amount demanded for each captured vehicle rose from US$150,000 in 2005 to $2.5 million in 2010.

In Somalia, whose waters are a hotspot for piracy, males have an average life expectancy of not much over 45 years and living standards are grim. The pirates are to some extent local heroes because they create jobs and can rescue communities from poverty. The risk of being shot is not great. As pirates, they are answerable to warlords, and the business is organised. For young men in the country, piracy is seen as cool and a way to attract girls as well as to get rich quickly.

The piracy problem, particularly in Somalia, has caused premiums in related insurance policies to rocket. So far, there is no standalone piracy cover on the market. Insurance is available, however, to cover hull and machinery risk, inclusive of piracy, but it is understood that the underwriters will pay on such claims only with reservations, and with extensive lawyer input.

Insurers find that the piracy culture is in discord with their modus operandi. In claims assessment, they are used to hard-nosed negotiations with parties, but the pirates in Somalia, Nigeria and elsewhere are not open to this approach.

Insurance may not be the complete solution for protection. Insurance brokers will send ship owners to armed and unarmed security specialists. There are several such security companies in the UK, and they take their fees separately from the insurers. Some insurers reduce their rates if security people are on board, but the success rate of this precaution in fending off piracy attacks is not advertised.

Pandemic

Another major risk to businesses is the pandemic. The H1N1 virus, known as swine flu, emerged as a threat in the United Kingdom and elsewhere in 2009 and was declared by the World Health Organization as a pandemic, but the impact proved less than it might. Risk consultants subsequently warned that businesses should consider the experience as a dress rehearsal for the next pandemic, which might be more widespread.

If there is a pandemic, research by Marsh has shown that businesses have a main concern about impact on the supply chain. As Lord Peter Levene, then Lloyd's chairman, said in a July 2009 speech at the NATO Strategic Concept Conference, organisations had become used to a 'just in time' model, with an optimal strategy that did not look so sensible if one threw a pandemic into the equation.

To prepare for such disruption, consultants advise businesses to consider how to keep themselves running, and that the plan has to run through the organisation. In a crisis, public and staff alike want to know what is going on in the business. If staff should all have to be working from home at once, consideration needs to be given to how, or whether, the business would function remotely.

> In a crisis, public and staff want to know what is going on in the business.

Climate change

Some risks seem more distant but are, nevertheless, inevitable. Climate change comes into this category, and presents an opportunity for insurers, in terms of developing new protective products. It is also a threat to their capital. Insurers hold more capital under Solvency II as a safeguard against exposure to inland flood losses in Britain, according to a 2009 Association of British Insurers report, *The Financial Risks of Climate Change*.

There is a legal framework for international action against climate change, in the form of both the 1992 United Nations Framework Convention on Climate Change, and the 1997 Kyoto Protocol. Of the two, the Kyoto Protocol is the most effective force, requiring industrialised countries to meet greenhouse gas emissions reduction targets for set periods.

One problem is that such countries have claimed they are reducing their emissions when, in reality, they have relied on goods imported from developing countries such as China that do not have binding emissions targets under Kyoto. Once this is taken into account, the emissions reductions are cancelled out many times over, according to campaigners.

The Kyoto Protocol expires at the end of 2012 and there have been attempts to follow up with a legal framework, but, so far, there have only been non-binding commitments. In broad terms, Europe has been considering a repeat exercise of Kyoto, but Japan, Russia and Canada have declined it, and the United States remains detached.

According to one academic, a lack of will to pursue necessary climate change initiatives seems deep rooted. In a draft conference paper, 'After illusion: realism, philosophy and hope in a seriously warming world', as presented at a March 2011 Lancaster University conference, *Climate Change and Philosophy at the Tipping Point*, John Foster, honorary research fellow at Lancaster University, noted that deadlines for addressing climate change priorities, as addressed at a 2009 Copenhagen summit, had been missed. He attributed this to a 'tacit, un-self-recognised strategy by interested parties for ensuring that nothing happens'.

In his paper, Foster expressed the view that the economic cost of tackling climate change would have an adverse impact on Western standards of living. Most people, like the decision makers on climate change, had a vested interest in maintaining these standards, however, and so were not committed to addressing climate change. In his view, the Western obsession with materialistic comfort and progress, driving the required standards of living, was an escape from confronting the inevitability and finality of death.

If this conspiracy-of-silence theory has some truth in it, the issue arises how far it may apply beyond climate change to other new risks. The lethargy that tends to surround business continuity planning assumes a potential new meaning.

Business continuity planning

Business continuity planning helps to identify uninsured and uninsurable risks, which arise from terrorism, weather, and other factors. The purchase of insurance is part of the process, but normally after other options had been considered. The FSA requires regulated firms to have a business continuity plan in place. In practice, many firms treat it as a box-ticking exercise.

Some are astoundingly unprepared, particularly when no one on the board sees the value of business continuity planning, as became clear in the chaos created by the April 2011 volcanic ash cloud that unexpectedly caused considerable stoppages in air transport for several weeks. In most cases, insurance policies do not provide cover against volcanic ash-related losses because they are not property damage, although the tide is starting to change.

Among the benefits of business continuity planning are a better chance of surviving, a potential reduction in insurance premiums and a higher credit rating from the rating agencies. It is an FSA requirement that business interruption arrangements should be regularly updated.

The way forward

Businesses should be adequately prepared for risks but, all too often, they are not. The preparation must come from the top, but some senior managers are more interested in turning a quick profit.

With risk comes opportunity, but to understand the risks can be an increasingly research-intensive task. There is always work for lawyers.

Firms should avoid the mentality of only tick-box business continuity planning. The worst can happen, with repercussions on the business that may include reputational damage, the subject of the next chapter.

The price of reputation

Introduction

Reputation is valuable to financial services institutions and listed companies, taking years to be built up. Reputation can, nevertheless, be destroyed by a few careless remarks from the top.

In this chapter, we will consider what reputation means to companies, and how it is protected. We will examine the impact of reputational damage.

The unpredictable risk

If a company loses reputation, the damage to its business can be enormous. An unexpected scandal implicating the company or a few wrong remarks by the chief executive can destroy reputation quickly, and a plan for damage limitation in such emergency circumstances needs to be in place. The risk of reputation loss could affect financial institutions or any listed company. As found in a June 2010 survey by Airmic, the not-for-profit association representing the interests of commercial insurance buyers and risk managers, risk managers are most likely to be kept awake at night by reputational risk exposures.

> An unexpected scandal can destroy reputation quickly, and a plan for damage limitation needs to be in place.

According to Airmic, reputational risk is the least predictable risk. The insurance industry has not done much work on quantifying it, and no major insurance solution is available.

One major issue with reputational risk is that it is hard to assess how great it is. The loss can be temporary. Outside financial services, best-selling author Jeffrey Archer served half a four-year prison sentence from 2001 on charges of perjury and perverting the course of justice. He turned the experience into published prison diaries and he continued subsequently to be lionised and feted in his profession.

I know of a former dealing manager and director of the controversial 1980s licensed dealer Harvard Securities. He later became a director of London & Norwich Investment Services, an even more dubious share-pushing company. These two companies lost investors substantial money on shares in companies that did not properly exist. This man is now a director of a respectable quoted company.

If in the long term, characters running disreputable enterprises can apparently turn respectable, in the short term reputational loss can have a bigger impact. As US investor Warren Buffett has put it, 'Lose money for my firm and I will be understanding; lose a shred of reputation for the firm, and I will be ruthless.' Enterprise risk management allows for reputational risk in its modelling, but how it is assessed and quantified must be a challenge for industries.

Contagion

Uncertain a phenomenon as it is, once reputational risk arises, it can spread rapidly to individuals and firms. When, in 2011, Rupert Murdoch closed down the best-selling Sunday newspaper *News of the World*, owned by his US-listed company News Corporation, it did much to mitigate scandals arising around the newspaper's phone hacking and other practices. The scandals still spread, but not to the extent that they would have done if the tainted newspaper had still been operating.

Murdoch's prompt action, coming at a time when he was ambitious to take over BSkyB, was probably, in retrospect, the best he could do by way of damage limitation. The *News of the World* scandals had highlighted the dangers of close relationships between business and politics. Here was a major warning to financial markets, if only not to get caught.

Such relationships can, of course, work in companies' favour, as some financial institutions found in the 2007–09 financial crisis. It is very arguable in the long run how far the big banks such as RBS, Lloyds TSB and Northern Rock have suffered reputational damage from the events. It may be that their relationships with the government, however temporary they were, had saved their reputation and that, in future years, memories of the crisis will fade, as they have now about major banks' past bad loans to third-world countries.

Containment

Taking a cue from Murdoch's closure of *News of the World* or from the government bailout of banks in the crisis, banks must act early to contain reputational damage if this is to stand a good chance of being effective. Financial institutions move accordingly to close down the accounts of risky customers. In December 2010, Visa and MasterCard suspended some dealings with WikiLeaks, the whistleblower web site, after they had scrutinised its compliance with their operating rules.

Containment can be as much about words as action, giving some real work, at this time like no other, to the corporate communications department. Firms typically speak through one or two media spokespeople only, which helps

> Containment can be as much about words as action.

to ensure a consistent message. Sometimes the approach is not enough. News International had used a media spokesman amidst its turmoil, but, if it had used a senior executive instead, difficult questions could have been answered more quickly, sending out more of a message that the group was putting the crisis high on its agenda.

Reputation risk is yet one more area of rich pickings for lawyers. They typically advise that senior management should attend to reputational risk, and that awareness of it is a team effort involving not just senior management and corporate communications, but also perhaps external PR, investor relations, lawyers, compliance, IT professionals and others.

Slip-ups

Of the reputational challenges that can arise for firms, from natural disasters to internal fraud, there is none more frustrating than a director's careless comments that could easily have been avoided. There is a ghastly tradition of senior executives saying the wrong things in one unguarded moment and watching their share prices plummet, perhaps never to recover. Commercial tact comes more easily to some than to others.

The impact of Gerald Ratner's remarks at the Institute of Directors on April 23, 1991 resonates today as a classic case study of the worst repercussions of mishandling public relations. Ratner said that the cut-glass sherry decanters with six glasses on a silver tray that he sold for £4.95 at Ratners were 'total crap' and that some of his earrings were cheaper than an M&S prawn sandwich but probably would not last as long. The media publicised his comments and the resulting public disgust nearly destroyed his listed company.

Tony Hayward, chief executive of BP, made a still more provocative gaffe in his public statements after the April 2010 explosion on the Deepwater Horizon oil rig, operated by BP. The incident had killed 12 people but, on 30 May, Hayward told a journalist, 'We're sorry for the massive disruption it's caused to their lives. There's no one who wants this thing over more than I do. I'd like my life back.'

Clearly, Hayward had meant nothing offensive, but this careless handling of the media, coupled with an optimism about the cleanup operation and his refusal to answer questions of a US congressional sub-committee, posed a major reputational challenge to BP. His participation in a yacht race instead of dealing with the oil spill gave the critics more ammunition. The oil group's plummeting share price served as a barometer of reputational damage as it was happening.

If ever anybody should doubt the impact of words and publicity on business, these two case studies should give food for thought. Here is evidence that presenting the right image to the public can be as important to the company's reputation as conducting the underlying business with integrity.

Regulatory fines

When financial services firms break the rules, a large regulatory fine and the accompanying publicity, not spared by the FSA, can have impact on their reputations. Some consultants argue for large firms that can easily afford the fine, reputational impact is the most severe part of the punishment. Certainly, large fines can have a deterrent effect, and, when some financial institutions were hit with large fines from mis-selling payment protection insurance between 2006 and 2009, it served as a warning across the industry that firms should comply not just with the regulator's detailed rules, but also with its high-level principles.

In practice, the impact of a fine may be minimal. The FSA has hit most large financial institutions with hefty fines, but their reputations in the long run seem to have remained intact, perhaps partly because such actions happen quite often. In addition, the firms have subsequently acted to limit the reputational damage. They have typically admitted the failings, and cooperated with the regulator, receiving a fine discounted by a third for early settlement. The FSA will have taken these steps into account in imposing the penalty. The firms have then issued short statements to the media, publicising their contrite actions and clarifying that they are taking remedial steps.

In August 2010, came a textbook example when the FSA fined Zurich UK, the UK branch of Zurich Insurance, £2.3 million for failure to have adequate systems and controls in place to prevent the loss of customers' confidential information. This was a large fine, but no major financial burden on such a large company. Zurich, by settling early and putting out gentle press statements, seemed to have forestalled most of the reputational damage. In such cases, the loss of management time devoted to dealing with the problem, and the need to reconstruct the relationship with the regulator, have typically been the major problem.

Individuals, however, have suffered far worse reputational hits than firms, and the FSA has warned it will be looking to hold more individuals personally accountable for their actions. Because their livelihood is at stake, individuals are less willing to settle with the regulator than firms.

The reputational challenge can be tough, even when it is based on unsubstantiated allegations. When in May 2011, Dominique Strauss-Kahn, managing director of the International Monetary Fund, was arrested on allegations of having forced his attention on a chambermaid in a luxury New York hotel, he resigned from his job. He entered a nightmare of controversial publicity until it was reported that the charges had been dropped.

Strauss-Khan and the IMF both emerged with a clean reputation, but the event will be remembered, at least for a while. His professional position had made him more sensitive to reputational assaults than most, and, with this, came a challenge to the IMF's reputation. This was a prime example of how a leader's reputation was enmeshed in his or her organisation, said Seamus Gillen, managing director, reputational risk practice, Reputation Institute (UK) at the May 2011 DIMA insurance forum in Dublin.

In some cases, however, the individual's loss of reputation is justified and, even when an employing institution is in the clear, publicity can cast unwelcome aspersions. In October 2010, Jérôme Kerviel, a rogue trader at Société Générale, was jailed for forgery, unauthorised computer use and breach of trust and was found to have been responsible for his own actions, but commentators questioned the robustness of the bank's line management.

The reverse can happen, and respectable individuals can become enmeshed in disreputable organisations. When crooks buy up a reputable firm in trouble, the original staff, if staying there, becomes swiftly associated with the acquiring ethos.

Technology risk

We have seen already that carelessness, as well as rogue activity, can lead to reputational loss. A more commonplace problem than unguarded comment by the chief executive is the lack of security around technology.

If a financial institution loses sensitive customer data held in its computer systems, it will suffer regulatory probes, media criticism and reputational damage. The firm will have to write to customers to alert them of any risks. The risk is very real because customer data is the perpetual target of hackers and fraudsters. The return on data theft can be huge, and the prestige value high.

> **Customer data is the perpetual target of hackers and fraudsters.**

The likely reputational damage in such cases is measurable by the share price decline, as happened to Sony after it announced in April 2011 that hackers might have stolen personal information of internet games users on its PlayStation Network and Sony Online Entertainment system.

Reputable companies may pay a substantial sum to avoid a hacking scandal. Some are understood to have paid off Eastern European gangs that have demonstrably hacked into their computer system and demanded a large sum if they are to refrain from damaging it. If the gangs should carry out their threat, it could impose severe, perhaps irreparable, damage, reputational as well as commercial.

The risks from technology abuse can come from within. Employees may use social media such as Twitter and Facebook to spread information confidential to the firm and which could become linked with it.

Ryan Rubin, director and head of security and privacy at Protiviti in the United Kingdom, told Thomson Reuters GRC that social media is an amplifier rather than a creator of risk, and firms have to instil awareness of it on a bottom-up as well as a top-down basis. Staff training can play a major part. In Rubin's view, corporate policies on new media and social networks should be neither Draconian nor wide open, but should establish a middle ground, and firms should regularly monitor them.

The disreputable

There exists a network of people whose reputations have been severely tarnished, but who still have financial services industry skills and talent. They operate behind the scenes as consultants to firms, typically at arm's length, but exercising leadership. The majority of financial services scams are subject to some such arrangement.

Even in some reputable firms, the call for profit can sway executives, provided that the appearance of respectability can be maintained, and sometimes it can. As Madoff proved for many years, reputation can be built up on appearance alone.

The way forward

Financial services institutions and listed companies have seen the impact of reputational damage in companies such as BP, and are keen to avoid it. Corporate communications is becoming increasingly sophisticated, and we are at a point where image can have more impact than the underlying reality.

The regulators can play their part in keeping reputation a sensitive issue but there is, and always will be, uncertainty around how it is valued.

19

Blow-up

Introduction

Systemic risk is about the collapse of our financial system and economy. The 2007–09 financial crisis showed how the activities of large financial institutions and their interconnectedness can create such risk.

In this chapter we will try to define systemic risk, examining how developed it might be, and its potential impact. We will examine how governments and supervisors are seeking to monitor and contain it.

Systemic risk

Systemic risk is not just the biggest challenge for financial markets. It is where some of the biggest bluff can be found, concealments of ignorance and uncertainty to match anything elsewhere in financial markets.

Everybody is agreed that this type of risk exists. Nobody knows quite what it is, however, or which firms are systemically risky, and how much such risk there is in the world. There are definitions focused on, for example, size, liquidity and interconnectedness, but subject to interpretation.

The financial crisis has proved a useful case study. Ahead of it, many had not foreseen the level of interconnected correlation. The near run on Northern Rock could have escalated across the banking sector if the government had not acted to guarantee deposits. The Lehman Brothers collapse in September 2008 had a major knock-on effect on financial markets, including derivatives counterparties. If AIG had later been allowed by the US government to collapse because of its investment banking activities, the systemic impact could have been far worse.

In combating the crisis, governments and supervisors stepped in with supportive measures, particularly quantitative easing. They worked this time, but were a shot in the dark. As always in financial services, most of the battle is about winning and keeping public confidence. It is a priority that the supervisors have taken on board.

> As always in financial services, most of the battle is about winning and keeping public confidence.

Further understanding of systemic risk seems an important next step. Regulators are addressing the issue in such areas as client money held by institutions, derivatives trading, and high frequency trading, but the scoping of systemic risk is yet in its infancy. They seek more capital from systemically risky firms, but this can be ineffectual if they do not target the right sectors and activities. Extra capital comes, of course, at a commercial cost to firms.

Specialist bodies

Specialist bodies focused on systemic risk have been established with great fanfare. The Financial Stability Board is directly answerable to the Group of 20, the international group of country leaders that has set a main priority on guarding against systemic risk. The FSB will not usually talk on a named basis to the press, and conceals its uncertainties with an air of secrecy. There is a widespread industry view that the secrecy is to avoid panicking the public; but it can backfire. Some are losing confidence in the organisation.

The other bodies seem, at least potentially, more transparent. The European Systemic Risk Board is a macro-economic monitoring body charged with alerting the European authorities to any emerging problems. It is in strong company, being part of the European System of Financial Supervisors, established from the start of 2011, which includes the newly empowered supervisory authorities for financial sectors (see Chapter 21). Critics fear, nevertheless, that the ESRB is toothless.

The UK makes its own contribution to systemic risk supervision through the Financial Policy Committee, which is part of its planned new regulatory regime (see Chapter 21). The FPC aims to monitor broad risks in financial markets, so filling a detected supervisory gap. Some of the principals involved are from the previous regulatory regime, which did not distinguish itself in handling the crisis, but maybe some lessons have been learnt. The committee is housed within the Bank of England, and one of the familiar faces is 'Merv the Swerve', known properly as Mervyn King, governor of the Bank of England, and now doubling up as chairman of the new committee. Other members include the two frontmen of the Financial Services Authority, its chief executive Hector Sants and its chairman Adair Turner.

The FSB, ESRB and FPC, a feast of acronyms, have different roles but in the same broad area of systemic risk, and fears of some overlap abound. There are disagreements on systemic risk issues between supervisors globally, and it is hoped that the planned advent of supervisory colleges will help address these. Clearly, the G-20's commitment to addressing systemic risk is not enough alone. It is also a lesson of history that nations joined together in crisis are not natural bed fellows. National regulators have typically rushed to protect their own boundaries when their own policy clashes with the international stance.

In our cross-border supervisory initiatives focused on systemic risk, we have, in short, parties that do not all agree, establishing policy on little-known matters, with an air of confidence that is hardly justified. If the FSB leads the way in the secrecy, the instinct to appear in control runs like a virus through the entire supervisory system and governments. It is a backhanded tribute to the power of investor temperament.

Lack of confidence

Public confidence in the financial system and in the ability of the authorities to stop systemic risk is limited, not least because the crisis has not fundamentally changed the culture of the markets. The banks are, of course, more wary than they were, but no less arrogant. Governments ultimately condone short-termism in financial markets because the activity contributes substantially to gross domestic product. Much of their apparent commitment to supervisory and governance development is lip-service.

The unspoken priority is to maintain reputation, and this is distinct, often enough, from ethics or standards. Here is a battle that financial markets and supervisors, cooperating uneasily in the great cause, are winning. It takes outsiders – represented by journalists, opposition politicians and prominent public figures – to protest against the hypocrisy. Their voices are not easily heard above the noise of the markets.

It is the financial markets, as opposed to their regulators, that disregard systemic risk in the interest of pursuing profit. It is unrealistic to expect companies, invested hugely as they all are in generating returns, to put more money than required into a form of risk that is industry wide. To take measures against the remote, ill-defined and industry-wide concept of systemic risk is in direct conflict with capitalism as financial markets know it. Institutions take a direct and personally interested approach to business.

The ancient Greek fable tells it best. In *Works and Days*, Hesiod tells us through his story of the hawk and the nightingale that the strong have absolute power over weak. The hawk grips the weeping nightingale in its talons and chides her for being distressed, saying he will eat her or let her go, as he wishes, and she is powerless to stop him. The message is that she is wasting her energy crying.

Financial markets have almost the same message. The institutions will invent and trade products as much as they wish, and capture market share at the expense of smaller institutions, if it suits them. They are not concerned about generating systemic risk, but rather about making money now.

Cultural perspectives

Governments are committed to keeping the financial markets going, which is perhaps why some definitions of systemic risk, and ideas on how to combat it, together receive far more attention than addressing the root causes. The disagreements on definition are, in fact, minor. Paradigm Risk, a consulting firm, has said that the FSB's officially unpublicised, but leaked, list of up to 30 global systemically important financial institutions, including insurers, must not be a one-stop focus. Systemic risk can arise in smaller firms as well as large, due to interconnectedness, it says.

Given the complexity of systemic risk, there is an increasing view that to achieve understanding, it is necessary to step outside financial services into disciplines such as biology and chaos mathematics, approaches not yet explored. The history of philosophy has its lessons. More than two and a half thousand years ago, the pre-Socratic philosophers of ancient Greece debated, among other things, how far the world was of one piece and whether there was movement in it, as discussed in Catherine Osborne's book *Presocratic Philosophy: A Very Short Introduction* (see recommended further reading, Appendix 5). The sense of experiment and the fumbling towards a theory about global interconnectedness were no less tentative than how today's national leaders and the supervisors debate systemic risk.

Systemic risk, as discussed at G-20 level, extends beyond the level of individual institutions and there is nothing new in this. In discussing cosmic cycles, the fifth-century philosopher Empedocles, prominent in his field, suggests that elements in the world become part of the one, and yet do not cease to be. Similarly today, earthquakes and volcanic ash remain individual risks, even as they pose systemic impact.

> Systemic risk extends beyond the level of individual institutions and there is nothing new in this.

Cosmic disintegration

On the linked principle, insurers work with banks, derivatives are linked with others in different institutions, and mortgages sold in Florida are bundled together to back bonds traded in London. When a crisis hits, however, the linked parts separate.

In a financial crisis, the bolting together of some parts of the financial services industry no longer makes sense. Post-crisis, AIG's financial products division, whose activities had led to the government bailout of the group, became incompatible with the insurance operations which were AIG's main activity. Across financial markets, risks taken off balance sheet in banks seemed incompatible with the rest of their activity. The change is one of perception.

When risks turn sour, the compatibility ceases to exist. As Osborne has noted in her book, Empedocles offers us a cosmic metaphor in his 'twofold birth of mortals'. Creatures emerge perhaps in unity and disintegrate perhaps in strife, and there is a point where the bodies are in bits.

In financial markets similarly, it seems clear that an incompatibility of juxtaposed products and activities across asset classes and geographies in the financial sector had always been potentially there but it takes a crisis, particularly in confidence, to reveal it. Such crises come in cycles, much like those in which Empedocles believed.

When a large bank such as Lehman Brothers collapses, derivatives exposures are ugly and scary until matched up with their partners in the chain. Comparably, ancient Greek mythology provided composite creatures such as the Minotaur, with a bull's head on a human body, and, as discussed in Osborne's book, Empedocles included some such monsters early and late in his cycles of human existence. The Greek philosopher refers to faces without necks, arms wandering naked without shoulders, and eyes in search of foreheads.

Solutions

Across industries, to prevent another financial crisis, coordination between national supervisors is crucial. There is an urgent need to gather and coordinate data more efficiently, but even this is only part of any solution.

Financial institutions have to play their part, including through adaptability. Empedocles said that offending spirits would have to wander for thirty thousand years from their loved ones, becoming all kinds of mortal creatures, experiencing hardships of sea, sun and tornadoes. Similarly financial institutions constantly assume new identities, often shaped by failures or corruption in the old.

Firms that were main sources of systemic risk in the 2007–09 financial crisis have reinvented themselves in this way.

Empedocles puts more emphasis on moral concerns such as good and evil, intention and free will than on science as explanations for his world of cosmic change, and such thinking has arisen in a new emphasis on ethics, bankers' bonuses and corporate governance.

The way forward

Systemic risk is the biggest risk, and to address it seems now the priority. There is some feeling that, if backed by the right practical action, this is the key to supervising financial markets effectively.

The problem is that systemic risk remains an unquantifiable concept, and methods of assessing it, from theory to data gathering, are not as advanced as they one day will be. For supervisors and theorists, there is a lot more fumbling in the dark. To put up a show of confidence that they have the matter in hand remains the priority.

The financial services industry is not fooled and nor does it particularly care about progress. Institutions will continue to pursue wealth as always, operating within the rules set.

The common interest, and perhaps ultimately the great hope, is that no one wants systemic collapse, at least in their business lifetime.

PART SIX

Rules or ruin

20

Decline and fall

Introduction

Financial services regulation changes so rapidly that it becomes old within a few years, more like a dog's life than a human's.

In Homer's *The Odyssey*, Odysseus, after 20 years of travelling, arrives home disguised as a beggar, and his old hound Argos, lying, full of fleas, on heaps of dung, recognises his master and wags his tail. He has not the strength to come closer.

Similarly, the Financial Services Authority, the UK financial services regulator, fawns on its masters, at the same time as wagging its tail as a gesture of independence. In its old age, as it were, it has become tarnished with some failure, but has dignity.

The FSA will live on in a metamorphosed form, as the Financial Conduct Authority in the pending new regulatory regime (see Chapter 21).

In this chapter, we will broadly assess the recent history of financial services regulation. We will then focus on the current regulator, the Financial Services Authority, and how it has performed.

Evolution of financial regulation

Financial regulation, like private City institutions, never really dies. One regime ends, and another arises, in an evolutionary process similar to those in the regulated industry. With all its faults, the

> Financial regulation never really dies. One regime ends, and another arises.

FSA has taken the development of UK financial services regulation some steps forward from its predecessor regime, which was a clumsy attempt at self-regulation.

Governments have always been well intentioned in this area. Margaret Thatcher, prime minister from 1979, had long been concerned about consumer protection in financial services. One problem, representative of the era, was in the licensed dealers of securities that operated as legalised boiler rooms in the UK, pushing dud shares on naive investors on a scale that ruined huge numbers of pensioners. There was limited redress.

The Financial Services Act 1986 created self-regulation within a statutory framework and, at the time, it seemed to some a combination of genius. The Securities & Investment Board oversaw five self-regulatory organisations, which created rules for, policed and controlled authorised firms. Their authority was statutory in all but name. The system was certainly a development from the lax regime that came before it, but, following implementation in February 2008, flaws became apparent. Some SROs were far too close to the industry. Many of the regulatory staff did not understand financial services, and at least one SRO was corrupt.

A few SRO staff considered regulation as a springboard to enter the industry. In one case, this led to insider dealing investigations, centred on an ex-regulator's activity at one regulated firm.

Along with the greed of staff to enter the industry they supervised, some of the SROs were chronically understaffed. There was a lack of coordination between them.

The FSA is born

In November 2001, the Financial Services and Markets Act 2000 came into force. The SROs and the SIB were abolished and the FSA became the single UK regulator for investment banking and insurance. The new system was about statutory regulation and it seemed a saviour, but, of course, it was not.

The FSA was given the power to write rules and principles, codes and provisions, and it had statutory immunity from being sued from action taken in official duties. The new regulator was accountable both to a committee of non-executive members and to consumer and practitioner panels.

The image remained all-important, with maintaining confidence in the UK financial system and promoting public understanding of it being two of the regulator's four statutory objectives. No less vague was the third objective of consumer protection, and perhaps the fourth, which was reducing scope for financial crime.

The regulator's power was clear. Any firm undertaking regulated activity in the UK had to be either authorised by the FSA or exempt, and individuals in key roles had to be approved. Over the years, the FSA has extended its regulatory reach to credit unions, mortgage advisers and insurance and the UK's central security depository, and to recognition of exchanges and clearing houses.

In exercising its powers, the FSA is dependent on its rules and it has constantly consulted on changes with the industry. The FSA knows its objectives but wants input from others on how to carry them out and on what is happening in the market.

In its younger days, like Argos, Odysseus' hunting dog, the FSA could catch some prey. Generally taking pride in its proportionate, risk-based approach to financial services regulation, the regulator has focused on the biggest threats to its statutory objectives and on the largest firms. At the same time, it has moved swiftly against smaller firms, often easier targets.

The regulator's boast has been that its regulation is principles-based, which has left much of the decision making, with the headaches that go with this, to the regulated firms. This supposedly advanced approach has reduced the burden on regulations and resources. The vagueness has given firms scope to find loopholes in the regulatory requirements.

The enforcement process has proved time-consuming, and often unfruitful, and the decisions have had a fair appeal system built in. Firms unsatisfied with a disciplinary action can refer the matter to the Financial Services and Markets Tribunal, run by the Lord Chancellor's department, which hears the case afresh.

The tribunal has proved itself to be independent, but the publicity to appellants can be damaging except where the FSA has been unable to make a case stick. In its lifespan, the FSA has admitted some weaknesses but never defeat. In July 2005, it said that it would be discounting its fines by as much as 30 per cent on firms that agreed an early settlement, so obviating the need for a long and expensive regulatory investigation. The move has saved it, and targeted firms, a lot of work.

Playing a lawyers' game

In adopting a principles-based regime, the FSA has emerged as a game player rather than the preserver of standards that it aspires to be. When faced with such regulation, firms are keen to defend their culture. They do not always cooperate with the FSA's recommendation that they should immediately confess problems. Instead they play a lawyers' game, presenting a case to the regulator, if it is necessary, only once they have assembled a plan for remedial action.

This works in their favour, providing ammunition to their strategic position that to work in financial markets is a game, where money is how one keeps score, and the regulator is the referee. The rules are not the same as standards. Ethics, over and above regulatory requirements, have played very little part in regulation, although they have come more under the FSA's radar since the 2007–09 financial crisis.

Rules are not the same as standards.

The FSA has not always had lawyers as good as those in the private sector. Its bigger weapons are adverse publicity about firms. The regulator has bullied some, but, quite often, is itself browbeaten.

In the aftermath of some failed supervision the FSA has admitted that it had concentrated on conduct of business but not enough on prudential regulation. In the Turner Review of global banking regulation, published in March 2009, Lord Turner, chairman of the FSA, stressed, among other things, that regulation and supervision should be based on a system-wide macro-prudential approach.

At about this time, the FSA changed its principles-based approach to the more aggressive outcomes-focused one. It was not enough to save the regulator from being folded into the Financial Conduct Authority.

The way forward

The FSA is big on self-promotion but weaker on action. It has sometimes gone for the easy, or wrong, targets. In the pre-crisis years, it made the mistake of believing too much in self-correcting markets. There are signs that it has learned from its mistakes, and the regulator, almost uniquely among its kind, does not shy from self-criticism.

The pending move from the FSA to a new regime is as much about restoring public confidence as about change. The reality is that some of the same people will stay in the regulatory regime, and some of the activity will not be much different. We will explore the ramifications in more detail in Chapter 21.

21

New rules, new City

Introduction

A new regulatory regime for UK financial services comes into force at the end of 2012. There will be three main regulatory bodies, like the three heads of Cerberus, the guard dog of the underworld, as represented in ancient Greek and Roman mythology.

In this chapter, we will see how the new regime, which replaces the Financial Services Authority, will work.

Overview

The new tripartite regulatory structure for UK financial services is a version of the 'twin peaks' approach that separates conduct and prudential supervision. Europe has avoided this approach, but it has worked well in Australia.

The system will pick up where the Financial Services Authority (see Chapter 20) has left off. In March 2009, Hector Sants, its chief executive, said that the industry should be very frightened of the regulator. In the new regime, the reign of terror will continue, and regulation will be more intrusive and interventionist.

The areas of responsibility are divided between the Financial Conduct Authority (FCA), which is the rump of the FSA, the Prudential Regulation Authority (PRA), and the Financial Policy Committee (FPC). There are echoes of the rather messy pre-FSA regime, which also had multiple regulators. Let us consider the component parts.

Prudential Regulation Authority

The Prudential Regulation Authority, a subsidiary of the Bank of England, has been created under the new regime to authorise, regulate and supervise banks, building societies, credit unions, investment banks and insurers, and Lloyd's and its managing agents. As supervisor of individual firms, the PRA will focus on the system's overall stability. As part of this remit, it will work closely with the Financial Policy Committee (see below).

In building on the FSA's intrusive and judgement-based supervision, the PRA is likely to expend more of its resources on reducing the *impact* of company failure than the FSA had done, and less on reducing its *probability*. All this is in line with the fashionable regulatory focus on addressing systemic risk (see Chapter 19).

Financial Conduct Authority

The Financial Conduct Authority is a separate body from the PRA, but will liaise closely with it, and there are concerns about potential overlap. The FCA takes over the FSA's conduct of business regulation and supervision of all firms, and is the prudential regulator of those regulated firms that the PRA does not cover.

As part of its interventionist approach, the FCA may ban unsuitable product at the early stages of the process. Many in the industry fear, however, that this misses the target. The problem can lie in the activity, and legitimate products such as credit default swaps can be abused.

The FCA will have a main aim of consumer protection, on a wide definition. As part of the process, the Authority will focus on the interplay between wholesale and consumer. There is a widespread fear that regulatory intervention could damage the interests of wholesale operations, which account in size for most of the London market's business. This could make London less competitive as a global financial centre.

> There is a fear that regulatory intervention could damage the interests of wholesale operations.

Financial Policy Committee

The Financial Policy Committee is a body sitting within the Bank of England which aims to identify, monitor and take action against systemic risks. The aim is to see the broad risk picture, which supervisory bodies had failed to do in the crisis. Adair Turner, chairman of the FSA, said at the regulator's June 2011 public meeting that he considered the FPC the government's most important innovation.

These are positive words, but there are concerns, not least around the backgrounds of external members of the FPC, including how much insurance representation there is, compared with banking.

One crucial aspect of the FPC's agenda is international liaison. The FPC will work with such bodies as the G-20, the Financial Stability Board the European Systemic Risk Board and local regulators.

The staffing challenge

To implement its agenda, the new regulatory regime needs high-calibre staffing, with strong academic skills or practical experience. Good staff do not come cheap. The FSA has already substantially raised its remuneration packages, but it has retained a reputation for employing young people who are many steps behind the industry in understanding, experience and knowledge.

Noise factor

The bigger the regulator, the more noise it can make, and noise can comfort consumers. The tripartite regulatory regime, not least because it is new, can appear as ferocious as Cerberus. The new regime, like its three-headed counterpart of classical mythology, may have weaknesses.

In Virgil's *The Aeneid*, Book 6, the Sybil, a prophetess, throws drugged sweet cakes at Cerberus as it guards the gates of hell. The creature snaps them up with his jaws, then falls into slumber, allowing her and Aeneas to get past him.

No real change

Cynics argue that the handover between the FSA's current regime to the new tripartite structure is largely cosmetic. Hector Sants, as both FSA chief executive and PRA chief executive designate, announced in a 13 December 2010 speech that it was important to signal to FSA employees quickly where they might be positioned in the future landscape.

European supervision

In Europe, the new regime has replaced the three previous European supervisory committees with the European Supervisory Authorities: the European Securities and Markets Authorty; the European Banking Agency; and the European Insurance and Occupational Pensions Agency. They have been operating since 1 January 2011 as part of the European System of Financial Supervisors, and have some extended powers.

The ESAs oversee the regulation of financial services across Europe and aim for a single EU rule book. They work with the European Systemic Risk Board, which is similarly part of the European System of Financial Supervisors (see Chapter 19), to enable financial stability.

If the ESAs should find that a national supervisor is failing to apply EU law, they have the power to investigate. They can make decisions binding on firms or market participants to ensure they comply with EU requirements, and can ban some financial activities temporarily. They have mediation powers.

How far the ESAs will exercise their powers still remains to be seen, but UK firms are scared of the potential impact. The system has removed some power and flexibility from the UK regulator, as from other national regulators. The FSA has had to back away in part from its principles-based approach to fit with the rules-based European regulations, perhaps enabling it to save some face. On the regulator's own admission, principles-based regulation has not been entirely successful.

Principles-based regulation has not been entirely successful.

Another possible convenience is that the FSA now no longer need justify all its decisions. If UK regulated firms object to any regulations, the FSA may sympathise but blame Europe. The FSA has input into Europe, but with limitations.

As always with Europe, the system has elements of a one-size-fits-all approach, having to cater for the newer European Union member states, and those that are more sophisticated. There is some gravitation to the lowest common denominator. Uniformity of regulation in Europe assists cross-border business and enables comparability, but the price can be high.

The way forward

The new UK tripartite regulatory regime seems to provide toughness, systemic focus, and coordination. The European regulatory regime will dictate to the UK regulators, hampering their decision-making but also taking some responsibility.

At the pan-European level, consumer protection and bureaucracy are becoming more prominent, neither of which bodes well for wholesale markets. The price may be worth paying. The opportunities that arise from cross-border trading could be enormous, and it is to this ideal that the industry clings.

22

Face-lift for the Old Lady

Introduction

The Bank of England, our central bank, has two core purposes – monetary stability and financial stability – and its powers are expanding. We will consider here its evolution, its role in the financial crisis, and subsequent changes. In the new regulatory regime, to be implemented from 2012, the Bank will take on the new role of prudential supervisor, and has new macro-prudential responsibilities.

In this chapter, we will assess the role and performance of the 'Old Lady of Threadneedle Street', as the bank is sometimes dubbed, and the facelift she is having under the new regime.

Bank supervisory issues

In the era until 1997, the Bank of England had been supervisor of the banks, and, from a separate department, government adviser on monetary policy. This was to change. On 6 May of that year, the Labour government, just in power, gave the Bank's operational independence over monetary policy.

The Bank of England was to lose its powers as a banking supervisor, however. After the July 1991 collapse of Bank of Credit and Commerce International, a report by Lord Justice Bingham found the Bank had not pursued the truth 'with the rigour which BCCI's market reputation justified'.

The Bank of England had never done anything dishonest, and was cleared of allegations of malfeasance made by BCCI's liquidator in a lawsuit that collapsed, but its efficiency was another issue.

When in 1995, Barings collapsed, the Bank of England's role as banking supervisor again came under scrutiny. Barings, as an investment and trading bank, had been required to seek authorisation from the Bank of England for its banking business, and from two other regulators. The mix had made supervision too difficult.

Regulatory reform was inevitable. In a sweeping change under the Bank of England Act 1998, the Financial Services Authority took over the role of authorising and supervising banks from the Bank of England. The exercising of this responsibility was to prove only a partial success. The 2007–09 financial crisis was a major trigger for regulatory reforms, including the return of a role for the Bank of England as a banking supervisor.

Lessons from the crisis

In the crisis, the Bank of England had emerged as a rescuer of the banking system, in keeping with its responsibilities. If a bank has liquidity problems which threaten the entire financial system, the Bank of England may choose to exercise its powers as the lender of last resort.

In September 2007, the Bank of England agreed to provide Northern Rock, a mortgage lending bank, with the funding it needed to survive. The bank's business model meant it obtained most of its funds from wholesale markets, where lending had frozen up due to US sub-prime mortgage failures.

The rescue put the Bank of England's rescue powers under scrutiny. Some queried whether 'the Rock' had posed systemic risk, given that this mortgage lender was only the fifth largest in the UK, and saw the rescue as encouraging moral hazard. Others believed that the move had been necessary for broader financial stability, and that, generally, the Bank should have injected liquidity earlier into the failing system, much like the European Central Bank and the US Federal Reserve.

The Bank of England did, however, provide its special liquidity scheme, prominent from early 2008 into 2009, which enabled building societies to swap their high-quality but illiquid mortgage-backed and other securities for tradable UK Treasury bills for up to three years.

The scheme overlapped, from March 2009, with the Bank's quantitative easing programme, which was essentially the electronic creation of money to buy, pumped into the economy. It was a successful programme in terms of its goals. The economy had survived, which was the main objective, although banks had not significantly increased their lending, which had been what was hoped.

Compared with previous years, the Bank of England was back in favour. Some City practitioners and politicians argued that banking supervision should never have been removed from the Bank, which, with its responsibility for monetary policy and as lender of last resort, understood financial markets better than the FSA. They found that the FSA had emphasised conduct regulation too much and prudential regulation not enough, and had not acted adequately on an October 2006 warning that Northern Rock was running its operation with high risk.

> The Bank of England was back in favour.

The then 'tripartite authorities', the FSA, the Bank of England and the Treasury, had not been cooperating, and this was a clear contribution to the crisis.

A new role

The Bank of England has regained some bank supervisory powers under the new regime through its new subsidiary, the Prudential Regulation Authority. The Financial Policy Committee monitors the economy, in cooperation with the Monetary Policy Committee (see Chapter 21 for more on both these bodies).The Bank's observations in one area can inform its activity in another.

Price stability

In addition to its new regulatory role, the Bank of England continues to monitor the overall stability of UK financial markets and price stability. The Chancellor of the Exchequer, acting for the Treasury, defines price stability and sets the annual inflation target, as measured by the Consumer Price Index. The Bank must keep inflation on target and so maintain monetary stability and, for this purpose, it has the power to change the repo (repurchase agreement) rate, the short-term rate at which the Bank of England lends to banks through repurchase agreements. In practice, this rate is interchangeable with the *base* rate.

In a monthly two-day meeting, the MPC determines whether to change the interest rate, taking into account economic indicators and surveys. If the economy is growing rapidly and employment is rising, the Bank may raise the rate to curb inflationary pressures but, if the economy is starting to slow, it will not. If the committee changes the rate, the retail banks quickly change their lending rates, often to a margin above the base rate. Higher rates slow consumer spending and make it more expensive for companies to borrow, which slows their growth. Investors may move their savings from shares into cash because they can get a higher return on their deposits, and this hits the stock market.

Should the MPC fail to keep the inflation target to within 1 per cent above or below target, the Governor of the Bank of England must write an open letter to the Chancellor to explain why, and what the Bank will do to bring inflation back within the parameters.

> The Bank of England publishes its own thinking on inflation in a quarterly inflation report.

The MPC's decisions are very public, and the Bank of England publishes its own thinking on inflation in a quarterly inflation report. Governor Mervyn King and other senior Bank officials constantly explain the Bank's strategy on interest rate decisions, including the need to think beyond the short term and make balanced judgements.

The Bank can influence the money supply not just by interest rate decisions, but also through its open market operations, by which it lends money to banks in the money markets, covering any imbalance in their books. The Bank uses its OMO to buy securities from banks daily, both outright and through repos, which means buying securities and later selling them back at a higher price. In the interests of stability, the Bank can intervene in the foreign exchange market.

The Bank manages the UK's gold and currency reserves on behalf of HM Treasury, and it oversees bank payment and settlement services. All the clearing banks keep accounts at the Bank, using them to settle differences between themselves through the cash clearing system provided.

Globally, the Bank liaises with such organisations as the International Monetary Fund and the Bank for International Settlements.

The way forward

The Treasury has made it clear that placing a single authority, the Bank, at the centre of the framework for preserving financial stability is its single most important UK regulatory reform. This is a sign of the respect that the Bank has gained over the years.

23

Corporate heartbeat

Introduction

Every crisis sets in motion corporate governance reform talk, and the 2007–09 events were no exception.

In this chapter we will examine what corporate governance is and how it works, both in the UK, and in Europe and the US.

Corporate governance

Corporate governance is about how a company conducts its corporate affairs and responds to stakeholders, employers, employees and society. The concept includes legislative and other rules specifying regulation and best practice.

Traditionally, UK corporate governance has operated on a voluntary 'comply or explain' basis, which has sometimes been ignored.

Since the financial crisis, governance reforms have shifted on to the global agenda. In a rethink, the UK's Financial Services Authority has moved towards bolstering the corporate governance rules for regulated firms. The European Commission has been discussing the strengthening of governance across all listed firms, including potential legislation.

Corporate governance remains controversial. The case that its implementation is profitable has found some backing in surveys but is far from watertight. Some companies prefer just to pay lip-service.

> Corporate governance remains controversial.

Even companies committed to corporate governance will set limitations on it. The conflict between rules and market freedom is ever present. Governance, like other aspects of regulation, has the capacity to quash individual flair and profitable activity, but it also helps to protect investors by making corporate abuse and misbehavior more difficult.

The UK evolution

The history of corporate governance is littered with scandals, including, in the 1980s, Robert Maxwell's theft from the Mirror Group pension funds and the Polly Peck collapse. The Cadbury Committee was set up in 1991 to combat the abuses. Under the Cadbury Code, implemented on a 'comply or explain' basis, a company should be run by its board, the chairperson should be separate from chief executive, and at least three independent non-executive directors should be on the board.

Subsequently, the Greenbury Committee produced a code on directors' pay, which focused on lack of transparency. Cadbury and Greenbury were consolidated in The Combined Code on Corporate Governance, now renamed the Corporate Governance Code.

Pension funds had come under scrutiny after Maxwell's death. The Myners Report, published in 2001, recommended that the funds should be more transparent and that trustees should voluntarily adopt best-practice principles for investment decision-making. These and related recommendations were implemented with only limited success.

In an extension of corporate governance to the Listing Rules, as required by the FSA, new listing applicants must ensure that directors are free from conflicts of interest, or manage these conflicts. With 'comply and explain', much again is left to the discretion of companies. The Model Code, an appendix to the Listing Rules, tries, not always successfully, to stop directors or employees of listed companies, and linked parties, from abusing unpublished price-sensitive information.

The United States heritage

In the United States some parts of the corporate governance regime have been rules-based, and inflexible. The obvious case has been the Sarbanes–Oxley Act 2002, which was phased in by emergency legislation after the Enron scandal, and remains broadly in force. The act aims to eliminate creative accounting and to reinforce the independent status of external auditors.

'Sarbox', as it is dubbed, has lost US exchanges much foreign company listing business to London. The London Stock Exchange welcomed the influx of new share issuance, boasting of the uprise in volumes, although the financial crisis subsequently led to a dip in numbers.

In light of representations about its severity and the commercial repercussions, Sarbox has been modified over the years. The act failed to prevent bad risk oversight by financial institutions, as the September 2008 collapse of Lehman Brothers showed, but this tough legislation has enhanced respect for US financial services regulation.

Corporate governance, including executive remuneration, is a major item on the agenda of the Dodd–Frank Wall Street Reform and Consumer Protection Act, which is introducing a raft of regulatory reforms into the US. There will be differences from the UK and continental European approaches, providing the industry with some opportunity for governance arbitrage.

Europe

So far, the European Commission has not introduced a single corporate governance code across the European Union, but it has common auditing and disclosure requirements applicable in the United Kingdom. The European Union Statutory Audit Directive aims to enhance confidence in companies' financial statements and annual reports, and the Company Reporting Directive requires listed companies to provide a corporate governance statement in their annual reports. Under the Companies Act 2006, the business review, to be included in the accounts of a company, has a statutory purpose, including to inform shareholders and to help them to assess how the directors had performed their duty under the Act.

In the aftermath of the financial crisis, there is more to come. In April 2011, the EC published a green paper on corporate governance for all listed companies, not just financial institutions. A major concern was that self-regulation of corporate governance and the 'comply and explain' regime were somewhat ineffectual.

According to the paper, national governance frameworks are becoming more important given increasing cross-border activity, and the crisis has shown a lack of effective governance, supervisory failures, and lack of challenges to boards.

The paper welcomed stewardship codes, as developed in, for example, the UK, which aim to enhance engagement between shareholders and companies, but acknowledges that short-term shareholders might have limited commitment to the cause.

In the paper, the EC questioned how effectively boards functioned, suggesting that they should be composed of a mixed gender group. To have more women on boards would be to broaden approaches, perhaps opening the floodgates to more questions being asked.

The paper noted that, under 'comply or explain', companies not complying with national standards were meant to explain why they deviated from them, but too often failed to do so. The paper asked whether there should be more detailed rules on those explanations, and whether national monitoring boards should have more say on companies' corporate governance standards.

As the green paper reflected, the thinking of authorities at European level is around a shift from self-regulation to more rules, more specific requirements and more detail. The UK thinking is broadly in line with this.

Ireland

Ireland's corporate governance code has achieved new standards in rules-based rigidity. In early 2011, shortly before the code was implemented, industry practitioners were expressing outrage at its prescriptive nature. In May 2011 at the DIMA European Insurance Forum in Dublin, Julia Carmichael, head of compliance at Aviva Re, said that the code had less latitude than European corporate governance developments, but both had to be complied with. The Irish code, under Central Bank of Ireland supervision, was subject to a 'comply or receive sanctions' approach, but had some subjective criteria. She queried whether such a code would allow good corporate governance to develop and foresaw a rise in the cost of director-level compliance.

Ireland's financial services industry and economy have had particularly severe problems, but whether this kind of approach will be helpful or just depress the industry's profits and motivation, as feared, remains to be seen.

The current UK approach

The United Kingdom has been far from idle in pursuing its own reforms. One milestone was the Walker Review, published in July 2009, which supported the Combined Code but included enhanced risk governance.

The review said that non-executive directors should properly understand a company so they can challenge the executive directors effectively. A risk committee should exist at board level, and its annual report should feature in the company's annual report. The chief risk officer should have a more significant role, and institutional investors should actively engage with the board. The review did not explicitly codify ethics, perhaps in recognition that this area remains subjective and unenforceable.

In June 2010, the Financial Reporting Council issued the UK Corporate Governance Code, a revised version of the Combined Code. The FRC found that the code's spirit had to be followed better and that shareholders should have better interaction with company boards, so having more impact on monitoring the code. 'Comply or explain' was, however, retained.

As part of the process, a new code, the Stewardship Code, replaced section E of the Combined Code to give guidance on good practice for institutional investors.

Regulatory interest

As a response to the financial crisis, the FSA found that boards needed to gain a better understanding of their company business model and of higher-risk activity and products, and to receive better management information. The executive needed to be challenged more.

In January 2010, the FSA said that its 'approved persons' regime should be intensified, and that there was insufficient segregation of key roles in the firm. For example, a person could move from being a marketing director to finance director without further FSA approval. On risk management, in line with the Walker review, the FSA proposed that larger banks and insurers particularly should establish a board risk committee to support their oversight of risk. Feedback to these and related FSA proposals was broadly supportive.

How far the FSA should extend its current intrusive approach to influencing the culture of regulated firms remains a matter of debate.

Remuneration

Before the financial crisis, banks paid out staff bonuses just after year-end results, as a percentage of revenues. As the FSA has noted, this approach subordinated depositors, creditors and shareholders to the interests of employees, fostering rather than controlling risk taking.

The European Union Capital Requirements Directive (CRD3) and the FSA's Remuneration Code, which covers remuneration aspects of the directive, have implemented changes, and UK banks are complying. Up-front bonuses have stopped and guaranteed bonuses have been curtailed. Payments must be at least half in equity, or equity-like, instruments. Bonuses are now subject to institutions' long-term performance.

The FSA has started seeking to ensure the aggregate amount of the bonus is consistent with the bank obligation to maintain adequate capital.

Shareholder engagement

In June 2011, Business Secretary Vince Cable launched an independent review into UK equity markets, led by Professor John Kay. This has been looking at, among other things, how to strengthen engagement between investors and companies, and boost company transparency, as well as the impact of fragmented share ownership.

Outsourcing risks

Companies that outsource back-office or other functions abroad run obvious risks.

Companies that outsource back-office or other functions to operations abroad run obvious risks. In booming markets, everybody focuses less on the corporate governance or other controls and, without a presence in the country, it is difficult to assess the standards.

The January 2009 fraud revelations at Satyam, the Indian outsourcing services provider, served as a warning. Three months before it happened, Satyam had received a Golden Peacock award from a group of Indian directors for excellence in corporate governance, a demonstration of how the appearance can belie the reality, a discrepancy not confined to India.

The way forward

So long as the business case for corporate governance remains uncertain, there will be companies that do not take it seriously.

It is partly in recognition of this that, in the aftermath of the financial crisis, corporate governance seems to be moving inexorably towards a rules-based approach.

Success is far from inevitable. If the cost burden of new corporate governance initiatives on business is too great, the initiatives may peter out once the economy and market are going through their next phase of sustained strength, if not before that.

PART SEVEN

Behind the façade

24

The day of the whistle-blower

Introduction

Whistle-blowers have never been popular, but, with feeling now running high about financial services misrepresentation and systemic risk, they are gaining more of a hearing.

In this chapter, we will look at the developing role of whistle-blowers, and how they are being accepted more into the mainstream.

The loyalty game

The City of London has always had the aura of a club. In recent past decades, anybody allowed in was expected to be absolutely loyal and discreet. As part of this culture, some firms have required employees to sign statements of confidentiality, but they have not had much force in practice. From firms' perspective, such a requirement has often not been necessary. Employees who talk out of turn are aware that they may pay the price of being ostracised from the City. Indeed, some have suffered this fate, typically to the detriment of their living standards.

> Employees who talk out of turn are aware that they may pay the price of being ostracised.

Within firms, an ethos of confidentiality has rather prevailed. The firm deals with problems internally, hushing them up to maintain reputation, and discussing them with regulators only where it has to, and then carefully. In the eyes of some firms, the less the employees know, the better, and, if they are found talking about problems or corruption within the company, they will be dismissed on a pretext.

The tide is turning. In recent years, firms and regulators have been forced to take whistle-blowing more seriously. Firms understand they cannot always ignore issues to which they have been alerted or the price to pay could be loss of reputation and more. An employee of a regulated firm with concerns about rule breaches may be more inclined in today's sensitive climate to take them elsewhere, if he or she cannot voice them internally.

Firms with effective internal whistle-blowing policies may, however, be able to obtain a reduction in rates on corporate insurance policies, and such a financial incentive carries some weight. The easier that whistle-blowing becomes, the greater is the risk that it is abused. Disgruntled or poorly performing staff may report on colleagues for destructive ends and managers may use the process as a form of workplace bullying or harassment. Often these opportunistic whistle-blowers will present an inaccurate case, which wastes the time of the company or regulator checking it out. If some wrongdoing is uncovered early, it comes at a price.

Notwithstanding, there are political pressures to encourage whistle-blowing and it is, on the purest level, the most direct and concentrated source of evidence and knowledge of internal goings on in a company, perhaps highly relevant to fraud or other issues of public importance. No doubt in keeping with such thinking, the Financial Services Authority has published guidelines encouraging firms to set up internal procedures to encourage workers to blow the whistle. The regulator even has a whistle-blowing desk to be used by people without workplace procedures, or who are not comfortable with using them or the result. The regulator seeks to protect whistle-blowers' identities, but it cannot guarantee anonymity, which is obviously a major disincentive.

Not every firm, even now, will rush to check the reports of whistle-blowers. For firms that may appear clean but are less than perfect within, whistle-blowers can present a high commercial risk. Once they are identified, they are often made pariahs, not just in their firms, but in the industry. A career in financial journalism or recruitment may beckon.

Some institutions, often dubious ones, will absolutely not tolerate whistle-blowers. I know of one penny share dealing firm whose dealing manager has told employees that if they ever talk to anyone, internally or externally, about the firm's share selling arrangements and tactics, they will find themselves no longer working in the firm or the industry.

Such pressures can arise in listed companies. The *News of the World*, a defunct Sunday newspaper, had employed almost any level of deceit to get its scandal-mongering stories. The newspaper had enticed many whistle-blowers with large cheques, but its internal culture was very different. The entire team of journalists knew better than to blow the whistle on a culture that included phone hacking and other dubious tactics.

Early alerts

If whistle-blowers had emerged early at the *News of the World*, unethical phone hacking and other activities could perhaps have been stamped out. On the same principle, if whistle-blowers had been given a proper hearing in financial services, the 2007–09 crisis could perhaps have been mitigated.

Such conclusions can be highly speculative, not least because there is every possibility that the whistle-blowers would not have been heeded. Whistle-blowers have not had a happy history of attracting a listening audience.

Regulators in the United States could have stopped the financial frauds of Bernard Madoff, arrested in December 2008, many years earlier if they had heeded a whistle-blower's warnings and evidence. Harry Markopolos, an independent investigator, had repeatedly alerted the Securities and Exchange Commission to the fund manager's dubious-looking schemes, but to not much avail. It is extraordinary how the SEC, by a few staff changes and new policies, coupled with careful statements amounting to a refusal to discuss the problems, has survived its failures and reconstructed its image.

The regulator had perhaps learnt from the techniques of some financial firms of the type it was supposed to supervise. Claims have been made on Madoff's behalf that he was pushed by the expectations of clients into lying to them while he maintained a Ponzi scheme at the expense of their savings. Madoff is rumoured to have offered his services from prison for the presentation of ethics courses at top universities, but there are no confirmed takers.

Most whistle-blowers are not lionised.

Markopolos gained retrospective credit for having blown the whistle on Madoff early and persistently, and has published a book on the subject. Most whistle-blowers are not so lionised. When in 2005, Paul Moore was made redundant from his job as risk manager at HBOS after he had warned his bank that it was lending recklessly in the credit bank, he found himself no longer working in the industry.

Financial incentives

Given that *bona fide* whistle-blowers are helpful in stopping wrongdoing, and understanding it, there is a case for encouraging them. Financial incentives might go a long way.

The case is sometimes made that one should blow the whistle as a matter of principle and not for financial gain. If the facts are important enough however, it can only be in the public interest that they come to light, which perhaps justifies a reward.

Under US legislation, whistle-blowers who report financial crime to the regulator, the Securities and Exchange Commission, will receive up to 30 per cent of any fine imposed on the wrongdoer that exceeds US$1 million.

In October 2010, the Chartered Institute for Securities & Investment reported survey findings that nearly two-thirds of financial services practitioners believed the United Kingdom should follow the lead of the United States in rewarding whistle-blowers to encourage greater exposure of fraud.

The way forward

We are in a society that seeks truth, and this is nowhere more so than in financial markets.

Whistle-blowing is obviously a major potential source of truthful information, but can also be manipulated or otherwise misused.

This is a matter for assessment for the authorities, but in general, whistle-blowing is becoming much more acceptable, taking its place and feeding into the work of regulators, newspapers and corporate compliance.

25

Media manoeuvres

Introduction

The media are the source of accurate information from financial markets, but also of much spin.

In this chapter, we will examine the role of public relations, investor relations, and financial media in the markets. We will examine how the news flow reflects, and influences, stock prices.

Media control

The media control the flow of information to UK investors. One factor is that regulated firms are required to disseminate price sensitive information publicly so that no individual or small group gets an unfair advantage, but the overwhelming principle is that the media has the widest access to the public.

The online editions of the national newspapers and trade press pick up many stories from the news agencies and, all too often, publish them with little or no change. It is partly for the labour-saving convenience of this service that they pay their agency subscriptions. For financial news, speed of publication has more value than depth of reporting, and accuracy counts more than absolute truth. Otherwise, the journalists may use material provided by the RNS, a main service for

> For financial news, speed of publication has more value than depth of reporting, and accuracy counts more than absolute truth.

regulatory news announcements, or by public relations agencies, or corporate communications of City firms and listed companies.

News ranging from the announcement of a takeover, or revisions in analysts' forecasts, is reported fast. The events covered include significant City moves, share placings, big insurance contracts, appointments as book runners to an IPO, fraud scandals, outcomes of regulatory investigations, and legislative developments.

If they have time, journalists will often report comment from the companies and brokers involved, but it is typically a prepared statement, unlikely to say anything profound or critical. Some of the coverage will outdate quickly. The smorgasbord of information flow may give retail investors the impression that they are being well and fairly informed. In reality, City firms dictate the agenda, conveying a tightly controlled message, on the timetable that suits them.

Given the time priorities as well as the economic constraints, the conventional media accepts uncritically the information that it repackages into news stories. Publications economise on their news flow, once the foundation of their business, by cutting their staff to a core of inexpensive journalists. Some of these professionals, particularly in the trade press, are surprisingly ignorant of the industry of which they write and are not very numerate.

Even the better informed reporters lack time to make phone calls and check sources. With the news factory production process under pressure to work ever faster, and on fewer resources, investigative journalism or impartial quality analysis have become luxury that the newspapers and trade press increasingly cannot afford. Nick Davies, an investigative journalist on *The Guardian*, documents such developments in *Flat Earth News* (see recommended further reading in Appendix 5).

Even so, there is still some excellent and informed comment, but the tide of economics is against it. In a best-case scenario, financial journalism can come closer to the truth than do the financial markets' own outputs.

Tipsters

On the message boards of financial news web sites, amateur share tipsters may spread false stories to encourage buying or selling of shares. Given that legal liability sits with the site as well as with the rumour monger, the policing of the message boards has improved. It remains far from foolproof.

Tipsters can gain a cult following, but may mislead their followers. Alexander Elder, a professional trader who had grown up in the Soviet Union in the Stalin area, said in his classic book *Trading for a Living*: 'When I was growing up in the former Soviet Union, children were taught that Stalin was our great leader. Later we found out what a monster he had been, but while he was alive, most people enjoyed following the leader. He freed them from the need to think for themselves.'

He said in his book that when he came to the US and started to trade, he was 'amazed to see how many traders were looking for a guru – their "little Stalin" in the market'. The professional tip sheets, often written by journalists, attract many such followers, but can be unscrupulous. The true insights are rarer than the promotional material claims. The self-publicity can be flamboyant. US technical guru Joseph Granville reached a pinnacle of fame in the 1970s and early 1980s. He argued that trading volume drives share price movement, a theory came to him when he was relaxing in his bathroom and gazing at the tile patterns.

There was some truth in Granville's attribution of importance to volume, but it was only one driver. His methods worked for a time. His canny self-publicity, coupled with some forecasting that came right, made him ephemerally famous. 'Everyone I touch I make rich,' said Granville at his peak. At his packed-out investment seminars across the US, he sang, and a trained chimpanzee would sometimes play the piano. When asked how he followed the market while travelling, Granville dropped his trousers, revealing stock quotes written on his underpants. When meeting clients, he appeared to walk on water.

Granville was attracting followers, but no guru is right for ever. The turning point came once when markets soared, and Granville warned his subscribers that a crash would happen, and they should sell. Stocks continued to rise, and he lost all his money, and ended up sleeping rough.

There is nothing new in an adverse outcome from attempts to persuade the public with speculative theories. The pre-Socratic philosopher Empedocles leapt into Mount Etna in an effort to prove that he was a god, but the subsequent retrieval of one of his sandals on the scene disproved his claim.

The tipsters, like the pre-Socratics before them, are focused on spin rather than lies. There is, of course, interplay. The PR agencies are experts at defining and never crossing the grey lines.

Public relations

Public relations is a tightly organised industry. A handful of PR agencies in the City of London control the content of the major stories on listed companies published in the press. The agencies are paid a small retainer by some clients, but up to hundreds of thousands of pounds a year by large listed companies. The business is far more profitable than the trade press that it largely controls. In-house PR for large companies can vary in quality but is essentially the same game. The PR industry puts across a one-sided message in a convincing and interesting way, packaged in a form that journalists can, and do, adapt comfortably for their readers.

The skills of the PR professionals are as old as civilisation itself. The sophists of fifth-century Athens were practitioners of essentially the same craft. Catherine Osborne, professor of philosophy at the University of East Anglia, in her book *Presocratic Philosophy: A Very Short Introduction*, has described the sophists of ancient Greece as the 'spin doctors of all time'. She notes that they had created a demand for the skills they were offering to sell to any who could afford to pay their high charges. Anybody had the right to speak in the assembly, and the sole source of influence was, in practice, the speaker's ability to persuade an audience.

Osborne says: 'Thus the Sophists, spin doctors of all time, dressed their windows in democratic colours to hoodwink the poor while milking the rich. In return, they taught clever talk designed to enable their pupils to manipulate popular opinion in their favour, and thereby maintain their plutocratic advantage in a system that was only nominally democratic.'

The discrepancy between appearance and reality continues in modern PR, where the spin has to be professional, but spin it undoubtedly is. By courtesy of the media, the stories spread like Chinese whispers, sometimes becoming more exaggerated as they build momentum, over weeks or days, with the PR man standing by like some kind of demented referee to channel the flow and dispel any doubts. Good PR never snatches the glory of the journalist, but is essentially an invisible hand of influence.

Spin has to be professional, but spin it undoubtedly is.

It is, indeed, part of their art that the major PR agencies are seen to operate with the utmost integrity. Invariably, listed companies, or companies launching an IPO cannot afford to be associated with dirty tricks.

PR for defensive purposes was put to good effect when it persuaded newspapers to write sympathetically about three executives for NatWest Bank, who were extradited to America in 2004, where they had been indicted on counts of wire fraud over Enron-related activities. Many argued that the 'NatWest Three' should face a trial in the UK, and that it was unfair that the United States could legally extradite them from Britain when its evidence was not tested in a British court, although if Britain was to extradite individuals from the US, it had to produce evidence to a US court.

The press had suggested strongly that the UK authorities should oppose the extradition but had not necessarily ascertained the full legal facts. As Robert Wardle, then head of the Serious Fraud Office, later noted, the evidence against the three men was in the United States and would have been sufficient to secure extradition.

The power of PR is such that it is prudent to respect it, as some have discovered to their cost. In February 2004, Jeffrey Skilling, the former CEO of Enron, was indicted on charges of fraud, insider dealing and other crimes in relation to Enron's activities, and is now serving a 24-year jail sentence in Colorado. In a press interview with CNN on 14 June 2010, he expressed regret about not having maintained relationships with the media and worked to change the reputation of his firm, which he believed could have had a positive outcome on his case.

Prisoners of the media

We have seen how the media machine works and how it is controlled by PR. The view that it feeds to the public is often one-sided. Retail investors are at the mercy of this news flow. They are modern equivalents to the prisoners chained up in the cave, as described in Plato's *The Republic*. They live their lives chained up to face a blank wall from which they cannot turn their heads. Behind them is a raised walkway where men pass carrying objects before a fire. The prisoners see only the shadows.

The objects carried are imitations, and the shadows are one step even further from the reality. The carriers are like sophists, who specialise in presenting the one-sided argument convincingly. Most retail investors, like the prisoners, lack access to the internal workings of the companies in which they hope to invest, and are removed from the financial markets. Instead, they trust in the news coverage, including online, that comes their way, but it is far removed from reality.

Plato's prisoners, if they are to stand a chance of experiencing reality, need to get beyond both the shadows and even a direct view of the men carrying objects, and leave the cave for the sunlight. Similarly, investors must see beyond those stories that the PR experts project in the media.

Institutional investors are better informed. As professionals they know more about the securities industry and have access to better information. They have research departments of their own and access to those of investment banks. They can gain know-how from investor relations, an industry sometimes run from PR agents.

Investor relations

Investor relations are about how a quoted company liaises with present and prospective investors. Through IR, the company tries to gain a fair valuation for its shares to keep investors loyal and the shares liquid. In addition, IR keeps the market informed of price-sensitive information without selective disclosure and provides capital markets feedback to the board for its decision-making.

To gain complementary assistance, the in-house IR team often sits close to the finance department and talks to analysts and investors. In general, it can have a major role in crisis management.

Some future trends

Investigative journalism

Investigative journalism is an expensive and legally risky branch of the trade, which is why it is declining in the traditional press. On the internet, however, it has acquired a new lease of life. WikiLeaks, dubbed by some the first stateless news organisation, indicates a direction in which investigative journalism may now be headed. Here is a web site to which anybody can submit documents anonymously; a team of reviewers, including WikiLeaks staff and mainstream journalists, decides what is published.

The site, which is funded by donations, uses advanced cryptograph techniques to protect sources, and fights off legal challenges. The infrastructure is hazy, with servers in several countries, including one in a Swedish nuclear bunker. There are more than 1,500 duplicate web sites aimed to stop any government from removing WikiLeaks from the Web.

WikiLeaks has stimulated debate on the public interest value of information leaks which are in the public interest, but also of the risks, such as when the publication compromises national security.

A turning point

Financial journalism, as an ideal, precludes manipulation or sensationalism. There has been a focus, including in testimony to Treasury sub-committees, on how far journalists' reporting had impact on the 2007–09 financial crisis. The independence of journalists has come under scrutiny.

A study, *What is Financial Journalism for? Ethics and Responsibility in a Time of Crisis and Change,* published in November 2008 by Polis, a media thinktank at the London School of Economics and Political Science, found that financial journalism needed an overhaul for reporting markets and the financial system. The definition of journalism and its responsibilities and aims were among the issues under focus. The study queried whether journalistic privileges should apply to, for example, bloggers.

Professional journalism, unlike the output of bloggers, can cost substantial money to produce. The funding needs to come from somewhere. There has been a lot of discussion about whether the public will pay for access to online newspapers, and, in a few cases, it is currently being put to the test.

> **Professional journalism can cost substantial money to produce.**

The way forward

The media are a poor representation of reality in financial markets, like the shadows in Plato's cave. The internet has narrowed the knowledge gap between investors and markets but also increased the confusion, by providing mixed quality data.

Even the highest-quality media access, online or otherwise, is not enough to help retail investors escape from the cave. Such an escape is, however, possible for those who want to know more, who engage deeply with the markets, who are willing to pay the price.

26

The power of perception

Introduction

Perception drives financial market, and, often becomes, at least in the short term, wildly divorced from the reality. In this chapter we will consider further how the professionals use suggestion and salesmanship to influence this perception.

We will examine the drive for truth from retail investors fed up with losing out to controlling markets, and how they are moving towards a new pact with the financial institutions.

Perception drives markets

There is agreement that the problems of the 2007–09 financial crisis are not over. The government's quantitative easing halted the contagion of the global debt problem but did not remove the debt. How far it is resolvable remains open to debate. Commentators say different things at any given time, often in accordance with their own commercial positions.

Analysts, strategists and, in their wake, salespeople are adept at packaging selective facts to present the case. The bite-sized expertise tailored to events is a component of the firm's broader long-term advisory package. A word from the expert can redirect the tide of money flows in an instant.

> The bigger the name of the investment bank that advises, the more likely are institutional investors to take heed.

The bigger the name of the investment bank that advises, the more likely are institutional investors to take heed. The recommendations, even if ill-founded, may well this way become a self-fulfilling prophecy. The analysts in big firms are known for making an immediate mark on their pronouncements.

This game may work only in the short term, but the following month, or week, or day, the analyst is likely to have a new story to tell on the same stock. The same adaptive principle applies on market and economic conditions for the strategy.

In this sense, market analysts and salespeople are like the Victorian novelists paid broadly on quantity, delivering their tales in instalments. The story must change with events, but their own imagination is allowed generous input. The reinventions would not be possible without the backing of governments and of greedy investors.

Inspired leadership

As market professionals drive perception, intense competition prevails, more in salesmanship than truth, although more of the latter can enhance sales. After all, financial markets are about forecasting, which is best based on truth, even if it is necessarily padded out with guesswork.

The reputation of the institution, and its placing power and size, are what give the forecasts credibility. If the forecasts are dramatically wrong but are backed by high-quality research, this can be represented as a compensating factor, or even as the most important attribute.

The bluff required in the game requires leadership, to make decisions about what is safe to say within regulatory requirements, and in line with the bank's commercial position, and which sales pitch to give individual clients at any given time.

The financial market leaders, in imbuing their pitches, including those they require of their underlings, with optimism, take a cue from our political leaders. They borrow from these stalwarts in their endless reinvention of stories, and in the convincing way they represent them.

Controlled negativity

Within the framework of positive investment promotions, led from the top, controlled negativity is leaked into forecasts and commentary, as part of a balancing act, to make what is said seem more credible, and to ensure expectations are not unreasonably high.

The negativity is typically measured to cover the financial institution making the recommendation if problems should arise after the clients have acted on it and bought. The aim is to keep the client satisfied that he or she is getting a good service.

Secret liaisons

Along with the release of negativity comes another controlling factor, the presentation of market relationships to maximise commercial credibility. The relationships that seem good on the outside, as between leaders of financial services firms, can be rancorous behind the scenes. The relationships between the industry and the regulators, inimical on the outside, can be amiable, even conniving, between them.

This double game might not be necessary if markets were not driven in the short term almost entirely by perception. As it is, investors like to see that markets must justify their actions, and there are forces in play to keep cavalier market behaviour in check. The markets have to be seen as in dispute with their regulators and having to justify their ways of operating. It is in the markets' interest that the regulators seem powerful and detached from the industry.

Calculated showmanship

The game of constant industry lobbying to regulators has therefore the element of showmanship. Just as the ancient Roman people were encouraged to attend their arenas where gladiators fought each other to the death or Christians were thrown to the lions, so retail investors are treated to the spectacle of clashes between the industry and the regulator, which claim their victims.

If the Romans had not been given the opportunity to sublimate their aggression into cheering on gladiator fights or similar, they could find more direct outlets for their dissatisfactions and energy. The emperors, who encouraged the contests, well understood how to keep their people's minds off their personal issues.

> **Markets are driven by the perceptions, above all, of confidence.**

Similarly, the financial services industry knows that, if it is not seen sometimes to be quashed by regulators, it could lose the confidence of retail investors. Markets are driven by the perceptions, above all, of confidence.

The regulatory regime is in turn created by the political interests that work closely with financial markets to ensure they continue to make a significant contribution to the country's gross domestic product. Retail investors are important because they, after all, buy the funds and insurance products, whose premiums are invested, from institutions, and they must therefore be kept informed a little and appeased substantially.

One way to reach them is through the press, and, in part to achieve this, the corporate communications teams of financial markets and their regulator are well resourced. The Financial Services Authority has a substantial and sophisticated press office, with a number of press officers specialising in different sectors, and providing an after-hours service as well. The same may be said for the Association of British Insurers, and for a number of other important trade associations.

Control scope

Leaders create perceptions that may exist partly in their own minds, measuring out negativity and positivity like ingredients in a cake they bake, representing reform.

When the control is exercised responsibly, it can work well. The expectations of retail investors can be managed in a realistic way. When, however, a bull market arises, and buying forces drive prices up, the control can become irresponsible.

Bad news may be suppressed and the good emphasised, as prices spiral even higher. We saw this phenomenon in the crisis, and it repeats itself in every bull market.

Pivot of reality

The secret of sustainability of the system is that the appearances are not incompatible with reality, even as they come, at the extreme, divorced from it. Reality is rather the pivot from which the appearance swerves.

Reality every so often breaks up the party in financial markets. The great pretenders are left standing exposed, law suits abound, and the regulators are forced to act.

Fraud becomes apparent

When markets collapse, misconceptions become apparent, and it is plain when some of the misrepresentations of the bull market have become dubious. No one will want to complain about unsuitable advice, however valid, if the investments entered into have soared in value and not yet retreated. If, however, an investment has plummeted, buyers will seek compensation if they stand a chance of getting it.

There is always some fraud that gets uncovered, such as conducted by the boiler rooms (see Chapter 4). Shares in some companies will prove worthless and may always have been. The fact that the boiler rooms employ many similar tactics, although cruder, as regulated firms creates a tapestry in which investors find it difficult to see the dividing lines between fraud, misrepresentation and optimistic salesmanship.

Chinese whispers

Markets have tried to resolve the confusion by inviting retail investors to trust them. They encourage them to buy the name, the ethos, and the tradition. The statistics and facts are not pushed so much.

Cults are built up around people and institutions and regulated status, and money is exchanged on investments far removed in value from fundamentals. This approach can work, for a while, perhaps.

Recycling

When markets crash, and the chain of Chinese whispers is broken up, and firms fail, and regulators step in, it is time for the City and financial markets, the greatest workers of, if you like, magic in the world today, to perform their finest trick, to reinvent themselves in terms so spectacular that it makes the great Houdini look an amateur.

The financial markets at such times undergo such upheaval that it is as if they had been melted down in a gigantic vault, reshaped and released on the world in a process so marvellous that it defies aging and contagion, and has a quality of the eternal.

In manifestations of the cyclicality, companies close and restart. The processes are akin to metempsychosis, part of the ancient Greek culture of beliefs. It is reminiscent of the myth of Er, the fable told by Plato at the end of his *The Republic*. Any person's life after death, as explained by Er based on his own visit to the afterworld, starts with 1,000 years of either heaven or hell, followed by a chosen new life on earth.

In Plato's myth, those who have just had the comfort of 1,000 years of heaven will be morally complacent in that choice. Those who have had 1,000 years of discomfort in hell will be more cautious. In financial markets today, institutions and individuals similarly react to experience. To take a prominent example, AIG, the US insurer that received a government bailout in the crisis, is unlikely in its new, restructured form to resume the reckless investment banking activity that had caused its near downfall.

Just as, in the myth of Er, characters before their rebirth on earth ritualistically lose their memory by drinking from the river of Forgetfulness, so investors become oblivious of past losses and of mis-selling by their stockbrokers.

Towards a new pact

Michel Foucault, the late social philosopher, has put the case that discourse of professions, of which jargon is a facet, is related to knowledge and power. One might say that the discourse of financial markets has helped to enable its practitioners to maintain power over investors. Politicians use their own discourse to support or to criticise financial markets.

The tide could be changing. Foucault died in 1984 but, since then, the internet has become prominent, and, with its clear decoding of jargon, has given retail investors an opportunity to seize back some control from the financial markets. Hence, the rise in popularity of execution-only online stockbrokers.

With this levelling of the playing field, there are signs that financial institutions have started a begrudging process of entering a new pact with investors. The regulators in Europe are playing their part by providing a new consumer-focused framework.

> **There are signs that financial institutions have started a process of entering a new pact with investors.**

The pact is about working together, rather than about fairness and decency. Retail investors are asking to be let into the secrets of financial markets, to play the game. The prisoners are looking to escape from the cave.

The way forward

Financial markets will continue to fluctuate in the short term on perception and not fundamentals, to work with regulators and politicians to present the most useful image to investors. When troubles come, the markets will continue to reinvent themselves.

The conciliatory nature of markets that have emerged after the crisis seems likely to subside once conditions have improved. In financial markets, history repeats itself, if never quite in the same way.

A final word

The business of dreams

We have talked in this book of cycles, of reincarnation, of how the City and financial markets can distance themselves from past problems. This is essentially the framework of the money myth, but it is not the full story. Every big lie carries in it the seed for redressing the balance. Take its time as it may, the law of compensation is at work.

To speed up the process is partly in our hands. Unfortunately, we do not always speak out as perhaps we should when we are required to be loyal to an institution. The truth can hurt image and respectability, which are commercial priorities for financial markets. Even so, natural justice can catch up with the wrongdoers.

I was struck by the truth of this finding when, in August 2011, a man was sentenced by the Crown Prosecution Service at Southwark Crown Court to nine years in jail for conspiracy to defraud investors through boiler rooms. His name was Tomas Wilmot and I took a particular interest in the case because, more than 25 years earlier, I had worked briefly as a share dealer at Harvard Securities, a firm of licensed dealers in the City, run by this man.

Harvard Securities had specialised in selling high-risk over-the-counter stocks to trusting investors. The young dealers had worked at the job from within days of being recruited, and it took them some months to realise how it worked, by which time they mostly left. The investors lost all or most of their money invested in the illiquid stocks the dealers recommended to them.

There was always an issue whether the stocks had been priced correctly, whether there was a genuine market in them, and what happened to the money the investors sent in. The paperwork provided warnings, but it was never enough. Investors lost most of their money, most of the time, although there were a few highly publicised winners.

It seemed impossible, even for the dealers, at the time to prove that anything untoward was going on and nobody did, at least in public. The dealing room hid behind the mantras of stockbroking, that shares are inherently risky, that markets are volatile, conditions can change quickly, and you win some, lose some, and similar. The company kept going, fighting legal actions, finding new clients, pushing more and more of its dubious stocks.

I will not dwell here on the years I spent providing clear evidence of fraud and wrongdoing to the regulators, politicians and the police, largely to no avail. The public outrage aroused by my book published in 1989, *The City Share Pushers*, was well documented, with a dedicated Channel 4 programme, and a serialisation in the biggest selling newspaper of the day. The fact that my former boss has been given a jail sentence, although not directly related to his activities covered in my book, seems at least a form of justice.

Why then do I feel some strange sympathy for Wilmot? Am I deeply corrupted, despite a straight career and life, or do I have some rational case, even if only small?

Let me gloss over the fact that Wilmot gave me a job in which, within six weeks, I'd more than quadrupled my previous modest schoolteacher's income. Nor need we dwell on the fact that the job was fun for the dealers, and for many of the clients, and that some of Wilmot's employees used the experience of Harvard Securities to develop respected careers in the City.

I think my mixed feelings are because, after leaving Harvard Securities and joining a 'respectable' stockbroker I came to realise that everyone in the industry was essentially up to the same game. As it now turns out, Wilmot got caught and many others have gone free.

There are distinctions, of course. Harvard Securities was a lot cruder than some of the large prestigious stockbrokers in the way it operated, but more ethical than the boiler rooms that Wilmot subsequently developed. In many cases, however, share dealing operations are along a continuum, the differences being of degree rather than kind.

If you invest directly in financial markets, you enter this free-for-all, something I have tried to show in this book. Rules and respectability are a veneer. They cannot be blatantly flouted with impunity, but, underneath, anything is possible. Once you understand how the game works, it is not so daunting. We can play it in our own way, and, yes, stick to the rules. We have chances. The stock market is, after all, the business of dreams.

Appendix 1

Twelve wake-up investment rules

1. Have the basics in place

Before you invest, have the basics in place such as a property of your own, a pension and life insurance. Keep some emergency cash in an accessible deposit account.

2. Conduct your research

Before you invest in a company, check fundamentals. Consider turnover, profits, earnings per share, P/E ratio, cash flow and return on capital employed. Compare with the sector and the broad market.

3. Question your stockbroker

Question your stockbroker on any investment recommendations. They may not be well thought out. Bear in mind that your broker has vested interests, if only on earning a commission on trades.

4. Do not rush into investments

Take at least half an hour to think about an investment before committing your money. You may lose some profit, but it is better than making a big mistake.

5. Allocate assets to suit your risk appetite

You should invest not just in equities, but in other assets such as property, bonds and cash, and commodities. There should be some non-correlation between, and within, asset classes, so if one investment declines in value, others may rise.

6. Switch to safe havens in a difficult market

When stocks are declining in value, consider switching to defensive stocks, to precious metals such as gold, or high-quality government bonds.

7. Consider fees and commission

When you invest, assess the impact of the commissions on trades and any fees. If you are receiving advice, you will pay for it in higher charges, so be sure that, as an investor, you are getting overall value for money.

8. Avoid the boiler rooms

When a boiler room salesperson tries to sell you shares, put down the telephone receiver on that person. If, in a weak moment, you agree to buy shares, break your commitment and do not send the money.

9. Think global, including exchange rates

As an investor, think global. The closing level on Wall Street will affect Asian stock markets overnight, both having impact on Europe the next morning. News affecting telecoms stocks in Italy or France will probably affect the same sector in the United Kingdom or Germany.

10. Follow the trend

Traders should follow the trend. If the market, or a sector, is rising, you buy, and if it falls, you sell. The trend continues until it is broken, at which point you sell.

11. Cut your losses and run your profits

Whether you invest for the medium to long term or trade for the short, you should cut your losses and run your profits. The winners tend to keep winning and losers losing.

As a guideline, in any portfolio of ten or twelve shares, there may be two or three winners, a similar number of losers and the rest in between.

12. Set a stop loss

Set a realistic stop loss, meaning a percentage level of decline below which you will sell your shares. This limits your losses and puts discipline into your trading.

Appendix 2

Twelve regulatory trends

1. Treating customers fairly

'Treating Customers Fairly' has been a main regulatory theme, but it has not worked well.

2. Move to fees-based advice

Fees are replacing commissions for financial advisers. The old, commission-based approach will remain in stockbroking.

3. Shift to European regulation

The UK regulator has lost some independence to centralised European supervision, but cross-border business is now much easier.

4. Living wills

Banks and some other financial institutions must have recovery and resolution plans in place. The idea is that, if things go wrong, they will not have to draw on the taxpayers' money, as some large banks did in the 2007–09 financial crisis.

5. Credible deterrence

Credible deterrence is a proactive approach by the regulator to take meaningful actions, including larger fines for miscreants.

6. Product intervention

To address concerns about product complexity and its potential for hidden risk, the UK regulator plans to focus on early product intervention where appropriate.

7. Capital adequacy

New regulatory requirements mean that banks and insurers will have, on balance, more capital. This provides some extra protection against insolvency, but the cost ultimately falls on the consumer.

8. Suitable individuals

The Financial Services Authority is rigorously interviewing individuals applying for key jobs in the City to assess their suitability. A debate has arisen on how far the regulator should influence the firm's culture.

9. Banking bonus restrictions

There are new regulatory restrictions on bankers' bonus arrangements, designed to remove the incentives for reckless, short-term trading.

10. Derivatives transparency and control

Derivatives are becoming more centralised and transparent, not least through a shift of some over-the-counter derivatives onto exchanges.

11. Systemic risk

There is a new urgent focus on detecting and preventing systemic risk. The concept has not yet, however, been adequately defined or quantified.

12. More rules-based corporate governance

Corporate governance is becoming more rules-based. The 'comply or explain' ethos, although still prevailing, is under scrutiny.

Appendix 3

Investment software checklist

1. Your need

Ask yourself whether you need investment/trading software. If you trade in small amounts, or only on a professional's advice, you may have little use for it.

2. Time investment

If you are to use trading/investment software effectively, you must take time to grasp its facilities.

3. Right facilities

Any software that you use should have the facilities essential for *you*. If you are a heavy trader, you need real time prices, which is at the more expensive end.

4. Ease of use

If you are not technically minded, opt for the most user-friendly software. This should enable you, for example, to enlarge a part of a graph by clicking on it.

5. Speed

Choose software that works fast.

6. Reliability

Use a reliable product. Some software often crashes. Read user reviews before you buy.

7. Alarms on charts

Look for an alarm on the charts to notify you of, for example, a trend breakout or when a support line is breached.

8. Chart scanning

Use a stock-screening facility to scan for chart patterns, such as engulfing on candlesticks charts, or new highs/lows, or signal crosses.

9. Help facility

The software should offer a help facility. If you want to understand what Stochastics is, you should be able to click on a definition.

10. Technical support

Technical support is crucial. Check that there is a users' help line and that it is not constantly engaged. You should be paying the cost of an ordinary call, and not a premium rate. Sometimes it can help to outline a complex problem by email and have a reply, and you should have this facility.

11. All-inclusive price

Check that the price for your software includes all that you need. A favorite trick of some promoters is to offer the basic product at a modest price, but with expensive add-ons.

12. Free trial

A free trial gives you a safety net, but make sure that this is *bona fide*. Companies have been known to renege, claiming that the users still have the software on their computers.

Appendix 4

Useful web sites

Accounting and corporate governance

ACCA, the global body for professional accountants, www.accaglobal.com
Financial Reporting Council, www.frc.org.uk
International Accounting Standards Board, www.iasb.co.uk
PricewaterhouseCoopers, www.pwc.com

Banking and building societies

British Bankers' Association, www.bba.org.uk
The Building Societies Association, www.bsa.org.uk
European Central Bank (English site), www.ecb.int
Association for Financial Markets in Europe, www.afme.eu

Bonds

Debt Management Office (gilts), www.dmo.gov.uk
International Capital Market Association, www.icmagroup.org

Collective investments and similar

Alternative Investment Management Association, www.aima.org
The Association of Investment Companies, www.theaic.co.uk
Investment Management Association, www.investmentuk.org

Morningstar, www.morningstar.co.uk
Standard & Poor's – funds website, www.funds-sp.com
Trustnet – a particularly good funds website, www.trustnet.com

Complaints and compensation

Department for Business Innovation & Skills, www.bis.gov.uk
Financial Ombudsman Service, www.financial-ombudsman.co.uk
Financial Services Authority – UK financial services regulator, www.fsa.gov.uk
Financial Services Compensation Scheme, www.fscs.org.uk
Office of Fair Trading, www.oft.gov.uk
Press Complaints Commission, www.pcc.org.uk

Credit rating agencies

A.M. Best, www.ambest.co.uk
Fitch Ratings, www.fitchratings.com
Moody's, www.moodys.com
Standard & Poor's, www.standardandpoors.com

Derivatives and commodities

The Futures and Options Association, www.foa.co.uk
Ice Futures, www.theice.com
London Metal Exchange, www.lme.com
NYSE Euronext, www.nyse.com/nyseeuronext
World Gold Council, www.gold.org

Economy

Bank of England, www.bankofengland.co.uk
HM Treasury, www.hm-treasury.gov.uk
International Monetary Fund, www.imf.org
National Statistics, www.statistics.gov.uk
Organisation for Economic Co-operation and Development, www.oecd.org
Samuel Brittan – economics commentator for *The Financial Times*, www.samuelbrittan.co.uk
David Smith, economics editor of *The Sunday Times*, www.economicsuk.com/blog/

Exchanges and MTFs

Borsa Italiana, www.borsaitaliana.it
Chi-X Europe, www.chi-xeurope.com
Deutsche Börse, www.deutsche-boerse.de
Federation of European Securities Exchanges, www.fese.be
London Stock Exchange, www.londonstockexchange.com
NASDAQ, www.nasdaq.com
Plus Markets Group, www.plusmarketsgroup.com

Insurance

Association of British Insurers, www.abi.org.uk
British Insurance Brokers' Association, www.biba.org.uk
Chartered Insurance Institute, www.cii.co.uk
International Underwriting Association of London, www.iua.co.uk
Lloyd's, www.lloyds.com

Investor relations

Investor Relations Society, www.irs.org.uk

Law enforcement and similar

City of London Police, www.cityoflondon.police.uk
Serious Fraud Office, www.sfo.gov.uk
Serious Organised Crime Agency, www.soca.gov.uk

Money laundering and fraud

Financial Action Task Force, www.fatf-gafi.org
Insurance Fraud Investigators Group, www.ifig.org
The Joint Money Laundering Steering Group, www.jmlsg.org.uk
Transparency International, www.transparency.org/

Money markets

Wholesale Markets Brokers' Association, www.wmba.org.uk

News, data and research

ADVFN, www.advfn.com
Bloomberg, www.bloomberg.com
Citywire, www.citywire.co.uk
City of London Corporation, www.cityoflondon.gov.uk
Digital Look, www.digitallook.com
The Economist, www.economist.com
Financial Times, www.ft.com
Hemscott, www.hemscott.com
Interactive Investor, www.iii.co.uk
Investors Chronicle, www.investorschronicle.co.uk
mergermarket, www.mergermarket.com
MoneyAM, www.moneyam.com
The Motley Fool UK, www.fool.co.uk
Reuters, www.reuters.co.uk
The Chartered Institute for Securities & Investment, www.cisi.org

Pensions

The Pensions Advisory Service, www.pensionsadvisoryservice.org.uk

Post-trade services

Euroclear UK & Ireland, www.euroclear.com
LCH.Clearnet Group, www.lchclearnet.com
SIX x-clear – the central counterparty service, www.ccp.sisclear.com

Private investors

Association of Private Client Investment Managers and Stockbrokers, www.apcims.co.uk
UKSA – UK Shareholders' Association, www.uksa.org.uk

Regulation and similar

Financial Services Authority, www.fsa.gov.uk
European Banking Authority, www.eba.europa.eu

European Insurance and Occupational Pensions Authority, https://eiopa.europa.eu/

European Securities and Markets Authority, www.esma.europa.eu

European Systemic Risk Board, www.esrb.europa.eu/

Competition Commission, www.competition-commission.org.uk/

Financial Stability Board, www.financialstabilityboard.org/

US Securities and Exchange Commission, www.sec.gov

International Association of Insurance Supervisors, www.iaisweb.org

International Organization of Securities Commissions, www.iosco.org

Reputation

Reputation Institute UK, www.reputationinstitute.com/contact

Risk management

Airmic, www.airmic.com

Federation of European Risk Management Associations, www.ferma.eu

Technical analysis

Bollinger Bands, www.bollingerbands.com

Building wealth through shares – the website of Colin Nicholson, technical analyst and teacher, www.bwts.com.au

Dorsey Wright & Associates, www.dorseywright.com (point and figure charting, including excellent free course)

International Federation of Technical Analysts, www.ifta.org

ShareScope, www.sharescope.co.uk

Society of Technical Analysts, www.sta-uk.org

StockCharts.com, www.stockcharts.com

Index